Behavior and Learning

Howard Rachlin

STATE UNIVERSITY OF NEW YORK AT STONY BROOK

Behavior and Learning

W. H. Freeman and Company
San Francisco

Library of Congress Cataloging in Publication Data

Rachlin, Howard, 1935–
    Behavior and learning.

    Includes bibliographies and index.
    1. Conditioned response. 2. Behavior modification.
I. Title. [DNLM: 1. Behavior. 2. Learning. LB1051
R119b]
BF319.R327   156'.3'15   76-2068
ISBN 0-7167-0568-0

Printed in the United States of America

9 8 7 6 5 4 3 2 1

To the memory of
Irving Rachlin

Contents

Preface

This book is intended as a middle-level undergraduate textbook on learning, with an emphasis on the area of learning usually referred to as conditioning or animal learning. It contains approximately enough material for a full one-semester course. Although the material will be easier to understand if the student has already had an introductory psychology course, nothing is taken for granted.

At the end of each chapter, except Chapter 1, an article or a group of articles is reprinted. The main purpose of these articles is to give the student practice in reading the psychological literature. The articles, generally, are much more detailed than the text. With the text alone the student might conclude that some of the issues addressed are simpler than they actually are. The articles should cure the student of this misapprehension. The articles are not intended to provide all of the background reading that a serious student will need, nor are they necessarily the "most important" in their area. But they all illustrate some point made in the text, and they provide an acquaintance with various aspects of the psychological literature.* Some of the articles are wholly theoretical, some are both empirical and theoretical, and some are wholly empirical. At the end of Chapter 8, a series of articles is included that illustrates how psychologists argue publicly with each other. After reading the text and the articles the student should be able to pick up an issue of a journal such as *Learn-*

---

*To preserve the flavor of the original sources, no attempt has been made to regularize capitalization, hyphenation, the style of references, and so forth, which vary somewhat from source to source.

ing and Motivation, Journal of Experimental Psychology: Animal Behavior Processes, Journal of the Experimental Analysis of Behavior, Journal of Applied Behavioral Analysis, or *Behavior Therapy* or the articles on learning in *Psychological Review* or *Psychological Bulletin* and read, understand, and criticize the articles.

The early chapters are purposely easier than the later ones. The first chapter and some subsequent sections are taken from my book *Introduction to Modern Behaviorism.* As the text proceeds, however, less and less of this introductory material is included. Throughout the text I have not hesitated to use hypothetical data (and so indicate) where it was convenient. Nor have I hesitated to sacrifice detail for comprehensibility. The journal articles provide some of the detail missing from the text.

I have not rejected any material or skirted any issue on the grounds that it is too difficult for an undergraduate to understand. Rather, I have attempted to supply the background first and then to approach the material in a way consistent with the background. Sometimes this process consumed more pages than the issue itself seemed to be worth, but I felt it to be worthwhile when the reasoning developed in a minor issue early in the text paralleled that of a major issue later on.

I apologize to all those psychologists whose work I have not cited but whose contributions to the field I have liberally made use of. I hope they will keep in mind that this is a textbook for undergraduates and not a reference book. I have tried to remedy this omission somewhat in the bibliographies at the end of each chapter, but these are obviously insufficient for the serious researcher.

Leonard Green, John Neale, and Barry Schwartz have all read and criticized parts of the text. I thank them for their valuable advice. Michael Cantor, Nancy Hemmers, Dennis Kelly, and I have discussed several of the issues dealt with in the text and the articles. Many of the ideas expressed in the text stem from these discussions. Finally, I thank Pat Carl, who typed, made coffee, and had patience beyond the call of duty.

November 1975   HOWARD RACHLIN

Behavior and Learning

Chapter 1

Background

Organisms try to influence the behavior of other organisms by a variety of means and for a variety of purposes. Indeed, much of the interaction among humans and other living creatures consists in efforts to influence behavior. Consider a cow nudging its newborn calf, or for contrast, a victorious alley cat driving an intruder from its territory.

Of course, not all interactions are so one-sided. Organisms often simultaneously modify each other's behavior. Even when one organism is clearly dominant over another, as in the relations between ant and aphid or doctor and patient, there may still be an element of mutual influence. If we examine the teacher–student relationship, which, in formal terms at least, seems rather one-sided, we may find that a given student is trying to get a good grade as actively as his teacher is trying to impart information and stimulate thinking. Thus what the teacher sees as learning on the part of the student may be, from the student's point of view, simply a means of influencing the teacher and obtaining a good grade.

Given a situation in which one organism is trying to influence the behavior of another organism, the purpose of the effort may not be readily apparent. A parent may spank a child to keep him from playing in the street. This punishment is intended "for the child's own good." On the other hand, if a parent spanks a child for not making his bed or cleaning his room, it may be the parent himself who hopes to benefit from the change in the child's behavior. Thus the motives behind the modification of behavior and the benefit to be derived from the modified behavior may critically determine the nature of a given interaction.

Let us consider one final example along these lines. A radio announcer may urge us to "Eat apples for health!" because he is paid to advertise apples. If the speaker were an apple grower, instead of a radio announcer, the same statement might be a form of benign propaganda. But if a nutritionist or doctor gives us this advice, the statement may express more concern for our health than for the selling of apples. The very same statement could be used in all three attempts to modify our behavior.

The type of relationship between organisms that will be discussed in this book is that of experimenter and subject. On the surface this relationship appears one-sided, with the experimenter observing, manipulating, and modifying the behavior of the subject. But in a deeper sense a truly reciprocal interaction occurs, for the subject helps determine the experimenter's behavior and causes him to modify old theories, to formulate new theories, and to design new experiments.

A look at the titles of articles by experimental psychologists in the field of learning yields clues to the objectives of learning studies. Here, for example, is a hypothetical set of titles corresponding to the experimental observations shown in Figure 1.1:

a. Variables influencing the rate of motor learning
b. The sense of time
c. A study of appetite
d. Anxiety as a determiner of performance

Although authors almost always qualify such broad titles in subtitles or introductions, the titles do reveal the questions that the experimental reports are meant to elucidate.

Psychologists seem to expect to be able to understand and explain all kinds of behavior. But looking at Figure 1.1, we see that they study narrowly defined bits of behavior in their laboratories. How, then, do they justify these grand expectations?

This chapter will be devoted to the theoretical and historical influences that have guided research in learning. Because the history of psychology is lengthy and complex, we shall concentrate primarily on one central problem: What kinds of events should a psychologist study? Through an understanding of some of the intellectual roots of modern psychology, we may come to understand the psychologist's purpose when he observes a human following a moving spot with a stylus, when he observes a pigeon pecking at an illuminated disk on the wall, when he observes a rat running down a straight alley to reach some food, or when he observes a man's sweating palm.

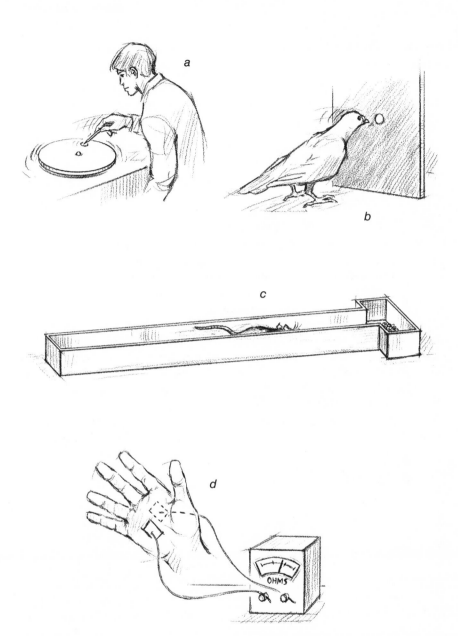

FIGURE 1.1
Four forms of behavior observed in the laboratory: (a) a man following a moving spot with a stylus, (b) a pigeon pecking at an illuminated disk on the wall, (c) a rat running down a straight alley with food at the end, (d) a change in electrical resistance due to sweat secreted on the palm of a hand.

CARTESIAN DUALISM

In the Middle Ages, the theology of Western Christendom viewed reason as a handmaiden to faith. Faith had resolved the essential nature of man; reason's job was to support faith. Clearly, the intellectual climate was not hospitable to the scientific study of human behavior.

At the dawning of the modern age, science began to question many traditional beliefs. For example, in 1616, Galileo Galilei (1564–1642) earned harsh censure from established authority for denying the theological truth that the earth was fixed at the center of the universe. René Descartes (1596–1650) was about twenty years old when the Church first censured Galileo. When Descartes later undertook to study the nature of man, he found a way to compromise with tradition rather than clashing with it head on.

Descartes was already a great mathematician and philosopher when he published his first essays concerning human and animal behavior. In these essays, he felt obliged to reconcile his findings with the fundamental precepts of theology. Descartes thus took the position—a position adopted by most subsequent philosophers*—that there are two broad classes of human behavior: voluntary and involuntary. Descartes said that voluntary behavior is governed by the mind (a nonphysical entity) and that involuntary behavior has nothing to do with the mind, but instead is purely mechanical—as mechanical as the behavior of animals. According to theology, animals had no souls; Descartes therefore considered them to be essentially like clockwork mechanisms. For this reason, their behavior could be studied directly.

Descartes may have gotten the idea that many human behaviors could also be mechanical from watching the movements of the mechanical statues constructed by ingenious seventeenth-century architects and hydraulic engineers. Many of these grotesque mechanical figures were activated, like the chimes of clocks, by internal forces, but some had a unique feature—they were triggered unknowingly by the observer of the mechanism. For instance, as the observer walked down a path he stepped on a hidden treadle that activated a hydraulic mechanism that, in turn, caused a grinning Saracen automaton to emerge from the bushes brandishing a sword. (Similar mechanisms are still to be found at amusement parks like Disneyland). To Descartes, this feature of the mechanisms, their response to a signal from the environment, was critically important. He reasoned that if human behavior could be simulated so well by these mechanical figures, then perhaps some of the principles on which the mechanisms operated also applied to the humans they were designed to imitate.

Figure 1.2 is a diagram by which Descartes showed operation of an involuntary, purely mechanical, act. The overall effect is that the fire (A), touching the foot (B) of the boy, causes him to withdraw his foot. The mechanism acts

---

*The term "scientist" was not coined until 1840.

FIGURE 1.2
This illustration from Descartes' *De Homine* was
designed to show the response of an organism to a
stimulus. [From Fearing, 1930.]

through the nerve. The lower end of the nerve is set in motion by the fire, and
this motion is transmitted upwards to the brain (de) ". . . just as, by pulling
one of the ends of a cord, you cause a bell attached to the other end to ring at
the same time." At the brain, a substance (which Descartes called "animal
spirits") is released from the cavity (F). The animal spirits travel back down
the nerve, swell the muscle in the calf, and cause the foot to be pulled back.
At the same time, animal spirits go to the eyes, head, and hand to direct them
toward the fire. Although this primitive explanation is crude by today's stan-
dards, it was a great departure from earlier conceptions of the workings of the
body in that it tried to explain the boy's action in physical terms—without
recourse to his will, his mind, or his emotions.

The dualism of Descartes' psychology is the feature that is essential to our
understanding of the history of psychology. As we have noted, both mind and
body were considered necessary to explain the totality of human behavior.
Figure 1.3 is a schematic diagram of human behavior as it was conceived by
Descartes. In his view, objects in the physical world affect the sense organs,
which send messages through the nerves to the brain. At the brain, two things

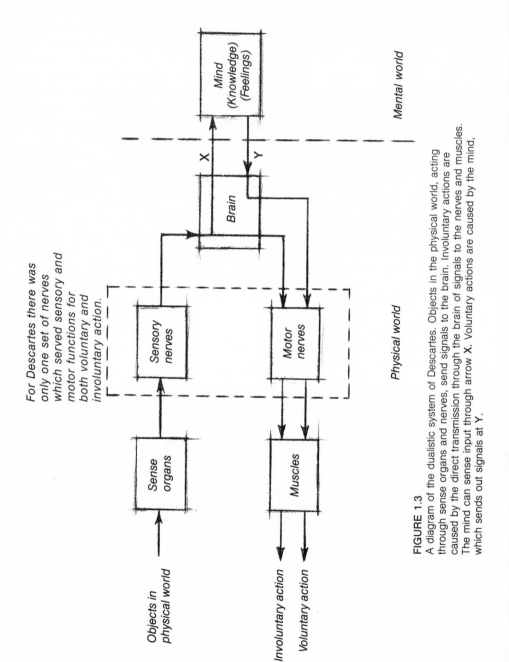

*For Descartes there was
only one set of nerves
which served sensory and
motor functions for
both voluntary and
involuntary action.*

FIGURE 1.3
A diagram of the dualistic system of Descartes. Objects in the physical world, acting through sense organs and nerves, send signals to the brain. Involuntary actions are caused by the direct transmission through the brain of signals to the nerves and muscles. The mind can sense input through arrow X. Voluntary actions are caused by the mind, which sends out signals at Y.

happen. First, in a purely mechanical way, the brain causes action by sending animal spirits through the nerves to the muscles. (This mechanical chain of effects from the sense organs to the brain and back to the muscles, by means of the nerves, eventually became known as a *reflex arc.*) At the same time, the body interacts with the mind at the pineal gland, near the center of the brain. This interaction allows the mind to be aware of both kinds of the body's actions—reflex, involuntary actions, over which it has no control, as well as voluntary actions, over which it exercises complete control. All actions involve the same nerves and muscles, but voluntary actions originate in the mind, a nonphysical realm, and involuntary actions originate in objects in the physical world. Only humans possess the extra pathway that leads to voluntary action (Figure 1.3). According to Descartes, since much behavior (including all animal behavior) is as mindless as the behavior of a stone, it can be considered subject to the same physical laws that govern a stone's behavior. On the other hand, the actions of the mind are not subject to physical laws but are determined by other laws, unknown, and perhaps unknowable.

The effect of Descartes' dualism was to divide up the study of behavior: involuntary behavior came to be studied by physiologists specializing in the study of the body; voluntary behavior remained in the realm of philosophers. These two branches of study had, at first, virtually nothing in common. They are of interest here because they gave rise to two distinct methods of collecting psychological data. We shall discuss first the mental branch of study and then the physical branch of study that grew out of Descartes' dualism.

THE MIND

Psyche is a Greek word meaning breath, spirit, or soul. Originally, psychology was that branch of knowledge that dealt with the human soul or mind. (Although "soul" and "mind" are not synonyms, the concepts are inextricably linked and the terms are often used interchangeably.) According to the dualism of Descartes, the mental world (which was identified with the soul) was the true realm of psychology, and the physical world—including the human body—was outside that realm.*

Introspection

In the age of Descartes, the concept of mind provided the very basis of philosophical speculation concerning human nature. How could the mind be studied? As we have noted, the study of mind through behavior was held to

---

*The modern psychologist turns these priorities around: for him, the object of psychology is to study behavior. He feels required to look for the explanation of all human and animal behavior wherever his quest takes him. His ultimate objective is to explain behavior. If the concept of mind is useful in that respect, it must be part of his explanation. If it proves not to be useful, he is free to ignore it.

be impossible because (1) involuntary behavior was not determined by the mind; (2) voluntary behavior, which was governed by the mind, was considered to be unpredictable, determined by man's free will. Since the only observation a philosopher could make of others was their behavior (speech being included as a form of behavior), the minds of others were closed to him.

The most that one can do, these philosophers contended, is to study one's own mind by looking inward. Such a study was thought to be reliable because the information carried from the body to the mind (arrow X, Figure 1.3) was considered to be orderly and to affect the mind in orderly ways.

To this day introspection remains a common technique for studying mental activity.

Innate Ideas

If we accept, for the time being, the notion that the mind can be examined by introspection, and that the object of the examination is to determine the nature and origin of its contents, we can focus on one of the key questions that troubled Descartes and the philosophers who came after him. That is, to what extent does the information entering the mind from the senses (arrow X in Figure 1.3) determine the contents of the mind? In other words, what is the effect of experience on ideas and emotions?

All philosophers agree that experience plays an important part in forming ideas. As we learn more about the world around us, our ideas change radically. A baby, for instance, sees a coin as a toy or as something to put in his mouth; an adult sees it quite differently. The question under debate was not whether experience modifies our ideas, but *to what extent* it modifies our ideas. Descartes himself, while believing that experience played a role in forming some of our concepts of the world, held that our most basic ideas are innate. That is, they are common to all human beings simply because they are qualities of the soul and because all human beings possess a soul. The idea of God, the idea of the self, the geometrical axioms, (for example, that a straight line is the shortest distance between two points), the ideas of space, time, and motion are thus all said to be innate; experience is thus believed to fill in the details. (For example, experience can tell you what sort of objects move fast and what sort of objects move slowly or stay still, but the basic idea of motion in the world is present before experience.)

Those who hold that there are innate ideas, or that innate ideas are more basic and important than what is learned from experience are called "nativists." Those who deny the existence of innate ideas or hold that the idea of innate ideas is relatively unimportant are called "empiricists." The controversy between nativists and empiricists is a theme that runs through philosophy and psychology to the present day. However, contemporary psychologists (who de-emphasize *mind* as an explanatory concept) argue not about innate ideas but about innate *patterns of behavior*. Note that the nativism-versus-empiricism dispute can apply to both halves of Descartes' bifurcated model of man. Although we have been discussing innate ideas, that is, inborn mental qualities, there are also innate physical qualities. Just as one can argue about the extent to which the idea of space is modified by experience, one can also argue about the extent to which the structure of the nervous system is modified by the environment. By and large, the beliefs of most contemporary psychologists fall somewhere between extreme nativism and extreme empiricism. Descartes, who is usually considered a nativist, played a role in the development of empiricism. For example, although he held that the idea of space was innate, he showed how experience might give rise to the ideas of size and distance.

The more extreme view, that all or almost all ideas are due to experience, was not formulated until after Descartes' death. The development of this more extreme form of empiricism took place in England, and its adherents came to be known as the "British associationists." This school of philosophy was a direct predecessor of experimental psychology, and we shall turn to it next (after a cautionary note).

WARNING

Because this chapter is about the historical background of behaviorism, we shall discuss a number of doctrines. So far we have mentioned mentalism, nativism, empiricism, and British associationism. Once we grasp the principles that underlie such doctrines, we are tempted to use "isms" as handy categories in which to group various philosophers and psychologists. This tendency should be resisted. Nativism and empiricism, for instance, should not be regarded as two boxes into which philosophers may be sorted. These two terms are better regarded as marking ends of a continuum that has an infinite number of gradations. Although, in our frame of reference; we see that philosophers X and Y are both relatively nativistic, X may have seen Y as an empiricist and may have spent most of his life arguing against Y's empiricism. The relativity of such perspectives is especially important when we discuss the British associationists. From our point of view, two centuries later, it seems that they had so much in common that their thinking can be labeled with one "ism." We therefore ignore many of their differences. Nevertheless, we must be aware that there *were* differences; that the differences were sometimes important; that when we class a given philosopher as a British associationist, we are not saying all there is to say about the characteristics of his individual philosophy.

Principles of Association

The British empiricists accepted Descartes' dualistic theory of human nature (Figure 1.3). They also accepted Descartes' belief that the seat of knowledge is the mind; they generally agreed with him that the proper subject for psychological study is the mind of man; they accepted his idea that the mind could be known by "reflection upon itself," in other words, by introspection. However, they did not accept Descartes' notion that man is born with a set of ideas. Their basic axiom was that all knowledge must come from the senses. Man may be born with the capacity to acquire knowledge, but everything we know, they held, comes from our experience. If we lived different lives, if our experiences were different, if we had been transported to a foreign land in infancy, then our knowledge would be different, and we would be, essentially, different people. This assumption is stated clearly by John Locke, one of the earlier associationists, in 1690 in *An Essay Concerning Human Understanding:*

> Let us then suppose the Mind to be, as we say, white Paper, void of all Characters, without any *Ideas;* How comes it to be furnished? Whence comes it by that vast store, which the busie and boundless Fancy of Man has painted on it, with an almost endless variety? Whence has it all the materials of Reason and Knowledge? To this I answer, in one word, From *Experience:* In that, all our Knowledge is founded; and from that it ultimately derives it self. Our observation employ'd either about *external, sensible Objects; or about the internal Operations of our Minds, perceived and reflected on by our selves, is that, which supplies our Understandings with all the materials of thinking.* These two are the Fountains of Knowledge, from whence all the *Ideas* we have, or can naturally have, do spring.

The empiricists held that all knowledge comes from the senses. But the senses, by themselves (unaided by innate ideas), could provide only sensations: eyes alone could detect a spot of color but could hardly provide the knowledge that the spot of color is a round red ball.

The empiricists faced a dilemma. If we have no innate idea of a book, how do we know that a patch of light that is before us is an object that can be opened and read? that when we open it we can expect to find print on the pages? that the pages will be numbered consecutively? How do we know, in fact, that this object will not disappear after we have touched it? that it is capable of being lifted up without falling apart? or, for that matter, that it won't bite us or explode and destroy us? In other words, how is the mere sight of the object associated with sensations we do not feel but can *expect* to feel once we have lifted the object, opened it, and started to read it?

What the empiricists needed to find was some sort of "mental glue" to hold together all of the sensations capable of being experienced from a given object. "Association"—hardly a new idea—served this purpose. Aristotle (384–322 B.C.) formulated one of the first sets of associationist principles. He said that we remember things together (1) when they are similar, (2) when they contrast, and (3) when they are contiguous. This last principle, that of "contiguity" is by far the most important, since all subsequent formulations of the principles of association contain it. It is perhaps worth stating formally:

> If two (or more) sensations are felt at the same time often enough, then one alone felt later can invoke the memory of the other (or others).

To summarize, then, the empiricists took as their basic axiom: All knowledge comes from the senses. Realizing that isolated sensations cannot convey the meanings or the connotations of objects, these philosophers adopted a further principle to explain how sensations are connected. This principle was the principle of association by contiguity: If sensations occur together often enough, one alone can cause the memory of the rest.

The task of the empiricists then became to explain how the principle of contiguity acts in particular instances to produce complex experiences from simple sensations.

Visual Distance

One kind of complex experience that concerned the associationists was the experience of distance. The world appears to us in three dimensions, yet the retina of the eye is a thin, fairly flat surface. How does the three-dimensionality of experience come from impressions on the retina? According to the associationist George Berkeley (1685-1753), one possibility was that our idea of visual distance comes from the sensation of moving the pupils of the eyes together. Here is Berkeley's argument. For closer objects we have to move our eyes closer together to focus the objects; for farther objects we must move them apart. The sensations in the muscles of the eyes correspond to the distance of the objects. Other, nonvisual sensations corresponding to distance are those involved in reaching for or walking to the object. These sensations of walking, reaching, and so forth, become attached to the sensations in the muscles of the eyes by association by contiguity. In other words, whenever we have to reach only a short distance to touch an object, our pupils have to move close together to focus on the object. Whenever we have to reach far to touch an object, our pupils must move farther apart. Thus, the movement of our pupils and the movement of our hands become associated, and when we look at an object without touching it and only our pupils move, we remember the other sensation—that of our hands moving. This memory of our hands' greater or lesser movement is, according to Berkeley, what we mean when we say an object is far away from us or near.*

Meaning

Another problem faced by the associationists was that of meaning. How do we learn, for instance, the meaning of the word "chair?" The solution of this problem by the associationist James Mill (1773-1836) was essentially an extension of Berkeley's solution of the problem of perceived distance. Here, in brief, is James Mill's reasoning. As we experience chairs in our lifetime,

---

*Berkeley seems to have favored different explanations at different times. This account of his argument is based on proposition 45 in "An essay towards a new theory of vision," Dublin, 1709. Reprinted in Berkeley, *Works on Vision* (Indianapolis: Bobbs-Merrill, 1963, p. 39).

we see them, touch them, sit on them, and so forth. All these activities in relation to chairs produce their own sensations as well as containing many sensations in common. The "sittableness" of a chair is an association of the visual experience of chairs with the kinesthetic sensation of sitting. Also, the simultaneous seeing and hearing of the word "chair" produces sensations that become associated with each other and with the sensations resulting from the sight and touch of chairs. These all mix together in a huge bundle so that when we hear the word "chair" the memories or ideas of all the other sensations come to our minds. These memories and ideas were conceived by Mill to be less vivid than the actual sensations, but otherwise identical to them. The meaning of a word would thus be nothing but the bundle or total sum of associated ideas called to mind when the word is spoken or read. (Figure 1.4 illustrates the process by which meaning is established.)

Mental Chemistry

A more sophisticated concept of meaning was advanced by James Mill's son, John Stuart Mill (1806–1873), whose thinking was clearly influenced by the advancing science of chemistry. The younger Mill suggested that simple ideas might interact in a way analogous to a chemical process rather than by simply mixing together like salt and pepper. John Stuart Mill argued that just as the properties of water differ from those of its elements, hydrogen and oxygen, the properties of the meaning or connotation of a word could differ from the properties of the sensations that went into forming it. As he wrote:

> When many impressions or ideas are operating in the mind together, there sometimes takes place a process, of a similar kind to chemical combination. When impressions have been so often experienced in conjunction, that each of them calls up readily and instantaneously the ideas of the whole group, those ideas sometimes melt and coalesce into one another, and appear not several ideas but one . . . [Mill, 1843]

The idea that the operations of the mind could be studied in an experiment was a direct outgrowth of such speculations by the British associationists. The groundwork for experimental psychology was laid when the apparent chaos of our thoughts, the infinitude of images and ideas that seem to float so haphaz-

---

FIGURE 1.4
(a) A common view of the way meaning becomes established through association. The sketch shows a child touching a chair and hearing his mother say the word "chair." The diagram shows the inputs to the various sensory systems of the child. The three sensations occur together and are associated with one another by the child. (b) This sketch shows the child at a later time, hearing the word "chair" when there is no chair present. The diagram shows that the word "chair" is now associated with past visual and tactile sensations.

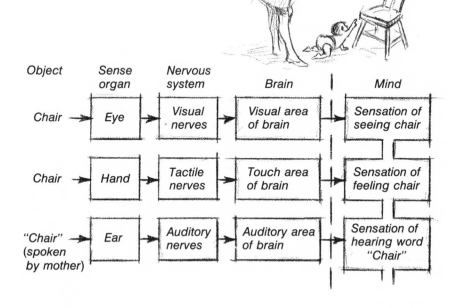

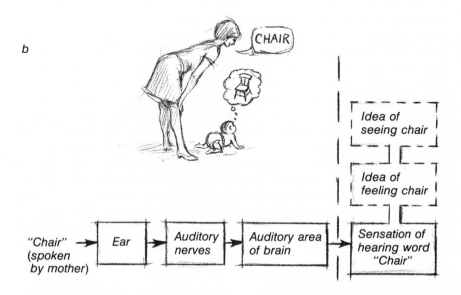

ardly in our minds, was seen to be a function of a restricted set of elements ("sensations") and of principles of association. The early experiments in mental experimental psychology took two forms: studies of sensations themselves and studies of their combination.

Studies of Sensation

The idea that a sensation, as it occurs in the mind, is not identical to a sensory process in the body had been present since ancient times, but the idea that sensation as a mental phenomenon could be studied and measured seems to have come into being in German universities in the nineteenth century. It is to that time and place that most experimental psychologists today trace the origins of their science.

The first psychological experiments sought to explain the way in which sensory impulses pass from the physical world to the mental world (arrow X in Figure 1.3). Two lines of investigation started separately and eventually fused. One line studied the intensity of sensations and the other studied the quality of sensations. Let us discuss each of them in turn.

Intensity of Sensations

To some early investigators, the mental world, in contrast to the physical world, seemed discontinuous. Consider the following hypothetical experiment. Imagine a light controlled by a dial capable of producing a continuous range of intensity from complete blackness to blindingly intense light (Figure 1.5). An experimenter, starting at zero, turns the dial up very slowly until a subject reports that he can see some light. The amount that the intensity must increase from zero before light is reported is called the *absolute threshold* (or "absolute limen"). Then the dial is turned farther, until the subject reports that the light is noticeably brighter than it was before. Then it is turned farther still, until the subject again reports an increase in brightness. Each interval of brightness between reports is called a *just noticeable difference* (jnd). As the light is continuously increased in physical intensity, the intensity of the sensation (brightness) seems to go up in discrete jumps, each jump corresponding to a jnd. It was noticed by Ernst Heinrich Weber (1795-1878) that for many different stimuli there was an orderly relation of jnd's to the magnitude of the stimulus. The bigger the stimulus, the bigger the increase required to notice that the stimulus increased. This relationship, in rough form, is quite obvious in everyday life. If a goldfish grows two inches longer overnight, its owner is likely to notice it the next morning; however, if an elephant grows two inches longer, no one is likely to notice it—even if it takes place in front of his eyes. Weber's significant contribution was quantifying this observation. He stated that the increase in the stimulus for one jnd was exactly proportional to the intensity (or size) of the stimulus. The importance of this correlation was seen by Gustav Theodor Fechner (1801-1887). He reasoned that since all jnd's had in common

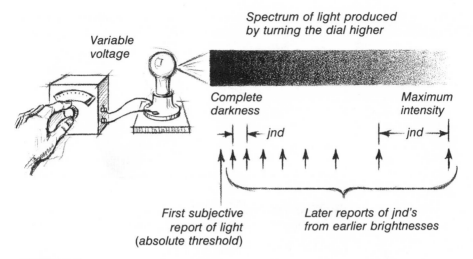

FIGURE 1.5
A light used to measure *just noticeable differences* (jnd's) of brightness. The arrows across the bottom of the brightness spectrum indicate points at which a subject reported a difference in brightness as the brightness was gradually increased. Note that the jnd's at the dark end of the spectrum are smaller than those at the bright end.

the fact that they were the smallest increment it was possible to see, then, as far as the subject who is watching for a change is concerned, any jnd is equivalent to any other (in other words, Fechner reasoned that all jnd's are subjectively equal). But, whereas the jnd's may be *subjectively* equal, they are not *physically* equal. If the jnd's vary in the physical dimension as Weber's theory states, and if all jnd's are subjectively equal, then the relation of subjective to physical size can be plotted (as in Figure 1.6). According to Fechner, in this relationship ". . . one has a general dependent relation between the size of the fundamental stimulus and the size of the corresponding sensation. . . . This permits the amount of sensation to be calculated from the relative amounts of the fundamental stimulus and thus we have a measurement of sensation [Fechner, 1860]." Fechner believed that this relation bridged the gap between the mental (psychic) and physical worlds (arrow X in Figure 1.3). Accordingly he chose the name *psychophysics* for this new science of the measurement of sensations, a name that persists today for the study of sensory magnitude.

Quality of Sensations

The theory of the associationists was that complex mental phenomena could be constructed from a limited group of elements. What, then, are the elements? How can they be distinguished from complex mental phenomena?

Johannes Müller (1801–1858), another German scientist, made the argument that the thing that distinguishes one sensation from another is not the stimulus

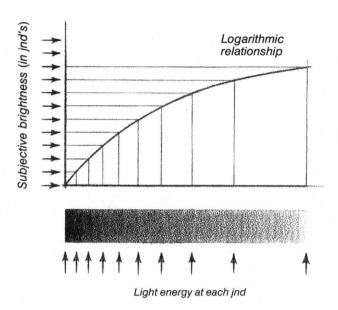

FIGURE 1.6
This graph shows the relationship between jnd's in
brightness and the magnitude of the stimulus (measured
by the voltage regulator). All jnd's are considered to be
subjectively equal.

itself, but the particular nerve stimulated. In other words, a sound seems
different to us from a light, not because sound energy is essentially different
from light energy, but because sound and light activate different nerves. Here
are Müller's views. The mind decides whether a given stimulus was a light or
a sound; if a light, what color; if a sound, what pitch. But the mind has no
contact with the light or sound itself. The mind can only be sensitive to the
nervous impulses leading from the receptors to the brain. The nerves alone tell
the mind what sort of stimulation is impinging on the body. Any one of a certain group of nerves can signal that a sound has occurred (the particular activated nerve corresponds to the pitch of the sound). The ear is constructed so
that it allows sounds of only that particular pitch to stimulate that particular
nerve. But, Müller argued, under certain circumstances the mind can be fooled.
If the energy that usually goes to our ears and causes us to hear a sound could
be made instead to stimulate the nerve that goes from our eyes to our brain,
we would experience the sound as a light. In fact any form of energy that
succeeds in striking the nerve that corresponds to a given sensation would be
capable of causing that sensation. He pointed out that electricity as well as
sound energy could cause us to hear sounds when it was applied to the nerves
of the ears. Müller's contention that the nerve rather than the stimulus deter-

mines the quality of sensation became the doctrine of *specific nerve energies*. This principle led to more questions. How many specific nerve energies are there? In vision, for instance, is there one for each color? In hearing, is there one for each tone?

A great deal of subsequent experimentation was directed towards answering such questions. In vision, for instance, all the colors were shown capable of being constructed by various combinations of three elementary colors, the primaries, red, green, and blue. These, then, could be the elementary sensations that reach the mind, and the vast array of colors that we see could be products of mental chemistry. Similar research was carried out for the other senses. Usually the method used was introspection and verbal report. Early experimental psychologists believed that a person could be trained to analyze his complex experience into its elements. For instance, an untrained observer experiences *wetness* as a unitary sensation, but observers experienced in introspection could analyze the experience of wetness into *pressure* and *cold*. As a check on this analysis it was shown that a dry, cold, uniform pressure on the finger, for instance, cannot be distinguished by a blindfolded observer from actual wetness.

Experiments in the analysis of sensations are still being carried on today, albeit in a more sophisticated way than those described here.

Secondary Laws of Association

Once it is accepted that simultaneously experienced sensations become associated in the mind, there is nothing more that the simple, unvarnished law of association has to say about them. How many times must they be experienced together before becoming associated? Which of several simultaneous sensations are more likely to become associated, or will they all become equally associated? Do sensations, once they become associated, remain so forever, or do they eventually separate again? These questions were not of great importance to the British associationists. However, the early experimental psychologists deemed them to be important because only by answering such questions would they be able to measure associations, and only by measurement would they be able to predict the occurrence of an association. It was the Scottish philosopher Thomas Brown (1778–1820) who first tried to answer these questions by formulating nine laws he called secondary laws of association (the three primary laws being those of Aristotle: contiguity, similarity, contrast). The secondary laws were held to modify the primary laws and to enable one to predict which sensations out of a group of sensations were more likely to become associated. Because of their importance for psychology it is worth listing Brown's secondary laws. They stated that association between sensations is modified by:

1. the length of time during which the original sensations endured
2. the intensity of the original sensations

3. the frequency of their pairing
4. the recency of their pairing
5. the number of other associations in which the sensations to be paired are involved
6. the abilities, capacities, and dispositions of the person experiencing the sensations
7. the emotional state of the person experiencing the sensations
8. the bodily state of the person experiencing the sensations
9. the similarity of the association itself to other, previously acquired, associations

The nine secondary laws of association set forth by Brown, as he himself recognized, contained no new facts but were merely a new way to organize facts that separately were well known. However, new facts about association did come from Hermann Ebbinghaus (1850–1909), who was the first to perform formal experiments in learning. His object was to study the quantitative relations implied by the nine secondary laws of association, particularly the third and fourth, which state that the mental association of two elements is modified by the frequency and recency of their pairing. Ebbinghaus chose nonsense syllables to be the elements he would use in his research and prepared lists of them to be memorized.

Ebbinghaus's nonsense syllables were three-letter combinations like BIV, RUX, JIC, and KEL, with the first letter a consonant, the second a vowel, and the third another consonant. It is worth knowing the claims Ebbinghaus made for nonsense syllables, because similar claims have frequently been made by psychologists about the kinds of material they use in their experiments and about the kinds of behavior they choose to study. In fact, the various, apparently trivial, observations depicted in Figure 1.1 are used in psychological experiments today for some of the same reasons that nonsense syllables were used in Ebbinghaus's classic studies. (Indeed, nonsense syllables themselves are still used in many studies of learning.) The advantages claimed for such materials are:

1. *They are relatively simple.* (It is important to understand the reason behind the search for simplicity in psychology. Many of the experiments that psychologists do will otherwise seem incomprehensible. Essentially, the reason that simplicity is sought is that psychologists hope that the underlying laws of behavior will prove to be simple and that the complexity we observe in everyday life will prove to be the result of the concatenation of simple basic processes. The reason for this hope is that in other sciences a similar hope has frequently been fulfilled. For example, it is virtually impossible for a physicist to predict the everyday behavior of physical objects except in a most general way. When a piece of paper is dropped in a room, it is impossible to predict the path it will take as it

flutters to the floor. But it is relatively easy to predict the path the paper would follow if it were dropped in a vacuum, a simplified environment where several second-order phenomena—like friction and air resistance—are not present. The vacuum is artificial, so is the nonsense syllable. The intent of scientists, however, is the same in both cases: to find an area in which laws operate simply and directly and in which behavior can be easily predicted. Psychologists are continually seeking to devise a test condition that is the psychological equivalent of a physical vacuum, and many of their methods reflect this effort. Just as the vacuum eliminates friction and air resistance, the nonsense syllable, according to Ebbinghaus, eliminates meaning. For Ebbinghaus, as for the earlier associationists, meaning was equivalent to the accumulation of sensations attached to a given word. Because the syllables he devised were not words, not associated with any objects, and therefore not associated with any particular sensations, they had no meaning.)

2. *They are relatively homogeneous.* (This means simply that no one nonsense syllable stands out from the rest.)

3. *They form an inexhaustible amount of new combinations, each of which can be compared to the other.* (In other words, a given list of ten nonsense syllables has no more meaning than any other list of ten nonsense syllables. Also, they may be compared in reverse. That is, CEV MEB has no more meaning than MEB CEV.)

4. *They are capable of quantitative variations, and may be divided at any point.* (The only difference between a list of five nonsense syllables and a list of ten nonsense syllables, no matter how they are arranged, is that the latter is twice as long. On the other hand, consider the differences between these two lists:

I	II
TOM	BUT
MEN	SIX
SIX	MEN
BUT	SAW
HIS	TOM
	GET
	HIS
	BIG
	RED
	CAR

The difference between them is not only that the second is twice as long, but that it is a meaningful sentence whereas the first is not. The second list, although twice as long as the first, is easier for most people to memorize because of its meaning.)

The object of Ebbinghaus's experiments was to use nonsense syllables in a quantitative analysis of the development of associations. He was not satisfied to know merely that greater frequency of pairing leads to greater association. He wanted to know exactly how much pairing was necessary before an association would be formed.

In the course of his investigations, Ebbinghaus studied many different aspects of association. To better understand his method, let us consider one of his experiments. The purpose of this particular experiment was to test the conception that an association is formed in the mind of a subject between all members of a list of nonsense syllables when he reads that list, and that the association is stronger for items on the list that are closer together and weaker for items on the list that are further apart. Consider the "original list" in Figure 1.7. According to Ebbinghaus, once the list is memorized, associations are formed between each item and all the other items. The association between

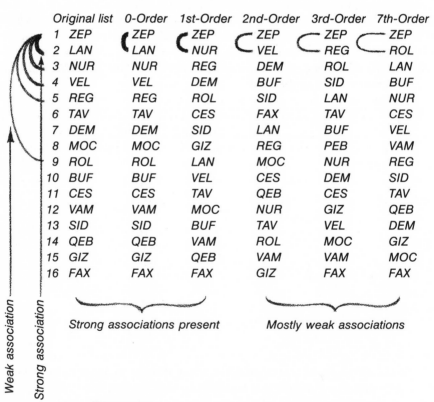

Order of remoteness from original list

Original list	0-Order	1st-Order	2nd-Order	3rd-Order	7th-Order
1 ZEP	ZEP	ZEP	ZEP	ZEP	ZEP
2 LAN	LAN	NUR	VEL	REG	ROL
3 NUR	NUR	REG	DEM	ROL	LAN
4 VEL	VEL	DEM	BUF	SID	BUF
5 REG	REG	ROL	SID	LAN	NUR
6 TAV	TAV	CES	FAX	TAV	CES
7 DEM	DEM	SID	LAN	BUF	VEL
8 MOC	MOC	GIZ	REG	PEB	VAM
9 ROL	ROL	LAN	MOC	NUR	REG
10 BUF	BUF	VEL	CES	DEM	SID
11 CES	CES	TAV	QEB	CES	TAV
12 VAM	VAM	MOC	NUR	GIZ	QEB
13 SID	SID	BUF	TAV	VEL	DEM
14 QEB	QEB	VAM	ROL	MOC	GIZ
15 GIZ	GIZ	QEB	VAM	VAM	MOC
16 FAX	FAX	FAX	GIZ	FAX	FAX

Weak association ⟶   *Strong association* ⟶

Strong associations present   *Mostly weak associations*

FIGURE 1.7
Lists of nonsense syllables prepared by Ebbinghaus.

neighboring items is strongest; the association between distant items is weak. This would imply, for instance, that ZEP LAN becomes strongly associated, ZEP NUR moderately associated, and ZEP ROL only weakly associated. In order to test this notion, Ebbinghaus invented what is called the *savings method*. He memorized several lists like those in the left-hand column of Figure 1.7; 24 hours later, he tried to relearn the same lists. The relearning of the lists, he found, took an average of 420 seconds less than the learning of the original list. The 420 seconds he saved he considered to be a measure of the strength of the associations 24 hours after they were formed. He reasoned that if he had forgotten the list completely he would have shown no saving (learning and relearning times would be equal), and if he had remembered the list completely he would have maximum saving (relearning time would equal zero). Thus, the amount of time saved would be an index of how well he had remembered the list.

Then he constructed, from the original list, a series of derived lists. "A derived list of zero order" is simply the original list. A derived list of the first order contains the items of the original list so arranged that all but one of the adjacent items in the derived list were separated by one item in the original list. A derived list of the second order is arranged so that most of the adjacent items in the new list were originally separated by two items. Higher order derived lists were constructed by the same principle. If, as Ebbinghaus theorized, the association on the original list was greatest for adjacent items, then a zero-order derived list, which retains the same adjacent items, should produce the most saving. A first–order derived list, which contains items from the original list spaced one item apart, should produce less saving. A second–order derived list with items spaced two apart should show still less, and so on. When the experiment was performed, this was exactly what Ebbinghaus found. A graph showing the decreasing amount of saving as the associations on the list became more remote is shown in Figure 1.8.

The experiments of Ebbinghaus were the first formal experiments in association, just as the experiments of Weber and Fechner were the first formal experiments in sensation. The goal of these experiments was to describe and measure scientifically the properties of the mind. The subjects were invariably human. The data collected was in the form of verbal reports. The preferred method of obtaining this data was by introspection on the part of the subject, although whether Ebbinghaus's experiments really relied on introspection is open to question. The introspective method in which the experimenter and subject are the same person was so influential, however, that even in his rather objective experiments, Ebbinghaus always served as his own subject.

For many years all scientists who called themselves psychologists were engaged in studying mental phenomena by methods like these. In the early part of the present century, however, such methods were seriously challenged by physiologists who claimed that pheomena such as memory, emotion, and

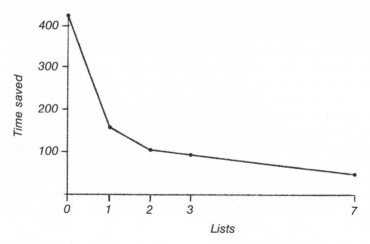

FIGURE 1.8
Results of Ebbinghaus's experiment. This graph shows that the amount
of time saved in relearning lists decreases as a function of their
remoteness from the original list (0). The time saved is the number of
seconds required to learn the original list minus the number of seconds
required to learn one of the derived lists 24 hours later.

knowledge, hitherto seen as mental, were actually capable of being explained
as bodily functions. Thus, they contended, the proper people to study such
phenomena were not psychologists trained in introspection, but physiologists
trained in analyzing the discrete and delicate functions of the body and, in
particular, the system of nerves that regulate bodily functions.

THE BODY

For a hundred years after Descartes, the methods of investigating the mind
and the body could not have been more widely separated. On one hand, the
British associationists and the German experimental psychologists studied
the mind of man by means of introspection. On the other hand, physiologists
studied the body by methods akin to those of physics. In general, the physiologists accepted Descartes' division: psychology, the study of the mind; physiology, the study of the body.

However, as their science gained precision, physiologists could account
for much of the behavior previously thought to be controlled by the mind.
For instance, in the seventeenth century, physiologists showed that after death
(when, presumably, the soul had left the body) hearts could be kept beating.
In fact, instances of hearts beating when removed entirely from the body were
reported. Today we know that the heart operates like a muscle and that muscles

can be activated by stimulating them appropriately even when they are detached from the body, but in the seventeenth century most people believed that the soul gave life to the heart. There are two possible resolutions to the problem that was posed by the observation that the heart, the muscles, and other organs were capable of functioning separately from the body. First of all, one could say that each of these organs had a soul—an animating force—of its own. This resolution was counter to the traditional belief that a human soul was in essence an *immortal entity:* such an entity obviously could not be divided up into several bits and pieces, some of which remained in human organs after death. The other solution to the problem was to deny that the soul had anything to do with the operation of the organs and to say that human organs worked "mechanically," like those of animals. This was the position that most physiologists took and the notion that is generally accepted today. (Not many people object to heart transplant operations on the grounds that they interfere with a patient's soul.)

With each new advance, the physiologists found mechanistic explanations for processes that were traditionally held to be controlled by the mind. Some people reasoned that physiology might continue to advance until it eventually captured the entire province of the mind. Might not all human behavior eventually be explained in mechanistic terms? By this reasoning, to say that a function was "controlled by the mind" was the same as saying that its causes were unknown, and that physiology had not yet advanced far enough to explain it. Perhaps Descartes' dualism was wrong, ran this mechanistic reasoning, and perhaps human behavior as well as animal behavior could eventually be explained without any reference to an animating force like the mind or the soul. In the words of Julian Offray De La Mettrie (1709-1751), one of the first thinkers to espouse a completely mechanical explanation of behavior:

> To be a machine, to feel, to think, to know how to distinguish good from bad, as well as blue from yellow, in a word, to be born with an intelligence and a sure moral instinct, and to be but an animal, are therefore characters which are no more contradictory, than to be an ape or a parrot and to be able to give one's self pleasure . . . I believe that thought is so little incompatible with organized matter, that it seems to be one of its properties on a par with electricity, the faculty of motion, impenetrability, extension, etc. [La Mettrie, 1748]

Most physiologists did not go so far as La Mettrie, preferring mechanical explanations for those functions of the body that they could bring under their scrutiny, and mental explanations for those functions that they had not yet investigated.

The subsequent physiological investigations that had the greatest effect on psychology were those that dealt with the reflex, that is, with the direct response of an organism to a stimulus in the environment. (We recall Descartes' example of the boy recoiling from the fire.)

As recently as the beginning of the twentieth century, there were still two principal areas of behavior that remained virtually unaffected by physiological research and almost wholly within the province of the mind:

1. Behavior seeming to arise from within the person himself, such as (*a*) an apparently voluntary raising of the arm for which no cause or stimulus can be found in the environment or (*b*) complex behavior (singing an operatic aria in the shower, for instance) for which no correspondingly complex environmental stimulus can be found.
2. Learning. Most reflexes seem to be permanently fixed in the body. How can they explain learning to sing a song, for instance, or learning a whole repertoire of songs?

However, it was in the late nineteenth century and early twentieth century that the Russian physiologists Ivan Michailovich Sechenov (1829–1905) and Ivan Petrovich Pavlov (1849–1936) asserted that even these two areas of behavior could be understood in terms of reflexes.

In the next several sections, we shall trace the history of the physiological investigation of the reflex. We shall see how the concept of the reflex has become vital in psychology, especially in the study of learning. Let us begin by returning to the world of Descartes to look for the origins of the concept of reflex action in early discussions of nervous conduction.

Nervous Conduction

In general, early theories of nervous conduction held that the mind governs behavior through the transmission of some kind of vapor or substance to the muscles. Such theories reflected both traditional doctrine and the state of knowledge in the physical sciences. For Descartes, nervous conduction was based on a hydraulic model. As we recall, his opinion was that the soul interacts with the body in the pineal gland, near the middle of the brain. This gland, he thought, directs "animal spirits" through the nerves to activate the muscles mechanically. In 1662, he wrote that even though animal spirits must be "very mobile and subtle, they nevertheless have the force to swell and tighten the muscles within which they are enclosed, just as the air in a balloon hardens it and causes the skin containing it to stretch." (See Figure 1.9.)

Descartes' views were highly influential. For a hundred years, controversy raged, not about whether animal spirits existed, but rather about what they consisted of. Some physiologists rejected Descartes' hydraulic model and adopted a pneumatic model; that is, they claimed that a gas, rather than a liquid, runs from the nerves to the muscles. Some (called iatro-physicists) claimed that there is a mechanical transmission of force, and others (called iatro-chemists) claimed that the phenomenon is basically a chemical process. This speculation was generally nonexperimental. A clear experimental advance, however, was made by Francis Glisson (1597–1677), who showed in 1677 that whatever

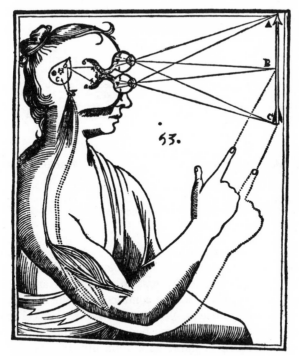

FIGURE 1.9
The central role of the pineal gland in Descartes'
physiology is shown in the diagram from *l'Homme*.
Images fall on retinas (5, 3, 1) and are conveyed to the
cerebral ventricles (6, 4, 2); these then form a single
binocular image on the pineal gland (H), the site from
which the soul controls the body. Stimulated by the
image, the soul inclines the pineal gland, activating the
"hydraulic system" of the nerves (8), causing a muscle
to move (at 7). [Courtesy of The Bodleian Library,
Oxford University.]

nervous conduction occurs when muscles contract, it does not consist of the
transfer of a substance, either liquid or gas, from the nerves to the muscles.
Glisson's experiment was simple. He had a subject put his hand in a tube full
of water, as shown in Figure 1.10, and then contract and relax his muscles.
When the muscles were contracted Glisson found that the height of the water
did not increase above the height for relaxed muscles, showing that no substance could be flowing into the muscles when they were contracted. From this
evidence, it followed that muscles work by themselves once they receive proper
stimulation. The question that remained was: what sort of stimulation do the
nerves supply to the muscles?

Actually, a more sophisticated experiment had been done by John Swammerdam (1637–1680), prior to Glisson's work, but had not become widely

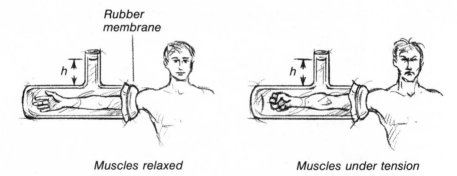

FIGURE 1.10
Glisson's experiment showing that muscles do not gain in substance when they are
contracted. The height of the water, h, is the same whether the subject's arm is tensed
or relaxed.

known. In 1660 Swammerdam had surgically isolated a nerve and muscle of
a frog and had shown that mechanical stimulation of the nerve was sufficient
to contract the muscle. In other words, no infusion of animal spirits or any
other substance was necessary for the contraction of the muscle; simple irritation of the nerve was sufficient. Whether such a mechanical irritation is the
actual process that takes place in the body when a muscle is contracted was
another question. Figure 1.11 shows some of the illustrations of Swammerdam's
experiments with nerves and muscles of frogs—experiments that have been
repeated by countless students of elementary physiology.

In general, until late in the eighteenth century, some kind of mechanical
conduction of energy was held to activate muscles, but the question of the
exact nature of the energy was not resolved. For instance, according to David
Hartley (1705–1766)—whose ideas we shall refer to again later—the nervous
impulse consisted of minute mechanical vibrations transmitted through the
nerve like a wave. By the beginning of the nineteenth century, physiologists
came to agree that however nerves might work, they were not adequately
explained by references to animal spirits, mind, or soul.

Around 1800 there was great interest in electricity and much fruitful study
of the subject. Some scientists speculated that nervous conduction might be
electrical. As research progressed in the middle of the nineteenth century, it
became increasingly clear that some form of electrical impulse was present in
the nerve. Today, the nerve impulse is thought to be a combination of electrical
and chemical events.

So we have, in the history of speculation about nervous conduction and
research into its nature, a progression of theories—hydraulic to pneumatic to
vibratory to electrical and chemical. These theories became more sophisticated
and complex as the physical sciences offered successively better ways to understand the way the human body functions.

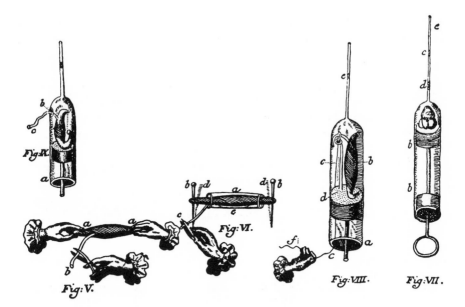

FIGURE 1.11
Early illustrations of Swammerdam's experiments. [From Fearing, 1930.]

The Reflex Arc

To those who have considered animal behavior (and much of human behavior) to be machinelike, the basic element of that machinelike behavior has been the *reflex arc,* the pathway leading from the sense organs through the nerves to the muscles. Descartes thought that sensory and motor signals travel through the same nerve. According to him, the sensory signal from the sense organ to the brain operated like a pull chain; the motor signal was hydraulic, consisting of the flow of animal spirits down through the nerve and into the muscle.

After Descartes' time, experimenters began to dissect animals to look for the organs necessary for various reflex functions. They found that certain parts of the nervous system (for instance, the cerebrum of the brain) could be entirely removed without destroying most reflexes; but they also found that severing some parts (notably, the spinal cord) immediately destroyed reflexes. This kind of investigation of the body may be compared to a mechanical investigation of an unknown machine. In order to discover whether a certain part of the machine is necessary for a certain function, you could remove or disconnect that part and see what functions are impaired. Does the carburetor of an automobile belong to its steering mechanism? One way to find out is to remove the carburetor and see if you can still steer the automobile. Because of experiments of this nature with animals, physiologists began to look upon the spinal cord and the base of the brain—but not the cerebrum—as necessary centers of reflex action. But what happens in the spinal cord or base of the brain between the input and output was still a matter for speculation. According to George Prochaska (1749-1820), an early reflexologist, "This part, in which, as in a centre, the sensorial nerves, as well as the motor nerves, meet and communicate, and in which the impressions made on the sensorial nerves are reflected on the motor nerves, is designated by a term, now adopted by most physiologists, the *sensorium commune* [Prochaska, 1784]." But it was not clear in Prochaska's time, nor is it fully clear today, exactly what occurs in the *sensorium commune,* now called the central nervous system.

Although information on the central nervous system was scanty in the eighteenth century, physiologists were able to make lists of types of behavior that they thought were governed by reflexes. Table 1.1 shows one made in 1749 by Hartley, classified according to the sense organ stimulated.

Table 1.1

Special Sense	Automatic Motion
1. "Feeling"—touch, pain	Crying, distortion of face, laughter following tickling, grasping, putting muscles into contraction following painful stimulation.
2. Taste	Sucking, mastication, deglutition, distortion of mouth, peristaltic motion of stomach and bowels, vomiting, hiccough, expulsion of faeces, spasms.
3. Smell	Inspiration of air to "increase" odor, contraction of the fauces and gullet, sneezing.
4. Sight	Motions of globe of eye, motions of the eyelid, contractions of the lacrymal glands, contractions of the muscular rings of the iris, and the ciliar ligaments.
5. Hearing	Contraction of small muscles of the auricle in adjusting to sound, contraction of muscles belonging to small bones of the ear.

In the early nineteenth century, physiologists began to develop a better picture of reflex mechanisms. In independent experiments with animals, Francois Magendie (1783-1855) and Charles Bell (1774-1842) discovered that when they cut the posterior branch of spinal nerves in an experimental animal, the animal could still move the innervated limb but did not react to a pinprick on the limb, whereas, when they cut the anterior branch of nerves, the animal responded to a pinprick but was not able to move the limb. This discovery established a clear distinction between nerves with a sensory function and nerves with a motor function. Meanwhile, lists of reflexes such as Hartley's were being expanded. Postural reflexes, such as those that allow a man to walk on a tilting ship, or allow a cat to land on its feet when dropped upside down, and tendon reflexes, such as the knee jerk, were studied in detail. However, no matter how the list of automatic actions was extended, there still remained a host of actions, including most of the complex actions of everyday life, such as speaking, reading, and writing, that were unexplained by the physiologists and therefore classified as voluntary acts. We now turn to the attempt by the Russian physiologists Sechenov and Pavlov to explain such complex acts mechanistically.

Complex Behavior

Although the notion that all behaviors could be classified as either voluntary or involuntary (automatic) was a basic legacy of the dualism of Descartes, many observable behaviors simply could not be fit into either classification. Sneezing and laughing seem involuntary enough, yet they can be suppressed; with much practice, some people have even learned to exert some control over the size of the pupils of their eyes. And what about breathing? We normally consider it to be quite automatic. But when a doctor puts a stethoscope to our chest we breathe in and out at his command; we can also hold our breath at will for short periods of time.

A different type of hard-to-classify behavior is represented by fast and accurate typing. Most skilled typists say that fast typing is automatic, and that they do not concentrate on the pressing of each individual key. In fact, if they try to think of each key, they slow down considerably. Yet, clearly, when someone starts learning to type, he or she must concentrate on each key that is struck. This voluntary effort seems to become involuntary with practice. A similar shift from voluntary to automatic behavior can be seen in the acquisition of almost any skill. As an advertisement for a standard-shift Volkswagen puts it, "After a while, it becomes automatic."

Recognizing (1) the tendency of many voluntary acts to develop into involuntary acts and (2) the modifiability of many involuntary acts, nineteenth-century physiologists had to admit that they knew little or nothing about many forms of behavior. Nevertheless, they persisted in their hope that the idea of reflexes would eventually explain all behavior of organisms.

It was Sechenov who attempted to show how complex, apparently voluntary acts, can, in a broad frame of reference, be understood to be essentially involuntary. To demonstrate this, Sechenov had addressed himself to the problem of energy. One of the most basic laws of physics is that of the conservation of energy: any energy that crosses the boundaries into a system must either remain in the system or come out in some other form. For instance, in an automobile engine, the energy contained in the gasoline that enters the engine eventually may leave it in the form of kinetic energy—the energy involved in the motion of the automobile—or in the form of heat lost to the environment, in the form of sound energy, and in the form of the chemical energy remaining in the exhaust gases. If you could keep a record of all the energy going into and coming out of the engine—or any system—you would find that the two amounts are equal.

Many movements of organisms are caused by direct stimuli in the environment. A tap on a human knee, for instance, causes a reflex jerk in the leg. The energy input here is great enough so that it does not stretch the imagination to attribute the energy output of the knee jerk to the energy input of the blow on the knee. This view of the operation of this reflex is illustrated in Figure 1.12. Even though we now know it to be a gross oversimplification, it was nevertheless possible for early physiologists to think of the knee jerk as a mechanism that connected the stimulus to the response by various linkages within the body, with the stimulus providing the energy for the response, just as a blow on a key of a standard typewriter provides the energy for a typebar to

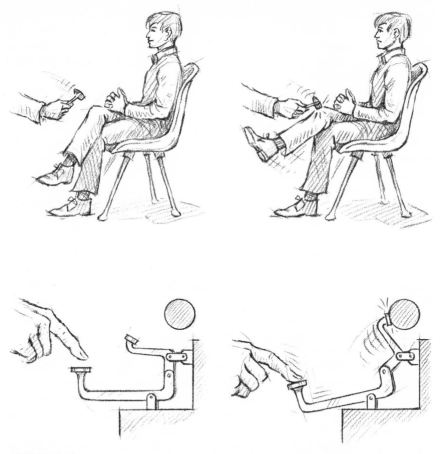

FIGURE 1.12
The reflex conceived of as a simple mechanism. *Above,* a high-energy stimulus from the environment causes a high-energy response in the form of a knee jerk. *Below,* a high-energy blow on a typewriter key causes a typebar to strike the roller.

strike the paper. But consider another reflex: a baby's sneeze. Where is the stimulus that provides the tremendous energy exhibited in a good satisfying sneeze? Could all that energy come from a mote of dust tickling the inside of the baby's nostril? It did not seem to Sechenov that it could. Instead, he proposed another kind of mechanism, one that we can compare to the electric switch that starts a fan. The energy that operates the fan is not supplied by the movement of the switch. The switch merely releases electrical energy to the fan, energy that is far greater than that required to turn the switch. While the switch is turned off, the pathway of electric current is blocked; turning on the switch removes the block. (In the nervous systems of organisms such blocking is called *inhibition,* and the stimulus that removes the inhibition is called a *releasing stimulus.*) Returning to the example of the baby's sneeze, we can think of the energy for the sneeze as stored up in the body of the baby, perhaps from milk drunk the previous day, ready to activate a sneeze at any moment—but normally inhibited from doing so. When the baby's nose is tickled, the energy is released and the baby sneezes. Figure 1.13 illustrates the mechanism. For a long time, explanations of complex behaviors had relied on the idea of inhibitory and releasing mechanisms, but Sechenov was among the first actually to locate them in the body.

In one series of experiments Sechenov measured the time taken by a frog to remove its foot reflexively when an acid stimulus was applied to its extended leg. Then he showed that this reflex could be modified by removing various portions of the frog's brain. Sechenov found, essentially, that the stimulus–response reaction time decreased when he removed certain areas of the brain—indicating that he had removed an inhibitory mechanism. When he put salt on parts of the frog's brain, the stimulus–response reaction time was increased—showing that he had excited an inhibitory mechanism. Figure 1.14 shows how Sechenov supposed this mechanism to work. In a series of experiments with humans, Sechenov showed that people's reflexes work more slowly when they are tickled than when they are not tickled; furthermore, the more tickling the slower the reflexes. In other words, tickling serves to increase the inhibition of reflexes.

Sechenov reasoned that if stimuli with little energy could trigger off and control such relatively violent reactions, then perhaps all of those complex actions that appear to be voluntary (controlled from within the organism by the mind) are actually controlled from outside the organism by stimuli that have so little energy that the organism is not aware of its responses to them. Although the reactions to low-energy stimuli may be slight, they are present, and are, according to Sechenov, purely mechanical. In other words, the small, unnoticed external stimuli have two functions. First, they cause reactions within the brain, reactions we have come to call thoughts. Secondly, they activate or release inhibitions on gross motor reactions. Sechenov says of this sequence:

It is generally accepted that if one act follows another, the two acts stand in causal relationship (post hoc—ergo propter hoc); *this is why thought is generally believed to be the cause of behaviour;* and when the external sensory stimulus remains un-noticed—which happens quite frequently—*thought is even accepted as the initial cause of behaviour.* Add to this the extremely subjective character of thought, and you will understand how firmly man must believe in the voice of self-consciousness, when it tells him such things. In reality, however, this voice tells him the greatest of falsehoods: *the initial cause of all behaviour always lies, not in thought, but in external sensory stimulation, without which no thought is possible.* [Sechenov, 1863]

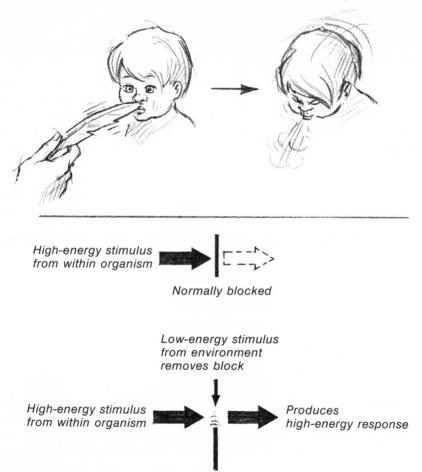

FIGURE 1.13
A low-energy stimulus can produce a high-energy response. This diagram suggests that the main source of energy is within the organism but that it is normally blocked. A low-energy stimulus may temporarily remove the block and thus permit a high-energy response.

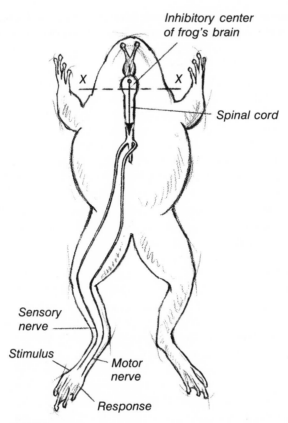

FIGURE 1.14
Sechenov's experiments on inhibition. Sechenov observed
that (1) salt applied to "an inhibitory center" in the frog's
brain slowed down the withdrawal of its leg from an acid,
and (2) severing the frog's nerves at X—X speeded up
the withdrawal.

By this reasoning, Sechenov attempted to draw all the complexity of behavior within the realm of reflexology. No longer was a reflex seen to be a simple chain from stimulus to response; instead, it was seen as a complex machinelike process modified by unnoticed signals from the environment—much like the process by which a radio receives low-energy electromagnetic waves and uses them to modify the high energy from its battery or from an electric outlet so as to generate signals loud enough to be audible.

But no matter how complex a radio may be, it is nevertheless fixed in its construction. If the signal to a radio is repeated, its response will be the same. In this respect, the behavior of an animal cannot be explained by Sechenov's theory. An animal does not always repond in the same way to a repeated stimulus. Its responses are modified, as we have seen, by experience; furthermore, the way in which responses are modified depends on the nature of the experience. It was another Russian physiologist, Pavlov, who was to show how reflexes could be modified by experience.

Pavlov realized that inborn reflex mechanisms, no matter how precise and complex, were not enough to explain the various adjustments that organisms make to their environments. In particular, such mechanisms could not explain the process that the psychologists who studied mental phenomena called *association.* For example, how could an inborn reflex explain the fact that people react strongly not only to heat on their skin, but to the sight of a fire, the smell of smoke, the word "fire" shouted in a loud voice, and the sound of fire engines in the street? Certainly it was too much to imagine that each of these stimuli is connected to an inborn reflex of its own; more likely, such groups of stimuli become associated through experience. But how? Pavlov's investigations were directed mainly towards this question.

The particular reflex that Pavlov and his students studied most closely was the salivary reflex in dogs. (We shall describe these experiments in more detail in Chapter 4.) In general Pavlov found that dogs salivate when any stimulus is presented, such as a bell, a light, the experimenter, or a geometrical pattern, provided that the stimulus has been presented together with food a sufficient number of times. There are parallels between Pavlov's work and Ebbinghaus's. Ebbinghaus presented two nonsense syllables together and observed association. Pavlov presented a neutral arbitrary stimulus (such as a bell) together with a stimulus (food) that was closely linked to a response. Like Ebbinghaus, Pavlov found that the more the paired stimuli are presented together, the greater is the strength of the association. The strength of the association was determined by Pavlov by measuring the amount of saliva secreted when the bell was sounded. As the amount secreted at the sound of the bell approached the amount secreted when food itself was present, the strength of the association was said to be increasing.

Pavlov decided that all organisms must possess two sets of reflexes:

1. *A fixed, innate set of relatively simple reflexes.* (According to Pavlov, the path of these reflexes runs from the sensory nerves through the spinal cord to the motor nerves; these simple reflexes can be modified by innate inhibitory mechanisms, as Sechenov had shown, but essentially they are fixed.)

2. *A set of acquired reflexes.* (These reflexes, called *conditioned* reflexes by Pavlov, are formed by pairing previously neutral stimuli with a stimulus that triggers off an innate reflex; the path of these acquired reflexes goes through the upper parts of the brain, the cerebral hemispheres; when these parts of the brain are removed, the acquired reflexes disappear, leaving only the simple innate reflexes.)

It was Pavlov's view that:

> the basic physiological function of the cerebral hemispheres throughout the . . . individuals life consists in a constant addition of numberless signalling conditioned stimuli to the limited number of the initial inborn unconditioned stimuli, in other words, in constantly supplementing the unconditioned reflexes by conditioned ones. Thus, the objects of the instincts [our desires for food and the like] exert an influence on the organism in ever-widening regions of nature and by means of more and more diverse signs or signals, both simple and complex; consequently, the instincts are more and more fully and perfectly satisfied, i.e., the organism is more reliably preserved in the surrounding nature. [Pavlov, 1955, p. 273]

Pavlov held that we (organisms) steer ourselves through our environments by means of signals conditioned through experience to remove us from trouble and to lead us to the things we need. He contended that all complex learned behavior is brought about through the combination of several simple conditioned reflexes, which are physiological—not mental—processes. He believed that through objective investigations, physiologists would eventually be able to predict all of the behaviors of animals and humans.

THE RELATION OF PHYSIOLOGICAL PSYCHOLOGY TO MENTAL PSYCHOLOGY

In regard to the associationists we pointed out that the parties to theoretical disputes are often seen from the perspective of time as essentially similar in basic outlook. To some extent, this applies to the reflexologists versus the associationists. The reflexologists, like Sechenov and Pavlov, thought that all complex behavior is mechanical; the associationists, like Ebbinghaus, thought that all complex behavior is influenced by the mind. Although these theorists differed in many obvious respects, they nevertheless retained several basic similarities.

Both the associationists and reflexologists believed that complex behavior is the result of the combination of simple elements. The associationists believed that the elements are simple sensations or ideas, that a complex idea is the combination of a group of simple ideas, and that the blending of simple ideas into complex ones takes place in the mind. The reflexologists believed that the elements are simple reflexes, that a complex action or behavior is the combination of a group of simple reflexes, and that the blending of simple reflexes into complex ones takes place in the brain.

The parallels between the basic concepts of these two outgrowths of Descartes' dualism, although often obscured, were not unnoticed at the time. Both the mentalists and Pavlov claimed that conditioned reflexes might shed light on the concept of association. Even as early as the eighteenth century, the associationist philosopher Hartley, who was also a physician and a physiologist, attempted to explain all of human behavior in terms of both association and physiology. He believed that mental and physical processes could exist side by side, that together they could account for all complex phenomena, each on its own terms, without interaction between them: in Hartley's book *Observations on Man* . . . (1750) the chapters alternate, one on the physical explanation of a phenomenon and the next on the mental explanation of that phenomenon. There is one chapter on the mental association of ideas and a tandem chapter—which anticipates Pavlov—on associative interactions within the brain.

An important point about both mental association and physiology as explanations of complex behavior is their common *structural* nature. Both systems have elements; the research pertinent to both systems has to do with the rules for the combination of these elements and the nature of the compound formed from the elements. In both systems the repeated pairing or grouping of stimuli attaches elements together in some way to build compounds. The general term for such systems is *structuralism.*

The next section is concerned with an alternative to and an attack on the structural method of analyzing behavior.

Molarism

So far, what we have said about psychology can be understood in terms of Figure 1.3, Descartes' system for understanding man. We have looked at the work of both the associationist Ebbinghaus and the physiologist Pavlov. Since both of these experimentalists relied on the idea that elements become combined into complex entities, both are described as structuralists.

Structuralism is surely not the only doctrine by which man may be understood. For example, consider again how we might come to understand such a complex entity as an automobile.

The engineer who built the automobile knows the relation between the temperature in the combustion chamber and the power output, and he knows the diameter of each opening in the carburetor. The mechanic who regularly repairs the automobile knows that it needs a little extra oil in certain areas where leaks occur, that the wheels are currently out of line, and that the exhaust system has another thousand miles to go. The driver knows that the car is hard to start that the steering is rather loose, that the back seat is cramped, and that the windshield washers and the clock do not work. If we offered $1000 to the person who knows the car best, who would be entitled to the prize?—the engineer, the mechanic, or the driver? They all "know" the car quite well, and no one area of knowledge is really more "basic" than the others. The engineer may argue that his knowledge is the most basic because without him the car wouldn't exist. But the driver might claim that since the ultimate purpose of a car is to be driven, to know how to drive an automobile well is to know an automobile in its most basic sense. There is much room for heated—and unproductive—

argument here. One must finally accept the fact that the ways in which the engineer, the mechanic, and the driver know the automobile are all valid ways of knowing automobiles, and that, in fact, there are other valid ways to know automobiles. Consider the traffic policeman, the road-builder, the city planner, the traffic engineer, the automobile salesman, and the pedestrian, to name a few.

Similarly, there are many ways in which the behavior of animals and man may be studied and known. The structural approach, whether mental or physiological, corresponds to an engineer's understanding of a car—the structuralist wishes to know the components and how they are put together. *Molarism* is another approach in psychology, one that attempts to know man as a whole. To return to our analogy, we might say that a driver has a molar view of a car's steering, acceleration, and braking characteristics. When a psychologist says he is a molarist, we can understand him to mean that he studies large units of behavior rather than looking for discrete "building blocks." The molarist also differs from the structuralist in the way in which he goes about his study and especially in the kind of data he collects and the kind of observations he makes.

The molarist observes a large psychological unit (like "personality") directly, without trying to break it into its elements, and, just as there are structuralists on both the mental and physical sides of Descartes' dualism (for example, Ebbinghaus versus Pavlov), there are also molarists on both sides. A group of molarists who addressed themselves to mental phenomena were the Gestalt psychologists.

Gestalt Psychology

In Germany in the early twentieth century the predominant approach in psychology was both mental and structural. The research was similar to that which had been done previously by Ebbinghaus, Weber, and Fechner, and mainly consisted in trying to discover laws pertaining to the association of mental elements such as sensations and ideas.

Gestalt psychology arose in reaction to the structural aspect of German psychology. The emphasis of the Gestalt psychologists was on the study of whole entities rather than parts. However, the Gestaltists did not object to the mentalism of earlier German psychology; in fact, they emphatically stated their desire to study the mind and consciousness. As mentalists, their chosen method of observation was introspection. As molarists, they did not try to analyze mental phenomena into elements but rather attempted to study properties of the entire mind as it interacted with the environment.

Let us consider a specific example of a phenomenon to which the Gestalt psychologists felt their argument was relevant: melody. The elements of a melody are tones. But, according to the Gestaltists, the essence of a melody is its organization. After all, a melody may be played in a different key (with different sets of tones). It may be sung by various singers, played on various instruments, and rendered in various styles. Yet it remains the same melody. •

If we try to break a melody down into discrete tones, we lose the very quality by which we can identify it—the way in which it organizes tones. It is fruitless, according to Gestalt psychologists, to study a complex process like a melody by trying to list its elements. We must instead listen to the melody as a whole and concentrate on its organization.

Let us consider another example offered by the Gestaltists. When we recognize a friend, we recognize him all at once. We don't stop to compare his eyes with our memory of his eyes, his nose with our memory of his nose, his mouth with our memory of his mouth, and so forth. According to the Gestalt point of view, we recognize our friend by comparing the whole organization of elements before us with an equivalent organization in our memory; this recognition of our friend's identity is primary and basic and does not depend on the analysis of what we see into particular elements. If we do analyze our recognition into elements, said the Gestaltists, we do it after it occurs, not before.

As we have indicated, the Gestaltists felt that data could be collected through introspection. After all, they studied the mind, and what better way was there to learn about the operations of the mind than for the mind to reflect upon its own operations? Instead of breaking down a stimulus, a geometrical figure for instance, into its elements of color, form, intensity, and so forth, the observer was asked to judge the stimulus simply and naively as it appeared to him along with other stimuli. The Gestalt psychologists realized that subjective judgments of qualities depend on relationships and patterns of organization. (For instance, the headlights of an oncoming car seem very bright at night when the surroundings are dim, but they seem less bright in the daytime when the surroundings are bright. The important determinant of the brightness of the headlights as we experience it is not the constant intensity of the headlights themselves, as structuralism might lead us to believe, but rather the relationship of that intensity to the intensity of the surrounding light. In other words, the total organization is what we experience.) Consider this experiment by the Gestalt psychologist Karl Duncker (1903–1940). In a dark room, the subject was shown only a spot of light located within a square frame. The frame was then moved while the spot was kept still. But the subject always thought that the spot moved within an immobile frame (Figure 1.15). Duncker called the apparent movement of the spot "induced movement." The Gestalt psychologists saw this experiment as proof that movement is seen subjectively in the relationship of an object (the spot) with its environment (the frame) and not in terms of isolated sensations. As regards their method of collecting psychological data, the Gestalt psychologists called themselves *phenomenologists;* the kind of introspection that tries to look at the contents of the mind as a whole, naively, without analysis, is called *phenomenology.*

The Gestalt psychologists were mentalists, to be sure, but they broke with tradition on an important point. Although they were studying the mind and although they maintained that the mind could influence behavior (as indicated by arrow Y, Figure 1.3), they also maintained that there were no "mental pro-

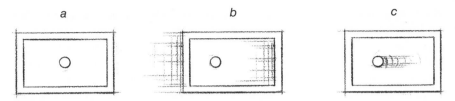

FIGURE 1.15
Duncker's experiment with "induced movement." (a) Spot of light within a frame in a dark room. (b) Experimenter moves frame slowly to the right, but (c) subject reports seeing spot move slowly to the left.

cesses." Recall the structuralist view: The mind receives isolated sensations, then (on the right side of the dotted line in Figure 1.3), these sensations are combined by the process of association—a mental phenomenon—that takes place in the mind but not necessarily in the brain. The Gestaltists denied the existence of such processes. According to them, consciousness is isomorphic to (has the same form as) processes in the brain. But if we have no conscious processes, if everything we think of or are aware of has a physical counterpart in our brains, how can we explain those instances where our consciousness does not reflect the real world? For instance, how can we explain the misperception of movement in Duncker's experiment (as illustrated in Figure 1.15)? Previous mental psychologists would have said that the misperception occurs in the mind, but the Gestalt psychologists explicitly denied that anything could occur in the mind. If we see the spot of Duncker's experiment as moving, its representation in our brains must be a moving representation, and the representation of the frame must be standing still. When the perception of things differs from reality, the distortion occurs in internal physical processes. The Gestalt psychologists went on to postulate certain physical processes in the brain that they believed might explain some of the phenomena they had discovered.

In the early twentieth century physicists had begun to study electromagnetic fields. The Gestalt psychologist Wolfgang Köhler (1887–1967) thought that many of the processes of electromagnetic fields had parallels in human perception of form and motion.

Physical Molarism

The influence of the Gestalt psychologists was not limited to their attack on the structural doctrine of the mental psychologists. The Gestaltists' idea that the best way to study any process is to look at the organization of that process as a whole was extended to the behavior of the body as well as that of the mind, as other psychologists, studying behavior in terms of discrete movements, began to question whether they could ever explain very complex behavior.

Let us consider how reflexologists might try to explain the path taken by Mr. X, who walks to work every morning. From the time he kisses his wife goodbye to the time he greets his co-workers, X's behavior can be described as a series of movements—of steps, left turns, right turns, stops, and starts—that might well be interpreted as a series of reflexes learned by constant repetition.

Yet suppose one morning there is construction on the street X usually takes, and that he must detour through a completely strange back alley. If he is a reasonably clever man, his detour will be successful and he will end up once more on the familiar street with the construction behind him. How could X have possibly made this detour if his behavior was running off mechanically as a series of reflexes, each triggered by a familiar stimulus? Some psychologists reasoned that such behavior could not be satisfactorily explained in terms of the kind of simple reflexes that the physiologists Sechenov and Pavlov studied. They claimed that X has, in fact, never acquired such reflexes, but rather that he has learned a *strategy*, an overall plan for getting to work, a sort of complex set of instructions to himself that takes into account, before they happen, the various possible environmental obstacles. What exactly the learning of such complex contingencies consists of remains a matter of dispute.

Some psychologists would say that the unifying theme of X's behavior is his purpose—getting to work—and that we must therefore study behavior in terms of purposes. They would contend that meaningful laws of behavior will never be expressed in terms of discrete reflexive actions—but always in terms of aims and goals. X's ordinary path and his detoured path have one thing in common—their destination. Change his destination and you will change his behavior in a fundamental sense; keep his destination the same and all paths to the destination can be studied as a single kind of behavior.

Still other psychologists see X's detour as evidence that explanations of behavior in purely physical terms will never succeed—that we must study man in terms of his mental life. What X acquires when walking to work is a cognitive or mental map of the path to work, and his detour is made with reference to the map that he has learned and carries around in his mind. One need not talk about his purpose in walking to work, these psychologists argue, for he would have acquired this mental map even while strolling aimlessly around the neighborhood.

The Gestalt psychologists themselves would have claimed that X's successful detour was a product of *insight*. One characteristic of conditioned reflex behavior is that it is gradually acquired by repeated pairings. Yet, according to the Gestaltists, the man's solution to the problem of the detour on his way to work was sudden and immediate. Insight is not something that is gradually learned by repeated pairings, but comes about by looking at a situation in a novel way, so as to grasp the structural and functional relationships of the problem.

Köhler, the Gestalt psychologist whose field theory of the brain we previously mentioned, was detained during World War I on Tenerife, an island that possessed a colony of apes for scientific study. Köhler performed a series of experiments with these apes that mainly consisted of setting problems for them and observing their solutions. Köhler almost invariably found that when they were given complicated problems the apes would persist in an incorrect solution or merely do nothing until they suddenly would perform the correct act without hesitation. Köhler ascribed this sudden change in the apes' behavior to insight—the seeing of a relationship between the elements of the problem. For instance, when a banana was hung out of reach of the chimpanzees in a room containing only an open box placed on the floor,

> All six apes vainly endeavored to reach their objective by leaping up from the ground. Sultan [one of the apes] soon relinquished this attempt, paced restlessly up and down, suddenly stood still in front of the box, seized it, tipped it hastily straight toward the objective, but began to climb upon it at a horizontal distance of half a meter, and springing upwards with all his force, tore down the banana. About five minutes had elapsed since the fastening of the fruit; from the momentary pause before the box to the first bite into the banana, only a few seconds elapsed, a perfectly continuous action after the first hesitation. Up to that instant, none of the animals had taken any notice of the box; they were all far too intent on the objective; none of the other five took any part in carrying the box; Sultan performed the feat single-handed in a few seconds. [Köhler, 1925, p. 40]

In Figure 1.16, we observe an ape faced with a somewhat more difficult problem.

FIGURE 1.16

The Gestaltists' objections to the analysis of behavior into discrete elements convinced most contemporary psychologists that although it was useful and important to study reflexes in the way that Sechenov and Pavlov had studied them, reflexes could not be regarded as the simple building blocks of all behavior (the behavior of Köhler's apes for example). Something more than the conditioned reflex was needed to account for truly complex behavior. It thus seemed necessary to modify radically the concept of the reflex or even to abandon it altogether as a basic mechanism of complex behavior. Most of the theoretical and experimental work on this problem was and is now being done by American psychologists, as we shall see in subsequent chapters.

The "Gestalt revolution" in psychology was only partially successful. Its negative purpose succeeded, for it demonstrated the inadequacy of a structural account of all behavior. However, its positive purpose failed, for it did not produce a completely molar account of behavior. Most psychologists see the value of both structural and molar analysis and are convinced that behavior can be understood on many different levels.

Functionalism

We have seen how Gestaltism, with its emphasis on the study of molar behavior, brought into question the premises of both physiological and mental structuralism. We now come to an even more influential doctrine, that of *functionalism,* which has flourished in the United States. The functional and molar revolutions in psychology overlapped considerably. Which came first is difficult to determine. Both made headway slowly, by fits and starts; the ultimate origins of both may be traced to historical arguments within philosophy and the physical sciences.

Functionalism stems from the theory of evolution put forward by the biologist Charles Darwin (1809–1882) a little over one hundred years ago. Darwin's theory, in capsule form, is that those organisms that are best able to survive in their environment tend to increase in number, and those that are least able to survive in the environment tend to decrease in number. Because organisms within a species naturally vary in physical qualities and behavior patterns, those organisms that are better able to survive than others will survive and reproduce —and their distinct adaptive qualities will tend to become preponderant; by this process the whole species will gradually change so as to become better fitted to cope with its environment.

Let us consider one common illustration of the action of evolution: the origin of the extreme length of the giraffe's neck. To begin with, (1) all giraffes, no matter how long their necks, depend on foliage for food, and (2) foliage is sometimes in short supply. In the course of natural variation, some early giraffes were born with longer-than-average necks—just as some humans are born very tall, even, occasionally, when they have parents of average height. Those giraffes with long necks were better able to eat leaves on the high trees in their environment and lived longer and produced more offspring. Those with short

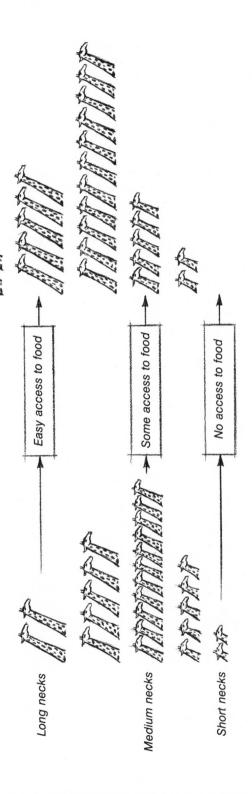

Long necks

Medium necks

Short necks

Easy access to food

Some access to food

No access to food

FIGURE 1.17
This graph shows how natural selection has altered the structure of the giraffe's neck. Leaves—the giraffe's food—have been in relatively short supply during the long history between the earlier and the later populations shown; thus the long-necked giraffes, which were able to reach higher leaves, had a better chance of surviving and reproducing than the short-necked giraffes. Since the offspring of long-necked giraffes had, on the average, longer necks than the offspring of the general population, there is a gradual increase in the proportion of long-necked giraffes. Note also the disappearance of short-necked giraffes.

necks were unable to reach the leaves on the upper parts of the trees and tended to die earlier and produce less offspring. Thus, as the generations went on, there were more and more offspring of long-necked giraffes, who tended on the average to be long-necked—just as the children of tall human parents tend on the average to be tall.

Darwin saw natural selection as a process similar to the artificial selection used by animal breeders; for instance, a race of plump chickens or turkeys can be created by breeding plump fowl and not breeding lean or stringy birds. Figure 1.17 shows how the process of natural selection works in the case of giraffes. Note that this process is contrary to the notion that (1) giraffes were constantly stretching their necks to reach the high leaves on trees, (2) this stretching made their necks longer, (3) they passed this trait on to their young.

A profound implication of the theory of evolution is that all living creatures share a common biological inheritance. After Darwin, species were no longer regarded as immutable, and there was no longer a sharp boundary separating "higher animals" from "lower animals"—or even men from animals. In regard to human life, evolution meant that the traits humans possess must have evolved from traits their ancestors once possessed.

One of the first effects of this principle of *biological continuity* on psychology was the acceptance of the notion that because humans have minds and consciousness, then other animals also have minds and consciousness, although of a more

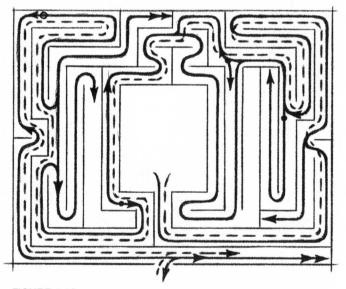

FIGURE 1.18
Floorplan of Small's maze. Small studied the "mental processes"
of rats with this wooden maze, which he based on the hedge
maze in the gardens of Hampton Court Palace in England.

rudimentary kind. This led psychologists who were studying the mentality of humans to become interested also in the mentality of animals. The evidence for mentality in animals had long rested on anecdotes about the clever actions of pets and farm animals. However, a group of American psychologists (the functionalists) began to investigate animal behavior in laboratories, especially at the University of Chicago. One of the tools they devised to study the mental processes of animals was the maze, and some of the first animals to be studied in mazes were rats.

In 1901, in a paper entitled "Experimental Study of the Mental Processes of the Rat," Willard Stanton Small (1870-1943) introduced the rat in the maze to psychology. Small's maze was modeled on the Hampton Court Maze, a garden maze created for the amusement of the English nobility. (These mazes are shown in Figures 1.18 and 1.19.) The object of Small's maze experiments was to determine the conscious state of an animal by observing its behavior. In the following description of a rat's behavior, Small's observations of behavior and his conclusions about the rat's conscious states are italicized. It might be instructive for the reader to try to list those italicized words that seem to him to be direct observations of behavior—as opposed to those that seem to express conclusions drawn by Small about the conscious state of the rat.

Analyses of Results

In appreciating the results of this series of experiments, . . . the [following] . . . facts come into view. . . . *the initial indefiniteness of movement* and the *fortuitousness of success;* the just *observable profit from the first experiences;* the gradually increasing *certainty of knowledge* indicated by *increase of speed and definiteness,* and the *recognition of critical points* indicated by *hesitation* and *indecision;* the lack of *imitation* and the improbability of *following by scent;* the outbreak of the instincts of *play* and *curiosity* after the edge of *appetite* is dulled. In addition are to be noted the further observations upon the contrast between the *slow* and *cautious entrance* into, and the *rapid exit* from the blind alleys, after the first few trials; the appearance of *disgust* on reaching the end of a blind alley; the clear indication of centrally excited *sensation* (images) of some kind; *memory* (as I have used the term); *the persistence of certain errors;* and the almost *automatic character of the movements* in the later experiments.

The historical importance for psychology of the notion of biological continuity is that it stimulated much research in comparative psychology—the study of the behavior of one species as compared to another species. At first the purpose of this research was to affirm or deny Darwin's theories by comparing the mental qualities of one species with those of another—to answer the question, for instance: Which animal has the higher-developed mentality, the dog or the horse?—and to thereby rank the various species in terms of the properties of their minds. Contemporary comparative research ignores the relative "mental development" of species and concentrates more on the comparison of various complex behavior patterns.

View from above

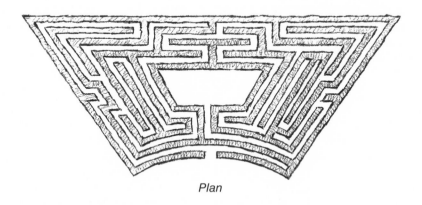

Plan

FIGURE 1.19
The Hampton Court maze. [Crown Copyright.]

The general principle that the process of natural selection embodies is critically important in modern psychology, as well as in other sciences; it is the principle of *feedback*. In a feedback system, a process is regulated through testing the actual state of the process against a selected potential state.

In Figure 1.20 the dotted lines represent a feedback loop whereby information about the actual state of an ongoing process is compared with information about a potential state of the process. In the case of the natural selection of long-necked giraffes, a potential state was signaled by the height of the leaves on the trees. Time after time, this potential state was compared with the actual state of the length of the giraffes' necks. The long-term result of this process was attainment of a new actual state: a population of long-necked giraffes.

Feedback is a very common process in everyday experience. Consider a household thermostat. In this case, a desired state is represented by the setting on the thermostat, say 72°. The actual state is the current temperature of the house, say 65°. The ongoing comparison of these two states controls a process—the burning of coal, gas, or oil to warm the house. As soon as the difference disappears—that is, as soon as the house becomes as warm as the setting on the thermostat indicates it should be—the heater or furnace is turned off. Figure 1.21 shows such a thermostat mechanism.

Such self-adjusting systems embody simple *negative* feedback (a term borrowed from engineering usage). The feedback is called negative simply because the ongoing comparison tends to decrease the difference between the actual state of the system and the selected potential state of the system. Both the system of natural selection and the thermostat can eventually reach *equilibrium* when the actual and signaled states are identical, and the process terminates. However, it is possible to have other kinds of feedback. *Postive* feedback tends to amplify the difference between the actual state and the selected potential state, producing a runaway process. Suppose, for instance, that the thermostat we have been considering got connected by mistake to the air conditioner instead of the furnace. Then, the difference in temperature between the desired

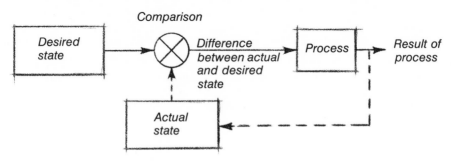

FIGURE 1.20
A diagram of a simple feedback system.

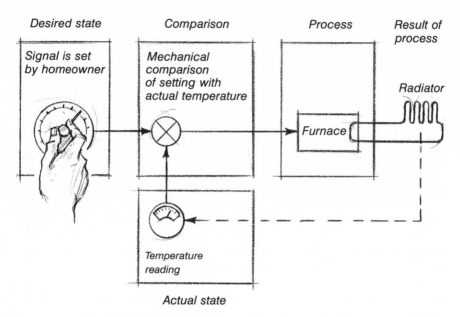

FIGURE 1.21
A diagram showing the operation of a household thermostat.

72° and the actual 65° would activate the air conditioner, causing the actual temperature to drop further, increasing the difference. The thermostat feeds more power to the air conditioner, which in turn decreases the temperature still further, and so forth. Positive feedback in everyday situations often causes havoc. A young man, for instance, thinks that a young woman is cool to him because he is not forward enough, whereas the reverse is actually true. He increases his forwardness and finds her cooler. He interprets this continued coolness as a sign that he is still not forward enough, increasing his advances in proportion to the degree of coolness his very advances are generating. Such miscalculations between persons can result in something unpleasant, like a slap on the face. In the case of an international arms race, they could lead to disaster.

The feedback principle, showing how a process could be controlled by a desired end or function, formed the basis for functional psychology. The functionalists, inspired by Darwin's theory, believed that mental processes had evolved to serve various useful functions for organisms struggling to cope with their complex environments. According to the philosopher and psychologist William James:

> Mental facts cannot be properly studied apart from the physical environment of which they take cognizance. The great fault of the older rational psychology was to set up the soul as an absolute spiritual being with certain faculties of its own by which the several activities of remembering, imagining, reasoning, willing, etc.,

were explained, almost without reference to the peculiarities of the world with which these activities deal. But the richer insight of modern days perceives that our inner faculties are adapted in advance to the features of the world in which we dwell, adapted, I mean, so as to secure our safety and prosperity in its midst. Not only are our capacities for forming new habits, for remembering sequences, and for abstracting general properties from things and associating their usual consequences with them, exactly the faculties needed for steering us in this world of mixed variety and uniformity, but our emotions and instincts are adapted to very special features of that world. In the main, if a phenomenon is important for our welfare, it interests and excites us the first time we come into its presence. Dangerous things fill us with involuntary fear; poisonous things with distaste; indispensable things with appetite. Mind and world in short have been evolved together, and in consequence are something of a mutual fit. [James, 1893, p. 4]

Notice that the adaptation between our minds and environments is said to take place *in advance*. That is, our emotions and desires, which help us survive, are inborn, so that we are interested in an object that is important for our welfare "the first time we come into its presence." Furthermore, note that the locus of our sense that the object is important is said to be in the mind—considered a separate "organ" whose properties are as subject to the action of evolution as the length of the giraffe's neck, but which, like Descartes' concept, is still not to be found in the physical world (see Figure 1.3).

From the notion that the mind (1) is subject to evolutionary changes and (2) develops in response to the environment, it follows that complex behavior, which the mind controls, also must change with the generations of species, so that individuals cope better with their environments. This notion gave rise to research such as Small's, in which the complex behavior patterns of various organisms were studied with a view towards determining their mental qualities. To return briefly to the principle of biological continuity, recall that this principle implies that consciousness is not a purely human trait—that if it is possessed by humans, it must be possessed by other animals, at least to some degree. By 1912, some American psychologists had discovered the other side of the same coin. They observed that since both biologists and physiologists were studying animal behavior fruitfully without recourse to the notion of consciousness, then perhaps much of human behavior could also be explained without having to analyze or even refer to consciousness. The Russian reflexologists had previously abandoned the idea altogether as an explanatory concept. The important point for our discussion is not whether there really is such a thing as consciousness, but that when attention was no longer focused on consciousness, introspection lost its position as the prime method of psychological investigation.

John Broadus Watson (1878-1958) studied at the University of Chicago when the functionalist school of psychology flourished there. He was trained to perform animal experiments similar to Small's experiments with rats in a maze. Watson soon became convinced that he could separate his observations into (1) those that could be verified by other psychologists and (2) those that could not be so verified. In the former category, he placed observations of the overt behavior of animals—where and how they moved. Watson knew that such observations yielded general agreement. In the second category, he placed observations of the conscious states of animals. He knew that these observations consistently failed to yield much agreement. (In other words, Watson found it far more likely that three observers would agree on whether a rat turned left or right in a maze than on whether the rat was happy or sad while it was turning.)

Whereas some functionalists faulted each other's introspective training, Watson held that introspection itself was the source of the prevalent disagreement about animals' mental states. Watson declared that introspection should be banished from psychology and that psychological observations should be restricted, like other scientific observations, to overt behavior.

Because Watson focused on observable behavior, he called himself a "behaviorist" and broke away from the other functionalists at Chicago. As Watson's position gained adherents, behaviorism emerged as a successor to functionalism. Both approaches share a common attitude toward biological continuity, and both stress the adaptive function of behavior, but wherea. functionalism was devoted to examining the *mental life* of men and animals, behaviorism is devoted to their *overt activities*. As time has gone by, behaviorism has become predominant in American psychology.

BIBLIOGRAPHY

The best way to get an idea of the history of psychology is to read the original sources. A good place to start is R. J. Herrnstein and E. G. Boring's *A source book in the history of psychology* (Cambridge, Massachusetts: Harvard University Press, 1965). The material that introduces each section is particularly illuminating. Most of the quotations in the present volume come from selections in Herrnstein and Boring. From the source book one can go to more comprehensive original sources.

There are two classic history books of experimental psychology by E. G. Boring: *A history of experimental psychology* (New York: Appleton-Century-Crofts, 1950) and *Sensation and perception in the history of experimental psychology* (New York: Appleton-Century-Crofts, 1942). The attitude toward the history of psychology in the present volume is basically that of Boring's two history books; the approach in these books is to follow the history of psychology from Descartes through the British associationists to modern psychology. For an approach centered around studies of behavior *per se*, see J. R. Kantor, *The scientific evolution of psychology* (2 vols., Chicago: The Principia Press, 1963-1969). For a history of studies on the reflex, see F. Fearing, *Reflex action* (New York: Hafner Publishing Company, 1930).

The material quoted in this chapter is from the following sources:

Descartes, René, *De homine*. Leiden: 1662. Reprinted in Herrnstein and Boring, p. 269.

Fechner, G. T., *Elemente de psychophysik*. Leipzig, 1860. Reprinted in Herrnstein and Boring, p. 75.

Hartley, David, *Observations on man, his frame, his duty, and his expectations*. London and Bath, 1749. Reprinted in Fearing, p. 86.

James, W. *Psychology*. New York: Henry Holt, 1893.

Köhler, W. *The mentality of apes*. Translated by E. Winter. New York: Harcourt, Brace and Company, 1925.

La Mettrie, J. O. de, *L'homme machine*. Leiden, 1748. Reprinted in Herrnstein and Boring, p. 278.

Locke, John, *An essay concerning human understanding: in four books*. London, 1690. Reprinted in Herrnstein and Boring, p. 584.

Mill, J. S., *A system of logic, ratiocinative and inductive, being a connected view of the principles of evidence, and the methods of scientific investigation*. London, 1843. Reprinted in Herrnstein and Boring, p. 379.

Pavlov, I. P., *Pavlov: selected works*. Translated by S. Belsky. Moscow: Foreign Languages Publishing House, 1955.

Prochaska, George, *De functionibus systematis nervosi*. Prague, 1784. Reprinted in Herrnstein and Boring, p. 294.

Sechenov, I. M., *Refleksy golovnogo mozga*. St. Petersberg, 1863. Reprinted in Herrnstein and Boring, p. 321.

Small, W. S., Experimental study of the mental processes of the rat. *American Journal of Psychology*, 1901, **12,** 218-220. Reprinted in Herrnstein and Boring, pp. 552-553.

Chapter 2

Environmental and Behavioral Events

In a psychological experiment the environmental events that are observed and recorded are called stimuli and the behavioral events that are observed and recorded are called responses. Stimuli and responses constitute the psychologist's data. His job is to discover relations between them.

Many of the disputes among psychologists center on what sort of environmental events can serve as effective stimuli and what sort of behavioral events can serve as meaningful responses. The nature of principles and laws that psychologists ultimately discover will depend on what sort of data they collect.

For one psychologist a stimulus may consist of a point of light on the retina of the eye; a response may consist of a muscle twitch. For another psychologist a stimulus may be a problem in algebra; the solution may be the response. The aspects of the environment that can be considered stimuli and the aspects of behavior that can be considered responses are unlimited in theory and, in practice, are limited only by the instruments used to measure these events.

After a cautionary note we shall take up the question of psychological data. Just what aspects of behavior should be observed, counted, and measured by psychologists.

WARNING

We are discussing data collection before discussing the theories that tell us what sorts of data to collect. On one hand, the data determine the theories that are constructed; on the other hand, the theories determine what sort of data should be collected. It's like the chicken and the egg. But we must start somewhere, so we shall start with data. Because we have not yet discussed theory the student may get the impression that data collection is arbitrary in psychology. This is *not* the case, as will become clear later on.

MOLAR VERSUS MOLECULAR DATA

As we noted in Chapter 1 some psychologists study relatively large units of behavior, whereas others look for discrete "building blocks." The first approach is molar, the second molecular. For instance, we might want to classify a bird's behavior into such categories as "courtship," "nest-building," "defending its territory," and "feeding." It might be difficult, as the bird flies from point A to point B, to tell which of the various categories this particular activity falls into, but ethologists and zoologists experienced in observing behavior of birds in their natural habitats can make such judgments consistently and accurately. These would be relatively molar classifications. On the other hand, we might want to analyze the individual movements of each of the bird's muscles. The observer is limited in the behavior he observes only by what he can measure. If we wanted to plot the movements of individual muscles we would need elaborate instruments. Usually (as in the classification of individual muscle twitches) molecular classifications require more elaborate instruments but this need not always be the case. It might take very complicated instruments to tell when a bird was migrating (a molar response).

Just as responses are classifications of the behavior of a subject by an observer, stimuli are classifications of the subject's environment by an observer.

Molar and molecular data actually form a continuum along an observational dimension. A point on the continuum is meaningful only *relative* to another point. To a psychologist, for instance, a physiologist seems to be investigating molecular phenomena, but to an atomic physicist the physiologist's data might seem molar. The molarity–molecularity dimension is especially important in psychology. Yet experiments and theories encountered in psychological journals often fail to point out their positions on the molarity–molecularity continuum. Thus the reader must be able to distinguish them himself. As a guide to this problem, we shall give a brief description here of the various types of molar and molecular analyses that appear in this book.

Analyses of Spatial Stimuli

A molecular analysis would say that any figure in a two-dimensional field (for instance) consists of nothing but a series of points arranged in various ways. According to such an analysis, the perception of a whole figure (such as a circle) is constructed from perception of the points that are its elements.

A molar analysis would consider a two-dimensional figure as perceived directly prior to consideration of its elements. This was an issue on which the

Gestalt psychologists concentrated. They considered themselves molarists, claiming that relationships in spatial fields could be perceived directly, prior to perception of the elements of the relationship.

Analyses of Temporal Stimuli

A molecular analysis would break up stimuli occurring over a period of time into instantaneous events. The state of an organism at a certain point in time would reflect the stimuli experienced at each prior instant. A molar analysis, on the other hand, would not attempt to sum up past events in the state of an organism at the present instant or to anticipate future events in terms of the present instant, any more than a point would be used to sum up or anticipate a circle. Rather, the entire temporal extent of a stimulus would be considered as a whole. For instance, if hearing a symphony affects the behavior of the listener, a molecular analysis would assume that each note of the symphony as it occurred gave rise to or modified a state in the listener, and that state then caused the behavior. A more molar view would study behavior in relation to various melodic lines. A still more molar view would look for causes of the behavior in the symphony as a whole.

A molecular analysis sees discrete environmental events, each having a separate effect upon an organism. Thus, if a rat were subjected to a series of discrete shocks, each shock would cause its own painful reaction, which would then fade away until the next shock augmented the residue of the prior shock in some way. The rate of shocks could affect behavior only by means of these separate changes in the organism's state. A high rate of shocks would have a different effect from a low rate of shocks because each individual shock at a high rate would occur while the organism was in one state, whereas individual shock at a low rate would occur while the organism was in another state. A molar analysis, on the other hand, might simply determine how behavior varied as a function of rate of shocks.

Analyses of Behavior

It was the psychologist Edwin R. Guthrie (1886–1959), who first made the distinction between acts and movements. Guthrie, a molecularist (like Sechenov, whose theories we discussed in Chapter 1), argued that all behavior, no matter how complicated, was made up of discrete muscular movements. An act, such as opening a door, was, according to Guthrie, nothing more than a series of movements. B. F. Skinner (b. 1904), arguing for a more molar view of behavior, proposed that acts, or what he called "operants," be considered the basic units of behavior. (We shall have more to say about operants later.) The difference between Skinner and Guthrie on the act-movement dimension might be illustrated by an experiment done by Guthrie and G. P. Horton. The experimenters put cats in a puzzle box from which they could escape by pressing lightly against a vertical pole in the middle of the box. The problem was absurdly easy for the cats. They all "solved" it almost immediately. However, Guthrie and Horton were interested in *how* the problem was solved. To discover this they took pictures of the cats at the moment that the pole was pushed and the door opened. It turned out that each cat had an idiosyncratic way of pushing the pole. If a cat got out of the box on the first trial by pushing the pole with its hindquarters, it tended to push the pole with its hindquarters on all trials thereafter. If a cat got out by pushing the pole with its nose, it kept pushing the pole with its nose on subsequent trials. To explain the differences in the cats' behavior, Guthrie suggested that each cat had learned something different in the puzzle box—that is, a particular series of movements. Skinner would argue that all of the cats had learned the *same* thing—that is, the act of pushing the pole. The difference in the individual movements made by the cats is irrelevant for Skinner. The important thing is that they all pushed the pole. Skinner would argue that the molar *act* of pushing the pole was the same for each cat and that in that sense all of Guthrie and Horton's cats learned the same thing. Obviously, in one sense the cats all learned the same thing and in another sense each cat learned something different. Both types of analysis are valid because they both tell us something about behavior. It would be wrong to say that one is more basic than the other.

DISCRETE EVENTS

A discrete event is one that takes place in such a brief time span that the time during which it occurs is insignificant compared with the time between successive occurrences of the event. Because of their uniformity, their ease of measurement, and their suitability for experimental manipulation, discrete events are frequently used by behavioral psychologists as stimuli and responses.

An example of a discrete environmental event might be a pistol shot, a flash of light, or a blow of a hammer on the patella tendon of the knee. Often the onset of a continuous event is itself considered a discrete event. Consider the onset of a tone: if it takes negligible time for the intensity of the tone to rise from zero to its maximum value, the tone's onset could be considered a discrete event, regardless of the duration of the tone.

On the behavioral side, a discrete event might be an eyeblink, the pressing of a lever by a rat, the pecking of a key by a pigeon, or a short verbal response such as "Yes" or "No."

For both behavioral and environmental events, the discreteness of the events in question is a convenient fiction. Obviously, an eyeblink takes time to occur, and although we can ignore this time for many purposes, we cannot ignore it for others. An example of how forgetting the arbitrariness of the designation "brief" can get investigators into trouble is the problem that arises in the presentation of brief tones. Frequently experiments require that a tone be presented repeatedly, with each presentation as much like the others as possible. Ordinarily, stimuli are perceived to be more alike when they are brief than when they are protracted. It might thus be assumed that one brief tone would sound pretty much like another. However, brief presentations of tones of long wavelength give exactly the opposite effect. Figure 2.1 illustrates what happens when a long wavelength tone is presented for too brief a period. The short interval of presentation allows only part of the wave to get through. The portions corresponding to (b) and (c) of Figure 2.1 actually sound different to the

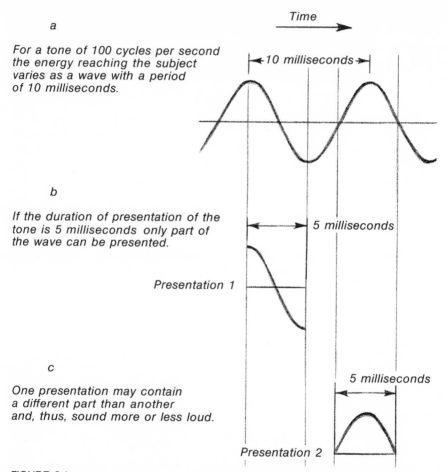

FIGURE 2.1
How making the presentation of a tone too brief can distort the characteristics of the tone. (a) For a tone of 100 cycles per second the energy reaching the subject varies as a wave with a period of 10 milliseconds. (b) If the duration of presentation of the tone is 5 milliseconds only part of the wave can be presented. (c) A second presentation may contain a different part of the wave and thus sound different. (In this figure we have ignored, for simplicity's sake, the presence of transient energy at the onset and offset of the tone.)

listener. If he hears only one portion, he gets a distorted picture of the whole—much as the legendary blind man, feeling only the trunk of the elephant, concludes that elephants are much like snakes.

In science "more molecular" often means "more accurate." But the example above shows that in psychology this is not always the case.

MEASUREMENT OF DISCRETE EVENTS

In discussing the measurement of events we shall confine ourselves largely to behavioral events—that is, responses—because these are most often the objects of measurement. But what we say about responses also applies to stimuli. Although stimuli are mostly produced by the experimenter and kept constant with easily definable parameters, they sometimes have to be measured. It is often not clear before an experiment starts what aspect of the stimulus will have the simplest, or most direct, effect on behavior. Sometimes stimulus parameters that are difficult to control but easy to measure may establish the simplest relationship between environment and behavior. For instance, we may be able to control the intensity of illumination of a light source but not the amount of light reaching the subject's eyes. It may turn out to be easier to measure this amount of light (say, by measuring the light reflected from the cornea) than to control it directly. And it would be the measured intensity at the eye rather than the intensity at the source that we would expect to influence behavior most.

Let us suppose, now, that in a given instance we have indeed found an event brief enough relative to the time between events that we can treat it as effectively instantaneous, and that by making it brief (in the case of a stimulus) or by only measuring a brief portion of it (in the case of a response) we do not distort it or lose too much of its character. What aspects of such an event are measurable?

Consider a rat that drinks by extending its tongue and licking at water. There is reasonable evidence that when a rat licks, it licks in bursts of very brief licks at a rate of 7 or 8 licks per second. Furthermore, this rate seems to be constant from rat to rat and fairly constant for an individual rat whether the rat has been deprived of water or not. When a rat has been deprived of water the bursts of licks are prolonged. When the rat has not been deprived bursts are short and the rat waits a long time between bursts, but within any burst the rate is always 7 or 8 licks per second. How can we check to see that this is correct? The first requirement is a means of determining when a lick has occurred. We could have an assistant stand and watch the rat, but if licks were really occurring at 7 or 8 per second it is doubtful that our assistant would be keen-eyed enough to catch every one. Fortunately a device is available—called a drinkometer—that will measure the rat's licks. Figure 2.2 shows how a drinkometer works. Water is fed to the rat through a narrow glass tube: each time the rat licks the tube a drop of water falls onto its tongue. The drinkometer

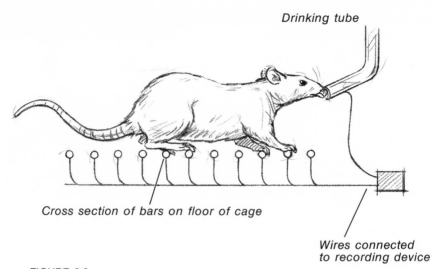

FIGURE 2.2
A drinkometer. Each time the rat licks the tube the electric circuit is closed and
the lick automatically recorded.

is wired so that a mild electric potential exists between the drinking tube and the
floor of the cage on which the rat stands. When the rat touches the tube with its
tongue it completes a circuit between the tube and the floor, and sensitive electronic equipment measures the current in this circuit (which is too mild for the
rat to feel) and indicates to the experimenter when a lick has occurred.

Now that we have the drinkometer to detect the lick, how can we measure
how fast licks are occurring? One device is the event recorder pictured in Figure
2.3. This recorder has a roll of paper that moves at constant speed under a pen.
Each time the rat licks at the tube the pen moves up and then back down rapidly.
The record that this machine leaves is a line with pips on it at intervals corresponding to the time between licks. The event record pictured at the left of
Figure 2.4 shows a pattern that might be obtained with a rat. This type of
record, besides giving us an overall picture of the rate of licking, also permits
us to identify individual licks and to separate periods of licking from periods of
pausing. Remember that 7 or 8 licks per second is the rate *when* the rat is licking. The overall rate might be quite a bit lower (like the income of the brick-
layer who makes $10 per hour *when* he is working but who may make less over
a year's time than the clerk who makes $3 per hour but works steadily all year).
In an event record it is the density of pips that reveals the rate at any point.

Time Between Discrete Events

For discrete events, which themselves are assumed to take no appreciable
time, the time between events—called interresponse time (irt) if the events

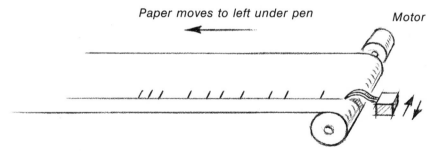

Paper moves to left under pen   **Motor**

FIGURE 2.3
An event recorder. A pen makes a regular tick for each response.

are responses—is the most molecular unit of measurement. An *interresponse-time distribution* would show the number of interresponse times falling within each of various time ranges. Returning to our example of a rat drinking from a tube, let us suppose that we have an event record of licking and want to construct from it an interresponse-time distribution of licking. The first thing we must decide about such a distribution is the range of interresponse times to lump together. This range is called a "bin" size. Figure 2.4 shows how such a distribution would look with various bin sizes.* The decision about bin size seems trivial at first, just a convention of plotting data, like choosing graph paper with big or little boxes, but actually it is of critical importance. When we decide bin size we are deciding how to go from molecular to molar data. An interresponse-time distribution may tell us something about licking that an event record does not because it pictures the data in a different way, but as soon as we lump several interresponse times together into a single bin we can no longer distinguish between them and consequently lose some of the detail of the data. Whether this loss is worth the gain in meaningfulness obtained through the picture the distribution gives us is one of the most critical decisions a scientist is called upon to make. Some of the distributions of Figure 2.4 are more meaningful than others. Some may be describable by relatively simple mathematical expressions, whereas others may require complex expressions. Which is the "best" distribution depends on the use to which the distribution is to be put. The distribution with the bin size 0.05 second would be best for our purpose, which is to check whether rats really lick at a rate of 7 or 8 licks per second. This distribution has a peak somewhere between 0.1 and 0.15 second. A series of licks 0.125 second apart would be occurring at the rate of 8 per second. Smaller bin sizes do not provide a single peak interval by which to summarize the rat's performance. Larger bin sizes yield a less precise measurement of that

---

*The data in Figure 2.4 are not real. They were made up by the author to demonstrate, more vividly than real data might, the importance of proper selection of bin size.

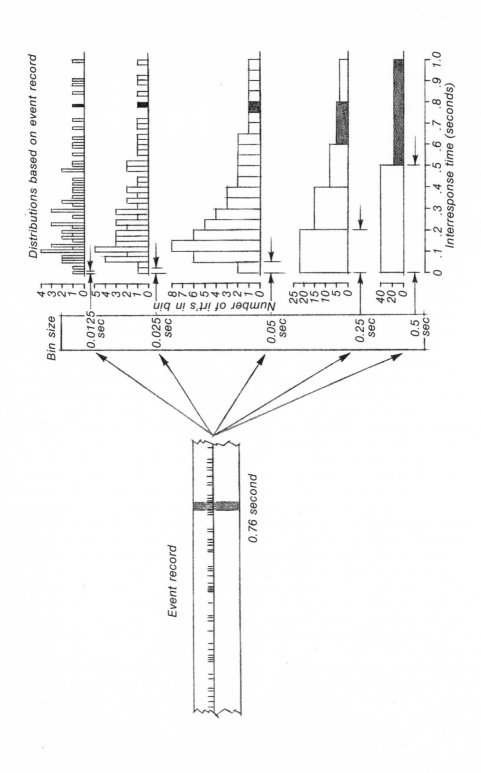

interval. It seems so far that the data we have made up exhibit a certain regularity—a rate of about 8 per second, due to the fact that the most common irt falls between 0.1 and 0.15 second. We shall see later (in Figure 2.10) that although this range of irt's is the most probable, it is by no means as dominant as would appear from Figure 2.4.

A potentially important sort of information that is discarded in going from the event record of Figure 2.4 to the interresponse–time distributions is the sequence in which the responses occurred. This is true whatever the bin size. If the rat was becoming significantly less thirsty with each lick and was pausing more between licks as it spent more time licking, the distributions of Figure 2.4 would not indicate this fact. When we rank–ordered the interresponse times in Figure 2.4 we ignored whether there were more or fewer long interresponse times at the beginning or the end of the period. A disadvantage of interresponse–time distributions is that they ignore such sequences.

Rate of Discrete Events

The rate of discrete events is technically the reciprocal of the time between events. If the time between events is 3 seconds, then the rate of those events is $1/3 = 0.33$ event per second. It is also true, technically, that any distribution of interresponse times can be converted to a distribution of rates by simply taking the reciprocal of the value of each bin. It would be a mistake, however, to think of rates of events wholly in these terms because in practice rates of events and times between events are very often measured differently. Times between events are more often expressed by the kind of distributions shown in Figure 2.4, which ignores sequences. Rates of events are frequently expressed in ways that do not ignore sequences.

To see how rates of events can be measured sequentially, let us return to the event record at the left of Figure 2.4 and analyze it in a different way. Now, instead of concentrating on amount of time between fixed events let us concentrate on number of events in fixed periods of time. Figure 2.5 shows how an event record can be analyzed in terms of unitary periods of time. Note that the plots of rate per unit time maintain sequences. If the rat was pausing more

---

FIGURE 2.4

At the left is a section of an event record of a rat's licking at a drinkometer. The time between any two successive licks is an interresponse time (irt). For instance, the shaded portion of the event record represents an irt of 0.76 second. There are 54 irt's in the event record. The distributions at the right show how many of the irt's fall within various ranges of time represented by bin sizes. For instance, when the bin size is 0.05 second (middle distribution) all the irt's between 0 and 0.05 second go in the first bin (2 irt's go in this bin), all the irt's between 0.05 and 0.1 second go in the second bin (6 irt's go in this bin), and so on. The 0.76 second irt (shaded in the event record) would go in the shaded bin of each distribution.

and licking less as the session progressed, that fact would be preserved in Figure 2.5, whereas it would have been lost in Figure 2.4.

The difficulty with the technique shown in Figure 2.5 for determining rates of events from an event record is that, since the fixed time periods will necessarily bridge periods of responding and periods of pausing, the rates of response obtained will include some elements of responding and some elements of pausing. If the rat of our example is indeed alternating between bursts of licking

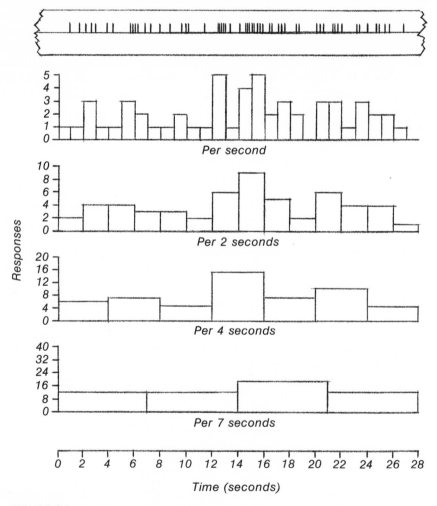

FIGURE 2.5
Rate of responding (number of responses per unit time) with different units of time. With small units of time (1 second) the rate is variable. With large units of time (7 seconds) the rate is fairly constant with a slight peak in the third quarter of the total 28-second period.

at 8 per second and not licking at all, some of the bins may contain bursts only (at a rate of 8 per second) and some may contain pauses only (at a rate of zero), but many will contain both bursts and pauses, giving a rate somewhere between 8 and 0 licks per second. However, since the rat (hypothetically, so far) is either responding at 8 licks per second or not at all, these bins will give a false picture of the rat's behavior.

One way of avoiding both the fault of the interresponse-time analysis of the event record as shown in Figure 2.4 (losing sequences) and the fault of the rate analysis of the event record as shown in Figure 2.5 (losing detail) is not to use an event record at all for collection of data but to use a cumulative record. Recording data cumulatively is a standard part of the repertory of scientific techniques, but this method of data recording was not applied to behavioral events until B. F. Skinner demonstrated its usefulness in 1938. Although this contribution may seem to be merely a minor change in apparatus, it has strongly influenced the course of psychological research. The importance of the cumulative recorder for behavioral studies is that it records patterns of behavior without sacrificing detail.

One problem with event records may be guessed from Figure 2.3. When the rate of events is high (for instance, 8 per second) but the pauses between events are long, we have to make a critical decision about how fast to move the paper. A fast-moving paper will give good discrimination between individual events, but during the long pauses the paper will roll furiously onto the floor. With an event recorder we have to choose: do we want a reasonable picture of events as they take place (such as rate of licks) or do we want a reasonable picture of pauses between events? Very rarely is it possible to pick up an event record and see the whole pattern of events and pauses.

The cumulative recorder reveals patterns more clearly. This device is shown in Figure 2.6. Like the event recorder, the cumulative recorder has a paper moving under a pen. But unlike the event recorder, the cumulative recorder's pen does not move up and down. Each event moves the pen up a notch, with the result that the immediate rate of events is indicated not by the density of pips but by the slope of the line generated. When the line is steep, events are coming rapidly; when the line is shallow, events are coming slowly. It is easier to judge the slope of a line than the density of a series of pips. Because of this, the cumulative recorder can move more slowly than the event recorder and still allow good measurement of very rapid events (such as licks at a rate of 8 per second).

A method for describing patterns of responding in a cumulative record was proposed by T. F. Gilbert in 1958. Gilbert's method is based on the assumption that when animals engage in any form of behavior, they do so rhythmically—that is, at a constant rate. Let us consider our hypothetical rat with the drinking tube. Gilbert calls the time between the availability of the tube and the rat's first lick the *latency*. After the latency period, suppose the rat starts licking at a constant rate. This rate Gilbert calls *tempo,* an appropriate name for

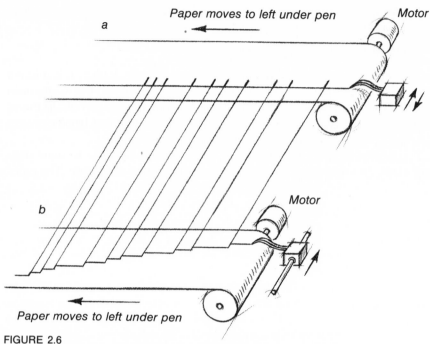

FIGURE 2.6
(a) An event recorder. A pen makes a regular tick for each response. (b) A cumulative recorder. A pen moves in one direction along a slide for each response and automatically drops back to the starting position when it reaches the edge of the roll of paper.

what is essentially a rhythmic activity. Finally, the rat stops licking and pauses. Then it starts licking again. Clearly the rat is distributing its time, spending some fraction of its time licking and the remainder pausing. (The rat may be engaging in other activities such as grooming, running, and eating during the "pause" period. It need not be standing still. However, all behavior that is not licking, for our present purposes, we lump together in the pause.) The ratio of the time spent licking to the total time, Gilbert calls *perseveration.* In other words,

$$\text{perseveration} = \frac{\text{lick time}}{\text{lick time and pause time}}.$$

For any given interval, we can find both tempo and perseveration.

When behavior is modified, the part of behavior that gets modified most easily is often perseveration—in other words, the distribution of time spent doing an activity versus not doing that activity. Hence perseveration is an important measure.

Figure 2.7 shows how latency, tempo, and perseveration of a response would be measured on a cumulative record.

Probability of Discrete Events

Probability is not something one can observe directly. Rather, it is inferred from the relative frequency with which things happen. When the weatherman says in the afternoon that the probability of rain tonight is 50 percent, he means that given a large number of afternoons with weather conditions like the present one, it will rain on about half of the following nights.

A relative frequency is a frequency that is specified relative to some standard event. In a dice game, the standard event is a throw of the dice. The prob-

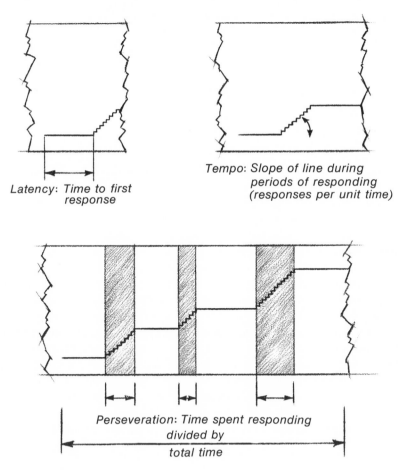

Latency: Time to first response

Tempo: Slope of line during periods of responding (responses per unit time)

Perseveration: Time spent responding divided by total time

FIGURE 2.7
How latency, tempo, and perseveration are measured in a cumulative record.

ability of throwing a four on a single die is one-sixth because out of a large number of throws one-sixth of them will be fours.

There are two kinds of standard units of measurement with which we are concerned in this book. One is the *trial*. The other is the *temporal unit* (whether second, hour or day). In a trial a set of environmental conditions is presented to the subject. The subject's behavior is observed to see whether a certain type of response is made. The fraction of the trials on which that response occurs reflects the probability of that response under those environmental conditions. To take a simple example, a child may be offered a piece of candy 20 times under similar conditions (that is, by the same person, at the same time after meals, and so on) and accept the candy within 10 seconds 15 times out of the 20 times it is offered. The probability of his accepting the candy, within 10 seconds, is $15/20 = 0.75$.

When the standard measure is a unit of time, probability is estimated in terms of rate of occurrence. The faster events occur in time, the more probable they are said to be.* To take another simple example, when a child takes cookies frequently from a cookie jar there is said to be a high probability of his taking cookies. If he takes cookies infrequently there is said to be a low probability of his taking cookies.

Random Events

With the cumulative recorder we can detect behavioral patterns that are sufficiently coarse, such as the pattern of licking of the rat. But some patterns of events may not show up in a cumulative record. If, within a burst of licking, the rat alternated between short and long interresponse times averaging 8 per second, a cumulative record would show the same average slope for the burst (the same tempo) as if the rat licked regularly at 8 per second, or as if the rat's licks occurred randomly but averaged 8 per second. For patterns within very rapid events, or for small differences between slower events, the cumulative recorder is inadequate. But before we discuss how to measure patterns of events precisely, we have to discuss the opposite of patterns—randomness.

What do we mean when we say that events are occurring randomly? We do not mean that they are infrequent or improbable. Birds may fly by in no particular temporal pattern, but we would hope (especially if we have just bought a house in the country) that their appearance is not infrequent. Consider two railroads in different countries, an efficient and an inefficient one. The time-tables read alike. Trains are supposed to come every hour on the hour. At both

---

*We are still assuming that the events are discrete—that is, that the time between events is much greater than the duration of the events themselves. When events are not discrete, the probability of starting the event must be evaluated separately from the probability of continuing the event once started. Often the two probabilities are quite different. For instance, it is hard to get my daughter to take a bath (low probability of starting), but, once she is in the bathtub, it is hard to get her out (high probability of continuing).

railroad stations 24 trains stop per day. At one, however, the trains are pretty much on time; at the other, the trains come randomly. When we make this distinction we may have in mind two functions of the kind shown in Figure 2.8. In the efficient railroad the probability of one train arriving right after the previous one is virtually nil. So is the probability of there being 2 hours between trains. A train might arrive a few minutes before or after the hour, but, except for rare disasters, the trains run on time. In the inefficient railroad all is chaos. They manage to get their 24 trains out each day but that's about all one can say about their schedule. A train is as probable when the previous train has just passed as when passengers have already been waiting for an hour and a half. There is no way to predict when a train will come. Of special importance is the fact that knowing when the previous train has come is absolutely no help. Another train is equally probable at any time. For the inefficient railroad we can truly say that trains are arriving randomly.

Now, generalizing to other events, namely stimuli or responses, we can say they are truly random when we can plot a function of probability versus time

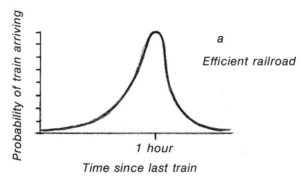

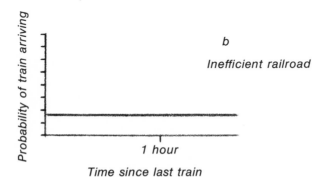

FIGURE 2.8
Probability of train arrivals as a function of time for two hypothetical railroads.

(or versus trials) that is horizontal. When the graph of probability versus time between events is not horizontal, but has one or more peaks, events are not random with respect to time but are occurring in a pattern. Thus, if we wanted to know whether events were random with respect to time or occurring in a pattern we would have to plot a graph on the order of those in Figure 2.8 to see whether it was flat or not. How can this be done?

In practice, drawing graphs like those in Figure 2.8 directly from observation is complicated. The reason is that the probability graphed on the y-axis of Figure 2.8 is a relative probability. The probability that a train will arrive, say, between 50 and 60 minutes after the previous train is the number of trains arriving between 50 and 60 minutes after the previous train divided by the number of times that the observer has already had to wait at least 50 minutes. The standard event (the denominator) by which probability is calculated is, in this case, the 50-to-60 minute period after a train has arrived. Whether another train arrives during that period (the numerator) is what determines the probability. To draw a probability graph directly, one would have to keep track of two things: (1) the number of times one had to wait for each period *and* (2) the number of times a train came during that period. The probability of a train arriving between 50 and 60 minutes is determined by dividing the second observation (number of arrivals between 50 and 60 minutes) by the first (number of times one had to wait at least 50 minutes).

Remaining with the railroad-station example, suppose there was an idler, perhaps an old railroad buff, who had nothing better to do with his time than to hang around railroad stations and watch trains go by. Let's say he suspected that the railroad was of the type exemplified in Figure 2.8b, an inefficient one. How could he confirm his suspicion? One method might be to take a piece of graph paper and a wristwatch to the station the next time he went. Then he could rule the paper as shown in Figure 2.9a and wait for the next train. As soon as the train left he would look at his watch and start timing. If 10 minutes went by without a train he would put an "O" in the lower left box. If another 10 minutes went by without a train he would put an "O" in the second box on the bottom line. He would keep putting O's in boxes on the bottom line until a train came. Then he would put an "X" in the box. (In Figure 2.9 a train comes between 30 and 40 minutes on his first observation.) Then he would

---

FIGURE 2.9
A technique for discovering whether events (in this case arrivals of railroad trains) are occurring randomly. (a) The observer puts an O on the bottom row when a train does not come in 10 minutes and an X when a train does come. Each time a train comes he starts over on a higher row. For example, on his first observation a train came between 30 and 40 minutes after the previous train. On his second observation a train came within the first 10 minutes. (b) Probability of a train coming in each 10-minute period. (c) X's only plotted. A distribution of times between trains.

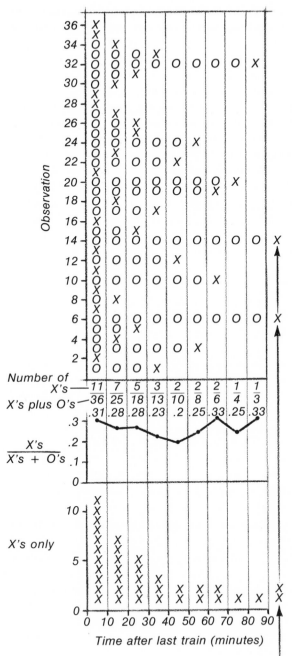

a

Observer puts an O on bottom row when train does not come in 10 minutes and an X when train does come. Each time a train comes he starts over on a higher row. For example, on his first observation a train came between 30 and 40 minutes after the previous train. On his second observation the train came within the first 10 minutes.

b

Probability of a train coming in each 10-minute period.

c

X's only plotted. A distribution of times between trains.

Time after last train (minutes)

More than 90-minutes wait

start over again with the next train on the next line. At the end of the day he might have a chart looking something like the one in Figure 2.9a. For each column he would then divide the number of X's by the number of X's plus the number of O's. The number of X's represents the number of trains in each 10 minutes. The number of O's represents the number of times the man had to wait at least that long. This quotient represents the probability of a train coming during that period. The quotients corresponding to each column of Figure 2.9a are shown in Figure 2.9b. Notice that the curve is rough (as curves of actual data tend to be). It does not form a smooth horizontal line. Nevertheless, there are no consistent peaks or valleys such as in Figure 2.8a, and there are no consistent upward or downward trends. The data tend to confirm the man's suspicions that the railroad trains are arriving randomly.

A somewhat easier way to do the same thing is shown in Figure 2.9c. The man might notice that each X in his original chart (Figure 2.9a) is preceded by a string of O's. Instead of putting down X's and O's he might just put down X's, each corresponding to the period when a train arrived. If he did that his graph would look like that of Figure 2.9c. But Figure 2.9c is nothing but an interevent time distribution with bin size equal to the width of the columns (10 minutes on the railroad buff's graph). That is, the total number of X's in each column is the number of instances when the time between trains was that given at the base of each column. To get from an interevent distribution such as that of Figure 2.9c to a probability distribution such as that of Figure 2.9b, the man has to divide the number of X's in each column by the number of X's in that column plus the number of O's that would have been in that column had he been recording them. He can find out exactly how many O's would have been in any column by adding up all the X's in all the columns to the right of the column in question. Since each X is preceded by a string of O's in Figure 2.9a, there would have been an O in any column for each X in all the columns to the right. For instance, in the third column there are 13 O's in Figure 2.9a and 13 X's in all the columns to the right of it in both Figures 2.9a and 2.9c. The reason that it is unnecessary for the man to mark down O's is that he can always count all the X's to the right of any point instead. The high number of short waits (as in Figure 2.9c) when events are occurring randomly may perhaps be surprising, but anyone who has waited for buses on Fifth Avenue in New York City knows that they frequently arrive all bunched together in packs, a sign that, however regularly they may have begun, traffic soon adds a random element to their interarrival times.

Returning to the example of a psychologist observing a rat licking a drinking tube, we can imagine the psychologist going through much the same charting procedure as the railroad buff. To get from an interresponse–time distribution to a probability distribution, the psychologist would have to go through the same steps that we outlined for going from the interevent distribution of Figure 2.9c to the probability distribution of Figure 2.9b.

Figure 2.10 shows how the interresponse–time distribution constructed in Figure 2.4 can be transformed into a probability function. The probability function for our made-up data, like the irt function, has a peak somewhere between 0.1 and 0.15 second, corresponding to a rate of about 8 responses per second, but the peak is much less pronounced. The 8-per-second rate is slightly more probable than others but, according to Figure 2.10, not vividly so. The probability function of Figure 2.10 is not very different from a horizontal line (after .1 second) showing that despite the regularity of the irt distribution there was a large element of randomness in the way the events of Figure 2.4 (which we made up) were occurring.*

We have already discussed the uses of an interresponse–time distribution. The main advantage of a probability distribution is that it allows us to test whether events are random with respect to time. Since random events form a horizontal line on a probability distribution, it is easy to measure randomness by determining whether, and by how much, a set of points (such as those of Figure 2.9b or 2.10b) deviates from a horizontal line. On the other hand, it is difficult to tell from an interevent-time distribution (such as those in Figure 2.9c or 2.10a) whether the behavior is random. (The form of an interevent distribution of random events is a downward sloping function, technically, an exponential function. It is difficult to tell when a set of points conforms to an exponential function.)

Probability functions like those of Figure 2.8, 2.9b, and 2.10b are sometimes called interresponse-times-per-opportunity functions (a term coined by Douglas Anger in 1956). This nomenclature reflects the fact that the probability of a given interresponse time is relative to the total number of occurrences of equal or longer interresponse times. An opportunity to respond at a given time after a previous response would only occur when the subject had waited at least as long as the given time. Then he would have the "opportunity" to respond or to wait still longer.

To see clearly why the word "opportunity" is used in this context, let us consider two extreme cases: (1) between 5 hours and 5 hours plus 10 minutes the probability of a train arriving is zero; (2) between 5 hours and 5 hours plus 10 minutes the probability of a train arriving is 1.0 (certainty). We can easily imagine both circumstances in real life—the first, if the conditions were such that the railroad would never allow a 5 hour wait unless a disaster had occurred, in which case no trains would be sent out at all that day—the second, if a 5-hour interval was the most that the stationmaster was to allow before using a reserve train on the siding next to the station. The reserve train would thus be a certainty if the wait had been as much as 5 hours.

---

*In any construction of a probability function from an irt function, as in Figure 2.9 and 2.10, there are more data (because more responses) in the early bins than in the later ones. Often the data in the later bins are too meager to be meaningful, as in Figure 2.10.

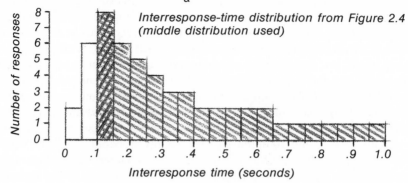

a

Interresponse-time distribution from Figure 2.4 (middle distribution used)

Probability of response at .1 − .15 = $\dfrac{\text{Number of responses at .1 − .15}}{\text{Sum of all responses at .1 and afterwards}}$ = $\dfrac{\blacksquare}{\blacksquare + \blacksquare}$

$= \dfrac{8}{46} = .17$

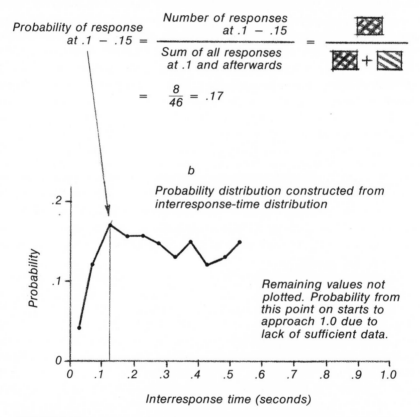

b

Probability distribution constructed from interresponse-time distribution

Remaining values not plotted. Probability from this point on starts to approach 1.0 due to lack of sufficient data.

FIGURE 2.10
Constructing a probability function from an irt distribution. (a) Interresponse-time distribution from Figure 2.4 (middle distribution), (b) Probability distribution constructed from interresponse-time distribution. Values after .5 are not plotted.' Probability from this point on starts to approach 1.0 due to the lack of sufficient data.

Now consider again the railroad buff. He doesn't know whether case 1 or case 2 is in effect (or whether some intermediate case applies with a probability between zero and 1.0). If, within the span of his observations he never has to wait as much as 5 hours he will never know which case is in effect.

One might say that he has had no opportunity to observe what happens between 5 hours and 5 hours plus 10 minutes or that the railroad has had no opportunity to show what it would do at that interval. If, on the other hand, there were 10 instances when the railroad buff had to wait as much as 5 hours between trains he would have these 10 opportunities to make an observation. If the train came within 10 minutes each time, his probability estimate would be 1.0 and he might guess that case 2 was in effect. Whatever the fraction of the 10 opportunities the train actually arrived would be the probability estimate during the interval from 5 hours to 5 hours plus 10 minutes. Similarly, with responses, the probability of responding during an interval can only be estimated when there have been a sufficient number of irts at least as long as the lower boundary of the interval. "Number of opportunities" is the denominator of the probability fraction with continuous responding just as "coin tosses" would be the denominator when calculating probability of heads on a series of tosses.

CONTINUOUS EVENTS

It would be handy for the psychologist if all environmental and behavioral events came in the compact discrete packages we have been discussing so far. Unfortunately, few environmental events are as easy to identify as single, sharp blows to the patella tendon of the knee, and few behavioral events are as easy to measure as the rat's licks at a drinking tube. In everyday life we experience such environmental events as the 6 o'clock news, the mingled odors of cooking, and the changes in the weather—and such behavioral events as riding a bicycle, writing reports, and playing football.

The work that psychologists do would be of little importance if it could not be extended, at least in theory, to the continuous events of everyday life.

There are several methods by which continuous events are dealt with by psychologists. By far the most common method is to analyze continuous events into discrete components. An example would be riding a bicycle. Instead of looking at this behavior as the continuous event that it is, we could look only at the number of revolutions of the pedals per minute. Considering the completion of each revolution as a separate event, we could analyze bicycle riding in the same way that we analyzed the rat's licking. In analyzing a football game, to take another complex example from everyday life, we might consider only the rate of touchdowns (discrete events) isolated from everything else that happens in the game. Still another example of how continuous events can be broken up into discrete events is the laboratory measurement of salivation.

Figure 2.11 shows a hypothetical graph of how salivation might vary with time. Animals salivate continuously. Yet Pavlov, in his studies of conditioning, almost always treated salivation as a discrete event. What he did was to consider *increases* of salivation beyond a certain point as *instances* of salivation. His measuring instruments were designed to record only abnormally high rates of salivation (say, only those above the dotted horizontal line of Figure 2.11) as instances of salivation. "Normal" salivation (below the dotted line) was ignored.

A second method of dealing with continuous events is to divide them into temporal intervals. Now it might seem that ignoring everything about a complex event except the time that it takes is to ignore everything that is interesting about the event, and sometimes this is certainly the case. Yet in a surprising number of instances such temporal information is useful or even critically important. In a football game it might be useful for the coach to know how much time his team spent on offense versus how much time on defense or how much time the game was being played on one end of the field versus how much time on the other end. The most interesting thing (for a scientist) about a bird's behavior over a given season might be how much time the bird spends nest-building versus how much time the bird spends looking for food. The relative durations of these activities may change significantly with the season or with other factors in the environment. An example of how such an analysis is done in practice is Martin Lindauer's study of worker bees. Lindauer marked individual worker bees when they were first born and watched them carefully through the first 24 days of their life. Figure 2.12 shows how he classified the behavior of one bee during this time. Note how much time the bee spends "resting." This was time when the bee seemed to Lindauer to be doing nothing in particular. But another observer might have classified this behavior as "guarding" or some other activity. If it were possible to calculate the energy expended per unit time at each of the activities, we could multiply the time

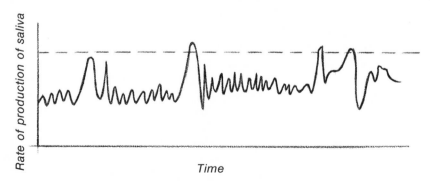

FIGURE 2.11
How the production of saliva might vary with time.

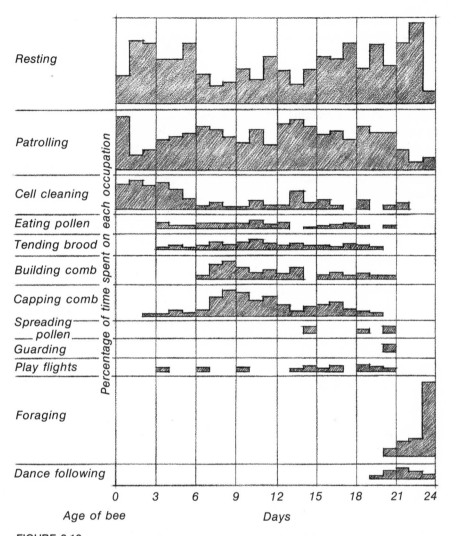

FIGURE 2.12
The distribution of effort by an individual worker bee observed over many hours of its life. Notice particularly the amount of time spent patrolling and resting. [From Lindauer, M. *Communication among social bees.* Cambridge, Mass.: Harvard University Press. Copyright © 1961 by the President and Fellows of Harvard College.]

spent at each activity by the energy expended per unit time and get a graph similar to that of Figure 2.12, but showing the bees' distribution of energy instead of time over the course of a day. We might find in such a case that the distributions were more even, the bee spending about equal energy at various activities. Resting for a long time might involve expenditure of energy equal to flying for a brief period. It is difficult to determine the energy spent in various activities, and where this has been tried it has not so far revealed much more about behavior than analysis simply in terms of time.

THE LOCATION OF EVENTS

Just as the temporal dimension of behavioral and environmental events can be divided into units for study, so can the spatial dimension. In fact, the spatial dimension can be measured more directly, without the help of event and cumulative recorders. Nevertheless, relatively few studies have focused on the spatial characteristics of events.

One study dealing with the spatial distribution of behavioral events is an experiment conducted by Richard Herrnstein with pigeons. In this experiment pigeons pecked at a strip of rubber, occasionally being rewarded for the pecking by access to grain (see Figure 2.13). The position of each peck was measured. The distribution of the pigeon's pecks in space can be analyzed in the same way as the distribution of similar events in time. Herrnstein found that pigeons tended to peck repeatedly at the same portion of the rubber strip rather than randomly across the strip even though reward was no more likely after pecking at one point than another. When the reward was removed, the pigeons tended to distribute their pecks more evenly across the strip. Thus, the spatial distribution of behavior depended on the environment—whether reward was or was not provided.

Usually, in experiments, the spatial extent of behavioral events is deliberately limited to facilitate the study of temporal relationships. For example, most studies of key-pecking of pigeons, because they are concerned with temporal characteristics of events, do not use the extended surface that Herrnstein did. Rather, the pigeon is given food only for pecks at a small key, and the temporal characteristics of those pecks are measured. Similarly, the physiologist interested in molecular muscle twitches usually confines his measurements to an extremely restricted spatial area and then studies events temporally within this area. He could, alternately, study the spatial distribution of muscle twitches, and this is sometimes, although not frequently, done.

The spatial and temporal characteristics of behavioral events are sometimes studied in conjunction. In our football example in the previous section, we considered both temporal and spatial characteristics of the team's behavior—that is, how much time it spent on each end of the field. Mazes, of which psychologists seem to be so fond, also allow both spatial and temporal interactions to be studied. An example of an actual study that combines temporal and spatial characteristics of behavior is the experiment by Fred D. Sheffield and Byron A. Campbell called "The Role of Experience in the 'Spontaneous' Activity of Hungry Rats." These investigators used a device called a stabilimeter to study the behavior of rats. The stabilimeter is illustrated schematically in Figure 2.14a. Each rat was kept in a single stabilimeter throughout the course of ex-

Access to food (when it was presented)
through hopper under key

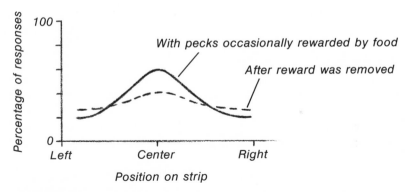

FIGURE 2.13
Example of a spatial distribution of responding. The long food hopper enabled
the pigeon to move its beak from the strip to the hopper with equal facility
wherever on the strip it was pecking.

periment. All of the rats were exposed to two environmental events each day:*
(1) the light in the chamber was turned off (for other rats the light was normally off and the event consisted of the light being turned on; these rats responded the same way as those we are considering) and (2) the rats were fed.
The critical experimental variable was whether the two environmental events
were presented together or separately. For one group of rats the feeding always

---

*Of course each rat experienced an infinite number of environmental events but the experi-
menters deliberately varied only two.

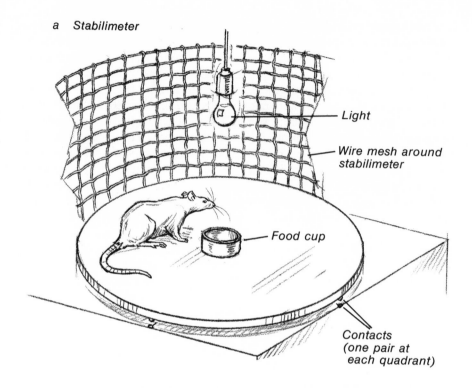

a Stabilimeter

Light

Wire mesh around
stabilimeter

Food cup

Contacts
(one pair at
each quadrant)

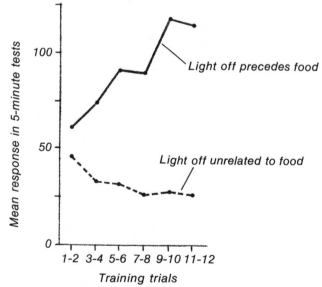

b   Function relating activity to pairings of light out and food.

Light off precedes food

Light off unrelated to food

Mean response in 5-minute tests

100

50

0

1-2 3-4 5-6 7-8 9-10 11-12

Training trials

came at the end of the light-off period. For the other group the feeding was randomly related to the light-off period. Sheffield and Campbell wanted to measure changes in the activity of the rats during the light-off period as the experiment proceeded. To measure activity they counted the number of times each rat moved from one quadrant of the chamber to the other during the light-off period. Whenever the rat moved across a quadrant of the chamber, that quadrant tilted, closing the contacts of a switch and thereby recording the move on a counter. The total on the counter for each rat was recorded after each light-off period and then the counter was reset. Figure 2.14b shows how these totals varied as the experiment progressed. The rats that had the events paired were more and more active during the light-off period as the experiment proceeded. The rats that did not have the events paired were active at first during the light-off period (perhaps because of the novelty of this event) but later this activity died out. For now we need only consider this experiment as an example of how temporal and spatial aspects of events interact. The periods of light-out are temporally defined, but the measured activity is spatially defined.

The location of environmental events is often of vital concern to the subject (for instance, the fox who must tell where the sound of the hunting horn is coming from) but it has been of surprisingly little concern, so far, to psychologists. Although there have been many studies of the ability of humans (and other animals) to locate sound sources, there is not much information yet on how the location of events affects behavior.

Environmental events can be treated as molar or molecular on the spatial dimension as on the temporal dimension. As an example of a molar spatial concept, consider the statement, "It is partly sunny outside." The truth of this statement requires that there be some spaces in the atmosphere with sunlight and some spaces without sunlight, but says nothing about what has to occur at any particular space. It cannot be partly sunny at any point in space. At a point in space (at a given time) there is either sun or shadow. To speak of partial sunlight we have to consider a spatial area larger than a point.

A molecular treatment of spatial events can be seen in the paintings of Seurat, whose images are made up of small points of various primary colors. When you look at a painting up close, all you can see is a field of many colored points; as you step back from the painting, figures and scenes emerge and the colors blend. The success of Seurat's technique suggests that everything we see may be analyzable into a series of discrete points in space, each of a different color and brightness. The complexity of our experience would then be expressable in terms of the interaction of points or groups of points with each other.

FIGURE 2.14
Sheffield and Campbell's experiment on the relation of temporal and spatial dimensions of behavior. (a) A stabilimeter. (b) Function relating activity to pairings of light off and food.

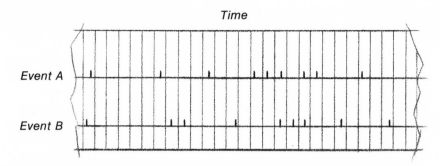

FIGURE 2.15
Two events, A and B, occurring at various times within the same time period. The
chart shows three instances of temporal contiguity.

With respect to spatial events the notion of molarity versus molecularity is
generally taken for granted. Everyone understands that an elephant, for instance, can only be defined over an extended spatial field. Knowing only what
is at a certain point you will never be able to tell whether an elephant is there.
But our everyday language does not so easily embrace the molar–molecular
distinction in temporal terms—except perhaps in music, which is why the
Gestalt psychologists were so fond of using musical examples to illustrate
molar–molecular distinctions.

TEMPORAL RELATIONSHIPS BETWEEN EVENTS

Contiguity

Let us suppose that we have a time period divided into arbitrary temporal
units as shown in Figure 2.15 and that two kinds of discrete events, A and B,
occur during this period. These could be any discrete events, behavioral or
environmental: bar-presses, brief electric shocks, licks, eyeblinks, gunshots,
or anything else, as long as A and B are different. For convenience let us assume
that the temporal units are small enough so that only one of each kind of event
could occur in each unit and also small enough so that when two different
events occur during the same unit they can be considered contiguous.* A
quick glance at Figure 2.15 reveals three instances of temporal contiguity.

It is temporal contiguity that the British associationists identified as the
relation between events responsible for learned behavior. For many psychologists today, temporal contiguity is still the key to learned behavior. When two

---

*In actual experimental situations the temporal units we are considering are often single
"trials" in which it is arranged that only a certain limited set of events can occur. But outside of
the laboratory, events exhibiting contiguous relationships occur freely at various intervals.If we
ignore the time between trials in an experimental situation, the duration of each trial can be
considered to be just like the time between events in Figure 2.15.

events occur at the same time, or in quick succession, they become associated. The more there are of these contiguous occurrences, the stronger the association. As philosophers, the British associationists were not generally concerned with the physical underpinnings of association. Only David Hartley attempted to explain association in terms of neural phenomena. His explanation, involving "vibrations" in the brain, anticipated Pavlov's theory of conditioning.

According to Pavlov's theory, "fields of excitation" are set up around centers in the brain where the nerves terminate. Figure 2.16 shows Pavlov's model. The excitation is strongest in a path from the part of the brain corresponding to the stimulus to the part corresponding to the unconditioned response it causes (Figure 2.16a). When a weaker stimulus is presented simultaneously with a stronger one (Figure 2.16b) the excitation from the weaker is deflected

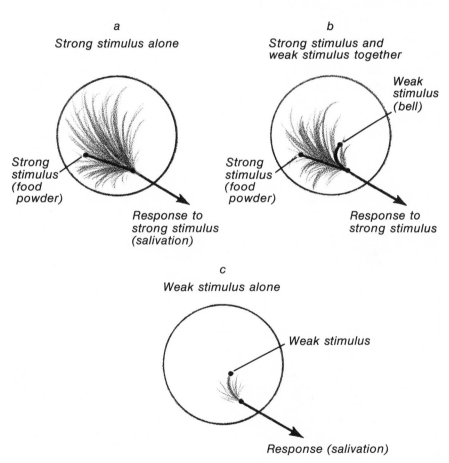

FIGURE 2.16
Hypothetical brain fields during classical conditioning.

toward the axis between the stronger stimulus and its response. As the two stimuli are presented together more and more, the brain changes so that the resistance to energy flow between the weak stimulus and the strong response becomes less and less. Finally, when the weak stimulus is presented alone (Figure 2.16c) its energy goes through the new low-resistance path to cause the strong response by itself. In most of Pavlov's experiments with dogs, the strong stimulus was food powder, the strong response was salivation, and the weak stimulus was a sound from a bell or a tuning fork. If the bell and the food powder were presented contiguously a sufficient number of times, the dogs would salivate when the bell was presented by itself.

A whole host of mechanisms similar to those described by Pavlov have since been hypothesized to explain the relationship between a stimulus-response connection and the reward or punishment which E. L. Thorndike claimed could "stamp in" or "stamp out" the connection. All of these models for simple association between two stimuli and for conditioning of various kinds rely on contiguity between the events becoming associated. According to these models if an association occurs between A and B when A and B are noncontiguous events, there must be a chain of mediating events between A and B linking the two together. In the experiment by Ebbinghaus in Chapter 1 (Figure 1.7) the connection between the noncontiguous items ZEP (item 1) and VEL (item 4) on the original list is not direct, but mediated by a chain of connections (in the mind) between LEP and LAN, LAN and NUR, and NUR and VEL, which are contiguous.

In real life (as opposed to the psychology laboratory) we are constantly forming associations between noncontiguous events. For instance, I associate eating with gaining weight even though there is rarely contiguity between my eating and weighing myself. Many psychologists, following the British asso-ciationists, contend that noncontiguous events can only be associated when they are bridged by a string of contiguous events. Thus, the invention of mediating mechanisms bridging noncontiguous events with contiguous events has been a large part of what these psychologists spend their time doing. In later chapters we shall discuss how some of these mediating mechanisms are supposed to work.

Contingency

If A and B happen at the same time they are contiguous. The relationship between events specified by contiguity is instantaneous. Contingency, on the other hand, cannot be judged in an instant. A contingent relationship is a prob-abilistic relationship, which requires a sample from which to judge. For a contingent relationship between A and B, not only do A and B have to happen together but the *absence* of A must also coincide with the *absence* of B. If I am wearing blue socks on the day I win a raffle I can say without hesitation that these events (the blue socks and the raffle winning) were contiguous. But I cannot say anything about contingency until I know what the probability is of my winning a raffle without blue socks and what the probability is of my wearing blue socks and not winning a raffle.

A contingency relationship between two events consists of four subevents expressed as contiguities. The table in Figure 2.17a shows these four contiguities for the events pictured in Figure 2.15. They are the contiguities of A and B, of not-A and not-B, of A and not-B, and of B and not-A. In Figure 2.17b the number of instances of each contiguity divided by the total number of units (27) yields probability. Thus, the upper left–hand probability of Figure 2.17b is the probability of A and B occurring at the same time (that is, contiguously) given the occurrence of a temporal unit as we have defined it. The numbers in the boxes of Figure 2.17 are exactly what one would expect on the basis of chance. That is, they are the numbers of coincidences one would expect between A and B if A and B were occurring randomly in time. Since 9 of the 27 units have an A in them and 9 of the 27 units have a B in them, the probability of a coincidence of A and B is $9/27 \times 9/27 = 1/9$. If A and B were items to be associated, and association occurred on the basis of simple contiguity, then the three instances of A and B occurring together as in Figure

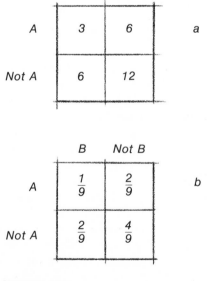

FIGURE 2.17
Contingency tables expressing relationship between events A and B pictured in Figure 2.15. Table (a) shows simple frequencies. Table (b) shows these frequencies divided by the total number of instances to form probabilities.

2.15 might be sufficient to cause some learning to take place. If, on the other hand, A and B were associated on the basis of contingency, then there should be no association between them because their relationship is random (non-contingent) as shown by the contingency tables of Figure 2.17. In order to learn anything on the basis of contiguity, attention need be focused only on an instant, the instant of the contiguity. But in order to learn on the basis of contingency, attention must encompass events over a considerable time span. In the case of the table in Figure 2.17, enough events must be sampled to fill the boxes in the table, and such sampling necessarily takes time. Again, the issue of molar versus molecular psychology arises. If the basis of all learning is molecular, then learning must be expressed in terms of contiguities. But if learning can be molar, that is, if its fundamental units can have duration, it would be possible for contingencies to be experienced directly, without prior learning of contiguities (as the Gestalt psychologists said that we experience a piece of music). Much of the research and theory of present-day psychology is centered around this issue.

It may be argued that because the contingency tables of Figure 2.17 consist merely of four contiguities there is a possibility that learning of contingencies is based on prior learning of the four contiguities involved. This possibility was explored with a model for learning based on contiguity developed by Allen Wagner and Robert Rescorla. The model will be discussed later, in the chapter on classical conditioning.

Correlation

If all of the assumptions we made upon drawing Figure 2.15 were correct, there would be no need to consider correlations. That is, if A and B were discrete events (if their durations and intensities were equal) and if temporal units could be selected so that they could contain an A and a B but not two A's or two B's, then contingency tables would suffice to show the relationship between these events. But often one or another of the above conditions does not fit the data being studied. In that case, the essential relationships between events expressed by a contingency table can be expressed instead by a correlation. Figure 2.18 shows a set of A's and B's that would be difficult to arrange like Figure 2.15. In Figure 2.18 the temporal units encompass several occurrences of A- and B-events. To determine the relationship between A and B the number of A-occurrences in each unit can be plotted against the number of B-occurrences. If we divided the number of occurrences, A or B, by the size of the temporal unit we would have the rate of event A plotted against the rate of event B. The division into equal temporal units is equivalent to providing a rate measure on the axes in Figure 2.18b. The scatter plot of Figure 2.18b shows that the rate of event A is positively correlated with the rate of event B. That is, when event A is occurring rapidly so is event B. An example of two real events positively correlated would be rate of eating pretzels and rate of

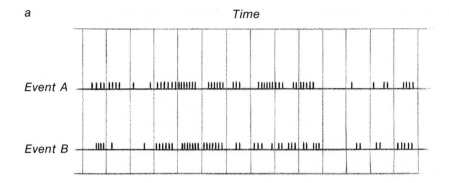

a

Time

Event A

Event B

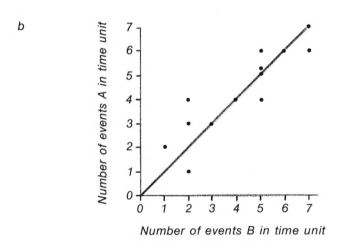

b

FIGURE 2.18
Correlation between event A and event B over time.

drinking. The positive correlation is shown by the upward sloping line, which is the line that best fits the points of the scatter plot. If the line were horizontal or vertical it would mean that the events were not correlated—that knowledge of the rate of A would not enable you to predict anything about rate of B and vice versa. If the line were sloping downward it would mean that the rates of A and B were negatively correlated; that is, the faster event A was occurring the slower event B was occurring. An example of two real events negatively correlated would be rate of drinking milk and rate of eating dill pickles.

A useful feature of correlations is that they can be made between two non-discrete events such as degree of deafness and loudness of speech or between a nondiscrete and a discrete event such as atmospheric temperature and rate of licking for a rat.

   As with contingencies it has been argued that correlations of various kinds
can be learned directly, and here again the issue is between molar and molecular
psychology. Rate of discrete events has no meaning at an instant of time. At
an instant the rat is either licking or it is not. The rate of licking has meaning
only over an extended temporal period. Similarly, on the stimulus side, rate
of electric shock or rate of food delivery has no meaning except over an extended interval of time. Thus, if two rates of discrete events are being compared or if the rate of a discrete event is being compared with something else
the rates themselves have no meaning in terms of temporal contiguity. Can a
molar entity such as rate of a discrete event be a fundamental psychological
unit, or must there be some more fundamental units that can be brought into
temporal contiguity?

   Suppose that some stimulus event is occurring as in the upper part of Figure
2.19 and some response event is also occurring as in the lower part of that
figure. The more molar psychologist would tend to say that the rates of the
stimulus and response are directly related—that the rate of stimulus is causing
the rate of response. The more molecular psychologist would notice that the
individual stimulus and response occurrences were not in temporal contiguity.
He would then assume that the stimulus was directly causing some state inside
the organism, which in turn was causing some tendency to respond. The two
mediating events inside the organism would then be in temporal contiguity
with each other and could thereby become associated. This, in a way, is the
core of the difference between molar and molecular psychology—a difference
we shall see frequently exemplified throughout the rest of this book.

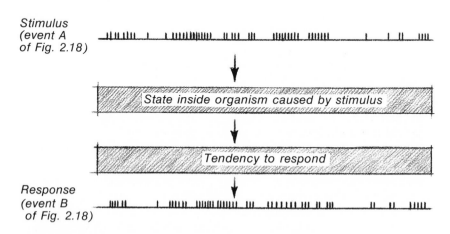

FIGURE 2.19
Events inside the organism hypothesized by molecular psychologist to mediate
between stimulus and response to bring them into temporal contiguity.

BIBLIOGRAPHY

The particular combination of material included in this chapter is somewhat unusual, so there is no single place the student could go to find out more about it. The best we can do is to suggest a few references for various aspects of what was covered in the chapter.

The general philosophy of being flexible in defining stimuli and responses comes from the work of B. F. Skinner. It is developed fully in his book *The behavior of organisms,* listed below. A more recent and shorter exposition of this same philosophy is to be found in Skinner's paper "Are theories of learning necessary?" (*Psychological Review, 57,* 193–216, 1950).

The distinction between *acts* and *movements* as subjects for learning comes from an early work by E. R. Guthrie, *The psychology of learning,* listed below. Guthrie's conclusion was that movements, rather than acts, are learned—just the opposite of the one espoused here. Nevertheless, the *distinction* between the alternatives is more important than which side one comes down on and Guthrie draws the distinction clearly.

The statistical aspects of the present chapter would be amplified considerably by any good statistics text. A treatment of methodological and statistical problems relevant to the research described here can be found in M. R. D'Amato's *Experimental psychology: Methodology, psychophysics and learning* (New York: McGraw-Hill, 1970).

Following is a list of articles and books referred to in this chapter:

Anger, D. The dependence of interresponse time upon the relative reinforcement of different interresponse times. *Journal of Experimental Psychology,* 1956, *52,* 145–161.

Gilbert, T. F. Fundamental dimensional properties of the operant. *Psychological Review,* 1958, *65,* 272–282.

Guthrie, E. R. *Psychology of learning.* New York: Harper & Row, 1935.

Guthrie, E. R., and Horton, G. P. *Cats in a puzzle box.* New York: Rinehart, 1946.

Hartley, D. *Observations on man, his frame, his duty, and his expectations.* London and Bath: J. Johnson, 1749.

Herrnstein, R. J. Stereotypy and intermittent reinforcement. *Science,* 1961, *133,* 2067–2069.

Lindauer, M. *Communication among social bees.* Cambridge, Mass.: Harvard University Press, 1961.

Pavlov, I. P. *Conditioned reflexes.* Translated by G. V. Anrep. London: Oxford University Press, 1927.

Sheffield, F. D., and Campbell, B. A. The role of experience in the "spontaneous" activity of hungry rats. *Journal of Comparative and Physiological Psychology,* 1954, *17,* 97–100.

Skinner, B. F. *The behavior of organisms: An experimental analysis.* New York: Appleton-Century-Crofts, 1938.

We have reprinted an article by Skinner taken from a speech to a group of psychiatrists in which the advantages and disadvantages of postulating events taking place *inside* the organism are discussed in relation to understanding human behavior.

Supplemental Reading for Chapter 2

WHAT IS PSYCHOTIC BEHAVIOR?
B. F. Skinner

Since my field of specialization lies some distance from psychiatry, it may be well to begin with credentials. The first will be negative. In the sense in which my title is most likely to be understood, I am wholly unqualified to discuss the question before us. The number of hours I have spent in the presence of psychotic people (assuming that I am myself sane) is negligible compared with what many of you might claim, and the time I have spent in relevant reading and discussion would suffer equally from the same comparison. I am currently interested in some research on psychotic subjects, to which I shall refer again later, but my association with that program in no way qualifies me as a specialist.

Fortunately, I am not here to answer the question in that sense at all. A more accurate title would have been "What is *behavior?*—with an occasional reference to psychiatry." Here I will list such positive credentials as seem appropriate. I have spent a good share of my professional life in the experimental analysis of the behavior of organisms. Almost all my subjects have been below the human level

From *Theory and Treatment of the Psychoses: Some Newer Aspects.* F. Gildea, editor. Washington University Press, 1956. The research described at the end of this article was carried out at the Metropolitan State Hospital at Waltham, Massachusetts. Dr. Harry Solomon, then of the Boston Psychopathic Hospital, collaborated with the author in setting up the laboratory. Dr. Ogden R. Lindsley took immediate charge and was responsible for much of the overall experimental design and the day-to-day conduct of the experiments.

Reprinted in B. F. Skinner, *Cumulative Record,* 3rd Edition, 1972, Meredith Corporation.

(most of them rats or pigeons) and all, so far as I know, have been sane. My research has not been designed to test any theory of behavior, and the results cannot be evaluated in terms of the statistical significance of such proofs. The object has been to discover the functional relations which prevail between measurable aspects of behavior and various conditions and events in the life of the organism. The success of such a venture is gauged by the extent to which behavior can, as a result of the relationships discovered, actually be predicted and controlled. Here we have, I think, been fortunate. Within a limited experimental arrangement, my colleagues and I have been able to demonstrate a lawfulness in behavior which seems to us quite remarkable. In more recent research it has been possible to maintain—actually, to sharpen—this degree of lawfulness while slowly increasing the complexity of the behavior studied. The extent of the prediction and control which have been achieved is evident not only in "smoothness of curves" and uniformity of results from individual to individual or even species to species, but in the practical uses which are already being made of the techniques—for example, in providing baselines for the study of pharmacological and neurological variables, or in converting a lower organism into a sensitive psychophysical observer.

Although research designed in this way has an immediate practical usefulness, it is not independent of one sort of theory. A primary concern has been to isolate a useful and expedient measure. Of all the myriad aspects of behavior which present themselves to observation, which are worth watching? Which will prove most useful in establishing functional relations? From time to time many different characteristics of behavior have seemed important. Students of the subject have asked how well organized behavior is, how well adapted it is to the environment, how sensitively it maintains a homeostatic equilibrium, how purposeful it is, or how successfully it solves practical problems or adjusts to daily life. Many have been especially interested in how an individual compares with others of the same species or with members of other species in some arbitrary measure of the scope, complexity, speed, consistency, or other property of behavior. All these aspects may be quantified, at least in a rough way, and any one may serve as a dependent variable in a scientific analysis. But they are not all equally productive. In research which emphasizes prediction and control, the topography of behavior must be carefully specified. Precisely what is the organism doing? The most important aspect of behavior so described is its probability of emission. How likely is it that an organism will engage in behavior of a given sort, and what conditions or events change this likelihood? Although probability of action has only recently been explicitly recognized in behavior theory, it is a key concept to which many classical notions, from reaction tendencies to the Freudian wish, may be reduced. Experimentally we deal with it as the *frequency* with which an organism behaves in a given way under specified circumstances, and our methods are designed to satisfy this requirement. Frequency of response has proved to be a remarkably sensitive variable, and with its aid the exploration of causal factors has been gratifyingly profitable.

One does not engage in work of this sort for the sheer love of rats or pigeons. As the medical sciences illustrate, the study of animals below the level of man is dictated mainly by convenience and safety. But the primary object of interest is always a man. Such qualifications as I have to offer in approaching the present question spring about equally from the experimental work just mentioned and from a parallel preoccupation with human behavior, in which the principles emerging from the experimental analysis have been tested and put to work in the interpretation of empirical facts. The formal disciplines of government, education, economics, religion, and psychotherapy, among others, together with our everyday experience with men, overwhelm us with a flood of facts. To interpret these facts with the formulation which emerges from an experimental analysis has proved to be strenuous but healthful exercise. In particular, the nature and function of *verbal* behavior have taken on surprisingly fresh and promising aspects when reformulated under the strictures of such a framework.

In the long run, of course, mere interpretation is not enough. If we have achieved a true scientific understanding of man, we should be able to prove this in the actual prediction and control of his behavior. The experimental practices and the concepts emerging from our research on lower organisms have already been extended in this direction, not only in the experiments on psychotic subjects already mentioned, but in other promising areas. The details would take us too far afield, but perhaps I can indicate my faith in the possibilities in a single instance by hazarding the prediction that we are on the threshold of a revolutionary change in methods of education, based not only upon a better understanding of learning processes, but upon a workable conception of knowledge itself.

Whether or not this brief personal history seems to you to qualify me to discuss the question before us, there is no doubt that it has created a high probability that I will do so, as shown by the fact that I am here. What I have to say is admittedly methodological. I can understand a certain impatience with such discussion particularly when, as in the field of psychiatry, many pressing problems

call for action. The scientist who takes
time out to consider human nature when
so many practical things need to be done
for human welfare is likely to be cast in
the role of a Nero, fiddling while Rome
burns. (It is quite possible that the fiddling referred to in this archetypal myth
was a later invention of the historians,
and that in actual fact Nero had called in
his philosophers and scientists and was
discussing "the fundamental nature of
combustion" or "the epidemiology of
conflagration.") But I should not be here
if I believed that what I have to say is
remote from practical consequences. If
we are now entering an era of research in
psychiatry which is to be as extensive and
as productive as other types of medical
research, then a certain detachment from
immediate problems, a fresh look at
human behavior in general, a survey of
applicable formulations, and a consideration of relevant methods may prove to
be effective practical steps with surprisingly immediate consequences.

The study of human behavior is, of
course, still in its infancy, and it would be
rash to suppose that anyone can foresee
the structure of a well-developed and
successful science. Certainly no current
formulation will seem right fifty years
hence. But although we cannot foresee
the future clearly, it is not impossible to
discover in what direction we are likely to
change. There are obviously great de-
ficiencies in our present ways of thinking
about men; otherwise we should be more
successful. What are they, and how are
they to be remedied? What I have to say
rests upon the assumption that the behavior of the psychotic is simply part and
parcel of human behavior, and that certain considerations which have been
emphasized by the experimental and
theoretical analysis of behavior in general are worth discussing in this special
application.

It is important to remember that I
am speaking as an experimental scientist.
A conception of human behavior based
primarily on clinical information and

practice will undoubtedly differ from a
conception emanating from the laboratory. This does not mean that either is
superior to the other, or that eventually a
common formulation will not prove useful to both. It is possible that questions
which have been suggested by the exigencies of an experimental analysis may not
seem of first importance to those of you
who are primarily concerned with human
behavior under therapy. But as psychiatry
moves more rapidly into experimental
research and as laboratory results take on
a greater clinical significance, certain
problems in the analysis of behavior
should become common to researcher and
therapist alike, and should eventually be
given common and cooperative solutions.

The study of behavior, psychotic or
otherwise, remains securely in the company of the natural sciences so long as we
take as our subject matter the observable
activity of the organism, as it moves
about, stands still, seizes objects, pushes
and pulls, makes sounds, gestures, and so
on. Suitable instruments will permit us to
amplify small-scale activities as part of
the same subject matter. Watching a
person behave in this way is like watching
any physical or biological system. We also
remain within the framework of the natural sciences in explaining these observations in terms of external forces and
events which act upon the organism.
Some of these are to be found in the
hereditary history of the individual, including his membership in a given species
as well as his personal endowment. Others
arise from the physical environment, past
or present. We may represent the situation as in Figure 1. Our organism emits
the behavior we are to account for, as our
dependent variable, at the right. To explain this, we appeal to certain external,
generally observable, and possibly controllable hereditary and environmental
conditions, as indicated at the left. These
are the independent variables of which
behavior is to be expressed as a function.
Both input and output of such a system
may be treated with the accepted dimen-

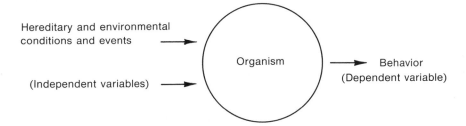

Hereditary and environmental
conditions and events

(Independent variables)

Organism

Behavior
(Dependent variable)

FIGURE 1

sional systems of physics and biology. A complete set of such relations would permit us to predict and, insofar as the independent variables are under our control, to modify or generate behavior at will. It would also permit us to *interpret* given instances of behavior by inferring plausible variables of which we lack direct information. Admittedly the data are subtle and complex, and many relevant conditions are hard to get at, but the program as such is an acceptable one from the point of view of scientific method. We have no reason to suppose in advance that a complete account cannot be so given. We have only to try and see.

It is not, however, the subtlety or complexity of this subject matter which is responsible for the relatively undeveloped state of such a science. Behavior has seldom been analyzed in this manner. Instead, attention has been diverted to activities which are said to take place within the organism. All sciences tend to fill in causal relationships, especially when the related events are separated by time and space. If a magnet affects a compass needle some distance away, the scientist attributes this to a "field" set up by the magnet and reaching to the compass needle. If a brick falls from a chimney, releasing energy which was stored there, say, a hundred years ago when the chimney was built, the result is explained by saying that the brick has all this time possessed a certain amount of "potential energy." In order to fill such spatial and temporal gaps between cause and effect, nature has from time to time been endowed with many weird properties, spirits, and essences. Some have proved helpful and have become part of the subject matter of science, especially when identified with events observed in other ways. Others have proved dangerous and damaging to scientific progress. Sophisticated scientists have usually been aware of the practice and alert to its dangers. Such inner forces were, indeed, the hypotheses which Newton refused to make.

Among the conditions which affect behavior, hereditary factors occupy a primary position, at least chronologically. Differences between members of different species are seldom, if ever, disputed, but differences between members of the same species, possibly due to similar hereditary factors, are so closely tied up with social and ethical problems that they have been the subject of seemingly endless debate. In any event, the newly conceived organism begins at once to be influenced by its environment; and when it comes into full contact with the external world, environmental forces assume a major role. They are the only conditions which can be changed so far as the individual is concerned. Among these are the events we call "stimuli," the various interchanges between organism and environment such as occur in breathing or eating, the events which generate the changes in behavior we call emotional, and the coincidences between stimuli or between stimuli and behavior responsible for the changes we call learning. The effects may be felt immediately or only after the passage of time—perhaps of many years. Such are the "causes"—the independent variables—in terms of which we may hope to explain behavior within the framework of a natural science.

In many discussions of human behavior, however, these variables are seldom explicitly mentioned. Their place is taken by events or conditions within the organism for which they are said to be responsible (see Figure 2). Thus, the species status of the individual is dealt with as a set of instincts, not simply as patterns of behavior characteristic of the species, but as biological drives. As one text puts it, "instincts are innate biological forces, urges, or impulsions driving the organism to a certain end." The individual genetic endowment, if not carried by body type or other observable physical characteristic, is represented in the form of inherited traits or abilities, such as temperament or intelligence. As to the environmental variables, episodes in the past history of the individual are dealt with as memories and habits, while conditions of interchange between organism and environment are represented as needs or wants. Certain inciting episodes are dealt with as emotions, again in the sense not of patterns but of active

causes of behavior. Even the present environment as it affects the organism is transmuted into "experience," as we turn from what is the case to what "seems to be" the case to the individual.

The same centripetal movement may be observed on the other side of the diagram (see Figure 3). It is rare to find behavior dealt with as a subject matter in its own right. Instead it is regarded as evidence for a mental life, which is then taken as the primary object of inquiry. What the individual does—the topography of his behavior—is treated as the functioning of one or more personalities. It is clear, especially when personalities are multiple, that they cannot be identified with the biological organism as such, but are conceived of, rather, as inner behaviors of doubtful status and dimensions. The act of behaving in a given instance is neglected in favor of an impulse or wish, while the probability of such an act is represented as an excitatory tendency or in terms of psychic energy. Most important of all, the changes in behavior which represent the fundamental behavioral processes are characterized as mental activities—such as thinking, learning, discriminating, reasoning, symbolizing, projecting, identifying, and repressing.

The relatively simple scheme shown in the first figure does not, therefore, represent the conception of human be-

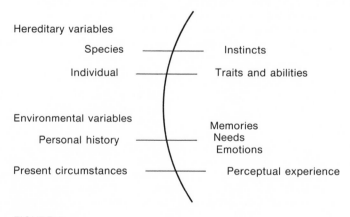

FIGURE 2

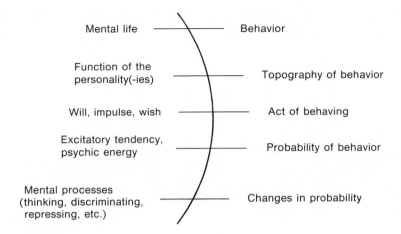

Mental life ———— Behavior

Function of the
personality(-ies) ———— Topography of behavior

Will, impulse, wish ———— Act of behaving

Excitatory tendency,
psychic energy ———— Probability of behavior

Mental processes
(thinking, discriminating, ———— Changes in probability
repressing, etc.)

FIGURE 3

havior characteristic of most current theory. The great majority of students of human behavior assume that they are concerned with a series of events indicated in the expanded diagram of Figure 4. Here the hereditary and environmental conditions are assumed to generate instincts, needs, emotions, memories, habits, and so on, which in turn lead the personality to engage in various activities characteristic of the mental apparatus, and these in turn generate the observable behavior of the organism. All four stages in the diagram are accepted as proper objects of inquiry. Indeed, far from leaving the inner events to other specialists while confining themselves to the end terms, many psychologists and psychiatrists take the mental apparatus as their primary subject matter.

Perhaps the point of my title is now becoming clearer. Is the scientific study of behavior—whether normal or psychotic—concerned with the behavior of the observable organism under the control of hereditary and environmental factors, or with the functioning of one or more personalities engaged in a variety of mental processes under the promptings of instincts, needs, emotions, memories,

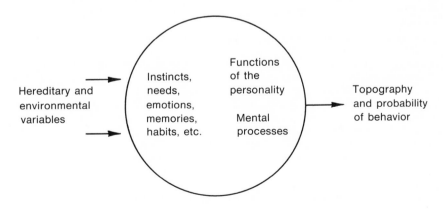

Hereditary and
environmental
variables

Instincts,
needs,
emotions,
memories,
habits, etc.

Functions
of the
personality

Mental
processes

Topography
and probability
of behavior

FIGURE 4

and habits? I do not want to raise the question of the supposed *nature* of these inner entities. A certain kinship between such an explanatory system and primitive animism can scarcely be missed, but whatever the historical sources of these concepts, we may assume that they have been purged of dualistic connotations. If this is not the case, if there are those who feel that psychiatry is concerned with a world beyond that of the psychobiological or biophysical organism, that conscious or unconscious mind lacks physical extent, and that mental processes do not affect the world according to the laws of physics, then the following arguments should be all the more cogent. But the issue is not one of the nature of these events, but of their usefulness and expedience in a scientific description.

It can scarcely be denied that the expansion of subject matter represented by Figure 4 has the unfortunate effect of a loss of physical status. This is more than a question of prestige or "face." A subject matter which is unquestionably part of the field of physics and biology has been relinquished for one of doubtful characteristics. This cannot be corrected merely by asserting our faith in the ultimately physical nature of inner processes. To protest that the activities of the conscious and unconscious mind are only in some sense an aspect of the biological functioning of the organism will not answer the practical question. In abandoning the dimensional systems of physics and biology, we abandon the techniques of measurement which would otherwise be a natural heritage from earlier achievements in other sciences. This is possibly an irreparable loss. If we come out flatly for the existence of instincts, needs, memories, and so on, on the one hand, and the mental process and functions of the personality on the other, then we must accept the responsibility of devising methods of observing these inner events and of discovering dimensional systems according to which they can be measured. The loss of the opportunity to measure

and manipulate in the manner characteristic of the physical sciences would be offset only by some extraordinary advantage gained by turning to inner states or conditions.

It is possible, however, to argue that these inner events are merely ways of representing the outer. Many theorists will contend that a habit is only a sort of notation useful in reporting a bit of the history of the individual, just as so-called "mental processes" are ways of talking about changes in behavior. This is a tempting position, for we may then insist that the only dimensional systems required are those appropriate to the terminal events. But if we are to take that line, a great deal still needs to be done to put our house in scientific order. The concepts which one encounters in current behavior theory represent the observable events in an extremely confusing way. Most of them have arisen from theoretical or practical considerations which have little reference to their validity or usefulness as scientific constructs, and they bear the scars of such a history. For example, Freud pointed to important relationships between the behavior of an adult and certain episodes in early childhood, but he chose to bridge the very considerable gap between cause and effect with activities or states of the mental apparatus. Conscious or unconscious wishes or emotions in the adult represent the earlier episodes and are said to be directly responsible for their effect upon behavior. The adult is said, for example, to be suffering from conscious anxiety generated when as a child he was punished for aggressive behavior toward a sibling. But many details of the early episode are glossed over (and may, as a result, be neglected) in attributing the disturbances in his behavior to a current anxiety rather than to the earlier punishment. The number of references to anxiety in treatises on behavior must greatly exceed the number of references to punishing episodes, yet we must turn to the latter for full details. If the details are not available, nothing can take their place.

Other kinds of independent variables provide similar examples. Everyone is familiar with the fact that, in general, organisms eat or do not eat depending upon a recent history of deprivation or ingestion. If we can establish that a child does not eat his dinner because he has recently eaten other food, there may seem to be no harm in expressing this by saying that "he is not hungry," provided we explain this in turn by pointing to the history of ingestion. But the concept of hunger represents quite inadequately the many features of schedules of deprivation and other conditions and events which alter the behavior of eating. In the same way the inner surrogates of hereditary variables function beyond the line of duty. We often have no other explanation of a given bit of behavior than that, like other features of anatomy and physiology, it is characteristic of a species; but when we choose instead to attribute this behavior to a set of instincts, we obscure the negative nature of our knowledge and suggest more active causes than mere species status warrants. Similarly, we accept the fact that individuals differ in their behavior, and we may, in some instances, show a relation between aspects of the behavior of successive generations, but these differences and relationships are optimistically misrepresented when we speak of hereditary traits and abilities. Again, the term *experience* incorrectly represents our information about a stimulating field. It has often been observed, for example, that some trivial incident generates a reaction altogether out of proportion to its magnitude. A person seems to be reacting, not to the physical world as such, but to what the world "means to him." Eventually, of course, the effect must be explained—for example, by pointing to some earlier connection with more important events. But whatever the explanation, it is almost certainly not adequately expressed by the notion of a momentary experience. There are obvious difficulties involved in representing a physical environment *plus a personal history* as a current psychological environment alone.

So far as our independent variables are concerned, then, the practice we are examinining tends to gloss over many important details and complexities. The conceptual structure conceals from us the inadequacy of our present knowledge. Much the same difficulty is encountered with respect to the dependent variable, when observable behavior takes second place to mental functionings of a personality. Just as the physical environment is transmuted into experience, so physical behavior comes to be described in terms of its purpose or meaning. A man may walk down the street in precisely the same way upon two occasions, although in one instance he is out for exercise and in another he is going to mail a letter. And so it is thought necessary to consider, not the behavior itself, but "what it means" to the behaving individual. But the additional information we are trying to convey is not a property of behavior but of an independent variable. The behavior we observe in the two cases *is* the same. In reading meaning or intention into it, we are speculating about some of its causes. To take another example, it is commonly said that we can "see" aggression. But we "see" it in two steps: (1) we observe the behavior of an organism, and (2) we relate it to observed or inferred variables having to do with injurious consequences and with the kinds of circumstances which make such behavior probable. No behavior is itself aggressive by nature, although some forms of behavior are so often a function of variables which make them aggressive that we are inclined to overlook the inferences involved. Similarly, when we observe two or more behavioral systems in the same individual and attribute them to different personalities, we gain a considerable advantage for certain descriptive purposes. For example, we can then describe oppositions between such systems as we would between different persons. But we have almost certainly suggested a unity which is not justified by the observed systems of behavior, and we have probably made it more difficult to represent the actual extent of any conflicts as well as to explain its origins. And when we observe that the behavior of a person is characterized by a certain responsiveness or probability of responding and speak instead of a given amount of psychic energy, we neglect many details of the actual facts and dodge the responsibility of finding a dimensional system. Lastly, mental processes are almost always conceived as simpler and more orderly than the rather chaotic material from which they are inferred and which they are used to explain. The "learning process" in experimental psychology, for example, does not give us an accurate account of measured changes in behavior.

We look inside the organism for a *simpler* system, in which the causes of behavior are less complex than the actual hereditary and environmental events and in which the behavior of a personality is more meaningful and orderly than the day-to-day activity of the organism. All the variety and complexity of the input in our diagram seems to be reduced to a few relatively amorphous states, which in turn generate relatively amorphous functions of the personality, which then suddenly explode into the extraordinary variety and complexity of behavior. But the simplification achieved by such a practice is, of course, illusory, for it follows only from the fact that a one-to-one correspondence between inner and outer events has not been demanded. It is just this lack of correspondence which makes such an inner system unsuitable in the experimental analysis of behavior. If "hunger" is something which is produced by certain schedules of deprivation, certain drugs, certain states of health, and so on, and if in turn it produces changes in the probability of a great variety of responses, then it must have very complex properties. It cannot be any simpler than its causes or its effects. If the behavior we

observe simply expresses the functioning of a personality, the personality cannot be any simpler than the behavior. If some common learning process is responsible for the changes observed in a number of different situations, then it cannot be any simpler than these changes. The apparent simplicity of the inner system explains the eagerness with which we turn to it, but from the point of view of scientific method it must be regarded as a spurious simplicity, which foreshadows ultimate failure of such an explanatory scheme.

There is another objection. Although speculation about what goes on within the organism seems to show a concern for completing a causal chain, in practice it tends to have the opposite effect. Chains are left incomplete. The layman commonly feels that he has explained behavior when he has attributed it to something in the organism—as in saying "He went *because* he wanted to go," or "He could not work *because* he was worried about his health." Such statements may have value in suggesting the relevance of one set of causes as against another, but they do not give a full explanation until it is explained *why* the person wanted to go, or why he was worried. Frequently this additional step is taken, but perhaps just as often these incomplete explanations bring inquiry to a dead stop.

No matter how we may wish to represent such a sequence of causal events, we cannot satisfy the requirements of interpretation, prediction, or control unless we go back to events acting upon the organism from without—events, moreover, which are observed as any event is observed in the physical and biological sciences. It is only common sense, therefore, as well as good scientific practice, to make sure that the concepts which enter into a theory of behavior are explicitly and carefully related to such events. What is needed is an operational definition of terms. This means more than simple translation. The operational method is commonly misused to patch up and preserve concepts which are cherished for extraneous and irrelevant reasons. Thus it might be possible to set up acceptable definitions of instincts, needs, emotions, memories, psychic energy, and so on, in which each term would be carefully related to certain behavioral and environmental facts. But we have no guarantee that these concepts will be the most useful when the actual functional relationships are better understood. A more reasonable program at this stage is to attempt to account for behavior without appeal to inner explanatory entities. We can do this within the accepted framework of biology, gaining thereby not only a certain personal reassurance from the prestige of a well-developed science but an extensive set of experimental practices and dimensional systems. We shall be prevented from oversimplifying and misrepresenting the available facts because we shall not transmute our descriptions into other terms. The practical criteria of prediction and control will force us to take into account the complete causal chain in every instance. Such a program is not concerned with establishing the existence of inferred events, but with assessing the state of our knowledge.

This does not mean, of course, that the organism is conceived of as actually empty, or that continuity between input and output will not eventually be established. The genetic development of the organism and the complex interchanges between organism and environment are the subject matters of appropriate disciplines. Some day we shall know, for example, what happens when a stimulus impinges upon the surface of an organism, and what happens inside the organism after that, in a series of stages the last of which is the point at which the organism acts upon the environment and possibly changes it. At that point we lose interest in this causal chain. Some day, too, we shall know how the ingestion of food sets up a series of events, the last of which to engage our attention is a reduction in the probability of all behavior previously reinforced with similar food. Some day we may even know how to bridge the gap between the behavioral characteristics common to parents and offspring. But all these inner events will be accounted for with techniques of observation and measurement appropriate to the physiology of the various parts of the organism, and the account will be expressed in terms appropriate to that subject matter. It would be a remarkable coincidence if the concepts now used to refer inferentially to inner events were to find a place in that account. The task of physiology is not to find hungers, fears, habits, instincts, personalities, psychic energy, or acts of willing, attending, repressing, and so on. Nor is that task to find entities or processes of which all these could be said to be other aspects. Its task is to account for the causal relations between input and output which are the special concern of a science of behavior. Physiology should be left free to do this in its own way. Just to the extent that current conceptual systems fail to represent the relationships between terminal events correctly, they misrepresent the task of these other disciplines. A comprehensive set of causal relations stated with the greatest possible precision is the best contribution which we, as students of behavior, can make in the cooperative venture of giving a full account of the organism as a biological system.

But are we not overlooking one important source of knowledge? What about the direct observation of mental activity? The belief that the mental apparatus is available to direct inspection anticipated the scientific analysis of human behavior by many hundreds of years. It was refined by the introspective psychologists at the end of the nineteenth century into a special theory of knowledge which seemed to place the newly created science of consciousness on a par with natural science by arguing that all scientists necessarily begin and end with their own sensations and that the psychologist merely deals with these in a different way for different purposes. The notion has been revived in recent theories of perception, in which it has been suggested that the study of what used to be called "optical illusions," for example, will supply principles which help in understanding the limits of scientific knowledge. It has also been argued that the especially intimate empathic understanding which frequently occurs in psychotherapy supplies a kind of direct knowledge of the mental processes of other people. Franz Alexander and Lawrence Kubie have argued in this manner in defense of psychoanalytic practices. Among clinical psychologists Carl Rogers has actively defended a similar view. Something of the same notion may underlie the belief that the psychiatrist may better understand the psychotic if, through the use of lysergic acid, for example, he may temporarily experience similar mental conditions.

Whether the approach to human behavior which I have just outlined ignores some basic fact, whether it is unable to take into account the "stubborn fact of consciousness," is part of a venerable dispute which will not be settled here. Two points may be made, however, in evaluating the evidence from direct "introspection" of the mental apparatus. Knowledge is not to be identified with how things look to us, but rather with what we do about them. Knowledge is power because it is action. How the surrounding world soaks into the surface of our body is merely the first chapter of the story and would be meaningless were it not for the parts which follow. These are concerned with behavior. Astronomy is not how the heavens look to an astronomer. Atomic physics is not the physicist's perception of events within the atom, or even of the macroscopic events from which the atomic world is inferred. Scientific knowledge is what people *do* in predicting and controlling nature.

The second point is that knowledge depends upon a personal history. Philosophers have often insisted that we are not aware of a difference until it makes a difference, and experimental evidence is beginning to accumulate in support of the view that we should probably not know anything at all if we were not forced to do so. The discriminative behavior called knowledge arises only in the presence of certain reinforcing contingencies among the things known. Thus, we should probably remain blind if visual stimuli were never of any importance to us, just as we do not hear all the separate instruments in a symphony or see all the colors in a painting until it is worthwhile for us to do so.

Some interesting consequences follow when these two points are made with respect to our knowledge of events within ourselves. That a small part of the universe is enclosed within the skin of each of us, and that this constitutes a private world to which each of us has a special kind of access can scarcely be denied. But the world with which we are in contact does not for that reason have any special physical or metaphysical status. Now, it is presumably necessary to learn to observe or "know" events within this private world just as we learn to observe or "know" external events, and our knowledge will consist of doing something about them. But the society from which we acquire such behavior is at a special disadvantage. It is easy to teach a child to distinguish between colors by presenting different colors and reinforcing his responses as right or wrong accordingly, but it is much more difficult to teach him to distinguish between different aches or pains, since the information as to whether his responses are right or wrong is much less reliable. It is this limited accessibility of the world within the skin, rather than its nature, which has been responsible for so much metaphysical speculation.

Terms which refer to private events tend to be used inexactly. Most of them are borrowed in the first place from descriptions of external events. (Almost all the vocabulary of emotion, for example, has been shown to be metaphorical in origin.) The consequences are well known. The testimony of the individual regarding his mental processes, feelings, needs, and so on, is, as the psychiatrist above all others has insisted, unreliable. Technical systems of terms referring to private events seldom resemble each other. Different schools of introspective psychology have emphasized different features of experience, and the vocabulary of one may occasionally be unintelligible to another. This is also true of different dynamic theories of mental life. The exponent of a "system" may show extraordinary conviction in his use of terms and in his defense of a given set of explanatory entities, but it is usually easy to find someone else showing the same conviction and defending a different and possibly incompatible system. Just as introspective psychology once found it expedient to train observers in the use of terms referring to mental events, so the education of experimental psychologists, educators, applied psychologists, psychotherapists, and many others concerned with human behavior is not always free from a certain element of indoctrination. Only in this way has it been possible to make sure that mental processes will be described by two or more people with any consistency.

Psychiatry itself is responsible for the notion that one need not be aware of the feelings, thoughts, and so on, which are said to affect behavior. The individual often behaves *as if* he were thinking or feeling a given way although he cannot himself say that he is doing so. Mental processes which do not have the support of the testimony supplied by introspection are necessarily defined in terms of, and measured as, the behavioral facts from which they are inferred. Unfortunately, the notion of mental activity was preserved in the face of such evidence with the help of the notion of an unconscious mind. It might have been better to dismiss the concept of mind altogether as an explanatory fiction which had not survived a crucial test. The modes of in-

ference with which we arrive at knowledge of the unconscious need to be examined with respect to the conscious mind as well. Both are conceptual entities, the relations of which to observed data need to be carefully reexamined.

In the long run the point will not be established by argument, but by the effectiveness of a given formulation in the design of productive research. An example of research on psychotic subjects which emphasizes the end terms in our diagram is the project already mentioned. This is not the place for technical details, but the rationale of this research may be relevant. In these experiments a patient spends one or more hours daily, alone, in a small pleasant room. He is never coerced into going there and is free to leave at any time. The room is furnished with a chair, and contains a device similar to a vending machine, which can be operated by pushing a button or pulling a plunger. The machine delivers candies, cigarettes, or substantial food, or projects colored pictures on a translucent screen. Most patients eventually operate the machine, are "reinforced" by what it delivers, and then continue to operate it daily for long periods of time—possibly a year or more. During this time the behavior is reinforced on various "schedules"—for example, once every minute or once for every thirty responses—in relation to various stimuli. The behavior is recorded in another room in a continuous curve which is read somewhat in the manner of an electrocardiogram and which permits a ready inspection and measurement of the rate of responding.

The isolation of this small living space is, of course, not complete. The patient does not leave his personal history behind as he enters the room, and to some extent what he does there resembles what he does or has done elsewhere. Nevertheless, as time goes on, the conditions arranged by the experiment begin to compose, so to speak, a special personal history, the important details of which are known. Within this small and admittedly artificial life space, we can watch the patient's behavior change as we change conditions of reinforcement, motivation, and to some extent emotion. With respect to these variables the behavior becomes more and more predictable and controllable or—as characteristic of the psychotic subject— fails to do so in specific ways.

The behavior of the patient may resemble that of a normal human or infra-human subject in response to similar experimental conditions, or it may differ in a simple quantitative way—for example, the record may be normal except for a lower overall rate. On the other hand, a performance may be broken by brief psychotic episodes. The experimental control is interrrupted momentarily by the intrusion of extraneous behavior. In some cases it has been possible to reduce or increase the time taken by these interruptions, and to determine where during the session they will occur. As in similar work with other organisms, this quantitative and continuous account of the behavior of the individual under experimental control provides a highly sensitive baseline for the observation of the effects of drugs and of various forms of therapy. For our present purposes, however, the important thing is that it permits us to apply to the psychotic a fairly rigorous formulation of behavior based upon much more extensive work under the much more propitious control of conditions obtained with other species. This formulation is expressed in terms of input and output without reference to inner states.

The objection is sometimes raised that research of this sort reduces the human subject to the status of a research animal. Increasing evidence of the lawfulness of human behavior only seems to make the objection all the more cogent. Medical research has met this problem before, and has found an answer which is available here. Thanks to parallel work on animals, it has been possible, in some cases at least, to generate healthier behavior in men, even though at this stage we may not be directly concerned with such a result.

Another common objection is that we obtain our results only through an over-simplification of conditions, and that they are therefore not applicable to daily life. But one always simplifies at the start of an experiment. We have already begun to make our conditions more complex and will proceed to do so as rapidly as the uniformity of results permits. It is possible to complicate the task of the patient without limit, and to construct not only complex intellectual tasks but such interactions between systems of behavior as are seen in the Freudian dynamisms.

One simplification sometimes complained of is the absence of other human beings in this small life space. This was, of course, a deliberate preliminary measure, for it is much more difficult to control social than mechanical stimulation and reinforcement. But we are now moving on to situations in which one patient observes the behavior of another working on a similar device, or observes that the other patient receives a reinforcement whenever he achieves one himself, and so on. In another case the patient is reinforced only when his behavior corresponds in some way to the behavior of another. Techniques for achieving extraordinarily precise competition and cooperation between two or more individuals have already been worked out with lower organisms, and are applicable to the present circumstances.

This project has, of course, barely scratched the surface of the subject of psychotic behavior. But so far as it has gone, it seems to us to have demonstrated the value of holding to the observable data. Whether or not you will all find them significant, the data we report have a special kind of simple objectivity. At least we can say that this is what a psychotic subject did under these circumstances, and that this is what he failed to do under circumstances which would have had a different effect had he not been psychotic.

Although we have been able to describe and interpret the behavior observed in these experiments without reference to inner events, such references, are of course, not interdicted. Others may prefer to say that what we are actually doing is manipulating habits, needs, and so on, and observing changes in the structure of the personality, in the strength of the ego, in the amount of psychic energy available, and so on. But the advantage of this over a more parsimonious description becomes more difficult to demonstrate as evidence of the effectiveness of an objective formulation accumulates. In that bright future to which research in psychiatry is now pointing, we must be prepared for the possibility that increasing emphasis will be placed on immediately observable data and that theories of human behavior will have to adjust themselves accordingly. It is not inconceivable that the mental apparatus and all that it implies will be forgotten. It will then be more than a mere working hypothesis to say—to return at long last to my title—that psychotic behavior, like all behavior, is part of the world of observable events to which the powerful methods of natural science apply and to the understanding of which they will prove adequate.

Chapter 3

Patterns of Behavior

In view of the adaptability of humans and other animals, it has proved remarkably difficult to modify their behavior in significant ways. Cats still scratch furniture, and most animals refuse to be domesticated at all. Despite alternately punitive and therapeutic treatment of criminals, crime continues to plague our society. Despite the certainty of wholesale suffering, nations keep fighting wars.

We cannot successfully modify behavior until we understand what is to be modified. Whoever desires to modify his own behavior or the behavior of another organism is in something like the position of a sculptor, who must understand the material he is working on. Just as wood must be carved according to its grain, behavior must be modified according to naturally occurring patterns. When modification is attempted that goes against these patterns, it will be difficult—if not impossible—to achieve.

Since the study of primary behavioral patterns has historically been the province of biology, much of the material in this chapter is of a biological nature. However, we shall concentrate on the questions most vital to psychology. For instance:

How "fixed" are fixed reflexes?
How does anatomy limit behavior?
To what extent is behavior based on instinct?
How may behavioral cycles be altered?

SIMPLE REFLEXES

One of the simplest types of behavioral patterns to study—and modify—is the reflex. In its classical conception the reflex was pictured as a simple connection between stimulus and response—modified perhaps by inhibition, as shown by Sechenov, or by experience, as shown by Pavlov. The models for this conception of reflex action were mechanical, electrical, or chemical, and they represented actual events believed to take place inside the organism: event A causes event B, which in turn causes event C, like a series of billiard balls—each caroming off the last. Prototypical reflexes for this simple stimulus-response conception are the kneejerk, the salivation reflex, and the eyeblink. For these reflexes, clearly defined stimuli can be found in the environment and clearly defined responses are exhibited in behavior—the stimulus always preceding the response, as it is supposed to do in a well-behaved mechanical device such as that of Figure 1.12. In reality, however, even the simplest reflexes do not operate in this way. Along all the paths taken by reflexes in the nervous system, there are numerous feedback loops and extensive mechanisms for monitoring and influence by other parts of the nervous system. Thus, when a physiologist cuts away everything but a single nervous pathway from stimulus to response, varies the stimulus, and measures the response, he is studying an abstraction that may or may not be observed as a behavioral event. In an intact organism, not "prepared" by having much of its nervous system cut away, the reflex might work quite differently. The nervous impulse might go to several different places, be fed back to govern its own input, be monitored and controlled by higher nervous processes, activate several other reflexes, and so on. Although this by no means detracts from the value of such a physiological investigation, it does show the value of a different approach—looking at organisms as behaving entities.

Modern psychologists define a reflex as the reliable occurrence of a particular behavioral event following a particular environmental event—determined experimentally by the correlation between the two events in time. If the presence of his girlfriend reliably causes a young man to remove his eyeglasses, then that act is as much a reflex as an eyeblink following a puff of air, although in the former case the physiological connections are complex and largely unknown and in the latter case they are relatively straightforward. In other words, psychologists define a reflex behaviorally rather than physiologically.

Habituation and Sensitization

Two familiar processes by which the action of a simple reflex can be altered are habituation and sensitization. Habituation is nothing more than getting used to something. The author spent much of his youth in an apartment house one block from an elevated train that made a tremendous noise at approximate ten-minute intervals, twenty-four hours a day. Apparently, no one who lived in the area minded, or even noticed, the noise. But outsiders found it completely distracting. The story is told of the man who moved into the neighborhood and could not sleep because of the noise from the trains. When he was told that he would get used to it in a couple of weeks, he went to stay—for two weeks—at his sister's house, where it was quiet. Unfortunately for him, there is no way to habituate a response to a stimulus without experiencing the stimulus.

Sensitization is the opposite of habituation: responses get more and more intense. Consider a person who experiences a mild shock and reacts mildly the first time but shows more pain each subsequent time he experiences it. Or consider people who "get on your nerves." At first their presence is not so bothersome, but each subsequent encounter becomes worse despite the fact that their behavior is no different from what it was at first.

If we think of learning as a change in behavior related to experience that turns out to be useful, then both habituation and sensitization can be considered examples of learning.* Both produce many biologically useful changes in behavior, which may help preserve the life of the organism or the species. Certainly it is useful for the response of riveters working on a high-rise building to habituate to the sight of twenty stories of open air below their feet. Since by its very nature habituation is something we do not notice, we are normally unaware of the large extent to which it goes on in everyday life. But if we noticed everything going on around us—that is, if our responses did not habituate—we would be unable to base our actions on the important things, which often are the unusual things.

A method for measuring habituation in humans invented by the Russian psychologists E. N. Sokolov and A. R. Luria makes use of the plethysmograph, a device for measuring blood volume. One type of plethysmograph has a sensor that shines a light on the skin and measures how much of the light is reflected; when blood volume is high, less light is reflected (a blush consists of a darkening of the skin caused by high blood volume). One sensor is attached to the finger and another to the head. The subject is seated in a dark room, and a baseline reading is taken on the two sensors. Then a stimulus is presented. Characteristically there is a decrease in the finger blood volume and an increase in the head blood volume. This difference in readings is found whenever the subject seems to be paying attention to something. The Russians call this an "orienting response." As the stimulus is repeated, the orienting response dies off. The subject presumably habituates to the stimulus (stops attending to it). If the stimulus is changed (say from a buzzer to a tone) the orienting response reappears.

---

*However, many psychologists restrict the term "learning" to processes requiring association between stimuli and responses. Under this more restrictive definition habituation and sensitization would not be examples of learning.

In one experiment Luria tested the orienting response with a group of children, first fitting the children with plethysmographs and then reading them a list of words. At first an orienting response was observed after each word, but gradually the orienting response habituated. After a series of words was read to the children without producing any orienting response (they were presumably paying no attention to the words) the children were told that when they heard a certain word they should press a button that sounded a buzzer. The children now recovered the orienting response, but only for the critical word; they still gave no orienting response to the other words. On some level they still must have been hearing the other words—they could tell what the words were *not*. So habituation of attention was not complete, but only sufficient to remove the orienting response to the noncritical words.

With animals, habituation has been studied extensively in the startle response of rats. Rats are placed in a cage with sensors that measure sudden movements but not gradual movements, even forceful ones. Then, a brief loud tone is presented to the rat. Almost always the rat reacts sharply, causing the sensors to measure a startle response. As the tone is repeated, the rat's startle response habituates. (However, when the stimulus is superimposed upon background noise within a certain range of intensities, the response increases—sensitizes— instead of habituating.) The course of habituation is rapid at first and then levels off, as shown in the idealized graph in Figure 3.1.

Habituation, as a simple form of learning, works in similar ways on the molar and molecular levels. R. F. Thompson made an intensive study of habit-

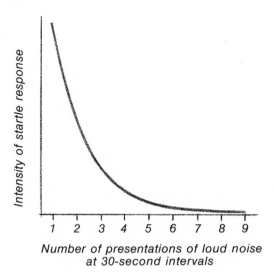

**Number of presentations of loud noise
at 30-second intervals**

FIGURE 3.1
Hypothetical function showing habituation of startle response with repeated presentation of loud noise.

uation on the molecular level, using the physiological preparation of a decerebrate cat. The connection between the upper spinal cord of the cat and its brain was cut so that the cat's brain could not influence the action of the reflex. The stimulus was an electric shock to the skin, and the response was the flexion of the cat's hind leg. Thompson noticed the following similarities between the cat's molecular reflex (the flexion response) and molar reflexes (such as the startle response, the orienting response, and my habituation to elevated trains):

1. *Given that a particular stimulus elicits a response, repeated applications of the stimulus result in decreased response (habituation). The decrease is usually a negative exponential function of the number of stimulus presentations.* (That is, the habituation function looks something like Figure 3.1.)

2. *If the stimulus is withdrawn, the response tends to recover over time (spontaneous recovery).* (That is, habituation is not permanent. If I returned to my old neighborhood after many years, I would again hear the elevated trains—assuming that they are still running.)

3. *If repeated series of habituation training and spontaneous recovery are given, habituation takes place more rapidly each time.* (If I did move back into my old neighborhood again, I would stop noticing the sound of the trains faster than I did the first time.)

4. *Other things being equal, the greater the frequency of stimulation, the more rapid or more pronounced is habituation.* (The more frequently the trains come, the sooner I will stop noticing them.)

5. *The weaker the stimulus, the more rapid or more pronounced is habituation. Strong stimuli may allow no significant habituation.* (Although I might be able to get used to trains, I might never get used to the window–rattling noise of jet planes if I lived next to an airport.)

6. *The effects of habituation training may proceed beyond the zero or asymptotic response level.* (One person has lived in the neighborhood for one year, another for ten years. Neither notices the trains. If they both leave the neighborhood for a year and then both move back again, the person who had lived in the neighborhood ten years might still not notice the trains, whereas the person who had lived there for only one year would have to habituate again—although he might do it faster this time. That is, those extra nine years were having an effect even though the ten-year resident had already habituated to the noise.)

7. *Habituation of response to a given stimulus exhibits stimulus generalization to other stimuli.* (After getting used to the trains, one might also not notice buses, garbage trucks, and other noisy vehicles.)

8. *Presentation of another (usually strong) stimulus results in recovery of the habituated response (dishabituation).* (If someone pinches me while a train is going by, I might suddenly notice the train.)

9. *Upon repeated application of the dishabituatory stimulus, the amount of dishabituation produced habituates. This might be called habituation of dishabituation.* (If they kept pinching me every time a train passed by, I would eventually stop noticing the trains again, in spite of the pinches—I would habituate to the pinches.)

Figure 3.2 shows some of these principles of habituation in a quantitative way. The graphs, representing leg flexion responses of decerebrate cats, come from a paper by R. F. Thompson and W. A. Spencer called, "Habituation: A Model Phenomenon."

The principles that apply to habituation also apply to many instances of more complex learning involving association. For instance, just as habituation occurs faster after each time the stimulus is reinstated, so does learning after each period of forgetting. After each summer vacation, a child forgets his multiplication tables and then has to relearn them in the fall. However, if he is normal, he relearns them more quickly each time.

Reaction Time

No environmental stimulus, no matter how directly it influences an organism's behavior, can produce an immediate response. Sometimes the response will not be observed until long after the stimulus has occurred. Such a delay between stimulus and response—referred to as *latency*—is generally attributed to the novelty or complexity of the stimulus, since the delay decreases with learning. In E. L. Thorndike's classic study of latency, which we shall discuss in Chapter 5, animals that were repeatedly shut up in puzzle boxes escaped more quickly each time. Yet even the quickest response took *some* time. That time over and above the time required for learning is called *reaction time,* and it is presumably determined by anatomical factors.

Reaction time first became of practical interest not in psychology, but in astronomy. The observer at a telescope had to count beats of a metronome and report the count when a star touched the crosshair of the telescope. Astronomers assumed that this task could easily be performed, yet they found that errors constantly crept into their calculations. One astronomer reported firing his assistant because of a consistent difference between the assistant's readings and his own. The astronomers' problem was that they did not take into account the time between the actual stimulus (the star touching the crosshair) and the response. When they finally discovered the source of their error, they called it "the human equation"—an error derived from the limitations of human anatomy. Even precise machines, no matter how carefully engineered, show a similar delay between input and output.

Reaction time gives the appearance of being a fairly simple variable, and, relatively speaking, it is. But so complex are most organisms that even this

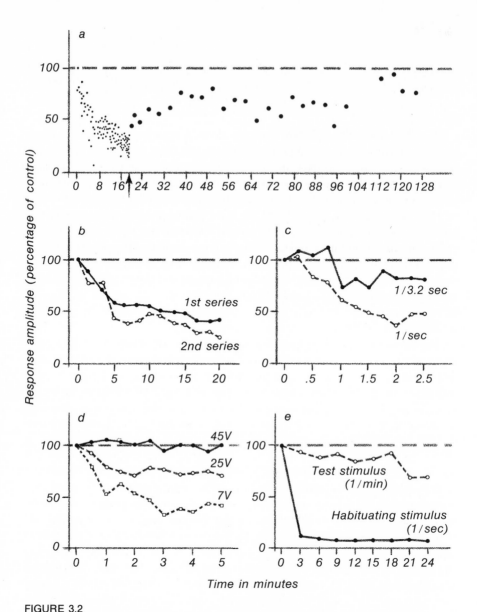

FIGURE 3.2

(a) Habituation (zero minutes to arrow) and spontaneous recovery (arrow to 128 minutes) of the hindlimb flexion reflex of the spinal cat in response to repeated skin shocks. (Stimuli were brief trains of shocks—5 in 50 milliseconds—delivered every 10 seconds during habituation and every 3 minutes during spontaneous recovery, except for a 12-minute period of no stimuli (at about 100 minutes). In this figure the response measured is tension developed by contraction of the tibialis anterior muscle, expressed as a percentage of mean initial-control response amplitude. (b) Effect of repeated-habituation and spontaneous-recovery series on degree of habituation. Response recovered to control level following first habituation series and was then rehabituated (second series). Conditions as in (a). Data are averages of 10-trial blocks (c) Effect of stimulus frequency on habituation. Single shocks given 1 per 3.2 seconds in one habituation series and 1 per second in the other to the saphenous nerve. Data are supposedly simple variable reveals a host of complications as soon as one thinks seriously about measuring it. As an illustration of how difficulties of behavior measurement are faced, and to some extent overcome, let us consider reaction time in more detail.

First, the difficulties. Since we have defined reaction time as minimum latency imposed by gross anatomical factors, we must make sure that there are no other factors contributing to the latency. Specifically, we must make sure, (1) that the stimulus is easy to detect, (2) that habituation to the stimulus has already taken place, (3) that the subject is experienced with the task, (4) that he is paying attention, and (5) that he is motivated to respond as quickly as possible. Most of these difficulties can be overcome by using appropriately vivid stimuli, providing ample practice, giving humans appropriate instructions, and giving animals appropriate rewards. But attention poses special problems. With even the best attitudes of humans and the biggest rewards for animals, it is difficult for subjects to pay attention for long periods of time—to be ready to make the response (in many experiments it is just pressing a button) as soon as the stimulus appears. Attention wanders.

To overcome wandering attention, it has become customary in reaction-time experiments to provide a warning a few seconds before the actual stimulus. The warning signal prepares the subject to respond as soon as the stimulus appears, just as the signals "On your mark—Get set" prepare the runner to respond to "Go." The problem with the warning is the same as the problem often found in a race: subjects respond to the warning signal. If you ever have occasion to start a race (and the circumstances are appropriate), try saying "On your mark—Get set" and then not saying "go." See how many runners will be half way down the track or how many swimmers will be in the water. The problem with the warning is this: it must come just before the stimulus, with a fixed time between the two, to ensure that readiness to respond will be at its peak when the stimulus occurs. But if the warning is too close and too regularly related to the stimulus, the subject will respond to the warning. For instance, if the warning comes two seconds before the stimulus, the subject can estimate when two seconds have elapsed after the warning and respond just about the same time as the stimulus comes on, with a measured reaction

---

averages of 10-trial blocks. (d) Effect of stimulus intensity on habituation. Brief trains of shocks, as in (a), were delivered every 10 seconds to the saphenous nerve with spontaneous recovery allowed after each series. Voltages refer to output of stimulator and were attenuated, but in the same ratios, when delivered to the nerve. Data averaged over 3-trial blocks. (e) Stimulus generalization of habituation. Single shocks to two separate branches of the saphenous nerve. The habituating stimulus to one branch was given 1 per second, and the test stimulus to the other branch was given 1 per minute. Data are averages over 3-trial blocks for response to the test stimulus and averages over the same periods of time for response to the habituating stimulus.) [From Thompson, R. F., and Spencer, W. A. Habituation: a model phenomenon for the study of neuronal substrates of behavior. *Psych. Review,* 1966, *73,* 16–43. Copyright 1966 by the American Psychological Assn.]

time close to zero. It does not solve the problem to strongly penalize responses that occur before the stimulus because this makes subjects over-cautious and can increase reaction time beyond what it would be if there were no warning at all.

An experimental attempt to get around this problem was made recently by Carol Saslow with monkeys as subjects. Each monkey was trained to press a button with its finger when a warning tone sounded, and when a flash of light (the stimulus) appeared one second later, to lift its finger from the button as quickly as possible. The monkeys were hungry, and would receive food occasionally if their responses were within a range of at least X seconds but not more than Y seconds after the stimulus. Figure 3.3a shows the experiment. At first the band of acceptable responses was very wide so that most of the responses produced food for the monkey. Gradually, the band was narrowed and brought close to the stimulus so that the monkey would have to respond faster and faster after the stimulus to get food. Both of the monkeys in Saslow's experiment did very well at getting food. Figure 3.3b shows that as the band was shifted closer to the stimulus, the monkeys responded faster. Saslow suspected, however, that when the band was very close to the stimulus the monkeys did not respond to the stimulus itself, because if they waited for the stimulus before starting to respond they could not possibly have responded fast enough to get the food. For very close bands, the monkeys must have been trying to estimate when the stimulus was going to appear by timing one second from the warning. The problem was how to tell when the monkeys were estimating the one second from the warning to the stimulus and when they were actually responding to the stimulus. Saslow reasoned that, other things being equal, it was more difficult to estimate one second than to simply respond to the stimulus—that the variability in estimations of when the second had elapsed would be greater than the variability in responses to the stimulus itself. She reasoned further that, because of the variability of their estimations, the monkeys would resort to estimating only when responding to the stimulus itself did not work to produce food—only when the end of the band was closer to the stimulus than the monkey's minimum reaction time. Thus there would be a point, as the band shifted closer and closer to the stimulus, where the monkeys' minimum reaction time would have been reached and it would be necessary for them to start estimating from the warning; this point should be marked by a sudden increased variability in the time between stimulus and response. Figure 3.3c shows that this was exactly what happened. The variability was low when the band was far away from the stimulus, but as the band was brought closer to the stimulus the variability suddenly increased. This was the point, Saslow reasoned, where the monkeys—who were responding as fast as they could to the stimulus and still could not get food—switched their strategy to one of estimation from the warning stimulus. Interestingly, the minimum reaction time of about 0.15 seconds corresponds to the minimum reaction time of humans under similar conditions.

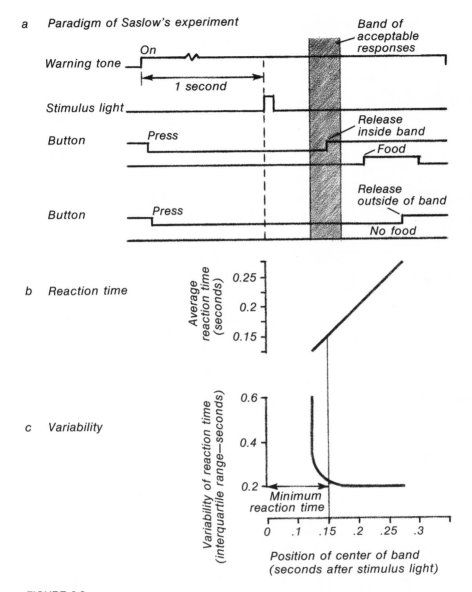

a   Paradigm of Saslow's experiment

Warning tone — On ~~~ | ← 1 second →| Band of acceptable responses

Stimulus light

Button — Press — Release inside band / Food

Button — Press — Release outside of band / No food

b   Reaction time

Average reaction time (seconds)

0.25
0.2
0.15

c   Variability

Variability of reaction time (interquartile range—seconds)

0.6
0.4
0.2

Minimum reaction time

0   .1   .15   .2   .25   .3

Position of center of band (seconds after stimulus light)

FIGURE 3.3
Behavior of a monkey in Saslow's experiment on minimum reaction time. Although the monkey's average reaction time stayed within the band (graph b) as the band was brought closer to the signal (to the left) the variability of reaction times increased sharply at about 0.15 seconds, showing that the monkey was estimating time from the warning instead of responding directly to the stimulus.

Of course, there is no true absolute minimum reaction time. Refinements of procedure, stronger stimuli, easier responses, and the use of drugs might reduce reaction time still further.

As a dependent variable, reaction time has had an interesting history within psychology. At first it was used by Hermann von Helmholtz (1821–1894) to measure the speed of nervous conduction. The stimulus was a touch on the body, and the response was pressing a button. When the stimulus was a touch on the sole of the foot, the reaction time was slightly longer on the average than when the stimulus was a touch on the thigh. Helmholtz reasoned that the difference in reaction time must be the time taken for the nervous impulse to get from the foot to the thigh. Dividing the distance between the foot and the thigh by the difference between reaction times should give the speed of the nervous impulse between foot and thigh. As measured by this method, the speed was about 100 meters per second—not far from that measured by modern electronic methods.

Reaction time has also been used to measure how long it takes to process various kinds of information. For instance, it takes people longer to react when there are two stimuli to decide between (for example, red stimulus—press left button, green stimulus—press right button) than when there is only one stimulus. The difference in reaction times might represent the time required to make a decision. Recent experiments have also shown that people can decide faster whether a positive sentence is true (for example, "the earth is round") than whether a negative sentence is true (for example, "the earth is not flat"). The difference might represent the time taken to change the negative sentence into a positive one. One pitfall of this method of subtracting reaction times is that it assumes that only one thing goes on at a time—that first the stimulus is perceived, then it is processed, then a response is started. But we know that these processes may overlap in time—in which case, simple subtraction of reaction times is an insufficient measuring device.

COMPLEX REFLEXES

The kneejerk, eyeblink, and salivation reflexes are relatively simple reflexes with responses largely measurable along a single dimension. But there is another class of reflexes which require observation of more complex responses. The responses characteristic of these reflexes are called *fixed-action patterns*, and they are much studied by ethologists. Let us look first at the response side of complex reflexes—ignoring for the moment the effective stimuli—and afterwards turn our attention to the stimulus side.

Fixed-Action Patterns

It has often been observed that various postural patterns of birds, once triggered off, are performed regardless of what happens afterwards. For instance, according to the ethologist R. A. Hinde in his book *Animal Behavior:*

> A female canary uses a special weaving movement to push loose strands of material into the cup of its nest. If the bird is given neither a nest site nor nest material, this movement may be performed on the floor of the cage and without nest material; its form then differs little if at all from that when it is performed in its normal functional context, and so stimuli from the nest cup or nest material can play little part in its control. [Hinde, 1970, p. 19]

Such cases are the exception, however. Most often, once a fixed–action pattern is begun, it is guided by external stimuli as well as by proprioceptive stimuli from the act itself. For example, many animals that herd or flock together have alarm calls that set off fixed patterns of flight. Although the flight is triggered by the alarm call, its *direction* is determined by the position of the predator, the direction of flight of the other animals, and other cues. The licking of rats at a waterspout, which we discussed so extensively in the last chapter, can also be considered a fixed-action pattern. Note that whereas the topography and the rate of licking are relatively fixed, the percentage of time spent licking is highly modifiable by environmental conditions and contingencies of reinforcement.

The patterns of movements made by fish swimming, dogs swallowing, locusts flying, and insects walking have been the subject of intensive investigation by physiological psychologists and ethologists. Because the nervous systems of some of these animals are relatively simple, it has been possible to trace their neural control mechanisms. But even these simple mechanisms can be elusively complex. For instance, it was originally thought that the flight movements of the locust were governed by a self-contained feedback system wherein the upward movement of the wings when carried to its extreme would inhibit further upward movement and set off the downward movement. Then, when the downward movement was at its extreme it would be inhibited and the upward movement set off, and so on. But it was found, when the stretch receptors were removed, that the rhythmic pattern of electrical activity corresponding to flight continued in the locust's nervous system. It was then found that wind on the head of the locust would modify both normal flight movements and electrical activity (stronger winds reducing them) and that even when the musculature and nerves of the wings of the locust were removed, the rhythmic nervous activity still appeared and was still governed by the wind on the head. Obviously the rhythm cannot have been generated solely by the peripheral muscles and receptors in the wings if the rhythm persists after these anatomical parts are removed. It is now suspected that the flight pattern consists of the action of several "central pacemakers" operating together and governing the flight movements, much as a coxswain governs the rowing rhythm of his crew. The pacemakers themselves are governed by visual input and other factors such as wind on the head and condition of the wings.

Fixed-action patterns tend to be rigid and relatively hard to modify. According to Hinde, "Each animal has a repertoire of these fixed-action patterns and only a limited ability for developing new ones." (Hinde, 1970, p. 22). What can be modified much more easily than the pattern itself are the particular stimuli that trigger off a given fixed pattern. Nevertheless in nature certain kinds of stimuli are much more likely than others to trigger off a given fixed-action pattern. We turn next to consideration of these stimuli.

Effective Stimuli

Ethologists have also investigated the stimuli that trigger various fixed-action patterns. In these investigations the response is held constant while the stimulus is varied. One of the most famous of these studies was N. Tinbergen's study of a fish called the three–spined stickleback. The male stickleback establishes his territory during mating season and attacks any other male stickleback that intrudes on his territory. But, if a female stickleback enters the territory, the male does not attack but rather engages in courting behavior. How does the male tell females from other males? To answer this question Tinbergen

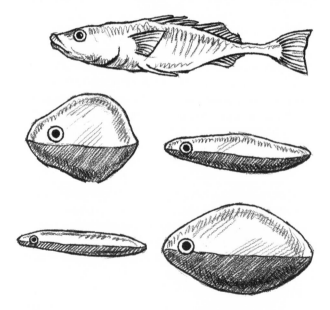

FIGURE 3.4
Models used for identifying the stimulus characters eliciting the aggressive behavior of the male three-spined stickleback. The four lower models, each of which has a red belly, all elicit aggressive behavior, whereas the upper model, which lacks a red belly but resembles a stickleback more closely in other respects, is relatively ineffective. [From Tinbergen, N. *The study of instinct.* New York: Oxford University Press, 1951.]

FIGURE 3.5
The model on the right elicits courting behavior from male sticklebacks. The one on
the left does not; it lacks the swollen abdomen of an egg-carrying female. [After
Tinbergen, N. *The study of instinct.* New York: Oxford University Press, 1951.]

constructed a series of models (shown in Figure 3.4) and moved them slowly
into the territory of a male stickleback. The male attacked models with red
undersides and ignored models without red undersides, however realistic they
looked otherwise. Thus, it must be the red underside of the male stickleback
that elicits attack behavior in another male.

But what is it about female sticklebacks that causes males to make courting
movements? It turns out that only models exhibiting an eye and a distended
belly (the belly characteristic of a female ready to lay eggs) will elicit courting
in the male (Figure 3.5). Other models, however realistic, will not elicit this
behavior. The male, his cylindrical nest already constructed, begins to swim
about in zigzag arcs. This "dance" may elicit a courting response in the female.
If so, she swims toward the male with her body upward, exposing her belly.
The male then leads the female toward the nest. He points with his head
towards the entrance. She enters. At this point he pokes under her tail with
his snout—an action which causes the female to release the eggs into the nest.
(Tinbergen found that poking with a glass rod would do as well as the nose of
a male stickleback). Along with the eggs a chemical is released that causes the
male to ejaculate as he follows the female through the nest, thus fertilizing the
eggs. This series of events and counter-events, which comprises the mating of
sticklebacks, is far from the simple mechanical process suggested by the notion
of reflexes. Effective stimuli provided by one partner give rise to fixed action
patterns on the part of the other. But at each stage many things may go wrong—
and often do. The female may become distracted and just swim off. The male
may occasionally attack the female. Hormones that make the courting behavior
possible in both partners may for some reason be lacking. We have barely
begun to scratch the surface of the complex causal factors in even such a relatively simple and well-studied phenomenon as the courting behavior of sticklebacks. How much less then, can we be expected to know about such behavior
in humans.

A controversial case in the investigation of what constitutes an effective stimulus is the response of turkeys to hawk-like stimuli. K. Lorenz and N. Tinbergen found that the stimulus pictured in Figure 3.6, when moved to the right above young turkeys' heads with the short end in front, caused the turkeys to run away—but when moved to the left did not cause the turkeys to run. Now, when moved to the right, the model looks something like a hawk (a predator of turkeys), and when moved to the left the model looks something like a goose (not a predator). Subsequent experiments have shown that the speed, direction, and angle of movement are much more important than the shape in causing the turkeys to run away. Another controversy regards whether the hawk-goose discrimination is innate or learned by the turkeys from experience with flying objects. The controversy is far from settled. It illustrates, however, how difficult it is to determine which responses to effective stimuli are innate. No animal is totally without experience (even the fetus has experienced its environment), and experience invariably has a strong influence on behavior.

Another problem is that "innate" behavior is not always the same thing as "natural" behavior. It is natural for a gull to recover an egg that has rolled out of its nest by reaching out with its beak and rolling the egg back in. One would think that the gull would be most likely to perform this rolling action with stimuli that most resemble its own egg. But it turns out that the bigger the egg, the more likely it is to be rolled in (artificial eggs several times natural size are preferred over real eggs). Thus, what is innate is not necessarily what is natural. Another example is the elaborate artificial lures used to catch fish. Often lures

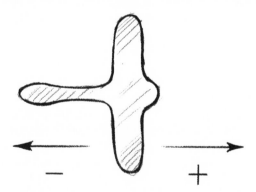

FIGURE 3.6
Cardboard model used to elicit escape reactions from young turkeys. It was effective when moved to the right but not when moved to the left. [After Tinbergen, N. *The study of instinct.* New York: Oxford University Press, 1951.]

FIGURE 3.7
Cardboard models used to elicit gaping
responses from nestling thrushes. The nestling's
response is directed towards the smaller
projection on the left-hand model and the larger
projection on the right-hand model, indicating
that its orientation is determined not by the
absolute size of the projection, but by its size
relative to that of the rest of the model. [From
Tinbergen, N. *The study of instinct.* New York:
Oxford University Press, 1951.]

which work best do not duplicate the fishes' natural food, but exaggerate some specific characteristic (such as shininess). Still another example is provided by the exaggerated female attributes of the models in Playboy.

Often it is not the absolute but rather the relative dimensions of stimulus objects that elicit behavior. Nestling thrushes gape at the heads of their parents so that the parents will put food in their mouths. Two crude models of parents with two heads each are shown in Figure 3.7. Tinbergen and D. J. Kuenen found that the nestlings gaped at the left head of the left model and the right head of the right model. The heads that elicited gaping had the same relative size to their bodies, though their absolute sizes were different.

An extensive series of experiments by T. G. R. Bower have shown that very young human infants already perceive relational characteristics of their world. The stimuli Bower used in one experiment are shown in Figure 3.8. First Bower showed the tilted rectangle to the babies. This was the standard. Then he showed a nontilted rectangle and a nontilted trapezoid to them. These were the test stimuli. He wanted to know which of the test stimuli the babies would perceive to be more like the standard. If the babies were seeing things according to their absolute dimensions they would pick the trapezoid (test 2) because the image on the eye's retina made by the trapezoid is identical to that made by the standard (the tilted rectangle). But if the babies could relate the shape of an object to its angular orientation (as adults do) they would see the rectangle of test 1 as the same rectangle they had seen as the standard and choose it over the trapezoid.

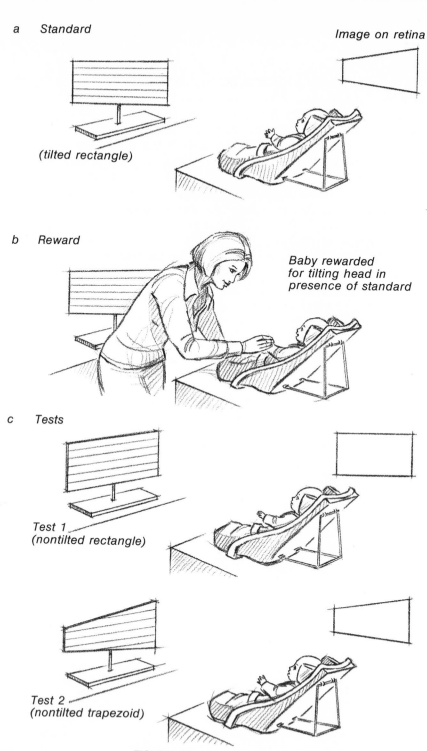

a   Standard

Image on retina

(tilted rectangle)

b   Reward

*Baby rewarded
for tilting head in
presence of standard*

c   Tests

Test 1
(nontilted rectangle)

Test 2
(nontilted trapezoid)

FIGURE 3.8
Bower's experiment with babies.

The experiment sounds simple, but how do you ask a baby only a few weeks old which of two objects looks more similar to a third? Bower devised an ingenuous method illustrated in Figure 3.8b. He trained the babies to tilt their heads from side to side by rewarding them each time they did so by a peek-a-boo from the baby's mother. Then he let the babies see the standard and only rewarded them for their head tilting when the standard was present. The babies soon learned to tilt their heads with the standard present but not to tilt their heads when the standard was absent. Finally, Bower showed the babies the three stimuli of Figure 3.8 one at a time without rewarding them. The babies, as might be expected, tilted their heads most frequently with the standard in front of them—but which of the other two stimuli caused more tilting? The babies tilted more for the rectangle (test 1) than the trapezoid (test 2), showing that they saw the rectangle as more similar to the standard than the trapezoid was. This means that the babies must have been able, at the age of a few weeks, to tell that an object is the same even when it is tilted at an angle and forms a somewhat different image on the retina. They must have been able to judge the relational qualities of their environment.

WARNING

A simple reflex, as we said earlier, is an abstraction. Rarely in anatomy or behavior, and almost never in human anatomy or behavior, does the chain of reflex action occur as a simple stimulus causing a simple response without feedback and influence from other sources. We do not simply *see* a stimulus—we *look* at the stimulus, so the behavior (of looking) occurs simultaneously with, or even prior to, the stimulus. Looking and seeing form a coordinated complex act. At the other end of the reflex, it is almost never the case that the nervous system triggers off a response and then forgets about it. Rather, the response is guided by the stimuli it produces. I do not throw my hand at a salt shaker (that is, I do not make a ballistic response); my reaching for the salt shaker is guided by the relative positions of my hand and the salt shaker as I see them and as I feel the position of my hand and body through proprioception. The model that best explains the process of reaching for a salt shaker is not a simple stimulus–response (S–R) model (see the salt shaker—reach for it), but rather a complex version of the tracking procedure we shall discuss next.

The danger of considering the reflex as a simple S–R connection was pointed out as early as 1896 by the psychologist John Dewey (1859–1952). Nevertheless, the simple S–R model was a tempting one for psychologists and has constantly appeared in one form or another throughout the history of psychology.

Human Tracking Behavior

A behavior which exemplifies the action of complex reflexes, and which has been studied extensively because of its practical importance, is *tracking*. Tracking is the following of a moving object with some part of the anatomy.

The first kind of tracking that animals do is to follow objects with their eyes. This behavior has been observed even in newborn infants. If an infant is placed before a train of moving stripes, his eyes will follow a stripe across his visual field, then suddenly jerk back and follow another stripe across the field, and so on. This back-and-forth movement of the eyes is called *nystagmus,* and the particular kind of nystagmus we have described is called *opto-kinetic nystagmus.* This type of tracking, like other behavior that develops early in life and receives virtually constant use, is difficult to modify—but not impossible. Changing the typical pattern of eye–movements in reading, for instance, is the basis for some speed–reading techniques.

Soon after following objects with their eyes, infants develop the ability to grasp objects in their visual fields. This act which requires tracking both object and hand, also requires the ability to control the movement of the hand so as to reduce the distance between hand and object. Eye-hand coordination has been studied in humans by means of several techniques, and in fact forms a whole field of inquiry in itself, which we cannot hope to cover here in any detail. Nevertheless, it might prove instructive to consider how experimenters have approached the study of this important type of tracking.

Consider a man operating a machine, say simply steering a car along a road (we could as well consider the task of adjusting the brightness or the sound of a television set). The interaction between man and machine can be diagrammed as the feedback system in Figure 3.9. The inputs at A and C to the box labeled "driver" represent, respectively, the path of the road and the position of the car. When the driver looks through the windshield he sees both of these, and his first job is to compare them as to alignment. If the car is not on the center of the proper lane the driver has to steer it. If he has learned this skill correctly, the system will show negative feedback; that is, the difference between the car's position and the lane's position will have decreased. The properties of the car itself (such as the looseness of the steering mechanism) will modify the feedback loop between B and C. The road will determine the input at A. In penny arcades there is a game that imitates this process. The player, at a steering wheel connected by remote control to a toy car, tries to keep the car on the road as the road moves erratically on a belt under it. Similar devices have been used by human-factors engineers (psychologists who study the interaction of men and machines) to study human tracking behavior.

A simplified drawing of two tracking devices is shown in Figure 3.10. In the device shown in Figure 3.10a, a spot moves up and down on a screen. The subject has a lever by means of which he can move a bar up and down. His task is to keep the bar on the spot. The spot is moved automatically. It can theoretically move in any manner, but three types of movement have become standard in psychological investigations: (1) the spot may start at one position and then move suddenly to another position (a step input), (2) the spot may start at one position and then move gradually to another position (a ramp input), or (3)

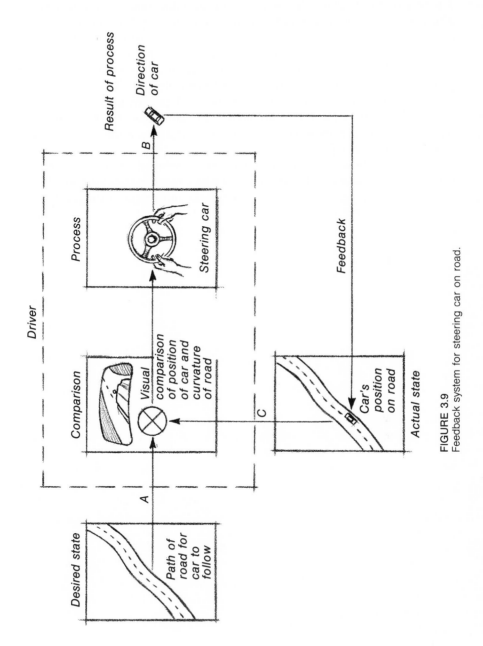

FIGURE 3.9
Feedback system for steering car on road.

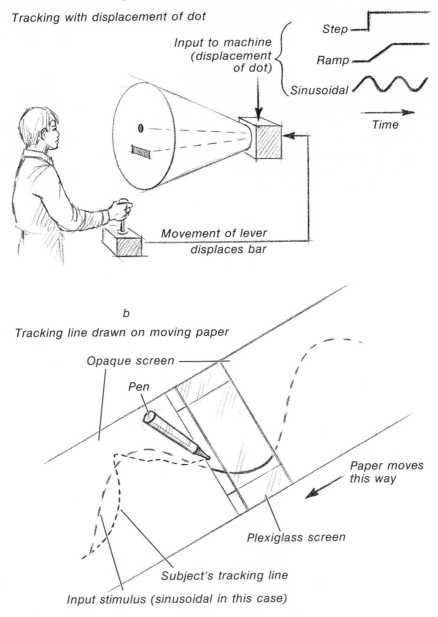

a

Tracking with displacement of dot

Input to machine
(displacement
of dot)

Step

Ramp

Sinusoidal

Time

Movement of lever
displaces bar

b

Tracking line drawn on moving paper

Opaque screen

Pen

Paper moves
this way

Plexiglass screen

Subject's tracking line

Input stimulus (sinusoidal in this case)

FIGURE 3.10
Two ways to study tracking. (a) Tracking with displacement of dot. (b) Tracking line
drawn on moving paper.

the spot may oscillate sinusoidally (that is, move up and down). The sensitivity of the bar on the screen to the movement of the subject's lever is called the *gain*. "High gain" means that a small displacement of the lever produces a large displacement of the bar. "Low gain" means that a large displacement of the lever produces a small displacement of the bar. If the gain is too high, tracking will be difficult because the sensitivity of the system will cause too much overshooting of the target. (Steering a car while going in reverse is a system with high gain. Imagine steering in reverse at 60 miles per hour!) If the gain is too low, tracking will be difficult because it will take too long to get the bar to move any appreciable distance. (Trucks and buses, especially the old-fashioned kind without power steering, have low gain in their steering mechanisms because of the comparatively heavy weight that has to be moved.)

Figure 3.10b shows a simpler device for studying tracking. The input is drawn by the experimenter directly on a sheet of paper that moves beneath a slot. The subject can see more or less of the input depending on the width of the transparent plexiglass screen. His job is to keep the pen on the track. Again, the inputs may be step functions, ramp functions, or sinusoidal functions.

Both of the devices in Figure 3.10 fit the feedback model of Figure 3.9. The input, either step, ramp, or sinusoidal, corresponds to the input at A in Figure 3.9. The output, either lever or pen, corresponds to B. The feedback, the changing position of the bar or the mark of the pen, corresponds to C. The gain of the system governs the feedback between B and C. The apparatus in Figure 3.10b, because of the direct transition from output (movement of pen) to feedback (mark of pen), is considered to have a gain of unity, neither amplifying the input as high gain would do nor attenuating the input as low gain would do.

The general finding with tracking tasks is that at first people tend to track the position of the input. That is, they pay attention only to where the input is at the moment. They move as rapidly as they can to where the input is, slowing down only when they reach it. This results, of course, in considerable overshooting of the target. Figure 3.11a shows the pattern a novice might make in performing the tracking tasks of Figure 3.10 with a step input. The reaction of the subject is rather like that of a spring, oscillating about its final resting point with ever-decreasing amplitude. With a ramp input (Figure 3.11b), the novice subject is always moving to where the input just was (but no longer is). As a result, he usually lags behind the input. Occasionally noting this lag, the subject will correct for it, suddenly catching up to the input, but soon he lags behind again. With a sinusoidal input (Figure 3.11c and d) the novice subject also lags behind. Note that when the frequency of the input is low (3.11c) a small lag does not result in much difference between input and output, but when the frequency of the input is high (3.11d) the same lag brings the output almost 180° out of phase with the input.

Novices at tracking tasks and other tasks involving manipulation of controls and reading of displays behave with stereotypic patterns. For instance, when

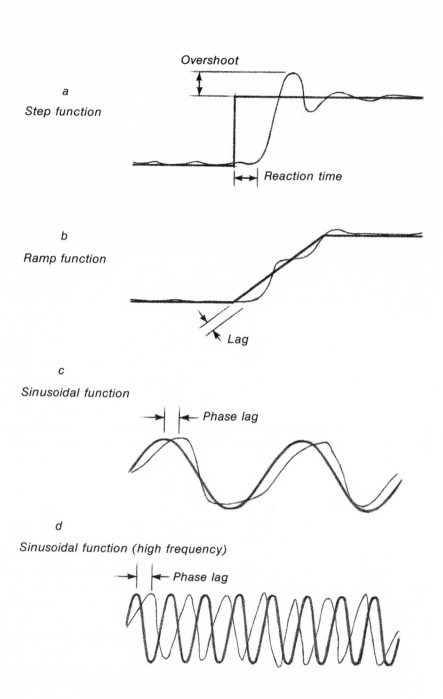

a
Step function

Overshoot

Reaction time

b
Ramp function

Lag

c
Sinusoidal function

Phase lag

d
Sinusoidal function (high frequency)

Phase lag

FIGURE 3.11
How a novice subject tracks various types of input.

you ask a person to turn an unfamiliar machine with an unfamiliar knob, he will almost invariably turn the knob clockwise. He will also assume that clockwise movement of a knob corresponds to upward rather than downward movement of a display indicator. These patterns are called *population stereotypes*. The term reflects the finding that representatives of a given population approach any new task with certain biases. Whether such biases are largely due to prior experience or to innate properties of the nervous system is not known.

With experience, subjects in tracking experiments come to do much better than those represented in Figure 3.11. They begin to respond to the input's movement over the course of time, rather than just to its position at the moment. Subjects learn to anticipate the sudden changes in the step function and to slow down before reaching the new position. With the ramp function, subjects soon learn to track the velocity, instead of the position of the input; they move at a constant speed, correcting only for occasional errors. With the oscillating movement, subjects come to respond to the frequency and amplitude of the input, making appropriate curves even with their eyes closed. This shows that subjects need not pay attention only to what is there at the moment. Their behavior, in its molar characteristics, corresponds to the molar characteristics of the input. We shall have occasion later to discuss this remarkable capability of human (and nonhuman) behavior to deal with environmental events occurring over broader and broader extents of time.

Tropisms

Tropisms are simple mechanical or chemical feedback processes or combinations of such processes that have the interesting property of looking like organized motivated behavior. Jacques Loeb (1859–1924), who first described tropisms in plants and simple animals, believed that the principle of the tropism could be used to explain all behavior—even behavior that seemed to be a product of the will. This was the time (around the turn of the century) when psychologists, inspired by Darwin's theory of biological continuity, were beginning to study mental processes in lower animals. In Loeb's work, the emphasis was reversed.

Take for instance, Loeb's study of certain caterpillars that emerged from their cocoons in the spring, climbed to the tips of tree branches, and ate the new buds. The then-current interpretation was that the caterpillars had an infallible instinct for self-preservation, and it was this instinct that led them somehow to the place where their food was waiting for them. Loeb showed that no such complicated ability was required to explain the caterpillars' behavior. The caterpillars are sensitive to light and have two eyes, symmetrically placed one on each side of the head. When the same amount of light comes into the two eyes, the caterpillars move straight ahead; but when one of the eyes gets more light, the legs on that side move more slowly. The result is that the caterpillars tend to orient toward the light—which in nature invariably is strongest at the tops of trees. Thus, whenever they move, they move toward the tops of the trees, ending up at the tip of a branch. When, in his experiments, Loeb put lights at the bottom of the trees, the caterpillars went down, not up, and would starve to death rather than reverse direction. When the caterpillars were blinded in one eye, they travelled in a circle like a mechanical toy with one wheel broken. The attraction of the caterpillars to the light was not the product of the caterpillars' will or desire for light, according to Loeb's interpretation, but of a mechanical feedback process—like the homing of a missile or a torpedo to its target.

Loeb's first experiments were with plants. He observed that sunlight on one side of certain plants retarded growth of that side relative to the other. Then, the other side grew until the plant tilted over and faced the sun. When the plant was facing the sun, it grew equally on both sides. Figure 3.12 shows how this process works. This process does not depend on reflexes carried through nerves because plants have no nerves.* Yet it appears to be a purposeful act. When we observe it, we tend to say that the plant is "seeking" the sun. However, Loeb's explanation is better because it allows us to predict and control the plant's behavior.

According to Loeb, the working of all tropisms can be explained with two principles: symmetry and sensitivity. Symmetry may exist as both morphological (structural) symmetry and dynamic symmetry. Generally these two types of symmetry work together as in the plant's growth.

Let us consider again the action of the caterpillars in response to the light. The first thing to notice about the caterpillar is that it is symmetrical. We may assume that, corresponding to the structural symmetry we observe, there is a dynamic symmetry of connections and interactions of eyes, nerves, and muscles. Let us now assume that the caterpillar starts off walking at an angle to the light. This will cause a greater amount of light to strike one eye than the other. The more light that is received, the more intense is stimulation in the optic nerve that leads from the eye to the (rudimentary) brain. The imbalance in the optic nerve will be transmitted (and cause a corresponding imbalance) to the motor nerves and, finally, to the muscles. The difference in muscle tonus causes a change in position of the head and a change in direction of movement until there is equal light in both eyes. Only when such a condition is established is there stability in direction of movement—but this will be the very moment when the caterpillar is headed straight toward the light.

Note that orientation to light does not depend on the specific qualities of the central nervous system. The important things are symmetry and sensitivity. The difference between the nervous system of the caterpillar and the protoplasmic reaction of the plant is that the nerves are quicker and more sensitive. The

---

*Current theory is that a plant's growth is medicated by enzymes, chemicals similar in structure to the hormones that regulate and mediate growth and behavior of animals.

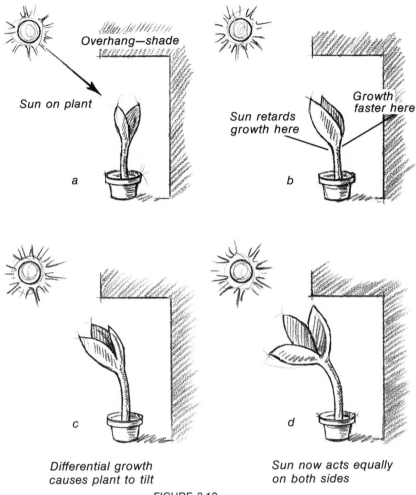

FIGURE 3.12
How plants seek the sun.

importance of symmetry in tropisms is demonstrated by the fact that cutting off an insect's leg generates strange orientations and spiral or oblique approaches to light—exactly what would be predicted by Loeb. According to Loeb, then, what the caterpillar inherits is not the desire to move toward the light, but the differential sensitivity to light in its nerve-muscle system.

The tropisms of simple organisms have been divided into two categories: *taxes* and *kineses*. Taxes involve orientation. The caterpillar's "attraction" to light is a taxis. Kineses, which are simpler, involve type—and particularly speed—of movement. The stimulus (which has been light intensity in our examples but can be gravitational fields, sounds, the direction of polarization of light, smells or other chemical stimuli, electrical or magnetic fields, and so on) usually produces more or less rapid movement or more or less rapid turning. Woodlice, for instance, tend to aggregate in moist places. This is because the more humidity there is, the less the woodlice tend to move. Thus, once a woodlouse finds itself in a moist place it stays there until the moisture is gone. It does not seek out moisture, but merely stays where moisture is.

The simple mechanistic picture of the action of kineses is complicated somewhat by the occurrence of adaptation to the stimuli for kineses. For instance, certain planaria (a single-celled organism) tend to aggregate in dark places because an increase in the intensity of light makes them change direction more frequently than they would otherwise. But they adapt to the light quickly. Thus a planarium coming from a dark place into light (of intensity X, say) changes direction rapidly (often going back to the dark where it came from). A planarium coming from more intense light into intensity-X light has already adapted to the light and so does not change direction. The upshot is that planaria coming from lighter to darker places keep going and wind up in still darker places; planaria coming from darker to lighter places change direction and also wind up in the dark.

Despite the success with which Loeb's account of certain movements of plants and lower animals predicts their behavior, most of the behavior of higher organisms does not fall into this pattern. This is because Loeb's mechanism does not account for learning. It accounts for certain innate behavioral patterns but not patterns acquired over the organism's lifetime. In some organisms, learning modifies much behavior that would otherwise be classified as tropistic. Loeb realized that tropisms as such could not explain complex behavior, since they were modified by learning (what he called associative memory). Nevertheless, he opened up the possibility that many actions now considered motivated, willful, or purposive have as their underlying basis a tropism such as possessed by plants and simple insects. We know, for instance, that rats avoid bright light. One might also consider human "attractions" and "repulsions" as tropisms modified by learning processes.

Loeb believed that even the learning process, when it came to be understood, would prove to have a chemical basis. Some recent work with simple organisms tends to bear this out. Recent experiments have suggested that certain chemicals might contain the essence of what is learned. For instance, when worms which had learned to contract during a signal that preceded electric shock were fed to another group of worms called "cannibal" worms, the second group learned to contract during the signal faster, apparently by virtue of having eaten the first group! There is still some question whether these results will stand up under further tests, but their serious consideration by most present psychologists indicates confidence in the eventual explanation of learning and memory as chemical processes.

BEHAVIORAL CYCLES

Many of our activities are geared to the clock or the calendar. We eat, sleep, and play at certain times of the day. To some extent the rhythms of our lives are simply conventional. A Martian landing in England might observe that humans had some innate tendency to have tea at 4 p.m. or, landing in a Moslem country, might note innate east-bowing tendency just before sunrise and sunset. But if these cyclic activities are conventional, many others are not. Figure 3.13 shows the activity cycles of a tropical millipede kept in a chamber with constant illumination, temperature, and humidity. The pattern of activity, showing a peak once a day, persisted until the millipede died on the twenty-fifth day of its captivity. Generally, daily cycles (called *circadian rhythms*) lose their exact 24-hour periodicity if animals are isolated from the natural phases of light and dark. The activity cycle of the millipede is about 24.8 hours in constant light and 23.0 hours in constant darkness.

The daily cycles of eating and drinking maintained by most animals provide a good example of cycles with both internal and external control. The internal control is the natural bodily rhythm of eating and becoming satiated, then becoming hungry again, eating again and so on. The light-dark patterns of the external environment, clocks, dinner bells, and the behavior of others are all examples of the plentiful external stimuli that also govern eating and drinking. Normally, the internal and external rhythms are in synchrony. Dinner is usually served when we are hungry enough to eat it. But, when in experiments, the external stimuli are removed—for example, when light-dark patterns are eliminated by putting people in rooms without windows for long periods of time—the internal cues gradually grow out of phase with the light-dark cycles of the outside world. People in such experiments come to ask for breakfast

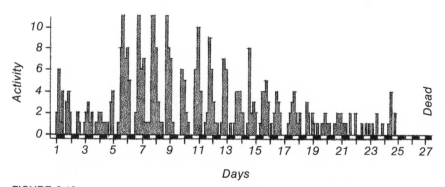

FIGURE 3.13
The activity of a tropical millipede kept in a chamber with constant illumination, temperature, and humidity. There is a peak in the activity of about once a day, until the animal dies on the twenty-fifth day. [From Cloudsley-Thompson. *Journal of Experimental Biology*, 1951, *28*.

foods at night and dinner foods in the morning. Nevertheless, a reasonable periodicity is maintained in the eating itself as a result of the internal rhythms of the activity, such as the periodic buildup and breakdown of chemicals in the bloodstream. However, with disuse, and under certain other conditions, even these internal cues may fail us. Stanley Schacter and his colleagues at Columbia University have done research on this topic. They have found that fat people depend on external rather than internal cues for eating. Fat people get hungry when passing delicatessens, but not when left alone in a room in which they are unaccustomed to eating. Experiments have shown that people of normal weight tend to report hunger when their stomachs are contracting with hunger pangs. Fat people, however, report hunger unrelated to the condition of their stomachs. According to Schacter, fat people never really feel hunger as an internal state. They say they feel hungry, but a little probing often reveals that the hunger occurred not because it had been a long time since eating, but because they had just passed a bakery or watched others eating.

Schacter, R. Goldman, and A. Gordon did an experiment that shows how independent fat people are of the internal stimuli usually associated with hunger. There were four groups of subjects in this experiment. All of the subjects were told to skip the meal (lunch or dinner) that preceded the experiment. Half of the subjects were fat and half normal. These in turn were divided into two subgroups. Half of the fat subjects and half of the normal subjects were fed roast beef sandwiches at the beginning of the experiment, and half were fed nothing. The remainder of the experiment was disguised as an experiment on taste. The subjects were told that they were judging the taste of various kinds of crackers. They were given several bowls of crackers and told to eat as many as they needed to make their judgments. They were left alone for 15 minutes with the crackers and their rating sheets. The actual dependent variable was how many crackers they ate. The results are shown in Figure 3.14. Normal subjects (subjects who weren't fat) did what might be expected. Those who had not eaten the roast beef sandwiches ate more crackers than those who had eaten roast beef sandwiches. For the fat subjects, it did not seem to matter whether or not they had been fed in advance. The crackers were in front of them and they ate them. In fact, the fat people who were given the roast beef sandwiches ate a few more crackers than those who were presumably hungry. The thing to remember about these experiments is that although the basic cycle of eating is caused internally, external cues gain control, and in some cases virtually complete control, by constant association with eating.

Cycles of activity—that is, of simple movement—are less stable than cycles of eating and drinking, perhaps because internal cues are less vivid. Sleep–wake cycles are somewhat more stable than the general activity cycles, but the sleep–wake cycles will fall out of synchrony with night–day cycles if external cues are absent. Long jet flights that place people suddenly in a shifted light–dark cycle disrupt behavioral patterns initially, but adjustment is fairly rapid. Airline pilots and others who travel frequently come to adjust still faster.

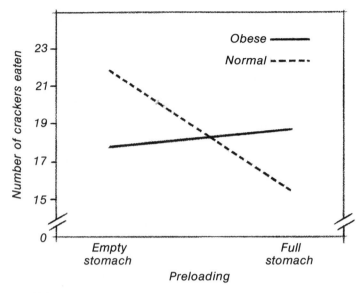

FIGURE 3.14
The effects of preloading on eating. [From Schacter, S. Some
extraordinary facts about obese humans and rats. *American
Psychologist,* 1971, *21,* 129–155. Copyright 1971 by the American
Psychological Assn.]

In most animals the cycles with a period of more than a few seconds but
less than a week, such as the eating, drinking, sleep, and activity cycles we
have just discussed, are most amenable to modification by factors in the environment. Very short and very long cycles are more difficult to modify. The
6-per-second lick rate of the rat is as we have seen a persistent consummatory
cycle whose period is difficult to modify. Whether licking occurs depends on
various environmental and experimental influences, but the rate of licking, once
it occurs, is relatively fixed.

Another example of events occurring with a very short rhythm is provided
by brain waves. If a person is placed comfortably in a quiet, dimly lit room,
with one electrode taped to a part of his head near the back (near the occipital
cortex) and another electrode taped to another part of his body (say his hand)
a small electric potential varying rhythmically with time will be measured
between the two electrodes. When the person is relaxed the period is about
one-twelfth of a second. This period is called the alpha rhythm. Figure 3.15
shows a recording of this rhythm. Biofeedback experiments have shown that
people can be trained to produce the alpha rhythm in their own brains. The
technique consists of a device to measure the brain waves and a signal such as
a light or tone to tell the person when his brain waves conform to the alpha
rhythm. His job is then to keep the signal on. It turns out that some people can
become very good at this. Since people generate alpha-rhythm brain waves

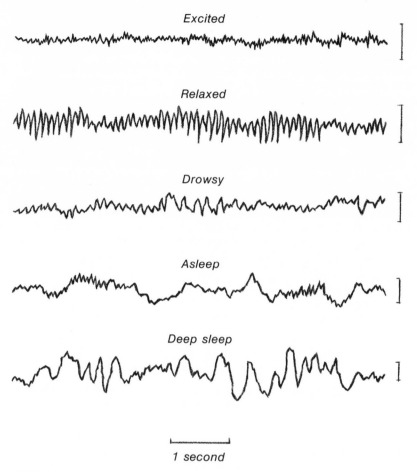

FIGURE 3.15
The electroencephalogram (EEG) of man. [From Jasper, in Penfield and Erickson. *Epilepsy and cerebral localization.* Springfield, Ill.: Charles C. Thomas, Publisher, 1941.]

when they are at rest, it has been reasoned that they are learning to relax when they learn to generate the alpha rhythm. Some researchers have reported that advanced practitioners of various types of meditation, such as Buddhist monks and Indian yogis who have meditated for many years, show a much greater than average ability to generate the alpha rhythm. This has led to attempts to use alpha-training as a shortcut to peace of mind, as a substitute for drugs, and as a cure for various stress-related illnesses. The results of these efforts are inconclusive at present. There probably is more to peace of mind than the alpha rhythm; indeed, reported subjective experiences of the alpha state do vary from subject to subject—some people even say they find it boring.

ENVIRONMENTAL RHYTHMS

In many situations, patterns of behavior are established and maintained mainly by periodic environmental stimuli. A fairly obvious example is the traffic light, which signals "stop" and "go" according to a predetermined pattern and which governs behavior accordingly. However, just as environmental stimuli intrude to influence many naturally occurring biological rhythms, so do biological factors influence behavior governed by periodic environmental stimuli.

In institutions such as jails and army posts, where significant events are rigidly scheduled, behavior takes correspondingly rigid forms. When people leave the institution their behavior continues for a while to conform to the schedule: they wake up, go to sleep, eat, rest, and exercise at the times determined by the institution until gradually a combination of variable exigencies of everyday life and variable biological rhythms take over again. The old soldier who cannot adapt to civilian life may be unable to adjust his rigid behavior to more flexible rhythms. He feels lost if food is not provided at fixed times every day and he wakes up at 6:30 each morning even though he has nothing to do at that hour.

A study of environmentally induced periodic behavior was made recently by John Staddon and Virginia Simmelhag at Duke University. The researchers studied the behavior of pigeons that were allowed access to food at short periodic intervals. Outside of the experimental chamber, the pigeons were fed only enough to maintain their weights at 80 percent of normal, or free-feeding weight, but permitted to drink water freely and swallow grit (small stones that a pigeon eats to help digest food). After being taken from their home cages and weighed, the pigeons were introduced, separately, into the experimental chamber. There a tray containing food was made available every 12 seconds for 2 seconds at a time. Thus, a complete cycle lasted 14 seconds and consisted of 12 seconds without food and 2 seconds with food. There were 64 of these cycles for each pigeon each day, adding up to an experimental session 15 minutes long. The pigeons were always hungry enough to eat whenever food was available. Their naturally occurring eating cycles were thus not a factor in this experiment, since the pigeons were never allowed to become satiated.

It was the pigeons' behavior during the 12 seconds between food presentations that interested Staddon and Simmelhag. Specifically, they wanted to see whether any behavioral patterns would emerge. One wall of the experimental chamber had a window through which the pigeon could be observed. The researchers were able to discern 16 types of behavior exhibited by the pigeons in this relatively sterile environment. Table 3.1 lists these activities and describes them.

Whenever a pigeon engaged in one of the 16 activities, the observer would press a button corresponding to that activity on the recording device and hold

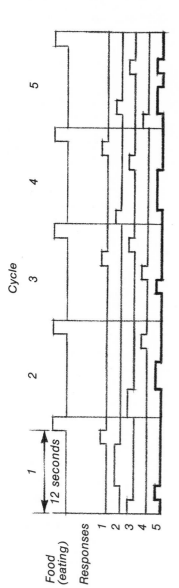

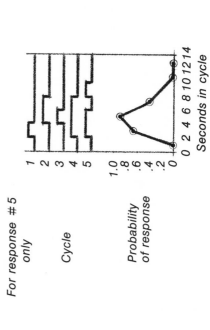

FIGURE 3.16
Simplified example of how Staddon and Simmelhag analyzed their data (see text, page 136).

Table 3.1 Description of Observed Activities

Response Number	Name	Description
R_1	Magazine wall	An orientation response in which the bird's head and body are directed toward the wall containing the magazine.
R_2	Pecking key	Pecking movements directed at the key.
R_3	Pecking floor	Pecking movements directed at the floor.
R_4	Quarter circle	A response in which a count of one quarter circle would be given for turning 90° away from facing the magazine wall, a count of two for turning 180° away, three for 270°, and four for 360°.
R_5	Flapping wings	A vigorous up and down movement of the bird's wings.
R_6	Window wall	An orientation response in which the bird's head and body are directed toward the door of the experimental chamber containing the observation window.
R_7	Pecking	Pecking movements directed toward some point on the magazine wall. This point generally varied between birds and sometimes within the same bird at different times.
R_8	Moving along magazine wall	A side-stepping motion with breast-bone close to the magazine wall, a few steps to the left followed by a few steps to the right, etc. Sometimes accompanied by (a) beak pointed up to ceiling, (b) hopping, (c) flapping wings.
R_9	Preening	Any movement in which the beak comes into contact with the feathers on the bird's body.
R_{10}	Beak to ceiling	The bird moves around the chamber in no particular direction with its beak directed upward touching the ceiling.
R_{11}	Head in magazine	A response in which at least the beak or more of the bird's head is inserted into the magazine opening.
R_{12}	Head movements along magazine wall	The bird faces the magazine wall and moves its head from left to right and/or up and down.
R_{13}	Dizzy motion	A response peculiar to Bird 49 in which the head vibrates rapidly from side to side. It was apparently related to, and alternated with, Pecking (R_7).

continued

Table 3.1 (*continued*)

Response Number	Name	Description
R_{14}	Pecking window wall	Pecking movements directed at the door with the observation window in it.
R_{15}	Head to magazine	The bird turns its head toward the magazine.
R_{16}	Locomotion	The bird walks about in no particular direction.

SOURCE: Staddon and Simmelhag, 1971.

it down until the activity stopped. The presence of food was also indicated on the recorder. To simplify things, Figure 3.16 shows what an event record might have looked like with 5 responses (instead of 16) and 5 cycles (instead of 64). The bottom part of Figure 3.16 shows how the data were analyzed to discern any consistent patterns. For each response all the cycles were superimposed over each other, and each 2–second period in the cycle was examined for the fraction of cycles in which that response occurred. This gives a curve showing probability of each response during each 2–second period.

Two patterns emerged. Some responses started with low probability right after food delivery and became more and more probable during the 12 seconds of the cycle—at the end of the cycle, just before food delivery, these responses were most probable. Other reponses reached maximum probability early in the cycle and then decreased to zero about halfway through the cycle. Figure 3.17 illustrates, in an idealized form, the two types of responses. The first kind were labeled *terminal responses.* The second kind were labeled *interim responses.* Figure 3.18 shows actual data for one pigeon.

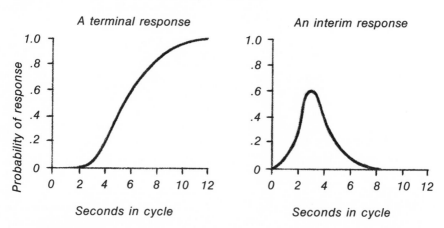

FIGURE 3.17
Idealized forms of terminal and interim responses in Staddon and Simmelhag's experiments.

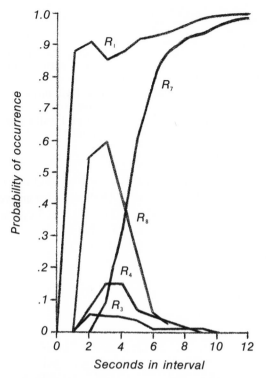

FIGURE 3.18
Probability of each behavior of one of Staddon and
Simmelhag's pigeons as a function of postfood
time averaged over three sessions of steady-state
responding. (Each point gives the probability that
a given behavior occurred in that second of
postfood time.) [From Staddon, J. E. R., and
Simmelhag, V. L. The superstition experiment: a
reexamination of its implications for the study of
adaptive behavior. *Psychological Review,* 1971,
78, 3–43. Copyright 1971 by the American
Psychological Assn.]

The responses that turned out to be terminal responses were usually an
orientation toward the wall of the chamber where the food tray would appear
(R_1) and a pecking movement of the head (R_7); the terminal responses of all the
birds were almost identical. Orienting toward the source of food and pecking
seem appropriate, moreover, to the coming of the food, and these responses
became highly probable as the food was about to appear. Interim responses, on
the other hand, varied considerably from bird to bird. These involved locomotion, pecking the floor (where stray grains of food sometimes fell), flapping
wings, preening, and so on. It is the theory of Staddon and Simmelhag (which

we shall discuss in more detail later) that each cycle is divided into two periods —an early period, when food is improbable, and a later period, when food is highly probable for the pigeons. During the early period, when food is improbable, the tendency of the pigeons is to escape the chamber and seek food elsewhere. Since they are prevented from doing this they seek satisfaction from other sources. Thus, they look on the floor for food, they preen, they flap their wings. If there were another pigeon in the chamber, this is when they would perform aggressive or sexual acts. If there were water in the chamber, this is when they would drink. As the time for food approaches however, their behavior becomes stereotyped—they engage in a fixed action pattern appropriate to a high probability of food.

How these two types of responses, terminal and interim, are influenced by learning, by rewarding certain of them and punishing others, will be discussed later. For now it is sufficient to note that a remarkable degree of patterning of behavior was established by simply presenting food at fixed intervals to hungry pigeons.

Adjunctive Behavior

Adjunctive behavior is another term for interim activities. Adjunctive behavior occurs when a strong environmental stimulus such as food (or electric shock) is presented at fixed or variable temporal intervals. In the sparse environment of Staddon and Simmelhag's experimental chamber, few such activities were available. But in everyday life—where the fixed pattern of meals and the sleep-wake cycle occur—many other activities are simultaneously available. What happens when other activities are made available in the experimental chamber? Obviously we cannot consider every conceivable activity, so let us briefly consider one (aggression) that has been studied in some detail.

It was discovered by a group of psychologists (Nathan Azrin, Donald Hake, and R. Hutchinson) at Anna State Hospital in Illinois that when two animals of the same species were placed together in a cage and subjected simultaneously to a brief but severe electric shock, they would turn on each other and fight, often severely injuring one another. When only one of the animals was shocked, the shocked animal would attack the unshocked animal. This attack behavior occurred reliably after each shock, and Azrin and his colleagues as well as other psychologists investigated it in some detail. They found that many species of animals, including rats, monkeys, pigeons, turtles, and people, exhibit aggression when exposed to a painful stimulus in the presence of another animal. Animals also attack models of other animals (see Figure 3.19) and even inanimate objects. The reliability and severity of the aggression depends on the intensity of the painful stimulus. Aggression is also found when food presentation is cyclical. In a situation in which an animal is fed part of the time and not fed another part of the time, it will often attack another animal during the period when the presentation of food is improbable.

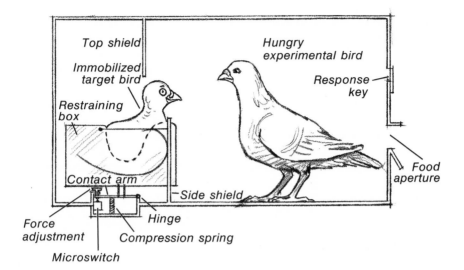

FIGURE 3.19
Schematic of the apparatus for measuring attack. The experimental chamber was 26 by 14 by 14 inches high. Plexiglas shields at the top and on the sides of the restraining box prevented the experimental pigeon from getting behind the target pigeon. [From Azrin, N. H., Hutchinson, R. R. and Hake, D. F. Extinction-induced aggression. *J. Exp. Anal. Beh.*, 1966, *9*, 191–204. Copyright 1966 by the Society for the Experimental Analysis of Behavior, Inc.]

Taking an anthropomorphic view, it might seem that the animal was fooled into thinking that the other animal was hurting him (or removing his food) and retaliated by attacking the other animal so as to get it to stop. In that case the aggression would be a reasonable way to reduce pain. But this view of aggression does not appear valid. When rats are trained to press a lever to escape shock, they tend to ignore the lever when another rat is present and spend their time attacking the other rat (which does nothing to reduce the shock) instead of pressing the lever that would reduce the shock. Thus, rats actually will tolerate greater pain in order to attack another rat. It has also been found that a shocked pigeon will work to produce a model of another pigeon and then attack the model. The model that the shocked pigeon attacks serves as a reward, similar to the food which a hungry pigeon eats.

So it seems as if animals have a very strong tendency to attack something, almost anything, between shocks or between food presentations. If an attackable object is available, they will attack that object even at the cost of more pain. If nothing is available to attack, they will seek something to attack and do work (peck a key, for instance) in order to get it.

Some experimentation has also been done on ways to reduce this sort of aggression. Certain drugs will decrease aggression, but it is not clear whether they reduce aggression directly or only reduce the effective intensity of the pain. It has been found possible to reduce aggression somewhat if each aggressive response is followed by a severe punishment—another shock. In this case, the punishment shocks, although they may augment the strong instinctive tendency to attack, effect a learned inhibition of attack. As we shall see in later chapters, severe punishment is one of the most powerful—though not necessarily one of the most useful—ways to modify behavior.

Another very vivid type of adjunctive behavior is *polydipsia*. It was discovered by John L. Falk (who coined the term, "adjunctive behavior"). When a rat is exposed to periodic food presentations, and water is simultaneously available, the rat will drink large amounts of water (much more, in fact, than it would ordinarily drink). As with aggression, the rat will do work in order to get the opportunity to drink; also, the temporal pattern of drinking is the same as that of aggression. Still other activities that follow the adjunctive-interim behavior pattern are *pica* (eating wood or other non-food material), wheel running, and sexual behavior.

In the experimental chamber we may observe a few terminal and interim activities by making one significant event (such as food) periodic and restricting the availability of other activities (such as drinking or aggression). In everyday life many significant events occur periodically, and may overlap, and many other activities are continuously or intermittently available.

BIBLIOGRAPHY

Most of the material in this chapter is treated in a comprehensive and informative way in R. A. Hinde's excellent book *Animal behavior*, listed below. This book, subtitled "A synthesis of ethology and comparative psychology," fulfills the promise of its title and should be read by anyone seriously interested in the material of this chapter. A much shorter coverage of similar material can be found in Van der Kloot's paperback, *Behavior*, listed below.

The following is a list of works referred to in this chapter:

Azrin, N. H., Hutchinson, R. R., and Hake, D. F. Extinction–induced aggression. *Journal of The Experimental Analysis of Behavior*, 1966, *9*, 191–204.

Bower, T. G. R. The visual world of infants. *Scientific American*, 1966, *215*, 80–92.

Dewey, J. The reflex-arc concept in psychology. *Psychological Review*, 1896, *3*, 357–370.

Hinde, R. A. *Animal behavior.* New York: McGraw–Hill, 1970.

Loeb, J. *Forced movements, tropisms, and animal conduct.* Philadelphia: Lippincott, 1918.

Luria, A. R. Speech development and the formation of mental processes. In *A handbook of contemporary soviet psychology*, ed. M. Cole and I. Maltzman. New York: Basic Books, 1969.

Saslow, C. A. Behavioral definition of minimal reaction time in monkeys. *Journal of The Experimental Analysis of Behavior,* 1972, *18,* 87–106.

Schacter, S. Some extraordinary facts about obese humans and rats. *American Psychologist,* 1971, *21,* 129–144.

Sokolov, E. N. Neuronal models and the orienting reflex. In *The Central nervous system and behavior: Transactions of the third conference,* ed. M. A. B. Brazier. New York: Josiah Macy Jr. Foundation, 1960.

Staddon, J. E. R., and Simmelhag, V. L. The superstition experiment: A reexamination of its implications for the study of adaptive behavior. *Psychological Review,* 1971, *78,* 3–43.

Thompson, R. F., and Spencer, W. A. Habituation: A model phenomenon for the study of neuronal substrates of behavior. *Psychological Review,* 1966, *73,* 16–43.

Thorndike, E. L. *Animal intelligence.* New York: Macmillan, 1911.

Tinbergen, N. *The study of instinct.* Oxford: Clarendon Press, 1951.

Van der Kloot, W. G. *Behavior.* New York: Holt, Rinehart & Winston, 1968.

We reprint the first part of the Staddon and Simmelhag article mentioned in the text. The article begins with a discussion of an experiment by Skinner on "superstition." Skinner provided food at fixed intervals to hungry pigeons. He noticed that certain stereotyped patterns of behavior emerged. One pigeon would flap its wings, another would turn in figure 8's, another would bob its head, and so on. Skinner attributed these patterns to the power of the food to "reinforce" or strengthen any behavior that preceded it. Since the food was given freely, it might come while the pigeon was doing anything. Each pigeon, according to Skinner, was thus "caught" adventitiously by the food delivery, which reinforced the behavior that happened to be occurring. Thus, each pigeon had a different behavior strengthened. As this idiosyncratic behavior was strengthened it would be more likely to be "caught" by the next reinforcement, and so on. Eventually each pigeon would exhibit some pattern of behavior, thus superstitiously learned. Staddon and Simmelhag challenge Skinner's explanation and provide one of their own based on the observation of interim and terminal responses described in the text. (The remainder of Staddon and Simmelhag's paper, in which their theory is expanded, is included at the end of Chapter 7.)

Supplemental Reading for Chapter 3

THE "SUPERSTITION" EXPERIMENT:
A Reexamination of its Implications
for the Principles of Adaptive Behavior
Part I

J. E. R. Staddon
Virginia L. Simmelhag

Replication and extension of Skinner's "superstition" experiment showed the development of two kinds of behavior at asymptote: *interim activities* (related to adjunctive behavior) occurred just after food delivery; the *terminal response* (a discriminated operant) occurred toward the end of the interval and continued until food delivery. These data suggest a view of operant conditioning (the terminal response) in terms of two sets of principles: principles of behavioral variation that describe the origins of behavior "appropriate" to a situation, in advance of reinforcement; and principles of reinforcement that describe the selective elimination of behavior so produced. This approach was supported by (*a*) an account of the parallels between the Law of Effect and evolution by means of natural selection, (*b*) its ability to shed light on persistent problems in learning (e.g., continuity vs. noncontinuity, variability associated with extinction, the relationship between classical and instrumental conditioning, the controversy between behaviorist and cognitive approaches to learning), and (*c*) its ability to deal with a number of recent anomalies in the learning literature ("instinctive drift," auto-shaping, and auto-maintenance). The interim activities were interpreted in terms of interactions among motivational systems, and this view was supported by a review of the literature on adjunctive behavior and by comparison with similar phenomena in ethology (displacement, redirection, and "vacuum" activities). The proposed theoretical scheme represents a shift away from hypothetical "laws of learning" toward an interpretation of behavioral change in terms of interaction and competition among tendencies to action according to principles evolved in phylogeny.

NOTE: Part II of this article appears at the end of Chapter 7.

Research was supported by grants from the National Institute of Mental Health, United States Public Health Service, and the National Science Foundation to Duke University and the University of Toronto. The authors thank Nancy K. Innis for advice and assistance. Janice Frank, Irving Diamond, Carl Erickson, Richard Gilbert, and Peter Klopfer kindly commented on earlier versions of this paper. A shorter version of the experimental part of this work was presented in partial fulfillment of the requirements for the MA degree at the University of Toronto (Simmelhag, 1968). Requests for reprints should be sent to J. E. R. Staddon, Department of Psychology, Duke University, Durham, North Carolina 27706.

From *Psychological Review*, V. 78, No. 1, pp. 3–16. Copyright 1971 by the American Psychological Association. Reprinted by permission.

The field of learning has undergone increasing fractionation in recent years. Interest in "miniature systems" and exact theories of local effects has grown to the detriment of any attempt at overall integration. Consequently, as one perceptive observer has noted:

At times, one senses a widespread feeling of discouragement about the prospects of ever getting clear on the fundamentals of conditioning. Attempts to arrive at firm decisions about alternative formulations rarely produce incisive results. Every finding seems capable of many explanations. Issues become old, shopworn, and disappear without a proper burial [Jenkins, 1970, pp. 107-108].

The present article outlines an attempt to redress this imbalance. It is organized around the problem of "superstitious" behavior, originated by Skinner some years ago, which plays a crucial part in the empirical and theoretical foundations of current views of learning. Discussion of a replication of Skinner's original experiment leads to an account of the relationships between evolution and learning, and a system of classification derived therefrom. The paper concludes with a theoretical account of "superstition" and some related phenomena.

THE "SUPERSTITION" EXPERIMENT

In his classic experiment on "superstitious" behavior, Skinner (1948) showed that the mere delivery of food to a hungry animal is sufficient to produce operant conditioning. The pigeons in that experiment were allowed 5-second access to food every 15 seconds, and food delivery was independent of their behavior. Nevertheless, nearly every pigeon developed a recognizable form of stereotyped, superstitious behavior that become temporally correlated with food delivery as training progressed.

Skinner's (1961) analysis of this phenomenon is a straightforward application of the Law of Effect:

The conditioning process is usually obvious. The bird happens to be executing some response as the hopper appears; as a result it tends to repeat this response. If the interval before the next presentation is not so great that extinction takes place, a second "contingency" is probable. This strengthens the response still further and subsequent reinforcement becomes more probable [p. 405].

Skinner's observations were quickly repeated in a number of laboratories. The apparent simplicity and reliability of the phenomenon, coupled with the plausibility of Skinner's interpretation of it, and the more exciting attractions of work on reinforcement schedules then developing, effectively stifled further study of this situation. However, both the experiment and his explication played a crucial role in advancing Skinner's theoretical view of operant behavior as the strengthening of unpredictably generated ("emitted") behavior by the automatic action of reinforcers.

Two kinds of data obtained in recent years raise new questions about "superstition" in this sense. First, experiments with time-related reinforcement schedules have shown the development of so-called "mediating" behavior during the waiting period, when the animal is not making the reinforced response. Thus, on schedules which require the animal to space his responses a few seconds apart if they are to be effective in producing reinforcement (spaced-responding schedules), pigeons often show activities such as pacing and turning circles. Similarly, on fixed-interval schedules, in which the first response t seconds after the preceding reinforcement is effective in producing reinforcement, pigeons may show a similar behavior during the postreinforcement "pause" when they are not making the reinforced response. Other species show activities of this sort in the presence of appropriate environmental stimuli; for example, schedule-induced polydipsia, in which rats reinforced with food on temporal reinforcement schedules show excessive drinking if water is continuously available (Falk, 1969). None of these activities is reinforced, in the sense of being contiguous with food delivery, yet they are reliably produced in situations similar in many respects to Skinner's superstition procedure. Possibly, therefore, some of the activities labeled superstitious by Skinner, and attributed by him to accidental reinforcement of spontaneously occuring behavior, may instead reflect the same causal factors as these mediating activities.

Second, a number of experiments have demonstrated the development of behavior in operant conditioning situations by a process more reminiscent of Pavlovian (classical) conditioning than Law of Effect learning as commonly understood. Breland and Breland (1961) reported a series of observations showing that with continued operant training, species-specific behavior will often emerge to disrupt an apparently well-learned operant response. In the cases they describe, behavior closely linked to food (presumably reflecting an instinctive mechanism) began to occur in advance of food delivery, in the presence of previously neutral stimuli ("instinctive drift"). Since these "irrelevant" activities interfered with food delivery by delaying the occurrence of the reinforced response, they cannot be explained by the Law of Effect. A description in terms of stimulus substitution—a principle usually associated with Pavlovian conditioning—is better, although still not completely satisfactory. More recently, Brown and Jenkins (1968) have shown that hungry pigeons can be trained to peck a lighted response key simply by illuminating the key for a few seconds before food delivery. Fewer than a hundred light–food pairings are usually sufficient to bring about key pecking. The relationship between this "auto-shaping" procedure and Pavlovian conditioning is further emphasized by an experiment reported by Williams and Williams (1969). They found that auto-shaped key pecking is maintained even if the key peck turns off the light on the key and thus prevents

food delivery on that occasion. All these experiments show the occurrence of food-related behaviors, in anticipation of food, under conditions more or less incompatible with the Law of Effect.

The auto-shaping procedure is operationally identical to Pavlovian conditioning with short delay (the light–food interval in these experiments is typically 8 seconds). Therefore the eventual emergence of food-related behavior, in anticipation of food delivery, is not altogether surprising—although the directed nature of key pecking has no counterpart in principles of conditioning that take salivation as a model response. The superstition situation is also equivalent to a Pavlovian procedure—in this case temporal conditioning, in which the UCS (food) is simply presented at regular intervals. Perhaps, therefore, prolonged exposure to this situation will also lead to the emergence of food-related behavior in anticipation of food. Possibly the superstitious behavior described by Skinner includes activities of this sort, that occur in anticipation of food, as well as mediating activities that occur just after food delivery.

The present experiment affords an opportunity to test these ideas. It provides comparative data on the effect of fixed versus variable interfood intervals on superstitious responding (Skinner used only fixed intervals), as well as allowing a comparison between response-dependent and response-independent fixed-interval schedules. The experiment also extends Skinner's work by recording in some detail both the kind and time of occurrence of superstitious activities. The emphasis is on the steady-state adaptation to the procedures, but some data on the course of development of superstition are presented.

We hope to show that careful study of the superstition situation makes necessary a revision of Skinner's original interpretation and, by extension, requires a shift of emphasis in our view of adaptive behavior.

METHOD

Subjects

Six pigeons were used: four white Carneaux, two with experimental experience (Birds 31 and 29) and two experimentally naive (Birds 47 and 49). Two other pigeons were of a local (Toronto, Ontario) breed and were experimentally naive (Birds 40 and 91). All the birds were maintained at 80% of their free-feeding weights throughout.

Apparatus

Two standard Grason-Stadler operant conditioning chambers were used. The response keys were covered with white cardboard except during the response-dependent condition when one key was exposed and transilluminated with white light. Data were recorded by a clock, digital counters, and an event recorder. Food delivery was controlled automatically by relays and timers. Behaviors were recorded via push buttons operated by an observer. A tape recorder was used to record comments and corrections. Except for the push buttons and the tape recorder, all programming and recording apparatus was located in a separate room. White noise was present in the experimental chamber and, together with the noise of the ventilating fan, served to mask extraneous sounds.

Procedure

Three schedules of food delivery were used: (*a*) A response-independent fixed-interval (FI) schedule in which the food magazine was presented at 12-second intervals. (*b*) A response-independent variable-interval (VI) schedule in which the food magazine was presented on the average every 8 seconds. The following sequence of interreinforcement intervals was used, programmed by a loop of 16-millimeter film with holes punched at appropriate intervals: 3, 6, 6, 12, 9, 7, 3, 10, 21, 6, 5, 11, 8, 5, 3, 9, 7, 9, 5, 13, 3, 8, 9, 4, 7, 12, 11, 3, 6, 5, and 9 seconds. (*c*) A response-dependent FI schedule in which

food was delivered (reinforcement occurred) for the first key peck 12 seconds or more after the preceding reinforcement.

Food delivery involved 2-second access to mixed grain. Sessions ended after the sixty-fourth food delivery and the pigeons were run daily.

Habituation sessions. All the birds were given a number of daily 10-minute sessions when no food was delivered; the birds were simply placed in the chamber and their behavior observed and recorded. The birds received the following numbers of such sessions: Bird 31, 3; Bird 29, 3; Bird 47, 15; Bird 49, 15; Bird 40, 7; Bird 91, 7. Note that the experimentally naive birds received more habituation exposure.

Response-independent training. Four of the pigeons were then given a number of sessions on each of the two response-independent procedures, either FI followed by VI, or the reverse. The birds received the procedures in the indicated order (number of sessions in parentheses): Bird 31: FI 12 (26), VI 8 (111); Bird 29: VI 8 (26), FI 12 (109); Bird 47: VI 8 (36), FI 12 (36); Bird 49: FI 12 (37), VI 8 (36).

Response-dependent training. Two of the birds already trained on the response-independent procedures were then switched to the response-dependent FI 12 for the following numbers of sessions: Bird 31, 37; Bird 47, 52. The two naive birds (40 and 91), after their habituation sessions, were given one session of response-independent FI 12 when the food magazine operated every 12 seconds, but contained no grain. This was to habituate these birds to the sound of the mechanism. The next day these two birds were placed in the experimental box with the food magazine continuously available for 10 minutes. The following day the two birds were introduced to the response-dependent FI 12-second schedule. A small piece of black tape was placed on the lighted response key, as an induce-

Table 1   Description of Observed Activities

Response no.	Name	Description
R_1	Magazine wall	An orientation response in which the bird's head and body are directed toward the wall containing the magazine.
R_2	Pecking key	Pecking movements directed at the key.
R_3	Pecking floor	Pecking movements directed at the floor.
R_4	$\frac{1}{4}$ circle	A response in which a count of one $\frac{1}{4}$ circle would be given for turning 90° away from facing the magazine wall, a count of two for turning 180° away, three for 270°, and four for 360°.
R_5	Flapping wings	A vigorous up and down movement of the bird's wings.
R_6	Window wall	An orientation response in which the bird's head and body are directed toward the door of the experimental chamber containing the observation window.
R_7	Pecking	Pecking movements directed toward some point on the magazine wall. This point generally varied between birds and sometimes within the same bird at different times.
R_8	Moving along magazine wall	A side-stepping motion with breastbone close to the magazine wall, a few steps to the left followed by a few steps to the right, etc. Sometimes accompanied by (*a*) beak pointed up to ceiling, (*b*) hopping, (*c*) flapping wings.
R_9	Preening	Any movement in which the beak comes into contact with the feathers on the bird's body.
R_{10}	Beak to ceiling	The bird moves around the chamber in no particular direction with its beak directed upward touching the ceiling.
R_{11}	Head in magazine	A response in which at least the beak or more of the bird's head is inserted into the magazine opening.
R_{12}	Head movements along magazine wall	The bird faces the magazine wall and moves its head from left to right and/or up and down.
R_{13}	Dizzy motion	A response peculiar to Bird 49 in which the head vibrates rapidly from side to side. It was apparently related to, and alternated with, Pecking (R_7).
R_{14}	Pecking window wall	Pecking movements directed at the door with the observation window in it.
R_{15}	Head to magazine	The bird turns its head toward the magazine.
R_{16}	Locomotion	The bird walks about in no particular direction.

ment to pecking, for this first session only. All the birds pecked the key during the first session of the response-dependent procedure. This rather elaborate key-training procedure was designed both to prevent the experimenter from shaping the naive birds' behavior, and to avoid the possibility of "superstitious" conditioning, which might be entailed by some form of auto-shaping. Bird 40 received a total of 45 sessions of the response-dependent FI 12-second schedule, Bird 91 received 38.

Response description and scoring. Response categories were arrived at on the basis of initial observation during the habituation sessions and were altered as necessary to accommodate new behaviors. The names, descriptions, and numbers of the categories appear in Table 1. Responses were scored (by pushing the appropriate button) in two ways, either discretely or continuously. If a response tended to occur in discrete units (e.g., pecking), then the appropriate button was pushed each time an instance of the response occurred. The observer was the same throughout (VLS), and the maximum recordable rate for discrete responses was 3–4 per second. A continuous response is one which took an indefinite amount of time (e.g., facing magazine wall); the appropriate button was pressed throughout the duration of a continuous response. Discrete responses were pecking (wall, key, or floor) and quarter circles, all the rest were continuous responses. In general, the response categories were mutually exclusive. The only exception is facing Magazine wall (R_1), which at various times occurred with Flapping wings (R_5), Moving along magazine wall (R_8), and Pecking (R_7).

RESULTS

The data of interest in this experiment are the kind and amount of behavior at different points in time following the delivery of food. As training progressed, a systematic pattern of behavior as a function of postfood time began to emerge. The properties of this steady-state pattern for VI and FI schedules is discussed first, followed by a description of the changes that took place during acquisition.

Steady-State Behavior

In the steady state, the behavior developed under both the FI and VI procedures fell reliably into two classes: (*a*) The *terminal response* was the behavior that consistently occurred just before food delivery. It began 6–8 seconds after food delivery on the FI procedures, and about 2 seconds after food on the VI procedure, and usually continued until food delivery. (*b*) A number of activities usually preceded the terminal response in the interval. These activities are probably indistinguishable from what has been termed mediating behavior, but we prefer the more descriptive term *interim activities*. These activities were rarely contiguous with food.

Figure 1 shows the performance averaged across the three sessions of steady-

state responding under all conditions for all the pigeons. The left-hand panels show the response-dependent FI schedule; the middle panels, the response-independent (superstitious) FI schedule; and the right-hand panels, the response-independent VI procedure, for the four birds exposed to each. The graphs show the probability (relative frequency) with which each of the activities occurred during each second of postfood time. Each bird shows the clear division between terminal and interim activities already alluded to. Excluding R_1, and the results for Bird 29 on VI, Pecking (R_7) was the terminal response for all the response-independent procedures. For Bird 29, the terminal response Head in magazine (R_{11}) became an interim activity following the shift from VI to FI and was replaced as terminal response by Pecking. Pecking remained the terminal response for this bird throughout a sequence of response-independent procedures after the ones reported here, lasting for a total in excess of 90 sessions. A curious idiosyncratic head movement accompanied pecking by Bird 49 (R_{13}: Dizzy motion) on response-independent FI, although it disappeared following the switch to VI. The locus of Pecking on the magazine wall differed from bird to bird and varied both across and within sessions for some birds. The stable features of this response were its topography and its restriction to the general area of the magazine wall. A variety of interim activities occupied the early parts of the FIs and the period within 2 or 3 seconds after food on the VI schedule: Pecking floor (R_3), $\frac{1}{4}$ circles (R_4), Flapping wings (R_5), Moving along magazine wall (R_8), and Beak to ceiling (R_{10}) were the most frequent. The interim activities were therefore more variable from bird to bird than was the terminal response.

The pattern of behavior characteristic of each interval was little affected by whether or not food was dependent on key pecking. The similarity between the patterns during response-dependent and

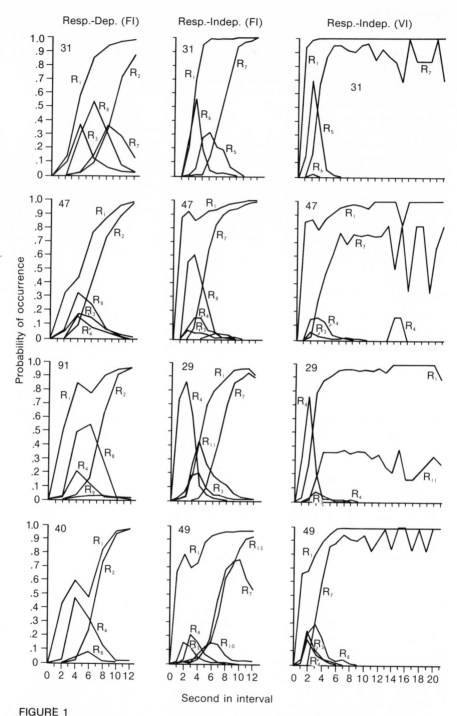

FIGURE 1

Probability of each behavior as a function of postfood time for all birds for all three experimental conditions, averaged over three sessions of steady-state responding under each condition. (Each point gives the probability that a given behavior occurred in that second of postfood time. Data for the response-dependent condition are averaged across 2-second blocks. Behaviors (R_i) are identified in Table 1.)

response-independent FI is particularly striking for Bird 47, who was switched directly from the response-independent to the response-dependent procedure. Bird 31, for whom the response-independent and response-dependent FIs were separated by response-independent VI, shows more variation in the interim activities under the two conditions. Birds 91 and 40, who were exposed only to the response-dependent FI, show a similar pattern of interim activities to the response-independent birds, although again there is some variation as to details. This similarity cannot be attributed to the procedure used to shape key pecking (see Procedure). After the imposition of the key-pecking contingency, Bird 31 retained the old Pecking response as an interim activity restricted to a period in the interval just before key pecking. Bird 47 showed a similar effect of his response-independent experience in that a high proportion of his key pecks failed to depress the key sufficiently to activate the automatic recording circuitry, although they were recorded as key pecks by the observer. Overall, these data provide no evidence for substantial changes in the pattern of terminal or interim activities traceable to the imposition of a key-pecking requirement.

The general pattern of terminal and interim activities during the response-independent VI schedule was similar to the FI procedures. Differences were restriction of the interim activities to the first 2 or 3 seconds of postfood time rather than to the first 6 or 7 seconds (with one exception, to be discussed), and the smaller number of interim activities, in most cases. Under both fixed and variable procedures, once the terminal response began in an interval, it continued until food delivery. The exception is Bird 47 who showed a drop in the probability of the terminal response (Pecking, R_7) accompanied by a transient increase in the interim activity of $\frac{1}{4}$ circles (R_4) at the 14–15-second postfood time. A similar slight drop in the probability of Peck-

ing, although not accompanied by an interim activity, was also shown by Bird 31. These differences are related to the properties of the VI schedule (see Discussion).

Sequential Structure

Figure 2 indicates something of the sequential structure of the behavior occupying each interfood interval for each bird during the response-independent procedures. The figure summarizes the two to five behavior sequences that account for most of the intervals during the three steady-state sessions. For simplicity, no account is taken either of interbehavior times or of the duration of each activity in this method of representation. The most striking characteristics of these sequences are: (a) that each bird showed only a small number of typical sequences (usually three or four); (b) that the sequencing was very rigid, so that although a given behavior might fail to occur during a particular interval, it never occurred out of sequence—this is indicated by the absence of return arrows ("loops") in these diagrams; and (c) that the variability of the sequences was greatest early in the interval and least at the end, in the period just preceding food delivery—this is indicated by the absence of "forks" (ambiguous transitions from one behavior to two or more others, as in the diagram for Bird 31 where $R_6 \rightarrow R_5$ or $R_6 \rightarrow R_7$ with approximately equal probability) late in the sequence of behaviors shown in the diagrams. This regular sequencing did not occur early in training, as indicated in Figure 4, discussed below.

An inviting possibility raised by these regular sequences is that this behavior may be described by some kind of Markov chain (cf. Cane, 1961). Although the argument cannot be presented in full here, this assumption cannot be sustained for a number of reasons, the most important of which are (a) that the duration of a bout of a given activity was shorter the later the activity began within an interval,

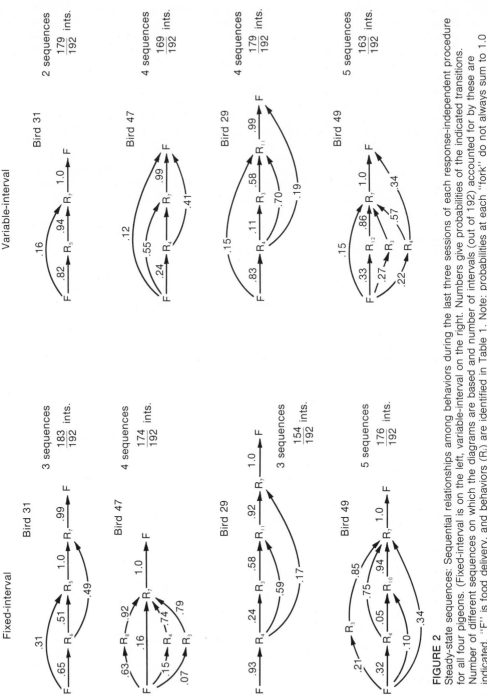

FIGURE 2

Steady-state sequences: Sequential relationships among behaviors during the last three sessions of each response-independent procedure for all four pigeons. (Fixed-interval is on the left, variable-interval on the right. Numbers give probabilities of the indicated transitions. Number of different sequences on which the diagrams are based and number of intervals (out of 192) accounted for by these are indicated. "F" is food delivery, and behaviors (R_i) are identified in Table 1. Note: probabilities at each "fork" do not always sum to 1.0 because not every sequence is accounted for.)

and (*b*) that the time between two successive activities was shorter the later in the interval the first activity ended. These and other considerations suggest that postfood time was the most important factor controlling both the onset and the offset of each activity in the sequence.

Acquisition

Figure 3 shows acquisition data for naive Bird 49, through and beyond the period which his behavior became stable on response-independent FI. The graphs show (as a function of sessions) the probability of the various behaviors in each of the six 2-second periods making up the FI. The most noteworthy characteristic of acquisition is the relatively sudden disappearance of the behavior Head in magazine, which was almost the only behavior to occur during the first few sessions for Bird 49, in favor of the terminal response Pecking on magazine wall. For Bird 49 this transition took place between the seventh and eighth sessions of FI without any prior history of pecking during earlier sessions. Once pecking became established as a terminal response, the only further change was a slow decline in the probability of the response during the early parts of the interval (e.g., between 3 and 8 seconds). The other birds showed similar results on their first exposure to the response-independent procedures; for each bird, pecking on the magazine wall first occurred during the following sessions: for Bird 31, on the first FI session; Bird 29, twelfth session of FI following the switch from response-independent VI; Bird 47, twenty-eighth session of VI; Bird 49, eighth session of FI. Thus, although one of the experienced birds pecked during the first response-independent session (31), the other did not until being switched to a different schedule (29). No bird shifted to a different terminal response once he began pecking; the total number of sessions of response-independent experience (FI and VI) for each of the four birds following the onset of

pecking was as follows: Bird 31, 140; Bird 29, 96; Bird 47, 45; Bird 49, 66. For Bird 29, the terminal response during the response-independent FI procedure (i.e., before the onset of pecking) was Head in magazine. As with the other birds, once pecking appeared it was in full strength almost immediately and further experience had the effect merely of restricting it more to the later parts of the interval.

Figure 4 shows sequence data, in the same form as Figure 2, for the first three sessions of the first response-independent schedule to which each bird was exposed. Approximately the same proportion of the total number of sequences observed within 192 intervals is accounted for by these diagrams as in the diagrams of Figure 2 for the last three sessions. The data for the first three sessions are much more variable, showing repetitions of a behavior within an interval and reversals of sequence; three out of four birds show no single terminal response. Thus, the regularities apparent in Figure 2 are evidently a real effect of training and not simply an artifact of this method of representation.

DISCUSSION

The results of this experiment confirm the suggestion that the "superstition" situation generally produces two distinct kinds of activity: interim activities that occur at short and intermediate postfood times, and the terminal response that begins later in the interval and continues until food delivery. It is not always clear from Skinner's original discussion just which kind of behavior he was observing. In one case, he briefly describes an experiment in which the interfood interval was 60 seconds, and the "superstitious" response (a "well-defined hopping step from the right to the left foot") was automatically recorded. In this case, the behavior was evidently a terminal response, since it occurred with increasing frequency through the interval:

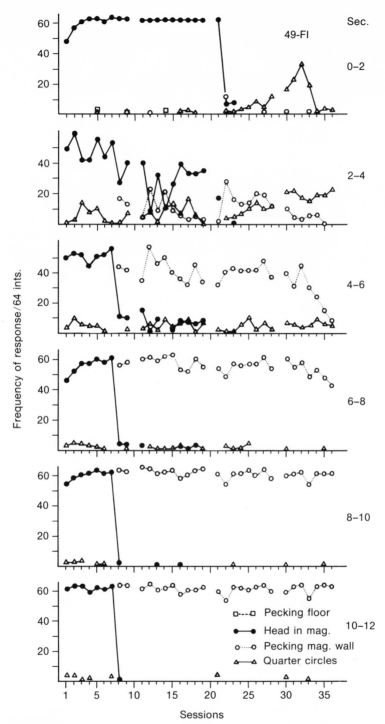

FIGURE 3

Development of the terminal response. (The graph shows, for Bird 49 on the response-independent fixed-interval procedure, the transition from Head in magazine (R_{11}) to Pecking (R_7) as terminal response, and includes one interim activity, $\frac{1}{4}$ circles (R_4), for comparison. Each panel covers 2 seconds of the 12-second interval and indicates the number of intervals (out of 64) in which a given response occurred in that 2-second block for each session over the first 36 sessions. Gaps indicate days for which data are not available. Bird 49 was not run for a 9-day period between Sessions 21 and 22.)

Fixed-interval   Variable-interval

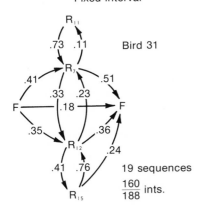

Bird 31

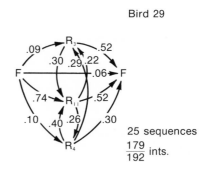

Bird 29

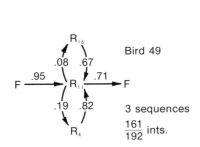

Bird 49

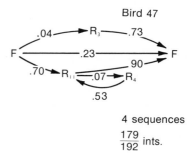

Bird 47

FIGURE 4

Sequence data, in the same form as Figure 2, for the first three sessions under the first response-independent procedure to which each bird was exposed (Details as in Figure 2.)

The bird does not respond immediately after eating, but when 10 or 15 or even 20 sec. have elapsed it begins to respond rapidly and continues until the reinforcement is received [Skinner, 1961, p. 406].

On other occasions, however, Skinner may have been observing interim activities, as, in our experience, they are sometimes much more striking than the terminal response, especially early in training when they may include actions like jumping in the air, vigorous wing flapping, and idiosyncratic head and limb movements. We have also sometimes observed interim activities during sessions when there was no obvious terminal response.

REFERENCES

BRELAND, K., & BRELAND, M. The misbehavior of organisms. *American Psychologist,* 1961, **16,** 661–664.

BROWN, P. L., & JENKINS, H. M. Auto-shaping of the pigeon's key-peck. *Journal of the Experimental Analysis of Behavior,* 1968, **11,** 1–8.

Cane, V. Some ways of describing behaviour. In W. H. Thorpe & O. L. Zangwill (Eds.), *Current problems in animal behaviour.* London: Cambridge University Press, 1961.

FALK, J. L. Control of schedule-induced polydipsia: Type, size, and spacing of meals. *Journal of the Experimental Analysis of Behavior,* 1967, **10,** 199–206.

JENKINS, H. M. Sequential organization in schedules of reinforcement. In W. N. Schoenfeld & J. Farmer (Eds.), *Theory of reinforcement schedules.* New York: Appleton-Century-Crofts, 1970.

SKINNER, B. F. "Superstition" in the pigeon. *Journal of Experimental Psychology,* 1948, **38,** 168–172.

SKINNER, B. F. *Cumulative record.* New York: Appleton-Century-Crofts, 1961.

WILLIAMS, D. R., & WILLIAMS, H. Automaintenance in the pigeon: Sustained pecking despite contingent non-reinforcement. *Journal of the Experimental Analysis of Behavior,* 1969, **12,** 511–520.

Chapter 4

Classical Conditioning

- You are walking home past a bakery and get a whiff of fresh hot apple pie. You start to salivate and you are reminded of how hungry you are. You rush home, anticipating supper.
- You pass a strange woman on the street. Her perfume smells familiar. You suddenly remember your kindergarten teacher, who wore the same perfume. You remember her fondly—or perhaps not so fondly.

In both of the above examples an automatic response is made to events in the environment that have little importance in and of themselves, but serve as signals for more important events. In the first example, the smell would not satisfy your appetite. In the second, it was not the teacher's perfume that made you like (or dislike) kindergarten. But both of these signals have, in the past, reliably accompanied an event that is important; the smell of a pie has accompanied the eating of it; the teacher's perfume has accompanied loving attention and kind words (or, perhaps, a slap on the wrist).

How we react to signals like the smell of pie, or the perfume, depends on our experience. Since we all have had similar experiences with the smell of pie and pie itself, we all react similarly when we smell the pie. But, since we have had different experiences in kindergarten we are likely, each to react uniquely to the smell of his teacher's perfume.

How certain signals come to be related to certain significant environmental events, and how we learn to behave differently in the presence of a stimulus after it has been used as a signal, is the subject of classical conditioning. It was first studied by the Russian physiologist, I. P. Pavlov around the turn of the century.

PAVLOV'S EXPERIMENTS

Seven decades ago Pavlov was studying the salivation reflex in dogs when he discovered that systematic changes in the dogs' reflexes were clearly linked to his own pattern of behavior in the laboratory. Pavlov began to study this intriguing phenomenon and subsequently produced the first empirical reports on the conditioned reflex.

Pavlov had initially set out to investigate the physiology of the secretion of various fluids within the mouth and stomach. By ingenious surgical techniques he was able to implant tubes, called catheters, leading from various points along the dogs' digestive tracts out through the skin. Part of the secretion of fluids in the digestive tracts passed into the tubes and was collected and its amount was measured. In effect, the questions that Pavlov asked were, "If I give the dog some food to eat, how soon will the food, acting as a stimulus, cause the mouth and the stomach to secrete their various digestive fluids?" "What is the mechanism that links the insertion of food in the mouth and the secretion of saliva?" "What is the function relating the amount of food and the amount of saliva secreted?" "As the food reaches the stomach, how long does the stomach take to secrete the acids necessary to digest the food?" Such physiological questions seemed unrelated to psychology.

However, in the course of his research Pavlov began to be plagued by an annoying phenomenon: as dogs became familiar with the experimental situation, they would often begin to salivate and secrete stomach acids as soon as Pavlov walked into the room. Pavlov called these premature secretions "psychic" secretions because he believed at first that they resulted from the dogs' psychic (mental) activity. Later, he realized that these "annoyances" bore certain similarities to the physiological reflexes he had been measuring, and he decided to study them.

One of the first of Pavlov's experiments on psychic secretions is particularly instructive. A dog's secretion of stomach acids, following the introduction of food into its mouth, increases and then decreases over the course of four hours, as shown in curve (a) of Figure 4.1. This curve represents (1) whatever was secreted as a direct result of the stimulation of food in the stomach *plus* (2) whatever was secreted before food reached the stomach (the "psychic secretions"). Pavlov wished to measure these two components of the curve separately. In order to plot the curve of direct secretions only, Pavlov introduced food not through the dog's mouth, but directly into its stomach through a tube, called a fistula, which bypassed the normal routes from the mouth to the stomach. When food was introduced through the fistula into the stomach, the gastric secretion was much less than when food was eaten in a normal way. Curve (b) in Figure 4.1 shows the amount of secretion under this special condition. This,

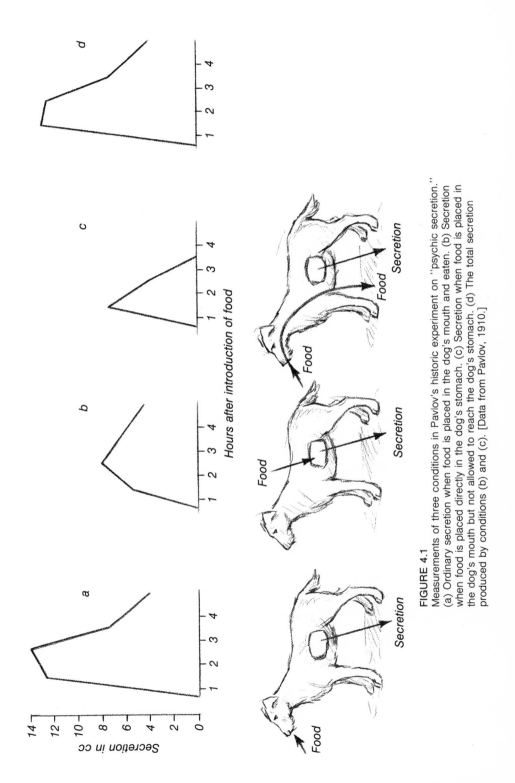

FIGURE 4.1
Measurements of three conditions in Pavlov's historic experiment on "psychic secretion." (a) Ordinary secretion when food is placed in the dog's mouth and eaten. (b) Secretion when food is placed directly in the dog's stomach. (c) Secretion when food is placed in the dog's mouth but not allowed to reach the dog's stomach. (d) The total secretion produced by conditions (b) and (c). [Data from Pavlov, 1910.]

then, represented one component of the total secretion—the secretion that followed direct stimulation of the stomach by food. The second component of curve (a) was determined by a method called *sham-feeding*. The dog ate food in the normal way, chewing and swallowing it, but the food was not allowed to pass into its stomach; instead, the food was removed through another fistula before reaching the stomach. Despite the fact that no food reached the stomach, there was a secretion of stomach acids as shown by curve (c). Curve (d), which is the sum of curves (b) and (c), is similar to curve (a). Thus, the experiment confirmed Pavlov's suspicion that total stomach secretion derived about equally from direct stimulation and "psychic" stimulation.

Now let us turn to another of Pavlov's experiments. Pavlov knew that his dogs began to salivate when they merely saw food, just as a hungry man begins to salivate when he passes a bakery. Pavlov wondered whether such premature salivation was caused only by the sight of food in particular or whether *any* stimulus, such as the sounding of a tone, would cause this premature salivation if followed often enough by actual eating. To answer this question, Pavlov constructed the apparatus shown in Figure 4.2. A hungry dog was isolated from as many extraneous stimuli as possible. Then Pavlov struck a tuning fork, which produced a tone, and after half of a second, fed the dog. He repeated these pairings of tone and food several times, measuring salivation all the while through a tube leading from the dog's cheek to a small container. At first, the dog salivated only after the food was inserted into its mouth. But it gradually salivated earlier and earlier in the procedure, until salivation finally appeared somewhat *before* the dog was fed, but after the tone. Pavlov found that such "psychic" secretions could be established in this manner for many kinds of stimuli.

It is important to recognize the difference between Pavlov's earlier experiment with sham-feeding and his later one with the presentation of a tone before feeding. In the first experiment, Pavlov observed a "psychic" secretion linked to food, a stimulus that had already been established and (for all Pavlov knew) could have been established even before the dog was born. In the second experiment, however, Pavlov observed a "psychic" secretion that followed a wholly new and arbitrarily chosen stimulus. This process—the forging of a connection between a new stimulus (like a tone) and an existing reflex (like salivation to food in the mouth)—Pavlov called *conditioning*.

ELEMENTS OF CLASSICAL CONDITIONING

It is worth examining Pavlov's classical procedure more closely, in order to learn the traditional nomenclature for its various elements.

The first necessary element is an established reflex. A reflex consists of a stimulus and a response, when the response is reliably elicited by the stimulus. In Pavlov's experiment the response was salivation and the stimulus was the

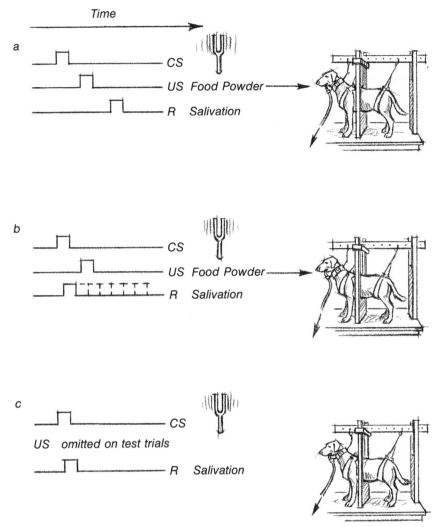

FIGURE 4.2
Classical conditioning. (a) Procedure for the establishment of conditioning. (b) One test for conditioning: Does the response come to precede the US? (c) Another test for conditioning: Does the response occur in the absence of the US?

presence of food in the mouth. The stimulus part of this reflex—the presence of food in the mouth—is traditionally called the *unconditioned stimulus,* or, more briefly, the US. The next requirement for classical conditioning is a neutral stimulus, anything that will not by itself cause the response before the experiment begins. This neutral stimulus is called the *conditioned stimulus* (CS). Besides tones, Pavlov used lights, pictures, and other objects as CS's. Indeed,

Pavlov himself became a CS for his dogs. (This was the bothersome effect that launched Pavlov's research into conditioning.)

The US–response connection and the CS are the two basic components of any classical conditioning experiment. The schematic sketches in Figure 4.2 show how they are related in time.

Often conditioned stimuli (CS's) are physically connected to unconditioned stimuli (US's), as the smell of bread is to bread. But sometimes conditioned stimuli (CS's) are quite arbitrary and different for different people. For instance, the word "lemon" might be a CS for salivation for an American, but not for a Frenchman, who would salivate when he saw "citron."

The end result of the conditioning procedure is the *conditioned reflex*. The conditioned reflex in Pavlov's experiments was salivation in response to a previously neutral stimulus. Parts (b) and (c) of Figure 4.2 show two measurable effects of classical conditioning, both of which were studied by Pavlov. Part (b) shows the salivation response occurring progressively earlier until it occurs before the US; part (c) shows the occurrence of the response with the US omitted. In order for the response to occur with the US omitted, the sequence in (a) is presented repeatedly—except that, according to a prearranged schedule, the US is occasionally omitted. As the experiment progresses, the usual observation is that the response without the US becomes almost, but not quite, as large in magnitude as the response with the US. Measurement of the effect shown in (b) emphasizes the *latency* of the response; measurement of the effect shown in (c) emphasizes the *magnitude* of the response. (As classical conditioning proceeds, one finds that the latency of the response to the CS becomes shorter and the magnitude becomes larger.)

Pavlov saw conditioning as the establishment of a new reflex by the addition of a new stimulus to the group of stimuli that are capable of triggering a response.

Classical conditioning, Pavlov believed, shed new light on the process of association. In association, as studied by Ebbinghaus with nonsense syllables, for instance, there are all the elements of classical conditioning. One syllable is presented to the subject first (the CS). Then another is presented to the subject (the US). These pairings are repeated, and, finally, the subject can say the name of the second syllable (the response) when he is presented with the first. Pavlov maintained that psychologists like Ebbinghaus who were studying the association of mental events were really doing experiments in classical conditioning, but with the stimuli and responses not as well controlled as they were in Pavlov's laboratory.*

---

*Currently, even psychologists most involved in the study of mental events recognize that some processes in the brain must correspond to these events. But nowadays the mental processes studied are often so complex that it proves difficult to trace their relationship to simple classical conditioning procedures. Thus, cognitive psychology and physiological psychology are two separate disciplines. Psychologists in both disciplines hope that one day they may be unified with a common set of principles.

Although Pavlov's original experiments used secretion of saliva in response to food as the basic reflex, to which a neutral CS was attached, the classsical conditioning procedure has since been carried out with many other kinds of reflexes. Mild electric shock has often been used as a US because it produces a host of measurable responses. For example, after electric shock the rate of breathing increases, the heart rate increases, and the part of the body being shocked is withdrawn. In one experiment performed by H. S. Liddell at Cornell University, sheep were shocked briefly on the foreleg, causing them to breathe faster and deeper and also to raise the leg (even though the wires delivering the shock were attached to it.) The experimenters decided to set a metronome ticking a few seconds before the shock was given. After this was done four or five times, a sheep would lift its leg and begin breathing faster as soon as the metronome started ticking. The shock was the US; the ticking metronome was the CS; the leg-raising and faster breathing were responses.

Pavlov believed that we are all born sensitive to a set of unconditioned stimuli that cause strong reactions in us innately—for example, fire causing us to pull away, food causing us to secrete saliva, or a hug or a pat on the head causing pleasurable feelings. Later in life we learn to associate signals that reliably precede these events with the events themselves. The signals become conditioned stimuli. According to Pavlov, learning is nothing more than the acquisition of more and more conditioned stimuli.

TECHNIQUES OF CLASSICAL CONDITIONING

At one time, textbook descriptions of classical conditioning techniques would typically list the various stimuli that have served as US's in conditioning experiments, together with the responses they elicit, and then mention a few common CS's, implying that any of the CS's paired with any of the US's according to certain temporal arrangements would produce conditioning of the responses to the CS according to certain rules. It would be almost as if we had two barrels, one containing CS's and one containing US's, into which the experimenter could blindly reach, pick out any items to pair, and be fairly certain as to the result. Unfortunately (for simplicity of presentation, at least) such substitutability of stimuli is not found. Recent experiments show that conditioning depends critically on the particular CS's and US's chosen. We shall thoroughly discuss this limitation on conditioning in Chapter 7. Meanwhile, the present section will simply enumerate a few common conditioning paradigms so that we can refer to them later without describing them in detail.

Salivary Conditioning

Salivary conditioning is Pavlov's original classical conditioning paradigm, first demonstrated with dogs and later with humans and other animals. The US must be something that unconditionally causes salivation. At first food powder, inserted through a tube into a dog's mouth, was used. Later experiments used dilute hydrochloric acid, with the sourness of very sour lemons, which also causes dogs to salivate. The salivation response of the dogs was measured through a catheter in the dog's cheek. With humans, absorbent cotton pads have been used for measurement of saliva. In all cases salivation is constantly going on and it is the sudden increase in salivation that constitutes the response. The conditioned stimuli that Pavlov used most frequently were auditory—first tones sounded on tuning forks, then bells or tones from speakers. When another stimulus was needed, it could be a brief light flash, the presentation of a card with a diagram on it, or a vibratory stimulus on the animal's skin.

Eyelid Conditioning

In eyelid conditioning, the US is a puff of air directed at the eye. The response consists of an eyeblink. An advantage of the eyeblink response is that it can occur very rapidly and can be measured precisely by photographic techniques. It is also common to many different organisms. With the eyeblink response the CS is often a sudden increase in the illumination of a disk that the subject watches. This increase itself causes a slight movement of the eyelid (called the *alpha* response); after conditioning, the light CS causes a much stronger blink than it would have if it had not been paired with the air puff.

Eyelid conditioning has been applied to humans, monkeys, dogs, rats, and, frequently, rabbits. The rabbit has a membrane between the eyelid and the eye called the *nictitating membrane.* This membrane opens and shuts like the eyelid and is also sensitive to the puff of air. In some recent experiments a mild electric shock has been used instead of the puff of air as the US. The advantage of using the shock is that it can be applied following the CS regardless of whether the rabbit blinks with its nictitating membrane. That is, its annoying effect cannot be avoided, as the air puffs can, by blinking.*

CS's other than the light increase have also been used with eyelid conditioning. Various tones and vibratory stimuli have been successfully used as CS's.

GSR and Heart-Rate Conditioning

The galvanic skin response (GSR) is a change in electrical resistance between one area of the skin and another. It is often measured between the front and back of the hand in humans (as shown in Figure 1.1). This change in resistance may be caused by sweating, but there is disagreement as to whether sweatiness is the only factor involved. In any case, the GSR reliably follows electric shock and other painful stimuli and is frequently the measured response in classical conditioning experiments with humans.

---

*A trial on which the US is avoided would not technically be a classical conditioning trial. It would more appropriately be classified as instrumental conditioning, as we shall see in the next chapter. Procedures that prevent the avoidance of the US are preferable for studying classical conditioning by itself.

Heart rate can also be conditioned in humans and other animals. The usual CS is a tone and the US is a shock. A peculiarity of heart-rate conditioning is that the initial response to the CS alone (the alpha response) is often opposite in direction to the unconditioned response to shock. For instance, a person's heart rate decreases to below normal when a tone is presented alone but increases to above normal after a shock. In such cases, will the eventual conditioned response to the tone be more like the unconditioned response to the tone or the unconditioned response to the shock? The problem is complicated by the effects of breathing and the variation of heart rate *during* the CS, but the bulk of the evidence seems to indicate that the eventual CR—the response to the tone —is more like the original response to the tone (the alpha response) than it is like the unconditioned response to the shock. Pairing of shock with tone seems to augment the alpha response rather than to create a new response to the CS. Nevertheless, it is clear that pairing of tone and shock changes the response to the tone. For some psychologists this is enough to earn the label "conditioning."

Conditioned Emotional Response (CER)

The conditioned emotional response differs sharply from other types of classical conditioning in that its measurement is indirect. The more conditioning, the less responding observed. Let us consider an example. A rat is trained to press a lever to get food and its rate of pressing is continuously monitored. Then a tone is sounded for several seconds. Initially the rat stops pressing when the tone comes on, but after a few tone presentations the rat presses the bar as fast during the tone as in its absence. (Habituation to the tone has occurred.) Then the tone, still periodically presented, is followed by electric shock. The rat will again suppress its bar-pressing during the tone, and although the suppression may not be as severe after a while as it was at first, the rat will continue to suppress its bar-pressing each time the tone comes on. This suppression is called a *conditioned emotional response* (CER). It is measured, not by what happens during the tone, but by what does not happen—the rat does not press the bar. A CER effect on a cumulative record of bar-pressing is shown in Figure 4.3*

The theory behind the use of this technique in classical conditioning is that the rat does make a response at the onset of the tone (CS)—an emotional response such as anxiety or fear. The emotional response is assumed to interfere with the rat's bar-presses, causing their rate to decrease. This decrease, then, is taken as the measure of emotional response. The more fear conditioned, the fewer bar-presses measured during the tone and vice versa. The concept of the

---

*This cumulative record also shows a "contrast effect," the temporary speeding up of responding just after the change from a relatively aversive to a relatively safe period. We shall discuss this effect in Chapter 9.

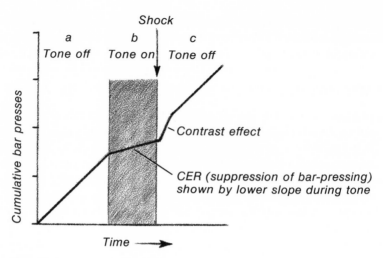

FIGURE 4.3
A cumulative record of the CER effect for a rat's bar-pressing. The rat's
bar-presses are occasionally followed by food (reinforced) during periods
(a), (b), and (c). (The periods of eating are not indicated on the cumulative
record.) In this example we assume that the rat has been previously
exposed to several tone–food pairings. The onset of the tone suppresses
the rate of bar-pressing. The shock halts bar-pressing briefly at the
beginning of period (c). Then the rat presses even faster (contrast effect)
and finally returns to a rate of pressing about equal to that of period (a).

emotional response serves as a mediator between the shock and the observed
suppression of bar-presses. Whether a concept such as fear is necessary to explain why the rat presses the bar more slowly is a subject of considerable debate
between psychologists. We shall discuss it further in Chapter 9. Those psychologists who prefer not to use the intermediary concept call this phenomenon
conditioned suppression, with the implication that the suppression itself is the
conditioned response. In any case, it is a widespread phenomenon occurring
with CS's other than tones, such as lights and even odors, with US's other than
shocks such as loud noises and short periods of darkness (blackouts), and with
responses other than bar-presses of rats, such as pecking of pigeons and jumping
of dogs. Its properties seem to be similar to those of other classical conditioning procedures.

Other Classical Conditioning Procedures

We shall have occasion in this and subsequent chapters to discuss other
classical conditioning techniques such as leg-withdrawal of dogs with electric-
shock stimuli, visceral conditioning of rats, and a process called "autoshaping,"
which is opposite to the CER effect just discussed in that various responses are
increased instead of decreased. We shall describe these procedures as they arise.

The reader should realize that systematic experiments in classical conditioning have been conducted for three-quarters of a century, that hundreds of techniques have been used, only a small fraction of which we can describe here.

TEMPORAL RELATIONS BETWEEN CS AND US

In practice the CS–US pairing of Figure 4.2 is often called *simultaneous conditioning*, even though the onset of the US occurs slightly after the onset of the CS. With Pavlov's procedures the optimum delay (the delay that provides the maximum conditioning as measured by the techniques of Figure 4.2b and c) is about 1/2 second. The strength of conditioning falls rapidly with shorter delays so that, when the CS and US are actually simultaneous, conditioning is less than one–third as strong as with the slight delay. With longer delays conditioning strength also falls from the maximum, although not as rapidly as with shorter delays.

Long delays may be programmed in two ways. In one, called *delay conditioning,* the CS is left on during the delay; in the other, called *trace conditioning,* the CS is turned on briefly and then turned off during the delay. (The two procedures are illustrated in Figure 4.4b and c.) With delays of around ten seconds some conditioning is obtained with both procedures. The pattern of responding is the same for both procedures although stronger responding is obtained with delay than with trace conditioning. Let us consider what this pattern of responding is with a tone as the CS, food powder as the US, and salivation as the response. At first salivation occurs only after food powder is delivered (stage 1, Figure 4.4). Then some salivation begins to occur at the onset of the tone (stage 2) so that we have two bursts of salivation, one right after the tone onset and one right after the food onset (conditioned salivation and unconditioned salivation). Then the conditioned salivation begins to appear later and later during the delay until finally it occurs just before the food powder is due (stage 3). According to Pavlov, this suppression of salivation until food powder is about to be delivered is a form of internal *inhibition;* he called it *inhibition of delay.* If a loud noise was sounded during the delay period it seemed to release the inhibition—the dog would salivate immediately. It was as if the dog were holding back its salivation, which the noise then released. This loud noise was said by Pavlov to be disinhibitory. We shall discuss disinhibition further when we take up the phenomenon of extinction.

Another form of conditioning used by Pavlov is called *temporal conditioning.* It is shown in Figure 4.4d. Temporal conditioning consists simply in presenting the US at fixed intervals with no external CS. The CS was assumed by Pavlov to be internal temporal stimuli. After prolonged exposure to temporal conditioning, the conditioned response usually occurs just before each US delivery. When, in the previous chapter, we discussed patterns of behavior with fixed intervals of stimulation, as in the Staddon and Simmelhag experiment, we were discussing temporal conditioning.

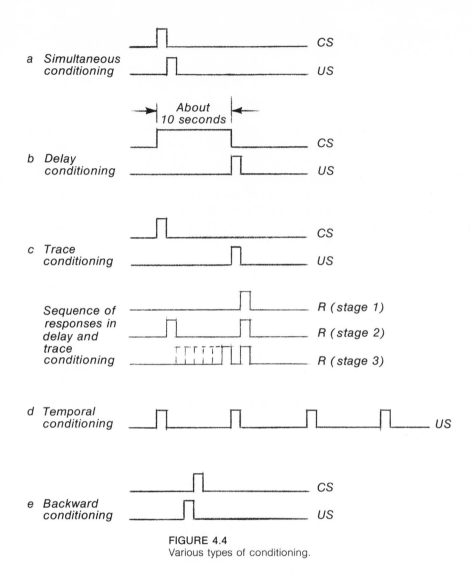

FIGURE 4.4
Various types of conditioning.

Finally we should mention *backward conditioning* (Figure 4.4e). With backward conditioning the delay between the CS and US is negative, so to speak. Remember that when the CS and US are actually simultaneous, little conditioning occurs. With backward conditioning, the strength of the conditioned response is still less. In fact there is some disagreement whether any conditioning occurs at all with this paradigm. At any rate, it is clear that, since the response would not precede the US, conditioning could not be measured by the method of Figure 4.2b. The method of Figure 4.2c, eliminating the US, would have to be used.

Figure 4.5 is an idealized function showing how strength of eyelid conditioning varies with the time between a discrete CS and US. Similar functions are often obtained with salivary conditioning. To the left of the vertical line (zero on the abscissa) is backward conditioning. Immediately to the right is simultaneous conditioning, and far to the right is trace conditioning. Note that trace conditioning is weak. This is not always the case. With certain CS's and US's (as we shall see in Chapter 7) trace conditioning of several hours is possible.

PSEUDOCONDITIONING

Suppose we select a CS and a US and, after pairing them and testing the results as shown in Figure 4.2, find that the unconditioned response is now elicited by the CS. Can we safely assume that conditioning has taken place? Unfortunately, no. In some cases, the US presentation may change the state of the organism so that the CS produces the response by itself without any necessary connection to the US. Consider, for example, an experiment using electric shock as the US and a vibratory tactile stimulus as the CS (see Figure 4.6). First vibrations are applied to one hand of a human subject. No effect is found. Then vibrations are paired with shock to the hand, and we observe a withdrawal of the hand. Then vibrations are applied alone, and again the hand is withdrawn. Is this effect the result of classical conditioning? The test is to get another subject, apply electric shock alone (unpaired with vibrations), then apply vibrations alone, and see if the hand is now withdrawn. If it is, we can be fairly sure that the shock merely made the hand more sensitive to the vibrations, and that we did not observe classical conditioning in the first subject.

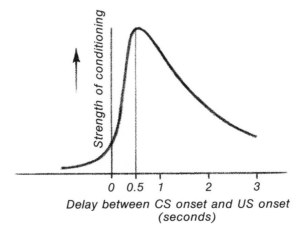

FIGURE 4.5
Idealized function showing typical strength of conditioning as delay between CS onset and US onset is varied.

Present vibrating stimulus alone
Observe no withdrawal

Classical conditioning?   *Pseudoconditioning test*

Pair V with S

Present S alone

Observe withdrawal

Observe withdrawal

Present V alone

Present V alone

Observe withdrawal

Observe withdrawal

FIGURE 4.6
An example of a test for pseudo classical conditioning. If the results of
these two procedures (*left* and *right*) are withdrawals similar in latency and
extent, then it is possible that none of the withdrawals is a classically
conditioned response. However, if there is no withdrawal after the test
procedure (*bottom right*) but a withdrawal after the classical conditioning
procedure (*bottom left*), then the response at bottom left is a genuine
classically conditioned response. In this case, "V" stands for a vibration
and "S" stands for a shock.

A critical test of classically conditioned behavior is to determine whether the *relation of the CS and US* is necessary to produce the behavior. When we perform a classical conditioning experiment and observe what appears to be a conditioned response, but then find that the relation between the CS and US is not necessary to produce that response, we have merely observed *pseudo-conditioning*. It is always important to test classical conditioning experiments to see if they can be explained on the basis of pseudoconditioning. Figure 4.6 shows the sequence of the pseudoconditioning test.

EXTINCTION

So far we have been talking about conditioning as if it were a one-way process. We have noted, for example, that by a procedure such as that shown in Figure 4.2 we can condition a dog's salivation response to a tone struck on a tuning fork. Is that dog fated, then, for the rest of its life, to salivate when it hears the tone? No, it is not. Any response can be eliminated if the CS occurs a sufficient number of times without the US following. We recall that the CS was occasionally presented alone in the test trials of part (c) of Figure 4.2. However, it was isolated like an island amid a sea of conditioning trials, like those in part (a) of Figure 4.2. Suppose we arranged large blocks of trials in which the CS was always presented alone. What would happen to the response? We would find that the response would begin to decrease in magnitude so that eventually it would cease to appear. This process is called *extinction* of the response. A typical extinction curve is shown in Figure 4.7.

Extinction is not simply forgetting, with the passage of time. For extinction to occur the relationship forged between the conditioned and unconditioned stimuli must be broken. Our emotional reaction to our kindergarten teacher's perfume will diminish faster if we smell the perfume many times after leaving kindergarten (extinction) than it will by the simple passage of years.*

The usual procedure for extinguishing a response is quite straight-forward. The US is simply omitted from the normal conditioning procedure.

In order to clarify the nature of the process of extinction, let us pay an imaginary visit to Pavlov's laboratory. Suppose we bring a dog with us, one that has never been exposed to any laboratory conditioning procedure; if Pavlov sounds his tuning fork, our dog will not salivate. Suppose another dog, one of Pavlov's, was previously conditioned so that it salivated to a tuning–fork tone but that its response was subsequently extinguished. When Pavlov sounds his tuning fork, his dog salivates as little as ours. It seems as though the conditioning of Pavlov's dog has been "wiped away" by the process of extinction and that no one could ever tell the two dogs apart on the basis of their behavior.

---

*There is some dispute over whether conditioning dissipates at all with simple passage of time. On the one hand, conditioned responses do attenuate with longer intervals between training and testing. On the other hand, the subject might have experienced stimuli during the interval, similar enough to the CS, to constitute inadvertent extinction trials.

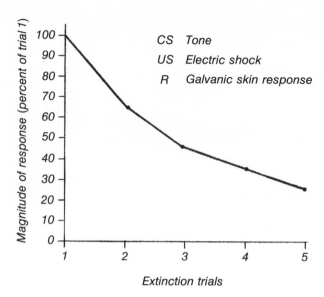

FIGURE 4.7
Typical extinction curve. Each extinction trial is a
presentation of the CS alone. In this case the curve shows
the extinction of the galvanic skin response following 24
conditioning trials. Each point represents the average
response of 20 human subjects. [Data from Hovland, 1936.]

In fact, Pavlov found that he *could* distinguish between two such dogs if he
presented the tone and then sounded a loud noise suddenly and unexpectedly.
The dog with the extinguished response (Pavlov's, in our example) would
salivate, and the other (ours) would not salivate. Pavlov reasoned that extinction did not simply "wipe away" conditioning, but that it added another force
equal and opposite to the force of conditioning. He called the force added by
extinction an *inhibitory force*. He thought that the sudden loud noise somehow
temporarily removed the inhibitory effect of extinction and allowed salivation to begin.

Pavlov had discovered that if the noise was sounded during conditioning it
stopped salivation. In other words, the noise acted in the opposite direction
to whichever process was going on. It could not do this if a response that had
been both conditioned and extinguished was identical to a response that had
never been conditioned in the first place. Pavlov called the extinction process a
form of *internal inhibition*. The action of the loud noise during extinction,
which produced salivation, he called *disinhibition*, or release of inhibition. The
action of the loud noise during conditioning, which inhibited salivation, he
called *external inhibition*.

The process of internal inhibition may be compared to a system of weights
and counterweights. Imagine a weight attached to a block of wood (as in

Figure 4.8) and tending to pull it towards the left (assume the weight of the scales themselves is insignificant). There are two ways to stop the block from moving towards the left. One is to cut the string or otherwise remove the weight (an analogy to "wiping away" conditioning). Another way is to add another weight on the other side (an analogy to a force of inhibition). Both procedures produce a stationary block (extinction). If the weights and strings are hidden from view, how can you tell which system applies? You can distinguish between conditions (b) and (c) in Figure 4.8 by cutting one of the strings

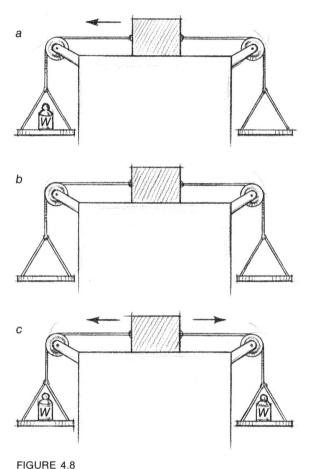

FIGURE 4.8
This system of weights shows how extinction might operate as either a negative or a positive process. (a) If conditioning is seen as the pull of a weight, extinction can be either (b) a negative process that simply removes the weight, or (c) a positive process that adds a new weight to the system to counterbalance the effect of conditioning.

(an analogy to the disinhibitory effect of the loud noise). If this is done to the apparatus shown in (b), nothing will happen to the block. But if it is done to the apparatus in (c), the block will move suddenly in one direction (this is analogous to the reappearance of the response).

One other phenomenon also discovered by Pavlov, deserves mention here. This is the phenomenon of *spontaneous recovery*. Suppose now a dog's salivation is conditioned with the tone, and then extinguished until it fails to occur with the tone. Suppose the dog is taken away and then, several weeks later, brought back to the laboratory. The tone is sounded and, even though salivation was completely extinguished, the dog salivates again. This is called spontaneous recovery of salivation, and Pavlov ascribed it to the difference between the temporal course of conditioning and inhibition in the brain. The inhibiting forces, he believed, tended to dissipate faster than the excitatory forces so that with time an initial balance between excitation (conditioning) and inhibition would be upset in favor of excitation.

GENERALIZATION AND DISCRIMINATION

There is bound to be some *generalization* in a process through which a new pattern of behavior is acquired. For instance, if a dog's behavior is modified in a laboratory so that the dog salivates when it hears a tone sounded by a tuning fork, another tone slightly higher or lower in pitch will also make it salivate. Generalization is also evidenced when a child, sometimes to the embarrassment of his parents, calls every man he meets "Daddy." Of course, the child will eventually learn to reserve the name "Daddy" for his male parent. When this occurs, we say he has learned to make a *discrimination*.

Let us consider an experiment performed in the United States in 1934 on the generalization of a classically conditioned response. The GSR (galvanic skin response) was conditioned in a group of college students: the US in the experiment was mild electric shock and the CS was a vibrating instrument applied to the skin. For some subjects the instrument was applied to the shoulder and for others it was applied to the calf. As training progressed, the amount of GSR measured on test trials (when the CS was presented without the shock) was seen to increase. Then, on later test trials, the instrument was occasionally applied at places on the skin *other* than where conditioning was originally established. The farther away the instrument was applied on these later test trials, the less was the response.* Figure 4.9 shows the magnitude of the response as a function of the distance from the original point of application. The kind of curve shown in Figure 4.9 is called a *generalization gradient.*†

---

*At the time, no pseudoconditioning test was performed, but subsequent research has indicated that a large part of the measured response was due to genuine conditioning.

†The specific spot at which the vibrating stimulus was applied was not important in determining the gradient; what was important was the distance from the original CS, wherever that CS may have been applied.

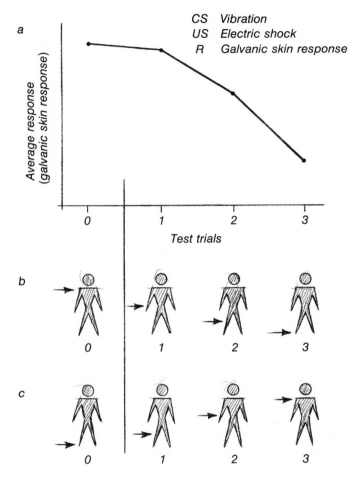

FIGURE 4.9
The generalization of a classically conditioned response. (a) This graph shows the decline of a galvanic skin response to vibration as the vibration is moved progressively farther from the original site of conditioning. (b) Some subjects were initially conditioned on the shoulder. (c) Some subjects were initially conditioned on the ankle. [Data from Bass and Hull, 1934.]

Generalization gradients like the one in Figure 4.9 are by no means unalterable. Suppose we have a set of several similar stimuli, only one of which we want to be a CS. Suppose that, even though we use only the desired stimulus as the CS in a classical conditioning experiment, we find that the subject generalizes and responds to the other stimuli too. How can we eliminate responses to these other stimuli but retain responses to the one we want to be a CS? We may try alternating conditioning trials that contain both the desired CS and the US with extinction trials that contain no US—only the unwanted stimuli. Our hope is that the organism will learn to discriminate the particular stimulus to which we want it to respond from the unwanted stimuli. This procedure works—but significantly, it works only up to a point.

We know Pavlov's view that extinction is an active process of inhibition, not just a matter of "wiping away" old conditions but more like adding counterweights to a hypothetical system of weights (Figure 4.8). Keeping this in mind, consider the following experiment, performed by one of Pavlov's students, Shenger-Krestovnikova. She trained dogs to salivate by a method similar to Pavlov's except that instead of a tone she used a circle drawn on a card as the CS. She found that after the salivation response had been conditioned in the presence of a circle, the response generalized to the extent that the dogs would also salivate when they saw an ellipse, like those in Figure 4.10. In order to condition discrimination between (a) and (b), (a) was presented with the US and (b) was presented without the US. Following this procedure, the dogs would salivate in response to (a) but not in response to (b). Then the same procedure was repeated with (a) and (c), then (a) and (d)—(d) being an ellipse very much like the circle. According to Pavlov, this is what happened when (a) and (d) were discriminated:

> In this case, although a considerable degree of discrimination did develop, it was far from being complete. After three weeks of work upon this differentiation not only did the discrimination fail to improve, but it became considerably worse, and finally disappeared altogether. At the same time the whole behaviour of the animal underwent an abrupt change. The hitherto quiet dog began to squeal in its stand, kept wriggling about, tore off with its teeth the apparatus for mechanical stimulation of the skin, and bit through the tubes connecting the animal's room with the observer, a behaviour which never happened before. On being taken into the experimental room the dog now barked violently, which was also contrary to its usual custom; in short it presented all the symptoms of acute neurosis. On testing the cruder differentiations they were also found to be destroyed. . . . [Pavlov, 1927, p. 291]

One cannot help but draw a parallel to the behavior of humans when they are required to perform for long periods of time at the limit of their discriminative capacities. Humans can make just so many discriminations, until, like

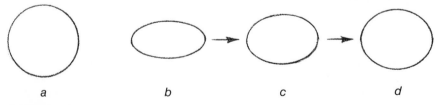

     a   *b*   *c*   *d*

FIGURE 4.10
Shenger-Krestovnikova's stimuli. Dog's responses were conditioned to a circle (a). Their responses to an ellipse (b) were extinguished. As the ellipse was gradually changed to look more like a circle, as in (c) and (d), the dogs' ability to discriminate broke down, and, in Pavlov's words, their behavior "presented all the symptoms of acute neurosis."

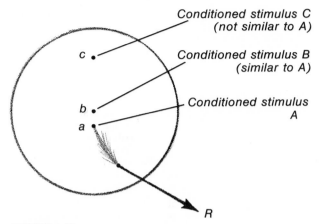

FIGURE 4.11
Pavlov's brain model (See Figure 2.16) extended to account
for generalization. The critical assumption is that similar stimuli
terminate near each other in the brain and so tend to elicit the
same response.

Pavlov's dogs, or rather like those of Shenger-Krestovnikova, they start making mistakes and are unable to perform tasks that were previously easy for them. In extreme cases they may develop the "symptoms of acute neurosis" to which Pavlov refers.

Pavlov's ideas about generalization and discrimination are consistent with his ideas of how the brain worked (Figure 2.16). Figure 4.11 extends this view to account for generalization. Stimulus A, let us suppose, has been a CS and now elicits response R. If stimulus B is similar to A, it will, according to Pavlov, terminate in the brain (at b) near where stimulus A terminates (at a) and so the energy from stimulus B will bridge the gap between (a) and (b) with little loss and elicit R in almost full strength. With stimulus C, different from A, and therefore terminating far from point (a) in the brain, much resistance impedes the path of the energy from (c) to (a) and so stimulus C elicits R with little strength.

If (b) is not too close to (a), discrimination training, with A repeatedly reinforced (the US presented) and B repeatedly unreinforced, can set up inhibitory forces in the path from (b) to (a) and prevent stimulus B from eliciting the response. If (b) is too close to (a), discrimination training will set up the opposing forces discussed above and cause experimental neurosis.

HIGHER-ORDER CONDITIONING AND CONDITIONED INHIBITION

Phase (a) of Figure 4.12 shows simple classical conditioning. CS_1 becomes capable of eliciting the response by virtue of its pairing with the US. Now

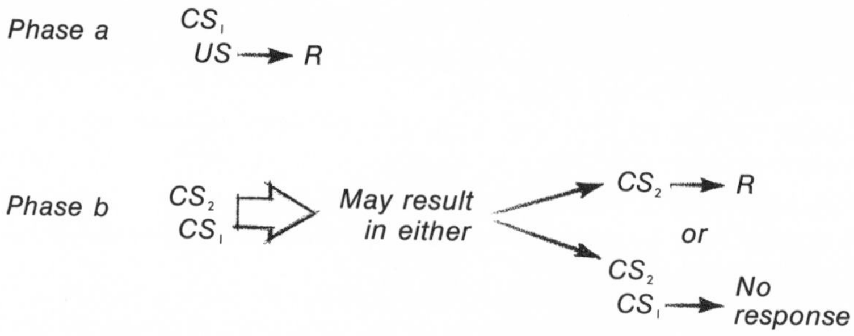

Phase a   CS₁
               US ——▶ R

Phase b   CS₂ ⟹   May result ——▶   CS₂ ——▶ R
               CS₁   in either   or

                                         CS₂
                                         CS₁ ——▶ No
                                                  response

FIGURE 4.12

Higher-order conditioning and conditioned inhibition as two possible results of
the same procedure. Phase (a) is simple simultaneous conditioning with CS₁
and a US. In phase (b) CS₂ is paired with CS₁ but without the US. When this
procedure gives CS₂ the capability of eliciting the response it is called
higher-order conditioning. When the compound in phase (b) fails to elicit the
response it is called conditioned inhibition.

suppose that after phase (a) is completed, another CS, CS_2, is presented before CS_1 and the US is eliminated, as in phase (b) of Figure 4.12. There are two possible results of this procedure. One is that CS_2, after being paired with CS_1, will come to elicit the response by itself. In this case, CS_1 serves as an effective US for CS_2, transferring its power to elicit the response to that new stimulus. When this happens the process is called *higher-order conditioning*. This process is the basis for the theoretical extension of classical conditioning to account for complex human behavior where no US is immediately apparent. According to Pavlov much human behavior is the product of higher-order conditioning. By extension of this procedure, the response should be transferable to a CS_3, CS_4, and so on. In the laboratory, however, higher-order conditioning beyond CS_2 has not been easy to obtain.

Another possible result of the pairing of CS_2 and CS_1 without the US, as in phase (b), is that no response at all will be observed. This result is especially likely if phases (a) and (b) are alternated frequently. Then, CS_2 becomes a signal that the US will *not* be presented—what Pavlov calls a *conditioned inhibitor*. A response is made to CS_1 if it appears alone, but no response is made to CS_1 if it is preceded by CS_2. For example, an attacking dog (CS_1) might make you run away, especially if the dog has previously bitten you (US→R). But the dog would not make you run away if you noticed first that it was tied to a post (CS_2).

In a given instance, which will be observed—higher-order conditioning or conditioned inhibition? It depends on the temporal relations between the stimuli. In the laboratory higher-order conditioning is an unstable phenomenon since it is superimposed on what is essentially an extinction condition. Higher-order conditioning is more likely during the first few pairings of CS_2 and CS_1. It is strengthened by longer intervals between CS_2 and CS_1, but even in this case it eventually disappears. The more training with phases (a) and (b), the more vivid the stimuli, and the closer the pairings, the more likely it is that conditioned inhibition will be observed.*

It is theoretically possible that in phase (b) both higher-order conditioning (a response between CS_2 and CS_1) and conditioned inhibition (no response after CS_1) could occur together. In this case, the original conditioned response would be inhibited, but another response, established on the basis of the now inhibited behavior, would occur.

STIMULUS SUBSTITUTION

In Chapter 2, and previously in this chapter, we briefly described Pavlov's speculations about what goes on in the brain during classical conditioning. According to Pavlov, the CS, after conditioning, acts through the same nervous pathways as the US. This hypothesis leads directly to the view of conditioning known as *stimulus substitution,* in which the CS is seen to elicit the same response as the US. The UR and CR may differ in strength as conditioning proceeds but cannot, according to the principle of stimulus substitution, differ in quality.

This view and an alternative view are illustrated in Figure 4.13. In View I (stimulus substitution), CR and UR are identical. According to this view, the

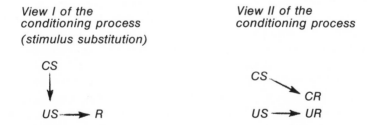

FIGURE 4.13
Two views of the associative process underlying conditioning. View I (stimulus substitution) holds that CS and US produce identical responses. View II allows the two responses to differ.

---

*In everyday life, higher-order conditioning may persist because occasionally CS_2, CS_1 and the US will all be paired together as when a weather report of rain (CS_2), cloudy skies (CS_1) and rain itself (US) occur in succession.

smell of bread reminds us of the bread, so we salivate. This view comes down to us, through Pavlov, from the British associationists and Ebbinghaus, who asserted that the representations of the stimuli in the mind (the ideas) themselves become associated.

The fact that the stimuli now have a common response would be only an indication that the association of ideas has taken place. Pavlov believed that the representations of the stimuli are events in the brain, not the mind, but still the common response would only be an indication that these representations had become associated.

View II allows the CR to differ from the UR. Often theorists who hold this view maintain that the CR that eventually occurs before the presentation of the US differs from the UR by being preparatory. In Pavlov's salivation experiment the CR is salivation because salivation prepares the dog for the food powder to be inserted in its mouth. As this example suggests, View II derives from functional psychology.

In most cases of classical conditioning the response that prepares an organism best for the onset of the US is the same as the response to the US. For instance, an eyeblink is the response to a puff of air to the eye and it is also the response that best prepares the organism for an oncoming puff of air if it is made before the air arrives. Salivation is the response to food powder in the mouth and it is also the response that best prepares the organism for the presentation of food powder. Withdrawal is the response to electric shock and it is also the response that best prepares the organism for an oncoming electric shock. All of these are common US's and R's in experiments on classical conditioning. The response to the CS (the CR) with all of them is the same in form as the response to the US (the UR). Is this because the actual UR is excited by the CS, as the stimulus-substitution theory would hold, or is it because the organism is preparing for the oncoming US after being warned by the CS? The same response would be observed in either case.

In 1937 K. Zener investigated this question by conducting a conditioning experiment with dogs. Instead of restraining the dogs, as Pavlov had in his experiments, Zener let them move freely about in a cage. He presented them with periodic signals followed by food and took motion pictures of the dogs' behavior during the signals and between signals. He found that though the dogs' glandular response, salivation, was the same (1) in preparation for food and (2) in the presence of food, their motor responses were different. In preparation for food, the dogs engaged in exploratory behavior with much motor activity. In the presence of food, the dogs' behavior was confined to chewing; they did not move about. Moreover, the dogs engaged in exploration, sniffing, and barking during the signal—but no chewing. The stimulus-substitution hypothesis would lead one to expect chewing too; if the signal excites the same motor responses as the food, the dogs should chew as well as salivate during the signal. Thus Zener's observations appear to constitute evidence against the stimulus-substitution hypothesis. Until recently, however, most psychologists believed that motor responses (as opposed to autonomic responses such as salivation and GSR) were not subject to classical conditioning techniques; consequently, Zener's findings did not seem relevant to classical conditioning. But many recent experiments have shown that classical conditioning of motor responses is possible and even, in some cases, easy to do. To the extent, then, that classical conditioning is a general phenomenon, Zener's findings demonstrate its mechanisms.

The hypothesis that the CR and the UR are different has gained added support from analyses, in salivary conditioning experiments, showing that the chemical content of dogs' saliva during the preparatory period (when only the CS is present) is actually different from the chemical content when food is present. In heart-rate conditioning, as we mentioned previously, the CR is often opposite in direction to the UR. In eyeblink conditioning as well, differences in blinking in response to the CS and US are observed. On the whole then, the stimulus-substitution hypothesis, at least in its strongest form, as in Pavlov's brain model, has been disproved—the CR does not equal the UR. Whether the CR is wholly preparation for the US or whether another physiological mechanism modifies the UR to create the CR is still unknown.

COMPOUND STIMULI

So far we have considered CS's and US's in isolation, ignoring the background against which these stimuli are presented. Now, however, we must abandon these simplifying assumptions and consider the background stimuli. In most classical conditioning experiments each trial consists of a single CS presentation. Between trials, we have so far assumed, nothing occurs. But, much as we might like to imagine that, subjects in conditioning experiments do not exist in a vacuum. Between and during trials, they experience a host of unmeasured stimuli, which we might call background stimuli. When the CS is presented it is actually a compound stimulus consisting of the CS superimposed on the background stimuli. Because the background stimuli are difficult to measure, compound stimuli are studied by superimposing one CS (say, a tone) upon another (say, a light). The importance of these studies lies in the fact that *any* conditioning situation, however simple, may be viewed as a compound-stimulus situation with the CS superimposed upon background stimuli. What we learn from deliberately compounding two external CS's (such as a light and a tone) may then be applied to basic conditioning paradigms such as those illustrated in Figure 4.4.

WARNING

The material in the next section is more complex than that in the rest of the chapter. Although the mathematics is kept simple, the student will have to carefully follow complex diagrams and keep a set of abstract symbols straight in his mind. It is worth the effort, however, because most current theories of classical conditioning are based on the Wagner-Rescorla model.

The Wagner-Rescorla Model for Compound Stimuli

Allen Wagner and Robert Rescorla, psychologists at Yale University, have recently proposed a model that, with relatively few assumptions, accounts for much of the data collected with compound stimuli. Originally their model was designed to account for a phenomenon called "blocking." This phenomenon, shown in Figure 4.14, was first reported by Leo Kamin at McMaster University in Canada. Kamin observed that when a US is paired first with one of a pair of CS's (as it is for the experimental group in phase (a) of Figure 4.14) and then with both CS's together (phase b), the first CS (CS_1) gains the power to elicit the response by itself (phase c), but the second CS (CS_2) elicits no response by itself, or only a very slight response (phase d). On the other hand, when for a control group the two CS's are presented with the US, without either one having first been presented alone with the US, a test presentation of either stimulus is followed by a response. It is as if, for the experimental group, the

	Experimental group	Control group
Phase		
a (conditioning)	CS_1 $US \longrightarrow R$	
b (conditioning)	CS_1 CS_2 $US \longrightarrow R$	CS_1 CS_2 $US \longrightarrow R$
c (test)	$CS_1 \longrightarrow R$	$CS_1 \longrightarrow R$
d (test)	$CS_2 \longrightarrow$ No response	$CS_2 \longrightarrow R$

FIGURE 4.14
Kamin's blocking experiment. For the experimental group the conditioning with CS_1 in phase (a) seems to block conditioning with CS_2 in phase (b) as shown by the test of phase (d). Without such treatment in phase (a) (the control group) there is conditioning with CS_2 in phase (b).

prior presentation of CS_1 in phase (a) blocked the subsequent association of CS_2 with the US. The blocking experiment was originally performed with the CER paradigm (suppression of bar-pressing in rats), but it seems to work with several classical conditioning paradigms and with various organisms.

At first the blocking phenomenon was explained, vaguely, in terms of "attention." The procedure in Figure 4.14a draws the attention of the subjects in the experimental group to CS_1. Later, these subjects do not notice the addition of CS_2 in phase (b) and so no conditioning takes place with the new CS. For the control group, CS_1 and CS_2 are presented together and so attention is paid to both CS's and conditioning takes place with both CS's. The problem with the concept of "attention" is that it is too vague to do much more than just describe what we observe. We all have a pretty good idea of what attention means, but it is difficult to quantify or to use to predict the results of new experiments.

Wagner and Rescorla have explained blocking in a more molecular way by means of a few key assumptions, which experimentation has now verified. First let us consider how they account for simple conditioning. Then we can apply the model to blocking. Wagner and Rescorla assume that with successive pairings of CS and US the strength of conditioning (as measured by the magnitude of the response the CS evokes by itself) grows as in Figure 4.15a. The rate of increase is determined by the salience (vividness) of the CS and the ability of the subject to learn. Salient stimuli and sensitive subjects will produce faster rates of increase. The asymptote of the curve is determined by the strength of the response elicited by the US. With repeated pairings, the CS becomes capable of producing a response more and more like that of the US.*

To be a bit more technical, the curve is determined by the following equation for the amount of conditioning on a given trial:

$$\Delta R_{CS} = c\,(R_{US} - R_{CS})$$

where ΔR_{CS} = increase of strength of response to the CS on that trial,

         R_{US} = strength of response to the US,

         R_{CS} = strength of response to the CS before the trial,

         c   = a fraction between 0 and 1 determined by salience of the stimulus and ability of subject to learn. This constant cannot be estimated in advance but must be determined from the shape of the conditioning curve.

---

*For convenience the theory accepts the stimulus-substitution hypothesis and assumes that the CR and UR are identical. However, this assumption is not strictly necessary. In the theory R_{US} may stand for whatever response is being conditioned, whether or not it actually equals the unconditioned response.

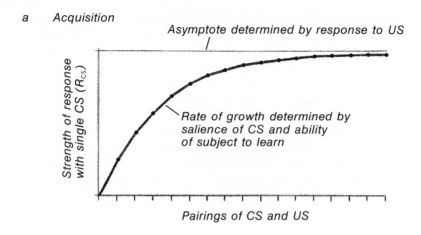

a   Acquisition

b   Extinction

FIGURE 4.15
Wagner and Rescorla's model of growth of classically conditioned response during
conditioning and decay during extinction. For simplicity we have assumed that rate of
growth and decay (the constant (c) in Equation 1) is 0.25. That is, on each trial, growth
(or decay) is 0.25 of the remaining distance to the asymptote.

What this equation says is that on any trial the amount learned (ΔR_{CS}) is
some constant fraction (c) of the amount still to be learned ($R_{US} - R_{CS}$). When
the amount already learned is low (the left part of the curve) a lot is learned
on a given trial. When the amount already learned is high (the right part of the
curve) very little more is learned on a given trial. Many learning curves actually
do look like the one in Figure 4.15a. They represent the common, everyday
experience of progressing rapidly when you first start learning something new
but then reaching a point where further practice only brings you up a small
notch. The curves might as well represent improvement with practice at
bowling or golf.

The extinction curve shown in Figure 4.15b is described by the same equation, except that $R_{US} = 0$, R_{CS} starts off at a high value, and each ΔR_{CS} is negative. In other words, extinction is thought of as a pairing of the CS with a US equal to zero. Thus, extinction and learning are symmetrical; extinction is learning to stop responding. This is similar to Pavlov's notion that extinction is an inhibitory force acting opposite to conditioning.

The functions of Figure 4.15 were not new with Wagner and Rescorla. They had long before been used to describe learning and extinction. Wagner and Rescorla, however, were the first to apply them to situations with compound stimuli. To do this they made the simple assumption that the strength of response to a compound is the sum of the strengths of response to each of its elements. In symbols:

$$R_{CS_1 + CS_2} = R_{CS_1} + R_{CS_2}$$

In conditioning trials with two CS's compounded together the strength gained will be distributed to the individual CS's in proportion to their salience. Column (a) of Figure 4.16 shows how conditioning to a compound would be distributed to two individual CS's of equal salience. Columns (b) and (c) show how conditioning with any individual CS strengthens the responses to the compound of that CS with any other CS even though the other CS may itself have no strength.

These assumptions are enough to account for blocking. Let us follow the strengths of R_{CS_1}, R_{CS_2}, and their compound through the blocking experiment diagrammed in Figure 4.14. Figure 4.17 shows how the conditioning strengths vary during the two conditioning phases. In the initial phase (phase a), for the experimental group, when CS_1 only is paired with the US both R_{CS_1} and the potential compound $R_{CS_1 + CS_2}$ gain in strength as Figure 4.16b indicates they should. Because the compound has already gained most of its strength in the first phase, little learning takes place in the second phase, and so there is little strength to distribute to R_{CS_1} and R_{CS_2}. For R_{CS_1} this hardly matters since it was strengthened in the first phase. But R_{CS_2} got no conditioning strength in the first phase and so when tested, hardly evokes any response.

For the control group, CS_1 and CS_2 (assuming equal salience) both get equal conditioning and both evoke the response (at about half strength) when tested.

It may seem to the reader that this is a roundabout way to explain a phenomenon that could be explained intuitively in terms of "attention." But the advantage of the more precise model is that those who master it can use it to make predictions of the results of other experiments, whereas those who do not are left with their intuition, which, often as not, will prove faulty.

Several obvious predictions follow from the Wagner-Rescorla model. One is that blocking should diminish with fewer trials during phase (a). A second is that blocking should diminish if CS_1 is less salient then CS_2. A third is that

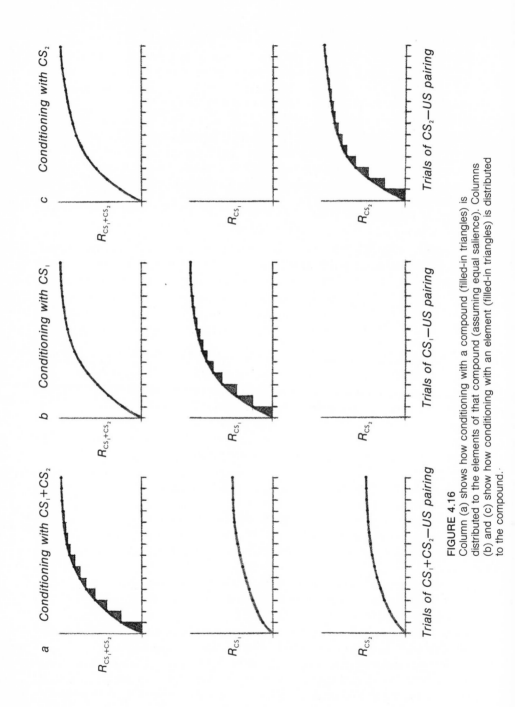

FIGURE 4.16
Column (a) shows how conditioning with a compound (filled-in triangles) is distributed to the elements of that compound (assuming equal salience). Columns (b) and (c) show how conditioning with an element (filled-in triangles) is distributed to the compound.

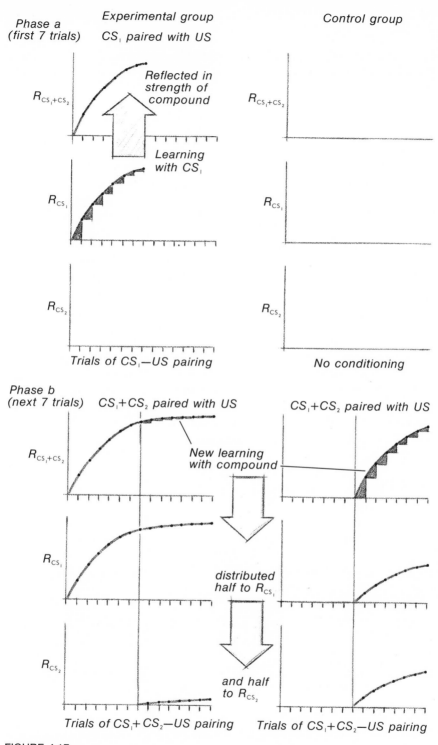

FIGURE 4.17
Blocking as explained by the Wagner-Rescorla model. The filled-in triangles show where conditioning takes place. The functions show distribution of conditioning strength to the compound and its elements. The result of the procedure is that R_{CS_2} acquires very little strength for the experimental group.

R_{CS_1} of the control group in phase (b) should be lower than R_{CS_1} of the experimental group. The reader can verify for himself from Figure 4.16 that these predictions follow from the model. When tested they have been confirmed.

In addition the model has been successful in predicting the results of a complicated series of experiments by Wagner and Saavedra, to which we shall turn next. Wagner and Saavedra did their experiments with eyelid conditioning in rabbits. The blocking effect had originally been studied with the CER paradigm in rats; nevertheless, the same theory handles both. There were three groups in the experiment. All three were exposed on every other trial to the compound stimulus, $CS_1 + CS_2$, paired with the US. They differed with respect to what happened on alternate trials as shown in Figure 4.18. For group 1, CS_1 was presented paired with the US; for group 2, neither CS_1 nor the US was presented; and for group 3, CS_1 was presented unpaired with the US. Then the three groups were tested for the strength of the response to CS_2. All groups were treated the same with respect to CS_2. Only what happened with CS_1 varied on alternate trials. Yet the three groups differed dramatically in their response to CS_2. (The last column of Figure 4.18 indicates that for group 1, CS_2 produced a low response, for group 2, CS_2 produced a medium response, and for group 3, CS_2 produced a high response.)

We shall trace through the conditioning process with the three groups presently, but first, to get an intuitive grasp of the Wagner–Saavedra experiment and to see that it is not inconsistent with the concept of "attention," consider an analogy to the experiment recast in terms of an everday problem of attention—paying attention to stop signs on the highway:

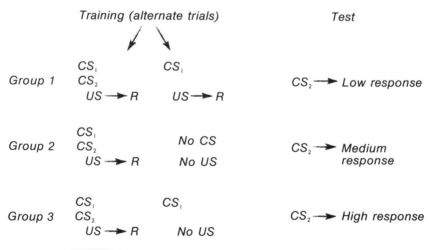

FIGURE 4.18
Procedure and results of the Wagner–Saavedra experiment.

Attention problem 1 (corresponding to group 1): Suppose you were driving through a foreign country with an unfamiliar alphabet. You come across two sorts of stop signs, one with red and green letters (corresponding to CS_1 + CS_2) and the other with just the red letters (corresponding to CS_1). Here you should pay attention to red letters only. If you paid attention to green at the expense of red, you might drive through the signs with red letters only. Since there are no signs with green letters only, you could safely ignore green. Let us say you would pay *low* attention to green letters (CS_2).

Attention problem 2 (corresponding to group 2): In another country all stop signs have both red and green letters. Here you could, with equal safety, pay attention to either red or green as you choose. Let us say you would pay *medium* attention to green letters.

Attention problem 3 (corresponding to group 3): In this country signs with red and green letters are still stop signs, but signs with the red letters alone are no-parking signs. You should *not* stop when you see red alone (corresponding to extinction of R_{CS_1}). Here you must pay attention to green, otherwise you would either be stopping at no-parking signs or running through stop signs. Let us say you would pay *high* attention to green letters.

The three degrees of attention to green letters in the three different countries correspond to the degrees of conditioning to CS_2 in the three groups of the Wagner-Saavedra Experiment.

Figure 4.19 shows how, according to the model, $R_{CS_1 + CS_2}$, R_{CS_1}, and R_{CS_2} vary with successive trials for the three groups. For convenience, we have assumed that $R_{US} = 1$ and c = 0.50* in the Wagner-Rescorla equation $\Delta R_{CS} = c (R_{US} - R_{CS})$; but the prediction of the model would be borne out for very wide ranges of the constants. In Figure 4.19, as before, a trial with a particular CS or compound is shown by a filled-in triangle, which represents the direct effect of conditioning. The distribution to the other CS or compound is also shown for all groups. Since there were never trials with CS_2 alone there are no filled-in triangles in the R_{CS_2} graphs.

Let us now trace the process of conditioning of each group. For group 1, which showed the lowest value of R_{CS_2}, the case is most complicated. Suppose the first trial is with CS_1 + CS_2 followed by the US. $R_{CS_1+CS_2}$ grows half the distance to the asymptote. (The first filled-in triangle in the upper left curve of Figure 4.19). This growth is split equally (assuming equal salience) between R_{CS_1} and R_{CS_2}. The next trial is with CS_1 alone followed by the US. Now R_{CS_1} increases, R_{CS_2} remains the same, and $R_{CS_1+CS_2}$, which must be the sum, R_{CS_1} + R_{CS_2}, grows along with R_{CS_1}. The third trial is with $R_{CS_1+CS_2}$ again and proceeds as the first with the growth split between R_{CS_1} and R_{CS_2}. On the fourth trial an interesting feature of the model becomes evident. $R_{CS_1+CS_2}$ has been

---

*In previous examples the constant, c, was 0.25 but a value of c = 0.5 makes R_{CS_2} for the three groups diverge more and shows the effect more vividly.

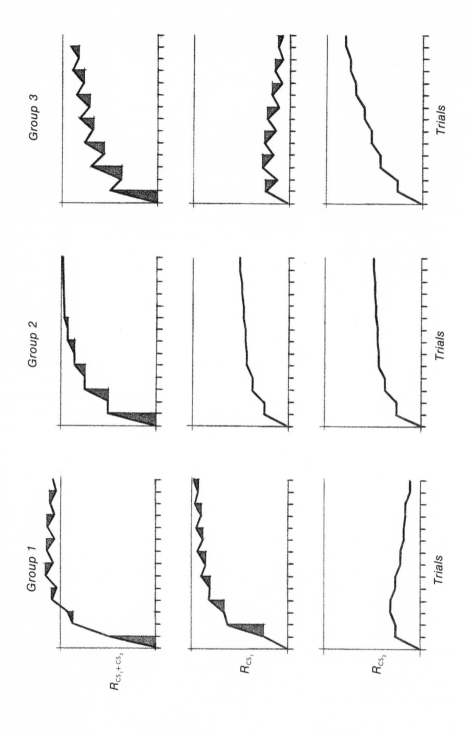

Group 1   Group 2   Group 3

$R_{CS_1 + CS_2}$

R_{CS_1}

R_{CS_2}

Trials   Trials   Trials

growing faster than R_{CS_1} since it gains full strength on all trials, whereas R_{CS_1} shares some strength with R_{CS_2} on $CS_1 + CS_2$ trials. By the third trial, $R_{CS_1+CS_2}$ has almost reached the asymptote. On the fourth trial, with R_{CS_1} alone, $R_{CS_1+CS_2}$ is pushed above the asymptote. Now according to the model, all conditioning trials will tend to bring response strength towards the asymptote, so further trials with $CS_1 + CS_2$ actually *decrease* $R_{CS_1+CS_2}$, bringing $R_{CS_1+CS_2}$ back down towards the asymptote. From the fourth trial on, a seesaw effect begins, with CS_1 trials being excitatory (R_{CS_1} still below asymptote) and $CS_1 + CS_2$ trials being inhibitory. The excitatory trials with CS_1 alone, however, have no direct effect on R_{CS_2}, which takes part only in the inhibitory effect of $R_{CS_1+CS_2}$, and so R_{CS_2} decreases slightly on $CS_1 + CS_2$ trials, heading slowly back down towards zero. Thus R_{CS_2} will be low in magnitude.

For group 2 in the Wagner-Saavedra experiment the model is much more straightforward. Each trial with $CS_1 + CS_2$ is distributed equally between R_{CS_1} and R_{CS_2}, so at the asymptote R_{CS_2} will be about half of R_{US} (assuming equal salience of CS_1 and CS_2).

For group 3, conditioning trials with $CS_1 + CS_2$ alternate with extinction trials with CS_1 alone. On conditioning trials half of the strength of conditioning goes to R_{CS_2}. But on extinction trials with CS_1 alone, R_{CS_2} is unaffected. In fact the extinction trials help R_{CS_2} to grow since they decrease $R_{CS_1 + CS_2}$. The further $R_{CS_1 + CS_2}$ is from its asymptote the more strength gained on the next conditioning trial with $R_{CS_1 + CS_2}$ and the more strength distributed to R_{CS_2}. Thus R_{CS_2} in this condition will grow fairly rapidly towards an asymptote equal to R_{US}.

The three groups, treated identically with respect to CS_2, had different strengths of R_{CS_2} depending on the different procedures with CS_1 on alternate trials. The model handles with equal ease other experiments with compound stimuli and is actively being explored by psychologists engaged in classical conditioning.

We should note that the model, as described here, would be relatively molecular as this term was defined in Chapter 2. CS's and US's are considered as

---

FIGURE 4.19

The three groups of the Wagner–Saavedra experiment. The filled triangles indicate direct conditioning. Conditioning with the compound ($CS_1 + CS_2$) always occurs on every other trial. On alternate trials group 1 receives conditioning with CS_1, group 2 receives a rest period, and group 3 receives extinction trials with CS_1. A conditioning trial (with $c = 0.5$ as we assume here) always brings the curve half way to the asymptote (upper horizontal line) even when the curve is above the asymptote (as in the upper left curve). An extinction trial always brings the curve halfway to the X-axis (as in the middle right-hand curve). Conditioning with the compound is distributed equally to the two elements. Conditioning with CS_1 is wholly reflected in the compound. As a result, R_{CS_2} attains low, medium, and high values for the three groups.

individual events to be paired or unpaired on individual trials. According to this model each contiguity of CS and US and each instance of CS and US alone would have its individual effect. These effects summate, in the manner we have just described, to yield a certain strength of response. If more molar measures—that is, contingency or correlation—are found to describe data of classical conditioning experiments, the model would ascribe such effects to the "more fundamental" contiguities, just as the molar physical effects of velocity and momentum of objects are ascribed to more fundamental motions of atomic and subatomic particles.

A MOLAR VIEW OF CLASSICAL CONDITIONING

Pavlov thought that even the most complex human behavior could be explained in terms of classical conditioning—that even such processes as solving a differential equation or composing a symphony would someday be proven to be simply concatenations of unconditioned and conditioned reflexes. He felt, though, that it was unfair to ask him to explain complex human behavior in the early stages of his science, just as it would have been unfair to ask Newton to predict or explain earthquakes. Since Pavlov's time, much effort has been expended on experimental applications of Pavlovian principles to more complex behavior. So far, however, little in the way of complex behavior has been generated in the laboratory by classical conditioning procedures.

A possibility for bridging the gap between the laboratory and everyday life lies in the molar conception of events, which we discussed in Chapter 2. With respect to classical conditioning, the molar approach deals, not with single contiguities of CS and US, but with contingent or correlative relationships between CS and US. To take an everday example, the reading on a thermometer in the window gains importance for us because its ups and downs signal corresponding feelings of hot and cold when we step outside. The thermometer reading (not a single value of it, but the whole range of values) serves as a conditioned stimulus. The temperature outside (again the whole range of values) serves as an unconditioned stimulus. The correlation between the two serves as a conditioning procedure. A few recent studies of classical conditioning have concerned themselves with contingencies and correlations rather than simple contiguities of stimuli. It has been found that such relationships (the intensity of a signal paired with the intensity of electric shock, for instance) are relatively easy for animals to learn; and in fact they bear a stronger resemblance to complex environmental events than do the one-to-one pairings of single CS's and US's.

Recent arguments have advanced the idea that classical conditioning actually depends on contingency, rather than on simple pairings of CS and US. The article reprinted here by Robert Rescorla on classical conditioning procedures elucidates this view and suggests that the proper control procedure for classical conditioning is not one in which the CS is presented without the US (unpaired), but rather one in which the CS is presented unrelated to the US (uncorrelated). An experiment by Rescorla that demonstrates the different effects of pairing and correlation is illustrated in Figure 4.20. For two groups of rats the CS (a tone) was periodically turned on and off. One group of rats received shocks (the US) randomly, regardless of whether the CS was on or off. Since the CS was on half of the time, half of those shocks were paired contiguously with the CS and half were unpaired; there was pairing but there was also unpairing of shocks and CS. A second group of rats received shocks only during the CS. If just pairing was sufficient for conditioning, both groups should have gotten the same conditioning because they were both exposed to the same number of CS-US pairings. That is, both groups got the same number of shocks during the CS. If correlation was important, only the second group should have gotten conditioning because only for this group were shocks *correlated* with the CS. When Rescorla tested for conditioning in a CER procedure by superimposing the stimuli on an ongoing bar-pressing task, he found that only the second group suppressed bar-pressing; therefore, only that group had received conditioning—even though they had received fewer shocks on the whole than the first group.

The interpretation of classical conditioning in terms of correlation forces us to redefine our concept of extinction. Traditionally, extinction consists simply of eliminating the US. But if conditioning is due to correlation (rather than contiguity) then any procedure producing a zero correlation between CS

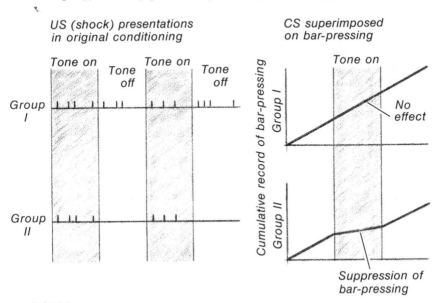

FIGURE 4.20
Pairing of tone and shock (group I) is not enough to cause tone to suppress bar-presses later. Absence of tone must also be paired with absence of shock (group II).

and US would be an extinction procedure. This includes the traditional extinction procedure (eliminating the US) as well as the control procedure (group I) of Figure 4.20. Throughout the rest of the book we shall maintain this view of extinction—that it consists of the breaking up of a relationship, regardless of whether that relationship is contiguity, contingency, or correlation. In classical conditioning, the terms of the relationship are CS's and US's. In instrumental conditioning, the terms are responses and rewards or punishers. We shall discuss the implications of this view of extinction in more detail in the next chapter.

Although Rescorla's experiment, illustrated in Figure 4.20, seems to support a molar, correlational view of classical conditioning, Rescorla himself has shown how it may be analyzed in more molecular terms by applying the Wagner-Rescorla model. Just as this model provided a more molecular explanation for the apparently molar phenomenon called "blocking," it also can account for the Rescorla experiment in molecular terms by treating it as an experiment with compound stimuli. Even though there is only one CS explicitly programmed, it is possible to consider the complex background stimuli consisting of the experimental apparatus and its surroundings as another single stimulus. Let us call this stimulus CS_1. *CS_1 is always present* in the experimental situation. The explicit CS used, the tone, may be superimposed on it or not. Let us call the tone CS_2. Referring to Figure 4.20, the CS going on and off would correspond to alternation of $CS_1 + CS_2$ and CS_1 alone. The first group of rats (group 1) would be exposed to $CS_1 + CS_2$ paired with the US, alternated with CS_1 also paired with the US. Turning back to Figure 4.19 we see that this corresponds to group 1 of the Wagner-Saavedra experiment. CS_2 for this group received little or no conditioning strength. Therefore, in the present Rescorla experiment, by the very same reasoning we applied with Wagner-Saavedra's group 1, it would also be expected to have little strength.

The second group of rats in the Rescorla experiment (group 2) would be exposed to $CS_1 + CS_2$ paired with the US, alternated with CS_1 alone, this time *not* paired with the US. Referring again to Figure 4.19 we see that this corresponds to group 3 of the Wagner-Saavedra experiment. CS_2 for this group received high conditioning strength. Therefore, in the present Rescorla experiment it would also be expected to have high strength.

The difference between the two groups of rats in the Rescorla experiment is thus explained by the same model that was applied to two groups of rabbits in another experiment with an entirely different conditioning procedure. This is excellent support for the Wagner-Rescorla model. It indicates that a molecular explanation is possible for some facts that seemed to require a molar explanation. This does not, of course, imply that the molar explanation is wrong. It is rather encouraging that both molar and molecular theories can fit the facts so well. It also indicates that experimental psychology is emerging as a science that can do more than give qualitative, post-hoc explanations of data.

APPLICATIONS IN BEHAVIOR THERAPY

The earliest attempts to apply the principles of learning to dysfunctional behavior made use of classical conditioning techniques, many of which are still in use. In a later chapter we shall discuss the implications of behavior therapy in general, the motivation of the psychologists engaged in its practice, and the rationale behind its use. This section will be confined to techniques using classical conditioning.

One of the first attempts to apply classical conditioning procedures to humans was an experiment by J. B. Watson aimed at showing how phobias might develop, rather than how to eliminate them. Watson and a colleague, Rosalie Rayner, conducted the experiment with a baby named Albert as their subject. Watson observed that few stimuli would cause Albert to cry; in other words, there seemed to be few unconditioned stimuli for a baby's crying. A stimulus that did cause such a reaction was a loud noise; it produced a startle reaction followed by crying. Watson decided to use the loud noise as an unconditioned stimulus and see whether he could, by a classical conditioning procedure, get Albert to react to a previously neutral stimulus as he did to the noise. For the neutral stimulus, Watson chose a white rat, one of a number of stimuli that did not elicit crying prior to the experiment. Watson showed Albert the white rat and immediately followed the presentation of the rat by a loud noise. Then he waited a while and paired the rat with the noise again. Only three or four such pairings were necessary before Albert started to cry when he saw the rat. Not only did Albert now cry when he saw the rat, but his crying generalized to other animals and to other furry objects (for example, a ball of cotton).

The fact that a human can learn to make emotional responses to previously neutral stimuli goes some way towards explaining human behavior. Most of our emotional behavior seems beyond our control. But when we realize that emotional reactions are often caused by conditioned stimuli—stimuli that were once neutral but that now, by virtue of prior pairing with unconditioned stimuli, can evoke powerful emotional behavior—we can often trace an emotional response back to its cause.

In this chapter we have not previously discussed whether conditioning occurs with or without awareness in humans. This is because the variables that influence conditioning often have little to do with whether the person being conditioned is aware (that is, conscious) of them. Sometimes we are aware of the CS but not the US, or vice versa. In many cases we can name the CS and US that become associated, as when we related the smell of bread to the bread. But imagine smelling the perfume (a CS) of your old teacher on a strange woman. You might suddenly feel nostalgic (the CR) and think the feeling had arisen by itself, when in reality it had been triggered by an external conditioned stimulus. Similarly, we often notice that we feel good (CR) before we notice the sunny day (CS) that caused our feeling. We often notice that we are afraid (CR) before we can identify the cause of our fear (the CS) in the environment. Oftentimes, the conditioned stimulus is so obscure or so obscurely related to the original unconditioned stimulus of our fearful reaction that we seek a professional psychologist to trace the connection.

Certain kinds of psychological therapy stress the conditioned-stimulus cause of dysfunctional behavior and try to counter it with conditioning procedures in the reverse direction, or with extinction procedures. For instance, Albert's fears might be extinguished by exposing him repeatedly to white rats without loud noises. But simple extinction might not be very effective. If the original conditioning were very strong, hundreds of extinction trials in different settings might be necessary. Furthermore, it has been found, with second-order conditioning, that extinction with the original CS (CS_1) does not necessarily apply to CS_2 as well. Further extinction trials with CS_2 are necessary. Thus, if Albert received second-order conditioning with a snake, say, paired with the white rat, his fear would have to be extinguished with the snake as well as with the white rat. Otherwise, it would be possible to re-establish fear of the white rat by pairing it with the snake (a stimulus that originally acquired its fear-eliciting properties by being paired with the now-neutral white rat). Similarly, any other stimulus, including background stimuli, might re-establish fear of the rat and undo the effects of extinction. Indeed, if extinction of fears worked in a simple way, no one would have to see a therapist.

It is usually proper to react to stimuli that signal certain conditions as you would react to the conditions themselves. If the conditions were then eliminated and your reaction to the signal died away, your behavior would be adaptive. But suppose the original conditions were removed and your reaction persisted to the signalling stimulus. For instance, to take the most pessimistic view, suppose Albert grew up morbidly afraid of white rats.* One method of reducing this fear is called *counterconditioning*. In a counterconditioning procedure Albert might be given something good to eat or a toy to play with. Then the rat would be introduced very gradually into his environment, first several feet away and then closer and closer. At the first sign of disruption of eating or play by crying, the rat would be removed and then slowly reintroduced again. The object of this procedure would be to associate the rat as a CS with US's other than noise (for example, eating or play) to interfere with the response (crying) previously made to the rat and, so to speak, crowd it out. This is likely to work better than simple extinction since it substitutes a specific response for the conditioned response rather than just allowing any other response to be substituted. This new response might then also appear in the presence of other stimuli that had been paired with the original CS.

-----

*Although the actual danger of such a result of Watson's experiment is slight, the experiment would not be done today because of the possibility that some permanent harm might be done to the child. In Watson's day occasional lasting effects of brief conditioning episodes were not suspected.

A similar therapeutic technique employing classical conditioning is called *systematic desensitization.* It was invented by Joseph Wolpe. Let us assume that Albert, now grown up, is still afraid of rats. Systematic desensitization would be applied in two stages. First Albert would be taught to relax his muscles deeply: he would be asked to lean back in a comfortable chair in a dark room, and the therapist would begin a sort of hypnotic routine, asking him to first tighten and then relax his hands and feet, then his arms and legs, then his deeper muscles, his spinal and neck muscles, and so on. Let us assume Albert learns to relax by this method. He is then ready for the second stage of systematic desensitization.

Prior to the relaxation sessions Albert and the therapist have constructed a series of sentences and paragraphs all involving rats. These are arranged in a hierarchy of increasing ability to cause disturbing behavior in Albert. The mildest might be the casual mention of the word "rat" in a sentence—for example, "The rats deserted the sinking ship." A stronger one would be something like, "They have just thrown you into a dark room and shut the door. There are scurrying sounds around you from the ceiling, floor, walls. You can sense many hungry rats fighting with each other for a piece of food—sometimes biting into each other's flesh. They are coming towards you, attracted by the smell of your body . . ." and so forth. The point of this procedure is to construct a gradient of stimuli, like a generalization gradient, with increasing ability to elicit the CR. Some of these verbal stimuli might actually elicit more signs of fear than the rat itself. The therapist then does with the sentences what he might have done with a real rat. While Albert is relaxed, the mildest stimulus is introduced. If Albert reports that his relaxation is disturbed (that is, that he makes a CR) he is asked to relax again and the sentence is reintroduced. This is repeated until Albert can hear the sentence without disturbing his relaxation. Now a new CR (relaxation) has been substituted for the old CR (fear). Once this is achieved the next sentence in the hierarchy is introduced, and then the next, until Albert can hear the most vivid scenes described without losing his relaxation. Then the therapist might proceed to real rats, and real-life situations. This technique works very well with all sorts of phobias and is now in common use. Its advantage over simple extinction is that, like counter-conditioning, a new CR is learned which can transfer to CS's other than the one originally used. Simple extinction tends to be too narrowly focused, too weak to overcome strong conditioning, and too easily overcome by reconditioning with the original US or even with other CS's not yet neutral themselves.

Masters' and Johnson's treatment of sexual dysfunction borrows some of its elements from systematic desensitization. A critical part of their technique involves relaxation and various degrees of sexual activity introduced gradually. (According to Masters and Johnson, sexual dysfunction arises from fears about performance.) At first the couple learns to gain pleasure from touching each other's bodies without engaging in actual intercourse. Rigid criteria of "sexual performance" are eliminated (in fact, intercourse is not allowed at early stages of treatment) so that failure is not experienced. The couple learns that sexual pleasure can be achieved without actual intercourse. Then, gradual approaches to intercourse are instituted with the provision that each step be accompanied by enjoyment for its own sake. The object is to make the entire complex of stimuli surrounding sexual behavior a CS for pleasurable reactions instead of fear. Other sorts of treatment and advice go along with the conditioning procedure, so it is difficult to pinpoint a single factor responsible for the success that Masters and Johnson have had. Nevertheless, conditioning seems to play a major part.

All of these examples involve establishing normal behavior by making the stimuli surrounding that behavior *less* aversive. Another technique involves making alternatives to the desired behavior *more* aversive. For instance, treatment of alcoholics often involves pairing of stimuli surrounding the act of drinking liquor with aversive stimulation. Also, homosexuals who want to change to heterosexual behavior have been treated by pairing pictures of men engaged in homosexual acts, with aversive stimulation. Although such procedures are often effective, there are ethical and practical problems with their use. The core of these problems lies in the unconditioned response to the aversive stimulus. When electric shock is used, for instance, the unconditioned response is much wider than simple suppression of drinking (of alcoholic beverages) or suppression of homosexual activity. It might include some behavior that neither the therapist nor the patient wants to occur. We shall discuss this problem further when we consider punishment and avoidance. For now, the reader should be aware that conditioning procedures cannot simply be lifted from the laboratory and applied to everyday life situations.

Like any technology, behavioral technology is applied piece-meal from theory. Only rarely can theoretical findings be taken intact and applied therapeutically. The behavioral engineer, like the mechanical, chemical, and electrical engineer establishes his own techniques and perfects them by trial and error. He borrows from the theorist his explanatory mechanisms, some of his specific devices, and his general approach towards his subject matter. The success of the theory then depends both on how well it explains what the engineer may be doing for purely practical reasons and on the success of the new techniques developed with reference to the theory.

BIBLIOGRAPHY

An excellent review of classical conditioning can be found in a chapter on the subject by H. S. Terrace in a textbook edited by J. A. Nevin and G. S. Reynolds called *The study of behavior* (Glenview, Ill.: Scott, Foresman & Co., 1973). Current thinking on the subject is handily summarized in two books that have emerged from symposia in which classical conditioning was discussed by experts in the field. The first is W. F. Prokasy (ed.), *Classical conditioning* (New York: Appleton-Century-Crofts, 1965). The second is A. H. Black and W. F. Prokasy (eds.), *Classical conditioning II* (New York: Appleton-Century-Crofts, 1972).

Following is a list of articles referred to in this chapter:

Bass, M. J., and Hull, C. L. The irradiation of a tactile conditioned reflex in man. *Journal of Comparative Psychology,* 1934, *17,* 47–65.

Kamin, L. J. Attention-like processes in classical conditioning. In *Miami symposium on the prediction of behavior: Aversive stimulation,* ed. M. R. Jones. Miami: University of Miami Press, 1968.

Liddell, H. S. The conditioned reflex. In *Comparative psychology,* ed. F. A. Moss. New York: Prentice-Hall, 1934.

Masters, W. H., and Johnson, V. E. *Human sexual response.* Boston: Little, Brown, 1966.

Pavlov, I. P. *Work of the digestive glands.* Translated by W. H. Thompson. Griffin, 1910.

Pavlov, I. P. *Conditioned reflexes.* New York: Dover, 1960. Originally published in English, 1927.

Rescorla, R. A. Pavlovian conditioning and its proper control procedures. *Psychological Review,* 1967, *74,* 71–80.

Rescorla, R. A., and Wagner, A. R. A theory of Pavlovian conditioning: Variations in the effectiveness of reinforcement and nonreinforcement. In *Classical conditioning II,* ed. A. H. Black and W. F. Prokasy. New York: Appleton-Century-Crofts, 1972.

Watson, J. B., and Rayner, R. Conditioned emotional reactions. *Journal of Experimental Psychology,* 1920, *3,* 1–14.

Wolpe, J. *Psychotherapy by reciprocal inhibition.* Stanford, Calif.: Stanford University Press, 1948.

Zener, K. The significance of behavior accompanying conditioned salivary secretion for theories of the conditioned response. *American Journal of Psychology,* 1937, *50,* 384–403.

We reprint here two articles by Robert Rescorla. The first, which is referred to in the text, argues that the proper control procedure for classical conditioning is a random pairing of CS and US. The second article is about conditioned inhibition. The article deals with the question of how to define an inhibitory process. The articles are related to each other in the sense that if conditioning depends both on the pairing and the *unpairing* of CS and US (as the first article argues) then the inhibitory process involved in the unpairing phase is just as important for conditioning as the excitatory process in the pairing phase. The second article then discusses the nature of this inhibitory process. The conclusion of the article is that inhibition, like excitation, is defined by a certain contingent or correlative relationship between CS and US; excitation is a positive contingency or correlation, inhibition is a negative contingency or correlation.

Supplemental Reading for Chapter 4

PAVLOVIAN CONDITIONING AND ITS PROPER CONTROL PROCEDURES

Robert A. Rescorla

The traditional control procedures for Pavlovian conditioning are examined and each is found wanting. Some procedures introduce nonassociative factors not present in the experimental procedure while others transform the excitatory, experimental CS–US contingency into an inhibitory contingency. An alternative control procedure is suggested in which there is no contingency whatsoever between CS and US. This "truly random" control procedure leads to a new conception of Pavlovian conditioning postulating that the contingency between CS and US, rather than the pairing of CS and US, is the important event in conditioning. The fruitfulness of this new conception of Pavlovian conditioning is illustrated by 2 experimental results.

The operations performed to establish Pavlovian conditioned reflexes require that the presentation of an unconditioned stimulus be contingent upon the occurrence of a conditioned stimulus. Students of conditioning have regarded this contingency between CS and US as vital to the definition of conditioning and have rejected changes in the organism not dependent upon this contingency (such as sensitization or pseudoconditioning) as not being "true" conditioning (i.e., associative). Therefore, in order to identify the effects due uniquely to the contingency between CS and US, a variety of control procedures have been developed. Each of these procedures attempts to

The preparation of this paper and the experimental work related to it were aided by United States Public Health Service Grant MH-04202 and National Science Foundation Grant GB-2428 to Richard L. Solomon and by a National Science Foundation predoctoral fellowship to the author. The author would like to express his appreciation to Vincent M. LoLordo and Richard L. Solomon for their advice and criticism of the ideas presented in this paper.

From *Psychological Review*, Vol. 74, No. 1, 71–80. Copyright, 1967 by The American Psychological Association. Reprinted by permission.

retain some features of the Pavlovian conditioning situation while eliminating the CS–US contingency.

This paper argues that, in fact, none of the conventional control procedures for nonassociative effects is adequate, either taken alone or in combination; it further argues that a new type of "random stimulus" control procedure does enable one to identify the role of the CS–US contingency in Pavlovian conditioning.

TRADITIONAL CONTROL PROCEDURES

The conventional control procedures for Pavlovian conditioning are quite familiar, so they will be described only briefly. In all of these descriptions, we assume that the conditioning or control treatment is administered, and then all groups are tested with a single (unreinforced) CS presentation. It is only the results of the test trial that are of interest. (Similar descriptions could be given when anticipatory CRs rather than test trial CRs are used as the index of conditioning.)

The various control treatments which are administered prior to the test trial in place of Pavlovian conditioning are listed below together with examples of their use.

1. CS-alone control. In this procedure a control subject (*S*) receives the same number of CS presentations as does an experimental *S*; however, no US is administered. This control is designed to evaluate the effects of familiarity with the CS and any changes in the organism due solely to that familiarity (Rodnick, 1937; Thompson & McConnell, 1955).

2. Novel CS control. In this procedure, no CS is given prior to the test trial. The test trial gives an estimate of the unconditioned effects of the CS (Rodnick, 1937; Wickens & Wickens, 1940).

3. US-alone control. Repeated presentations of the US alone are made in order to control for sensitization by, or habituation to, the US (Notterman, Schoenfeld, & Bersh, 1952; Wickens & Wickens, 1940).

4. Explicitly unpaired control (sometimes called the random control). In this procedure, *S* receives unpaired presentations of CS and US. This can be done in a variety of ways, but the most typical is presentation of both CS and US in the same session in random order but never close together in time (Bitterman, 1964; Harris, 1943).

5. Backward conditioning. The CS and US are paired, but the US is always presented prior to the CS (Kalish, 1954; Spence & Runquist, 1958).

6. Discriminative conditioning. One stimulus (CS+) is paired with the US and the other (CS−) is not. In this way CS− receives a treatment similar to that of CS+ except that the contingency with the US is an "explicitly unpaired" one. Differences between the reactions to CS+ and CS− are taken to indicate Pavlovian conditioning (Solomon & Turner, 1962).

The very variety of control procedures which have been developed attests to the inadequacy of any one. But it may be worthwhile to point briefly to the pitfalls of each procedure because some of these have not been widely recognized. We take as the logical criterion for an adequate control procedure that it retain as many features as possible of the experimental procedure while excluding the CS–US contingency. In general, each of the control procedures, although attempting to eliminate the CS–US contingency, can be shown to do considerably more. The result is that a variety of other differences, both associative and nonassociative, between experimental and control procedures is confounded with the absence of the CS–US contingency. Some of the confoundings are pointed out below.

1. CS-alone control. Quite obviously, an *S* treated in this way does not have the same number of US experiences as the experimental *S* does; therefore, any differences between *S*s can be attributed to this difference in experience with the US. But worse, repeated CS presentations in the absence of all USs may not lead to the same rate of CS habituation as does repeated CS presentation in a chamber in which the US also occurs.

2. Novel CS control. It is useful to know the unconditioned properties of the CS, but it is not clear what relevance this has for identifying "true" Pavlovian conditioning. The experimental *S has* experienced the CS a large number of times prior to the test trial and it is no longer novel to him. Why compare him to an *S* for whom the CS is novel? Comparison with a novel CS group allows one to assess the total change in reaction to the CS produced by the conditioning procedure but does not permit isolation of those changes due uniquely to the occurrence of Pavlovian conditioning.

3. US-alone control. This procedure has faults similar to those of the novel CS procedure. An *S* with this procedure

receives a novel CS at the time of test, while the experimental S receives a CS which it has experienced many times.

4. Explicitly unpaired control. In many ways this procedure comes closest to being an appropriate control, and it has become increasingly popular in recent years. However, it contains flaws which cannot be overlooked. Although it escapes the criticisms of Procedures 1, 2, and 3, it, too, does not simply remove the contingency between CS and US; rather, it introduces instead a *new* contingency, such that the US *cannot* follow the CS for some minimum time interval. Instead of the CS being a signal for the US, it can become a signal for the *absence* of the US. Although this is an interesting procedure in itself, it does not allow a comparison between two groups, one with a CS–US contingency and one without it. We are, instead, in the position of having two different CS–US contingencies which may yield different results. How can we know which group showed Pavlovian conditioning?

5. Backward conditioning. The relevance of this procedure rests upon the assumption that in Pavlovian conditioning not only the CS–US contingency but also their temporal order of presentation is important. It is not clear whether this should be taken as part of the definition of Pavlovian conditioning or as an empirical result. Nevertheless, some investigators have suggested comparison with a backward conditioning group to evaluate the traditional experimental group. For the purposes of analysis, let us assume that the CS and US do not overlap in this procedure. We then have a sequence of events: US–CS . . . US–CS . . . US–CS . . . in conditioning. This procedure produces the same difficulty as does the explicitly unpaired procedure: The occurrence of the CS predicts a period *free from the* US. Again presentation of the US *is* contingent upon CS occurrence but the contingency is a *negative* one. Of course, if the CS begins during the US in this procedure, CS oc-

currence predicts the *termination* of the US, which, in turn, introduces another contingency and further complications. It is worth noting that Konorski (1948) considered the backward conditioning paradigm as the prime example of an inhibitory conditioning procedure.

6. Discriminative conditioning. By now it should be clear that this control procedure falls prey to the same criticisms as do Procedures 5 and 6. CS− is explicitly unpaired with the US. In fact, the discriminative conditioning procedure can be viewed as the simultaneous administration to the same S of the experimental procedure and Control Procedure 4.

We can conclude that each of the proposed control procedures either confounds some important nonassociative change with the disruption of the CS–US contingency or changes the contingency from a positive to a negative one. Furthermore, there is no obvious way in which combined control procedures can be used to eliminate confoundings. Therefore, we are in the unfortunate position of being unable to evaluate "true" Pavlovian conditioning by the use of any or all of the conventional control procedures.

AN ADEQUATE ALTERNATIVE

There is, however, a control procedure which solves the problems raised above. We shall call this procedure the "truly random" control procedure. In this procedure, both the CS and the US are presented to S but there is *no contingency whatsoever* between them. That is, the two events are programmed entirely randomly and independently in such a way that some "pairings" of CS and US may occur by chance alone. All CS and US occurrences for the control group are the same as for the experimental group except that the regular temporal contingency between CS and US is eliminated. The occurrence of the CS provides *no information* about subsequent occurrences of the US. This procedure is similar in conception to the explicitly unpaired procedure, (4), except that it eliminates the contingency of that procedure which allows the CS to signal nonoccurrence of the US.[1]

There are a variety of ways of arranging a truly random control condition. Two major alternatives are: (a) Present the CS as in the experimental group but randomly distribute USs throughout the session; (b) conversely, present USs as in the experimental group but randomly distribute CSs. Note that, in order for there to be *no* contingency, the distributions must be such that CS occurrences do not predict the occurrence of USs at *any* time in the remainder of the session. If the CS predicts the occurrence of a US 30 minutes later in the session, an appropriate random control condition has not been achieved.

Despite the apparent adequacy of these alternatives, they actually add other confoundings. In the usual Pavlovian conditioning procedure, several time intervals other than the CS-US interval are kept relatively constant. Thus time intervals between successive CSs and successive USs are of some (relatively large) minimum value. Each of the two truly random controls would violate one of these relations and thus introduce changes other than removal of the CS-US contingency. Fortunately, this can be avoided if we depart from the traditional conditioning procedures and use a wide variety of intertrial intervals for the experimental Ss. Then it is possible to arrange truly random presentations of CS and US for the control Ss while preserving the inter-US and inter-CS intervals of the experimental condition. For instance, one could program CS-US pairings for the experimental group with a random-interval programmer. Then a truly random control would be arranged by using two independent random-interval programmers with the same pa-

rameters as that of the experimental group—one to deliver CSs and one to deliver USs.

We do not wish to understate the importance of a variety of nonassociative factors which do occur in Pavlovian conditioning. It is respect for their effects that leads to the advocacy of the truly random control for contingency-produced effects. One great advantage of the truly random control is that it holds constant between the experimental and control procedures *all* of the factors extraneous to the CS-US contingency *without demanding that we be able to specify in advance what factors might be operating.* In contrast, the customary control procedures have often been developed only to deal with one supposed nonassociative factor.

It is also important to realize that the actual results obtained with the truly random control procedure are irrelevant to the present argument. It may be that in some conditioning situations, Ss treated with the truly random control procedure will show strong changes in behavior when the CS is presented. This simply means that important changes not dependent upon a CS-US contingency occur in this situation; effects due to that contingency still must be evaluated as deviations from the effects produced by the truly random procedure.

Traditionally, the prime concern of American investigators has been the excitatory processes, and the inadequate conventional control procedures have reflected this concern. As noted above, many of these control procedures are biased toward the inhibitory side because of the explicit nonpairings of the CS and US. But the inhibitory effects of conditioning deserve attention in their own right. Clearly, we need an appropriate base condition against which to compare *both* the inhibitory and excitatory kinds of conditioning relations. The truly random sequence of CSs and USs provides an unbiased control procedure for both positive and negative contingencies be-

---

[1] A similar control procedure has been suggested by Jensen (1961) and by Prokasy (1965).

tween CS and US. In fact, if we are going to retain the conceptual terms "conditioned excitatory" and "conditioned inhibitory" stimuli, the truly random control procedure will provide a base line against which to *define* these effects.

In addition to serving as a control condition for Pavlovian conditioning, the truly random presentation of CS and US provides an unbiased *extinction* procedure. To the degree that our concern in extinction of Pavlovian CRs is with how the animal loses its *associative* connection, simply removing the US from the situation is an inappropriate extinction procedure. Simple removal of the US eliminates not only the CS–US contingency but also whatever nonassociative effects the US might have. However, using the truly random presentation of CS and US as an extinction procedure permits examination of the loss of contingency-dependent learning independently of these other effects. Furthermore, the truly random procedure serves as an unbiased procedure for extinction of *both* excitation and inhibition. If inhibition can be acquired it seems reasonable that it can be extinguished. The truly random presentation of CS and US is the most natural extinction procedure for inhibitory as well as excitatory effects.

OBJECTIONS TO THE "TRULY RANDOM" PROCEDURE: TWO THEORETICAL VIEWS OF CONDITIONING

It seems certain that our arguments will not be entirely convincing. All conventional control procedures have a common feature: They never allow forward pairings of the control CS and US. The reluctance which one might feel toward accepting a truly random control procedure stems in part from the close temporal pairings of CS and US which *will occur by chance* in that condition. One may thus argue that the truly random control procedure itself allows Pavlovian conditioning because of those few chance trials which pair CS and US; if so, it can

hardly be considered a "pure" control condition. According to such an argument, the same processes may be operative in both the experimental and control procedures, but to a lesser degree in the latter.

This objection runs deep and is worthy of extensive examination. It rests upon an assumption, often not made explicit, that the temporal *pairing* of CS and US is the sufficient condition for "true" Pavlovian conditioning. It views Pavlovian conditioning as a one-sided affair in which conditioning is either absent or excitatory; the number of CS–US pairings determines the degree to which conditioning is excitatory. It is this view which dominates American notions of conditioning and which has been influential in preventing inhibitory processes from playing a major role in our thinking. A good example of this position is the Guthrian claim that the reinforcing event in Pavlovian conditioning is simple contiguity between CS and US. From this point of view, a reasonable control procedure for Pavlovian conditioning is one in which *S* "is not taught that the US follows the CS." This has been interpreted to include the possibly quite different learning that "the CS is *not* followed by the US." With this type of bias, it might be reasonable to conclude that the "explicitly unpaired" and the discriminative conditioning procedure are appropriate controls for Pavlovian conditioning.

An alternative theoretical view of Pavlovian conditioning, and one which has not often been distinguished from that in the previous paragraph, is that the temporal *contingency* between CS and US is the relevant condition. The notion of *contingency* differs from that of *pairings* in that the former includes not only what *is* paired with the CS but also what *is not* paired with the CS. Thus the truly random procedure contains *no* contingency between the CS and US, even though it does contain some chance CS–US pairings. From this point of view the appropriate control condition for Pavlovian conditioning is one in which the animal is taught that "the CS is irrelevant to the US." Deviations from this base condition can be either positive (CS is followed by US) or negative (CS is followed by absence of US). This view of conditioning has the advantage of separating out, from the simple absence of conditioning, a conceptualized inhibitory process which has a status equal to that of excitatory processes. Intuitively it seems clear that learning that the US does not follow the CS is different from failing to learn that the US follows the CS or learning that the CS is irrelevant to the US. In this sense, at least, the contingency view of conditioning, and the truly random control procedure which it generates, is more in the spirit of Pavlovian theory.[2]

The idea of contingency used here needs explication. By it we mean the degree of dependency which presentation of the US has upon prior presentation of the CS. This is clearly a function of the relative proportion of US events which occur during or at some specified time following the CS. Thus, in the truly random condition no dependency exists, but in the standard Pavlovian conditioning situation the dependence is complete. The control condition is brought closer to the experimental condition as we increase the proportion of USs occurring in the presence of the CS. When, at the other extreme, all USs occur in the absence of the CS, the inhibitory end of the continuum is reached. These proportions can be stated in terms of the probability of a US occurring given the presence of a CS (or given that the CS occurred at some· designated prior time), and the probability of a US occurring given the absence of the CS (cf. Prokasy, 1965).

The dimension of contingency is then a function of these two probabilities; if Pavlovian conditioning is dependent upon the contingency between CS and US, it, too, will be a function of these two probabilities. However, no attempt is made here to specify a particular function which relates these two probabilities to a continuum of contingencies.[3]

If two conditioning procedures have the same probability of reinforcement in the absence of the CS, but have different probabilities in the presence of the CS, they differ in what is usually called the degree of partial reinforcement. Whether or not this affects the degree of contingency depends upon the function of these two probabilities that we choose to describe degree of contingency. We suggest that the contingency dimension, rather than the number of CS–US pairings, is the theoretically fruitful dimension in Pavlovian conditioning.

As soon as one admits a symmetry of inhibition and excitation in the Pavlovian conditioning situation, the CS–US pairing view of conditioning begins to lose appeal. Pavlovian conditioning consists of a sequence of CSs and USs arranged in a particular temporal pattern. Suppose, now, that one is primarily interested not in excitatory processes but in inhibitory processes, or in how an animal learns that the CS signals a period free from the US. From the point of view that the pairing of CS and US is the important Pavlovian event, the truly random control procedure is inadequate for a reason that is exactly the opposite to what it was for excitatory conditioning; now it contains a number of *nonpairings* of CS and US. Therefore, from such a view we are forced to conclude that the symmetrical control proce-

[2]It is worth pointing out that the argument advanced in this paper has direct analogues for instrumental training. Whatever faults it might have, the yoked-control procedure was introduced precisely to determine what effects are uniquely due to instrumental reinforcement contingencies. Similarly, the distinction between pairing and contingency views has recently been examined for operant conditioning by Premack (1965).

[3]These probabilities can be calculated whatever the number of CS and US events. If, for instance, there is only one CS–US pairing, there is a high degree of contingency since the probability of a US following a CS is one and the probability of a US in the absence of the CS is zero. However, it may turn out empirically that with only a few CS and US events the relative importance of single parings is greater.

dure for the study of inhibitory processes is to consistently *pair* CS and US. This, it seems, is less than sensible.

It may also be argued that the truly random control procedure does more than simply remove the contingency of Pavlovian conditioning. It might, for instance, introduce a new process of its own such as increasing the likelihood that S will ignore or habituate to the CS since it bears no relation to the US. This is, of course, possible; but it means that the arrangement of a contingency affects the rate at which S comes to "ignore" a CS. Thus this ignoring of a CS is governed by its associative relation to the US and is a proper part of the development of a CR. From the point of view of this paper, then, the truly random control procedure still provides the appropriate control.

Another objection to the truly random control procedure rests again upon the notion that the pairing of CS and US is the significant event for Pavlovian conditioning. One can claim "what is random for the experimenter may not be random for S." Such an objection argues that if we use the truly random control, we should arrange it so that the relation between the CS and US is phenomenally random. One suspects that, at least in part, this objection is based upon the notion of pairing of CS and US. The statement implies that even though CS and US are not related, S will behave as if the CS predicts the US. Those who make this claim are rarely concerned that S will behave as if the CS predicts no US!

It is, of course, possible that some process which normally produces Pavlovian conditioning when the US is made contingent upon the CS is operative even when the CS and US are presented in random fashion. Such a process might fail to operate only when there is a slight inhibitory, or only when there is a slight excitatory, contingency between CS and US. In its most general form, this argument says that the limits of our operational procedures do not necessarily define the limits of psychological pro-

cesses in the organism. It is difficult to disagree. On the other hand, this is not an objection which applies uniquely to the truly random control procedure. For instance, it applies also to the traditional controls for Pavlovian conditioning: What is explicitly unpaired for E may not be explicitly unpaired for S. A solution to this problem requires an ability, which we do not yet have, to identify psychological processes; until we do, there is little choice but to associate psychological processes in Pavlovian conditioning with experimental operations.

A major advantage of the contingency view of Pavlovian conditioning is that it provides a continuum of CS–US contingencies along which a zero point can be located. In the long run, the location of this zero with respect to process is not crucial; if we discover that the assumed correspondence between experimental contingency and psychological process is in error, it may be that results can be brought into line by relocating the point of "zero contingency."

TWO EXPERIMENTAL PREDICTIONS

The truly random control has led to the consideration of two theoretical views of Pavlovian conditioning, the pairing view and the contingency view. The difference between these two theoretical conceptions of Pavlovian conditioning is partly semantic. From our present knowledge it is arbitrary whether we wish to have a point of "zero" conditioning with deviations on both sides or a zero point from which deviations can occur only in one direction. On the other hand, the difference is also partly empirical, and in this framework the question is whether the *number* of CS–US pairings, or the *relative probabilities* of US in the presence and absence of the CS, is the determinant of Pavlovian conditioning. A comprehensive empirical answer to this question requires an extensive program of research, but two specific predictions can be extracted for illustrative purposes.

The area of most blatant disagreement between the two conceptions of conditioning is the notion of inhibition. (*a*) The *pairing* viewpoint fails to distinguish between *S*s failing to learn and *S*s learning that the CS and US are explicitly unpaired. Experimentally, in accord with the pairing view, a CS which has been repeatedly presented alone should not differ from one which has been explicitly unpaired with the US. (This simple statement of the prediction neglects the operation of such factors as sensitization which would produce more CRs in the explicitly unpaired condition.) (*b*) From the viewpoint that CS-US *contingencies* are the important determinants of Pavlovian conditioning, repeated CS presentations may result in failure to condition; but, explicitly unpairing CS and US should lead to the development of inhibitory phenomena. Thus, under some circumstances, the contingency viewpoint predicts a difference between the outcomes of these two treatments and the pairing view does not. But it is important to note that the contingency approach *only* predicts this difference when the CS is tested in the presence of some other excitatory stimulus. Inhibitory effects can be measured only when there is some level of excitation to be reduced. Again, at the risk of being pedantic, it is important not to confuse the question of the presence or absence of inhibition with the question of the ability to measure inhibitory effects.

The conditions for testing the empirical fruitfulness of the contingency view were met in an experiment by Rescorla and LoLordo (1965). In that experiment, two groups of dogs were trained on a Sidman avoidance task. Both groups were then confined and given Pavlovian conditioning treatments. While confined, one group received repeated tone presentations without any shock USs, while the other group received tones and shocks explicitly unpaired in the manner of Procedure 4 above. Later presentation of these tonal stimuli during the Sidman avoidance performance led to a substantial reduction in avoidance rate during the CS in the explicitly unpaired group and little change in rate during the CS for the group that received only tones. Because previous experiments supported the assumption that avoidance rate is in part a function of the level of fear, these results were interpreted to indicate that explicitly unpairing the CS and US led to the development of Pavlovian inhibitory processes capable of reducing fear. Merely presenting the tones did not lead to this result. The outcome of this experiment is consistent with the theoretical view that CS-US contingency, rather than simply CS-US pairing, determines the outcome of Pavlovian conditioning procedures.

The two contrasting views of Pavlovian conditioning also make differential predictions for the outcomes of excitatory conditioning procedures. Suppose that we condition one group of *S*s with a type of truly random conditioning procedure in which USs are delivered on a variable interval schedule and CSs are randomly distributed throughout the session. A second (experimental) group receives the identical treatment except that the preprogrammed USs are allowed to reach *S* only if they come in a 30-second period following a CS onset. Thus, for this group a switch permits the delivery of the independently programmed USs only for a period just after each CS. USs which are programmed for the truly random *S*s during other periods of the session never occur for the experimental group. The *S*s in this experimental group receive at least as many CS-US pairings as do *S*s in the truly random group, but USs can occur *only* following CSs. If the number of CS-US *pairings* is important, then this procedure should produce results similar to those of the truly random control. However, if the CS-US *contingencies* are important, then a considerably greater number of CRs should occur in the experimental group.

This conditioning procedure was used in a paradigm like that of the Rescorla and LoLordo experiment (Rescorla, 1966). All dogs were trained on a Sidman avoidance schedule. Then, separately, half of the animals received the truly random control treatment while the other half received the modified treatment of the experimental group described above. Shock was the US and tones served as CSs. After these conditioning treatments, the tones were presented during performance of the avoidance response. The CS of the truly random group had little effect upon performance, while the CS of the experimental group showed marked fear-producing properties, increasing the avoidance response rate. Again, this result supports the view that the important dimension in Pavlovian conditioning is the CS–US contingency rather than CS–US pairing.

These are but two examples of the kinds of experiments which the contingency view of Pavlovian conditioning generates. The fact that the results of these experiments support the fruitfulness of the contingency view suggests a program of research varying the relative probabilities which form the basis of the CS–US contingencies. In this way we can explore the relations between CS–US contingencies and Pavlovian conditioning.

In summary, we have argued that the conventional control procedures for Pavlovian conditioning are inadequate in a variety of ways. An alternative procedure, in which the CS and US bear no relation to each other, was proposed. It was argued that the failure previously to use this procedure stems from a particular, and probably inadequate, conception of Pavlovian conditioning. Taking seriously the truly random control procedure, we proposed an alternative theoretical view of Pavlovian conditioning in which the CS–US contingency is important rather than the CS–US pairing. The empirical usefulness of this alternative view has been illustrated.

REFERENCES

BITTERMAN, M. E. Classical conditioning in the goldfish as a function of the CS–US interval. *Journal of Comparative and Physiological Psychology*, 1964, **58**, 359–366.

HARRIS, J. D. Studies of nonassociative factors inherent in conditioning. *Comparative Psychological Monographs*, 1943, **18** (1, Whole No. 93).

JENSEN, D. D. Operationism and the question "Is this behavior learned or innate?" *Behavior*, 1961, **17**, 1–8.

KALISH, H. I. Strength of fear as a function of the number of acquisition and extinction trials. *Journal of Experimental Psychology*, 1954, **47**, 1–9.

KONORSKI, J. *Conditioned reflexes and neuron organization*. New York: Cambridge University Press, 1948.

NOTTERMAN, J. M., SCHOENFELD, W. N., & BERSH, P. J. Partial reinforcement and conditioned heart rate response in human subjects. *Science*, 1952, **115**, 77–79.

PREMACK, D. Reinforcement theory. In D. Levine (Ed.) *Nebraska symposium on motivation: 1965*. Lincoln: University of Nebraska Press, 1965. Pp. 123–180.

PROKASY, W. F. Classical eyelid conditioning: Experimenter operations, task demands, and response shaping. In W. F. Prokasy (Ed.), *Classical conditioning*. New York: Appleton-Century-Crofts, 1965.

RESCORLA, R. A. Predictability and number of pairings in Pavlovian fear conditioning. *Psychonomic Science*, 1966, **4**, 383–384.

RESCORLA, R. A., & LoLORDO, V. M. Inhibition of avoidance behavior. *Journal of Comparative and Physiological Psychology*, 1965, **59**, 406–412.

RODNICK, E. H. Does the interval of delay of conditioned responses possess inhibitory properties? *Journal of Experimental Psychology*, 1937, **20**, 507–527.

SOLOMON, R. L., & TURNER, L. H. Discriminative classical conditioning in dogs paralyzed by curare can later control discriminative avoidance responses in the normal state. *Psychological Review*, 1962, **69**, 202–219.

SPENCE, K. W., & RUNQUIST, W. N. Temporal effects of conditioned fear on the eyelid reflex. *Journal of Experimental Psychology*, 1958, **55**, 613–616.

THOMPSON, R., & McCONNELL, J. Classical conditioning in the planarian, *Dugesia dorotocephala*. *Journal of Comparative and Physiological Psychology*, 1955, **48**, 65–68.

WICKENS, D. D., & WICKENS, C. A study of conditioning in the neonate. *Journal of Experimental Psychology*, 1940, **26**, 94–102.

(Received March 29, 1966)

PAVLOVIAN CONDITIONED INHIBITION

Robert A. Rescorla

The notion of conditioned inhibition is examined and a definition is suggested in terms of the learned ability of a stimulus to control a response tendency opposed to excitation. Two techniques of measuring inhibition are outlined: (*a*) the summation procedure in which an inhibitor reduces the response that would normally be elicited by another stimulus and (*b*) the retardation-of-acquisition procedure in which an inhibitor is retarded in the acquisition of an excitatory conditioned response (CR). Examples of the use of these procedures are given for a variety of unconditioned stimulus (US) modalities. Several possible operations for generating conditioned inhibitors are reviewed: extinction following excitatory conditioning, discriminative conditioning, arrangement of a negative correlation between a conditioned stimulus (CS) and a US, use of an extended CS–US interval, and presentation of a stimulus in conjunction with US termination. A review of the literature on these operations suggests that conditioned inhibitors are not generated either by simple extinction procedures or by pairing a stimulus with US termination. By contrast, for both salivary and fear conditioning the other procedures do appear to generate inhibitors. Most of the procedures generating conditioned inhibitors can be described as arranging a negatively correlated CS and US.

In his work on conditioned salivation, Pavlov (1927) found that he could endow a neutral stimulus with the power either to elicit or to inhibit salivation, depending upon the temporal relations which he arranged between that stimulus and food. American psychologists have tended to emphasize the acquisition of the ability to elicit salivation, so-called excitatory conditioning, and to ignore what Pavlov himself discussed at length, that some relations between a neutral stimulus and food lead to the development of inhibition.

The present paper is concerned with the logical and empirical procedures involved in identifying Pavlovian conditioned inhibition.[1] The paper has three objectives: first, to provide at least a working definition of the concept of conditioned inhibition; second, to examine at some length the procedures available for identifying a stimulus as a Pavlovian conditioned inhibitor; and third, to review the scanty evidence on the conditions necessary to establish a stimulus as a conditioned inhibitor.

The defining properties of a conditioned inhibitor are not well specified in the psychological literature. But a few points of agreement are clear. First, the power of a conditioned inhibitor to produce changes in behavior is acquired as a result of the past experience of the organism; that is, its inhibitory function is conditioned in the most general sense of the term. Second, the outcome of this

Preparation of this manuscript was supported in part by National Science Foundation Grant GB-6493. Requests for reprints should be addressed to Robert A. Rescorla, Department of Psychology, Yale University, 333 Cedar Street, New Haven, Connecticut 06510.

From *Psychological Bulletin*, Vol. 72, No. 2, 77–94. Copyright 1969 by the American Psychological Association. Reprinted by permission.

[1] The review concentrates on Pavlovian conditioning. No attempt is made to discuss in detail the role of inhibition in instrumental learning; however, analogous findings from that literature are occasionally mentioned.

past experience is that a stimulus becomes capable of reducing some behavioral change which is normally attributed to excitation.

The criteria defining conditioned excitation (more commonly called a conditioned response) are somewhat more clear than those for conditioned inhibition. Typically, conditioned excitation is defined by satisfaction of two conditions; an operation relating the conditioned stimulus (CS) and the unconditioned stimulus (US), such as a pairing of the two or the arrangement of a positive contingency between them, and a change in behavior resulting from this operation. The most common example is the increase in salivation resulting from the operation of presenting in sequence a neutral CS and a food US. If the conditioning operation is performed and no change appears in the behavior of the organism, ostensibly no conditioning has occurred. Conversely, if that operation is not performed, and still changes in the organism are found, such changes are identified not with conditioning but with some nonassociative change in the organism. Excitatory conditioning is thus defined in terms of both an operation and a consequent change in the behavior of the organism. Although the laws which a conditioned response (CR) follows, including those specifying the nature of the change which will count as a Pavlovian CR, may eventually be included in the definition of conditioned excitation, the present definition is silent on this point. Nothing is said about the nature of the behavior change. Should one wish to exclude, for instance, changes in which the CRs are unlike the unconditioned response (UR) in form, this will only limit somewhat the scope of the present discussion.

Parallel attempts to specify conditioned inhibition have not been so sharply laid out. In the first place, the operation involved in setting up a conditioned inhibitor is rarely specified. In a subsequent section, several possible defining operations are reviewed. Second, a variety of effects upon behavior which might result from such an operation have been suggested; however, no single effect has been generally accepted. Again, in a later section, the usefulness of some of these possibilities is discussed. For the present, conditioned inhibitors are specified only in terms of the general kind of change that they produce in behavior. First, an acceptable conditioned excitor is specified in terms of an operation relating CS and US and the resulting behavioral change. A stimulus, then, is called a conditioned inhibitor if, as a result of experience of the organism with some operation relating that stimulus to the US, the stimulus comes to control a tendency opposite to that of the conditioned excitor. Notice that there are two important parts to this definition: (*a*) The experience must be with the same US as that forming the basis for the conditioned excitor; thus explicit counterconditioning with another US does not establish a stimulus as a conditioned inhibitor as the term is used here; (*b*) the tendency controlled by the supposed conditioned inhibitor must be opposite to that controlled by the conditioned excitor (cf. Jenkins, 1965). If the excitor produces an increased probability, decreased latency, and increased vigor of a particular response, then a conditioned inhibitor should decrease its probability, increase its latency, etc. Furthermore, the conditioned inhibitor should be specific to the behavior controlled by the excitor; the discussion is concerned only with stimuli which inhibit specifically the responses generated by excitatory conditioning with a particular US, not with stimuli that suppress all behavior. The intention here is to demand a specificity parallel to that which is attributed to conditioned excitation. When excitatory conditioning is performed with a given US, the pattern of conditioned responding should depend upon the particular US employed. One would not expect a general decrement in all the organism's responses from a conditioned inhibitor any more than one would expect a general increment in all responses from performing excitatory conditioning with a particular US.

For the present, the question of which specific past experiences might generate conditioned inhibitors is left open. This is primarily an empirical question and is dealt with in a later section. But notice that even at this point, deciding whether or not a stimulus is a conditioned inhibitor depends upon the operation specified to obtain a conditioned excitor as well as upon the outcome of that operation. This point is discussed later.

Thus, a conditioned inhibitor has been defined as a stimulus which through learning comes to control a tendency which is opposite to that of a conditioned excitor.[2] Any further properties which might accrue to conditioned inhibitors are to be discovered empirically. It may turn out that inhibitory tendencies are more fragile than excitatory tendencies (as Pavlov indeed assumed), or they may be more robust. Similarly, inhibition may dissipate with time (as again Pavlov assumed), or it may not. Conditioned inhibitors may be positive or negative reinforcers, aversive or appetitive stimuli. These are possible properties of a conditioned inhibitor but they are not central to its definition. The definition here is made purely in terms of control of a tendency opposite to that of an excitor.

THE MEASUREMENT OF INHIBITION

In most conditioning situations, it is considerably easier to measure conditioned excitation than it is to measure

---

[2]It may be noted that the term "conditioned inhibition" as used here differs from the usage of Pavlov. The term "conditioned" is used in the general sense of "learned" so that "conditioned inhibition" applies generally to learned inhibition. Pavlov applied the phrase "conditioned inhibition" to inhibition acquired as a result of a particular training paradigm. The present use of "conditioned inhibition" corresponds roughly to Pavlov's phrase "internal inhibition."

conditioned inhibition. For instance, in salivary conditioning, excitation is measured by the occurrence of drops of saliva to a CS after repeated conditioning trials. The change that takes place is that the CS now comes to produce drops of saliva, whereas it did not before. If this increase in the probability of salivation is the excitatory reaction, then by the definition given above, a conditioned inhibitor should produce a decrease in the probability of salivation. Immediately, there is an asymmetry between the measurement of excitation and inhibition. Prior to conditioning, the CS elicits no salivation; it is thus difficult to demonstrate the presence of conditioned inhibition through decreases in the amount of salivation elicited by the CS. And surely, the continued failure of a CR to occur is not sufficient grounds for asserting that the CS is a conditioned inhibitor.

One source of the problem is relatively clear: Typically the experimenter selects as "neutral" CSs those stimuli which prior to conditioning do not produce any evidence of *excitation;* that is, stimuli which normally elicit little or no response. It is then difficult to measure the degree to which a stimulus acquires control over a tendency to decrease the response. This is not to say that conditioned inhibition does not develop to such stimuli, only that it is difficult to detect its presence. Difficulty in observing conditioned inhibition should not be mistaken for its absence.

To bypass this problem of detection, a variety of special measurement procedures have been developed. What follows is a brief summary of such procedures together with mention of some experiments illustrating their use.

Summation

Pavlov (1927) suggested what is perhaps the most direct method of measuring inhibition. Suppose that there is a stimulus S_0 which is a known excitor of a response, then one can tell whether or not S_1 is a conditioned inhibitor of that response by comparing the response elicited by S_0 alone with that elicited by the combination of S_1 and S_0 presented together. If the combination produces a reduced response compared with that to S_0 alone, S_1 is declared an inhibitor. The notion is simply that S_0 elicits a given amount of excitation; excitation and inhibition are algebraically additive; thus if S_1 reduces the amount of responding that would normally occur to S_0, S_1 is an inhibitor. A similar logic applies to the demonstration that S_1 is a conditioned excitor; under those circumstances it should enhance the responding to S_0. However, this test is rarely applied except in the case that S_0 is the null stimulus which elicits little responding.

Notice two important things about the summation technique for demonstrating an inhibitor. First, it has built into it the assumption that excitation and inhibition produce directly opposite effects; S_1 is termed an inhibitor if it reduces the response normally elicited by the excitor S_0 no matter whether the response to S_0 involves an increment or a decrement in behavior. This is important since many excitatory CRs actually reflect themselves as behavior decrements. Second, it emphasizes the fact, which is obvious upon reflection, that it is impossible to demonstrate that a stimulus is an inhibitor of something unless there is something present to inhibit.

The summation procedure has been used with a variety of kinds of stimuli playing the role of S_0, the known elicitor of behavior.

1. Reduction of behavior elicited by an excitatory CS: The most common summation procedure employed by Pavlov involved showing that a suspected inhibitor reduced the CR elicited by a second, excitatory CS, based on the same US. For instance, in one experiment he examined the reduction in salivation to an excitatory CS when it was presented in conjunction with a stimulus which had repeatedly been presented to the dog but

had never been followed by food (Pavlov, 1927, p. 77). He found this reduction greater than that produced when the excitatory CS was presented in conjunction with a novel stimulus. Pavlov concluded that a CS repeatedly not followed by food became a conditioned inhibitor. Similar demonstrations of conditioned inhibitors using this technique with an excitatory CS occur throughout Konorski's (1948) book. A more recent example is found in a salivary conditioning experiment by Szwejkowska (1957).

This technique has recently been used in the demonstration that a stimulus consistently followed by the absence of shock can become an inhibitor of fear. Bull and Overmier (1968) showed an increase in avoidance latency in response to a positive conditioned stimulus (CS+) for shock when the CS+ was also accompanied by a negative conditioned stimulus (CS−) for shock. Similarly, in an experiment by Hammond (1967), a combination of a CS− for shock with a CS+ for shock showed less conditioned emotional response (CER) suppression than the CS + alone. With the GSR, Rodnick (1937) has used the summation technique to detect inhibition during the early part of a long-delay CS for shock. Rodnick's experiment is notable because it found transfer of conditioned inhibition between two aversive USs.

Finally, a parallel procedure has evolved for demonstrating control of nonresponding in an operant situation. Both Brown and Jenkins (1967) and Cornell and Strub (1965) presented negative stimuli (Ss−) in conjunction with discriminative stimuli for operant behavior. They interpreted reductions in the operant behavior produced by these stimuli as evidence that they are conditioned inhibitors.

2. Reduction of behavior elicited by a US: Several authors have used an unconditioned stimulus as S_0 in examining the reduction in behavior produced by an $S_1 S_0$ combination. With salivary condi-

tioning, Sergeev (1961) found that following extinction, a formerly excitatory CS now reduced the flow of saliva normally elicited by food. In contrast, during conditioning, presentation of this CS had enhanced the UR. Findings of the effects of conditioned and extinguished stimuli upon the GSR and eyeblink URs which conflict with those of Sergeev for salivary conditioning have been reported by Kimble and Ost (1961) and Kimmel (1966). With those responses, conditioned excitatory CSs seemed to inhibit the UR. It is interesting that this finding, too, has been interpreted by some as evidence for conditioned inhibition.

With stimulation of the motor cortex as the US, Tchilingaryan (1963) and Wagner, Thomas, and Norton (1967) used shifts in threshold value of the US needed to produce a UR as a measure of conditioned inhibition. Tchilingaryan found an extinguished CS (which had formerly been paired with motor cortex stimulation eliciting paw flexion) raised the intensity of the US necessary to produce the UR. A similar report was made by Wagner et al. for a CS— which had never been paired with motor cortex stimulation. Both of these authors used symmetrical downward shifts in UR threshold as a measure of conditioned excitation.

3. Reduction in the general level of conditioned excitation: Rescorla and LoLordo (1965) detected conditioned inhibitors of fear by their effect in reducing unsignalled avoidance behavior. This behavior may be thought of as maintained by a general level of conditioned fear for which an explicit stimulus is unidentified, S_X. Superimposition of stimuli upon unsignalled avoidance then amounts to presentation of $S_X S_1$ combinations. Reductions in behavior produced by such superimpositions have been interpreted as evidence that stimuli followed by absence of shock or used in a long-delay conditioning procedure with a shock US become inhibitors of fear (Rescorla, 1967a; Rescorla & LoLordo,

1965). Similarly, stimuli increasing the avoidance rate have been called conditioned excitors. Novel stimuli did not produce such changes in avoidance.

4. Stimulus generalization of inhibition: Following the establishment of a potential conditioned inhibitor, several authors have tested for inhibition by presentation of stimuli along a continuum of similarity to the supposed inhibitor. For instance, Krasnagorski (1927) established several points along the skin of a dog as conditioned excitors for salivation and then extinguished the response to one point. Stimulation of this set of points following extinction showed a differential response tendency which was minimal at the extinguished point. From these data, Pavlov reasoned that there was a fixed level of excitation along the continuum defined by these points; inhibition differed among the points and the gradient was a result of summation of a fixed level of excitation with different levels of inhibition. Hovland (1937) performed a similar experiment with GSR and gave his results a similar interpretation. In an operant-conditioning situation, some authors (e.g., Kalish & Haber, 1963) have examined modifications in excitatory stimulus generalization gradients produced by nonreinforcement of one point on the continuum. They interpreted such changes as indices of inhibition.

All of these generalization tests are perhaps best considered special cases of a summation procedure. A level of excitation is established across some continuum, either explicitly or through stimulus generalization; inhibition is then produced at one point of the continuum and the resulting changes in the excitatory gradient reflect the summation of excitation and inhibition at each point of the dimension. In tests of generalization of inhibition, comparison is made between the reduction produced by some supposed inhibitor and that produced by a variety of stimuli not treated so as to produce inhibition but varying in similarity with that inhibitor. It should be noted that if the *magnitude* of inhibition is to be measured in this way, considerably fewer metric assumptions about the summation of excitation and inhibition are necessary if the amount of the excitation is uniform throughout the continuum.

Jenkins (1965) recently added an important refinement to the generalization procedure within an operant setting. He suggested that to demonstrate that $S-$ is an inhibitor, the continuum of stimuli in the generalization test must be orthogonal to any dimensions spanning $S-$ and any $Ss+$. Otherwise what appear as inhibitory generalization gradients might be due to variations in excitation around some $S+$. The assumption seems to be that if the points on a generalization continuum are "equally" distant from $S+$, as is assumed to be the case if the dimension is orthogonal to the $S+$ dimension, they should all have some uniform tendency to respond (excitation) which can summate with different degrees of inhibition which they also elicit. This technique recently has been successfully used by Hearst (1968) and Farthing and Hearst (1968). Failure to meet the Jenkins criterios in most of the generalization-of-extinction experiments mentioned previously (e.g., Hovland, 1937; Krasnagorski, 1927) makes it impossible to identify the decrement observed in those experiments as inhibition.

The problem, of course, is to find dimensions which *are* orthogonal to one another; this may not be as easy as it first sounds. Although the dimensions described by the experimenter may be independent, these may not be the stimuli to which the animal is responding. Absence of a line may not have a sensible place on a dimension described by line orientation, but perhaps it does fit on a dimension describing the probability of seeing a black area at the top of the visual field when the head is primarily held erect. This difficulty in specifying the relevant dimension is particularly troublesome since it is reasonable to expect that dis-

crimination training may itself determine the dimensions to which the organism is responding.

Unless the level of excitation along the stimulus dimension can be safely specified, the use of this generalization technique is hazardous. For if either the degree of excitation is nonuniform or if it is zero along this dimension, then variations in responding to stimuli similar to $S-$ are not accurate indices of inhibition. It is of particular importance to demonstrate independently the presence of *some* level of excitation at each point of this continuum if lack of inhibitory control is to be inferred from failure to find an inhibitory gradient (cf. Farthing & Hearst, 1968; Terrace, 1966).

The use of any of these summation techniques is not without its problems. A frequently raised difficulty is that the test presentation of the S_0S_1 combination simply involves presentation of a stimulus complex which varies in similarity to the conditioned S_0; such decrements as may be observed can then be attributed to stimulus generalization decrement with reference to inhibitory control of S_1. It is clear that such effects of S_1 can be assessed by appropriate control procedures designed to identify the treatment of S_1 necessary to make it an inhibitor. This general problem of control procedures is discussed in a subsequent section.

A more subtle problem of presenting S_1 in conjunction with S_0 arises from the possibility of differential attention to the two stimuli. The treatment designed to make S_1 an inhibitor may lead the organism to attend to S_1 to the detriment of attention to S_0. Then S_1 might decrement the response to S_0 by drawing attention away from stimuli normally maintaining the response without actively controlling a tendency opposite to that controlled by S_0. Presumably if this is the case, S_1 would disrupt the normal response to S_0 largely without regard to the nature of the response it controlled or what US generated that response. Thus, in some cases it may be important to demonstrate that the inhibitory power of S_1 is relatively specific to a particular CR elicited by S_0.

Retardation of the Development of CRs

A second class of procedures which have been used to demonstrate conditioned inhibition focuses on the acquisition of responses resulting from excitatory conditioning. The argument here is that if conditioned inhibition and excitation are subtractive of one another, then setting up inhibition to a stimulus either prior to or simultaneously with excitatory conditioning should retard the development of an overt CR. Pavlov (1927, p. 302) reported an experiment by Rickman in which acquisition of a salivary CR to former CS− was greatly retarded.

Konorski, (1948) made particular use of this criterion for the demonstration of conditioned inhibition. In an extended series of investigations, workers in Konorski's laboratory repeatedly interpreted treatments which lead to retardation of the development of subsequent CRs to a CS as having established conditioned inhibition to that CS. Examples of retarded development of a salivary CR to a former CS− for food can be found in Konorski and Szwejkowska (1952b), Szwejkowska (1959), and Szwejkowska and Konorski (1959).

Using a CER procedure, Hammond (1968) interpreted retardation of the development of conditioned suppression to a former CS− for shock as evidence that the CS− had developed into a conditioned inhibitor. Similarly, Carlton and Vogel (1967) found interference with subsequent CER conditioning induced by repeated CS presentation prior to conditioning; this might be interpreted as evidence for conditioned inhibition. Precursors to the Carlton and Vogel finding can be found in the phenomenon of "latent inhibition" explored by Lubow and Moore (1959) and Lubow (1965). In both of these studies the authors measured inhibition through retardation in the

development of subsequent leg-withdrawal conditioned responses in sheep and goats.

Similar interpretations have been made of some instrumental learning experiments. For instance, Bower and Grusec (1964) and Trapold and Fairlie (1965) performed discriminative Pavlovian conditioning with food reinforcement in rats. They then trained the rats to bar press in the presence of either the former CS+ or the CS− for food. Although their interpretations are cautious, they have suggested that retardation in learning to bar press in the presence of CS− might indicate that it is a conditioned inhibitor for some Pavlovian conditioned incentive-motivation state.

In all of the above studies, procedures thought to produce conditioned inhibition have been administered *prior* to trying to set up a CR. Recently, Rescorla (1968b) reported that presentation of shock USs in the intertrial interval *during* excitatory fear conditioning can interfere with the development of that CR. He suggested that one interpretation might be that such shocks lead to the conditioning of inhibition to the CS, thus disrupting the appearance of the overt CR. Here the development of inhibition occurs simultaneously with the establishment of a CR.

One problem of the retardation of learning as an index of conditioned inhibition is that such learning decrement might result from other processes. A particularly popular alternative lies in a selective-attention mechanism. There is now considerable evidence which indicates that various conditioning procedures not only establish conditioned responses but also lead animals to attend selectively among stimulus events. It is reasonable to expect that an organism which comes to the experimental setting attending to stimulus dimensions other than that of the CS will be retarded in the development of a CR. For instance, in the latent-inhibition experiments, the repeated presentation of a CS in the absence of USs might lead the organism to cease attending to the CS without that CS gaining any control over tendencies opposite to subsequently established CRs. If such were the case, then the summation technique would presumably fail to show any inhibitory effect of the CS despite the fact that *development* of a CR to the CS is retarded.

A final comment should be made about the retardation and summation techniques. They both determine whether or not a stimulus is a conditioned inhibitor in the sense of having a net response tendency directly opposite to conditioned excitation. It is entirely conceivable that a stimulus have conditioned to it both excitation and inhibition; it would only be deemed a conditioned inhibitor by these assessment techniques if the conditioned inhibition is greater. Naturally, similar considerations apply to the identification of a conditioned excitor. At this point it seems likely that identification of such "hidden" response tendencies requires the use of a theory of inhibition. The assessment techniques discussed below make such additional theoretical assumptions about inhibition.

Criteria Dependent upon Special Properties of Inhibition

In addition to the above two criteria for detecting conditioned inhibition, several more specialized techniques have been proposed. These depend upon phenomena which were important to Pavlov in postulating an inhibitory process but which are not central to the notion of conditioned inhibition as defined here.

Pavlov noticed that following extinction of a formerly excitatory CR, a rest period allowed the CR to recover much of its strength. He termed this finding "spontaneous recovery" and argued from it that the excitatory tendency must have persisted through extinction; else, how could it reassert itself after a rest period, without further training? Similarly, Pavlov found that if a novel stimulus was presented in conjunction with an extinguished CS, some of the excitatory

CR reappeared, so-called disinhibition. Again, this was taken as evidence that the excitatory tendency persisted through extinction and was simply overcome by a superimposed inhibitory tendency. By this account, presentation of the novel stimulus disrupted the inhibition, leading to an increased response.

The deduction from these findings that the CS has inhibitory properties depends upon the assumption that conditioned inhibition is somehow less stable and more easily disrupted by external stimuli or the passage of time than is conditioned excitation. This may in fact be the case, but there is little empirical evidence that demands this assumption. Furthermore, this interpretation of spontaneous recovery and disinhibition depends upon the assumption that even though conditioned inhibition has developed to a stimulus, the excitatory tendency has survived whatever operations lead to the development of inhibition. It is this assumption, rather than the presence of conditioned inhibiton, to which the phenomena appear most relevant. It is perhaps more reasonable to account for these phenomena as special cases of stimulus generalization rather than as demonstrations of inhibition. In any case, it is clear that conditioned inhibition in the sense of controlling a tendency opposite to an excitor could develop to a stimulus and be detectable by, for instance, the summation technique in the face of failure to demonstrate either spontaneous recovery or disinhibition. These phenomena depend upon the two further assumptions that conditioned inhibition is less stable than excitation and that conditioned excitation persists through conditioned-inhibition treatments.

A third phenomenon has often been interpreted as evidence for inhibition: induction. Induction was first described by Pavlov as the enhancement of the reaction to a conditioned excitor when it is presented just subsequent to a conditioned inhibitor. The argument is that removal of a supposed inhibitor has an aftereffect which is opposite to the inhibitory process itself. This in turn summates with the excitor, thereby enhancing its response. An analogous wave of inhibition was supposed to follow the termination of a conditioned excitor. A modern parallel to this Pavlovian observation can be found in behavioral contrast in operant situations. Here the introduction of a nonreinforced S− leads to the enhancement of responding to a reinforced S+. Several authors have been tempted to attribute to S− inhibitory properties as a result of this observation.

The status of that inference is somewhat unclear. Pavlov had in mind a particular model of the operation of inhibition in which this overshooting aftereffect played an integral role. But there seems to be no logical necessity for such overshooting into excitation to follow conditioned inhibition. Furthermore, Pavlov himself often described the converse effect, so-called inhibitory aftereffect, in which termination of a conditioned inhibitor could *reduce* the response to a subsequent CS+. This, too, he interpreted as evidence for conditioned inhibition. This overshooting seems not central to the present conception of conditioned inhibition but rather tied to a particular theory of inhibition. It remains an empirical question whether induction covaries with inhibition as measured by the summation and retardation techniques.

In summary, several techniques for the measurement of conditioned inhibition have been reviewed.[3] Some of these techniques depend upon properties of a conditioned inhibitor other than its ability to produce a tendency opposite to that of a conditioned excitor. The inference from these procedures is accordingly less secure. The summation and the retardation-of-the-acquisition-of-a-CR techniques remain as relatively direct measures of conditioned inhibition. They most straightforwardly measure the ability of a stimulus to control a tendency opposite to excitation.

Finally, some comment should be made about the relationship between the concepts of conditioned inhibition and attention. As pointed out previously, in many instances, shifts in the attention of the organism among various stimuli will produce effects which are similar to those of conditioned inhibition. Conceptually the notions are clearly separable. Conditioned inhibition refers to an effect which is specifically opposite to conditioned excitation; a conditioned inhibitor is specific to the reduction of a particular response. In contrast, attention, as the term is typically used, refers to the effectiveness of a stimulus in producing a response, regardless of what that response may be. Given a stimulus S_0 which elicits a response, a second stimulus S_1 producing a shift in attention will modify the effectiveness of S_0 independently of the nature of the response that S_0 elicits and the US upon which it is based. However, an S_1 controlling conditioned inhibition should affect the response to S_0 maximally when related USs are used to set up the response to S_0 and the inhibition to S_1. Of course a particular treatment may endow a stimulus with both con-

---

[3]The assessment techniques reviewed here all concern the ability of a CS to *evoke* responses. It should be acknowledged that in some cases excitation and inhibition might be assessed through the ability of a CS to *reinforce* responses. Particularly in the case of Pavlovian fear conditioning, issues have grown up over the establishment of positive conditioned reinforcers through relationships a CS might bear to an aversive US. In some cases (e.g., Beck, 1961; Rescorla, 1969b, Weisman, Denny, & Zerbokio, 1967), the conditioning procedures are similar to those discussed here as setting up conditioned inhibitors; however, the results of the conditioning are assessed through the ability of the stimulus to reinforce responses. One way of viewing many of these experiments assumes a level of excitation (fear) maintained by other stimuli in the situation, the presentation of the treated stimulus upon execution of a response inhibits that fear and thus reinforces the response. However, the question of positive conditioned reinforcement in this kind of situation involves an extensive literature of its own which cannot be discussed in detail here.

ditioned-inhibition and attention-shifting properties.

It is experimentally possible to make a rough evaluation of conditioned inhibition and shifts in attention; if the effect of S_1 in modifying S_0's reaction depends heavily upon the nature of that reaction, then S_1 is primarily a conditioned inhibitor rather than a stimulus controlling shifts in attention. Evidence on the specificity of conditioned inhibition has been reported in salivary conditioning by Konorski (1967). Konorski reported retardation in salivary conditioning to a former CS− for food but rapid defense conditioning to the same CS. The retarded conditioning to CS− was dependent upon the nature of the response being conditioned, thus indicating that conditioned inhibition rather than attention was responsible for the retardation. Similarly the author has unpublished data indicating that a conditioned inhibitor based on shock, although retarded in the subsequent acquisition of fear, is not retarded in developing a discriminative stimulus (S^D) function for food-reinforced bar pressing.

Rescorla and Solomon (1967) reviewed various studies of conditioned excitation and inhibition resulting from use of positive and aversive USs. In these studies, which assess Pavlovian CRs through their effects on instrumental behavior, the effect of a Pavlovian conditioned inhibitor was not independent of the reinforcer maintaining the instrumental behavior. Thus conditioned inhibitors derived from shock disrupt shock-motivated avoidance behavior but facilitate or leave unaffected food-motivated behavior. Each of these effects is specifically opposite to the effect of a conditioned excitor based on shock. Furthermore, conditioned inhibitors based on food have quite different effects in these situations. Thus, for some kinds of conditioned inhibitor, there is evidence that the inhibitor is not a general disrupter of behavior but has relatively specific effects. Unfortunately, cases in which an investigator of conditioned inhibition reports this sort of evidence are rare.

Even within the two measurement techniques for conditioned inhibition discussed here it may be possible to distinguish between conditioned inhibition and attention. It seems reasonable that a stimulus to which the organism does not attend will be retarded in acquisition of an excitatory CR but will produce little effect in the summation procedure. On the other hand, a stimulus which attracts attention might be expected to produce decrements in the summation testing procedure but to lead to facilitated acquisition of an excitatory CR. Thus if a stimulus affects the attention of the organism it should not behave like a conditioned inhibitor in *both* the summation and retardation-of-acquisition test procedures. For this reason when attentional accounts seem plausible, it may be valuable to have information from both of these procedures for a stimulus thought to be a conditioned inhibitor.

PROCEDURES LEADING TO THE DEVELOPMENT OF CONDITIONED INHIBITION

A variety of different procedures have been thought to produce conditioned inhibitors. In this section, the evidence concerning some of those procedures is reviewed briefly.

First, however, another question must be considered: How do we identify an inhibitor as conditioned? The previous section reviewed procedures for asserting that a particular stimulus was an inhibitor but paid little attention to the question of how it became an inhibitor. What criteria must be satisfied in order to assert that a stimulus acquires its inhibitory power through a *conditioning* process? The view taken here is that conditioned inhibition is an associative process, resulting from some relation arranged between CSs and USs in much the same way that conditioned excitation is an associative process resulting from such a relation. To be called a *conditioned* inhibitor, a stimulus must acquire its inhibitory power through some relation it bears to a US in the past experience of the organism.

If conditioned inhibition is an associative process, then it needs to be evaluated against the background of nonassociative changes that normally take place in conditioning experiments. The problem here is parallel to that in excitatory conditioning. How do we know that the changes produced when we arrange relations between CS and US depend upon those relations? Perhaps, instead, the observed changes in the reaction to the CS could be generated, for example, by simply presenting the US repeatedly. The use of both the summation and the retardation-of-learning techniques must include comparisons with the effects that control CSs produce in these situations. This problem of controls for nonassociative changes has been dealt with for years in the case of excitatory conditioning, but little attention has been paid to the problem of nonassociative effects in the evaluation of inhibitory conditioning.

Recently, Rescorla (1967b) reviewed the problem of specifying nonassociative control procedures for excitatory conditioning. He suggested a reformulation of excitatory conditioning operations and a novel, companion control procedure for those operations. According to this suggestion, the critical operation for excitatory conditioning is a positive contingency between the CS and US. Such a positive contingency results when the probability of a US is greater following CS onset than at other times. On this view, the appropriate control procedure for nonassociative processes during conditioning is one involving presentation of both CS and US but with no contingency whatsoever between them, that is, one in which the probability of the US is equal in the presence and absence of the CS. This is best accomplished by randomly distributing CS and US events in time. This control procedure, the "truly random" procedure, might well serve as a

control for nonassociative factors in both excitatory and inhibitory conditioning. Within this scheme, it is reasonable to expect that operations involving a negative contingency between the CS and US would result in the development of conditioned inhibition.

It should be noted that this view of Pavlovian conditioning differs from that most frequently encountered. According to most accounts, it is the pairing of CS and US rather than the contingency of one upon the other that counts in conditioning. On the pairing view, the most appropriate control procedure for nonassociative effects during excitatory conditioning would involve presentation of CS and US without pairing them. The most popular procedure for doing this might be called the "explicitly unpaired" procedure. In this procedure, a subject receives both the CS and the US, but their occurrence is restricted to times when the other is not present. The pairing view of Pavlovian conditioning does not specify an operation leading to the development of inhibition nor a control procedure appropriate to such operations.

In good part, the difference between the two views of conditioning centers around their handling of conditioned inhibition. On the contingency view, the "explicitly unpaired" control procedure meets the conditions for the development of inhibition; in contrast, from the pairing viewpoint, it is simply a condition in which excitation fails to develop. This is partly a semantic matter, it being arbitrary where on a contingency continuum a "neutral" point is placed. However, the contingency viewpoint does seem to generate predictions which do not easily follow from the pairing view. For this reason, parts of the remainder of this section are presented with the contingency view in mind.

Most of the experiments reviewed here have not been conducted from the contingency viewpoint. Consequently, it is often the case that what is considered an appropriate nonassociative control from that viewpoint is not available. Instead comparison will have to be made with more traditional control procedures. This in itself may not be too serious since something is known of the properties of some of those control procedures. The most frequently used control procedures in the following studies are comparison with a novel CS or with a CS which has simply been repeatedly presented to the subject in the absence of all US events. It should be clear that these procedures are *not* equivalent to the experimental procedure in all respects except the relation between a CS and US. For instance, neither involves prior experience of the organism with the US, while the experimental procedures discussed do. A similar criticism applies to the use of generalization gradients as a control; other stimuli on the dimension are simply examples of the novel CS control. In the absence of further controls it cannot be asserted that the orderly gradient is due to a *conditioning* procedure and not simply familiarity with the original CS.

Particular notice should be made of the control procedure involving repeated presentation of the CS in the absence of all USs. This procedure is often called the "latent inhibition" procedure because in some situations it has been found to retard the development of a subsequently conditioned excitor. From the point of view adopted here this procedure cannot properly be said to produce a conditioned inhibitor; the reason for this is that the stimulus does not attain its inhibitory power through any relation with the US. How can this inhibition result from learning a relation between the CS and US when no US has been presented? Furthermore, prior to the attempt to produce excitatory conditioning, there is nothing in the latent-inhibition procedure which is specific to the particular US and CR that will be used. It is difficult to believe that such a stimulus could control a tendency specifically opposite to the excitation about to be set up, no

matter which excitation it is. Rather than speak of such retardation of the acquisition of an excitatory CR as due to conditioned inhibition, it may be better to consider it as due to some general tendency elicited by the stimulus such as failure to attend to the CS. In this connection it may be noted that the evidence for the latent inhibition comes exclusively from studies using retardation of the development of excitatory CRs as the measure of inhibition.

Nonreinforcement of a Previously Reinforced CS

One of the early phenomena which led Pavlov to postulate an inhibitory process was the extinction of a CR with the omission of the US following the CS. He conceived of this as the building up of inhibition to the CS which subtracted from a maintained level of excitation. Although recently this conception of extinction has not been popular, there remains the empirical possibility that with extinction a formerly excitatory CS becomes a conditioned inhibitor. Indeed, in the foreign literature, extinguished CSs are often described as inhibitory stimuli.

There is only meager evidence bearing on this question. Although Pavlov claimed that an extinguished CS was a conditioned inhibitor, he in fact never presented evidence which satisfies the definition adopted here. He never mentioned evidence showing that an extinguished CS reduces the CR elicited by a known excitor or that an extinguished CS is harder to recondition than a fresh CS. There are isolated Russian studies (e.g., Sergeev 1961; Tchilingaryan, 1963) claiming that an extinguished CS will reduce the UR in a salivary conditioning situation. Unfortunately, insufficient control procedures are reported for us to be certain that prior conditioning and extinction of the CS is required for a stimulus to have this effect. Furthermore, in most eastern European studies, extinction of a CS is carried out in a context of continued reinforcement of other CSs. Thus, in effect, the CS is a discriminative stimulus, CS−; this is perhaps quite a different operation than simple omission of all reinforcement.

A few American studies have used a summation technique to evaluate extinguished fear-eliciting CSs (e.g., LoLordo & Rescorla, 1966; Rescorla, 1967a). Typically, these have found that extinguished CSs do not become inhibitors of fear but simply return to the status of preconditioned stimuli.

The evidence from studies of retardation of learning is more clear. There seems to be little question that a formerly conditioned stimulus, no matter how much extinction intervenes, will recondition faster than a novel stimulus condition. In simple salivary conditioning, for instance, Konorski and Szwejkowska (1950, 1952b) provided ample evidence for this assertion. Pavlov himself (1927, p. 59) reported not retarded but rapid conditioning of an extinguished CS.

Once again, care must be taken in interpreting negative evidence from such relearning studies as unequivocally against the inhibitory proposition. Animals previously conditioned to a CS presumably have learned to attend to that stimulus dimension; it is not unreasonable to expect this to facilitate subsequent reacquisition even to the point of overcoming inhibition. Second, the presence of the US within an experiment is an important component of the functional CS. Simple reoccurrence of the US may lead to reappearance of the CR even in the absence of a reinforcing relation between the CS and the US. Inhibition may not have been built up to *that* part of the stimulus complex. Thus although an extinguished CS might become a conditioned inhibitor, a relearning procedure might fail to detect it. Nevertheless, in the absence of any strong positive evidence for conditioned inhibition being elicited by an extinguished CS from summation studies, the strong negative evidence from relearning studies seems particularly damaging. We can conclude only that there is no reason to believe that an extinguished CS is a conditioned inhibitor.

Discriminative (CS−)

A second procedure which Pavlov suggested established a CS as a conditioned inhibitor is discriminative conditioning in which CS+ is consistently followed by the US and CS− is not. Under these circumstances, Pavlov claimed that CS− came to control a tendency opposite to that of CS+. Using a summation technique, Pavlov himself demonstrated that CS− would reduce the salivation elicited by CS+; he further showed this reduction to be greater than that produced by a novel CS. Since that time a great deal of additional positive evidence has accumulated. Below are listed a few examples illustrating that a CS− in Pavlovian conditioning takes on conditioned inhibitory properties.

The evidence for the conditioned inhibitory properties of CS− in salivary conditioning comes mainly from Konorski's laboratory. Using a summation technique with CS+ for food as the known response elicitor, Szwejkowska (1957) and Szwejkowska and Konorski (1959) both found that presentation of CS− depressed the flow of saliva. However, neither of these studies reported evidence that the CS− required any special treatment to serve as an inhibitor; presumably it did not have this effect prior to its contrasted presentation with food, but such evidence is not reported. In a study with the retardation-of-conditioning procedure, Konorski and Szwejkowska (1952b) however did find that a CS− for food could be transformed into a CS+ for food only with considerably more training than that required by a novel stimulus. They cited in support of their results the experiments of various other eastern European authors.

As mentioned earlier, Bower and Grusec (1964) and Trapold and Fairlie

(1965) found a CS— for food retarded in acquisition when used as an S^D for food-reinforced bar pressing. However, comparison was made only between a CS— and CS+ for food; acquisition for the CS— might not have been retarded when compared with appropriate controls. More recently, Trapold, Lawton, Dick, and Gross (1968) reported that a CS— for food developed more rapidly as an S$^\Delta$ for food-reinforced bar pressing than did a control stimulus. However, they did not find parallel retardation when that CS— was used as an S^D. These results have been taken by the authors as evidence that this stimulus was an inhibitor of a Pavlovian incentive motivator involved in instrumental behavior.

One study with paw flexion and motor cortex stimulation by Wagner et al. (1967) found evidence for inhibition from a CS—. A CS— for cortical stimulation raised the threshold value of the cortical US necessary to produce a UR. Prior to conditioning, the CS did not have this effect.

Perhaps the best evidence for inhibition to a discriminated stimulus comes from studies using peripheral electric shock as the US. Hammond (1967), using a CER procedure in which fear is measured by disruption of ongoing appetitively motivated behavior, found a CS— reduced the suppression normally elicited by a CS+. Furthermore, the effect of the CS— was greater than the effect of a stimulus treated in a "truly random" control procedure. Hoffman (1968) measured inhibitory generalization gradients around CS—. When stimuli varying in similarity to CS— were superimposed on CS+, appropriate variations in disruption of CER suppression were observed. Using summation with a base-line level of excitation in a Sidman avoidance schedule. Rescorla and LoLordo (1965) found that a CS— inhibited fear in the sense of disrupting the avoidance response. Within that situation, a variety of controls have been shown to disrupt the avoidance very little: novel CS, CS alone,

truly random CS. Grossen and Bolles (1968) repeated these results with rats, and Bull and Overmier (1968) obtained similar findings using summation with an S^D for signalled avoidance. Hammond has found that a CS— for shock produced an analogous increase in the ongoing level of appetitively maintained bar pressing. A control stimulus produced no change in bar pressing.

Gluck and Rowland (1959) studied the effects of CS+ and CS— for shock upon EEG pattern in sleep-deprived cats. They found that CS+ produced signs of activation; CS—, in contrast, induced spindling (a sign of relaxation) in some cases when superimposed on CS+. This latter effect was not obtained prior to using the stimulus as a CS— for shock. Grings and O'Donnell (1956) found a CS— for shock reduced the GSR normally elicited by a CS+ in humans. A novel CS produced less decrement in the reaction to CS+.

Evidence for inhibition with a shock US also comes from several studies on retardation of the subsequent acquisition of fear. For instance, Hammond (1968) reported that a former CS— for shock is harder to establish as a CS+ for shock than either a truly random control stimulus or a stimulus simply presented in the total absence of shock.

In sum, the evidence that a CS— for food is a conditioned inhibitor for salivation is sparse. Such a stimulus does produce inhibition as measured by both the summation and retardation-of-CR techniques; however, appropriate control results are not always available to indicate that this inhibition is learned. On the other hand, the more recent studies with conditioned inhibition when a shock US is used are better controlled. These studies give strong support to the attribution of conditioned inhibition to a CS— for shock. Beyond these two USs, tests for inhibition to CS— have rarely been performed. The most common observation is that some difference in response occurs to CS— and CS+, but it is not common to test for the inhibitory properties of CS− compared with the effects of a control stimulus. Thus for many US modalities we simply do not have the appropriate evidence to decide whether or not a CS− is a conditioned inhibitor.

Stimuli Negatively Correlated with the US

It is often said that discrimination learning consists, in part, of a combination of conditioning and extinction; for this reason CS− is often treated in the same fashion as an extinguished CS+. As pointed out above, CS− is much more than that; it is a stimulus consistently followed by no US despite the continued occurrence of the US at other times. It is worth asking whether it is this aspect of CS− that might give it its inhibitory properties. Consider a situation in which a US can occur at various times but never occurs during or closely following a CS. Under these circumstances the CS and US are negatively correlated in time; the CS predicts the absence of the US. According to the contingency notion of conditioning such a stimulus (of which CS− is an example) should take on inhibitory properties.

Kosteneckaja (cited in Konorski & Szwejkowska, 1952b) found a CS not followed by food in a situation in which unsignalled food is otherwise occurring becomes a conditioned inhibitor. Here difficulty in the subsequent establishment of a CR was the index of inhibition.

Virtually all of the recent evidence for the assertion that a conditioned inhibitor results when a stimulus is negatively correlated with the US comes from situations using a shock US. One special case of such a stimulus is that generated by the "explicitly unpaired" procedure in which the US neither precedes nor follows the CS closely in time. Rescorla and LoLordo (1965) used summation with a base line of fear maintaining Sidman avoidance in dogs to assess the inhibitory properties of such a stimulus explicitly unpaired with shock. They found that a CS kept temporally distant from shock during independently administered Pavlovian conditioning subsequently produced depression of the avoidance rate. They inferred from this that it was a conditioned inhibitor of fear. As mentioned earlier, a variety of control procedures, including the truly random procedure, yield stimuli which have little effect in this kind of summation test procedure.

Rescorla (1966) used a similar procedure to examine a more general case of negative CS-US contingency. In that experiment a CS predicted the nonoccurrence of shock in a context of otherwise randomly occurring shocks. Here shocks could precede that CS, but the CS forecast a time of decreased shock probability. Again the conditioned inhibitory properties of that CS were indicated by its ability to disrupt ongoing avoidance behavior. Furthermore, in a recent parametric investigation, Rescorla (1969a) found that greater negative contingencies between a CS and shock made that CS a stronger conditioned inhibitor. This result occurred in a summation procedure with CER conditioning in rats.

Retardation of the acquisition of fear to a CS has also been used to assess the degree of inhibition conditioned to a stimulus negatively correlated with shock. Rescorla (1968b) performed CER conditioning on rats with a variety of probabilities of shock during a CS+. For different groups, shock also occurred with various probabilities in the absence of the CS+. He found that as the probability of shock in the absence of the CS increased, the amount of fear elicited by the CS decreased. One way of viewing this finding is that the non-CS shocks are setting up conditioned inhibition to the CS and thus retarding the development of an overt fear CR. In a second experiment, Rescorla (1969a) made more explicit use of the retardation technique. He compared the development of conditioned suppression to CSs which had a history of negative correlation with shock.

The CS had forecast the absence of shock in the context of otherwise randomly occurring shocks; the probability of shocks in the non-CS period varied among the groups. The notion was that greater conditioned inhibition should accrue to a stimulus predicting absence of a higher shock probability. Truly random and US-alone procedures were used in control groups. At the values used, a stimulus previously contrasted with a higher probability of shock was harder to condition as a CS+ for shock. As with the summation assessment procedure, the retardation technique indicates not only that negative CS–US contingencies yield conditioned inhibitors but also that the magnitude of the conditioned inhibition is greater with greater negative contingencies.

With CSs negatively correlated with shock, as with CS–, the evidence on inhibition is rare largely because the appropriate tests have not often been made. This, of course, is particularly true of the "explicitly unpaired" procedure because its extensive use as a control procedure shifts interest away from it as a procedure important in its own right. However, at least with a shock US, there is now accumulating evidence that under some circumstances such stimuli become conditioned inhibitors of fear.

Inhibition of Delay

If an extended CS–US interval is used in conditioning, it is often observed that the CR becomes confined to the later part of the CS. Pavlov (1927) interpreted this finding as indicating that the early portion of an extended CS becomes inhibitory. According to Pavlov's interpretation, the early part of the CS elicits both excitation and inhibition; with continued training the amount of inhibition becomes greater than that of excitation. He supported this interpretation with a variety of kinds of evidence, for example, disinhibition, and decrease in salivation to CS onset over trials. In the present context, the most relevant evidence is that the early portion

of such a CS reduced the salivation which would normally have been elicited by a second excitatory CS. There is very little additional evidence on the inhibitory control of the early part of such a CS. Barkhundarian (1960) found that the onset of a long-delay CS for food decreased the response normally produced by a second CS. However, the absence of relevant control procedures makes this finding difficult to interpret.

With shock as a US, only two studies have reported evidence relevant to the notion of inhibition as used here. Rodnick (1937) found the early portion of a CS+ for shock in GSR conditioning with humans reduced an air-puff-based eyeblink CR normally elicited by another CS. A control group indicated that without prior conditioning this CS did not affect the eyeblink. The second set of studies (Rescorla, 1967a) involved changes induced in avoidance rate by a CS previously paired with shock after an extended CS-US interval. Such a long-delay CS induced avoidance rate depression at its onset; as the CS continued the rate grew monotonically to a maximum well above the pre-CS rate. Comparable results were obtained with long CS–US intervals in a trace-conditioning procedure (Rescorla, 1968a). Rescorla interpreted these results as indicating that the onset of the CS was a conditioned inhibitor of fear. CS– alone and "truly random" control procedures did not yield CSs whose onset depressed the avoidance rate. Thus there is scattered evidence for both salivary and fear conditioning that the early portion of a long-delay CS is a conditioned inhibitor when the summation technique is used.

Very few experiments have assessed the inhibitory effects of the early part of a long-delay CS using the retardation-of-learning procedure. Presumably the proper experiment would find it more difficult to condition a CS with a short CS–US interval if the CS had a history of extensive conditioning with an extended CS–US interval. Konorski and

Szwejkowska (1952b) cited several eastern European studies in which this kind of result was obtained for salivary conditioning. However, there appears to be no more recent evidence on this point.

Stimuli Signalling US Termination

An active line of research in the field of reinforcement has concerned whether stimuli signalling the termination of a US become reinforcers. Equally, one may ask whether such stimuli become inhibitors of CRs based on US onset. This is of particular interest since Konorski (1948) suggested that the paradigm for establishing a conditioned inhibitor is pairing a CS with a fall in level of excitation. Segundo, Galeano, Sommer-Smith, and Roig (1961) reported that stimuli signalling the termination of a long duration shock produce behavioral relaxation and corresponding EEG changes in cats. Prior to this conditioning such CSs did not have these effects.

Two experiments related to this problem have been performed by Zbrozyna (1958a, 1958b). In those experiments, stimuli preceded the withdrawal of food. The basic finding was that during such stimuli the dog stopped eating in anticipation of food removal. Possibly this reflects inhibition of the response normally elicited by the food US. However, no data are presented on inhibition of a Pavlovian salivary UR.

Braud (1968) recently associated stimuli with the termination of a CS+ for shock rather than with the termination of the US itself. Such stimuli, when subsequently made response contingent, reduced the suppression normally elicited by fear CSs. Since response-independent CS presentation was not used, it is not clear whether these results should be interpreted in terms of conditioned inhibition or conditioned reinforcement.

An interesting confounding arises in most of the experiments involving stimuli signalling the termination of a US. When a stimulus precedes the end of the US it signals not only US termination but also the coming of the intertrial interval. It generally forecasts not only the end of the present US but also a time free from the onset of the next US. In that sense, the CS bears a close resemblance to the explicitly unpaired procedure. One may then ask whether the inhibition which may become conditioned to such a CS results from its preceding US termination or from its preceding a period which is free from the onset of the next US. Recently, Moskowitz and LoLordo (1968) addressed just this issue. After finding that stimuli bearing a backward-conditioning relation to a shock US become conditioned inhibitors of fear, they attempted to tease these variables apart. They found that a stimulus signalling a period free from shock served as an inhibitor whether or not it was associated with US termination. But a stimulus associated with US termination only became a conditioned inhibitor if it preceded a period relatively free from shock. The upshot is that presenting a stimulus in conjunction with the termination of a US may yield a conditioned inhibitor primarily because of this confounding with prediction of a period free from shock, that is, because it is negatively correlated with shock onset.

SUMMARY AND CONCLUSIONS

The present paper has reviewed the notion of conditioned inhibitor and has suggested that it is best viewed as a stimulus which comes, through learning, to control a tendency directly opposite to that of a conditioned excitor. To qualify as a conditioned inhibitor, the action of a stimulus must be largely confined to responses normally elicited by conditioned excitors based upon the same US. Furthermore, conditioned inhibitors are viewed as resulting from associative relations between a CS and US in a way parallel to conditioned excitation. Conditioned inhibition comes about as the result of learning relations among CSs and USs.

Two techniques of measuring conditioned inhibition are suggested: summation, the reduction in the response normally elicited by an excitatory CS; and retardation of excitatory conditioning to the supposed inhibitor. Other procedures for measuring conditioned inhibition are discarded because they fail to measure the ability of a stimulus to control a tendency opposite to conditioned excitation.

A variety of procedures thought to establish stimuli as conditioned inhibitors have been reviewed. In both salivary and fear conditioning, some relations between CS and US lead to the development of conditioned inhibition to the CS as measured by both the retardation-of-excitatory-conditioning and the summation procedures. For other kinds of conditioning the evidence is too scattered to make a positive statement. As yet there is not sufficient experimental analysis to make final assertions about the critical conditions for producing conditioned inhibition. Extinguished CSs and CSs preceding US termination do not seem to become conditioned inhibitors; on the other hand, discriminative stimuli, stimuli negatively correlated with the US, and possibly long-delay CSs do become inhibitors.

Most of the experiments which have generated conditioned inhibitors can be described as using procedures in which the CS and US are negatively correlated in time. That is, most conditioned inhibitors seem to be stimuli which forecast a decrease in the probability of occurrence of the US. This general statement applies to the case of discriminative stimuli, stimuli explicitly unpaired with the US, and those positive results with stimuli preceding the termination of the US, as well as to situations in which a negative relation was explicitly arranged. This conclusion encourages the view that Pavlovian conditioning is best described as arising from the contingencies arranged between CS and US. According to such a view, positive CS–US contingencies lead to the development of conditioned

excitation and negative contingencies lead to the development of conditioned inhibition. This view receives further encouragement from the finding that greater negative correlations between CS and US result in greater conditioned inhibition; this parallels the superior excitatory conditioning found with greater positive correlations between CS and US. If viewed in this way, conditioned inhibition has a status equal to that of conditioned excitation. Both kinds of learning result from variations on a CS–US contingency continuum. Indeed, the definition of conditioned inhibition may be reformulated in terms more parallel to that of conditioned excitation. Conditioned inhibition could be defined in terms of the operation of arranging a negative CS–US contingency and the outcome of a particular change in behavior.

REFERENCES

BARKHUNDARIAN, S. S. The physiological mechanism of disinhibition in relation to interaction between different forms of internal inhibition. *Pavlov Journal of Higher Nervous Activity*, 1960, **10**, 744–755.

BECK, R. C. On secondary reinforcement and shock termination. *Psychological Bulletin*, 1961, **58**, 28–45.

BOWER, G., & GRUSEC, T. Effect of prior Pavlovian discrimination training upon learning an operant discrimination. *Journal of the Experimental Analysis of Behavior*, 1964, **7**, 401–404.

BRAUD, W. G. Diminution of suppression by stimuli association with the offset of fear-arousing cues. *Journal of Comparative and Physiological Psychology*, 1968, **65**, 356–358.

BROWN, P. L., & JENKINS, H. M. Conditioned inhibition and excitation in operant discrimination learning. *Journal of Experimental Psychology*, 1967, **75**, 255–266.

BULL, J. A. III, & OVERMIER, J. B. Additive and subtractive properties of excitation and inhibition. *Journal of Comparative and Physiological Psychology*, 1968, **66**, 511–514.

CARLTON, P. L., & VOGEL, J. R. Habituation and conditioning. *Journal of Comparative and Physiological Psychology*, 1967, **63**, 348–351.

CORNELL, D. M., & STRUB, H. A technique for demonstrating the inhibitory function of S. *Psychonomic Science*, 1965, **3**, 25-26.

FARTHING, G. W., & HEARST, E. Generalization gradients of inhibition after different amounts of training. *Journal of the Experimental Analysis of Behavior*, 1968, **11**, 743-752.

GLUCK, H., & ROWLAND, V. Defensive conditioning of electrographic arousal with delayed and differentiated auditory stimuli. *Electroencephalography and Clinical Neurophysiology*, 1959, **11**, 485-496.

GRINGS, W. N., & O'DONNELL, D. E. Magnitude of response to compounds of discriminated stimuli. *Journal of Experimental Psychology*, 1956, **52**, 354-359.

GROSSEN, N. E., & BOLLES, R. C. Effects of a classical conditioned "fear signal" and "safety signal" on nondiscriminated avoidance behavior. *Psychonomic Science*, 1968, **11**, 321-322.

HAMMOND, L. J. Increased responding to CS− in differential CER. *Psychonomic Science*, 1966, **5**, 337-338.

HAMMOND, L. J. A traditional demonstration of the properties of Pavlovian inhibition using differential CER. *Psychonomic Science*, 1967, **9**, 65-66.

HAMMOND, L. J. Retardation of fear acquisition when the CS has previously been inhibitory. *Journal of Comparative and Physiological Psychology*, 1968, **66**, 756-759.

HEARST, E. Discrimination learning as the summation of excitation and inhibition. *Science*, 1968, **162**, 1303-1306.

HOFFMAN, H. S. Discrimination processes as related to aversive controls. In R. M. Gilbert & N. S. Sutherland (Eds.), *Animal discrimination learning*. London: Academic Press, 1968.

HOVLAND, C. I. The generalization of conditioned responses: I. The sensory generalization of conditioned responses with varying frequencies of tone. *Journal of General Psychology*, 1937, **17**, 125-148.

JENKINS, H. M. Generalization gradients and the concept of inhibition. In D. I. Mostofsky (Ed.), *Stimulus generalization*. Stanford: Stanford University Press, 1965.

KALISH, H. I., & HABER, A. Generalization: I. Generalization gradients from single and multiple stimulus points. II. Generalization of inhibition. *Journal of Experimental Psychology*, 1963, **65**, 176-181.

KIMBLE, G. A., & OST, J. W. P. A conditioned inhibitory process in eyelid conditioning.

Journal of Experimental Psychology, 1961, **61**, 150-156.

KIMMEL, H. D. Inhibition of the unconditioned response in classical conditioning. *Psychological Review*, 1966, **63**, 232-240.

KONORSKI, J. *Conditioned reflexes and neuron organization*. Cambridge: Cambridge University Press, 1948.

KONORSKI, J. *Integrative activity of the brain*. Chicago: University of Chicago Press, 1967.

KONORSKI, J., & SZWEJKOWSKA, G. Chronic extinction and restoration of conditioned reflexes. I. Extinction against the excitatory background. *Acta Biologiae Experimentalis*, 1950, **15**, 155-170.

KONORSKI, J., & SZWEJKOWSKA, G. Chronic extinction and restoration of conditioned reflexes. III. Defensive motor reflexes. *Acta Biologiae Experimentalis*, 1952, **16**, 91-94. (a)

KONORSKI, J., & SZWEJKOWSKA, G. Chronic extinction and restoration of conditioned reflexes. IV. The dependence of the course of extinction and restoration of conditioned reflexes on the "history" of the conditioned stimulus (The principle of the primacy of first training). *Acta Biologiae Experimentalis*, 1952, **16**, 95-113. (b)

KRASNAGORSKI, N. I. Studies upon central inhibition and upon the localization of the tactile and motor analysers in the cortex of the dog. Cited by I. P. Pavlov, *Conditioned reflexes*. London: Oxford University Press, 1927.

LoLORDO, V. M., & RESCORLA, R. A. Protection of the fear-eliciting capacity of a stimulus from extinction. *Acta Biologiae Experimentalis*, 1966, **26**, 251-258.

LUBOW, R. E. Latent inhibition: Effects of frequency of nonreinforced preexposure of the CS. *Journal of Comparative and Physiological Psychology*, 1965, **60**, 454-457.

LUBOW, R. E., & MOORE, A. V. Latent inhibition. The effect of frequency. *Journal of Comparative and Physiological Psychology*, 1959, **52**, 415-419.

MOSKOWITZ, A., & LoLORDO, V. M. Role of safety in the Pavlovian backward fear conditioning procedure. *Journal of Comparative and Physiological Psychology*, 1968, **66**, 673-678.

PAVLOV, I. P. *Conditioned reflexes*. London: Oxford University Press, 1927.

RESCORLA, R. A. Predictability and number of pairings in Pavlovian fear conditioning. *Psychonomic Science*, 1966, **4**, 383-384.

RESCORLA, R. A. Inhibition of delay in Pavlovian fear conditioning. *Journal of Comparative and Physiological Psychology*, 1967, **64**, 114–120. (a)

RESCORLA, R. A. Pavlovian conditioning and its proper control procedures. *Psychological Review*, 1967, **74**, 71–80. (b)

RESCORLA, R. A. Pavlovian conditioned fear in Sidman avoidance learning. *Journal of Comparative and Physiological Psychology*, 1968, **65**, 55–60. (a)

RESCORLA, R. A. Probability of shock in the presence and absence of CS in fear conditioning. *Journal of Comparative and Physiological Psychology*, 1968, **66**, 1–5. (b)

RESCORLA, R. A. Conditioned inhibition of fear resulting from negative CS–US contingencies. *Journal of Comparative and Physiological Psychology*, 1969, **67**, 504–509. (a)

RESCORLA, R. A. Establishment of a positive reinforcer through contrast with shock. *Journal of Comparative and Physiological Psychology*, 1969, **67**, 260–263. (b)

RESCORLA, R. A., & LOLORDO, V. M. Inhibition of avoidance behavior. *Journal of Comparative and Physiological Psychology*, 1965, **59**, 406–412.

RESCORLA, R. A., & SOLOMON, R. L. Two-process learning theory: Relations between Pavlovian conditioning and instrumental learning. *Psychological Review* 1967, **74**, 151–182.

RODNICK, E. H. Does the interval of delay of conditioned responses possess inhibitory properties? *Journal of Experimental Psychology*, 1937, **20**, 507–527.

SEGUNDO, J. P., GALEANO, C., SOMMER-SMITH, J. A., & ROIG, J. A. Behavioral and EEG effects of tones "reinforced" by cessation of painful stimuli. In J. F. Delafrensaye (Ed.), *Brain mechanisms and learning*. Oxford: Blackwell, 1961.

SERGEEV, B. F. On the localization of inhibition in the extinction of conditioned reflexes to chain stimuli. *Pavlov Journal of Higher Nervous Activity*, 1961, **11**, 695–700.

SZWEJKOWSKA, G. The effect of a primary inhibitory stimulus upon the positive salivary conditioned reflex. *Bulletin De L'Academie Polonaise Des Sciences*, 1957, **5**, 393–396.

SZWEJKOWSKA, G. The transformation of differentiated inhibitory stimuli into positive conditioned stimuli. *Acta Biologiae Experimentalis*, 1959, **19**, 151–159.

SZWEJKOWSKA, G., & KONORSKI, J. The influence of the primary inhibitory stimulus upon the salivary effect of excitatory conditioned stimulus. *Acta Biologiae Experimentalis*, 1959, **19**, 162–174.

TCHILINGARYAN, L. I. Changes in excitability of the motor area of the cerebral cortex during extinction of a conditioned reflex elaborated to direct electrical stimulation of that area. In E. Gutman & P. Nhik (Eds.), *Central and peripheral mechanisms of motor functions*. Prague: Academy of Science, 1963.

TERRACE, H. S. Discrimination learning and inhibition. *Science*, 1966, **154**, 1677–1680.

TRAPOLD, M. A. Reversal of an operant discrimination by noncontingent discrimination reversal training. *Psychonomic Science*, 1966, **4**, 247–248.

TRAPOLD, M. A., & FAIRLIE, J. Transfer of discrimination learning based upon contingent and noncontingent training procedures. *Psychological Reports*, 1965, **17**, 239–246.

TRAPOLD, M. A., LAWTON, G. W., DICK, R. A., & GROSS, D. M. Transfer of training from differential classical to differential instrumental conditioning. *Journal of Experimental Psychology*, 1968, **76**, 568–573.

WAGNER, A. R., THOMAS, E., & NORTON, T. Conditioning with electrical stimulation of motor cortex: Evidence of a possible source of motivation. *Journal of Comparative and Physiological Psychology*, 1967, **64**, 191–199.

WEISMAN, R. G., DENNY, M. R., & ZERBOKIO, D. J. Discrimination based on differential nonshock confinement in a shuttlebox. *Journal of Comparative and Physiological Psychology*, 1967, **63**, 34–38.

ZBROZYNA, A. W. On the conditioned reflex of the cessation of the act of eating: I. Establishment of the conditioned cessation reflex. *Acta Biologiae Experimentalis*, 1958, **18**, 137–162. (a)

ZBROZYNA, A. W. On the conditioned reflex of the cessation of the act of eating. II. Differentiation of the conditioned cessation reflex. *Acta Biologiae Experimentalis*, 1958, **18**, 163–164. (b)

(Received August 13, 1968)

Chapter 5

Instrumental Conditioning: Basic Principles

THORNDIKE'S EXPERIMENTS

Whatever can be learned can be fitted into two broad categories: (1) the relationship of various events in the environment with each other (classical conditioning) and (2) the relationship of various events in the environment to behavior. Learning of the latter kind is called *instrumental conditioning*.

When a child learns the relationship between the sight of bread and the smell of bread, that learning is an instance of classical conditioning. When the child learns the relationship between his own behavior of lifting the bread to his mouth and the taste of bread, that learning is an instance of instrumental conditioning. But these two broad categories also cover more complex kinds of learning. For instance, the relationship between the subject and predicate of a sentence is a relationship between events in the environment, between sounds we hear or figures we see on a paper; learning about grammar thus falls under the rubric of classical conditioning. But the relationship between saying, "Pass the salt." and actually getting the salt is between behavior and environment and is instrumental conditioning.*

---

*Other names for classical conditioning include *Pavlovian conditioning,* and *respondent conditioning.* Instrumental conditioning is also known as *instrumental learning* and *operant conditioning.* Some psychologists distinguish between instrumental conditioning, instrumental learning, and operant conditioning on the basis of the kind of response (locomotor versus nonlocomotor) or the procedure (trial-by-trial versus continuous observation of behavior). There is more similarity than difference among these techniques, however, and we will treat them alike here under the rubric of *instrumental conditioning.*

There has been much debate among psychologists whether instrumental conditioning is merely a form of classical conditioning, whether classical conditioning is merely a form of instrumental conditioning, or whether they are two completely separate types of learning, each with laws of its own. We shall discuss aspects of this debate throughout the book, but in this chapter we will concentrate on distinguishing between the two types of conditioning.

About the same time as Pavlov was working in Russia, laying down the principles of classical conditioning, the American psychologist E. L. Thorndike was doing the same for instrumental conditioning. Thorndike was concerned about the relationship between the behavior of animals and significant environmental events (rewards or punishments).

The Law of Effect

In 1898, Thorndike laid the groundwork for a simple but important principle, which he named the "law of effect." Here is a paraphrase of his principle: one effect of a successful behavior is to increase the probability that it will occur again in similar circumstances. Thorndike based this conclusion on experiments in which cats, dogs, and chicks were confined repeatedly in puzzle boxes like the one shown in Figure 5.1. In order to escape from the box and get the food that was within view, the hungry animal had to step on a lever or pull out a bolt, or perform some other mechanical task. Thorndike found that the animal, in the course of its behavior in the box, would sooner or later make the correct move-

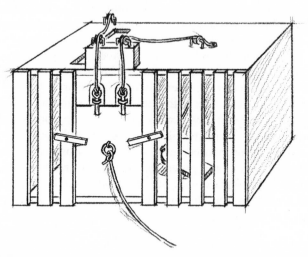

FIGURE 5.1
Thorndike's puzzle box. Cats that were placed inside this box learned to unbolt the door and then to press the door outward to escape. [From Thorndike, E. L. *Animal intelligence.* New York: Macmillan Publishing Co., 1911.]

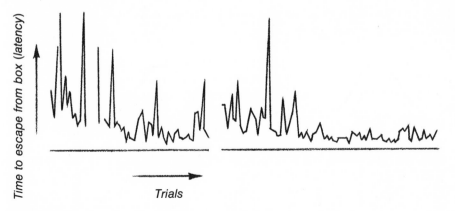

FIGURE 5.2
These two graphs show the performances of two cats in Thorndike's puzzle box. [From Thorndike, E. L. *Animal intelligence.* New York: Macmillan Publishing Co., 1911.]

ment and get out of the box. He measured the latency of the correct movement—how long it took the animal to escape—and continued to measure latency for each successive trial. Thorndike found that, in general, there was a negative correlation between the number of times an animal had escaped from the box and the length of time it took to escape—the more trials, the less time to escape. After many repeated trials, the animal would solve the puzzle and get out of the box almost immediately. (The graphs in Figure 5.2 show how latency decreased with repeated trials.)

Now let us consider the following hypothetical experiment, which is rather similar to Thorndike's and may further clarify the "law of effect." Suppose we construct a puzzle box like Thorndike's, except that we make the ceiling somewhat higher. And suppose that we now put a cat into the box, but that instead of letting it out after it solves a puzzle, we simply observe its behavior, particularly its jumping. Thorndike reported that one common behavior of a hungry cat in a box is jumping.) If we measure the heights of the jumps and plot them as a distribution (see the lower left portion of Figure 5.3), the curve will probably be bell-shaped, showing some very low jumps and some very high jumps but mostly medium jumps. Suppose that we open the door to the box after each jump greater than some arbitrary height, a little above average, say 13 inches, and feed the cat before putting it back into the box. At first, we find the usual number of 13-inch jumps. But as the experiment progresses, we find more and more jumps of 13 inches and above. In fact, the distribution will probably change to one resembling that at the lower right of Figure 5.3. The gradual increase in the height of the cat's jumps is analogous to the gradual increase of the necks of giraffes over generations as illustrated in Figure 5.3. Indeed, the "law of effect" is simply natural selection at work within the life history of a single organism.

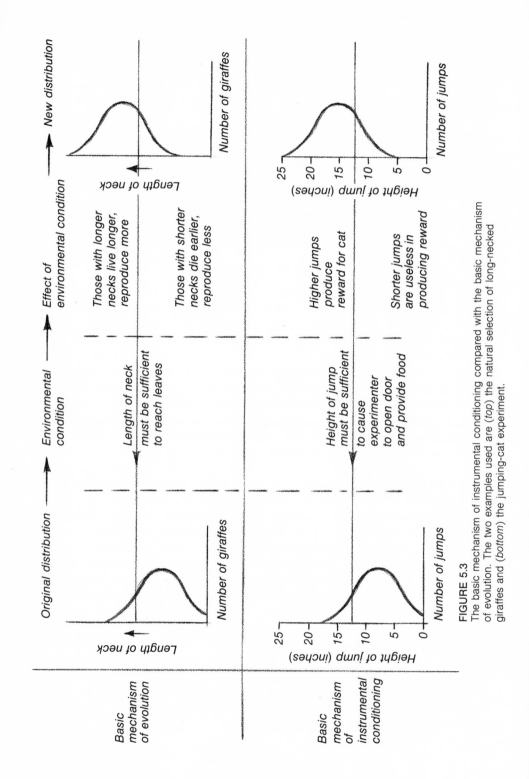

FIGURE 5.3

The basic mechanism of instrumental conditioning compared with the basic mechanism of evolution. The two examples used are (top) the natural selection of long-necked giraffes and (bottom) the jumping-cat experiment.

Because an action cannot be rewarded or punished unless it occurs, the mechanism of the "law of effect" can only strengthen acts that do already occur. In our hypothetical experiment with the jumping cat, we would have to wait a very long time for a jump over 20 inches to occur when the cat is first put into the box. Thus, if we tried to strengthen 20-inch jumps by rewarding them initially, we might not succeed. If, however, we first rewarded 12-inch jumps, we see from the revised distribution at the lower right of Figure 5.3 that 20-inch jumps would become fairly frequent. *Then,* if we rewarded 20-inch jumps we would be likely to succeed in strengthening them. By this method we could finally train the cat to consistently jump at the very limits of its capacity.

The use of such a procedure of successive approximations to train an organism to make a certain response is called *shaping.* This is the procedure usually followed in the laboratory when teaching a rat to press a bar or a pigeon to peck a key.

Like evolution, which results in very complex structures of species by means of gradual changes, shaping can result in very complex behaviors. A child first learns to grasp objects, then to throw a ball at a stationary target, then to throw a ball at a moving target, then to throw a ball while he himself is moving and finally, perhaps, to be quarterback on a football team. All this is achieved by gradual shaping, each new act built upon the repertory of acts previously acquired. Shaping of complex behavior conforms in various proportions to the demands of nature and the demands of other people. The quarterback's throw must take into account the natural rules relating to the intersection of its trajectory with the path of the pass receiver as well as the rules of the game of football itself. Thus, both the natural environment and other people set the tasks and provide rewards during the shaping process.

Thorndike and Pavlov

Like Pavlov, Thorndike was a molecular psychologist. He believed that each act was produced by a specific connection in the nervous system between a stimulus and a response. Each stimulus could be connected to several responses, but the connections would have different strengths. These connections could thus be ordered in a hierarchy—called a *habit-family hierarchy*—according to the probability of their occurrence. A habit-family hierarchy is illustrated in Figure 5.4. Reward would strengthen the connection it followed and raise the response in the hierarchy. Punishment, on the other hand, would weaken the response and lower it in the hierarchy.* In the lower part of Figure 5.3 the distribution on the left represents the hierarchy of connections between the stimulus of the box and various jumping responses before the action of reward. Reward rearranges the hierarchy to that on the lower right.

---

*Punishment was at first seen by Thorndike as the opposite of reward—weakening connections as reward strengthened them. The action of punishment was known as the *negative* law of effect. Later Thorndike gave up this view and adopted a form of the two-factor theory of punishment, a theory which we shall discuss in Chapter 9.

a

Each stimulus is connected to several
responses in a hierarchy. The highest
connections represent the most
probable responses.

b

If the experimenter selects one of the
weaker connections and follows it
(when it occurs) by reward the
connection is strengthened,

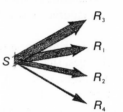

c

and its position in the hierarchy
is raised.

FIGURE 5.4
Thorndike's habit-family hierarchy.

While Thorndike agreed with Pavlov that behavior depended on specific stimulus–response connections, he explained the connections differently. For Pavlov a connection (a conditioned reflex) was strengthened if the conditioned stimulus was contiguous with the unconditioned stimulus (this is called *reinforcement* of the conditioned reflex). For Thorndike a connection (a habit) was strengthened if the response was contiguous with a reward to the animal (this is called *reinforcement* of the habit).

From Chapter 2 we know that molecular relationships are defined in terms of contiguities. In both instrumental and classical conditioning, reinforcement enters into these contiguities. The difference, illustrated in Figure 5.5a and b, lies in what the reinforcer is contiguous with. In instrumental conditioning the experimenter (or the environment) provides contiguities between reinforcer and *response*. In classical conditioning the experimenter (or the environment) provides contiguities between reinforcer and (conditioned) *stimulus*.

The two types of reinforcement can also be described in molar terms, as shown in Figure 5.5c and d. In instrumental conditioning, it is the contingencies and correlations between response and reward that reinforce the stimulus-response relation; in classical conditioning, it is the contingencies and correlations between conditioned and unconditioned stimuli. The values in the contingency tables and correlation plots represent molar equivalents of the individual reinforcements in instrumental conditioning (immediately after each

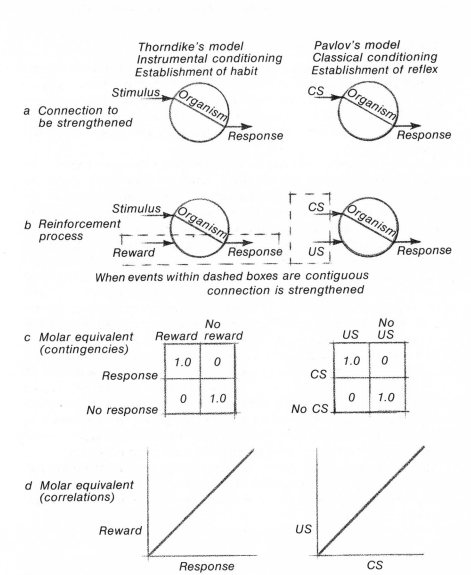

FIGURE 5.5
The difference between instrumental and classical conditioning. Parts (a) and (b) distinguish between the molecular models of Thorndike and Pavlov. Parts (c) and (d) distinguish between more molar conceptions of instrumental and classical conditioning.

response) and classical conditioning (immediately after each CS). A critical question in instrumental conditioning is whether learning is best expressed in terms of the connections of Figure 5.5a and b or the contingencies and correlations of Figure 5.5c and d.

Thorndike and Skinner

Thorndike's conclusion that rewards reinforce stimulus–response connections was challenged in 1938 by B. F. Skinner's claim that rewards reinforce operant responses directly, not their connection to a prior stimulus. As we noted in Chapter 2, Skinner defined a response, not as a set of specific movements, but as an act, or "operant," that produces a specific effect on the environment.*

According to Skinner we need not limit ourselves to behavior known to be elicited by certain stimuli. We are free to work with any behavior that the organism will emit. The only requirement is that we be able to measure the behavior so as to reward or punish the organism when the behavior is emitted. For example, the behavior "constructing a building" can be measured, and reinforcement can be programmed for it. The builder's contract, which determines the conditions of his reward, sets forth only specifications for the completed building. How the building is built is up to the builder. There may be an infinite number of ways in which this contract could be fulfilled. Similarly, in training a rat to press a bar, an experimenter programs reinforcement for bar-pressing, but without specifying how the bar must be pressed. The rat may press the bar with its left paw, its right paw, its head, its tail, or any other part of its body. What these different actions of the rat have in common is that they all change a certain portion of the environment in the same way—they all succeed in moving the bar through a certain angle, and they all may produce reward. Any instance of a class of behavior that produces such a common effect on the environment is called an *operant*. In this chapter, we shall deal with several operants, including bar-pressing, key-pecking, door-opening, the breaking of photocell beams, and even running from one place to another.

Most psychologists today follow Skinner in using the term "reinforcement" to refer to the action of reward on operants directly, without implying the corresponding strengthening of stimulus–response connections that Thorndike suggested.

KINDS OF INSTRUMENTAL CONDITIONING

There are four basic principles used in instrumental conditioning, all of which are related to the evolution of individual behaviors. In capsule form, we can describe the four principles as *reward, punishment, escape,* and *omission.* Figure 5.6 shows the contiguous, contingent, and correlational relationships when a response is followed by various events.

---

*In Thorndike's experiments each trial reset the stimulus and provided the opportunity for a response. In Skinner's experiments there were no discrete trials. The subject could respond or not respond freely (like the rat licking the tube in Chapter 2) so the particular stimulus for each response seemed unimportant.

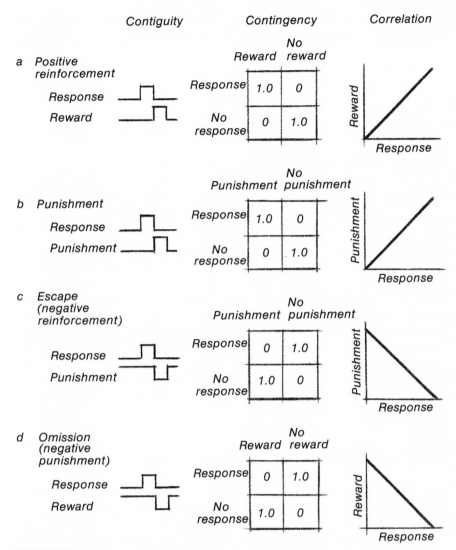

FIGURE 5.6
The four basic kinds of instrumental conditioning, classified by the consequences of a response.

1. The principle of reward was stated in Thorndike's "law of effect"—a reward tends to increase the probability that the response to which it is related will recur.* In conditioning experiments, reward is called *positive reinforcement.*

---

*Thorndike would have replaced the phrase ". . . to which it is related . . ." by ". . . which it follows . . . ," but we use the more general term which could refer to either contiguity, contingency, or correlation.

2. The principle of *punishment* is the inverse of Thorndike's law—an aversive, or noxious, stimulus tends to decrease the probability that the response to which it is related will recur.

3. In what is called *escape conditioning,* a particular response is related to escape from an aversive stimulus. Escape from an aversive stimulus increases the probability that the response will recur. For example, Thorndike found that his cats would often learn to solve the puzzle in the box even when they were not fed afterwards. In other words, they learned to respond solely in order to escape confinement. This type of conditioning is also called *negative reinforcement.*

4. *Omission* of reward occurs when the absence of a reward, otherwise present in the environment, is related to the response. Like punishment, the omission of a reward tends to decrease the probability that the response will recur. This type of conditioning is also called *negative punishment.*

We shall adopt the convention here of referring to rewards and punishments as environmental events that may impinge on the organism. Reinforcement (in instrumental conditioning) is neither an environmental nor a behavioral event, but a relationship between the two that tends to increase responding by either positive or negative means as described above. Punishment, likewise, is a relationship that tends to decrease responding by either positive or negative means. In one case we have two words, "reward" referring to the event in the environment and "reinforcement" referring to the relationship between that event and the response—a distinction that is obscured in the other case by the use of the word "punishment" for both the environmental event and the relationship.

The following nomenclature will be used in this book hereafter. (Although it is, admittedly, confusing, it is the system in general use and must be understood in order to make sense out of the psychological literature):

1. The relationship between the environmental event and the response is called REINFORCEMENT or PUNISHMENT. (Reinforcement and punishment may be POSITIVE or NEGATIVE.)

2. The environmental event is sometimes called a REWARD (or a REINFORCER) and sometimes an AVERSIVE STIMULUS (or a NOXIOUS STIMULUS or a PUNISHER).

3. The organism is REWARDED or PUNISHED.

4. The response is REINFORCED or PUNISHED.

METHODS OF MEASUREMENT

Techniques for measuring behavior are the tools of the psychologist's trade; they are as important to him as a hammer and saw are to a carpenter. Indeed, at times they seem so important that psychologists become more interested in the operation of the tools themselves than in the functions they have been designed to perform. But it is important to have a general understanding of these tools and what they measure.

Instrumental-conditioning responses are grouped according to their common effect on the environment. In the laboratory, this common effect is determined by the experimenter. Hence the problem of measurement in instrumental conditioning is not to *discover* the response to a stimulus, as it is in classical conditioning, but to *invent* a device that will be sensitive to changes in organism's behavior produced by the learning process. The latitude for such inventions is great, and there have been many widely different kinds of apparatus used. We shall describe a few of the most common kinds of measurements here.

Latency

The latency of any sort of behavior is the time between some signal and the occurrence of the behavior. The latency of an instrumental response will depend on the condition of the subject as well as on the reinforcement being presented. For instance, when a mother calls her little boy to dinner, he is likely to come faster when he is hungry than when he is not, faster for hamburgers than for liver, and faster on rainy days than on sunny days. Latency has been a popular dependent variable for instrumental-conditioning experiments and was, in fact, the measure of learning used by Thorndike in his original instrumental-conditioning experiments. Thorndike measured the interval from the time the animal was put into the puzzle box until it solved the puzzle and got out.

Since Thorndike's time, puzzle boxes have been simplified. One modification of the puzzle box has been the shuttle box invented by Neal Miller and O. Hobart Mowrer. A form of this device is a box with a barrier in the center. Instead of solving a puzzle and escaping to freedom and food, the animal jumps over the barrier from one side of the box to the other. The experimenter may put food in the other side of the box or he may put some aversive stimulus in the side with the animal. The most common aversive stimulus is electric shock. When electric shock is used, the animal jumps over the barrier into, say, the right side of the box to escape the shock on the left side, and the experimenter is able to measure the time between the onset of the shock and the jump. Then the animal is shocked on the right and the time between shock and jump is measured again. One would expect an animal to become experienced with this procedure and jump faster and faster to escape shock. This is exactly what happens. In fact if a signal precedes the shock, the animal does not wait for the shock to come on, but eventually learns to jump at the signal so that it avoids the shock altogether.

The shuttle box has two big advantages over the puzzle box. First of all, the behavior of the animal can be measured without the experimenter handling the animal between trials. (When the experimenter handles the animals he is likely to affect their behavior.) Secondly, the response of jumping is fairly discrete, in the sense that the response takes only a split second, so the latency from a signal to the beginning of the jump is about the same as the latency to the end of a jump.

Another isolation chamber in which latency can be measured is the lever box, or Skinner box, invented by B. F. Skinner (see Figure 5.7). Here, instead of shuttling over a divider, the animal presses a lever to escape shock. In a Skinner box, the response takes even less time than in the shuttle box. A further convenience of the Skinner box is the fact that the lever can be connected to a switch automatically delivering food or stopping electric shock.

Rate of Response (Tempo)

In many forms of behavior, each response is preceded by a signal (or stimulus). The running of a race, for instance, is formally started by the sound of a gun. In that case, the proper measure of responding is the time between the signal and the completion of the response. Sometimes, however, a certain form of behavior is repeated many times in the presence of a single signal. For instance, suppose that the little boy in our previous example has finally come home to dinner. He begins to eat, lifting a forkful of food. The signal for this first forkful is a plate of food, which remains present during repeated instances of the same response. Although we can measure the latency of his first forkful of food, we must turn to *rate of response* if we want to quantify the rest of his eating. His rate of eating (like his latency in coming home) may be expected to vary with his hunger and his food preferences. When he is hungry he needs no coaxing to eat heartily, but when he is not hungry he is likely to eat listlessly or not at all.

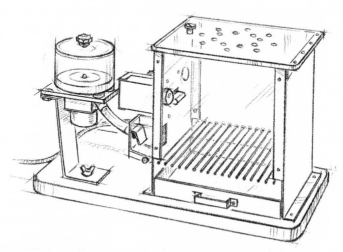

FIGURE 5.7
A lever box, or Skinner box. [Courtesy of Ralph Gerbrands Co., Arlington, Mass.]

FIGURE 5.8
A running wheel. [Courtesy of Wahmann Manufacturing Co., Baltimore, Md.]

Perhaps the simplest way to measure rate of response in the laboratory is to measure the speed with which an organism gets from one point to another. One device used for this purpose is called a *straight alley* and is, indeed, nothing but an alley with a box at either end. The animal runs from one box to the other, and its rate of running (its speed) can be measured automatically as it interrupts the light beams of a series of photocells. The straight alley is good for measuring the speed with which an animal runs toward a goal or away from a painful stimulus. However, if we were interested in continuously measuring an animal's running speed 1, 2, and 3 hours after an injection of a drug such as caffeine, we would need an impossibly long straight alley to allow a rat to run as far as it could. In order to measure rate of running over such long periods we use a device called a *running wheel* (Figure 5.8). As far as the animal (usually, a rat) is concerned, the running wheel is an infinitely long straight alley; its convenience for the experimenter is that no matter how fast or far the rat runs, it remains in the same place. The rat's speed of running is easy to obtain by timing the wheel's revolutions.

The Skinner box is frequently employed to study rate of responding as well as to measure latency. To use this device to measure rate of responding, we leave the signal on continuously and stipulate that, while the signal is on, pressing the lever will be reinforced.

We have discussed methods of measurement for two of Gilbert's three variables: The three variables, described in Chapter 2, are latency, tempo, and perseveration. The third variable, perseveration, has to be calculated from event or cumulative records. There is no easy way to measure it directly. Indirect methods of measuring perseveration will be discussed in Chapter 10.

EXTINCTION IN INSTRUMENTAL CONDITIONING

In classical conditioning, extinction consists in the removal of the conditioning relationship (contiguity, contingency, or correlation) that has been set up between conditioned stimulus and unconditioned stimulus. Similarly, in instrumental conditioning, extinction consists in the removal of the conditioning relationship between response and reward (or punishment). We shall discuss extinction in terms of correlations because they are easiest to diagram, but what we say can be translated also into the language of contiguities or contingencies.

A correlation of zero between response and reinforcement defines extinction. There are several ways in which a correlation of zero may be brought about. Figure 5.9 shows how zero correlations can occur with many rewards, few rewards, or no rewards. Essentially, the lack of correlation in extinction represents lack of control of reward by the response. Consider how pressing the accelerator pedal of a car usually controls the car's speed—the further down the pedal is pressed, the faster the car goes (a process analogous to positive reinforcement). But when the pedal is broken and control breaks down the car may stop (if you are lucky) or plunge wildly ahead. Either case is analogous to extinction, where control has broken down.

Once a response loses control over reinforcement it is, by definition, useless; assuming it costs some effort to make the response, we should expect the organism to stop responding. Usually this is exactly what happens. However, there are three important exceptions to this rule, instances where despite one or the other of the extinction procedures of Figure 5.9, responding does not die down to zero. These exceptions are (1) lack of discrimination, (2) superstition, and (3) pseudoconditioning. We shall consider them in turn.

Lack of Discrimination

Consider the positive–reinforcement training procedure of Figure 5.10, in which there is a correlation between responding and reward such that more responding results in more reward, though without strict one–to–one contiguity of events. An example might be the relationship between studying and good grades. Presumably, for an individual student there is a strong correlation between the two. Suppose a student has been studying at a level X, indicated on the abscissa of Figure 5.10a, and receiving grades Y according to that function. Now suppose that without any warning the teacher (perhaps out of laziness) decides not to read any more of the student's papers but to simply continue giving him the same grade he was getting before, regardless of his

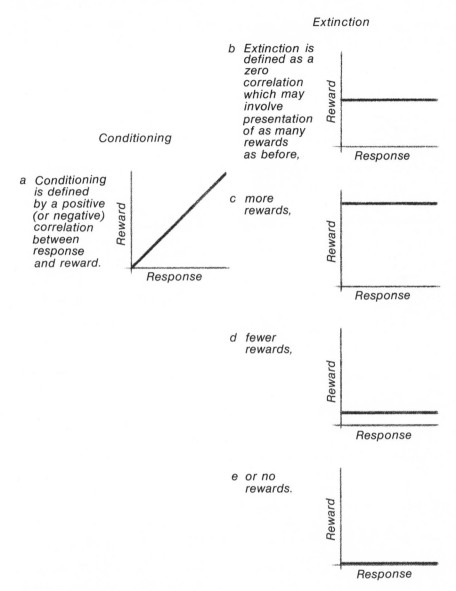

FIGURE 5.9
Positive reinforcement and several ways of programming extinction.

performance. The function now has been changed to that of Figure 5.10b. But if the student has been working at a steady rate with little variability, there will be no difference whatsoever in his experience. He is still studying at rate X and getting grade Y. If, however, the response has had some significant variability,

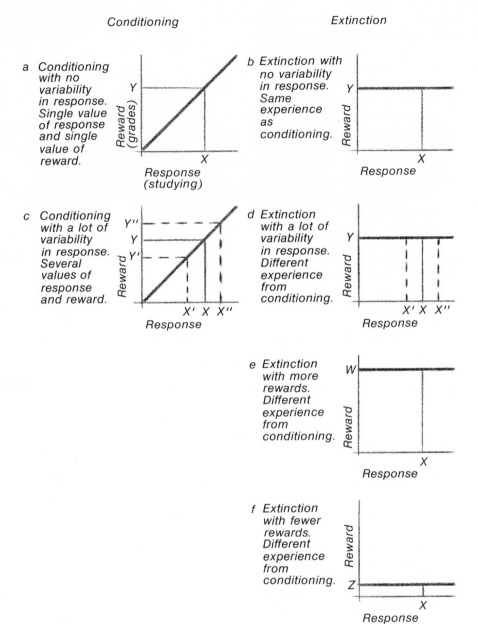

Conditioning   Extinction

a *Conditioning with no variability in response. Single value of response and single value of reward.*

Reward (grades)

Response (studying)

b *Extinction with no variability in response. Same experience as conditioning.*

Reward

Response

c *Conditioning with a lot of variability in response. Several values of response and reward.*

Reward

Response

d *Extinction with a lot of variability in response. Different experience from conditioning.*

Reward

Response

e *Extinction with more rewards. Different experience from conditioning.*

Reward

Response

f *Extinction with fewer rewards. Different experience from conditioning.*

Reward

Response

FIGURE 5.10
A subject's experience is identical in conditioning and extinction when reward is programmed as in (a) and (b) and when responding does not vary. If responding does vary, as in (c) and (d), or if extinction contains more or fewer rewards than conditioning, as in (e) or (f), the subject's experience is different in conditioning and extinction.

as in Figure 5.10c (varying between X' and X"), there would be a difference between training and extinction as far as the student is concerned. Instead of fluctuating between Y' and Y" (Figure 5.10c) the graphs would remain steady at Y (Figure 5.10d). With the conditions of Figure 5.10a and b we would expect the extinction procedure to have little effect on responding—the student would keep on studying and obtaining the same grade despite the teacher's new policy. On the other hand, with variability, if (as in Figure 5.10d) the student occasionally studied less or more (varied between X' and X") and still received the same grade (Y) we might expect him to gradually stop studying (assuming that grades are the only reward in the situation). Often, with training procedures that are fairly regular and extended, variability of responding is not high, and there is a possibility that a change to an extinction procedure that maintains a constant rate of reward will not reduce responding.

Extinction procedures that sharply increase or decrease the rate of reward (such as those of Figure 5.10e or 5.10f) are clearly discriminable from the original reinforcement conditions, and tend to sharpen discrimination even further by increasing variability. If the teacher in our example decided arbitrarily to always give the student a much higher grade (W) or a much lower grade (Z) than usual, the student's studying would be expected to vary at first and eventually to decrease.

Any sudden change in stimulation tends to increase variability. Thus, if extinction is accompanied by an external stimulus change, responding will decrease faster. In our example, the teacher, after changing the conditions from those of Figure 5.10a to those of 5.10b, might behave differently. He might act absentminded, lose copies of examinations, and so on. Any change from the usual pattern would tend to increase the variability of the student's behavior and decelerate responding.

It is important to note that extinction of positive reinforcement is only a special case of a change in the relationship between response and reward (a change from positive to zero correlation). Other changes could also be programmed, such as a change from positive to negative reinforcement, or a change from positive reinforcement to omission, or (as in the case we shall discuss shortly) a change from extinction to positive reinforcement. There are two processes required for an effective change in instrumental reinforcement: first, the change must be discriminated, and second, the new correlation conditions must have an effect. Usually these two processes occur together, but they can be separated, as, for example, when a new teacher takes over the grading. Now the conditions of reinforcement may differ, but exactly what those new conditions will be is still to be determined.

More direct evidence that extinction may be retarded when conditions of reinforcement and conditions of extinction are not discriminable is that when cues are provided during extinction, the extinction process is speeded up. For instance, in a Skinner box, if the color of the illumination of the test chamber is changed when reinforcement is withdrawn, extinction is faster. Any signal that is present during extinction and not present during conditioning will speed up extinction.

Superstition

The phenomenon of "superstition" occurs because in any finite temporal interval the relation between any two events cannot really be random. Although we may program a set of rewards to be completely independent of responding (as in Figure 5.9b) the rewards will fall in *some* relation to the responses whether we want them to or not. Only in an infinite interval of time can we be sure that no one relation is more probable or less probable than another. Thus, there will be accidental correlations (and accidental contiguities and contingencies) between response and reward even though no such relation is deliberately programmed. For instance, the pips of events A and B in Figure 2.15 are uncorrelated in the long run, but if a subject were exposed to only the first two periods he would find an accidental correlation and might behave (at least for a while) as if that correlation existed in the long run. When such correlations occur accidentally, they are apt to evoke the same behavior they would if they had been deliberately programmed. This behavior may then persist, perhaps because of lack of discrimination, even when the correlation has disappeared.

To give a concrete example, suppose a baseball player is in a slump, getting no hits. Then one day his bat is missing and he has to borrow a teammate's bat. On this day he gets four hits. Now, it may be purely accidental that the new bat was used on the day he happened to break out of his slump (let us assume that it is, in fact, accidental), but the coincidence is so striking that the baseball player buys his teammate's bat and uses it continuously thereafter. That is, the relation between the particular bat used and the number of hits is something like the function of Figure 5.10f during the slump (hits being analogous to rewards) and something like that of Figure 5.10e after the slump, resulting in a temporary accidental function looking like Figure 5.10a. The temporary accidental relation leads the player to stick with the new bat. This is the part played by "superstition." Once the ballplayer is using the new bat and getting a lot of hits he is much like the student who is studying hard and getting good grades even though no one is looking at his papers. His behavior persists through lack of discrimination.

Accidental correlations (contiguities or contingencies) alone can only account for temporary changes in behavior.* But accidental correlations combined with lack of discrimination may be responsible for much of the behavior that, in everyday life, we label superstitious.

---

*This is the point of Staddon and Simmelhag's argument that much of the behavior of pigeons when food is periodically given to them independent of behavior is due to pseudoconditioning, not superstition.

Pseudoconditioning

Consider the following hypothetical experiment. The experimenter puts a rat in a chamber, which has a bar protruding into it. Eventually, the rat, in the course of its normal movements about the chamber, will press the bar. When this happens the experimenter injects the rat with the drug adrenalin. This drug causes increased activity. The rat now moves more vigorously about the chamber. Because of this vigorous movement the rat hits against the bar sooner than before and the experimenter records a reduced latency of bar-pressing. After the second press, the experimenter again injects the rat with adrenalin, causing still more movement and, hence, an even faster rate of bar-presses. This continues until the rat is exhausted. Can we say that adrenalin is rewarding to the rat and that we have here a genuine case of instrumental conditioning of the bar-press response? We cannot, until we have tested for pseudoconditioning.

How can we perform such a test? In order to test for pseudoconditioning we have to find out whether the same response would occur without the critical element, the relation between response and reward. In the case of the rat and the adrenalin it would be easy to prove that adrenalin was not instrumentally conditioning bar-presses. We would merely take another rat and place it in an identical chamber. This time we would ignore the bar and just inject the rat periodically with adrenalin. Here no systematic relation of injections and bar-pressing would be established.) If this rat's rate of pressing increased as much as the first rat's, we could assume that the increase in pressing we observed for the first rat was not a result of the pairing of responses with reinforcement but merely an artifact of the adrenalin itself. This, then, would be a case of pseudoconditioning.

Thus, lack of discrimination, superstition, and pseudoconditioning all produce responding without a relationship between responding and reward (without an *instrumental* relationship). In the case of *lack of discrimination* this is because the lack of an instrumental relationship cannot be discriminated from some prior condition when there was an instrumental relationship. In the case of *superstition* it is because of an accidental temporary instrumental relationship. In the case of *pseudoconditioning* the relationship has nothing to do with responding, but the particular reward itself causes the response to be made.

Our discussion of extinction has focused on extinction of reinforcement, but the same principles apply to extinction of punishment. Suppose that response is maintained at a high rate (it may be maintained externally by positive or negative reinforcement or it may be rewarding in itself, as running in a wheel is for a rat or playing with a puzzle is for a monkey). Now suppose that a punishment relationship is imposed so that more responding increases the frequency or intensity of a noxious stimulus such as electric shock. This would reduce the rate of the response until subsequent removal of the punishment relationship (extinction of punishment) allowed the response to increase to its previously high rate. This increase in responding with removal of the punishment relationship corresponds to the decrease in responding found with extinction of reinforcement. If the punishment relationship is removed but the electric shock is maintained we may see retardation of the increase in rate of response to its unpunished value by virtue of lack of discrimination, superstition, or pseudoconditioning. For instance, when a rat's running in a wheel is first reduced by punishment with electric shock and then the punishment relationship is removed but electric shocks are still delivered randomly, the rat's running may not return to its unpunished rate either (1) because of lack of discrimination between the unpunished and punished conditions, (2) because running still occasionally is paired with shock (superstition), or (3) because the free shock itself causes the rat to freeze (pseudoconditioning).

We shall have occasion later to discuss extinction as it applies to specific cases, such as negative reinforcement and partial reinforcement.

LEARNED HELPLESSNESS

According to the view of conditioning and extinction in Figure 5.10, extinction will be slower when the behavior during extinction results in the same experience of the reinforcer (or punisher) as during prior conditioning. This equivalence of experience, which fails to provide discrimination between conditioning and extinction, is shown in Figure 5.10a and b. Now suppose that *extinction is presented first,* prior to conditioning, and that the behavior during conditioning subsequently results in the same experience of the reinforcer (or punisher) as during extinction. This also fails to provide discrimination between extinction and conditioning and should therefore retard conditioning. In experiments that have programmed such a sequence, with extinction first, conditioning has indeed been retarded. Occasionally, with aversive stimulation, the effect has been so strong that conditioning does not occur at all with the usual procedures. This failure to acquire a response after exposure to an extinction procedure is called *learned helplessness.* The reference experiment in this area was done by three researchers at the University of Pennsylvania, Steven Maier, Martin Seligman, and Richard Solomon.

On the first day of the experiment, dogs were exposed to electric shocks programmed independently of their behavior. Nothing the dogs could do prevented the shock or enabled them to escape it (each shock lasted five seconds). Any responses the dogs made were completely uncorrelated with electric shock (the extinction procedure). On the next day, the dogs were put into a shuttle box and again shocked. This time, however, the shocks were preceded by a signal, and the dogs could jump over a barrier to escape the shock (or, if they were fast enough, to avoid it). Most of the dogs in this experiment did not learn to escape. The dogs seemed to "give up" and passively "accept" the shock. Some of the dogs learned to escape after they were dragged by the experimenters across the barrier. Even then, some of them did not learn. In this respect their behavior contrasted vividly with dogs that had not been previously exposed to the inescapable shock. These dogs quickly learned to escape, and then to avoid, the shock in the shuttle box. Obviously the prior exposure to the extinction procedure with inescapable shock had a strong effect on the dogs' subsequent behavior in the shuttle box. It severely retarded their learning to avoid the shocks.

Once again, it is tempting to draw analogies to human behavior. Often, when people are put into situations where they cannot avoid pain no matter what they do, and then the situations are changed so that they can avoid pain, they have a difficult time learning the proper avoidance responses. A child who is beaten regularly no matter what he does may not learn to "behave well" when conditions are changed so that beatings only follow "bad" behavior. What is it, then, about the initial extinction conditions, with responses and shocks uncorrelated, that affects behavior later when they are correlated? The dogs learned in extinction that nothing they did could affect the shock. It was Maier, Seligman, and Solomon who gave the vivid name *learned helplessness* to this effect. Later, when the dogs were exposed to a situation where they could avoid shock, they had to "unlearn" the helplessness that they had previously acquired. In our terms, the dogs first learned the zero correlation between shock and responding; then, when exposed to the negative correlation they failed to react to the change in correlation.

The evidence provided by the Maier, Seligman, and Solomon experiment is that correlations, even when they are zero correlations, are learned (in the sense that they have a potent effect on behavior). It would be difficult to explain this experiment in terms of connections because the important feature of the first stage of the experiment, when shocks and responses were uncorrelated, was that there were no connections established. If there were no connections, what could have been learned? In terms of correlations, however, the experiment is easy to explain because zero correlations exist on the same continuum as positive correlations. There is no reason why they cannot be learned just as easily as positive correlations. Then, the zero correlation, already learned, interferes with the effect of the positive correlation imposed later.

The sequence of events is shown in Figure 5.11. At first responding with the extinction condition has wide variability (Figure 5.11a) but eventually the response settles down to that involving least effort (Figure 5.11b). There is a dispute among researchers in the field as to why the ultimate response settles down at zero. Some psychologists argue that once the zero correlation is learned, zero responding reflects least effort. Why respond at all when all responses result in equal aversive stimulation? Other psychologists feel that the zero measured responding reflects the acquisition of some other internal or external behavior that actually minimizes the effect of the shock. Although the subjects at the stage of the experiment represented by Figure 5.11b do exhibit charac-

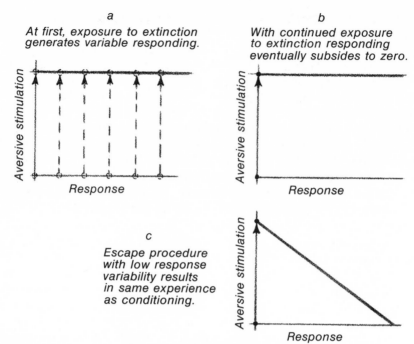

FIGURE 5.11
How prior exposure to extinction can retard conditioning. Subject learns zero
correlation during extinction. Initial high variability of responding (a), as shown by
the various positions of the dotted lines on the response axis, disappears and
responding subsides to zero (b). Escape procedure (c) provides same
experience as extinction procedure. Conditioning is retarded.

teristic behaviors, these seem to resemble attitudes of passive acceptance of the
shock rather than any attempts to actively minimize it. In any case, the response
to be conditioned later (jumping over a barrier in Maier, Seligman, and
Solomon's dogs) was certainly at zero level by the time the next stage was
presented. This next stage is illustrated in Figure 5.11c. Now, jumping over
the barrier would reduce the shock, but with no variability the experience of the
dogs is exactly the same in Figure 5.11c as it was in Figure 5.11b, and, just as
in Figure 5.10 they were retarded in extinction, so in Figure 5.11 the subjects
are retarded in conditioning.

If the dogs were exposed to the conditions of Figure 5.11c first while behavior was still variable, as it was in Figure 5.11a, they would have experienced
the negative correlation between their behavior and the aversive stimulation
and they would have quickly learned to escape.

Let us now add one more complication to the procedure. Suppose we expose
dogs first to the conditions of 5.11c, then to 5.11b, then to 5.11c again. Here
the dogs first learn to escape, and then escape responses are extinguished. Can

they learn to escape again? When this procedure has been tried, with the same apparatus as used to demonstrate learned helplessness, the dogs have learned to escape the second time. Evidently some learning acquired during the first exposure to the escape procedure persists through the extinction so that relearning of escape is not retarded. Recall a similar phenomenon in habituation. If habituation has occurred once and is then lost, it tends to be acquired more quickly the next time. According to Seligman, the initial escape learning provides a sort of *innoculation* against the deleterious effects of the extinction procedure and prevents the acquisition of learned helplessness.

Seligman has drawn interesting parallels between learned helplessness and depression in humans, which we shall consider at the end of this chapter.

SCHEDULES OF REINFORCEMENT AND PUNISHMENT

One of the earliest experiments relating to schedules of reinforcement was done more or less by accident by B. F. Skinner around 1932. In order to study the eating behavior of rats, he trained them to press a lever to receive a pellet of food and measured their rate of pressing, hence, their rate of eating, after various periods of food deprivation. One day, Skinner found that his supply of pellets was low. This inspired him to set up the apparatus so that instead of every press producing reinforcement, only one press a minute would be reinforced, no matter how many times a rat pressed the lever.

Not only did the rats keep pressing the lever, but their rate of pressing was considerably higher than when every press was reinforced. This increase in rate of responding is evidence against the notion that less reinforcement would simply produce less responding. Skinner inferred that the schedule (or rule) according to which reinforcement is presented could be a powerful way to control behavior. The name for the particular reinforcement schedule used by Skinner is a "fixed-interval" schedule.

The presentation of reinforcement on a prearranged schedule, such as a fixed–interval schedule, must not be confused with correlation between responses and reinforcement. Traditionally, when a schedule of reinforcement is programmed, a specific response (but not every response) produces reinforcement immediately. In a situation where reinforcers are correlated with or contingent on responding but not strictly contiguous with responses, reinforcers come between responses or just before responses as well as immediately after responses. The only relation required for a positive correlation is that increased responding somehow produce increased reinforcement. Reinforcement delivered on a schedule will always give rise to some correlation function and some contiguity relation between responding and reinforcement; however, reinforcement correlated with or contingent on responding does not imply that any particular schedule of reinforcement is in effect. The same applies, of course, to schedules of punishment. Let us now consider a method for expressing, in graphic form, the requirements of a schedule and the animal's performance with this schedule. We shall discuss schedules of positive reinforcement mostly, but the techniques can be applied as well with other instrumental procedures.

Fixed-Interval Schedules

In order to diagram fixed–interval (FI) schedules of reinforcement, we construct a graph with number of responses on the vertical axis and time on the horizontal axis, as in Figure 5.12a. We represent the conditions of reinforcement by vertical lines intersecting the times on the horizontal axis at which reinforcement is available. In Skinner's experiment, the requirement is that one minute elapse since the last reinforcement. Assuming that the rat presses the lever often enough, one response would be reinforced every minute. Starting at the origin, then, we can draw a cumulative record, as in Figure 5.12b, of the responses between reinforcements. Each response raises the cumulative record another step. The width of the step is the time between responses. When the first minute is reached, reinforcement is given (represented by a downward slash on the graph) after the next response and so on for the other intervals. If we project the slashes across to the vertical axis, as in Figure 5.12c, we get a picture of the number of responses between reinforcements. In a one-minute fixed-interval schedule (an FI-1′ schedule), the organism has only to respond once every minute to receive the maximum reward. Any additional responses during the minute have no effect. The kind of behavior often observed with fixed-interval schedules, and shown by the cumulative records of Figure 5.12, is a pause after reinforcement and then an increase in rate of responding until a high rate is reached just as the interval is about to end. This pattern (called scalloping) is found with many organisms and many responses. (An example of human behavior that conforms to the same pattern might be the frequency with which one looks at a pot of water when one is impatient for it to boil, or the frequency with which one opens the oven door to test the turkey while a hungry family is waiting.*

Fixed-Ratio Schedules

Another kind of schedule much studied in the laboratory is the fixed-ratio (FR) schedule. Here, the organism is rewarded only after making a certain fixed number of responses. For instance, a rat may be rewarded for every fourth

---

*Recent experiments have shown that in many fixed-interval schedules the change from pausing to rapid responding is quite sudden.

FIGURE 5.12
Cumulative record of lever-presses by a rat reinforced on a one-minute fixed-interval schedule. (Ticks mark reinforcements.) (a) The vertical lines mark the locus of each reinforcement; reinforcement is available once at the end of each minute no matter how many times the rat presses the lever. (b) Cumulative record of responding, showing reinforcements received by the rat. (c) Projection of the results to the vertical axis. The distances between the horizontal lines show how many responses occurred for each reinforcement.

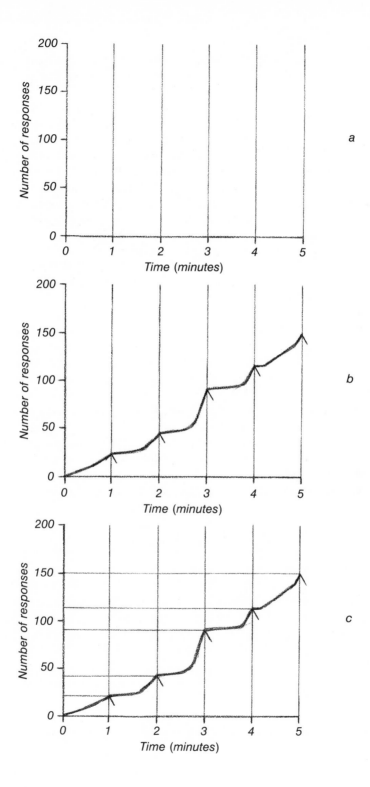

press instead of for every press. Figure 5.13a shows a cumulative record of a pigeon rewarded with three seconds of access to food for every 50 pecks at an illuminated disk. (This is called an FR-50 schedule.) The lines showing the loci of reinforcement are horizontal instead of vertical, reflecting the fact that fixed numbers of responses rather than intervals of time determine the availability of reinforcement. Each response raises the cumulative record a small step. When the step is reached corresponding to the ratio, reinforcement is given; reinforcement is represented by a slash on the graph. If we project the slashes downward to the horizontal axis, as in Figure 5.13b, we get a picture of the rate of reinforcements in time. If the reinforcements are close together, they are coming rapidly; if they are far apart, they are coming slowly. Note that after each reinforcement the pigeon pauses before beginning to respond again. This pattern of a rapid burst of responding, which fulfills the ratio, and then a pause after reinforcement is found for pigeons pecking a disk, rats pressing a lever, monkeys pressing a disk, humans tapping a telegraph key, and innumerable other responses.

Compound Schedules

The basic fixed-interval and fixed-ratio schedules may be combined in various ways. In the fixed-ratio, a certain *number* of responses must appear before reinforcement occurs. In the fixed-interval, a fixed *time* must elapse. Suppose we specify that a fixed number of responses must occur *or* a fixed time must elapse before reinforcement. This type of schedule is diagrammed in Figure 5.14a. The patterns of behavior shown by the two cumulative records would be rewarded at points (p) and (q). Pattern (p) would be rewarded sooner, but at the cost of more responses; pattern (q) would be rewarded later, but with fewer responses.

If we were to stipulate that both the interval *and* ratio requirements must be met for reinforcement to occur we would have the situation diagrammed in Figure 5.14b. Responding would be reinforced not at (p) or (q), where only the ratio or interval requirements are met, but at (r) or (s), where both requirements are met.

A third, and more complex kind of compound schedule is the interlocking schedule diagrammed in Figure 5.14c. For this schedule, the requirement is that a certain *sum* of responses and seconds must occur before a response will be reinforced. This schedule works on the same principle as a taximeter, which adds the time of the ride to the distance travelled to determine the fare. In the schedule, the time is added to the number of responses. When they reach a certain sum, reinforcement will be available at the next response.

Variable Schedules

The fixed patterning of responses that occurs when fixed–interval or fixed–ratio schedules are imposed does not occur with variable-interval or vari-

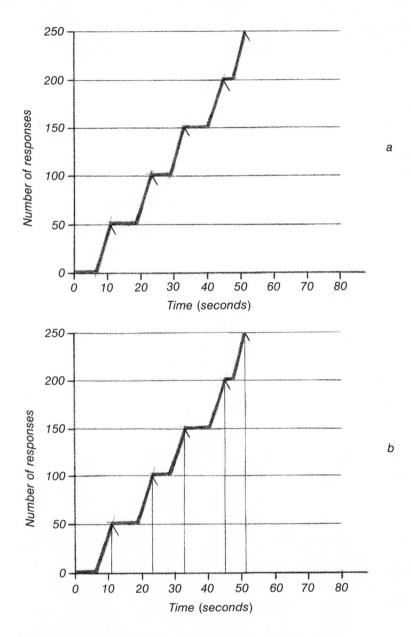

FIGURE 5.13
Cumulative record of pecks by a pigeon reinforced on a fixed-ratio
schedule of one reinforcement for each 50 pecks. (a) Cumulative
record with horizontal lines marking the locus of each reinforcement
and ticks representing actual reinforcements. (b) Projection to the
vertical axis, showing time between reinforcements.

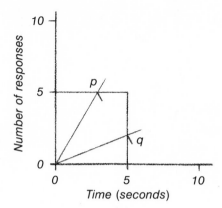

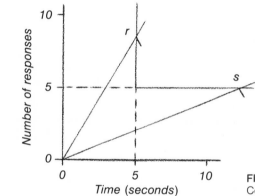

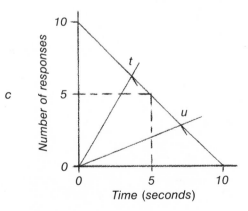

FIGURE 5.14
Compound schedules of reinforcement. (a) Locus of reinforcement for 5 responses *or* a 5-second interval. At p, behavior is reinforced after 5 responses in less than 5 seconds. At q, behavior is reinforced after 5 seconds and fewer than 5 responses. (b) Locus of reinforcement for 5 responses *plus* a 5-second interval. At r, behavior is reinforced after more than 5 responses in 5 seconds. At s, behavior is reinforced after 5 responses in more than 5 seconds. (c) Locus of reinforcement for 10 responses or 10 seconds or any number of responses and seconds totalling 10. At t, behavior is reinforced for 6 responses in 4 seconds. At u, behavior is reinforced for 3 responses in 7 seconds.

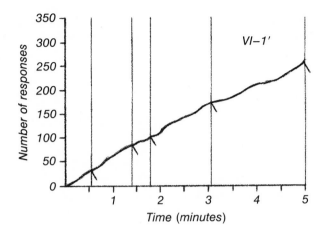

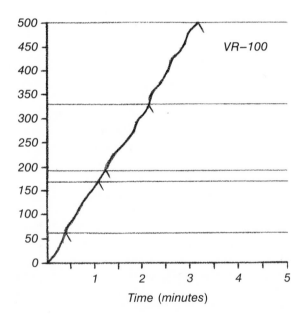

FIGURE 5.15

Loci of reinforcements and cumulative records for variable-interval and variable-ratio schedules of reinforcement of a pigeon's pecking. (Ticks mark reinforcements.) VI-1': This graph shows a variable-interval schedule in which a reinforcement is available at the average rate of once per minute. VR-100: This graph shows a variable-ratio schedule in which a reinforcement is available at the average ratio of one per 100 responses.

able-ratio schedules. A variable-interval (VI) schedule makes reinforcement available sometimes after short intervals and sometimes after long intervals. Figure 5.15 shows cumulative records of a pigeon's key–pecking for variable-interval and variable-ratio schedules of reinforcement. When we refer to a fixed-interval schedule of one minute (FI-1′), we mean that each reinforcement is made available after a one-minute interval. When we speak of a variable-interval schedule of one minute (VI-1′), we mean only that the *average* of the intervals used in that schedule is one minute.

When variable-interval and variable-ratio schedules are used, responses usually occur at a fairly constant rate. Note that the rate of responding with the variable-ratio schedule in Figure 5.15 is quite a bit faster than the rate for the variable-interval schedule. Because of the slow, steady rate of responding on variable-interval schedules, these schedules are often used as baselines to gauge the effects of other variables on behavior. A rat on a variable-interval schedule, for instance, responds more rapidly after being given an injection of dexedrine, a stimulant, than after being given an injection of pentobarbital, a depressant.

Drl and Drh Schedules

Drl (differential reinforcement of low rates) schedules have been devised which reward the subject *only* after long interresponse times (irt's). For instance, a drl 3-second schedule provides reinforcement for each response, provided it is preceded by a 3-second pause. If the subject responds before 3 seconds the interval starts over again. With this schedule, if responses were made every 2.5 seconds they would never be reinforced. Drl schedules tend, as one would suspect, to yield slow overall rates of responding, but, perhaps surprisingly, most irt's on drl schedules are shorter than the limit and therefore go unreinforced. With pigeons and rats on drl schedules it is not unusual for the ratio of reinforced to unreinforced responses to be less than one in a hundred. Humans are among the least efficient subjects in drl experiments. The author has seen college sophomores pressing buttons for hours on a drl 10-second schedule of reinforcement (points exchangeable for prizes) and collecting only one or two rewards and even in one case no rewards at all.

Other schedules, called *drh* schedules, provide reinforcement only if the irt is shorter than some specified limit or only if the subject makes some minimum number of responses within a given interval. Such schedules tend to produce very high rates of responding.

Extinction After Partial Reinforcement

Extinction, as we defined it, is the removal of the reinforcement relationship (contiguity, contingency, or correlation). The most common extinction procedure is to simply remove the reward entirely (as in Figure 5.9e). We have seen how extinction affects responses conditioned under a schedule of constant reinforcement (where each response is reinforced). But what happens when extinction is imposed after a schedule of reinforcement—that is, after partial reinforcement? Our line of thinking might run as follows: The more reinforcement for a response, the stronger that response should be. The stronger a response is, the better it should resist extinction. The better a response resists extinction, the more responses one should observe after reinforcement has been withdrawn. This line of reasoning seems logical, but, as a matter of fact, exactly the opposite holds true. When a response has been constantly rewarded, extinction is usually much faster than when the same response has been rewarded only part of the time. This result so surprised psychologists that they called it "Humphreys' paradox" (after Lloyd G. Humphreys, the man who first demonstrated it experimentally). This seeming paradox is a most reliable, reproducible, and significant effect.

Perhaps we can gain an insight into Humphreys' paradox from this example:

There are two hypothetical Coke machines. One, in building A, produces a drink for every dime inserted. The other, in building B, is partially broken. Occasionally, when a dime is inserted, nothing happens. The people in building B complain repeatedly, if ineffectually, about the situation, but they seem to be willing to lose their dimes once in a while as long as they eventually get a Coke. Now, suppose both machines break down completely. Which one will receive more dimes before the dimes stop altogether? Probably the machine in building B, which has been only partially reinforcing the "dime-inserting behavior." It will take a while before the people in building B realize that the machine is completely inoperative. The people in building A, on the other hand, will immediately realize that there is something wrong and stop inserting dimes.

The Coke-machine example shows that, for extinction to occur, organisms must learn to discriminate between conditions of reinforcement and conditions of extinction, and that anything that helps them to do this will speed up extinction. Partial reinforcement on some schedules is more like extinction than is constant reinforcement and, hence, harder to tell from extinction. To the extent that conditions of reinforcement resemble conditions of extinction, there will be more responses during extinction.

Evidence that extinction in partial reinforcement is a discrimination problem is provided by the finding that extinction is faster for fixed-interval and fixed-ratio schedules than for variable-interval and variable-ratio schedules. In the fixed schedules, disruption of the pattern of regular reinforcements signals extinction; in the variable schedules, there is no pattern to disrupt.

The assumption in the original reasoning that led to Humphreys' paradox is that strong conditioning of a response would produce more responses in extinction. This assumption is based on the notion that latency of response, magnitude of response, and resistance to extinction are all measures of the same thing, namely, the "strength" of the response. Apparently responses in extinction are not exclusively determined by the "strength" of a response—but also reflect a failure to discriminate between conditions of extinction and conditions of reinforcement. Where enough cues to this discrimination are provided, there are relatively few responses after reinforcement is withdrawn.

On a molar level, lack of discrimination is responsible for Humphreys' paradox. We shall discuss more molecular explanations in a later chapter on the two-factor theory (Chapter 9).

Schedules of Punishment, Negative Reinforcement, and Omission

Almost all studies of schedules have been made with schedules of positive reinforcement. This is partly historical accident and partly a matter of convenience, positive reinforcement being easy to program. However, punishers may also be arranged to follow responses on some schedule. To observe patterns of responding with schedules of punishment, the response must either be of such intrinsic value that it will be maintained despite punishment (like rats' wheel-running) or the response must be maintained by reward with punishment superimposed. The latter procedure is more common. The reward is usually presented on a variable-interval schedule, which generates uniform responding (a straight-line cumulative record), punishment is superimposed, and the pattern of responding observed. The pattern of responding with fixed-interval punishment is usually an acceleration right after the punishment and then suppression of responding just before punishment is due. Fixed-ratio punishment usually suppresses the tempo of responding generally, with no pauses as there would be with fixed-ratio positive reinforcement.

A schedule of negative reinforcement (escape) might be, for example, shocking a rat until it had completed some schedule requirement such as a fixed-ratio of 10 responses, then reducing the shock for a period of time and then increasing it again until the rat satisfied the schedule requirement. With escape, unlike punishment, no other means of maintaining the response is required. The main finding with schedules of escape with several species and several responses is that if more than a few seconds is required to satisfy the schedule requirements, responding becomes erratic and finally ceases altogether. This is probably because the aversive stimulus, most often electric shock, interferes with the response.

A schedule of omission would consist of providing continuous reward and then taking it away when the schedule requirements were satisfied. As with punishment, the response would have to be of high intrinsic value or maintained by another reward. Omission has been infrequently studied. The effects of schedules of omission are unknown.

PARAMETERS OF REWARD AND PUNISHMENT

Because of their simplicity, the devices most frequently used to measure the parameters of reward and punishment are the Skinner box with a single manipulandum (a manipulandum is a mechanism by means of which an environmental variable can be influenced by an organism's motor response) and the straight alley. One might think of the straight alley as a type of Skinner box in which each step the rat takes is a response. If the length of the alley is fixed, the running responses of the rat in the alley are reinforced on a fixed-ratio schedule. The straight alley is most appropriate for studying behavior in space, and the Skinner box is most appropriate for studying behavior in time. A rat's running at a certain place in the alley can be compared with its lever pressing at a certain time in the Skinner box. In fact, patterns of behavior are often similar with similar schedules of reinforcement and types of instrumental conditioning in straight alleys and Skinner boxes.

The experiments described in this section do not involve choice, or at least they involve only Hobson's choice—take it or leave it. (We shall reserve discussion of symmetrical choice for Chapter 10).

Rate and Amount of Reward

Rate of reward can be varied in straight-alley experiments by increasing or decreasing the length of the alley. It can be varied in Skinner-box experiments by changing the ratio of responses to rewards. Reducing the ratio usually increases the rate of reward, though rate of reward with ratio schedules depends entirely on how fast the animal responds. The surest way to vary rate of reward is to change the value of an interval schedule of reinforcement. An interval schedule is constructed in such a way that the rate of reinforcement is about the same regardless of how fast or how slowly the animal responds. A variable-interval schedule is like the mail, which comes at intervals (often fairly variable) regardless of the rate of the response of looking in the mailbox. Figure 5.16 shows how the rate of reward varies with rate of responding on a VI-1′ schedule

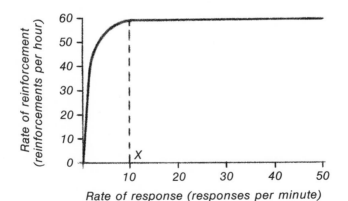

FIGURE 5.16
Rate of reinforcement as a function of rate of response on a variable-interval 1-minute schedule of reinforcement. Beyond point X, rate of reinforcement is virtually constant at 60 per hour.

of reinforcement. The figure might equally well serve for frequency of finding mail as a function of frequency of opening the mailbox. With zero responding, there is zero reward, but with almost any responding at all the rate of reward jumps to its asymptotic value and stops there. It would not matter if you looked in the mailbox five times a day or ten times—the rate of mail delivery (the value of the VI schedule) determines how frequently mail comes. Note that the function of Figure 5.16 says nothing about what the behavior of the subject will be. It just says that *if* the behavior is the value on the x-axis, the rate of reward will be the value on the y-axis. If in Figure 5.16 the rate of responding were anywhere above point X, the rate of reward would be close to 60 per hour. With interval schedules rate of reward can be an independent variable—it can be under the experimenter's control. With ratio schedules, rate of reward is under the control of the subject. It is a dependent variable like rate of response.

Amount of reward can be varied by giving a rat a greater or lesser number of pellets in the goal box of an alley or the magazine of a Skinner box or letting the hungry rat or pigeon eat for a longer or shorter time when reward is given. These techniques involve not only changes in the amounts of reward made available but also corresponding changes in consummatory responding. One way that has been used to vary reward and keep consummatory responding constant is to vary the concentration of the rewarding substance (such as sugar) in a solution, but give constant amounts of the solution.

Much research has been done to determine once and for all the function relating rate or amount of reward to rate of pressing a bar or pecking a key in a Skinner box or rate of running in a straight alley. On one hand, the various functions obtained show a similarity in shape. They all look pretty much like the function drawn in Figure 5.17. With no reward, responding is zero or very close to it; then as reward increases, the rate of response increases, at first very

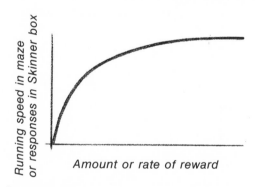

FIGURE 5.17
An idealized average function showing how responding often varies with amount or rate of reward. Actual functions for individual subjects would look much less smooth.

fast, then more slowly.* In general, reward parameters must be increased by large factors (from five to ten times) for responding to increase by a factor of 50 percent. Unfortunately there is no single function that precisely describes response rate as a function of various parameters. Logarithmic, exponential, and power functions have been proposed, and they all can be made to fit some of the data, but none of them fits all of the data. To give the reader an idea of the variability of such functions, Figure 5.18 shows functions of rates of pecking for six individual pigeons, each exposed to several rates of reward on variable-interval schedules. In general, all the pigeons pecked faster when the rate of reward was higher, but the variability from pigeon to pigeon was so great that no obvious quantitative conclusions can be made although we shall discuss, in Chapter 10, an attempt to fit these data with a mathematical function.

Delay of Reward

There are two questions one might ask about delay of reward as a independent variable: (1) What is its effect on learning? (2) What is its effect on the rate of a response once the response has been learned?

Delay of reward as an independent variable has a clear meaning only for a contiguity theory of learning. If contiguity between response and reward is necessary for instrumental conditioning, then delay between responding and reward should sharply reduce learning or even eliminate it entirely. Delay of reward seems, at first, an easy variable to test. Simply arrange that reinforcement be delayed after responding and study how well various responses are learned with various delays.

Such a seemingly simple problem turns out to be very difficult in practice. The main problem for an experimenter is to define the delay interval experimentally. He must decide what sort of thing he wants to happen during the delay period. According to one point of view, nothing at all should happen during the delay. But, if nothing happened—if in a strict sense all motion of any kind were suspended and all processes halted—then by definition delay could have no effect. Any effect must be the result of some process (be it "forgetting" or "interference by other responses") during the delay period.

Another alternative is to allow responses to occur during the delay period. For instance, consider the hypothetical experiment illustrated in Figure 5.19. The rat presses the lever, which is connected to a pellet dispenser located some distance away. The lever operates the pellet dispenser immediately,[†] but it

---

*This is true provided each function is obtained with a single schedule of reinforcement. Schedule of reinforcement affects behavior more strongly than the parameters we are considering here. Depending on the schedule it is possible to obtain very high rates of responding with low amounts of reinforcement and vice versa.

†Operation of the dispenser immediately after a lever-press does not necessarily involve operation after each lever-press. Lever-presses may still be reinforced intermittently with, for instance, a VR or VI schedule of reinforcement.

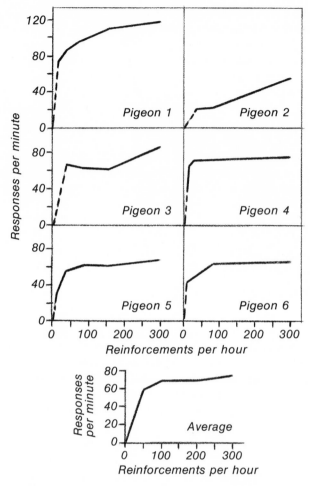

FIGURE 5.18
Rate of response for individual pigeons as a function of
rate of reinforcement. Rate of reinforcement was varied by
using variable-interval schedules of different values. The
average of the individual functions is also shown. These
functions have opposite coordinates from the function of
Figure 5.16. That function shows what rate of reinforcement
would theoretically be obtained with various rates of response
on a single VI schedule. Each function here shows rate
of response and rate of reinforcement *actually* obtained with
several VI schedules. [Data from Catania and Reynolds, 1968.]

takes some time for the pellet to be delivered, along a conveyor belt, into the
rat's cup. The time taken for the pellet to reach the rat is the delay of reward.
But while the rat is waiting it can press the lever and operate the pellet dispenser again and again.

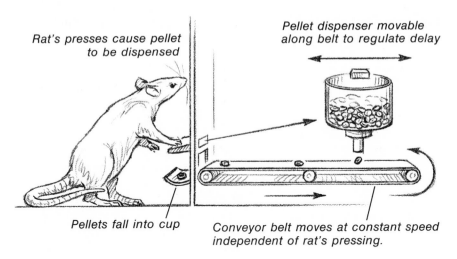

FIGURE 5.19
Hypothetical delay-of-reward experiment. Delivery of pellets is delayed by distance
between dispenser and cup. This technique would allow many accidental contigencies
between bar-pressing and pellet delivery.

The problem with this technique is that a pellet (actually dispensed after a previous response) may be delivered immediately after the rat has pressed the lever. According to the contiguity theory of learning, it should not matter which press actually produced the pellet—any reward immediately after a response will reinforce that response. That is, the accidental contiguity between response and reward might cause superstitious responding. Thus, the contiguity theory would claim that the delay produced by the procedure of Figure 5.19 might not always retard learning, although it might retard learning somewhat since the first lever-presses would not be followed immediately by reward.

A solution to the problem of superstitious responding would be to remove the lever during the delay period. Then, no responses could be made during that period and no responses could be accidently reinforced. This gives rise, unfortunately, to another problem. The very withdrawal of the lever serves as a signal that reward is coming. The role of such signals will be discussed later in detail when we come to the topic of secondary reinforcement. Meanwhile it suffices to say that the withdrawal of the lever acts like a promissory note: if this signal is invariably followed by reward, as it would be in our hypothetical experiment, it becomes "as good as reward" in its power to reinforce responding. Even though the actual rewards (the pellets) may be delayed by the experimenter, the signal that reward is coming (the withdrawal of the lever) is itself contiguous with the response and may immediately reinforce that response. When delay is varied in such an experiment, it may be as a parameter of classical conditioning (the relation of the signal to the reward) rather than instrumental conditioning (the relation of the response to the reward). In experiments with delay of reinforcement it has been found that the more vivid, the more distinctive from the conditions of responding, the delay period is, the less delay will retard learning. In alleys, for instance, where rats run to a distinctive goal box, are held there for the delay period, and then fed, delay hardly retards learning at all. That is, rats reach their asymptotic speed of running as fast when reward is delayed as when reward is immediate. When they are kept for the delay period in an antechamber that resembles the alley, however, delay slows down learning.

Accepting the limitations of the study of delay as a measure of learning by contiguity, we may nevertheless ask what effect delay has on rate of response once the response is learned. The function of Figure 5.20 shows how rate of running in an alley varies with delay of positive reinforcement (food pellets) and negative reinforcement (shock reduction). Running speed falls off sharply at first and then more gradually as delay is increased.

Studies with Skinner boxes have found similar functions. When each reinforcement is preceded by a blackout (all lights out and manipulanda unavailable) the rate of responding has been slower the longer the blackout duration.

Studies with delay of punishment have found symmetrical results. The longer punishment is delayed, the less suppressive effect it has. What to do while the punishment is being delayed poses the same problems as what to do while reward is being delayed.

As with amount of reinforcement, there have been attempts to fit curves such as that of Figure 5.20 with mathematical functions. Again, no clear agreement has been reached on a single function that, with small parametric variation, would fit all experimental data.

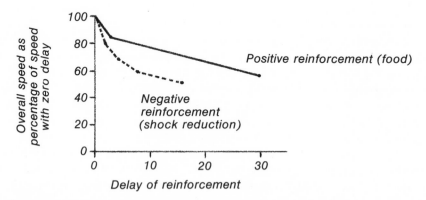

FIGURE 5.20
How delay of reinforcement affects running speed in an alley. The functions shown are of asymptotic running speed (after several weeks of daily sessions at a given delay). A different group of rats was run at each delay. Each point is an average for all the rats in the group. [From Logan, 1960, and from Fowler and Trapold, 1962 (Copyright 1962 by the American Psychological Association.)]

We now have to ask what delay of reinforcement means when responses and rewards are not in 1:1 relationship (contiguous) in the first place. Figure 2.18 shows two events correlated over time. Suppose event A is a response (such as a lever-press) and event B is a reward (such as delivery of a pellet). The function shows that the two events are correlated, but no 1:1 contiguity is present. What does delay of reinforcement mean in this situation? Delay here means shifting the entire sequence of rewards (the entire line B) over to the right. The more the rewards are shifted, the more the delay. But shifting the rewards will change the relation, not of one response and one reward, but of all the responses and rewards.

With responses and rewards that are noncontiguous in the first place, it is impossible to specify a separate response period and reward period. The two overlap. Therefore, the subject must be allowed to respond during the delay.

For instance, there is a correlation between exercise and pulse rate that is fairly strong and immediate. Suppose now that increases of pulse rate were delayed so that exercise one day would not increase pulse rate until the next day. Because pulse rate and exercise are continuous activities, there is no way to remove the response during the delay period (without introducing a new relation between the two events).

So far, the temporal relation of correlated noncontiguous events has not been studied experimentally. It would seem to have some practical interest, however, since delayed correlations abound in everyday life. Delayed correlations between eating and weight gain, exercise and health, sexual intercourse and signs of pregnancy, and so on, where there is a delay between an activity and its correlated consequences, govern much of our behavior.

The Relation Between
Delay, Amount, and Rate of Reward

Delay, amount, and rate of reward are separable independent variables. It is possible to vary delay, without varying rate or amount, by scheduling reward infrequently (say on a VI schedule) and delaying the reward so that the delay period (between response and reward) is small in comparison with the average period between rewards (the rate of reward). Thus, large variations in delay will involve only small variations in rate. However, this is not always done, so sometimes reports of the influence of delay on behavior may be attributed to the influence of rate.

When rate is varied, amount (per reinforcement) is usually kept constant. Thus, overall rate and overall amount vary together. Two reinforcements per minute usually amount to twice as much total reinforcement as one reinforcement per minute. Similarly, when amount is varied, rate is usually kept constant.

It is reasonable to ask whether amount and rate are really a single variable, which might be expressed as total reinforcement accumulated in a period of time. To put it another way, what is the difference between providing a lot of small meals and providing a single big meal? Obviously, at the extremes there is a difference. For instance, a single big meal once a week might be too much for the animal to eat at once and might result in starvation later on.

With respect to schedules of reinforcement, amount of food per reinforcement makes much less difference than rate of reinforcement or schedule of reinforcement in its influence on pattern or rate of response, so long as the animal gets some food and not so much as to cause satiation. With respect to choice, animals seem to be indifferent whether they get a lot of food all at once or a little at a time, but discussion of this will be reserved for Chapter 10.

ESCAPE (NEGATIVE REINFORCEMENT)

In the typical escape-conditioning experiment, an aversive stimulus is presented and the experimenter waits until the subject performs some act that the experimenter has specified in advance. When the act is performed, the aversive stimulus is removed. For example, a dog may be placed in a shuttle box (one with a hurdle in the middle that the dog can leap over). When the dog is on one side of the box, it may be shocked until it leaps over the hurdle. Dogs in such situations quickly learn to jump over the hurdle.

Negative reinforcement is a synonym for escape. Although the word "escape" vividly describes what is happening in a typical negative reinforcement experiment, we use the phrase "negative reinforcement" to remind us of the relation between this process and that of positive reinforcement. Both kinds of reinforcement will strengthen whatever acts they follow. Positive reinforcement reinforces by adding a positive stimulus; negative reinforcement reinforces by taking away a negative stimulus. The line between these two processes is not always easy to draw. (Is turning on the heater on a cold day reinforcing because it gives us warmth or because it removes our feeling of cold?)

One theory of reinforcement (the need-reduction theory, which we will discuss in the next chapter) holds that all reinforcement is negative reinforcement. The eating of food, for instance, is thus "escape from hunger," and the drinking of water is "escape from thirst."

Nevertheless, the behavior of animals exposed to aversive stimuli is different from that of animals deprived of food or water. A pigeon that is being shocked will jump around the area in which it is confined and flap its wings violently; a pigeon deprived of food will engage in more deliberate searching and pecking movements. The main difference between aversive stimuli (such as electric shocks or loud noises) and such feelings as hunger or thirst may be that the former originate suddenly outside the organism, whereas the latter originate gradually within it.

Because of the nature of aversive stimuli, it is usually difficult to program long intervals between negative reinforcements. For instance, when a rat is required to make several lever–presses in the presence of intense shock in order to terminate shock, the rat often stops pressing entirely. Thus, rate of negative reinforcement has not been much investigated.

The effects of varying amount and delay of negative reinforcement have been investigated. Amount of negative reinforcement in an alley can be manipulated by keeping the intensity of shock in the alley constant and varying the amount by which the shock is reduced when the rat reaches the goal box. Negative reinforcement can be delayed by withholding the shock reduction until the rat spends a certain amount of time in the goal box. As one would expect, speed of running increases with amount and decreases with delay of negative reinforcement. Parameters of negative reinforcement have also been investigated with rats swimming in alleys. The water in the alley is cold and the rat swims to the goal box where the water is warmer. The function relating amount of negative reinforcement to responding is usually more linear than that of Figure 5.17. That is, proportional increases of negative reinforcement tend to generate proportional increases of responding, whereas with positive reinforcement larger increments in reinforcement do not generate proportional increments in responding.

Another way to study negative reinforcement is by "titration." The intensity of electric shock (or another aversive stimulus) is increased periodically. The subject's responses (usually a rat pressing a lever in a Skinner box) then reduce the shock by a given amount. The procedure is somewhat like pumping the water out of a leaky boat, the increasing shock corresponding to the increasing water level in the boat. With the titration procedure the rat controls the level of shock. Figure 5.21 shows how shock intensity is controlled by a rat. The

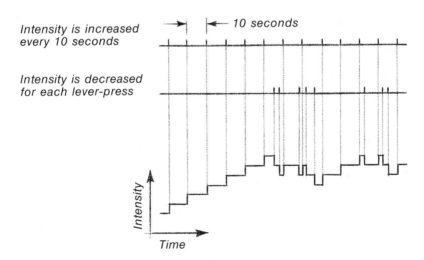

FIGURE 5.21
How the titration procedure in negative reinforcement works. Intensity of aversive stimulus is increased periodically. Responses decrease intensity.

rat allows the intensity to rise above its minimum level but presumably keeps it below painful levels. There is a trade-off between the work of pressing the bar and the pain of the shock. When the pain is severe enough it becomes worthwhile to expend the effort necessary to escape from it. Titration schedules have been useful for studying the effect of drugs on pain. When a rat is given an analgesic such as morphine, and then put in a titration-of-shock experiment, it keeps the shock at a higher level than it does without the morphine. The higher level of shock now seems to be less painful than it was before.

Titration has also been used extensively to study regulation of other stimuli such as temperature. If the air is heated uncomfortably but each response, say, pressing a bar, lets in a little cold air, the subject's regulation of ambient temperature can be studied. Any stimulus that becomes painful when increased beyond a certain intensity (including almost all stimuli that can be varied in intensity) can be studied with a titration procedure. Minute electrical stimulation of certain areas of the brain, for instance, which can be a reward at low intensities, is painful at high intensities. A rat will press a lever to regulate the intensity of brain stimulation by a titration procedure.

It is a property of titration procedures that in order to keep the stimulus (be it shock, temperature, brain stimulation, or another stimulus) constant, the rate of response must eventually take on just the value that will reduce the intensity by one unit each time it is increased by one unit. This rate, called the *critical rate of response,* is the same regardless of the intensity at which the stimulus is kept by the subject. (You would have to pump water out just as fast as it was coming in in order to keep the water level constant. It would not matter whether this level was at three inches or two inches. Pumping faster would lower the level. Pumping slower would raise the level.) Titration is thus a powerful way to generate a steady controlled rate of responding.

PUNISHMENT

Just as positive reinforcement tends to increase the rate at which a behavior is emitted, punishment tends to decrease the rate. The amount of suppression depends on the intensity of punishment. Figure 5.22 shows how the intensity of punishment determines the suppression in the rate at which pigeons peck a key. At higher intensities of shock, the rate of responding can be suppressed to zero.

At the beginning of this chapter, we discussed pseudoconditioning in instrumental conditioning experiments, referring to the hypothetical example of adrenalin as a reinforcer for bar-pressing behavior in a rat. The test of adrenalin as a pseudoreinforcer is whether the same increases in bar-pressing occur when the injection of adrenalin is dependent on, and independent of, a bar-press. If the adrenalin causes just as many bar-presses when it is delivered

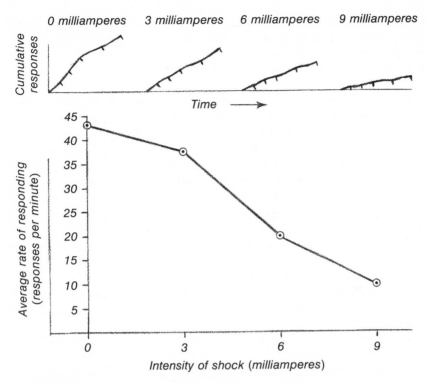

FIGURE 5.22
The effect of punishment on key-pecking in pigeons. Top: cumulative records
of pigeons pecking a key for reinforcement on a VI-1' schedule. (Ticks mark
reinforcements.) The graph at left shows a no-shock condition; the second graph
shows the effect of a 3-milliampere shock; the third graph shows the effect of a
6-milliampere shock; the fourth graph shows the effect of a 9-milliampere shock.
Bottom: a function showing that the rate of responding decreased as the intensity
of the electric shock increased. [Data from Schuster and Rachlin, 1968.]

randomly as when it follows each bar-press, then we do not have a case of
instrumental conditioning.

It is possible that the process of punishment may not be a form of instrumental conditioning at all. With positive reinforcement we are trying to train
the animal to *do* something. With punishment we are trying to train the animal
not to do something. When a hungry animal is presented with food, the behavior that one observes is eating. In order to get the animal to perform some
act other than eating (like pressing a bar), the food must be made dependent
on the bar-press. When an animal is shocked, the behavior that one observes
is jumping or running, or freezing in position, but *not* bar-pressing. In other
words, shock can itself produce "nonperformance" of bar pressing, the very
effect we are trying to condition. In order to get the animal to *stop* pressing

a bar, all one needs to do is shock the animal. But we said previously that true instrumental conditioning must involve a *relation* between responding and its consequences, not simple presentation of those consequences. It is at least conceivable that shock may reduce responding even without a contingency relation being established.

The question then is whether aversive stimulation delivered independently of responding suppresses behavior as much as aversive stimulation delivered only when a response is made. If it does, then punishment does not have the properties of instrumental conditioning. If it does not—if aversive stimulation must follow responding to have its maximum effect—then punishment does have the properties of instrumental conditioning. Many experiments have been performed to answer this question, and their almost unanimous answer has been: aversive stimulation delivered independently of responding has some suppressive effect, but not nearly as much as when it is dependent on responding.

To the extent that there is a difference, then, between the effects of response-produced aversive stimulation and response-independent aversive stimulation, punishment is a form of instrumental conditioning.

Curve B in Figure 5.23 shows rate at which a pigeon pecked a key when pecks were reinforced with food on a one-minute variable-interval schedule,

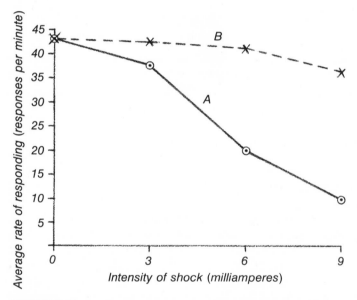

FIGURE 5.23
Curve A is repeated from the bottom portion of Figure 5.22, showing the rate of response as punishment increases. Curve B shows the rate of response under the same conditions of reinforcement but with the shocks delivered independently of the responses. The rate of delivery of the independent shocks was 120 per minute. [Data from Schuster and Rachlin, 1968.

and inescapable shocks were delivered twice per second. As the intensity of shock increased, the rate of pecking decreased slightly. Curve A in Figure 5.23 is a repetition of Figure 5.22, showing the rate at which another pigeon pecked a key when pecks were reinforced with food on the same schedule but shock was delivered only when the pigeon pecked the key. As the intensity of shock increased, the rate of pecking decreased sharply. The difference in the slopes of these two curves shows the instrumental effect of shock.

AVOIDANCE

Avoidance is escape, not from a noxious stimulus itself, but from a situation in which noxious stimuli are presented. For instance, coming in out of the rain is *escape,* but moving to Arizona because it is less rainy there is *avoidance.* Avoidance is thus a form of escape—escape from a molar condition of the environment.

WARNING

Avoidance, largely by historical accident, has played a major part in the dispute between molar and molecular views of instrumental conditioning. One must take some position from which to view this topic. In this chapter (except where indicated otherwise) events and relationships are viewed as relatively molar entities. In a later chapter we shall discuss these same topics (and positive reinforcement as well) from a more molecular point of view, that of two-factor theory.

Avoidance poses a problem for psychologists who believe that contiguity between response and reward is necessary for instrumental conditioning. There seems to be no event contiguous with an avoidance response that reinforces it. The man who moves to Arizona may well leave on a sunny day and still be avoiding rain. What, then, is the event contiguous with moving that reinforces the move? For psychologists willing to consider molar, or long–term, events as units, avoidance is no more of a problem than escape is. Thus, the man in our example could be influenced by such molar events as the high rainfall in his home state during the past year and the low annual rainfall in Arizona. If a low rainfall is more valuable to him than a high rainfall, the move is rewarded by the lower rainfall even though nothing important happens on the day of the move.*

---

*To anticipate a little, the difference between the molar and molecular views of avoidance centers on the role of those stimuli that *do* change when the avoidance response is made. (In our example, the appearance of the desert scenery of Arizona would be such a stimulus.) For the molar psychologist this stimulus change is not essential, though it may serve as a cue that the situation has changed. For the molecular psychologist the stimulus change is essential since it serves as the reward itself. The mechanism by which the stimulus change could acquire rewarding properties is that of classical conditioning. We will discuss this mechanism in more detail in the context of two-factor theory.

Avoidance has been studied with two different procedures. One, called *discriminated avoidance,* provides a specific warning signal that precedes the aversive stimulus. The other, *nondiscriminated* avoidance, provides no warning signal.

Discriminated Avoidance

An experiment by Richard Solomon and L. C. Wynne illustrates discriminated avoidance. The experimenters trained dogs in the shuttle box diagrammed in Figure 5.24. When the dogs were in side A, they were severely shocked. The electricity remained on until the dogs jumped to side B. However, 10 seconds before each shock, a light in the box went out. Gradually, the dogs were conditioned to jump when the light went out, *before* the shock came on, thus avoiding the shock altogether.

For some of Solomon and Wynne's dogs, the transition from escape of shock to avoidance of shock was rapid (for example, dog A of Figure 5.25); for other dogs this transition was more gradual (for example, dog B).

Nondiscriminated Avoidance

A type of nondiscriminated avoidance procedure (an avoidance procedure that provides no signal before the aversive stimulus) was invented by Murray Sidman and is called *Sidman avoidance.* In Sidman avoidance, brief shocks are programmed according to two predetermined intervals—a shock-shock (S–S) interval and a response–shock (R–S) interval. At the beginning of the experiment, shocks are governed by the S–S interval. If this interval were 1 second, as in Figure 5.26a, brief shocks would come every second as long as the subject (a rat in Figure 5.26) did not respond (press the lever). A response cancels all shocks for a period of time governed by the R–S interval. If the R–S interval were 10 seconds, as shown in Figure 5.26b, the rat would get a 10 second shock-free period for each lever press. Responses during the shock-free period postpone shock further. Thus, if the rat responded every 9 seconds, it would receive no shocks regardless of the S–S interval.

Note that with a zero S–S interval (continuous shock) Sidman avoidance is the same as escape conditioning, each response providing a shock-free R–S interval. With a zero R–S interval, Sidman avoidance would be equal to a punishment procedure. Responding with an R–S interval of zero could only increase the number of shocks received, regardless of the S–S interval.

Actual responding on a Sidman avoidance schedule strikes a balance between shocks received and response effort. When the R–S interval is very long (say 2 minutes) rats respond at a low rate because even a rate as low as 1 response every 1 minute and 59 seconds would prevent all shocks. When the R–S interval is close to zero, rats do not respond because the procedure is effectively punishment. As the R–S interval increases from zero, rats begin to respond, beginning faster and responding more with shorter S–S intervals. Figure 5.26c shows rate

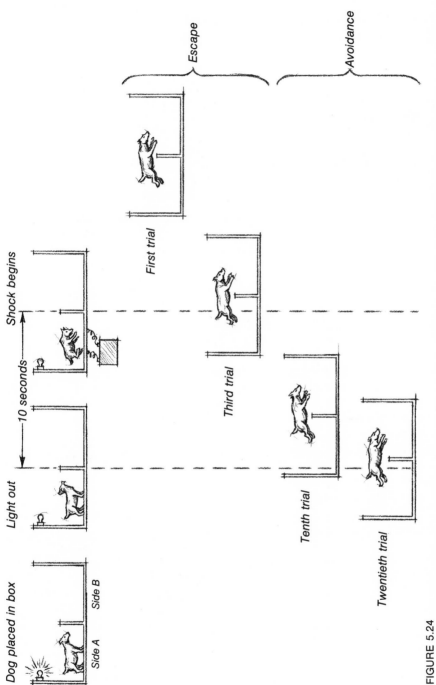

FIGURE 5.24

Solomon and Wynne's avoidance experiment. First trial: Dog jumps over barrier long after shock begins. Third trial: Dog jumps immediately after shock begins. Tenth trial: Dog jumps between signal and shock. Twentieth trial: Dog jumps immediately after signal appears.

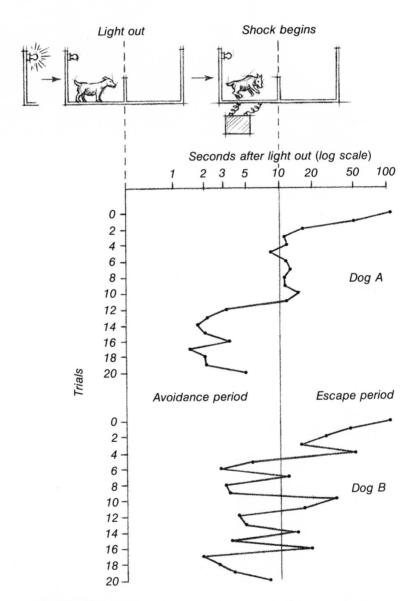

FIGURE 5.25
Graph showing the performance of the two dogs in Solomon and Wynne's experiment. (Each point represents a jump over the barrier.) Dog A shifted rapidly from escape to avoidance. Dog B shifted gradually from escape to avoidance. [Data from Solomon and Wynne, 1953.]

a

*Shocks received
with no response*

Shock–shock interval = 1 second

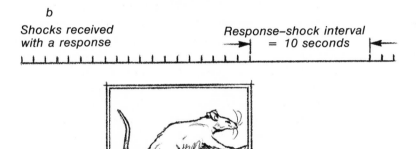

b

*Shocks received
with a response*

*Response–shock interval
= 10 seconds*

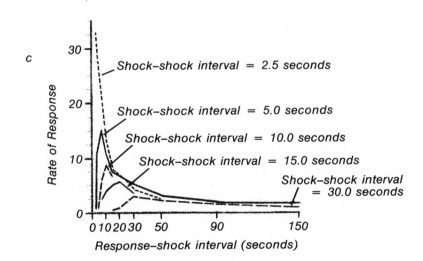

c

Rate of Response

30

Shock–shock interval = 2.5 seconds

20

Shock–shock interval = 5.0 seconds

Shock–shock interval = 10.0 seconds

10

Shock–shock interval = 15.0 seconds

*Shock–shock interval
= 30.0 seconds*

0

0 10 20 30   50   90   150

Response–shock interval (seconds)

FIGURE 5.26
Sidman avoidance. Shocks received when S–S interval = 1 second and
R–S interval = 10 seconds, are shown in (a), with no responding, and in
(b), with a single response. The curves in (c) show rate of response as a
function of the R–S interval with S–S interval as a parameter. [Data from
Sidman, 1953.]

of response as a function of the R–S interval with the S–S interval as the parameter.

It may be argued that Sidman avoidance is really a discriminated avoidance procedure because, although it provides no external warning stimulus before each shock, it does program shocks at fixed temporal intervals, so that internal temporally correlated stimuli could come to signal shock. A more truly non-discriminated avoidance procedure was designed by Richard Herrnstein and Philip Hineline, using rats in a Skinner box containing a lever and a grid floor (see Figure 5.27). There were two machines that could deliver shock to the rat through the grid floor, but only one was connected at a time. The shocks delivered by each machine were fairly intense, very brief, and programmed at irregular intervals. The only difference between the two was that machine A produced shocks at a fairly rapid rate and machine B produced shocks at a fairly slow rate. In other words, the probability of shock at any time was greater with A than with B. Ordinarily, machine A, which produces shocks at a high rate, is connected at first, and machine B is not connected. A press of the lever, however, disconnects machine A and connects machine B, which stays connected until a shock is delivered at which time it is disconnected and machine A is connected. Machine A is like the S–S timer of Sidman avoidance except that here the shocks come at variable instead of fixed intervals. Machine B is like the R–S timer of Sidman avoidance, again with variable instead of fixed intervals. It is possible under these conditions that immediately after a lever-press, machine B would produce a shock (this would happen if the rat pressed the lever at X–X in Figure 5.27). Thus, pressing the lever would not prevent shocks completely. All it would do is change conditions so as to decrease the overall rate of shocks. In the Herrnstein and Hineline experiment, all the rats learned to press the lever for such molar negative reinforcement.

Extinction of Avoidance

When extinction of avoidance is carried out in a way parallel to extinction of positively reinforced behavior, the reinforced response disappears quite rapidly. For instance, suppose one of Solomon and Wynne's dogs learned to jump over a barrier to escape—and then to avoid—shocks. Suppose we want to extinguish this behavior. During extinction the jumps would no longer be reinforced by escape or avoidance—we would shock the animal no matter what it did. When this procedure is followed, the jumps eventually stop. In fact, responses extinguished in this manner are often extinguished so thoroughly that it is difficult to get the animal to respond again, even when extinction is discontinued and conditioning is reinstated.

Attempts to reduce the rate of avoidance behavior by simply withdrawing the aversive stimulus have produced exactly the opposite results. Suppose again that an animal has learned to jump over a barrier to avoid shocks, as in the Solomon and Wynne study. Then, suppose the experimenter maintains the

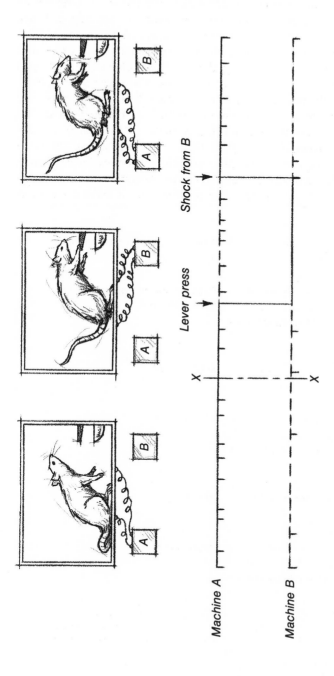

FIGURE 5.27
Herrnstein and Hineline's nondiscriminated-avoidance experiment. At top, three sketches show (from left to right): (a) a rat in a Skinner box to which machine A is attached; (b) the rat presses a lever that disconnects machine A and connects machine B; (c) the rat receives a shock from B, which now disconnects B and connects A. At bottom, two horizontal lines with vertical ticks show the electric shocks programmed by machine A and machine B. Solid line shows which machine was connected to the box at a given time and thus which shocks were actually received. (This means, for instance, that if the rat had pressed the lever at point X—X, it would have been shocked immediately.)

same conditions—the same box, the same signal, and the same jump before the shock comes on—except that the shock apparatus is unplugged. When Solomon and Wynne tried unplugging their electrical apparatus, they found that the dogs kept jumping; the dogs would jump literally hundreds of times after shock had been discontinued. Eventually, the avoidance behavior slowed down and stopped under these conditions, but the process was a lengthy one, especially as compared to the normal extinction procedure. It is easy to understand why the second extinction process was so inefficient if we remember what was said about extinction of positively reinforced responses: *The easier it is to discriminate the reinforcement situation from the extinction situation, the faster extinction will be.* In the case of the two extinction processes for avoidance, the first is easily distinguished from reinforcement. As soon as the dog makes the previously reinforced jumping response, and the shock is maintained never-

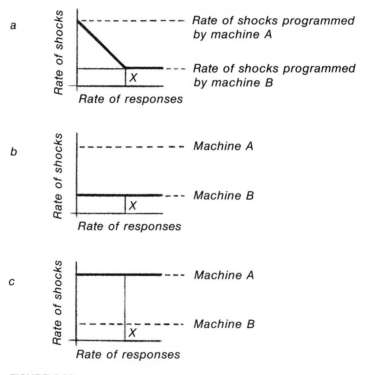

FIGURE 5.28
In Herrnstein and Hineline's avoidance procedure, faster responding results in fewer shocks as shown in (a). If extinction is programmed as in (b) with machine B always connected, the same rate of responding (x) results in the same rate of shocks as in (a). If extinction is programmed as in (c) with machine A always connected, the same rate of responding (x) results in a higher rate of shocks.

theless, the conditions of reinforcement are obviously at an end. However, in the second procedure, when the dog jumps and is not shocked, the conditions are identical to those of reinforcement. With the second method of extinction, as long as the reinforced response is maintained, the conditions of reinforcement and extinction are identical. Figure 5.28 shows why extinction is more rapid with the first method. Figure 5.28a shows the relationship between rate of responding and rate of shocks in the Herrnstein-Hineline experiment. No responding at all results in a high rate of shock programmed by machine A. As the rate of responding increases, the rate of shock decreases until it reaches the low value programmed by machine B. If a rat learns to avoid shocks in this procedure, it will press at, or maybe slightly above, rate X, keeping shocks at the minimum. If extinction is programmed as shown in Figure 5.28b, with shocks still coming at the low rate (machine B connected continuously), the rat will keep responding because the rate of response and shock are still as they were before. If extinction is programmed as shown in Figure 5.28c, with shocks now coming at the high rate (machine A connected continuously), the conditions will have suddenly changed and the rat's behavior will become more variable. The increased variability, in turn, exposes the rat to the new correlation (of zero) and the rat stops responding.

APPLICATIONS IN BEHAVIOR THERAPY

In the laboratory we are concerned with complex contingencies of reinforcement and with quantifying the variables that control behavior. We tend to take for granted the basic principles by which such control is gained—the principles outlined in this book. At several institutions, however, researchers have been resolutely applying these principles to the treatment of dysfunctional human behavior. These applications have been successful as measured against results with more traditional methods of treating behavioral disorders.

WARNING

Engineers, familiar with the physical sciences and with machines and their operation, develop practical applications of scientific findings. In regard to the behavioral sciences, we are all engineers in a sense. We are, ourselves, behaving organisms and we sometimes feel a pressing need for rules that will tell us how to behave. There is thus a strong temptation to extrapolate from pigeons to people—to attempt to apply laboratory data directly to our everyday lives. However, the behavior of an organism in response to the simple contingencies of an isolated laboratory environment may be quite different from the behavior of an organism exposed to the complex contingencies of a nonlaboratory environment. We hope to eventually apply what we have learned in the laboratory to the problems of everyday life. But such application must be undertaken with the utmost care.

Perhaps the greatest danger of premature application of the findings of behavioral science to the complex world outside the laboratory is that it gives us the illusion that we are acting scientifically when, in reality, our behavior is no more effective than it would be if it were guided simply by tradition. Since we know little of the complex effects of spanking on children, it is no more scientific to tell ourselves we are spanking a child "to reduce his maladaptive behavior" than to spank him "because we are mad at him." (It is for this reason that the examples that are drawn here from everyday life should not be regarded as direct guides to action.)

One way to look at dysfunctional behavior is to regard it as behavior that has evolved "out of synchrony" with changes in the environment. According to this view, when the environment changes too suddenly or drastically, an organism may not be able to "keep up"—to compensate adequately, to behave so as to maximize reward under the changed contingencies.

Someone who is unhappy about his behavior may seek help from a therapist. It is up to the therapist to provide the appropriate environmental gradations that will reward the patient for approximations to the desired behavior.

Sometimes it is society, rather than the person himself, that desires a change in his behavior. Murder is an obvious example of a dysfunctional behavior that harms human society. Then there are people who cannot function in the particular society in which they live. Some cannot hold a job; some cannot interact with other people; some cannot communicate rationally; others cannot even eat or attend to their own bodily needs without constant assistance. In the United States alone, more than a quarter of a million criminals are locked up in federal and state prisons, and more than half a million mental patients are institutionalized. The basic question regarding an institutionalized person is: Do we want to use the most effective means we know to change his or her behavior for the better (that is, to bring it into conformity with the environmental contingencies)? If we refuse to try, we continue to expose the inmate to the contingencies of reinforcement in our present institutions. This course of action often does provide a crude but effective means of modifying behavior—for the worse.

The techniques used in behavior modifications are varied. At present, behavior modification outside the laboratory is more of an art than a science; each therapist evolves his own techniques for application of behavioral principles. Let us consider some examples:

Revising Contingencies of Reinforcement

In a mental hospital (as in any hospital or institution where boredom is a strong factor) the attention of the staff is a potent reinforcer. Almost every mental hospital is "short staffed" and there is a tendency for staff members to pay most attention to those patients who give the most trouble. Thus, a behaviorist would contend that there is a built-in mechanism in most mental hospitals to reinforce trouble-making and disturbances of various kinds. An easy way for a patient to get personal attention under these circumstances is to refuse to eat. In fact, in many mental hospitals there is a large number of patients who must be coaxed to enter the dining room and once there, who must be fed like infants. A vicious circle develops. Patients refuse to eat, becoming the center of attention. This, in turn, reinforces their refusal to eat and gets them more attention. Clearly, positive feedback is at work in the situation.

In a report published in 1962, Teodore Ayllon and Erick Haughton, on the staff of a hospital in Saskatchewan, Canada, described a technique they devised to break the vicious circle. They selected a group of thirty schizophrenic women with a history of refusal to eat. Several attendants usually took thirty minutes to get the women into the dining room. Ayllon and Haughton then changed the contingencies. The attendants were instructed to ignore the patients. A bell sounded to announce that the dining room was open. Thirty minutes later the doors of the dining room were closed and patients were no longer allowed in. Whoever did not enter within 30 minutes did not eat that meal. Although, at first, few patients entered the dining room within the allotted time, eventually almost all of them did. Then the time was decreased from 30 minutes to 20 minutes to 15 minutes to 5 minutes. Finally, almost all of the patients entered the dining room within five minutes of the bell without the assistance of the attendants. Next, Haughton and Ayllon made entrance to the dining room contingent on dropping a penny (which the patients received from a nurse) into a slot. Then, in order to receive the coin, each patient had to press a button simultaneously with another patient at another button. At the end of the experiment, all the patients, selected originally for their refusal to eat, were engaging in cooperative behavior in order to obtain admission to the dining hall. Here is an example of making one reinforcer (attention from staff) independent of a behavior (refusal to eat) and making another reinforcer (food) dependent on a behavior (sharing a task with another person). The first reinforcer lost its effect on the patient's behavior and the second reinforcer gained effectiveness.

Shaping

A second example also involves the gradual shaping of a response, this time a verbal response of a *catatonic schizophrenic* patient who had been completely mute for nineteen years prior to the incidents reported here. To say the least, the patient, referred to as S (for Subject), was withdrawn and exhibited little psychomotor activity. The case history that follows is not unique. It is from a report published in 1960 by Wayne Isaacs, James Thomas, and Israel Goldiamond of Anna State Hospital in Illinois.*

> The S was brought to a group therapy session with other chronic schizophrenics (who were verbal), but he sat in the position in which he was placed and continued the withdrawal behaviors which characterized him. He remained impassive and stared ahead even when cigarettes, which other members accepted, were offered to him and were waved before his face. At one session, when E removed cigaretts from his pocket, a package of chewing gum accidentally fell out. The S's eyes moved toward the gum and then returned to their usual position. This response was chosen by E as one with which he would start to work, using the method of successive approximation. (This method finds use where E desires to produce responses which are not present in the current repertoire of the organism and which are considerably removed from those which are available. The E then attempts to "shape" and available behaviors into the desired form, capitalizing upon both the variability and regularity of successive behaviors. The shaping process involves the reinforcement of those parts of a selected response which are successively in the desired direction and the nonreinforcement of those which are not. For example, a pigeon may be initially reinforced when it moves its head. When this movement occurs regularly, only an upward movement may be reinforced, with downward movements not reinforced. The pigeon may now stretch its neck, with this movement reinforced. Eventually the pigeon may be trained to peck at a disc which was initially high above its head and at which it would normally never peck. In the case of the psychotic under discussion, the succession was eye movement, which brought into play occasional facial movements including those of the mouth, lip movements, vocalizations, word utterance, and finally verbal behavior.)
>
> The S met individually with E three times a week. Group sessions also continued. The following sequence of procedures was introduced in the private sessions. Although the weeks are numbered consecutively, they did not follow at regular intervals since other duties kept E from seeing S every week.
>
> *Weeks, 1, 2.* A stick of gum was held before S's face, and E waited until S's eyes moved toward it. When this reponse occurred, E as a consequence gave him the gum. By the end of the second week, response probability in the presence of the gum was increased to such an extent that S's eyes moved toward the gum as soon as it was held up.
>
> *Weeks 3, 4.* The E now held the gum before S, waiting until he noticed movement in S's lips before giving it to him. Toward the end of the first session of the third week, a lip movement spontaneously occurred, which E promptly reinforced. By the end of this week both lip movement and eye movement occurred when the gum was held up. The E then withheld giving S the gum until S spontaneously made a vocalization, at which time E gave S the gum. By the end of this week, holding up the gum readily occasioned eye movement toward it, lip movement, and a vocalization resembling a croak.

---

*In case histories, the subject is often referred to as S, the experimenter as E.

Weeks, 5, 6. The E held up the gum, and said, "Say gum, gum," repeating these words each time S vocalized. Giving S the gum was made contingent upon vocalizations increasingly approximating gum. At the sixth session (at the end of Week 6), when E said, "Say gum, gum," S suddenly said, "Gum, please." This response was accompanied by reinstatement of other responses of this class, that is, S answered questions regarding his name and age.

Thereafter he responded to questions by E both in individual sessions and in group sessions, but answered no one else. Responses to the discriminitive stimuli of the room generalized to E on the ward; he greeted E on two occasions in the group room. He read from signs in E's office upon request by E.

Since the response now seemed to be under the strong stimulus control of E, the person, attempt was made to generalize the stimulus to other people. Accordingly, a nurse was brought into the private room; S smiled at her. After a month, he began answering her questions. Later, when he brought his coat to a volunteer worker on the ward, she interpreted the gesture as a desire to go outdoors and conducted him there. Upon informing E of the incident, she was instructed to obey S only as a consequence of explicit verbal requests by him. The S thereafter vocalized requests. These instructions have now been given to other hospital personnel, and S regularly initiates verbal requests when nonverbal requests have no reinforcing consequences. Upon being taken to the commissary, he said, "Ping pong," to the volunteer worker and played a game with her. Other patients, visitors, and members of hospital-society-at-large continue, however, to interpret nonverbal requests and to reinforce them by obeying S.

It is important to note that the behavior shaped here is not wholly new. Rather, an old behavior is reinstated. Similarly, when a pigeon's behavior is shaped to produce key-pecking, the experimenter is not teaching the pigeon to peck. Rather, he is directing pecking just as Goldiamond was directing the patient's speech.

Some nonbehaviorists object to this kind of direct treatment of dysfunctional behavior on the grounds that it treats "only the behavioral symptoms of the disorder" rather than "the underlying disorder," which is said to exist in "the mind" of the patient. These critics contend that as long as the basic psychological problem is not found by subtle and sophisticated techniques and revealed to the patient, elimination of one symptom will tend to be replaced by the substitution of another. In actual instances of behavioral treatment, however, dysfunctional behaviors have been eliminated, and such a hypothetical substitution of symptoms is virtually never found.*

---

*Even if the critics were correct, and behavioral therapy treated only symptoms, surely it would be better to get rid of the symptoms and not the underlying disease than to "cure" the disease and leave all the symptoms intact. (A man would not worry about a cold without its symptoms to tell him that he has it. Similarly, he would worry a great deal if the symptoms of runny nose, headaches, sneezing, and high temperature persisted even though his "basic cold" had been cured.

But will a successful treatment in a mental hospital (or therapist's office), where the environment is largely under control, persist when a person returns to the normal complex environment outside of the institution? Behavioral modifications wrought in an institution could easily be extinguished in other environments. Clearly, it is important that appropriate behavior continue to be rewarded in the "outside world."

Often dysfunctional behavior seems to be subject to the effect of positive feedback. For some reason a man has a mild behavioral disturbance; his relatives and friends overreact to the mild disturbance and upset him; this increases the disturbance, which, in turn, provokes stronger reactions. A behavioral therapist's treatment of such behavior would be designed to break this pattern in a direct fashion. Relatives who have refused to have a patient home for visits because they are upset by the patient's strange appearance or behavior may change their attitude when the patient's appearance and behavior are less strange. Their changed attitude may well reinforce normal behavior outside the institution.

Extinction and Depression

Several psychologists have surmised that many of the clinical symptoms of depression in humans arise from a form of extinction—a lack of reward in the environment. Martin Seligman has extended this speculation to cover extinction of all kinds—not simply a lack of reward but a lack of correlation between reward and behavior. Thus, depression in humans is like learned helplessness in animals. Seligman makes a very strong case for the relationship between the two phenomena. He summarizes his argument as follows:

> As for symptoms, learned helplessness is characterized by passivity in the face of trauma and difficulty at learning that responding produces relief; it dissipates in time, may be associated with anorexia, and norepinephrine depletion. Depression is characterized by passivity and negative expectations about the effectiveness of one's actions; it, too, is thought to dissipate in time, and may be associated with loss of libido and norepinephrine depletion. Learned helplessness is caused by experience in which responding cannot control reinforcers, and reactive depression may have its roots in loss of control over gratification and alleviation of suffering. Helplessness can be cured by repeated exposure to responding that produces relief, and changing the patient's perception of himself as helpless to a set in which he believes that he can control reinforcement may be central to the successful treatment of depression. Learned helplessness can be prevented by immunizing experiences with control over trauma, and it is speculated that a life history of control over reinforcers may make individuals more resilient from depression.*

*M. E. P. Seligman, Depression and learned helplessness. In R. J. Friedman and M. M. Katz, eds. *The Psychology of Depression: Contemporary Theory and Research*, in press.

Anorexia is loss of appetite. Norepinephrine is a chemical present in the central nervous system that aids in the transfer of neural impulses from one nerve to another. Its depletion in humans with depression is not a proven fact. However, depressives treated with drugs that increase norepinephrine in the nervous system are sometimes relieved of their symptoms, and normal people given drugs that decrease norepinephrine in the nervous system sometimes develop symptoms of depression. In a study of learned helplessness in animals, rats that could control shocks and rats that could not control shocks were sacrificed and their brains examined. The rats that could control shocks had more norepinephrine than the others.

Several forms of therapy have been effective in treating depression (although there is no invariably effective cure). Seligman believes that they have in common their attempt to induce the patient ". . . to see that he can control important reinforcers by his own actions."

BIBLIOGRAPHY

This chapter is the core of the present book. There is no single place that the reader can look for an expansion of the material it contains. But he should be prepared by now to read many of the articles on animal learning in such journals as *Psychological Review, Journal of The Experimental Analysis of Behavior, Learning and Motivation,* and *Journal of Experimental Psychology: Animal Behavior Processes.* Recent issues of these journals contain articles on the topics of this chapter. A review of several areas in operant conditioning is contained in W. K. Honig (ed.), *Operant behavior: Areas of research and application.* (New York: Appleton-Century-Crofts, 1966). A newer edition of Honig's book, edited by Honig and J. E. R. Staddon, is in press now.

An extensive discussion of schedules of reinforcement and many examples of cumulative records with various schedules can be found in C. B. Ferster and B. F. Skinner's *Schedules of reinforcement* (New York: Appleton-Century-Crofts, 1957).

Following is a list of articles referred to in this chapter:

Ayllon, T., and Haughton, E. Control of the behavior of schizophrenics by food. *Journal of The Experimental Analysis of Behavior,* 1962, *5,* 343–352.

Herrnstein, R. J., and Hineline, P. Negative reinforcement as shock-frequency reduction. *Journal of The Experimental Analysis of Behavior,* 1966, *9,* 421–430.

Fowler, H., and Trapold, M. A. Escape performance as a function of delay of reinforcement. *J. Exp. Psych.,* 1962, *63,* 464–467.

Isaacs, W., Thomas, J., and Goldiamond, I. Application of operant conditioning to reinstate verbal behavior in psychotics. *Journal of Speech and Hearing Disorders,* 1960, *25,* 8-12.

Logan, F. A. *Incentive.* New Haven: Yale University Press, 1960.

Maier, S. F., Seligman, M. E. P., and Solomon, R. L. Pavlovian fear condi-
tioning and learned helplessness. In R. Church and B. Campbell (Eds.),
Aversive Conditioning and Learning. New York: Appleton-Century-
Crofts, 1969.

Seligman, M. E. P. Depression and learned helplessness. *The psychology of
depression: Contemporary theory and research,* ed. R. D. Friedman and
M. M. Katz. In press.

Schuster, R., and Rachlin, H. Indifference between punishment and free shock:
Evidence for the negative law of effect. *J. Exp. Anal. Beh.,* 1968, *11,*
777–785.

Sidman, M. Two temporal parameters of the maintenance of avoidance behavior
by the white rat. *Journal of Comparative and Physiological Psychology,*
1953, *46,* 253–261.

Solomon, R. L., and Wynne, L. C. Traumatic avoidance learning: Acquisition
in normal dogs. *Psychological Monographs,* 1953, *67,* No. 354.

Additional material on behavior therapy may be found in many sources. An excellent undergraduate text on abnormal psychology that emphasizes behavioral analysis
and treatment is G. C. Davison and J. Neale's *Abnormal psychology: An experimental
clinical approach* (New York: Wiley, 1974). Two recent texts, more advanced, are:

Krasner, L., and Ullman, L. P. *Research in behavior modification.* New York:
Holt, Rinehart and Winston, 1965.

O'Leary, K. D., and Wilson, G. T. *Behavior therapy: Application and outcome.*
Englewood Cliffs, N.J.: Prentice-Hall, 1975.

The most important behavior therapy articles are reprinted each year in:

Franks, C. M., and Wilson, G. T. *Annual review of behavior therapy: Theory
and practice.* New York: Brunner-Mazel.

Finally, entertaining informative books on practical applications of behavior
therapy in everyday life are published by an organization called "Behaviordelia,"
located in Kalamazoo, Michigan.

We reprint a section of a long paper by A. Charles Catania and G. S. Reynolds
illustrating how behavioral experiments are designed, performed, and analyzed. Note
that the experiments are not designed specifically to test hypotheses but merely to
find out how varying the parameters of a schedule affects performance. Yet these
results are the data which must be accounted for when formulating any hypothesis
about how behavior changes as a function of frequency of reinforcement. This work
has been much more valuable for psychologists (as judged by the number of citations
in the literature) than many more theoretically ambitious articles.

Supplemental Reading for Chapter 5

A QUANTITATIVE ANALYSIS OF THE RESPONDING MAINTAINED BY INTERVAL SCHEDULES OF REINFORCEMENT

A. Charles Catania
G. S. Reynolds

Interval schedules of reinforcement maintained pigeons' key-pecking in six experiments. Each schedule was specified in terms of mean interval, which determined the maximum rate of reinforcement possible, and distribution of intervals, which ranged from many-valued (variable-interval) to single-valued (fixed-interval). In Exp. 1, the relative durations of a sequence of intervals from an arithmetic progression were held constant while the mean interval was varied. Rate of responding was a monotonically increasing, negatively accelerated function of rate of reinforcement over a range from 8.4 to 300 reinforcements per hour. The rate of responding also increased as time passed within the individual intervals of a given schedule.

This research was supported by NSF Grants G8621 and G18167 (B. F. Skinner, Principal Investigator) to Harvard University, and was conducted at the Harvard Psychological Laboratories. Some of the material has been presented at the 1961 and 1963 meetings of the Psychonomic Society. The authors' thanks go to Mrs. Antoinette C. Papp and Mr. Wallace R. Brown, Jr., for care of pigeons and assistance in the daily conduct of the experiments, and to Mrs. Geraldine Hansen for typing several revisions of the manuscript. We are indebted to many colleagues, and in particular to N. H. Azrin, who maintained responsibility for the manuscript well beyond the expiration of his editorial term, and to D. G. Anger, L. R. Gollub, and S. S. Pliskoff. Some expenses of preparation of the manuscript were defrayed by NSF Grant GB 3614 (to New York University), by NSF Grants GB 316 and GB 2541 (to the University of Chicago), and by the Smith Kline and French Laboratories. Expenses of publication were defrayed by NIH Grant MH 13613 (to New York University) and NSF Grants GB 5064 and GB 6821 (to the University of California, San Diego). Reprints may be obtained from A. C. Catania, Department of Psychology. New York University, University College of Arts and Sciences, New York, N.Y. 10453.

From *Journal of the Experimental Analysis of Behavior*, Vol. 11, No. 3 Part 2, 327–383. Copyright 1968 by the Society for the Experimental Analysis of Behavior.

The statement that responses take place in time expresses a fundamental characteristic of behavior (Skinner, 1938, pp. 263-264). Responses occur at different rates, in different sequences, and with different temporal patterns, depending on the temporal relations between the responses and other events. One event of fundamental interest is reinforcement, and the rate at which responses occur and the changes in this rate over time are strongly determined by the schedule according to which particular responses are reinforced (*e.g.*, Morse, 1966).

An interval schedule arranges reinforcement for the first response that occurs after a specified time has elapsed since the occurrence of a preceding reinforcement or some other environmental event (Ferster and Skinner, 1957). In such a schedule, the spacing of reinforcements in time remains roughly constant over a wide range of rates of responding. The schedule specifies certain minimum intervals between two reinforcements; the actual durations of these intervals are determined by the time elapsed between the availability of reinforcement, at the end of the interval, and the occurrence of the next response, which is reinforced. The patterns and rates of responding maintained by interval schedules usually are such that this time is short relative to the durations of the intervals.

Ferster and Skinner (1957, Ch. 5 and 6) have described in considerable detail some important features of the performances maintained by interval schedules. In a fixed-interval (FI) schedule, the first response after a fixed elapsed time is reinforced, and an organism typically responds little or not at all just after reinforcement, although responding increases later in the interval. In a variable-interval (VI) schedule, the first response after a variable elapsed time is reinforced, and a relatively constant rate of responding is maintained throughout each interval. Detailed examination shows, however, that this responding may be modulated by the particular durations of the different intervals that constitute the schedule. In other words, the distribution of responses in time depends on the distribution of reinforcements in time. For example, responding shortly after reinforcement increases with increases in the relative frequency of short intervals in the schedule (Ferster and Skinner, 1957, p. 331–332). Thus, it is important to study not only the rate of responding averaged over the total time in an interval schedule, but also the changes in the rate of responding as time passes within individual intervals. (The former, a rate calculated over the total time in all the intervals of a schedule, will be referred to as an *overall* rate; the latter, a rate calculated over a period of time that is short relative to the average interval between reinforcements, will be referred to as a *local* rate. The terms will be applied to reinforcement as well as to responding. The terminology has the advantage of pointing out that both reinforcement and responding are measured in terms of events per unit of time.)

In a VI schedule, a response at a given time after reinforcement is reinforced in some intervals but not in others. The probability of reinforcement at this time is determined by the relative frequency of reinforcement at this time, which may be derived from the distribution of intervals in the schedule. The distribution of intervals in a VI schedule may act upon behavior because the time elapsed since a preceding reinforcement (or since any other event that starts an interval) may function as a discriminable continuum. Skinner (1938, p. 263 *ff.*), in his discussion of temporal discrimination, included the discrimination of the time elapsed since reinforcement as a factor in his account of the performances maintained by FI schedules. The major difference between FI and VI schedules is that an FI schedule provides reinforcement at a fixed point along the temporal continuum, whereas a VI schedule provides reinforcement at several points. The present account analyzes performances maintained by different interval schedules in terms of the local effects of different probabilities of reinforcement on the local rates of responding at different times.

Within interval schedules, reinforcement may be studied as an input that determines a subsequent output of responses (*cf.* Skinner, 1938, p. 130). In this sense, the study of the performances maintained by interval schedules is a study of response strength. The concept of response strength, once a reference to an inferred response tendency or state, has evolved to a simpler usage: it is "used to designate probability or rate of responding" (Ferster and Skinner, 1957, p. 733). This evolution is a result of several related findings: that the schedule of reinforcement is a primary determinant of performance; that different measures of responding such as rate and resistance to extinction are not necessarily highly correlated; that rate of responding is relatively insensitive to such variables as amount of reinforcement and deprivation; that rate of responding is itself a property of responding that can be differentially reinforced; and that rate of responding can be reduced to component interresponse times (*e.g.,* Anger, 1956; Ferster and Skinner, 1957; Herrnstein, 1961; Skinner, 1938). Nevertheless, the relationship between reinforcement and responding remains of fundamental importance to the analysis of behavior. Many studies of response strength have been concerned with the acquisition of behavior (learning: *e.g.,* Hull, 1943) or with the relative strengths of two or more responses (choice: *e.g.,* Herrnstein, 1961). The present experiments emphasize reinforcement as it determines performance during maintained or steady-state responding, rather than during acquisition, extinction, and other transition states, and are concerned with absolute strength, rather than with strength relative to other behavior.

EXPERIMENT 1: RATE OF RESPONDING AS A FUNCTION OF RATE OF REINFORCEMENT IN VARIABLE-INTERVAL SCHEDULES

The relation between the overall rate of reinforcement and the overall rate of a pigeon's key-pecking maintained by interval schedules may be thought of as an input-output function for the pigeon. In Exp. 1, this function was determined for VI schedules over a range of overall rates of reinforcement from 8.4 to 300 rft/hr (reinforcements per hour). Each schedule consisted of an arithmetic series of 15 intervals ranging from zero to twice the average value of the schedule and arranged in an irregular order. Thus, the relative durations of the particular intervals that made up each schedule were held constant.

Method

Subjects and Apparatus. The key-pecking of each of six adult, male, White Carneaux pigeons, maintained at 80% of free-feeding body weights, had been reinforced on VI schedules for at least 50 hr before the present experiments.

The experimental chamber was similar to that described by Ferster and Skinner

(1957). Mounted on one wall was a translucent Plexiglas response key, 2 cm in diameter and operated by a minimum force of about 15 g. The key was transilluminated by two yellow 6-w lamps. Two white 6-w lamps mounted on the chamber ceiling provided general illumination. The operation of the key occasionally produced the reinforcer, 4-sec access to mixed grain in a standard feeder located behind a 6.5-cm square opening beneath the key. During reinforcement, the feeder was illuminated and the other lights were turned off.

Electromechanical controlling and recording apparatus was located in a separate room. A device that advanced a loop of punched tape a constant distance with each operation (ratio programmer, R. Gerbrands Co.) was stepped by an electronic timer, and intervals between reinforcements were determined by the spacing of the holes punched in the tape. Thus, the absolute durations of the intervals depended on the rate at which the timer operated the programmer, but the relative durations were independent of the timer.

The punched holes in the tape provided a series of 15 intervals from an arithmetic progression, in the following order: 14, 8, 11, 6, 5, 9, 2, 13, 7, 1, 12, 4, 10, 0, 3. The numbers indicate the durations of the intervals between successive reinforcements in multiples of t sec, the setting of the electronic timer. (To permit the arrangement of a 0-sec interval, in which reinforcement was available for the first peck after a preceding reinforcement, the ratio programmer was stepped at each reinforcement as well as at the rate determined by the electronic timer.) In this series, the average interval of the VI schedule was 7t sec; with t equal to 6.5 sec, for example, the average interval was 45.5 sec.

At the end of each interval, when a peck was to be reinforced, the controlling apparatus stopped until the peck occurred; the next interval began only at the end of the 4-sec reinforcement. Thus, the apparatus arranged a distribution of minimum interreinforcement intervals; the actual intervals were given by the time from one reinforcement to the next reinforced response. In practice, the rates of responding at most VI values were such that differences between the minimum and the actual interreinforcement intervals were negligible.

Stepping switches that stepped with each step of the ratio programmer and that reset after each reinforcement distributed key-pecks to the 14 counters, which represented successive periods of time after reinforcement. The time represented by each counter was t sec, and each counter recorded responses only within interreinforcement intervals equal to or longer than the time after reinforcement that the counter represented. For example, the first counter cumulated responses that occurred during the first t sec of all intervals except the 0-sec interval (the 0-sec interval was terminated by a single reinforced response). Correspondingly, the seventh counter cumulated responses during the seventh t sec of only those intervals 7t sec long or longer. The fourteenth counter cumulated responses only during the fourteenth t sec of the 14t-sec interval, the longest interval in the series. Thus, response rates at early times after reinforcement were based on larger samples of pecking than response rates at later times.

Procedure. Seven VI schedules with average intervals ranging from 12.0 to 427 sec (300 to 8.4 rft/hr) were examined. Each pigeon was exposed to VI 12.0-sec, VI 23.5-sec, and VI 45.5-sec, and to a sample of the longer average intervals, as indicated in Table 1. (Occasional sessions in which equipment failed have been omitted; none were within the last five sessions of a given schedule.) Each schedule was in effect for at least 15 daily sessions and until the pigeon's performance was stable, as judged by visual inspection of numerical data and cumulative records, for five successive sessions. With few exceptions, the rate of responding in each of the last five sessions of a given schedule was within 10% of the average rate over those sessions.

The first peck in each session was reinforced and the VI schedule then operated, beginning at a different place in the series of intervals in successive sessions. Thus, each scheduled interval, including the first in the session, began after a reinforcement. Sessions ended after each interval in the series had occurred four times (61 reinforcements). Thus, the duration of a session ranged from about 16 min (12 min of VI 12-sec plus 61 reinforcements) to about 431 min (427 min of VI 427-sec plus 61 reinforcements).

Results

The overall rate of key-pecking as a function of the overall rate of reinforcement is shown for each pigeon in Fig. 1. The functions were, to a first approxima-

Table 1   Mean intervals (sec) of the arithmetic variable-interval schedules arranged for each pigeon, with number of sessions for each schedule shown in parentheses.

			Pigeon		
118	121	129	278	279	281
108 (52)	45.5 (52)	108 (29)	23.5 (35)	427 (52)	23.5 (35)
45.5 (29)	23.5 (29)	216 (35)	12.0 (17)	216 (29)	45.5 (17)
23.5 (22)	12.0 (58)	427 (29)	45.5 (29)	108 (22)	12.0 (29)
12.0 (36)	108 (22)	23.5 (22)	216 (22)	23.5 (36)	427 (58)
323 (37)	23.5 (15)	45.5 (36)	108 (36)	12.0 (22)	45.5 (22)
108 (28)		12.0 (22)	45.5 (22)	45.5 (15)	12.0 (43)
		23.5 (15)	427 (15)	108 (29)	
		108 (28)	427* (26)		

*Reinstated after interruption.

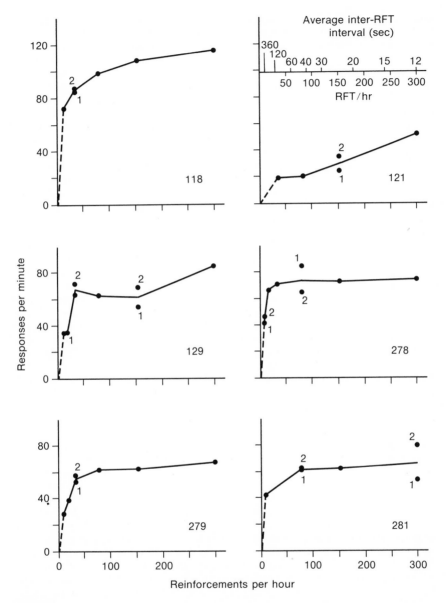

FIGURE 1
Rate of key-pecking as a function of rate of reinforcement for six pigeons. Key-pecking
was maintained by VI schedules consisting of 15 intervals in an arithmetic progression of
size, but arranged in an irregular order. Each point is the arithmetic mean of the rates of
responding over the last five sessions of a given schedule. Numerals 1 and 2 indicate
first and second determinations. Some representative average interreinforcement
intervals, proportional to reciprocals of the rates of reinforcement (rft/hr), are shown on
the scale at the upper right.

tion, monotonically increasing and negatively accelerated, perhaps approaching an asymptotic level for some pigeons. With increasing rates of reinforcement, the rate of responding increased more rapidly at low rates of reinforcement (for most pigeons, to roughly 50 rft/hr) than at higher rates of reinforcement. The shapes of the functions differed in detail from pigeon to pigeon: Pigeon 118, for example, produced a fairly smooth increasing function; Pigeon 121, an almost linear function; and Pigeons 278 and 279, a rapid increase to a near invariance in the rate of responding. This near invariance might be called a "locked rate" (Herrnstein, 1955; Sidman, 1960), a term that has been applied to the occasionally observed insensitivity of a given pigeon's rate of responding to changes in the parameters of an interval schedule of reinforcement.

Despite the near invariance, the functions appear in general to increase over their entire range. (Reversals, as for Pigeon 129 at 33.3 rft/hr, were within the limits of variability implied by the redeterminations, which generally produced higher rates of responding than the original determinations.) The average rate of responding maintained by 300 rft/hr was higher than that maintained by 153 rft/hr for all pigeons. In addition, rates of responding at higher rates of reinforcement may be spuriously low, because the contribution of the latency of the first response after reinforcement to the overall rate of responding was greatest at the higher rates of reinforcement. A correction for this latency would slightly increase rates of responding at the higher rates of reinforcement (300, 153, and, perhaps, 79 rft/hr), but would have virtually no effect at the lower rates of reinforcement. Despite the small changes at high rates of reinforcement, it seems reasonable to conclude that overall rates of responding increase monotonically (perhaps approaching an asymptote) as overall rate of reinforcement increases.

Within individual intervals between two reinforcements, the rate of key-peck-ing increased with increasing time since reinforcement, as shown for each pigeon in Fig. 2, which plots local rates of responding against the absolute time elapsed since reinforcement. The functions reflect in their vertical separation the different overall rates maintained by each schedule (Fig. 1).

Data obtained with each arithmetic VI schedule for each pigeon are plotted against relative time since reinforcement in Fig. 3. The functions have been adjusted by multiplying local rates of responding by constants chosen to make the average rate of responding for each function equal to 1.0. When the differences in overall levels of the functions were removed by this adjustment, the local rate of responding within intervals grew as approximately the same function of relative time after reinforcement in most VI schedules studied with most pigeons. The major exceptions were some pigeon's data from the shorter VI schedules: Pigeon 121 at 12.0 and 23.5 sec; Pigeon 278 at 23.5 and 45.5 sec; and Pigeon 281 at 12.0 sec. It may be relevant that only in these schedules were rates of responding sometimes low enough to produce large differences between the minimum and actual interreinforcement intervals. For the remaining functions, there appeared to be no systematic ordering from one pigeon to another of the slopes or degrees of curvature of the several functions. . . .

As with overall rates of responding (Fig. 1), the functions differed in detail from pigeon to pigeon, even if the atypical data from the shorter VI schedules are ignored. For a given pigeon, however, the functions in Fig. 1 and in Fig. 3 were generally similar: fairly smooth increasing functions for Pigeon 118, almost linear functions for Pigeon 121 except for data from the shorter VI schedules, and rapid increases to a near invariance for Pigeons 278 and 279. The similarity is debatable for Pigeon 281 even when the 12.0-sec function is disregarded, and no simple relationship is evident between the two sets of data for Pigeon 129. The possible significance of the similarities is that the same variables may have operated to produce changes in both the local rate of responding, as time passed within interreinforcement intervals, and in the overall rate of responding, when the overall rate of reinforcement was changed.

A cummulative record of the responding of Pigeon 118 is shown in Fig. 4. Upward concavity, which indicates an increasing rate of responding, is evident in almost every interval between reinforcements. The averaging of rates of responding across intervals assumed that there was no systematic change in the responding within intervals from one interval to another. No consistent sequential effects were evident in the cumulative records; if present, they constituted a relatively minor effect that, for the present purposes, will be ignored.

Discussion

Overall rates of responding. Individual differences among pigeons were considerable, but the functions relating overall rate of responding to overall rate of reinforcement were generally monotonically increasing and negatively accelerated. The general nature of this relationship is well supported by the literature on both VI and FI schedules. Both pigeons and rats have been studied in a variety of experimental contexts, usually over a narrower range of rates of reinforcement than was studied here. Monotonically increasing and negatively accelerated functions have been obtained from rats by Skinner (1936; data obtained early in the acquisition of FI performance), Wilson (1954; FI schedules), Clark (1958; VI schedules at several levels of deprivation), and Sherman (1959; FI schedules). The same relationship may hold for schedules of negative reinforcement (Kaplan, 1952; FI schedules of escape). Similar functions have been obtained from pigeons by Schoenfeld and Cumming (1960) and by Farmer (1963). . . . Other data have been obtained from pigeons by Cumming (1955) and by Ferster and Skinner (1957). In Cumming's ex-periment, rates of responding did not increase monotonically with rates of reinforcement, but rates of responding may not have reached asymptotic levels and the VI schedules alternated with a stimulus-correlated period of extinction. Ferster and Skinner presented data in the form of cumulative records selected to show detailed characteristics of responding; the data therefore were not necessarily representative of the overall rates of responding maintained by each schedule.

Monotonically increasing and negatively accelerated functions relating total responding to total reinforcement in concurrent schedules (Findley, 1958; Herrnstein, 1961; Catania, 1963a), in which VI schedules were independently arranged for pigeons' pecks on two different keys, have been discussed by Catania (1963a). Additional data are provided by experiments with chained schedules (Autor, 1960; Findley, 1962; Nevin, 1964; Herrnstein, 1964), in which reinforcement of responding in the presence of one stimulus consists of the onset of another stimulus in the presence of which another schedule of reinforcement is arranged (*cf.* the review by Kelleher and Gollub, 1962).

Evidence for substantial individual differences among pigeons has been noted in the literature. Herrnstein (1955), for example, varied the overall rate of reinforcement provided by VI schedules in an experiment concerned with the effect of stimuli preceding a period of timeout from VI reinforcement. Monotonically increasing, negatively accelerated functions were obtained from two pigeons (S1, 6 to 120 rft/hr, and S3, 6 to 60 rft/hr), but the third pigeon's rate of responding was roughly constant over the range of reinforcement rates studied (S2, 6 to 40 rft/hr: this pigeon provided the basis for a discussion of "locked rate"). Individual differences among pigeons were also observed by Reynolds (1961, 1963), who obtained monotonically increasing, negatively accelerated functions when different VI schedules in the presence of one stimulus were alternated with a constant

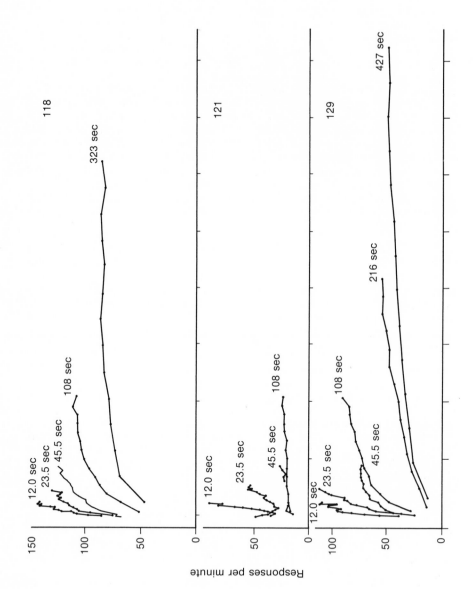

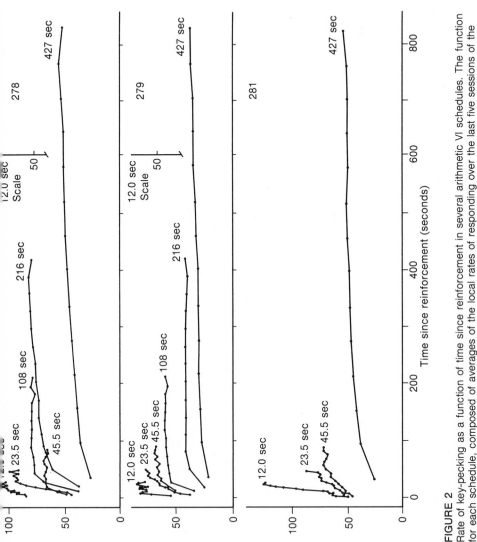

FIGURE 2

Rate of key-pecking as a function of time since reinforcement in several arithmetic VI schedules. The function for each schedule, composed of averages of the local rates of responding over the last five sessions of the schedule, is identified by the mean interreinforcement interval. Two of the 12.0-sec functions have been displaced on the ordinate, as indicated by the inserted scales (Pigeons 278 and 279). For those schedules arranged twice for a given pigeon, only one function, chosen on the basis of convenience of presentation, has been plotted.

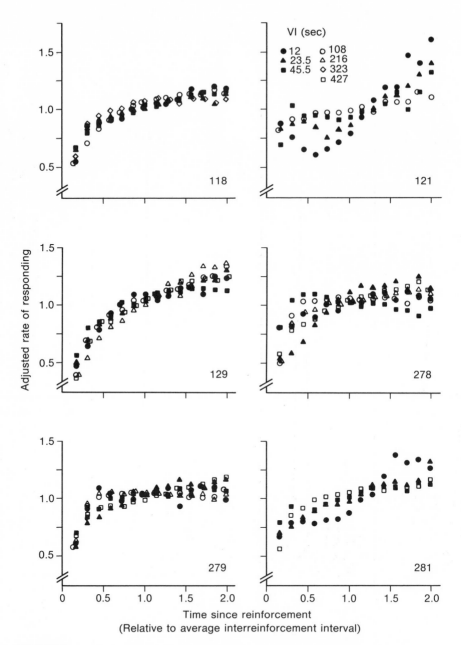

FIGURE 3
Rate of key-pecking, adjusted so that the average rate of pecking equals 1.0, as a function of relative time since reinforcement in several arithmetic VI schedules. For those schedules arranged twice for a given pigeon, only the first determination has been plotted.

118   Arithmetic VI 108-sec

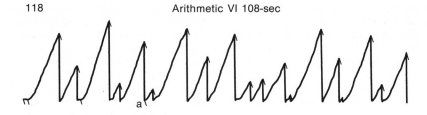

FIGURE 4

Cumulative record of a full session of key-pecking maintained by an arithmetic VI schedule with a mean interreinforcement interval of 108-sec (Pigeon 118). The recording pen reset to baseline after each reinforcement, indicated by diagonal pips as at *a*, a reinforcement after a zero-sec interval. Curvature can be seen most easily by foreshortening the figure.

VI schedule in the presence of a second stimulus (multiple schedules).

The derivation of a mathematical function describing the relationship between reinforcement and responding for all pigeons is complicated by the idiosyncratic character of each pigeon's data, particularly if the functions are restricted to those involving simple transformations of the ordinate and/or abscissa and are limited in the number of arbitrary constants. In an earlier version of this paper (Reynolds and Catania, 1961; Catania and Reynolds, 1963), a power function was proposed, on the basis of a fit to average data for the group of pigeons (see also Catania, 1963*a*). This function, of the form: $R = kr^{0.2}$, where R is rate of responding, r is rate of reinforcement, and k is a constant depending on the units of measurement, was chosen in preference to a logarithmic function, of the form: $R = k \log r + n$, where n is a constant and the other symbols are as above. The choice between these two functions was based more on logical considerations, *i.e.*, that rate of responding should approach zero as rate of reinforcement approaches zero, than on the superiority of the fit of the power function to the data. This mathematical representation, however, does not provide an adequate fit to the data from individual pigeons. Fits to data from individual pigeons are possible (*cf.* Norman, 1966), but they are not essential for the present purposes and will not be considered further here.

Local rates of responding. It has been noted (Results) that the idiosyncratic characteristics of the present data from each pigeon were reflected, to some extent, in the changes in the local rate of responding with the passage of time since reinforcement. This relationship is not mathematically determined; a given overall rate of responding could have been produced by a variety of different temporal distributions of responses within the intervals of a given schedule. Aside from a few atypical functions at high rates of reinforcement, local rates of responding generally increased monotonically as time passed since reinforcement (Fig. 3). For a given pigeon, the adjusted local rates of responding at different relative times after reinforcement remained roughly invariant over a wide range of overall rates of reinforcement.

The changes in local rates of responding cannot be accounted for solely in terms of time since reinforcement. The distribution of responses throughout a given period of time since reinforcement can be manipulated within VI schedules by changing the distribution of intervals (*e.g.,* from an arithmetic to a geometric progression of intervals; Ferster and Skinner, 1957). A variable that may operate together with time since reinforcement, however, is probability of reinforcement or some derivative of this probability. If a responding organism reaches a time after reinforcement equal to the longest interval in a VI schedule, the probability that the next response will be reinforced is 1.0. If, however, the organism has not yet reached that time, the probability is less than 1.0, and depends on the number of intervals that end at or after the time that the organism has reached. In the present arithmetic VI schedules, therefore, probability of reinforcement increased as time passed since reinforcement.

. . . It is sufficient to note here that both probability of reinforcement and local rates of responding increased as time elapsed since reinforcement. The overall-rate functions (Fig. 1) and the local-rate functions (Fig. 3) may therefore be similar because the changes in the overall rate of reinforcement provided by an interval schedule also changed the probability of reinforcement for responses within any fixed period of time. Thus, the overall- and the local-rate functions may depend on the same relationship between probability of reinforcement and subsequent responding.

Relationship between overall and local rates of responding. This relationship between local and overall rates of responding suggests that a given overall rate of responding may not be determined directly by an overall rate of reinforcement. Rather, a schedule may produce a given overall rate of responding through its effects on local rates of responding at different times after reinforcement. The way in which local rates of responding contribute to overall rates of responding must therefore be considered.

An overall rate of responding is a weighted average of the local rates of responding at successive times after reinforcement. The early times after reinforcement are weighted more heavily than the later times because the early times represent a larger proportion of the total time in the schedule. For example, within the first t sec after reinforcement in the arithmetic VI schedules, responding was possible 14 times as often as within the last t sec (first and last points on each function in Fig. 2 and 3; *cf.* Method). Thus, a consistent change in the local rate of responding early after reinforcement would produce a greater change in the overall rate of responding than the same consistent change late after reinforcement. An alternative measure, therefore, is the average of the successive local rates of responding maintained by a particular schedule (*e.g.*, the average of all the points on a given function in Fig. 2), because this measure does not weight early local rates more heavily.

When local-rate functions are similar at different rates of reinforcement (as to a first approximation for Pigeons 118, 129, and 279 in Fig. 3), the substitution of average local rate for overall rate of responding does not alter the functional relation between rate of responding and overall rate of reinforcement (Fig. 1); the average local rates and the overall rates of responding will differ slightly, by a multiplicative constant. This is not necessarily the case, however, when the local-rate functions are dissimilar. For example, in the 12.0-sec and 23.5-sec functions for Pigeon 121, the 23.5-sec function for Pigeon 278, and the 12.0-sec function for Pigeon 281 in Fig. 3, the local rates of responding shortly after reinforcement were relatively low compared to the local rates within other schedules for the same pigeons. The values of t in the 12.0-sec and 23.5-sec VI schedules were roughly 1.7 and 3.4 sec, respectively, and although rates of responding were high, occasional short pauses that occurred immediately after reinforcement reduced the number of responses in the early t-sec periods after reinforcement. Because these pauses were weighted more heavily in the overall rate of responding than in the average local rate, the overall rate was lower, relative to the average local rate, in these than in the remaining schedules. Inversely, the local rate of responding was relatively high after reinforcement for Pigeon 278 at VI 45.5-sec (Fig. 3), and the overall rate was higher, relative to the average local rate, in this than in the remaining schedules.

Figure 3 shows data from the initial determination of performance on each schedule. In three of the above cases (Pigeon 121 at VI 23.5-sec, Pigeon 281 at VI 12.0-sec, and Pigeon 278 at VI 45.5-sec), data from a redetermination were available. The redetermined local-rate functions (not shown in Fig. 3) deviated considerably less from other local-rate functions for the same pigeon than did the initial local-rate functions. These three cases represent three of the four largest discrepancies between initial and redetermined overall rates of responding (see Fig. 1), and it is of interest that the three discrepancies are each reduced by about 5 resp/min if initial and redetermined average local rates of responding are substituted for initial and redetermined overall rates of responding.

This observation is consistent with the assumption that the overall rate of responding is not directly determined by an overall rate of reinforcement. Reinforcement does not produce a reserve of responses that are emitted irrespective of their distribution in time. Rather, a given rate of reinforcement produces a given overall rate of responding through its effects on local rates of responding at different times after reinforcement. . . .

REFERENCES

Anger, D. The dependence of interresponse times upon the relative reinforcement of different inter-response times. *Journal of Experimental Psychology,* 1956, **52,**145–161.

Autor, S. M. *The strength of conditioned reinforcers as a function of frequency and probability of reinforcement.* Unpublished doctoral dissertation, Harvard University, 1960.

Catania, A. C. Concurrent performances: Reinforcement interaction and response independence. *Journal of the Experimental Analysis of Behavior,* 1963, **6,** 253–263. (*a*)

Catania, A. C. and Reynolds, G. S. A quantitative analysis of the behavior maintained by interval schedules of reinforcement. Paper presented at the meeting of the Psychonomic Society, Bryn Mawr, 1963.

Clark, F. C. The effect of deprivation and frequency of reinforcement on variable-interval responding. *Journal of the Experimental Analysis of Behavior,* 1958, **1,** 221–228.

Cumming, W. W. *Stimulus disparity and variable-interval reinforcement schedule as related to a behavioral measure of similarity.* Unpublished doctoral dissertation, Columbia University, 1955.

Farmer, J. Properties of behavior under random interval reinforcement schedules. *Journal of the Experimental Analysis of Behavior,* 1963, **6,** 607–616.

Ferster, C. B. and Skinner, B. F. *Schedules of reinforcement.* New York: Appleton-Century-Crofts, 1957.

Findley, J. D. Preference and switching under concurrent scheduling. *Journal of the Experimental Analysis of Behavior,* 1958, **1,** 123–144.

Findley, J. D. An experimental outline for building and exploring multi-operant behavior repertoires. *Journal of the Experimental Analysis of Behavior,* 1962, **5,** 113–166.

Herrnstein, R. J. *Behavioral consequences of the removal of a discriminative stimulus associated with variable-interval reinforcement.* Unpublished doctoral dissertation, Harvard University, 1955.

Herrnstein, R. J. Relative and absolute strength of response as a function of frequency of reinforcement. *Journal of the Experimental Analysis of Behavior,* 1961, **4,** 267–272.

Herrnstein, R. J. Secondary reinforcement and rate of primary reinforcement. *Journal of the Experimental Analysis of Behavior,* 1964, **7,** 27–36.

Hull, C. L. *Principles of behavior.* New York: Appleton-Century-Crofts, 1943.

Kaplan, M. The effects of noxious stimulus intensity and duration during intermittent reinforcement of escape behavior. *Journal of Comparative and Physiological Psychology,* 1952, **45,** 538–549.

Kelleher, R. T. and Gollub, L. R. A review of positive conditioned reinforcement. *Journal of the Experimental Analysis of Behavior,* 1962, **5,** 543–597.

Morse, W. H. Intermittent reinforcement. In W. K. Honig (Ed.). *Operant behavior: areas of research and application.* New York: Appleton-Century-Crofts, 1966. Pp. 52–108.

Nevin, J. A. Two parameters of conditioned reinforcement in a chaining situation. *Journal of Comparative and Physiological Psychology,* 1964, **58,** 367–373.

Norman, M. F. An approach to free-responding on schedules that prescribe reinforcement probability as a function of interresponse time. *Journal of Mathematical Psychology,* 1966, **3,** 235–268.

Reynolds, G. S. and Catania, A. C. Response rate as a function of rate of reinforcement and probability of reinforcement in variable-interval schedules. Paper presented at the meeting of the Psychonomic Society, New York, 1961.

Schoenfeld, W. N. and Cumming, W. W. Studies in a temporal classification of reinforcement schedules: Summary and projection. *Proceedings of the National Academy of Sciences,* 1960, **46,** 753–758.

Sherman, J. G. *The temporal distribution of re-responses on fixed interval schedules.* Unpublished doctoral dissertation, Columbia University, 1959.

Sidman, M. *Tactics of scientific research.* New York: Basic Books, 1960.

Skinner, B. F. The effect on the amount of conditioning of an interval of time before reinforcement. *Journal of General Psychology,* 1936, **14,** 279–295.

Skinner, B. F. *The behavior of organisms.* New York: Appleton-Century-Crofts, 1938.

Wilson, M. P. Periodic reinforcement interval and number of periodic reinforcement as parameters of response strength. *Journal of Comparative and Physiological Psychology,* 1954, **47,** 51–56.

Chapter 6

Instrumental Conditioning: Mechanisms

THEORIES OF
REINFORCEMENT AND PUNISHMENT

It is relatively easy to make a list of our own rewards and punishers although sometimes we are surprised at the things that can reinforce or fail to reinforce our own behavior. (Witness the businessman who claims he is working for money but upon retirement cannot stop returning to the office. Rewards other than money must be supporting his behavior.) It is less easy to list the things that may reward or punish another person. When a man bemoans the fact that he doesn't understand women it is often because he has failed to identify what sorts of things can reinforce or punish their behavior. It is still less easy to list the rewards and punishers for a non-human. In the latter case intuition fails us completely and we must rely wholly on observation. One way to find out what sorts of things reward a given organism is to try them out in an instrumental conditioning experiment. If a given event is made contingent on a given behavior and the behavior thereby increases in frequency then the event is a reward for the organism. This procedure would result in a list of items for each organism that could serve as rewards. But do the items on a given list have anything in common other than their ability to reinforce a given behavior? Is there some test, other than trying them out in a conditioning situation, to distinguish rewards (and punishers) from all the other events that an organism can experience? Theories of reinforcement and punishment are attempts to provide such a test. Without such theories, definitions of reinforcement and punishment are circular: Q. What is reinforcement? A. Reward contingent on behavior. Q. What is reward? A. Whatever reinforces behavior.

Q. Then what is reinforcement? A. Reward contingent on behavior . . . and so on, ad infinitum.

In most cases the theories of reinforcement and punishment that attempt to break this circle are biological, asserting that reinforcers and punishers can be distinguished from other events by their biological effect upon the organism.

Before we discuss these theories, we should note that each seems to contain at least a grain of truth but that none has succeeded, by itself, in accounting for all of the ways in which a response can be reinforced.

Need Reduction

Organisms need certain things to survive—for example, food and water, oxygen, and specific temperature ranges. It has been argued that all reinforcers must ultimately reduce one or another of these basic physiological needs. (In other words, if the psychologist wants to know whether a certain substance is rewarding to a certain organism, it would seem that all he has to do is call up the biology department of his university and ask whether the substance satisfies a physiological need. If it does, then it must be rewarding. If the biolgist tells the psychologist that a platypus needs the chemicals found in bananas in order to survive, then bananas must be rewarding to the platypus.) Unfortunately, this theory is inconsistent with several well-known facts. Take the case of saccharin. There is no question that artificial sweeteners such as saccharin can be rewarding. Rats will learn to run down the alley of a T-maze leading to a goal box with a saccharin solution in it even when they have plenty of water available. Rats will learn to press a bar to receive a saccharin solution and humans will gladly put a dime in a slot to receive a cupful of carbonated water mixed with artificial flavoring and saccharin even when a water fountain is nearby. Yet, such artificial sweeteners are passed through the body virtually unchanged. This is but one of many rewards that do not appear to satisfy any vital need.

Tension Reduction

Another theory of reinforcement, closely related to "need reduction," is that whatever immediately lessens tension of some kind in the organism is a reward, and, conversely, whatever increases tension is a punisher. Hunger, for instance, can be seen as a kind of tension that is lessened by eating. The trouble with this theory is that many things that seem to immediately increase tension are rewarding. For instance, it may seem like cruel and unusual punishment to allow a male rat to copulate with a female and then to remove him before he has a chance to ejaculate. Nevertheless, male rats will repeatedly run down the alley of a T-maze leading to such treatment, when the alternative is lacking female rats altogether. Animals of all kinds will work hard at tasks that lead to no more startling reward than the sight of another animal or the opportunity to do a more complex task. For instance, isolated monkeys will press a bar repeatedly to open a window that allows them to see activity in the laboratory. Monkeys will also solve puzzles with no reward other than the solution of the puzzle. It is difficult to classify all of these rewards in terms of tension reduction. If anything, presentation of some rewards seems to increase tension.

Brain Stimulation

In 1954, two physiologists, James Olds and Peter Milner, found that a rat would press a lever in order to deliver a mild electric shock to a certain area of its brain, the midbrain generally. The experiment is shown in Figure 6.1. The rat was enclosed in a cage with a lever attached to an electrical switch that sent current through a wire to certain areas of its brain. Each time the rat pressed the lever, a very mild current (of about $1/10,000$ ampere) was turned on for less than half a second. Olds found that rats would press the bar thousands of times an hour for periods of 12 hours or more to receive this

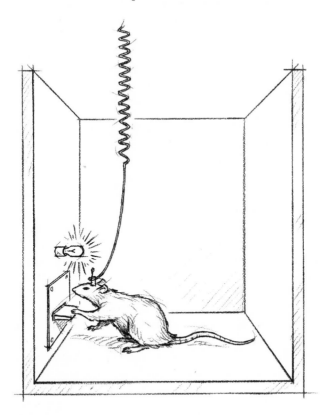

FIGURE 6.1
Olds' self-stimulation experiment. [After Olds, James. Pleasure centers of the brain. Copyright ©1956 by Scientific American, Inc. All rights reserved.]

stimulation. Evidently the current in the rat's brain was rewarding. This experiment led to the speculation that perhaps a common element in all rewards is an ability to stimulate certain locations in the brain. Olds called these areas "pleasure centers," reasoning that anything that stimulated them resulted in the feeling of pleasure. Similarly, stimulation of other areas, called "pain centers" served to punish bar-pressing and other responses.

The brain is so complicated and knowledge of its functioning so limited, that we cannot tell whether any given stimulus branches to a pleasure center or a pain center. In other words, we still have no operation that will predict what will or will not be reinforcing. Old's experiment seems to promise an eventual answer, but it may be a long time before the promise is fulfilled.

Consummatory Responses

Although it is convenient to regard rewards as stimuli, some psychologists argue that it would be more accurate to regard them as responses. (Thus they might say "eating the pudding is a reward," rather than saying "the pudding is a reward.") This theory, that reinforcement lies in the *act* of consuming a needed substance, rather than in the substance itself, is called a *consummatory-response* theory. According to this theory, certain acts and the sensations involved in performing these acts are said to be innately rewarding to organisms. The reason that bar-presses of a hungry rat will increase when they are followed by food is not that the bar-presses produce food, but that they give the rat the opportunity to eat. Thus, *eating* and *drinking* are sources of reinforcement, as opposed to food and water themselves.

This theory, unlike the need-reduction theory, is consistent with the reinforcing powers of substances like saccharin, since the act of consuming saccharin and the sensations involved therein are the same as the act of consuming other substances that actually reduce needs. Although sugar and saccharin are different with respect to their abilities to reduce basic needs, they are similar with respect to the *consummatory responses* they elicit.

The argument against the consummatory-response theory is that reinforcement often can be achieved by bypassing any response. Normally, when food is used as reward, the presentation of food and eating of the food go together. It is possible, however, to separate them. When food is delivered without eating, by being injected directly into the stomach, the food is still rewarding. Rats will learn to press a lever that results in the injection of food into their stomachs. Also, animals will learn to press a lever to get a higher proportion of oxygen to carbon dioxide in the air of a stuffy room, despite the fact that more oxygen in the air causes less breathing—in other words, less consummatory responding. We must conclude, then, that animals can be rewarded in ways other than by making a response.

Premack's Theory of
Reinforcement and Punishment

David Premack, in 1965, published a theory of reinforcement (and in 1971 extended it to punishment) that differs radically from the earlier theories. For all the theories of reinforcement we have so far considered, the central question was the biological basis for differences in reinforcement value of various events. Need reduction, tension reduction, brain stimulation, and consummatory response are all speculative answers to the question, why should one event be more valuable than another for a given organism? Premack's theory is silent on this point, simply assuming that there is a hierarchy of events at any time, ordered according to value. Like the earlier theories, however, Premack's theory represents an attempt to provide a way of telling in advance whether a given event will reinforce a given response. The test provided is not biological, as in other theories, but wholly behavioral.

Let us consider the theory. The first step, as we indicated above, is the assumption that all environmental and behavioral events, whatever they may be, can be ordered in a hierarchy of value for a given organism.* For instance, watching television, playing baseball, sleeping, hearing a concert, smelling a rose, writing a poem, being punched in the nose, and so on, are events that according to Premack should all fit within a hierarchy of value.

Reward and punishment are determined by relations between events in the hierarchy. Any event in the hierarchy (as long as there is a lower event) can be a reward. Any event in the hierarchy (as long as there is a higher event) can be a punisher. The critical relationship is the contingency of one event on the other. When a higher event is contingent on the occurrence of a lower event, the higher event serves as reward and the lower event becomes reinforced. When a lower event is contingent on a higher event, the lower event serves as a punisher and the higher event is punished.†

For example, imagine a boy who likes ice cream best, spaghetti next best, and spinach least. (For Premack it does not matter whether all or some of these foods are biologically good for the boy or whether all or some of them are pleasurable or painful to him, as long as they can be ordered in terms of value to the boy). Now, his mother might institute a program of reward for eating

---

*This hierarchy differs somewhat from Thorndike's habit-family hierarchy, which is a hierarchy of strength of connection between one stimulus and several responses. Thorndike's hierarchy can have only responses in it, whereas Premack's can have stimuli or responses, since both can serve as rewards and punishments.

†The relationship almost always imposed in Premack's experiments and those of his students is strict contiguity. When a reward or punisher is programmed, it is made to come directly after the response upon which it is dependent. But nothing about the theory limits reinforcement and punishment to contiguous relations. Contingencies and correlations other than those resulting from strict contiguity should also be effective or ineffective depending on the positions in the hierarchy of the events of which they are composed.

spinach by allowing him to eat some spaghetti provided he first ate some spinach. Or she could reinforce eating spinach by allowing him to eat some ice cream provided he first ate some spinach. According to Premack, reward works best when the items are furthest apart on the hierarchy, so rewarding the boy with ice cream should work better (get him to eat more spinach) than rewarding him with spaghetti. It would also be possible to reinforce eating spaghetti with ice cream, but of course impossible to reinforce eating anything higher on the hierarchy with anything lower.*

When a lower event is made contingent on a higher event, it punishes the higher event. For instance, if the mother made her boy eat some spinach each time he ate ice cream she would be punishing the eating of ice cream (and thereby causing the boy to eat less ice cream). A single event (such as eating spaghetti) may sometimes serve as a reward (as when it is contingent on eating spinach) and sometimes serve as a punisher (as when it is contingent on eating ice cream).

The events in the hierarchy can be stimuli or responses or, most frequently, combinations of both (for example, eating apples combines the stimulus of apples with the response of eating). Thus a rewarding or punishing event can be anything in the hierarchy. But the event reinforced or punished (upon which the reward or punisher is made contingent) must contain a response so that the behavior of the organism can increase or decrease in frequency. Thus, events such as running or eating can be either reinforced or reinforcing, punished or punishing, but electric brain stimulation cannot be reinforced or punished unless it is combined with some response (such as pressing a lever) that makes its presence dependent on behavior.

A crucial part of Premack's theory is the initial determination of the hierarchy of events. If this hierarchy, which serves as the basis for reinforcement and punishment relationships, can be determined independently of such relationships, then the circularity of the definition of reinforcement and punishment will have been broken.

The operation suggested by Premack for ordering the values of two events is a free-choice experiment. Properly, discussion of such experiments belongs in the chapter on choice, but in order for Premack's theory to be understood, we must introduce the issue here. In the case of the boy eating food, if we did not know the order of spaghetti and spinach in his value hierarchy, we could put him in a room with two large bowls, one containing spaghetti and the other containing spinach. If he spent more time eating spaghetti, then spaghetti would have a higher value than spinach. That is, in a subsequent test, we could get the boy to eat more spinach by making spaghetti contingent on spinach and we could get him to eat less spaghetti by making spinach contingent on spaghetti.

---

*This is true under ordinary circumstances. However, we shall discuss an exception to this at the end of the section.

Premack and his students have been exploring the implications of his theory. Most of their experiments have been performed to demonstrate to other psychologists that *any* events—even events that would not be classed, intuitively, as rewards—can nevertheless act as rewards when they are contingent on events still lower in the hierarchy. For instance, in one experiment Premack allowed several children free access to candy and to pinball machines. He found that many of the children spent a greater proportion of time playing the pinball machines than eating the candy. He reasoned that, for these children, playing with the machines was more valuable than eating the candy. According to his theory a more valuable event should reinforce a less valuable one. When he tested this by allowing the children to play with the machines only after they had eaten a certain amount of candy, he found that eating candy increased. In other words, playing with pinball machines reinforced eating. Note that this is a reversal of the usual situation, in which eating is the reinforcer and some other act is reinforced.

Similarly, Premack has shown that when a rat has been allowed to drink all the water it can drink and is then given a free choice between drinking and pressing a lever, the rat will press the lever for a longer time than it will drink. In this situation the theory predicts that when availability of the lever is made contingent on drinking, the rat will increase its rate of drinking. That is, lever-pressing will serve as a reward for drinking—just the opposite of the relationship usually studied in psychology laboratories. In tests of this prediction the rat did increase its drinking when it was rewarded by the opportunity to press a lever.

In a free-choice experiment where one alternative is electric shock (say, a box with electrified grids on one side) and the other choice is almost anything else, most animals will spend no time at all on the electric-shock side. In Premack's terms, electric shock is so low on the value hierarchy that when it is made contingent on other events it almost always reduces their frequency—that is, punishes them. But punishment, as we indicated, may occur with any event on the hierarchy as long as there is a higher event that it can punish. For instance, running in a wheel is usually ranked fairly high in a rat's value hierarchy. But if the rat is thirsty enough, drinking is higher (that is, in a 'free-choice experiment the thirsty rat will spend more time drinking than running). Thus, drinking should be punishable by running. Premack tested this prediction using a running wheel fitted with a drinking tube. The thirsty rat, confined in the motor-operated wheel, was forced to run for 5 seconds after every 15 licks at the tube. This contingency sharply decreased licking for the four rats tested. Thus, running, which is normally a high-value event, punished a still higher-value event (licking, for a thirsty rat).

According to Premack the free-choice measure—the time devoted to one activity or another—really reflects a more basic probability of events. That is, the relative value of two events determines their relative probability, which in turn determines the relative time during which the subject engages in each of them. The advantage of referring to values in terms of probabilities (rather than times) is that relative probabilities can vary from moment to moment, whereas relative time spent in an activity must occur over at least the time spent observing the activity. But there is really no difference between relative probabilities as measured by relative times and relative times themselves. Probabilities may be conceptually instantaneous, but operationally they take time to measure. So we shall stick to the language of relative time. The reader may translate relative time into probability if he feels more comfortable with the latter term. It makes no difference.

Let us now consider two practical problems in applying Premack's theory. The first regards events whose value changes drastically from one time period to another. The second regards the determination of how much time of the lower-value event we should require before allowing the higher-value event to occur, and then how much time of the higher-value event we should allow, in order to assure reinforcement.

Events that vary drastically in value from time to time seem to be an exception to Premack's theory. The example most commonly cited is sex. On one hand, animals (humans included) spend only a small amount of their time engaging in sexual activity. This, it would seem, should give sex a low position on the value hierarchy. On the other hand, sex seems to be a powerful reward. Rats will increase their lever-pressing or alley-running to high levels if rewarded by presentation of a sexual partner. Humans will devote great amounts of effort, not to mention money, to impress a member of the opposite sex. There seems to be a contradiction here. A low-value event should not be a powerful reward, except with still lower-value activities. But lever-pressing and running are not extremely low-value activities for a rat and yet they can be reinforced by sex. The explanation is that sex is a low-value activity only when the period over which value is calculated (the base period) is long. When the base period is short, sex can be a high-value activity. The problem is similar to that of Figure 2.5, where various intervals produced various distributions. Similarly, various base periods will produce various relative-time distributions. Let us suppose, for instance, that a rat is put into a chamber with a sexual partner and a running wheel. The rat can engage in sexual activity, run, or do neither. An observer marks down what the rat is doing every second. The rat is observed for 60 minutes. Thus there will be 3600 observations. Several analyses of the observer's record (completely hypothetical) are shown in Figure 6.2. To get percentage of time spent in running and sex, so as to compare them, we must decide on a temporal interval, a base period (like the periods of Figure 2.5) that will best reflect the values of the various activities. If we make our base period 1 second, obviously the relative time spent in sex or running will be either 100 percent or 0 percent and will vary too frequently to be useful for reinforcement or punishment relationships. Figure 6.2 shows several alternative base periods.

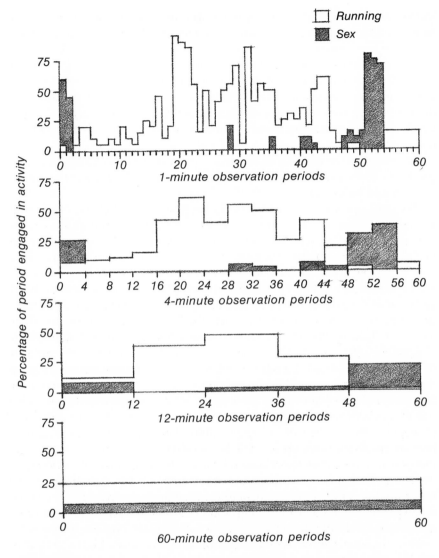

FIGURE 6.2
Percentage of time over the course of an hour that a rat engages in running and
sexual behavior (hypothetical data). The base periods used for the upper and middle
graphs give the best indication of the periodic change in relative value of these two
activities for the rat. With very large base periods, it seems as if running is always of
higher value than sex.

The curves indicate that at the beginning and near the end of the hour, sex is more valuable than running, whereas for most of the hour running is more valuable.* If the base period were the whole hour, sex would seem to be a lower-value activity than running. But with smaller base periods we see that sex has a very high value at times and can then be used as a reward for running. It is a matter for experimentation to determine exactly what biological events govern the appearance of a high value for sexual activity. Undoubtedly the way in which certain hormonal states vary with time since the previous sexual activity is an important factor.

Now we turn the question of how much of an activity should be required to produce a reward or punishment and then, how much of the reward or punishment should be given.

We must consider now what actually happens in a free-choice experiment. Let us again refer to our example of the boy and the food, and, this time, give him a free choice between spaghetti and ice cream only. Suppose we discover in the experiment that he eats four times as much ice cream as spaghetti, as Figure 6.3a shows. According to Premack's theory, this means at least two things: (1) that the values of ice cream and spaghetti are in the ratio of 4 to 1, and (2) that the particular distribution of Figure 6.3a is the preferred distribution. The boy prefers it over any other distribution, *including one with more ice cream.* That is, the free-choice experiment has revealed that although the boy prefers ice cream 4 to 1 over spaghetti he would rather have some spaghetti than no spaghetti at all. To put it another way, even though ice cream is preferred to spaghetti, it is not exclusively preferred. This means that after a certain period of ice-cream-eating, the value of ice cream temporarily falls below that of spaghetti and the boy switches to spaghetti. Then, after a certain period of spaghetti-eating, the value of spaghetti falls below that of ice cream and the boy switches back to ice cream. The boy's behavior in the free-choice experiment (as in most choice experiments, as we shall see) consists of shuttling between activities as they lose or gain in value. True, the boy takes a longer time to get tired of eating ice cream than to get tired of eating spaghetti (four times as long, in fact) but (as with running and sex in Figure 6.2) the relative values are constantly shifting (otherwise, why would the boy ever eat spaghetti?)

Now we know that ice-cream-eating, because it is valued higher, should reward spaghetti-eating, and this will generally hold. But if too much ice cream is given as a reward or too little spaghetti-eating is required to produce the reward of ice cream, the boy may be able to achieve a 4:1 ratio of ice cream to spaghetti without increasing his rate of eating spaghetti above that of the free-choice experiment. To put it another way, suppose the boy's mother wanted to get the boy to eat more spaghetti by rewarding him with ice cream. Suppose the

---

*The curves do not add up to 100 percent since obviously the rat does other things than run and engage in sexual activity.

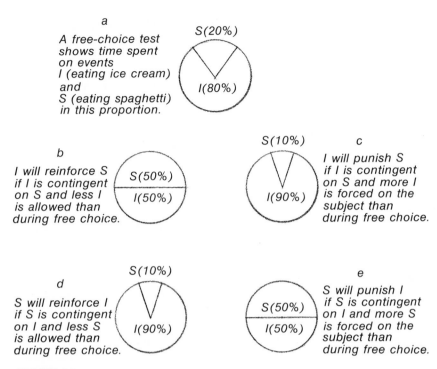

FIGURE 6.3
A free-choice test shows that a subject spends 80% of his time in activity I and 20% in activity S. In a contingency relationship, reinforcement will occur when the subject is permitted less time than he would ordinarily spend in the contingent activity. Punishment will occur if the subject is forced to spend more time than he would ordinarily spend in the contingent activity.

boy, left to himself, ate only one forkful of spaghetti at each meal and for dessert ate a whole bowlful of ice cream. If the mother then rewarded the boy for eating one forkful of spaghetti by giving him a whole bowlful of ice cream she would be doing nothing that the boy would not have done himself and her reward program would not increase the boy's eating of spaghetti. She would have to do one of two things: either make the boy eat more spaghetti to get the ice cream or give him less ice cream than a bowlful (say only a spoonful) for each forkful of spaghetti. Both of these methods would be likely to increase the boy's spaghetti-eating. Figure 6.3 illustrates the relationship that must prevail between the reinforced and reinforcing events for reinforcement to occur and extends the analogy to punishment. As the figure shows, it is even possible to reinforce eating ice cream by giving spaghetti, provided enough ice-cream-eating is required and very little spaghetti is offered as reward (the ratio must be less than 4:1). In our example, if the mother wanted to reinforce ice-cream-eating by spaghetti she would have to require the boy to eat, say, two bowlfuls of ice cream to get, say, only half a forkful of spaghetti. According to Premack this change in reinforcement potential occurs because as the boy eats more and more ice cream its value sinks to below that of the spaghetti of which he is now deprived.

To summarize, Premack's theory has two major elements. The first is the idea that reinforcement and punishment are relationships between events in a hierarchy of value. This differs from previous theories that a reward or punishment was something fixed—that certain events could be rewards, others were neutral, and still others could be punishers. In Premack's theory we know if an event is a reward or punisher only when we know its position in the hierarchy relative to the event upon which it is contingent.

The second element of Premack's theory is the idea that the hierarchy of value can be determined by wholly behavioral means (that is, by free-choice experiments). The second idea is independent of the first. It may someday be possible to determine the hierarchy by physiological measurement (perhaps brain waves of a certain sort will be stronger for events higher in value or the amount of some chemical in the blood will correspond to the value of events). But this would not affect the first idea, that reinforcement and punishment are defined wholly as contingent relationships among events higher or lower in value.

So far Premack's theory of how reinforcement and punishment work has been the most successful of all those proposed, in the sense that it has stood up best under empirical testing. We shall have more to say in Chapter 10 about some of the issues raised here.

THEORIES OF RESPONDING

No theory has yet been offered that accounts for patterns and rates of response on all schedules of reinforcement, let alone those few we have described in the previous chapter. Nevertheless, a few general principles have been advanced, some molecular and some molar, which may help us to understand why the various schedules and other parameters of reinforcement generate the behavior they do. We shall discuss several principles of responding on schedules, using a pigeon pecking a key as an example.* Then we shall consider some implications of these principles for interresponse-time and probability distributions.

---

*This example is by far the most common experimental preparation used for studying schedules of reinforcement. But the procedures we use to analyze pigeons pecking keys also apply to rats running in mazes and, indeed any other situation in which schedules of reinforcement may be applied. The pigeon's key-peck is a discrete response, continuously available. For nondiscrete responses, such as salivation, or intermittently available responses, such as as running in a maze, appropriate transformations must be made (see Chapter 2).

Differential Reinforcement of
Interresponse Times (Irt's)

Most of the schedules we have described in the previous chapter provide differential reinforcement for various interresponse times. Drl and drh schedules (see p. 256 for a description of these schedules) specifically reinforce long and short irt's. Variable-interval schedules would reward the subject with higher probability after long interresponse times. Figure 6.4 shows how variable-interval schedules tend to provide more reward for long irt's. The longer the subject waits before responding, the more likely it is that the variable-interval timer has programmed a reinforcement for the next response. For the same reason fixed-interval schedules also tend to differentially reinforce long irt's.

Occasionally there have been attempts to explain responding under various schedules of reinforcement wholly on the basis of how the schedules reinforce irt's of various durations. More long irt's mean slower measured rates of response. It is possible that the slow rates of response with variable-interval schedules are a direct result of the reinforcement of long irts. But differential reinforcement of irt's cannot wholly explain performance on schedules. If VI schedules reinforce long irt's with high probability, they will reinforce longer irt's with higher probability. What sets the limit on how long irt's can get? With ratio schedules, any irt has an equal probability of being reinforced. Why are there so many short irt's (very rapid responses) with ratio schedules? What causes the patterning of responses with fixed-interval and fixed-ratio schedules?

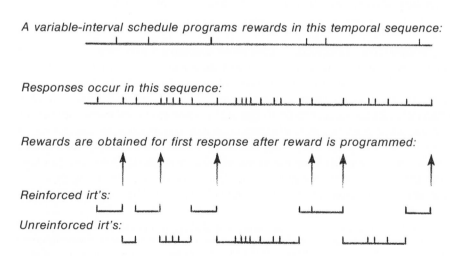

A variable-interval schedule programs rewards in this temporal sequence:

Responses occur in this sequence:

Rewards are obtained for first response after reward is programmed:

Reinforced irt's:

Unreinforced irt's:

FIGURE 6.4
How a variable-interval schedule selectively reinforces long irt's. Note that most of the long irt's are reinforced, while most of the short irt's are unreinforced.

These questions cannot be answered purely in terms of differential reinforcement of irt's. Other principles must be invoked.*

Reward versus Cost

The principle of reward versus cost says that behavior will take the form that provides the most reward for the least effort in the long run. In the previous chapter, Figure 5.16 showed how rate of reinforcement increases with rate of responding in a variable-interval schedule. As responding increases from zero, rate of reinforcement increases very quickly and then levels off. Soon the point of diminishing returns is reached, where large increases in rate of response yield only small increases in rate of reinforcement. The reward-versus-cost theory explains the slow responding on a variable-interval schedule as a direct result of this function. Up to point X of Figure 5.16 a slight increase in rate of response causes a large increase in rate of reinforcement. Beyond point X, responses, which presumably cost effort, buy very little additional reinforcement and are therefore not worth expending. With ratio schedules, on the other hand, the faster the responding, the more the reinforcement in direct proportion. Thus a reward-versus-cost analysis would predict the fast responding that is found with ratio schedules. This analysis says little about patterns of responding. It is best applied to variable-interval schedules and variable-ratio schedules, where responding occurs at a uniform rate. With fixed-interval and fixed-ratio schedules, the theory by itself does not explain why responding is high at one point and low at another. With drl schedules, the theory predicts much slower responding than is actually found. Usually much more effort is expended than necessary with drl schedules of reinforcement.

Temporal Discrimination

The patterns of responding with various schedules may be viewed in terms of temporal discrimination. This theory says that when a pigeon's sense of time tells it that reinforcement is probable, the pigeon is likely to peck. When reinforcement is improbable, pecks are unlikely. Slow responding on a variable-interval schedule is, according to this theory, due to the improbability, at any instant, of a peck being reinforced. The analogy, previously mentioned, of looking into the oven to see when the turkey is done, is most applicable with a theory of performance based on temporal discrimination. A response (looking into the oven) is seen as a guess, based on temporal discrimination, that reinforcement is available (the turkey is ready to be eaten). The pattern of responses

---

*More sophisticated versions of the theory of differential reinforcement of irt's suggest that irt's are reinforced not according to their probability but according to their probability times their duration (the rate of reinforcement per irt). For instance, if a 10-second irt is reinforced once out of five times, the rate of reinforcement is one per fifty seconds, or 1.2 reinforcements per minute for that irt. The higher the rate of reinforcement for an irt, the more that irt should be emitted.

with a fixed-interval schedule fits this theory well. Immediately after reinforcement, when further reinforcement is unlikely, responding is slow. As the interval progresses, reinforcement becomes subjectively more likely and responding increases until the end of the interval, when reinforcement is most likely.

The temporal-discrimination theory, in its simple form, implies that rate of response can vary continuously, with slow rates for low probabilities of reinforcement and fast rates for high probabilities of reinforcement. Let us call this the *continuous temporal-discrimination theory*. Another version of this same theory allows only a limited number of discrete response states. A *two-state temporal-discrimination theory* would have the organism either not responding or responding at a fixed rate. Measurements of medium rates would contain a certain amount of pausing and a certain amount of responding, like a mixture that contains a certain amount of salt and a certain amount of pepper. Just as the overall mixture would be a darker grey with more pepper and a lighter grey with more salt, the overall rate of response would be higher with more responding and lower with more pausing. But just as the salt and pepper mixture would contain no actually grey particles, the response and pause mixture would contain no medium rates of response (that is, no rates of response other than the fixed, high, rate). The two-state theory would predict more extended periods of responding (relative to pausing) as reinforcement became more probable. Thus, in a fixed-interval schedule the subject would be more likely to be pausing at the beginning of the interval and responding at the end. Three-state, four-state, five-state, and more complex models of responding are also possible but have rarely been proposed.*

Temporal-discrimination theories are generally good at explaining patterns of response with various schedules. For fixed-interval schedules they also explain the fact that as a subject grows more and more experienced with the schedule, responses come to be confined to the period at the end, just before reinforcement is due (because more training would sharpen temporal discrimination). But these theories do not explain the difference in rate of response between interval and ratio schedules that deliver the same rate of reinforcement (responding is faster with ratio schedules). In fact they have difficulty, in general, in accounting for behavior with ratio schedules.

The arguments among those who support the various theories could fill a whole book by themselves. None of these principles accounts fully for behavior on all schedules of reinforcement. Most likely, none of them acts to the exclusion of the others. They should be considered more as factors, all of which can influence behavior, than as exclusive theories competing with each other. Some of them do, however, imply that certain sorts of interresponse-time distribu-

---

*Limited-state theories (for example, two-state theories) are also logically possible with differential reinforcement of irt's and reward-versus-cost models, but they have seldom been proposed in those contexts.

tions will be found with various schedules of reinforcement. We shall discuss these distributions now, using the variable-interval schedule as an example.

THE DISTRIBUTION OF RESPONSES

The simplest theory that has been advanced to explain how responding is distributed states that responding is random. Recall the example of the inefficient railroad from Chapter 2. Knowing when the last train arrived was no help at all in predicting when the next train would arrive. A random temporal distribution of responses means that knowing when the last response occurred would be no help in predicting when the next response would occur. If responses were occurring randomly, the irt probability (irt's/op) function would be horizontal (Figure 6.5a, right side). As we pointed out in Chapter 2, this means that the distribution of irt's would be exponential, as shown at the left of Figure 6.5a. With a variable-interval schedule, where the reinforcements themselves are randomly distributed in time, the *continuous temporal discrimination theory* of responding would predict that responses, having no basis for any particular temporal distribution themselves, should also be randomly distributed in time. The *reward-versus-cost theory,* which makes predictions only on a molar level, might imply that on a molecular level responding should be random (although a molar theorist might claim that any distribution of irt's that yielded a particular overall rate of response would not be inconsistent with his theory).

A simple version of the *differential-reinforcement-of-irt's theory* predicts how irt's should be distributed in a variable-interval schedule. Since long irt's are reinforced with higher probability than short irt's, the irt probability function should increase continuously as irt's get longer. This theory predicts the functions shown in Figure 6.5b. Finally, the *two-state temporal-discrimination theory* predicts that irt probability functions will have two maxima, as shown in Figure 6.5c. The left maximum is the most common irt when the subject is responding at its fixed rate. The right maximum is the average pause between bursts of responding. The mix of bursts and pauses would produce a continuously varying overall rate of response.

To return to Gilberts' terminology (see Figure 2.7) the two-state theory implies that perseveration of responding varies from one schedule of reinforcement to another, while the tempo of responding stays constant. The other theories imply a change in tempo of one kind or another. As an illustration of the distinction between variation of tempo and perseveration, consider two ways of varying speed when travelling from one city to another. One way is to vary the speed continuously. If you wanted to get there fast you might drive 60 miles per hour. If you were not in a hurry, you might drive 30 miles per hour. Another way to vary speed is to drive always at 60 miles per hour but to stop more frequently for rests. The first method changes the tempo (the instan-

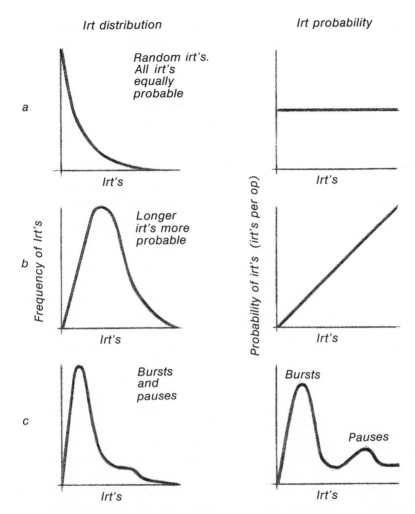

FIGURE 6.5
What irt and irt's/opportunity distributions would look like, ideally, if (a) all
irt's were equally likely, (b) long irt's were more likely than short ones, and
(c) bursts and pauses characterized the response patterns, with long and
short irt's more likely than medium ones. For the relation of an irt
distribution to an irt's/opportunity distribution see Figure 2.10 and
accompanying text.

taneous rate). The second method changes the perseveration. How does responding actually vary? How do actual distributions of irt's look, and which
theory do they confirm? Unfortunately, irt distributions vary considerably in
shape, as well as particular parametric values, depending on the response, the
organism used as a subject, and other particulars unrelated to the theories we
are considering here.

Some facts about irt distributions, however, do seem to emerge from the data. For instance, tempo of responding may occasionally vary. Different drl and drh schedules of reinforcement result in responding of different tempos. Within a fixed-interval schedule of reinforcement the scallops on the cumulative record indicate that tempo varies continuously (although after a subject has had extensive training on fixed-interval schedules, the cumulative records look more like those obtained with fixed-ratio schedules—a pause and then a constant rate of responding). Also, various schedules of punishment vary the tempo of responding.

But more frequently, tempo varies very little, and perseveration varies considerably as overall rate of responding changes. This is true for various schedules of reinforcement and also for other parameters such as rate and amount of reinforcement within a schedule. Figure 6.6 shows irt distributions and probability (irt's/op) distributions for three pigeons on a VI-1' schedule of reinforcement. As we implied above, the distributions are ambiguous. One pigeon has a single mode in its probability distribution, which suggests that tempo might vary for this pigeon as schedule parameters varied. For the other two pigeons, the probability distributions are bimodel as predicted by the two-state temporal-discrimination theory. The first mode, "bursts," is usually constant as parameters of the schedule are varied. The second mode, "pauses," tends to change with parametric changes. For these pigeons it is likely that the speed of responding would vary in perseveration rather than tempo.

With rats running in alleys and mazes the pattern of responding is often similar to that of the two pigeons whose probability distributions showed two modes. Many studies have shown that animals tend to change their overall speed of running by varying perseveration. Tempo is relatively insensitive to the sorts of variables we are discussing in this chapter.

Thus, when a rat runs a maze more quickly on one trial than another, it is usually because the rat is stopping less frequently, not because its actual speed of running changes. Another way to put it is that changing parameters of reward or punishment changes the way the rat distributes its time—running at a constant rate versus not running—rather than changing any characteristic of the running itself.

CONFLICT

The effects of punishment on responding are described graphically by the *conflict model* of reinforcement and punishment. This model, first proposed by the Gestalt psychologist Kurt Lewin, was systematized and tested experimentally by Neal Miller and his students at Yale University. The model was developed with reference to events in space (for which the straight alley would be the appropriate experimental tool), but it applies as well to events in time (for

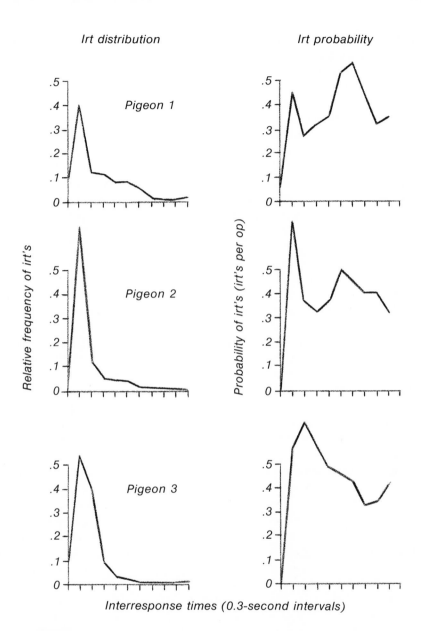

Irt distribution

Irt probability

Pigeon 1

Pigeon 2

Pigeon 3

Relative frequency of irt's

Probability of irt's (irt's per op)

Interresponse times (0.3-second intervals)

FIGURE 6.6
Actual irt and irt/opportunity distributions for three pigeons. Key-pecks were reinforced on variable-interval 1-minute schedules. Of the three pairs of theoretical distributions of Figure 6.5, the burst–pause pattern is most like that of the lower pair of distributions. [From C. P. Shimp, Reinforcement of short interresponse times. *J. Exp. Anal. Beh.,* 1967, *10,* 425–434. Copyright 1967 by the Society for the Experimental Analysis of Behavior, Inc.]

which the Skinner box would be the appropriate experimental tool).* In a trans-lation of the model from spatial to temporal terms, an event nearer or farther away in space could become an event nearer or farther away in time. A stimulus that serves as a cue to tell a rat how far it is from the goal box (a spatial cue) could become a stimulus that tells the rat how long it will be until a reinforce-ment arrives (a temporal cue). A stronger or weaker tendency to respond at a point in the alley could become a stronger or weaker tendency to respond at a point in time.

According to the conflict model the organism is a point in a spatial field somewhat like a magnetic field. Objects in that field exert attractive or repulsive forces. The objects that attract the organism correspond to events (either stimuli or responses) we have been calling rewards. The objects that repel the organism correspond to events we have been calling punishments.† The attractive and repulsive forces both act at a distance, but they are weaker the farther away they are and stronger the closer they are. That is, the closer the organism is to the reward, the greater is the tendency to approach it. The closer the organism is to the punishment, the greater is the tendency to avoid it. Thus, from each attractive or repulsive object in the field there extends an approach or avoidance gradient. Conflict arises from the interaction of these gradients. Figure 6.7 shows approach and avoidance gradients for a rat in an alley. The theory makes no prediction about the exact shape of the gradients (they are usually drawn as straight lines for convenience). When there are two rewards at different points in the field, both exert attractive forces. These may cancel each other out and result temporarily in movement toward neither reward, but this *approach-approach* conflict condition is unstable since the slightest movement toward either reward increases its attractive force and decreases that of the other. Imagine that you are walking down the center of a street and come upon two bakeries, one on either side. You might hesitate for a second, but as you started in the direction of one bakery its smell would become more enticing and you would continue in that direction.

Avoidance-avoidance conflict arises when two punishers are at two different points in the field. Both repel the organism. When the repulsive forces are equal, movement stops. Avoidance-avoidance conflict is more stable than approach-approach because movement in either direction increases the re-pulsive force in that direction and tends to send you back where you came from. (Imagine now that there are two disreputible-looking characters, possible muggers, on either side of the street.)

---

*Although most spatial models can easily be translated into temporal terms (as when an alley is translated into an FR schedule) it is sometimes awkward to do the reverse (an alley equivalent of a VI schedule would be awkward, although not impossible to arrange). This is why most experiments in animal learning nowadays use Skinner boxes rather than mazes or alleys.

†Premack's theory that the efficacy of rewards and punishments depends on their value relative to that of the response would be reconcilable with conflict theory to the extent that the value of the reward remained higher and the value of the punishment remained lower than locomotion re-sponses in the spatial field.

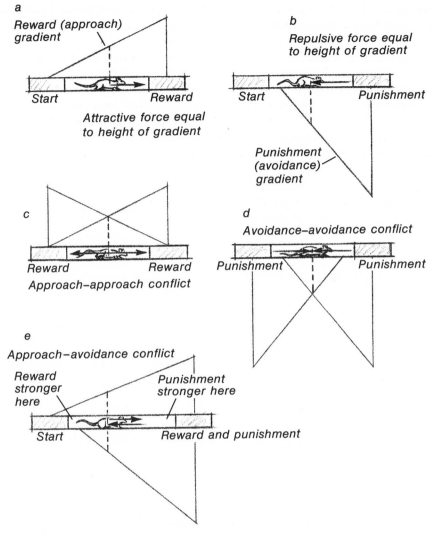

FIGURE 6.7
The conflict model. (a) shows a reward gradient. (b) shows a punishment gradient. (c), (d), and (e) illustrate three kinds of conflict. Gradients are equal at point where rat is standing, so rat has equal tendency to move in either direction.

Approach-avoidance conflict occurs when the reward and punisher are in the same direction so that the same movement brings you closer to both. This, of course, is the standard punishment paradigm, in which a response is both rewarded and punished, and it is by far the most frequently studied conflict situation. (Imagine now, a mugger standing in front of a bakery on one side of the street.) According to the conflict model the shallower reward gradient is dominant when the organism is far away and it generates approach behavior, but the steeper avoidance gradient becomes relatively more and more dominant until at some point approach and avoidance cancel out.

Variations in training, amount of reward, amount of punishment, amount of deprivation, and other variables raise or lower the height but not the steepness of the gradients.

Subjects should run towards reward faster and with more force the closer they are to the reward. Subjects should run away from punishment faster and with more force the closer they are to the punishment. With reward and punishment together, subjects should approach to a certain point and then stop (the

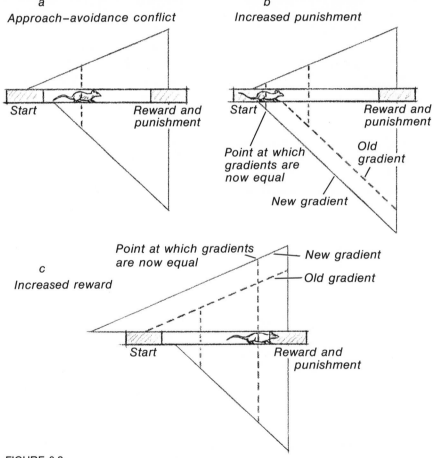

FIGURE 6.8
Approach–avoidance conflict. Increasing punishment moves point of equilibrium (equal gradients) back towards start of alley. Increasing reward moves point of equilibrium forward towards goal box.

point at which the gradients are equal). Increasing reward or decreasing punishment should bring the point at which they stop closer to the point at which the reward and punishment are being applied. Figure 6.8 shows how some of these predictions follow from the model.

The model has been tested with mixed results. On one hand, rats in alleys running to goal boxes where they have been both fed and shocked do tend to run part way and stop. They run further if they have had more training with food, if they are given more food in the alley, and if they have been shocked fewer times. They also tend to run faster (both towards and away from the goal box) when they are closer to the goal box—as the model predicts. The critical prediction that punishment gradients are steeper than reward gradients has, however, proven difficult to test. The steepness of gradients, whether reward or punishment, seems to depend more on discriminative cues within the alley or on the schedule of reinforcement or punishment (in temporal experiments) than on whether the event in the goal box was a reward or a punishment. Nevertheless, the conflict model remains an interesting descriptive model for behavior when experimental conditions are manipulated to strengthen two incompatible responses. Note that the model says nothing about whether the "conflict" of responses is mirrored inside the organism by a physiological state or a mental state. The gradients need not represent anything inside the organism; they are merely symbols for the way in which external stimuli affect behavior. In this respect, the conflict model is a wholly behavioral model.

An interesting corollary to the conflict model is the concept of *displacement*. If we imagine a rat in an alley, displacement consists of a tendency for the rat to move out of the alley altogether. With approach–approach conflict there is no tendency for displacement. (In the two-bakeries example there is a tendency to stay in the neighborhood of the bakeries.) With avoidance–avoidance conflict the tendency for displacement is very strong. (Consider the two-muggers example, or try to push your two index fingers together, end to end, and see what happens.) With approach–avoidance conflict there is also a tendency for displacement (for example, a tendency to get around the mugger and into the bakery). According to the model, displacement should be strongest where conflict is strongest (i.e., where reward and punishment gradients are equal). When experiments have allowed rats to escape from the alley with approach-avoidance conflict, they have found that rats do run part way down the alley and then escape (presumably at the point where conflict is strongest).

MOTIVATION

In many textbooks on behavior, "motivation" plays an important role. The organism is pictured as being similar to a car, with a drive mechanism (motivation) and a steering mechanism (learning). A more appropriate analogy, from the viewpoint of this book, might be an analogy to a rowboat, in which drive and steering are combined in the same mechanism. Much of what we have already covered under other rubrics would be covered traditionally under motivation; for instance, theories of reinforcement such as Premack's are usually treated as theories of motivation. In fact, Premack's earliest systematization of his theory was presented at the Nebraska Symposium on Motivation in 1965. Chapter 3 of this book, dealing with patterns of behavior, would ordinarily be called "motivation."

In nonbehavioristic textbooks, motivation plays a still more important role. Mentalistic theories of behavior such as Freud's rely heavily on the role of motivation as the driving force behind behavior. Physiological theories see motivation as characteristic states of certain physiological variables.

For our purposes, however, "motivation" will be restricted to the parameters of those variables that provide the context for reinforcement. For instance, when food is used as positive reinforcement, motivation is the deprivation of food; when electric shock reduction is used as negative reinforcement, motivation is the shock level before reduction. The more hours of deprivation, the more intense the shock, the greater the motivation. A psychologist's definition of motivation will depend on his definition of reinforcement. A drive-reduction theorist would define motivation in terms of drive, a tension-reduction theorist, in terms of tension, and so forth. In Premack's theory, motivation is what is measured in the free-choice experiment. The value-hierarchy, once established, would constitute the motivational state of the organism, that is the context in which reinforcement can act.

WARNING

Although it is not necessary to infer that food deprivation causes hunger and that shock causes pain, in everyday life and, to some extent, in scientific discourse (including parts of this book) psychologists talk about animals being hungry or stimuli being painful. But there is a danger in using these terms—we may forget their definitions in terms of the operations of deprivation and reinforcement and assume the existence of underlying physiological or mental states that have not been measured. We may assume that another person or another animal, because of superficial similarities to ourselves, has a similar underlying motivational structure or because of superficial differences, has a different underlying motivational structure. Empathy on the basis of superficial similarity rather than on the basis of measurable behavioral similarity may lead us to offer rewards when they are not wanted or to withhold rewards when they are wanted.

It is a fairly safe generalization that the degree of motivation for positive and negative reinforcement tends to affect behavior in the same way that the amount of positive or negative reinforcement affects behavior, with functions similar in appearance to those of Figure 5.17. Figure 6.9 shows lever-pressing

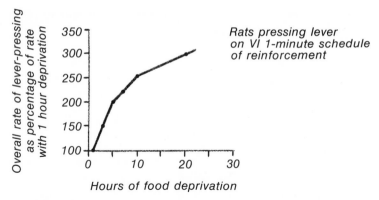

FIGURE 6.9

Average increase in rates of responding by rats pressing levers as a function of hours of food deprivation. Rate of responding with 1-hour deprivation is taken as a standard. Rates at other deprivations are taken as percentages of the rate at 1-hour deprivation. [From Clark, R. Some time correlated reinforcement schedules and their effects on behavior. *J. Exp. Anal. Beh.,* 1959, 2, 1–22. Copyright 1959 by the Society for the Experimental Analysis of Behavior, Inc.]

as a function of hours of food deprivation. The curve of Figure 6.9, which reflects averages, tends to increase more gradually than corresponding curves for individual rats. For individuals, the motivation curves tend to rise sharply from zero and level off suddenly, as do the individual curves for rate of reinforcement of Figure 5.18. Average curves, in general, vary more gradually than the individual functions of which they are composed.

The Yerkes–Dodson Law

In 1908, R. M. Yerkes and J. D. Dodson performed an experiment with mice that led to a new understanding of the relation between motivation and performance. In the experiment, a mouse was put into a box with two doors—one white and one grey. The white door led to a compartment where the mouse was shocked. The grey door led to a compartment without shock and from which the mouse could escape back to the start box. The mouse was forced (pushed by hand) to go forward through one of the doors. Yerkes and Dodson varied (a) the darkness of the grey door from very light grey (difficult to discriminate from white) to black (easy to discriminate from white) and (b) the intensity of shock behind the white door. Figure 6.10 illustrates their findings. For the easy task (white versus black), the more intense the shock, the better the mice became at choosing the black door. For a medium task (white versus grey), at first increases in shock intensity increased performance, although not as much as they did in the easy task; then, further increases started to decrease performance. In the hard task (white versus very light grey) this pattern was

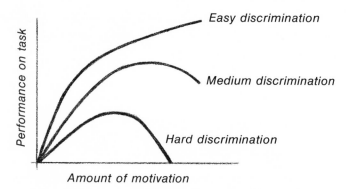

FIGURE 6.10
Illustration of the Yerkes–Dodson law, relating performance to
motivation, with discrimination difficulty as a parameter. Note
that the maximum (optimal performance) is at lower motivation
for more difficult discriminations.

accentuated. The point of maximum performance was at a lower intensity of
shock for the hard than for the medium task. For the easy task, if there was a
maximum it was higher than the intensities used.

Although the experiment performed by Yerkes and Dodson dealt with choice
(and the shock that was varied was punishment, as we have defined it, not motivation), the experiment is pertinent to this section because the results have been
applied to nonchoice as well as choice situations* and to motivation as we have
defined it as well as to punishment. The Yerkes–Dodson Law says that as
motivation is increased, performance first increases and then decreases, the
decrease occurring sooner the more difficult the task is.

The Yerkes–Dodson findings fit well into the conflict model, which pictures
the organism as a point in a field, attracted and repelled by objects in the field.
With strong motivation, attraction toward the object is strong and the tendency
to go straight toward the object is increased. When a barrier is placed between
the organism and the object, as might happen with a difficult task, the strong
motivation directs the organism up against the barrier and prevents backing-
off to go around it. For instance, a hungry dog might not back up to go around
a fence as quickly as a less hungry dog. The hungry dog would stay at the fence,
closest to the food. Similarly, a human faced with a task requiring complex
discriminations (such as playing a piano concerto) would do well not to dwell
too much on the reward (applause) he is to receive afterwards. Overly strong
motivation would interfere with the difficult task at hand (playing the piano).
On the other hand, with a task requiring easy discriminations (say, running
a race) it would seem the more motivation the better.

---

*We shall see in Chapter 10 (on choice) that all behavior may be considered choice behavior.

Experimental tests of the Yerkes-Dodson law have sometimes failed to find a downturn in performance at high levels of motivation. But at the extreme, there must be a downturn, since very high levels of motivation (hunger or shock, for instance) are damaging to the organism. If we extended deprivation we would expect a downturn in performance sooner or later even for the easy tasks used in the experiment of Figure 6.10.

Incentive and Motivation

In straight-alley experiments, the word "incentive" refers to parameters of reward in the goal box. When we vary the amount of food in the goal box we are varying incentive. We know from observations such as those that gave rise to Figure 5.17 that a rat will run faster down an alley with higher incentive.

The word "motivation" refers to the context of reward and therefore, to conditions outside the goal box. Usually this means hours of deprivation of whatever is in the goal box, but it could refer to conditions in the alley itself such as aversive temperature or confinement. We know from observations such as those that gave rise to Figure 6.9 that a rat with higher motivation will run faster down an alley.

We thus have two basic methods of experimental manipulation (incentive and motivation) but a single behavioral result (running faster). Do these two methods of experimental manipulation correspond to two mechanisms within the organism? An analogy could be made here to a similar question in perception. Figure 1.15 shows that there are two ways to make a spot seem to move to the left in a frame. One way is to move the spot to the left. The other is to move the frame to the right. Here also are two experimental manipulations. Do they correspond to two processes in the organism or to a single process (the relative movement of the spot in the frame)? The question is difficult to answer experimentally. If we regard reinforcement as a *change* in conditions from runway of an alley to goal box (or, more abstractly, from point A to point B) then there is only *one* variable—the amount of change. The diagrams of Figure 6.11 show that both reward and punishment may be increased in either of two ways, by increasing incentive or by increasing motivation. Whether these ways are equivalent depends on whether point A represents a neutral state. If so, there is a difference between varying reward by incentive and varying it by motivation (by making the reward better or the lack of reward worse). But if A is just some arbitrary point on a scale of value (as Premack's theory implies) then there is no fundamental difference between increasing the value of reward and decreasing the value of lack of reward. The *change* would be the same.

Are incentive and motivation two separate variables? Would it be possible, for example, to classify all the ways of manipulating running speed into these two categories on the basis of functional differences? Consider three ways of increasing running speed: (1) increasing shock in the alley, (2) decreasing shock in the goal box, and (3) increasing food in the goal box. The first is considered

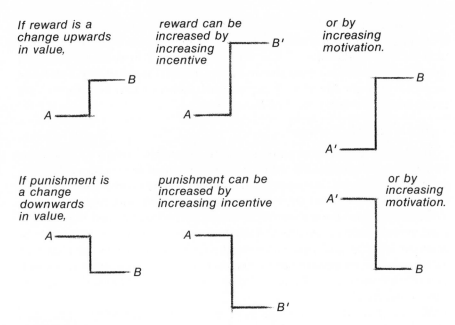

FIGURE 6.11
Increases or decreases in the value of the contingent event or its context in instrumental conditioning determine whether motivation or incentive is varied for both positive reinforcement and punishment.

a motivational variable and the second two, incentive variables. If motivation and incentive are separate, one ought to be able to determine how they interact. Do they add together or multiply together to determine running speed, or is running speed some other function of their interaction? So far attempts to determine the relationship between motivation and incentive have produced differing results, depending on the particular experimental methods used (for example, pellets of food and concentration of sucrose have different effects). For our purposes, therefore, we shall simply consider incentive and motivation as two ways of varying running speed (and, analogously, of varying the rate of any response) and leave open the question of *how* they affect responding.

Transient and Steady-State Effects

So far in this chapter we have been dealing with steady-state effects. The functions of Figures 5.17, 5.18, 5.20, 5.22, 5.23, 6.9, and 6.10 show performance after it has stabilized under a given set of conditions. Each point on the functions of Figure 5.18, for instance, represents the average of several sessions. In order for these points to be determined, pigeons first had to be trained to eat from the magazine feeder in the Skinner box when they were hungry. Then they were trained to peck the response key (an illuminated disk) to operate the magazine. Then each pigeon was exposed to a different schedule of reinforcement. Each day one session was run for each pigeon until 60 rewards had been obtained (each consisting of 4 seconds' access to grain from the magazine). The same schedule was used each session for each pigeon until the rate of pecking (total number of pecks divided by session times minus time spent eating the food) was about the same from day to day. It took anywhere from 15 to 60 days for the rate of pecking to stabilize. Once the response rate was stable for a given pigeon on a given VI schedule of reinforcement, the average of the last 5 sessions for the pigeon was plotted as a point on Figure 5.18. Then the pigeon was switched to another VI schedule until rate of pecking stabilized on that schedule, and another point was obtained. This continued (with several returns to the same schedule to see if the rate of pecking remained the same) until all the schedules were covered. It was a very slow process. The rates of responding obtained are steady-state rates of responding. But what are the transient effects when conditions are suddenly switched in the middle of a session? The difference between the investigation of steady-state and transient behavior phenomena is like the difference between looking at, on one hand, the behavior of people born rich versus poor and, on the other hand, the behavior of someone who has just won or lost a million dollars. Figure 6.12 shows, on the left, hypothetical steady-state functions for motivation and incentive with reward and punishment. What happens to response rate when conditions are *suddenly* changed from X to Y or from Y to X? The right-hand functions show what often happens. When reinforcement is suddenly increased (or punishment decreased), responding rises above the steady-state level at which it will ultimately settle. When punishment is suddenly increased (or reinforcement decreased), responding falls below the steady-state level at which it will ultimately settle. Corresponding effects may be found when motivational variables are suddenly varied, but it is usually difficult to vary motivation for positive reinforcement suddenly. For instance, an animal cannot be suddenly switched from 1-hour deprivation of food to 24-hour deprivation of food (although by physiological techniques, such as stimulation in various sites in the brain, sudden shifts in hunger may be obtained)*.

The sudden rise in responding when reinforcement is increased (or punishment decreased) is called *positive contrast*. The sudden decrease in responding when punishment is increased (or reinforcement decreased) is called *negative contrast*.

Contrast effects are by no means always obtained, and when they are obtained, positive and negative contrast do not always come and go together when conditions are switched back and forth. For instance, with pigeons pecking

---

*Some psychologists believe that the only difference between positive and negative reinforcement is the fact that, in nature, motivation for positive reinforcement (for example, hunger) increases slowly, whereas motivation for negative reinforcement (for example, pain) increases suddenly.

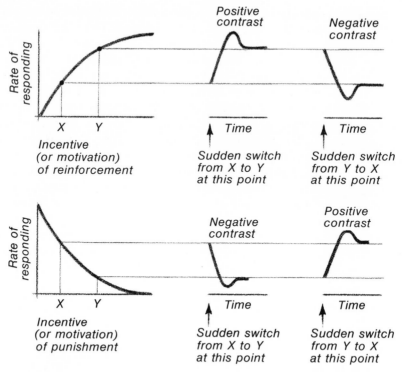

FIGURE 6.12

Transient effects found when conditions of incentive or motivation are suddenly changed. Positive contrast consists of a temporary elevation above the steady-state point. Negative contrast consists of a temporary depression below the steady-state point.

keys for food reward, positive contrast is frequently observed when reward is suddenly increased, but negative contrast is not observed when reward is decreased. When rats run in alleys for food reward, negative contrast is frequently observed when reward is decreased, but positive contrast is not observed when reward is increased. We will discuss the possible mechanisms underlying the contrast effect in Chapter 9.

BIBLIOGRAPHY

Within the past seven years or so several symposia have been organized to discuss the topics presented in this chapter. A partial list of the reports of these symposia follows:

Boakes, R., and Halliday, M. S., eds. *Inhibition and learning.* London: Academic Press, 1972.

Campbell, B. A., and Church, R. M., eds. *Punishment and aversive behavior.* New York: Appleton-Century-Crofts, 1969.

Gilbert, R. M., and Millenson, J. R., eds. *Reinforcement: Behavioral analysis.* New York: Academic Press, 1972.

Glazer, R., ed. *The nature of reinforcement.* New York: Academic Press, 1971.

The reader who is interested in conflict theory can find more information in A. J. Yates' *Frustration and conflict* (London: Methuen, 1962). But first he should read Chapter 9 of the present book.

Following is a list of articles referred to in this chapter:

Miller, N. Experimental studies of conflict. In *Personality and the behavior disorders,* ed. J. M. Hunt. New York: The Ronald Press, 1944.

Olds, J., and Milner, P. Positive reinforcement produced by electrical stimulation of the septal area and other regions of the rat brain. *Journal of Comparative and Physiological Psychology,* 1954, *47,* 419–427.

Premack, D. Reinforcement theory. In *Nebraska symposium on motivation,* ed. D. Levine. Lincoln: University of Nebraska Press, 1965.

Premack, D. Catching up with common sense or two sides of a generalization: Reinforcement and punishment. In Glazer, *op. cit.*

Yerkes, R. M., and Dodson, J. D. The relation of strength of stimulus to rapidity of habit formation. *Journal of Comparative Neurology and Psychology,* 1908, *18,* 459–482.

We reprint an article by William Timberlake and James Allison on "response deprivation". Response deprivation is the idea (as expressed in Figure 6.3 and the accompanying legend) that reinforcement of a response is possible only when the subject is permitted less time than he would ordinarily spend in the response-contingent activity. That is, the subject must be deprived of the response before the opportunity to make that response can serve as a reward. In this article Timberlake and Allison discuss a simple mathematical expression of response deprivation (first proposed by Eisenberger, Karpman and Trattner in 1967) and subject the model to several tests, finding the model supported.

At one point Timberlake and Allison argue against estimating overall probability from too large an observation period. Later, even momentary probabilities are held to be inadequate. The argument here is very subtle, hinging on how one estimates probability from measures such as those of Figure 6.2 and the relationship between the duration of the free-choice period (which they call the baseline), the duration of the response to be reinforced and the duration of access to the reinforcer. The reader may want to skip this argument (indicated by editor's footnotes). As we indicated on p. 308 probability is not measured directly. It may be defined in such a way that it conforms or fails to conform to any direct temporal measure. The argument in the text is thus, not between temporal measures and probability but between one temporal measure and another.

RESPONSE DEPRIVATION:
An Empirical Approach to Instrumental Performance

William Timberlake

James Allison

The empirical law of effect is criticized as an incomplete step in the development of empirical laws of instrumental performance. An alternate approach to the prediction of performance is developed which follows Premack in relating instrumental performance to empirical measures of operant behavior. However, it is concluded that instrumental performance is not determined by a probability differential in operant baseline between the instrumental and contingent responses, but by the condition of response deprivation. This condition depends on the terms of the schedule as well as operant baseline measures. The response deprivation condition occurs in a contingency if, in performing the instrumental response at operant baseline, the subject would perform less than his operant baseline of the contingent response. Instrumental performance appears directly related to the amount of response deprivation. Response selection and the application of the response deprivation approach are discussed.

Learning theorists of the most disparate persuasions agree that the consequence of an instrumental response is an important determinant of the subsequent probability of that response. While it is generally acknowledged that some consequences increase the probability of an instrumental response, and others do not, there is not much agreement on what property of the consequence produces the increase. Failure to resolve this theoretical issue, combined with the

Preparation of this paper was supported in part by National Science Foundation Grant GB-36209 to the authors. We have profited from the suggestions of many people. We thank especially David Birch, Eliot Hearst, Connie Mueller, David Premack, Frank Restle, and Edward Walker. Requests for reprints should be sent to William Timberlake, Department of Psychology, Indiana University, Bloomington, Indiana 47401.
From *Psychological Review*, Vol. 81, No. 2, 146–164. Copyright 1974 by the American Psychological Association. Reprinted by permission.

success of Skinner's (1938, 1950) atheoretical approach, produced a pragmatic approach to instrumental learning. The empirical law of effect ignored conflicting theoretical views and simply asserted that some consequences have a response-increasing property, and other consequences do not. Spence (1956) expressed the law:

Responses accompanied or followed by certain kinds of events (namely, reinforcers) are more likely to occur on subsequent occasions, whereas responses followed by certain other kinds of events (namely, non-reinforcers) do not subsequently show a greater likelihood of occurrence [p. 33].

We will contend that in spite of its longevity, the empirical law of effect is an inadequate empirical guide to the prediction of instrumental performance. It is useful only under a restricted set of conditions, and is based on a questionable model of instrumental learning. We will suggest an alternative approach to instrumental performance which has a more adequate empirical base.

INADEQUACY OF THE EMPIRICAL LAW OF EFFECT

The inadequacy of the empirical law of effect as a predictor of instrumental performance was first pointed out in a criticism that the law is circular (Postman, 1947). The probability of the instrumental response is the only independently defined variable in the empirical law of effect. The other variable, the reinforcer, is defined by the effect it is assumed to have on the probability of the instrumental response. If a particular consequence is associated with an increase in the probability of the instrumental response, then it is a reinforcer; otherwise, it is not. Employed in this fashion, the empirical law of effect only defines a reinforcer; it is not a law.

In a classic defense, Meehl (1950) suggested that the empirical law of effect escaped the problem of circularity if reinforcers were treated as transituational in their effects. A reinforcer identified in one situation can be predicted to increase the probability of an instrumental response in other situations. Meehl's solution provides the empirical law of effect with empirical content (Hilgard & Bower, 1966) but is objectionable on at least two grounds. First, though probably intended only as an interim solution, the concept of transituationality appears to have hindered the development of more adequate laws of instrumental performance. Researchers have limited their efforts to cataloging events which increase instrumental responding (Miller, 1963). Such a catalog is a first step in the development of scientific laws, but the next step, discovering the attributes of the events which determine their effect, is overdue in the case of the empirical law of effect.

Second, the transituational hypothesis of reinforcers is successful in predicting commonly investigated phenomena, such as bar pressing for food by hungry animals. However, this predictive success appears more related to a fortuitous, situational consistency than to an analysis of the basic laws involved.[1] An analogy will clarify this distinction.

A well-known physical law states that the pressure of a gas in a fixed space is a direct function of its temperature. Suppose, however, that the concept of temperature were not known but that researchers had cataloged "pressurizing agents" which increased the pressure of gas systems to which they were added. If all gas systems considered had similar initial temperatures, then all pressurizing agents would be transituational in their effects. However, if the gas systems differed in initial temperature, then a given pressurizing agent might increase, decrease, or have no effect on the pressure of a system to which it was added. Such phenomena can be understood and predicted only by developing the concept of temperature and the associated gas laws.

If the problem of identifying reinforcing agents is at all analogous to the problem of identifying pressurizing agents, then there should be many exceptions to the transituational property of reinforcers. Reinforcers should increase, decrease, or have no effect on responses which they follow. In fact, there are widely known exceptions to the transituational property. For one, a food consequence will not typically increase instrumental responding in a satiated rat. This result is so intuitively obvious that little has been made of it. Instead of modifying their approach to deal directly with this exception, researchers have treated hunger as a boundary condition for the application of the empirical law of effect. One defense of this boundary condition is that the animal must eat the food in order for an effect to occur. Since

---

[1]See Staddon (1973) for an interesting discussion of related issues.

a satiated rat does not eat food, no reinforcement will occur.

However, this escape clause does not apply to a series of studies reported by Premack (1965). Premack combined two known reinforcing responses in the same schedule, one as the instrumental response, and the other as the contingent response. One such schedule involved manipulation responses in monkeys (Premack, 1959, 1963b), and another, wheel running and licking in rats (Premack, 1962, 1965). In each schedule both responses had a nonzero operant level, and each closely followed the other. The empirical law of effect therefore appears to predict that each should reinforce the other. The results showed that, at most, only one response in a given contingency increased in probability.

PROBABILITY-DIFFERENTIAL HYPOTHESIS

Premack (1959) was able to predict which response would increase by comparing the relative probabilities of the two responses in a paired operant baseline. He formalized his discovery in the probability-differential hypothesis: "For any pair of responses, the more probable one will reinforce the less probable one [p. 132]." Response probability is determined from the duration of the instrumental and contingent responses in a paired operant baseline. Duration of responding is used rather than rate on the grounds that the clock does not move faster or slower as a function of the particular response involved. The paired baseline session is identical to the contingency session in terms of all stimulus, organismic, and procedural conditions, except that access to both responses is free rather than regulated by a schedule.

The probability-differential hypothesis provides a testable alternative to the empirical law of effect and surpasses it in ability to predict instrumental performance before the fact. The probability-differential hypothesis is potentially

applicable to any response without prior experience in using it as a reinforcer. Further, this hypothesis predicts the outcome of contingencies between two known reinforcers and accounts for the failure of a food consequence to increase bar pressing in a satiated rat. Eating is not a high-probability response in a satiated rat.

Despite its advantages, the probability-differential hypothesis has generated a relatively small number of studies and has only slowly entered the mainstream of reinforcement theory (Kling & Schrier, 1971). Most textbooks of learning continue to feature the empirical law of effect as the preferred technique for predicting instrumental performance (Deese & Hulse, 1967; Hall, 1966; Hilgard & Bower, 1966).

The reasons for this are complex. The probability-differential hypothesis has been criticized for making mistaken predictions, though some of these claims appear to be based on misunderstanding rather than experimental disproofs.[2]

_____

[2]One of the most frequently cited criticisms of the probability-differential approach was raised by Miller (1963). He pointed out that a high probability of wheel running could be obtained by shocking a rat in a running wheel, but he doubted that the animal would therefore perform an instrumental response to turn on the shock and run. Miller's thought experiment violates a basic procedure of the probability-differential approach. The contingency should change only the rules for access to the contingent response. Any other part of the stimulus situation or the organismic variables eliciting approach to the contingent response should remain constant. Miller's suggested procedure is analogous to measuring eating when a rat is food deprived but imposing a schedule when the rat is satiated. To complete the analogy, if the rat performed the instrumental response, it would be simultaneously deprived and given food. It is possible that such a schedule might produce an effect, but to predict its outcome from the probability-differential approach would require a different baseline than the type Miller suggested. A schedule appropriate to Miller's baseline would make wheel running contingent upon an instrumental response in the presence of constant shock. Under these circumstances, it seems probable that the rat would learn to release the wheel to run.

Other problems include comparing the probability of different responses in commensurable units and assessing the baseline of reinforcing stimuli which are not related to clearly specified responses (e.g., brain stimulation). However, Premack (1965, 1971) has suggested solutions to these difficulties, and none of them seems greater than those surrounding the use of the empirical law of effect.

In our opinion, the major obstacle to replacing the empirical law of effect is its acceptance as the empirical form of a basic law of instrumental learning. Unique events (called reinforcers) exist, and they increase the performance of responses which they follow. In the view of many researchers, further work will contribute to the empirical law of effect only by specifying the unique physiological or biobehavioral qualities of a reinforcer. The basic form of the law is fixed.

There appear to be two bases for this belief. One, which was previously discussed, is the consistency of results acheived by using reinforcers within certain boundary conditions. The second is the pervasive influence of a particular theoretical model of instrumental learning, the reinforcement model. In the next section we will examine the evidence for the reinforcement model and its relation to the empirical law of effect.

REINFORCEMENT MODEL AND THE STRENGTHENING PROCESS

At the heart of the reinforcement model is a learning-reinforcement process—specifically, a strengthening process (Thorndike, 1913). This strengthening process is assumed to be initiated by the presentation of a unique stimulus event, a reinforcer, closely following the to-be-strengthened response. The frequency and contiguity with which a reinforcer follows a response determine the final strength of that response.

The empirical law of effect and the reinforcement model share a common heritage, Thorndike's law of effect. As a result, they are virtually identical in their assumptions. Some versions of the empirical law of effect contain no reference to learning or strengthening; however, many do (e.g., Skinner, 1938, 1971), and there seems little doubt that strengthening is generally assumed to be the basis for an increase in instrumental responding (Herrnstein, 1970). To displace the empirical law of effect, it will be necessary to displace the reinforcement model and its strengthening process as well.

Despite its plausibility and widespread acceptance, the appeal of the strengthening process is primarily intuitive; the process itself is a mystery. The work of Lashley (1950) and more recent researchers (John, 1967, 1968) reveals no simple analog of strengthening in the brain. Further, since its antecedents can be determined only by example, the conditions for strengthening can be inferred only after the fact of instrumental performance is established.

The reinforcement model does provide a unitary basis for response selection, storage of information, and performance in its strengthening process; but the advisability of such a simplification is questionable. Low intercorrelations between different measures of performance (Kimble, 1961), the phenomena of latent learning (Blodgett, 1929; Kimble, 1961) and all-or-none learning (Restle, 1965), the effects on performance of incentive shifts, intermittent reinforcement, and overlearning (Hall, 1966; Walker, 1964, 1969), all suggest the existence of multiple processes in instrumental learning. More recently, Estes (1969, 1971), Atkinson and Wickens (1971), and Longstreth (1972) argued for multiple processes by claiming that a reinforcer may affect learning by virtue of its contiguity with the instrumental response but that it has no direct effect upon performance. Perkins (1968), too, suggested that different variables and laws determine acquisition and asymptote of instrumental responding.

Far from discrediting the reinforcement model, these problems have set the stage for its elaboration. Concepts such as r_g-s_g (the fractional anticipatory goal response), r_j-s_j (the fractional anticipatory frustrative response), and attentional processes have been added to the model, largely without an increase in its empirical ties.[3] The reinforcement model has become a paradigm in Kuhn's (1964) sense of the term—a model which directs experimentation and interpretation but cannot itself be tested. It can only be displaced by an alternative model.

In addition to those above, there are two further arguments for displacing the reinforcement model, arguments which we feel suggest the direction a new model should take. First, the reinforcement model fails to set any a priori limit on asymptotic performance. Such a limit would seem to be a prerequisite for a model of performance. The absence of such limits in the reinforcement model points up its focus on the hypothetical learning-reinforcement process instead of on performance.

The second criticism disputes the assumption of the reinforcement model that a contingency affects performance only by providing contiguity between the instrumental response and a reinforcer. Premack (1965) reasoned that if this assumption were true, then any condition in which a high-probability response quickly and repeatedly followed a low-probability response should produce an increase in the low-probability response. As a test of this assumption, Premack examined paired-baseline sessions of licking and wheel running in

rats in which licking was the higher probability response. He defined as a contiguous pairing any occasion on which licking followed wheel running within two seconds. On the average these pairings occurred more than 18 times in a 15-minute session, but no increase in wheel running occurred.

In searching his data for other possible functions of a contingency, Premack observed that schedules which produced instrumental performance also reduced the contingent response below its paired baseline. To test the importance of this reduction, Premack set up a schedule between wheel running and licking which required only a small amount of the less-probable running response for access to a large amount of the more-probable licking response. This schedule did not reduce the contingent response: By running at baseline level, the animal was able to gain access to its baseline level of licking. Premack reasoned that if reduction of the contingent response is necessary for instrumental performance, then no increase in running would occur, despite the fact that the contingent licking response had a higher operant probability than running.

This schedule produced no increase in running, nor did running decrease when the opportunity to lick was withdrawn in an extinction test (Premack, 1965). The only difference between this schedule and previous schedules which did produce instrumental running (e.g., Premack, 1962) was that previous schedules reduced the contingent response below its baseline, and this schedule did not.

Premack (1965) concludes:

Apparently an invariant though unrecognized component of a contingency is a decrement in the amount of responding that occurs to the contingent stimulus, relative to what would occur were the stimulus free. Our results suggest that this reduction is vital, that reinforcement cannot be initiated without it. We are thus led to suppose that although the reduction is not a necessary feature of the contingency,

[3]The concepts of r_g-s_g and r_j-s_j are related to the empirical phenomena of anticipatory consummatory responses and anticipatory emotional responses, respectively. However, independent measures of these phenomena have not correlated particularly well with the course of instrumental learning. In practice, r_g-s_g and, to a lesser degree, r_j-s_j are used without reference to an empirical base other than their assumed effects on learning and performance.

it nonetheless occurs as a routine part of the reinforcement procedure. It would be preferable to elevate this factor from its obscure status as a hidden concomitant to that of a public operation where its consequences for theory can be examined [pp. 172–173].

In the next section we will present an alternative to the reinforcement model. This alternative suggests the development of empirical laws more adequate than the empirical law of effect. Both the model and the suggested laws are directed at the prediction of asymptotic performance under a schedule. Insofar as is possible, our intention is to isolate the determinants of instrumental performance from those of response selection and acquisition. We assume that the subject is able to learn what-leads-to-what in a given schedule. Our primary interest is the initial formulation of empirical laws of asymptotic instrumental performance.

TOWARD AN ADAPTIVE MODEL OF PERFORMANCE

Two major assumptions underlie the adaptive model. The first is that instrumental performance is a result of conflict between the freely occurring behavior of the animal and the restrictions of a schedule. The effects of a schedule cannot be understood or predicted by considering the contingency situation alone. A consequence is not merely the presentation of an isolated stimulus event but is better viewed as access to a response (the contingent response), which, along with the instrumental response, shows characteristic levels and patterns of performance in a free behavior baseline. A schedule imposes sequential and quantitative constraints which typically conflict with the patterns of free behavior. Asymptotic instrumental performance represents a resolution of this conflict.

The most common conflict produced by a schedule is a restriction of access to the contingent response. One way of imposing this restriction is to require the animal to perform a relatively large amount of the instrumental response in order to gain access to a relatively small amount of the contingent response. An increase in instrumental responding reduces the conflict between the contingency schedule and the free-responding baseline by increasing access to the contingent response.

Though the adaptive model in this general form does not predict the amount of increase in the instrumental response, it does suggest a limit to this increase. In general, the subject should not perform more of the instrumental response than is necessary to return the contingent response to its baseline. To exceed the baseline of the contingent response would necessitate increasing rather than decreasing the degree of conflict between baseline response levels and those in the contingency session.

For example, if a hungry rat is given free access to food and a bar in a baseline session, it will spend considerably more time eating than bar pressing. In a typical contingency, the schedule demands that the rat perform a large proportion of its baseline amount of bar pressing for access to a small proportion of its baseline amount of eating. By the time the rat has bar pressed its baseline amount, it will have gained access to only a small fraction of its baseline amount of eating. Additional bar pressing produces more food, thereby allowing the animal to approach its baseline amount of eating. From the point of view of reducing conflict, the rat should press the bar more than its baseline but not more than the amount necessary to reproduce its baseline amount of eating.

The second major assumption of the adaptive model is that resolution of the conflict between the determinants of free behavior and the requirements of the schedule is based on the biological equipment and capacities of the animal involved. An adaptive outcome is not necessarily most efficient (profitable) in obtaining access to the contingent response (Herrnstein, 1970). In the example above, the rat may perform responses other than bar pressing in reaction to the scheduled restriction of food. It might escape its cage, eat sawdust, nibble its pellets more efficiently, alter its metabolism of fats, bite the experimenter, or gnaw the bar. These outcomes are not equally profitable, but all are adaptive in that they follow from the organism's functioning as a biologically evolved system and in response to the imposition of the schedule.

Animals would be expected to show efficient performance only if their phylogenetic and ontogenetic programming provided the possibility of such a solution to the conflict imposed by the schedule. The fact that much behavior under a schedule appears to take the form of efficient instrumental responding is probably due primarily to a judicious selection of apparatus, animal, and procedure, and only secondarily to the general effect of a reinforcer.

In our development of an empirical approach to performance under a contingency, we will restrict ourselves to the prediction of asymptotic instrumental performance in single response, instrumental schedules. Multiple schedules will not be considered. Instrumental performance is defined as an increase in the amount of the instrumental response over its paired baseline. An instrumental schedule is one in which the amount of contingent response earned is uniquely and directly related to the amount of the instrumental response performed.

The restrictions in our exposition are intended to allow the development of empirical laws of performance without the prior necessity of a theory of response selection. Though the use of instrumental schedules does not guarantee that the subject will perform the response designated by the experimenter, it does make selection more likely than if the schedule did not designate an efficient response. Performance under the latter type of schedule probably would be based on mechanisms specific to an individual or species.

The paired baseline, in which both responses are freely and simultaneously available for the duration of subsequent contingency sessions, is used to determine the operant probabilities of the instrumental and contingent responses. The paired baseline provides the best estimate of what the subject would do if it were not for the schedule, and thus provides the best standard for judging the conflict imposed by the schedule.

The typical procedure of measuring only the single baseline of the instrumental response is inappropriate because it provides no estimate of the operant performance of the contingent response. It is interesting that experimenters have typically guaranteed a known relation between the baselines of the instrumental and contingent response through their procedures. For example, rats required to perform the low probability response of bar pressing to obtain food are deprived of food, thereby ensuring a high baseline probability of eating. Such procedures can be seen as an imprecise (though convenient) substitute for the direct measurement of the paired baseline of the instrumental and contingent responses.

RESPONSE DEPRIVATION CONDITION

If it is assumed that conflict between the schedule-imposed behavior and the free-responding baseline determines instrumental performance, it is important to state precisely the circumstances necessary for this conflict. The concept of response deprivation provides such a statement. For a given instrumental schedule, the condition of response deprivation is defined to occur if the animal, by performing its baseline amount of the instrumental response, is unable to obtain access to its baseline amount of the contingent response.

Eisenberger, Karpman, and Trattner (1967) defined this condition more formally.[4] The response deprivation condition is satisfied if

$$\frac{I}{C} \times \frac{O_c}{O_i} > 1,$$

where I and C are the terms of the schedule, and O_i and O_c are the paired operant baselines of the instrumental and contingent responses. The I term of the schedule is the instrumental requirement for access to the contingent response, and C is the amount of access to the contingent response earned by performing I.

A more easily appreciated expression can be obtained by multiplying both sides of this inequality by O_i/O_c, yielding

$$\frac{I}{C} > \frac{O_i}{O_c}$$

as a definition of the response deprivation condition. To determine the existence of the response deprivation condition, the two responses need not be measured in identical units. It is only necessary to measure I in the same units as O_i, and C in the same units as O_c.

If the animal in a contingency session performs the instrumental response at or below its baseline, then Equation 1 necessitates that the contingent response be performed below its baseline. Each time the animal performs Amount I of the instrumental response, then Amount C of the contingent response, the subject necessarily performs a greater proportion of O_i than of O_c. By the time the subject performs O_i of the instrumental response, it will have performed less than O_c of the contingent response.

Deprivation of the contingent response can be shown more formally by defining N as the number of times in the contingency session that the subject completes the instrumental requirement and gains access to the consequence. Total instrumental responding and total access to the contingent response in the contingency session can be approximated by multiplying top and bottom of the left side of Equation 1 by N, yielding

$$\frac{NI}{NC} > \frac{O_i}{O_c}.$$

If the subject performs at its baseline of the instrumental response ($NI \simeq O_i$), the numerators can be canceled and the terms rearranged to produce $NC < O_c$, thereby demonstrating deprivation of the contingent response.

The assumption that the response-deprivation condition determines instrumental performance disagrees with Premack's contention that a probability differential between two responses is the important condition (Premack, 1959, 1965).* In some circumstances, the two hypotheses make similar predictions. Many contingencies that satisfy the response-deprivation condition satisfy the probability-differential condition as well. For example, if a hungry rat must bar press to eat food (a high-probability contingent response), and the amount of food presented is small, the contingency will also deprive the subject of eating relative to its baseline. One bar press would have to produce at least 100 45-milligram pellets in order for the contingency schedule not to satisfy Equation 1 in a half-hour session (W. Timberlake, unpublished data, 1973, for 90-day-old rats at 85% of body weight).

Both approaches also predict that a contingency will increase only one of the two responses. The probability-differential hypothesis makes this prediction because only a high-probability response is assumed to be an effective contingent response. The response-deprivation approach makes the prediction on the

---

[4]Eisenberger et al., (1967) refer to this condition as response suppression. Premack called it contingent-response reduction; we prefer the term response deprivation.

*[Here begins the argument against probability measures.]

grounds that a given contingency schedule can satisfy the response-deprivation condition for only one of two responses. This prediction can be seen by rewriting Equation 1 in terms which do not prejudge which of the two responses is instrumental and which is contingent. If

$$\frac{A}{B} > \frac{O_a}{O_b},$$

then it is true that

$$\frac{B}{A} < \frac{O_b}{O_a}.$$

In words, if the contingency schedule deprives the subject of Response B, it cannot also deprive the subject of Response A.

Despite these predictive similarities, there are differences which compel us to accept the response-deprivation condition as the more important of the two conditions. First, Premack (1965) himself showed that a schedule which did not satisfy the response-deprivation condition produced no instrumental performance despite the fact that the operant baselines of the two responses satisfied the probability-differential condition. Hence, the response-deprivation condition is necessary for instrumental performance. What Premack failed to clarify is whether the probability-differential condition is also necessary for instrumental performance (Eisenberger et al., 1967). If both conditions must be present, then instrumental performance will occur only if the response-deprivation condition is satisfied *and* the contingent response has the higher operant probability. If only the response-deprivation condition must be present, instrumental performance will occur if the schedule satisfies the response-deprivation condition, even if the contingent response has the lower probability.

Eisenberger et al. (1967) attempted to evaluate these two possibilities in a series of experiments with humans. In the paired-baseline session of Experiment 4,

college students were instructed to manipulate a lever, or a knob, or both lever and knob, or neither, as they saw fit. The 12 critical subjects performed both responses, but the knob response had a higher operant probability than the lever response. The baseline session was followed by a contingency session in which the opportunity to engage in the less probable lever response was contingent upon performance of the more probable knob-manipulating response. The schedule for the critical subjects satisfied the response-deprivation condition but not the probability-differential condition. The results showed that the response-deprivation condition was sufficient for instrumental performance. Despite the lower probability contingent response, subjects increased instrumental knob manipulating.

Allison and Timberlake (1974) performed a series of experiments on saccharin licking in rats which also show that the probability-differential condition is not necessary for instrumental performance in schedules which satisfy the response-deprivation condition. In one experiment rats spent more time licking .4% saccharin solution than .3% saccharin solution in paired-baseline sessions. The baseline phase was followed by contingency sessions in which the more probable response (licking .4% saccharin) was the instrumental response and the less probable response (licking .3% saccharin) was the contingent response. The contingency schedule required 80 seconds of .4% licking for each 10-second access to the .3% solution ($I = 80$ seconds, $C = 10$ seconds). This schedule satisfied the response-deprivation condition and produced an increase in .4% saccharin licking.

Two subsequent experiments with rats using .4% and .1% saccharin provided further evidence for the importance of the response-deprivation condition for instrumental performance. If the response-deprivation condition alone produces instrumental performance, then it should be possible to increase either response by changing the terms of the schedule to produce deprivation of the other. But, if the probability-differential condition is necessary for instrumental performance, then only one of the two responses can be increased unless the operant probabilities of the two responses are changed. The schedule in the first experiment deprived the subject of .4% saccharin licking and produced an increase in instrumental .1% saccharin licking. The schedule in the second experiment deprived the subject of .1% saccharin licking and produced an increase in instrumental .4% saccharin licking. These results show that the probability-differential condition is not necessary for instrumental performance, provided that the schedule satisfies the response-deprivation condition.

Timberlake and Allison (1973) showed additional support for this conclusion in an experiment, with seven female albino rats, which employed saccharin licking and wheel running as the two responses. This experiment used reciprocal schedules (Allison, 1971), which require the subject to perform a specific amount of each response in order to receive access to the other response. One schedule required 30 $\frac{1}{4}$-turns of the wheel for access to saccharin and 10 licks to unlock the wheel. This schedule satisfied the response-deprivation condition with respect to running as the instrumental response and produced an increase in running. Another schedule required 60 licks to unlock the wheel and 5 $\frac{1}{4}$-turns of the wheel for access to saccharin. This schedule satisfied the response-deprivation condition with respect to licking as the instrumental response and produced an increase in licking. (See Figure 1.)

In summary, the evidence reviewed here indicates that the probability-differential condition is neither necessary nor sufficient for instrumental performance. Instrumental performance occurs only if the contingency schedule satisfies the response-deprivation condition.

RESPONSE DEPRIVATION AND MOMENTARY PROBABILITY DIFFERENTIAL*

Premack (1971) recently advanced the concept of momentary probability differential to account for instrumental performance. He has employed this concept in two contexts: in paired baseline to call attention to changes in the relative probabilities of responses during the session, and in the contingency to refer to inferred changes in relative response probabilities produced by the schedule. This section compares the concept of momentary probability differential with that of response deprivation.

Premack (1971) pointed out that in paired-baseline sessions, ". . . *average* response probabilities may badly misrepresent momentary response probabilities [p. 129]." As an example he cites data in which the probability of licking a 32% sucrose solution was higher than the probability of running during the initial part of the baseline session but lower during the latter part. Thus, according to the probability-differential hypothesis, it should be possible to increase instrumental running with contingent licking during the first part of a contingency session, while the reverse would occur during the latter part.

We agree that a complete account of instrumental performance will consider fluctuations in baseline, but it should be noted that baseline variability does not necessarily discredit predictions from the response-deprivation hypothesis. For every experiment reported in this paper, it is possible to define intervals in the baseline during which the relative probabilities of the responses reversed. Despite these reversals, the predictions of the response-deprivation hypothesis, based on average probabilities, were confirmed. Further, the response-deprivation hypothesis makes different predictions

---

*[Here begins the argument against momentary probability.]

than the momentary probability hypothesis. The latter predicts reversal of the roles of the instrumental and contingent responses only if their probabilities shift during the baseline session. The response-deprivation hypothesis predicts reversal based on schedule changes alone at any point in the baseline (so long as both responses have above zero probabilities).

Premack (1971; personal communication, 1973) has also applied the concept of momentary probability differential to the contingency session, arguing that response suppression (deprivation) is simply a way of producing an eventual probability differential in favor of the contingent response. This eventual (residual) probability differential is in turn responsible for increased instrumental responding.

This application of momentary probability differential is particularly interesting because it implies that a contingent response of lower average probability can increase an instrumental response of higher average probability. If a schedule satisfies the response-deprivation condition, then each time the subject performs I and C, the subject approaches O_i more rapidly than O_c. At some point in the session the subject will approach O_i more closely than O_c. From this point on, the contingent response will have a greater probability than the instrumental response. For this latter section of the contingency session the momentary probability-differential hypothesis predicts that the contingent response should increase instrumental responding. A numerical example of this type of contingency can be found in Table 1, Case 1.

This use of probability differs from Premack's previous procedures in that it is inferred rather than directly measured.

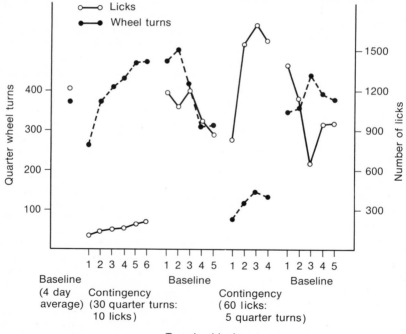

FIGURE 1

Mean number of $\frac{1}{4}$-wheel turns and saccharin licks. (The first schedule deprived the subject of licking, the second schedule deprived the subject of running.)

To be consistent with his previous work, it would be necessary to measure a paired baseline at the point in the contingency session at which the momentary probabilities are assumed to reverse. Whatever the outcome of such a procedure, there are much stronger reasons for doubting the efficacy of the momentary probability-differential hypothesis. Premack (1965) himself reported data which contradict the momentary probability-differential view while supporting the response-deprivation view. When a high-probability response (licking) was contingent on a low-probability response (wheel running), no increase in running occurred if the schedule did not satisfy the response-deprivation condition. Eisenberger et al. (1967) obtained similar results in their work on manipulatory behavior in humans.

The importance of these results lies in the fact that the schedules which produced no increase in the instrumental response did not satisfy the response-deprivation condition but did produce a theoretical probability differential in favor of the contingent response. A numerical example of this type of contingency can be found in Table 1, Case 2. Thus, it appears that the response-deprivation condition is distinguishable from the momentary probability-differential condition and that the evidence favors response deprivation as the more adequate predictor of instrumental performance. The probability-differential hypothesis must undergo further revision before it can account for the above data. (See Allison & Timberlake, 1974, for further discussion of this point.)*

AMOUNT OF RESPONSE DEPRIVATION AND INSTRUMENTAL PERFORMANCE

To this point we have demonstrated the importance of the response-deprivation condition for instrumental per-

*[Here ends the argument about probability versus time.]

Table 1 Examples of Changes in Residual O_c and O_i during the Contingency Session

	Case 1				Case 2		
Baselines: $O_i = 16$; $O_c = 8$				Baselines: $O_i = 8$; $O_c = 16$			
Schedule: $I = 4$; $C = 1$				Schedule: $I = 2$; $C = 4$			
N^a	Residual O_i	Residual O_c	Larger residual	N^a	Residual O_i	Residual O_c	Larger residual
1	12	7	O_i	1	6	12	O_c
2	8	6	O_i	2	4	8	O_c
3	4	5	O_c	3	2	4	O_c
4	0	4	O_c	4	0	0	—

NOTE: Abbreviations: O_c = baseline of the contingent response, O_i = baseline of the instrumental response, I = instrumental requirement, C = access to the contingent response.

[a]Number of times the subject has performed I and then C in the contingency session.

formance. This section examines the possibility of a quantitative relation between amount of response deprivation and performance under instrumental schedules. As a tentative working hypothesis, we propose that amount of instrumental performance will be a monotonically increasing function of the amount of response deprivation. This hypothesis does not necessarily follow from the hypothesis that the response-deprivation condition is necessary for instrumental performance. The quantitative hypothesis depends on further assumptions concerning the way in which schedule-produced conflicts are resolved. Given the potentially complex manner in which a subject can adapt to a schedule, it seems likely that our hypothesis will not hold for all amounts of response deprivation or all types of schedules. For example, high amounts of response deprivation may produce emotional responses which interfere with instrumental performance. The primary function of the quantitative hypothesis is to provide a simple, empirically testable groundwork for the development of more complex laws of instrumental performance.

The amount of response deprivation produced by a schedule can be defined as the amount of reduction in the contingent response that would occur if the subject performed the instrumental response at its baseline level. This measure can be

written as
$$D_c = O_c - NC,$$

where N is the largest number of repetitions of I such that $NI \leq O_i$. Since $N \simeq (O_i/I)$, then

$$D_c \simeq O_c - \frac{O_i C}{I}. \qquad [2]^5$$

It can be seen from Equation 2 that in an instrumental contingency the amount of response deprivation is an increasing function of the baseline of the contingent response (O_c) and the instrumental requirement (I) but a decreasing function of the baseline of the instrumental response (O_i) and the amount of access to the contingent response (C). Since our working hypothesis assumes that instrumental performance is a monotonically increasing function of the amount of response deprivation, we predict that instrumental performance will be a similar function of these variables. In other words, instrumental performance should be a monotonically increasing function of I and O_c and a monotonically decreasing function of C and O_i. We will review evidence for these predictions in the next few paragraphs.

The Instrumental Requirement

Many studies have shown that instrumental performance is directly related to I, the instrumental requirement for access to the contingent response. Increasing the size of the ratio in fixed-ratio schedules

produces an increase in the rate of key pecking in pigeons (Ferster & Skinner, 1957) and bar pressing in rats (Boren, 1961; Collier, Hirsch, & Hamlin, 1972) and monkeys (Hamilton & Brobeck, 1964). Schaeffer (1965) varied the number of licks required for 10 seconds of running in a wheel and found that the rate of sucrose licking increased as the fixed ratio increased from 5 to 41. We have obtained similar results with instrumental licking of .1% saccharin for contingent 10-second access to .4% saccharin. Licking .1% saccharin increased as the instrumental requirement increased from 5 through 25 seconds.

Some of these studies have shown a limit to the effect of the instrumental requirement on instrumental performance. Beyond a certain point performance stops increasing or even decreases with higher instrumental requirements (e.g., Hamilton & Brobeck, 1964). A possible interpretation of such results is that other adaptive responses occur which compete with the instrumental response (e.g., emotional behavior or escape behavior). A complete account of contingency-produced behaviors must include these behaviors as well. For the present, it can be concluded that this prediction holds only within a certain range of values of I.

The Baseline of the Contingent Response

Several studies have shown that instrumental performance is an increasing function of O_c, the baseline of the contingent response. Premack (1963a) varied O_c by varying the contingent response—running in heavy wheels or light wheels and licking various concentrations of sucrose. Instrumental bar pressing for contingent running or licking was directly related to O_c. Brownstein (1962), using instrumental and contingent sucrose licking in rats, and Premack (1963b), using instrumental and contingent manipulatory responses in monkeys, also found that instrumental performance was an increasing function

---

[5]D_c is measured in the same units as the contingent response. The instrumental response can be measured in different units because O_i and I appear as a ratio in Equation 2, so the units cancel. However, if comparisons are to be made between the effects of different amounts of response deprivation, it will be necessary to be consistent in the measurement of instrumental and contingent responding. Expressing the same schedule in different units will change the value of D_c. The prediction that instrumental performance will be a monotonically increasing function of amount of response deprivation should hold only within a set of schedules (and baselines) measured in consistent units.

of O_c. Indirect evidence also supports this prediction. For example, food-rewarded bar pressing in rats increases with food deprivation (Batten & Shoemaker, 1961)—a manipulation known to increase the amount eaten when food is made freely available (Dufort & Wright, 1962). Similarly, prefeeding the rat decreases the subsequent amount of food-rewarded bar pressing (Skinner, 1938), and we have found (unpublished data, May 1968) that prefeeding decreases the subsequent amount eaten.

Access to the Contingent Response

The variable C, access to the contingent response, has been manipulated infrequently in free-responding experiments (see Kimble, 1961). Several studies reported by Collier (1972) clearly support the prediction that instrumental performance is a decreasing function of C in an instrumental contingency. Collier placed rats under a 24-hour fixed-ratio contingency schedule whereby they obtained all their food by pressing a bar. He found that the number of bar presses per day decreased as the size of the food pellet increased. Other studies have found mixed results (Kling & Schrier, 1971; Weissman, 1963); however, most of these studies have used interval schedules in which the amount of the contingent response obtained is not related to the amount of instrumental responding. The results of such schedules are not clearly predictable at the simple level on which we are employing the response-deprivation concept.

The Baseline of the Instrumental Response

The last prediction, that instrumental performance is a decreasing function of O_i, the baseline of the instrumental response, has received mixed support. Holstein and Hundt (1965, Experiment 2) studied bar pressing in rats for contingent access to sucrose solution. They manipulated O_i, the baseline of bar pressing, by accompanying each bar press with elec-trical stimulation of the brain in the high O_i condition and no stimulation in the low O_i condition. One subject showed less instrumental bar pressing under the high O_i condition than under the low O_i condition, as the hypothesis predicts. The other subject showed no difference between the two conditions.

Schaeffer (1965) reported contradictory results in an experiment on instrumental licking and contingent wheel running in rats. He varied O_i by presenting different groups with one of two different sucrose solutions, water, or an empty tube and found that instrumental licking increased as O_i increased. However, Schaeffer's procedure provided inadequate control of the instrumental requirement, I. The nominal schedule (the terms stated by the experimenter) required the subject to lick five times to free the wheel for 10 seconds; however, once the animal had licked five times, it was allowed to continue licking while the wheel was free. Each time the animal completed another five licks, access to the wheel was reset for 10 seconds. Under these circumstances the subjects continued to lick following completion of I; the amount of extra licking was directly related to O_i (Schaeffer, 1962). Consequently, the actual value of I increased with O_i. From Equation 2 it can be seen that if the actual value of I increased at a greater rate than O_i then the amount of response deprivation also increased with O_i.

In an experiment which investigated this effect, two groups of rats licked either saccharin or water as the instrumental response and received access to wheel running as the contingent response. Half of each group worked under a schedule which replicated Schaeffer's procedure by allowing the subject to terminate instrumental licking (subject-terminated requirement). The other half worked under a schedule in which the experimenter controlled I by withdrawing the tube upon completion of the requirement (experimenter-terminated requirement).

The results of the first schedule were similar to Schaeffer's findings. The group with the higher baseline of the instrumental response showed the largest increase in the instrumental response. The results of the second schedule conformed to the predictions of our working hypothesis; the group with the higher baseline of the instrumental response showed the smallest increase in the instrumental response. Table 2 summarizes these data. These findings illustrate the necessity of defining the schedule precisely in order to apply the response-deprivation hypothesis.

Additional predictions can be generated from Equation 2 by manipulating combinations of the four variables on the right. At least one of these predictions is quite interesting. Since Equation 2 shows the amount of response deprivation to be dependent on the ratio of I to C, identical I/C ratios should produce identical amounts of instrumental performance, regardless of the absolute values of I and C. This prediction was tested in an experiment on .1% and .4% saccharin licking in rats (Allison & Timberlake, 1974). Four schedules employed different values of I and C, but the I/C ratio was a constant 10 .4% licks to 1 .1% lick (IC = 400/40, 300/30, 200/20, or 100/10). All schedules satisfied the response-deprivation condition and produced statistically identical increases in .4% saccharin licking.

The evidence reviewed in this and the preceding sections supports the contention that response deprivation is a key condition of instrumental performance in free-responding experiments. The amount of response deprivation appears directly related to performance in instrumental contingencies. The predictions of our working hypothesis are compatible with available data and suggest new lines of research. Many of the results are not readily interpretable within the Reinforcement Model but fit nicely with an adaptive model in which instrumental

Table 2 Average Increase in Instrumental Licks as a Function of Baseline of the Instrumental Response (O_i) and Type of Schedule

Requirement	Saccharin (high O_i)	Water (low O_i)
Subject terminated	361.4	133.4
Experimenter terminated	122.3	247.8

NOTE: The nominal schedule was I = 30 licks, C = 10 seconds. Entries represent the mean score of seven animals over six days of asymptotic performance. Abbreviation: O_i = baseline of the instrumental response.

performance is conceived as a response to the conflict produced by deprivation of the contingent response.

An important problem for the present approach is how to assess the baseline of a consequence not associated with a specific or easily measured response. The next section discusses this problem in the context of escape and avoidance, but our conclusions are applicable to appetitive contingencies as well.

ESCAPE AND AVOIDANCE CONTINGENCIES

The major problem in generalizing the response-deprivation approach to escape and avoidance behavior is that of measuring the baseline level of the contingent response. This problem occurs because the consequence is not defined in terms of an environmental event, such as relief or relaxation, but these responses are either poorly specified or technically difficult to measure.

Terhune and Premack (1970) suggested one solution to this problem of baseline measurement. They measured the operant level of escape from forced running in a wheel by allowing the rat to press a bar to stop the wheel during baseline. In the contingency session the opportunity to press the bar and stop the wheel was made contingent on an instrumental licking response.

The present authors used a similar technique to measure the baseline of escape from and avoidance of shock in rats (unpublished manuscript, March 1973).

In the 10-minute baseline sessions shock was turned off during the time the subject spent holding one of two bars, Bar *C* (an average of 594 seconds). The time spent holding the ineffective bar, Bar *I*, was also measured. In the contingency sessions, holding Bar *C* did not turn off the shock unless the subject had first held Bar *I*. The instrumental response was thus holding Bar *I* in the presence of shock, and the contingent response was holding Bar *C* in the absence of shock. Holding Bar *I* for *x* seconds earned a certain amount of shock-free time, a constant multiple of *x*, which the subject could use by holding Bar *C*.

Three schedules employed *I/C* ratios of *x/x*, *x/2x*, and *x/10x*, where *x* was the amount of time the subject held Bar *I* prior to holding Bar *C* (*I/C* = 1.0, .5, and .1, respectively). All schedules satisfied the response-deprivation condition, and the amount of response deprivation increased with *I/C* (see Equation 2).[6] The predictions were that all schedules would be directly related to *I/C*. Both predictions were confirmed (see Table 3).

These data suggest that the response-deprivation analysis can be applied successfully to escape and avoidance behavior

---

[6]If O_i is zero, Equation 2 does not predict any effect of varying *I* and *C* because the term containing *I* and *C* goes to zero. A solution is to assume that O_i is not zero but is some fraction less than one.

by defining the contingent consequence in terms of a specific response. This approach should be generalizable to other contingencies in which the contingent response is difficult to specify (e.g., brain stimulation).

RESPONSE SELECTION

The response-deprivation analysis does not provide a complete analysis of instrumental learning but deals only with instrumental performance. In order to restrict attention to performance, it was necessary to learn the contingency (what-leads-to-what) and perform the appropriate instrumental response. In this section we will defend these assumptions and suggest mechanisms of response selection compatible with the adaptive model.

It is easy to take for granted that the subject will perform the appropriate instrumental response in a contingency. Experimenters are skilled in choosing apparatus and contingencies which produce selection and performance of a particular response. This success appears to result from two rules of thumb. First, the experimenter makes sure that the instrumental response is the most salient and the most efficient way of gaining access to the contingent response. Second, the experimenter relates the instrumental response to the behavioral repertoire which the subject displays under the conditions of the contingency. If the rat will

---

Table 3   Asymptotic Time (in seconds) Spent Pressing Bar *I*

Subject	First paired baseline	Schedule (*I/C* = .1)	(*I/C* = .5)	(*I/C* = 1.0)	Second paired baseline
1	0	79	160	205	3
2	0	74	129	220	4
3	1	54	142	232	0
4	0	43	113	194	0
5	2	49	127	182	0
6	1	52	122	188	0
7	5	43	144	190	15
M	1	56	134	202	3
Mdn	1	52	129	194	0

NOTE: Abbreviations: *I* = instrumental requirement   *C* = access to the contingent response.

not lift a bar, it is required to press it or run a maze. If a pigeon will not press a bar, it is required to peck a key. The work on autoshaping of key pecking in pigeons and bar manipulation in rats highlights the ability of experimenters to hit upon instrumental responses that are closely related to the animal's ready-made repertoire (Brown & Jenkins, 1968; Moore, 1971; Peterson, Ackil, Frommer, & Hearst, 1972; Staddon & Simmelhag, 1971). In the case of key pecking and bar manipulation, instrumental-like responses appear to be elicited directly by cues which predict the delivery of the consequences. Failure to use such highly "prepared" responses (Seligman, 1970) may result in great difficulty in learning (Bolles, 1970, 1972; Breland & Breland, 1961, 1966; Shettleworth, 1972).

From the success of these two rules in determining the instrumental response, it is possible to infer the existence of two related mechanisms of response selection. These response-selection devices can be characterized as (a) a comparator mechanism which selects the response most efficient in gaining access to the consequence, and (b) a set of species-typical response mechanisms which result in instrumental-like anticipatory responses to cues predicting the consequence. Both types of devices can be viewed as comparators. The first is an efficiency comparator promoting individual survival. The second is a phylogenetic comparator promoting species survival. These mechanisms act simultaneously. They may select the same response (as in fixed-ratio key pecking in the pigeon), or they may select conflicting responses (as in omission training in autoshaping; Williams & Williams, 1969). Whatever the contingency, response selection should be the result of an interaction between these two types of mechanism.

This brief discussion of response-selection mechanisms should support our contention that the factors which determine response selection can be partly isolated from those which determine

performance. The adaptive model and the response-deprivation approach are compatible with ethological, cognitive, and information-processing approaches to response selection.

APPLICATION NOTES

The following application notes will make explicit some of the experimental procedures and assumptions underlying the present approach.

Baseline Assessment

We assumed that the prediction of instrumental performance depends on the accurate measurement of the instrumental and contingent responses in a paired-baseline session. The paired-baseline assessment was chosen on the grounds that it provided the best estimate of what the subject would do if it were not for the constraints imposed by the schedule. By referring to paired-baseline responding, it should be possible to discover the degree of conflict produced by imposing the schedule.

An alternative to the paired-baseline procedure is the measurement of two separate baselines, one for the instrumental and the other for the contingent response. However, in our opinion the use of two single baselines does not allow as accurate a judgment about the conflict imposed by the schedule as does the paired baseline. In single-baseline sessions the instrumental or contingent response competes for expression only with activities such as exploration, pausing, or grooming. In paired-baseline sessions the instrumental and contingent responses must compete for expression with each other as well. To go from single-baseline sessions to the contingency involves two types of conflict, one imposed by the necessity of two responses sharing the same time period, and the second imposed by the terms of the schedule. The use of paired baseline resolves the time-sharing conflict prior to imposing the schedule, thereby allowing a better estimate of the effects attributable to the schedule alone.

This conclusion does not eliminate the use of other baselines. The response-deprivation condition, defined in relation to the paired baseline, produces a conflict which is probably resolved by a combination of adaptive reactions. We have referred to these reactions collectively as instrumental performance. However, a more complete analysis would begin to divide instrumental performance into several components by employing different baselines, control groups, and measures. In such a task, there is no one baseline, control group, or measure that is appropriate to the analysis of all components of instrumental performance (cf. Seligman, 1969). Each procedure allows the assessment of different aspects of adaptive behavior. We have chosen the paired baseline as a starting point because it appears best suited to define the conflict imposed by a schedule.

The Schedule

To apply our analysis accurately, it is important that the nominal schedule (the one stated by the experimenter) reflect the schedule performed by the subject. The most typical discrepancies between nominal and actual schedules involve greater than I amount of instrumental responding (the subject overshoots the requirement) or less than C amount of the contingent response (the subject fails to use all access time to the contingent response). Neither effect is damaging to most predictions since both errors increase the size of the nominal I/C ratio, thereby leading to the prediction of a larger increase in instrumental responding than would be anticipated from the assumed schedule.

However, as shown by Schaeffer's (1965) results, the difference between nominal and actual schedules can be very important. The strictest control of the schedule parameters is provided by a reciprocal schedule (Allison, 1971) in which the subject must perform amount I

to gain access to the contingent response and then perform amount C of the contingent response in order to regain access to the instrumental response. This schedule ensures that the assumed ratio and the actual ratio experienced by the subject are identical.

One other obvious limitation is that neither I nor C be larger than the animal can perform. Changes in very large I or C values would be expected to have no effect on performance.

A general limitation of the schedules in this paper was their restriction to instrumental schedules—those in which the amount of performance of a clearly defined instrumental response is directly related to the amount of the contingent response obtained. There are many schedules, some quite popular in the literature, which do not meet this test (e.g., variable-interval and fixed-interval schedules). The adaptive model can still be applied to these schedules because they may impose a conflict with baseline responding. The conflict is not easily measured in advance but does depend on the difference between the amount of contingent responding allowed in the contingency and the baseline amount of contingent responding ($O_c - NC$). Clear predictions of performance are more difficult than in instrumental contingencies because no efficient instrumental response is available. The performance of the subject will probably be based on species-typical responses to predictive and frustrative cues.

A related difficulty in applying the present approach occurs when noninstrumental responses available to the subject present the possibility of an alternative resolution to the contingency-imposed conflict. For example, W. McIntosh (unpublished data, August 1972) recently tested the effect of a freely available .1% saccharin solution upon a rat's instrumental nose poking for access to a .4% saccharin solution. When the .1% solution was absent, the subject increased instrumental nose poking over baseline. However, when the .1% solution was available the subject licked it rather than perform the nose-poking response for access to the .4% solution. A complete account of contingency-produced behavior must include considerably more complexity than the present instrumental version of the response-deprivation analysis.

SUMMARY

Some consequences increase the probability of instrumental responses which they follow, and other consequences do not. The empirical law of effect has been used to distinguish these consequences but in a post hoc fashion. The empirical law of effect is challenged as an unfinished step in the development of empirical laws; it is shown to make incorrect predictions and to be closely related to an untestable model of instrumental learning, the reinforcement model.

We suggest that the empirical law of effect and the reinforcement model should be abandoned, and instrumental learning should be separated into several different processes rather than united with one strengthening process. We focus on the prediction of instrumental performance and develop the adaptive model and the concept of response deprivation to account for instrumental performance. The adaptive model views instrumental performance as the result of conflict between baseline responding and the response relations imposed by the schedule. Response deprivation represents a way to quantify the amount of conflict produced by an instrumental schedule.

The data reviewed from free-responding experiments showed that instrumental performance is generally a direct function of the amount of response deprivation, no matter how it is produced. The response-deprivation analysis can be generalized to escape and avoidance contingencies and is compatible with several models of response selection. We conclude that response deprivation is an important and quantifiable determinant of instrumental performance.

REFERENCES

ALLISON, J. Microbehavioral features of nutritive and nonnutritive drinking in rats. *Journal of Comparative and Physiological Psychology*, 1971, **76**, 408–417.

ALLISON, J. & TIMBERLAKE, W. Instrumental and contingent saccharin licking in rats: Response deprivation and reinforcement. *Learning and Motivation*, 1974, **5**, in press.

ATKINSON, R. C., & WICKENS, T. D. Human memory and the concept of reinforcement. In R. Glaser (Ed.), *The nature of reinforcement*. New York: Academic Press, 1971.

BATTEN, D. E., & SHOEMAKER, H. A. The effects of deprivation and incentive palatability on a conditioned operant response. *Journal of Comparative and Physiological Psychology*, 1961, **54**, 577–579.

BLODGETT, H. C. The effect of the introduction of reward upon the maze performance of rats. *University of California Publications in Psychology*, 1929, **4**, 113–134.

BOLLES, R. C. Species-specific defense reactions and avoidance learning. *Psychological Review*, 1970, **77**, 32–48.

BOLLES, R. C. Reinforcement, expectancy, and learning. *Psychological Review*, 1972, **79**, 374–409.

BOREN, J. J. Resistance to extinction as a function of the fixed ratio. *Journal of Experimental Psychology*, 1961, **61**, 304–308.

BRELAND, K., & BRELAND, M. The misbehavior of organisms. *American Psychologist*, 1961, **16**, 681–684.

BRELAND, K., & BRELAND, M. *Animal behavior*, New York: Macmillan, 1966.

BROWN, P. L., & JENKINS, H. M. Autoshaping of the pigeon's keypeck, *Journal of the Experimental Analysis of Behavior*, 1968, **11**, 1–8.

BROWNSTEIN, A. Predicting instrumental performance from the independent rates of contingent responses in a choice situation. *Journal of Experimental Psychology*, 1962, **63**, 29–31.

COLLIER, G. Reinforcement magnitude in free feeding. Paper presented at 13th Annual Meeting of the *Psychonomic Society*, St. Louis, Mo., 1972.

COLLIER, G. H., HIRSCH, E., & HAMLIN, P. H. The ecological determinants of reinforcement in the rat. *Physiology and Behavior*, 1972, **9**, 705–716.

DEESE, J., & HULSE, S. H. *The psychology of learning*. (3rd ed.) New York: McGraw-Hill, 1967.

DUFORT, R. H., & WRIGHT, J. H. Food intake as a function of duration of food deprivation. *Journal of Psychology,* 1962, **53,** 465-468.

EISENBERGER, R., KARPMAN, M., & TRATTNER, J. What is the necessary and sufficient condition for reinforcement in the contingency situation? *Journal of Experimental Psychology,* 1967, **74,** 342-350.

ESTES, W. K. Reinforcement in human learning. In Jack T. Tapp (Ed.), *Reinforcement and behavior.* New York: Academic Press, 1969.

ESTES, W. K. Reward in human learning: Theoretical issues and strategic choice points. In R. Glaser (Ed.), *The nature of reinforcement.* New York: Academic Press, 1971.

FERSTER, C. B., & SKINNER, B. F. *Schedules of reinforcement.* New York: Appleton-Century-Crofts, 1957.

HALL, J. F. *The psychology of learning.* New York: Lippincott, 1966.

HAMILTON, C. L., & Brobeck, J. R. Hypothalamic hyperphagia in the monkey. *Journal of Comparative and Physiological Psychology,* 1964, **57,** 271-278.

HERRNSTEIN, R. J. On the law of effect. *Journal of the Experimental Analysis of Behavior,* 1970, **13,** 243-266.

HILGARD, E. R., & Bower, G. H. *Theories of Learning.* (3rd ed.) New York: Appleton-Century-Crofts, 1966.

HOLSTEIN, S. B., & HUNDT, A. G. Reinforcement of intracranial self stimulation by licking. *Psychonomic Science,* 1965, **3,** 17-18.

JOHN, E. L. *Mechanisms of memory.* New York: Academic Press, 1967.

JOHN, E. L. Electrophysiological studies of conditioning. In G. C. Quarton, J. Melnechuk, & F. O. Schmitt (Eds.), *The neurosciences—A study program.* New York: Rockefeller University Press, 1968.

KIMBLE, G. A. *Hilgard and Marquis' conditioning and learning.* New York: Appleton-Century-Crofts, 1961.

KLING, J. W., & SCHRIER, A. M. Positive reinforcement. In J. W. Kling & L. A. Riggs, *Woodsworth & Schlosberg's experimental psychology.* (3rd ed.) New York: Holt, Rinehart & Winston, 1971.

KUHN, T. *The structure of scientific revolutions.* Chicago: Phoenix, 1964.

LASHLEY, K. S. In search of the engram. *Symposia of the Society for Experimental Biology,* 1950, **4,** 454-482.

LONGSTRETH, L. E. A cognitive interpretation of secondary reinforcement. In J. K. Cole (Ed.), *Nebraska Symposium on Motivation: 1972.* Lincoln: University of Nebraska Press, 1972.

MEEHL, P. E. On the circularity of the law of effect. *Psychological Bulletin,* 1950, **47,** 52-75.

MILLER, N. E. Some reflections on the law of effect produce a new alternative to drive reduction. In M. R. Jones (Ed.), *Nebraska Symposium on Motivation: 1963.* Lincoln: University of Nebraska Press, 1963.

MOORE B. R. On directed respondents. Unpublished doctoral dissertation, Stanford University, 1971.

PERKINS, C. C. An analysis of the concept of reinforcement. *Psychological Review,* 1968, **75,** 155-172.

PETERSON, G., ACKIL, J. E., Frommer, G. P., & HEARST, E. S. Conditioned approach and contact behavior toward signals for food or brain-stimulation reinforcement. *Science,* 1972, **177,** 1009-1011.

POSTMAN, L. The history and present status of the law of effect. *Psychological Bulletin,* 1947, **44,** 489-563.

PREMACK, D. Toward empirical behavior laws: I. Positive reinforcement. *Psychological Review,* 1959, **66,** 219-233.

PREMACK, D. Reversibility of the reinforcement relation. *Science,* 1962, **136,** 255-247.

PREMACK, D. Prediction of the comparative reinforcement values of running and drinking. *Science,* 1963, **139,** 1062-1063. (a)

PREMACK, D. Rate differential reinforcement in monkey manipulation. *Journal of the Experimental Analysis of Behavior,* 1963, **6,** 81-89. (b)

PREMACK, D. Reinforcement theory. In D. Levine (Ed.), *Nebraska Symposium on Motivation: 1965.* Lincoln: University of Nebraska Press, 1965.

PREMACK, D. Catching up with common sense or two sides of a generalization: Reinforcement and punishment. In R. Glaser (Ed.), *The nature of reinforcement.* New York: Academic Press, 1971.

RESTLE, F. The significance of all-or-none learning. *Psychological Bulletin,* 1965, **64,** 313-325.

SCHAEFFER, R. W. Contributions of the operant level of the instrumental response to the reinforcement relation. Unpublished doctoral dissertation. University of Missouri, 1962.

SCHAEFFER, R. W. The reinforcement relation

as a function of instrumental response base rate. *Journal of Experimental Psychology,* 1965, **69**, 419–425.

SELIGMAN, M. E. P. Control group conditioning: A comment on operationism. *Psychological Review,* 1969, **76**, 484–491.

SELIGMAN, M. E. P. On the generality of laws of learning. *Psychological Review,* 1970, **77**, 406–418.

SHETTLEWORTH, S. J. Constraints on learning. In D. S. Lehrman, R. A. Hinde, & E. Shaw (Eds.), *Advances in the study of behavior.* Vol. 4. New York: Academic Press, 1972.

SKINNER, B. F. *The behavior of organisms: An experimental analysis.* New York: Appleton-Century-Crofts, 1938.

SKINNER, B. F. Are theories of learning necessary? *Psychological Review,* 1950, **57**, 193–216.

SKINNER, B. F. *Beyond freedom and dignity.* New York: Knopf, 1971.

SPENCE, K. W. *Behavior theory and conditioning.* New Haven: Yale University Press, 1956.

STADDON, J. E. R. On the notion of cause, with applications to behaviorism. *Behaviorism,* 1973, **1**, 25–64.

STADDON, J. E. R., & SIMMELHAG, V. L. The "superstition" experiment: A reexamination of its implications for the principles of adaptive behavior. *Psychological Review,* 1971, **78**, 3–43.

TERHUNE, J. G., & PREMACK, D. On the pro-portionality between the probability of not-running and the punishment effect of being forced to run. *Learning and Motivation,* 1970, **1**, 141–149.

THORNDIKE, E. L. *The psychology of learning.* New York: Teacher's College, 1913.

TIMBERLAKE, W., & ALLISON, J. Interchangeability of instrumental response and reinforcer based on schedule changes. Paper presented at the meeting of the midwestern Psychological Association, Chicago, May 1973.

WALKER, E. L. Psychological complexity as a basis for a theory of motivation and choice. In D. Levine (Ed.), *Nebraska Symposium on Motivation: 1964.* Lincoln: University of Nebraska Press, 1964.

WALKER, E. L. Reinforcement—the one ring. In J. T. Tapp (Ed.), *Reinforcement and behavior.* New York: Academic Press, 1969.

WEISSMAN, A. Behavioral effects of pairing an S^D with a decreasing limited-hold reinforcement schedule. *Journal of the Experimental Analysis of Behavior,* 1963, **6**, 265–268.

WILLIAMS, D. R., & WILLIAMS, H. Automaintenance in the pigeon: Sustained pecking despite contingent non-reinforcement. *Journal of the Experimental Analysis of Behavior,* 1969, **12**, 511–520.

(Received May 29, 1973)

Chapter 7

Limits of Behavior Change

It is tempting to assume that conditioning occurs automatically whenever environmental and behavioral events are properly correlated. If this were the case, an experimenter could pick any conditioned stimulus and any unconditioned stimulus (for classical conditioning) or any response and any reward (for instrumental conditioning) and by correlating their presence and absence produce an association between them according to the general rules of conditioning. Unfortunately, no such regularity exists, even for the simple stimuli and responses dealt with in the laboratory. The experiments described in this chapter demonstrate vividly the limits of behavior change. Some of these experiments arose out of the ethological research discussed in Chapter 3. Others arose out of research by learning theorists looking for general rules of behavior change, but finding their efforts plagued by the unique nature of the organism they happened to be studying.

We shall start with a relatively brief discussion of the ethological investigation of developmental changes in a single organism that make it more or less receptive to various environmental influences at different periods in its life. Next we shall consider the degree to which fixed-action patterns of various kinds limit or facilitate conditioning. This will lead us to the problem of differences in associability in classical conditioning—specifically, the finding by John Garcia that there are modalities of unconditioned stimuli and conditioned stimuli that are easily associated by a given organism (for example, rats associate tastes with sickness) and others that, with identical procedures, are not easily associated (for example, rats do not associate tastes with peripheral pain). We shall then turn to a similar finding in instrumental conditioning.

Finally, we shall present two theoretical accounts of how behavior change is limited. One, advanced by Martin Seligman at the University of Pennsylvania, applies to each association a degree of "preparedness"—a dimension that indexes the conditionability of that association. Another, advanced by John Staddon and Virginia Simmelhag at Duke University, attempts to separate that part of behavior governed by biological factors peculiar to each organism from that governed by environmental contingencies.

DIFFERENCES IN RECEPTIVITY

After a duck is hatched, there is a period of a few days, called a *critical period,* when it will attach itself faithfully to almost any large moving object. In nature this object is almost always its mother—which explains the strings of ducklings trailing after their mothers around a pond. But the duckling will follow the moving object if it is a goose or even a human being, instead of a duck. Ducklings tend to follow round objects more readily than square objects, but they will follow square objects too. In laboratory experiments ducklings have even followed painted blocks of wood. Whatever the duckling follows during its first few days it is likely to continue to follow, rejecting all other followable objects. If a duckling once starts to follow a human being, it will usually continue to follow that same person even though other people or other animals, including its natural mother, are available. This phenomenon, called *imprinting,* was first identified and studied extensively by the ethologist Konrad Lorenz. Lorenz found that if a duckling was imprinted with a goose during the early critical period and then after several weeks removed and put among other ducks, the next year it would direct its mating activity towards geese (the species with which it had been imprinted) rather than ducks, its own species, with which, moreover, it had spent all of its life except the first few weeks.

Some of these observations about imprinting fit neatly into the conditioning paradigms discussed previously. The first few days of life are bound to be upsetting, to say the least, and it is not unreasonable to suppose that any behavior would be reinforced that provides environmental stability (visual and otherwise). This would include, presumably, a duckling following its mother so as to maintain a single object in its visual field. When, as in nature, this object is also associated with food and warmth, it is not hard to understand why following occurs early in life, why the object followed is a source of reinforcement, and why the reinforcement might be expected to be strong and persistent. What is difficult to explain in terms of conditioning is why the critical period is so rigidly limited to the first few days and why this particular source of reinforcement and not any of the others subsequently experienced should determine future sexual behavior. In the nineteenth century, William James speculated that instincts and learning were inextricably intertwined. The facts of imprinting are a case in point.

The discovery of critical periods for animal learning has given rise to speculations that similar critical periods also exist for human learning. For instance, is there a critical period for the acquisition of language, prior to which language is impossible to learn and subsequent to which it is very difficult to learn? Does experience during some critical period determine once and for all whether we will be "basically" heterosexual or homosexual? As we have indicated previously, American psychology has been largely empiricist in orientation and has tended to answer these questions negatively. Acquisition of language, reading, sexual preferences, and other types of human behavior have been thought to be mostly due to experience—their predictability being attributed more to similar experience than to similar developmental processes.

After many years of comparative neglect, the work of the European ethologists is now having a strong effect on American psychology. This is probably because other limits of behavior change have been discovered by psychologists working within the American empiricist tradition, which have caused them to appreciate more corresponding findings of their European colleagues. It is to these limits, discovered by the empiricists themselves, that we turn next.

DIFFERENCES IN MOTOR REACTIONS

E. L. Thorndike, the American most responsible for the view that learning is automatic, simply a matter of trial and error, observed himself that not all responses could be conditioned equally well. Certain stimuli, responses, and reinforcers seemed to "belong together" more than others for animals of a given species. Thorndike's experiments with cats in a puzzle box illustrate the sensorimotor aspects of *belongingness*. In most of his experiments Thorndike trained cats to pull strings or press levers to get out of the box. In one experiment, however, Thorndike tried to train a cat to yawn to get out of the box. This training proved to be exceedingly difficult. Finally, when Thorndike succeeded, the yawn produced by the cat was an artificial parody of what a yawn should be. The cat opened and closed its mouth but did not really yawn. Evidently yawning and getting out of a box do not "belong together." Thorndike met with similar failures in trying to train a cat to scratch itself to get out of the box. The problem may have been that Thorndike's cats did not naturally yawn or scratch when confined. Rather, they tended to explore the cage and poke their paws and noses into corners. Because the cats did not yawn or scratch Thorndike might have had difficulty teaching them these acts with *any* reward.

Negative Reinforcement

Since Thorndike, similar phenomena have periodically turned up in the psychological literature. Rats can be trained to jump forwards to escape shock

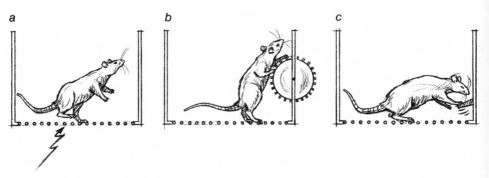

FIGURE 7.1
Why is it easier to teach a rat to escape and avoid shock by turning a wheel than by pressing a bar? (a) Rat's natural reaction to shock is to climb over the wall of its box. (b) Turning a wheel is similar to climbing and, hence, an easy avoidance response to teach and stable once taught. (c) Pressing a bar is not similar to climbing and, hence, a difficult avoidance response to teach and unstable once taught.

to their rear paws and to jump backwards to escape shock to their front paws, but not to jump in the opposite direction, which in nature would be into instead of away from the place of danger. In avoidance studies it has been found easier to train rats to turn a wheel to avoid shock than to press a lever. Turning a wheel resembles the scrambling a rat would do to get out of the box, whereas pressing a lever involves orientation toward the lower part of the box, where the shock is coming from (see Figure 7.1). The movements an organism would normally make to escape from shock or other painful stimuli have been called, by the psychologist Robert Bolles, *species-specific defense reactions.* Each species has a repertoire of such responses ranging from freezing in place, to running away, to attacking. Bolles speculates that the responses corresponding to those the organism would normally emit in the presence of the aversive stimulus are the ones that can be taught as avoidance responses. If one attempts to teach an animal to avoid an aversive stimulus by making a response it would not ordinarily make in the presence of such a stimulus, the animal will learn the avoidance response only very slowly, the response will be unstable, and the performance of the response will look artificial, like the cat's yawning. When the response in an avoidance task is actually antagonistic to a species-specific defense reaction, it will be impossible or nearly impossible to teach. It is no accident, Bolles argues, that many avoidance studies deal with dogs or rats jumping over hurdles to avoid shock. Jumping over a hurdle is just what these animals would do naturally to escape a painful stimulus, so this is a convenient response to study. There is nothing wrong with this as long as it is realized that the association between jumping and avoidance of shock is far from arbitrary, and that any results obtained with this species-specific reaction must be scrutinized carefully before they can be generalized to other responses or other species.

It was once part of the lore of the animal conditioning laboratory that pigeons could not learn to escape or avoid aversive stimuli. What was meant by this piece of shorthand was that pigeons could not be taught to escape or avoid shock by pecking a key. Pigeons can avoid certain stimuli very effectively, as anyone can testify who has tried to catch one on the street. But pecking a key was a convenient response to use with positive reinforcement (we shall see why in a few pages when we discuss autoshaping), and there did not seem to be any reason that pigeons should not learn to escape or avoid shock as they had learned to obtain food. If instrumental conditioning were simply a matter of associating an arbitrarily chosen response with an arbitrarily chosen reinforcer, it would indeed be a mystery if pigeons could not learn to escape or avoid shock by pecking a key. But the mystery disappears as soon as it is realized that the typical species-specific defense reaction of pigeons to sudden, intense shocks, such as those used in escape or avoidance experiments, is running or flying away. Thus it was found that head raising (a movement preparatory to flying) could be taught to pigeons as an escape or avoidance response. Similarly, pigeons could be taught to escape shock by walking to the other side of the chamber. Pecking remained an impossible response to teach until shock was increased gradually instead of applied suddenly. When pulses of shock are introduced gradually, their intensity raised in slow steps from zero to the values usually used, the species-specific defense reaction of pigeons is different form the reaction to sudden, intense shock. With sudden shock the pigeons flee; with gradual shock they attack. When shock is introduced gradually it is in fact unnecessary to specifically train pigeons to peck a key to turn it off. If the key is suddenly illuminated after the shock reaches its maximum value, pigeons will attack the key. Figure 7.2 shows one pigeon pecking the key (actually a button illuminated and extended slightly into the chamber) and another hitting the key with its wings. Both of these responses occurred without any specific training. When the response in question is actually instrumental in turning off the shock it tends to occur earlier and earlier (at less intense shocks) and to be made more efficiently. Instead of attacking the key the pigeon now calmly brushes the key with its wings (if wing-flapping was the initial response) or calmly pecks the key (if pecking was the initial response). The response undergoes a metamorphosis from a natural species-specific defense reaction to an instrumental response that resembles the initial reaction only superficially (as the instrumental yawn of Thorndike's cats resembled a real yawn only superficially).

The physiological psychologist Philip Teitelbaum has speculated that a corresponding metamorphosis occurs in the nervous system as organisms grow

FIGURE 7.2
(a) Pigeon pecking key to escape shock. (b) Pigeon hitting key with wing to escape shock.

older and as they recover from brain damage. In immature or damaged brains, according to Teitelbaum, reflexes are relatively unmodifiable. As brains mature or recover from damage, these fixed reflexes change and become more flexible in function and subject to modification by the techniques of classical or instrumental conditioning.

The species-specific defense reactions described by Bolles are a subcategory of the ethologists' fixed-action patterns, which we discussed in Chapter 3. The species-specific defense reactions are fixed-action patterns that occur in the presence of aversive stimuli. According to Bolles, any responses learned to escape or avoid aversive stimuli are derived from these fixed-action patterns. One need not accept entirely this strongly nativist view to recognize the significant role that fixed patterns of behavior play in negative reinforcement.

Positive Reinforcement

In positive reinforcement, fixed patterns of behavior also play an important role in determining what behavior can and cannot be modified. As in negative reinforcement, these patterns can help or hinder the process of conditioning, depending on whether the conditioning is or is not in harmony with the patterns. Let us first consider how fixed patterns of behavior may hinder conditioning.

Keller Breland set out, after receiving training at Harvard University in animal learning, to apply in a practical setting the principles he had learned. He and his wife Marian trained animals to do various tricks for advertising purposes and for exhibits at state fairs, shopping centers, and the like. The training was accomplished with the use of instrumental conditioning principles. For instance, one exhibit, activiated by a customer putting a quarter into a slot, consisted of a chamber containing a chicken, a miniature basketball basket located a miniature foul-shot away from the chicken, and a short vertical tube a few inches in diameter located between the chicken and the basket. About a second after the chamber was illuminated, a continuous stream of air started from the tube and a ping pong ball popped out of the tube and hung suspended in the air stream. The chicken pecked at the ping pong ball and sent it in the direction of the basket, more often than not into the basket, scoring a point and receiving a short delivery of food from a hopper in the rear of the cage. After three points were scored, the chamber darkened and the show was over. After several such exhibitions the satiated chicken was retired for the day, and a hungry one replaced it. Tricks such as these, taught not only to chickens but also to reindeer, cockatoos, porpoises, and whales, helped confirm the principles discovered in animal laboratories.

In 1961, however, after about fifteen years of this sort of endeavor, the Brelands published a paper called "The Misbehavior of Organisms," in which they recounted some of their failures. The failures all took the same form: an animal would be taught some simple act and would learn the act quickly, but later another response would intrude into the act, becoming more and more frequent until it dominated the animal's performance so strongly that the food reward was delayed or not attained at all. For instance, consider the Brelands' description of the behavior of a pig:

> Here a pig was conditioned to pick up large wooden coins and deposit them in a large "piggy bank." The coins were placed several feet from the bank and the pig required to carry them to the bank and deposit them, usually four or five coins for one reinforcement. (Of course, we started out with one coin, near the bank.)
>
> Pigs condition very rapidly, they have no trouble taking ratios, they have ravenous appetites (naturally), and in many ways are among the most tractable animals we have worked with. However, this particular problem behavior developed in pig after pig, usually after a period of weeks or months, getting worse every day. At first the pig would eagerly pick up one dollar, carry it to the bank, run back, get another, carry it rapidly and neatly, and so on, until the ratio was complete. Thereafter, over a period of weeks the behavior would become slower and slower. He might run over eagerly for each dollar, but on the way back, instead of carrying the dollar and depositing it simply and cleanly, he would repeatedly drop it, root it, drop it again, root it along the way, pick it up, toss it up in the air, drop it, root it some more, and so on.
>
> We thought this behavior might simply be the dilly-dallying of an animal on a low drive. However, the behavior persisted and gained in strength in spite of a severely increased drive—he finally went through the ratios so slowly that he did not get enough to eat in the course of a day. Finally it would take the pig about 10 minutes to transport four coins a distance of about 6 feet. This problem behavior developed repeatedly in successive pigs.

The Brelands describe the interfering behavior of the pigs as *instinctive drift*. By this they mean that the pigs instinctively root (dig in the ground with their snouts), that the experimental situation with food and small wooden objects provided the conditions for exhibiting this behavior, and that the instinctive behavior came to predominate over the instrumentally reinforced behavior. We might call the rooting of the pigs a *species-specific appetitive reaction*, to parallel the species-specific defense reaction described by Bolles. Both the appetitive and defense reactions are subcategories of the fixed-action patterns we have previously discussed.

Now let us turn to situations where fixed patterns of behavior work for, rather than against, conditioning. In Chapter 5 we discussed the concept of instrumental pseudoconditioning. In the example cited there, adrenalin delivered after each bar-press caused the rat to be more active and hence press the bar more often—so adrenalin, although it increased bar-presses, may not have done so via the mechanism of instrumental conditioning. But suppose the reward used is truly rewarding (when tested against a pseudoconditioning control) but *also* elicits some behavioral pattern that enhances measured responding. This is often the case with food—the behavior elicited by feeding enhances the particular response that food is supposed to reinforce.

In Chapter 3, in discussing the experiment of Staddon and Simmelhag, we noted that with pigeons, periodic free presentation of food generates pecking of one kind or another, usually pecking at the wall of the cage. If there is an illuminated key on the wall and periodic reinforcements are dependent on pecking the key (as with a fixed-interval schedule of reinforcement), many of the pecks on the key can be attributed to the periodic food presentations themselves rather than to the instrumental dependency of the food presentations on pecking. In other words, in many instrumental-conditioning situations a positive feedback process is at work. The food causes a pattern of behavior, which (as the experimenter has arranged) will produce more food, which in turn produces more of the behavior, and so on. In the Staddon and Simmelhag experiment, the pattern of pecking was the same in the group for which food deliveries were coming freely at fixed intervals as it was in the group for which food (also at fixed intervals) was dependent on pecks at a key. The only difference between the dependent and independent groups was the location of the pecks: the dependent group pecked at the key and the independent group pecked at the wall. For the dependent group (on an ordinary fixed-interval schedule), the positive feedback process must have been working—pecks produced food, which produced more pecks—the pattern of pecking corresponding to the pattern of food as it did for the group for which reinforcement was independent of pecking. The Staddon and Simmelhag experiment shows that a hungry pigeon pecking a key to produce food hardly represents an arbitrary instrumental-conditioning situation. Just as a shocked dog or rat will jump over a hurdle, a hungry pigeon will peck something. The instrumental contingency served in the Staddon and Simmelhag experiment to direct the pecking onto the key, but as we shall see in a moment, directed pecks can occur even without instrumental contingencies, provided the stimulus conditions are changed somewhat.

An experimental procedure that shows vividly how fixed patterns of behavior can interact with instrumental responding is the procedure called *autoshaping*. Autoshaping is a recent discovery and has not yet been defined precisely.

But its basic message is clear: behavior can be "shaped" rapidly when species-specific reactions and associations are brought into play.

In ordinary instrumental conditioning experiments, shaping is a lengthy process. The experimenter first waits until the animal orients towards the response manipulandum, then he presents food. This increases the probability of such orientation in the future. The next time that the experimenter observes the orientation he withholds food until the animal comes somewhat closer to the manipulandum, then closer and closer in successive approximations until the desired response is emitted. (Figure 7.3a shows how a pigeon's behavior is shaped to peck a key. Recently, however, it has been discovered that not only do pigeons tend to peck when food is presented freely, but they will also direct their pecks at a response key if illumination of the key is paired with food. In 1968 Paul L. Brown and Herbert M. Jenkins published the first report of the phenomenon. Their basic finding was that when a hungry pigeon was exposed to periodic free presentations of food, each preceded by a brief (3- or 8-second) illumination of the response key, most pigeons would peck the key after about 40 to 50 such presentations. (Figure 7.3b shows how autoshaping is used to get a pigeon to peck a key, without reinforcing successive approximations, by automatically pairing the key illumination with food.)

The process shown in Figure 7.3c is called *negative autoshaping.* It was first reported by David and Harriet Williams. Until the first peck at the key, the process is exactly the same as positive autoshaping shown above it. When the pigeon pecks the key, however, food is not delivered. Thus, there are two processes working in opposition in negative autoshaping. Pecking is stimulated by the autoshaping procedure, which acts as long as the pigeon does not peck. When the pigeon does peck, however, food is withheld—an instrumental contingency equivalent to *omission,* which tends to decrease pecking. The result of the negative autoshaping procedure is that pigeons peck (as they do with the positive autoshaping procedure) and continue to peck at a slow rate, sometimes going for many trials without food because they pecked the key. Evidently autoshaping is a strong process since it overcomes the omission contingency and keeps the pigeon pecking the key. How does autoshaping work? The matter is in some dispute. At first, it was thought that successive approximations to a key-peck were being adventitiously reinforced by the food presentations. (The word "autoshaping" is derived from this theory. It connotes an automatic shaping of the response. We shall, however, use the word to refer to the procedure, not the theory.) But this simple instrumental-conditioning theory cannot really account for autoshaping because when the obvious test is made, of looking to see whether the pigeon is moving closer and closer to the key on successive trials, no such observation is made. There is also some evidence that the duration of the key-peck (the time that the pigeon's beak is in contact with the key) in autoshaping, especially negative autoshaping, is shorter than in regular instrumental conditioning. Another line of evidence against this theory

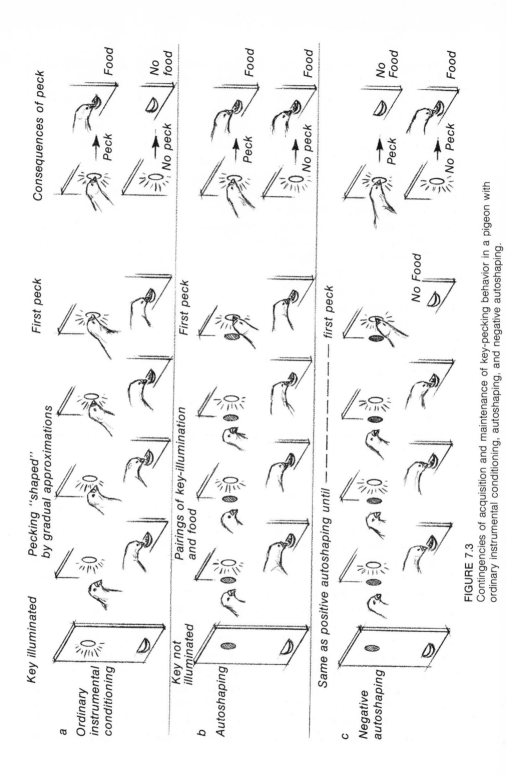

FIGURE 7.3
Contingencies of acquisition and maintenance of key-pecking behavior in a pigeon with ordinary instrumental conditioning, autoshaping, and negative autoshaping.

is that in negative autoshaping pecking persists after the first peck. To explain such maintenance the adventitious instrumental reinforcement that is supposed to reinforce pecking would have to overcome the explicit instrumental omission contingency arranged to reinforce nonpecking. It seems unlikely to most experienced researchers that this could be the case. Whatever maintains pecking in this situation would have to be stronger than adventitious reinforcement would be.

A better explanation for the pigeons' behavior in this situation is an innate tendency to peck in a situation where food is probable. The onset of the key light just before food delivery provides a signal delineating the period of high food probability. This signal acts as what ethologists would call a *releaser* for the peck. To some extent the signal is a *learned* releaser; in classical conditioning, a signal (a conditioned stimulus) by virtue of pairing with the unconditioned stimulus comes to cause a response ordinarily elicited by the unconditioned stimulus. This would explain the pigeon's tendency to peck during the signal (as it does at the food itself), but it does not explain why the pigeon directs its peck at the key. To some extent the onset of the key light must also be an *innate* releaser for pecking (provided there is an already established tendency to peck). The key itself perhaps resembles the food to some extent and releases pecks just as, in nature, the sight of a grain of food releases pecks.

Autoshaping, easy as it is to establish, depends on a number of conditions. (1) The pigeon should be hungry. Although autoshaping may work with relatively satiated pigeons, it works better with hungry ones. (2) Food should be presented occasionally in the situation. Turning the key light on and off does not work if no food is present. (3) The key light must be turned on and off. Continuous illumination does not work even with food present. (4) The key light should signal a high probability of food; that is, it should come on just before the food, and it should be on for a brief time relative to the time it is off (the inter-trial intervals). As the key light loses its power to signal reinforcement (by being left on too long, for instance) it also loses its power to autoshape pecking.

Autoshaping works with water reward as well as food. The peck at the key with water reward has a different topography from that with food reward: the pigeon seems to be sipping at the key instead of pecking at the key as it does with food reward. Autoshaping also works with electric-shock reduction. Pigeons will peck at a key when the key light is turned on just before electric shock is reduced. This may be because the shock, turned on gradually, elicits attack at the lit key. Responses of animals other than pigeons can also be autoshaped. Monkeys, for instance, have been trained by autoshaping to press a lit panel.

Autoshaping is a phenomenon that is being studied intensively now in several laboratories. New information may change the picture, but it seems now as

	1 Positive rein-forcement	2 Auto-shaping	3 Negative auto-shaping	4 Auto-shaping with negative rein-forcement	5 Negative rein-forcement	6 Negative rein-forcemer
I Organism	Pigeon	Pigeon	Pigeon	Pigeon	Pigeon	Pigeon
II Reinforce-ment	Food (pigeon hungry)	Food (pigeon hungry)	Food (pigeon hungry)	Shock reduction (gradual shock onset)	Shock reduction (sudden shock onset)	Shock reductio (sudden shock onset)
III Stimulus conditions	Key light on con-tinuously	Key light precedes food	Key light precedes food	Key light precedes shock reduction	Chamber con-tinuously illuminated	Key ligh on con-tinuousl
IV Behavior elicited	Pecking, but not at key	Pecking at key	Pecking at key	Pecking at key. Flapping wings at key	Flight	Flight
V Instrumental response required	Pecking at key	—	Not pecking at key	—	Head raising	Pecking at key
VI Resultant behavior	Instru-mental response easy to shape	Same as IV	Pecking at key (at low rate)	Same as IV	Instru-mental response easy to shape	Instru-mental response difficult to shape

FIGURE 7.4
How patterns of behavior interact with various conditioning procedures.

if the autoshaped peck emerges from a combination of innate patterns of be-havior, innate releasing stimuli, and classical conditioning.

Why is autoshaping important? It may seem as if we have spent too much time on this phenomenon. Why worry about the responses of a seemingly insignificant organism in an artificial environment? But autoshaping is impor-tant for several reasons. On one hand it has shown psychologists that the sup-posedly simply case of a pigeon pecking a key in a Skinner box is actually much

7	8	9	10	11	12
Negative rein-forcement	Negative rein-forcement	Positive rein-forcement (secondary)	Positive rein-forcement	Classical con-ditioning	Classical con-ditioning
Rat	Rat	Pig	Cat	Rat	Rat
Shock reduction (sudden shock onset)	Shock reduction (sudden shock onset)	Food (pig hungry)	Escape from puzzle box	Sickness (from X ray or LiCl)	Sickness (from X ray or LiCl)
Chamber con-tinuously illuminated	Chamber con-tinuously illuminated	Tokens present	Inside of box	Tasty water	Bright-noisy water
Climbing out of cage	Climbing out of cage	Rooting	Explor-atory, manipu-lative behavior	Sup-pression of drinking during sickness. Avoidance of water	Sup-pression of drinking during sickness. No avoidance of water
Turning wheel	Pressing lever	Placing tokens in piggy bank	Yawning	———	———
Instru-mental response easy to shape	Instru-mental response difficult to shape	Instru-mental response learned but gradually replaced by rooting	Instru-mental response very difficult to shape	Same as IV	Same as IV

more complicated than it at first appears. The activity of pigeons studied in the Skinner box is not purely instrumental but is superimposed on the innate behavior patterns of the pigeon and "contaminated" by classical-conditioning effects. On the other hand, autoshaping offers a unique opportunity to study how these various types of conditioning interact with each other and with the organism's behavior patterns under conditions in which behavior is more easily observed and measured than in most other experimental environments and certainly more than in the natural environment. The Skinner box offers the possibility that the various components of behavior can be studied in inter-action and the contribution of each evaluated. Finally, autoshaping is worth studying because it involves the basic components of all learning—human and otherwise—innate patterns shaped to a greater or lesser extent by environmental contingencies. Autoshaping, as an instance of such an interaction, takes its place among the other activities we have considered in this chapter on the limits of learning. Figure 7.4 (columns 1–10) arranges several of these activities to show how innate patterns can interact with conditioning.

DIFFERENCES IN ASSOCIABILITY

In classical conditioning the CS-US relationship gives rise to an altered re-sponse. In instrumental conditioning the response-reinforcement relationship gives rise to an altered response. The limitations we have so far been discussing refer to the influence of the situation in which learning takes place on the alter-ation of the response. Motor reactions to the situation either facilitate or hinder the response (as columns 1–10 of Figure 7.4 illustrate). Now we turn to a more fundamental type of limitation—a limitation of the associability inherent in the CS-US and response-reinforcement *associations* themselves. It turns out that associations, like motor reactions, are by no means arbitrary. That this is so can perhaps best be illustrated by describing an experiment by John Garcia and Robert A. Koelling published in 1966. In previous experiments it had been found extremely easy to train rats to form an association between sickness (usually caused by X-radiation) and taste (that is, rats would avoid the food they had eaten before becoming sick), but it had been difficult to train rats to form an association between sickness and visual or auditory stimuli. These experimental results fitted in with what was known about rats' natural avoid-ance of poisons. For centuries man has been trying to get rid of rats by poi-soning them, but without much success. For instance, if the basement of a butcher shop containing barrels of salted meats were infested with rats, the owner might poison a small dish of sugar and leave it out for the rats. But the rats would each eat only a drop of the sugar (even though it tasted good), would become sick, and would thereafter avoid sugar. They would keep eating the meat, they would not die, and they would not leave the cellar. This phenom-enon, of tasting a bit of new food and then, if becoming sick, avoiding it there-after, is known as bait-shyness. It is an annoying habit of rats, which on their part is quite adaptive since it makes them difficult to poison. What Garcia and Koelling wanted to investigate was the relative ease with which rats associ-ated sickness with taste, but not with sights or sounds.

Garcia and Koelling tested four groups of rats in classical conditioning experiments, diagrammed in Figure 7.5. All the rats were given the same CS, what the experimenters called "bright-noisy-tasty water." By means of a drink-

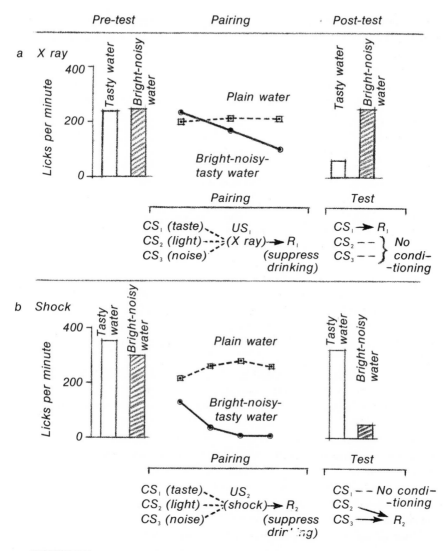

FIGURE 7.5
Garcia and Koelling's association experiment, with X ray and shock used as the aversive stimuli.

ometer (see Figure 2.2) each lick at a tube was counted and followed by a brief flash of light and a click. The water in the tube was flavored with saccharin (or salt for some of the rats), so each lick was followed by a gustatory, a visual, and an auditory stimulus. This combined CS was then paired with different aversive stimuli (US's) for the four groups of rats. Two groups were given aversive stimuli that made them sick; one sickness group was given X rays while they were drinking and the other given the poison lithium chloride in the drinking water (not shown in Figure 7.5). The other two groups were shocked—one immediately after each lick and the other with the shock delayed slightly (only the immediate-shock group is shown in Figure 7.5). Interspersed with the conditioning trials (each conditioning trial consisted of a 20-minute daily period of drinking paired with the aversive stimulus) were trials on which plain water was presented, without the aversive stimulus. In addition, prior and subsequent to the pairing of CS and US, each group was tested with the tasty water and bright-noisy water separately. Figure 7.5 shows the results for one sickness group and one shock group (the other groups followed suit). During the pre-test, the rats in both groups drank large quantities of both the bright-noisy water and the tasty water, in about equal proportions. During the experiment proper, both groups of rats gradually came to stop drinking the bright-noisy-tasty water (although on alternate days they drank plenty of plain water). Evidently both sickness and shock caused the rats to stop drinking. But on the post-tests, the rats that had been made sick did not drink the tasty water and did drink the bright-noisy water, and the rats that had been shocked did not drink the bright-noisy water but did drink the tasty water. Although both sickness and shock suppressed drinking, each became associated with only some of the stimuli accompanying drinking. Sickness became associated with taste (and not with lights and sounds), whereas shock became associated with lights and sounds (and not with taste).

These results clearly show that one cannot simply pair CS's and US's arbitrarily and expect conditioning to occur. Whether conditioning occurs will depend on which CS's are paired with which US's. For the rat, tastes and sickness "belong together."

Columns 11 and 12 of Figure 7.4 show how this procedure compares with the others we have discussed. In other noninstrumental paradigms (signified by no entry in row V) the behavior elicited is relatively simple (pecking or wing flapping), but with this procedure the behavior elicited relates to the particular stimulus used. Here it is not the response alone that is observed, but the association of the response with a given stimulus.

Other experiments have shown that for other animals the belongingness of taste and sickness is not so strict as for rats. For instance, the quail quite readily associates visual stimuli with sickness. This makes sense from a biological point of view since the rat has poor vision and eats many different kinds of food with many different tastes, but the quail has excellent vision and eats very few kinds of food, mostly consisting of hard grain, which it swallows whole and therefore hardly tastes. If the quail had to depend on taste to avoid poisoned food it would have a great deal of difficulty surviving.

Learned taste aversions have been invoked to explain why animals tend to select a diet that keeps them supplied with sufficient vitamins. The theory is that a vitamin-deficient diet actually makes animals sick and that the taste of it thereby becomes aversive. The animals then eat other foods instead, until they find foods that do not make them sick (that contain the lacking vitamin). Paul Rozin at the University of Pennsylvania has found that rats will avoid a vitamin-deficient diet that has made them sick even when they are hungry and no other food is available.

If animals show an avoidance of tastes associated with sickness, they might also be expected to show a preference for tastes associated with recovery from sickness. Although this complementary effect is not so strong or all-pervasive as the taste–sickness effect, some studies have found preferences in rats for foods associated with recovery from sickness.

A peculiarity of taste–sickness associations is that they are best formed with novel tastes. Rats can learn to associate familiar tastes with sickness, but only after many trials and with a difficulty commensurate with that of associating sights and sounds with sickness.

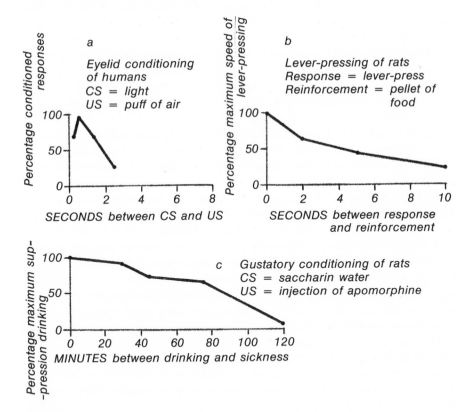

FIGURE 7.6
How delay affects conditioning with classical, instrumental, and gustatory procedures. [Data for (a) from Reynolds, 1945; data for (b) from Perin, 1943; data for (c) from Garcia, Ervin, and Koelling, 1966.]

Perhaps the most remarkable difference between taste–sickness association and the other types of learning that have been studied is the long delay possible between CS and US with the taste–sickness effect. To give an idea of the difference, Figure 7.6 shows, in parts (a) and (b), two standard delay functions, the first for classical and the second for instrumental conditioning, and in part (c) a delay function for taste–sickness learning. The various functions found in various laboratories differ in detail but there has been general agreement that the optimum delay between CS and US in classical conditioning is about 0.5 second, and that in instrumental conditioning, immediate reinforcement is best. The delay function in Figure 7.6c, published by Garcia, Ervin, and Koelling, is of quite a different order, with conditioning at a high level even after a 1-hour delay. In this study each group of rats was given a sweet solution and then made sick later after a period indicated on the abscissa. There were five pairings of taste and sickness for each rat. Then the rats were tested for how much sugar solution they would drink. Even the group with 3-hours delay drank less than the controls. Subsequent studies have found taste–sickness conditioning with delays between CS and US of up to 6 or 8 hours.

The question of why such delays are possible with taste–sickness conditioning and seemingly not possible with other combinations of CS and US has not been finally settled. One theory is that tastes are not interfered with by other stimuli during the delay period, whereas stimuli such as sights and sounds are. Another theory is that tastes linger in the mouth during the delay period so that they are still there when sickness comes on. But control experiments show that despite intervening tastes, even novel ones, rats still associate sickness with tastes experienced several hours earlier. The theory that tastes linger in the mouth is also not confirmed. Taste–sickness associations are formed when sufficient plain water is drunk during the intevening interval to wash away the taste. More significantly, rats learned to discriminate between high and low concentrations of a sour solution when one concentration was followed by sickness and the other was not, by avoiding the particular concentration paired with sickness. Since the two concentrations have similar aftertastes it would be hard to explain taste aversions as aversions formed for aftertastes. Again, a mechanism useful for survival has been found. Long delays between CS and US help the rat to survive. Otherwise the rat would not learn to associate slow-acting poisons with their tastes and poisoning rats would be an easy job.

Psychologists studying the taste–sickness association speculate that a separate physiological system governs this important type of association. It is as if when a rat becomes sick, this mechanism looks back over the past several hours and if any novel foods have been eaten, provides the rat with an aversion for those foods. This physiological mechanism, whatever it might be, is a primitive structure. Taste aversions have been taught to deeply anesthetized rats. In an anesthetized rat the higher nervous centers are presumably not functioning.

Pre-established associative tendencies play a part also in instrumental conditioning. The Polish psychologist Jerzy Konorski and his students have found, in experiments testing various discriminative stimuli with instrumental responses of dogs, that certain stimuli, responses, and reinforcers seem to work together better than others. For instance, "go–no go" response alternatives, in which the reinforcer follows the response but is withheld if the response is withheld (for example, food reinforces lifting of the paw in the presence of the stimulus) work best with a discriminative stimuli that vary in intensity or quality (for example, a metronome signals reinforcement availability; a buzzer signals that reinforcement is unavailable, even if response is made). Under these conditions dogs will learn to respond (lift a paw) or withhold response under appropriate stimulus conditions. If, instead of buzzer versus metronome, the "go–no go" response is taught with a single stimulus, say the buzzer, coming from in front of the dog to signal reinforcement availability and from behind the dog to signal unavailability, the dog learns slowly, if at all, to respond and withhold its response appropriately.

Conversely, when the response is itself directional (for example, lifting the left paw followed by food in the presence of one stimulus, lifting the right paw followed by food in the presence of another stimulus), then directional stimuli (buzzer from the front or from the rear) are quite appropriate (the dog learns fast) but stimuli differing in intensity or quality are inappropriate (the dog learns slowly or not at all). Konorsky believes that the ease or difficulty of discrimination with various arrangements of stimuli, responses, and reinforcers is due to the properties of the nervous system. The behavior of his dogs cannot be explained simply in terms of their orientation to various stimuli or to other responses elicited by the discriminative stimuli or the reinforcer (that is, in a way that would fit easily into Figure 7.4) since the dogs can be trained fairly easily to respond in a direction opposite to the direction of the stimulus (for example, raising the right paw when the buzzer comes from the left), which should be difficult if orientation toward the stimulus were the critical determinant of ease of learning in his experiments.

The fact that in both classical and instrumental conditioning certain types of stimuli and responses are seemingly easier to associate than others probably has something to do with the structures of the nervous system, particularly the brain (with classical conditioning, primitive brain structures; with instrumental conditioning, perhaps more complicated structures). If learning is mediated by the brain it stands to reason that, whatever mechanisms the brain uses, it will be more disposed to some sorts of learning than others because they are more suited to those mechanisms. The mechanisms themselves are almost completely unknown at the present time. To what extent they are innate structures and to what extent they are formed by experience is undetermined as well. It may be, for instance, that some early common experience with tastes and sickness by rats, conceivably during nursing and weaning or possibly even during the fetal stage, lays down the pattern of the mechanism; or it may be that the mechanism is inherited by the rat, just as its two eyes, four legs, and tail are inherited. But most likely, the adult rat's tendency to associate taste and sickness derives from a combination of biological evolution and experience. The same would hold for other sorts of associative tendencies, such as those discovered by Konorski.

THEORETICAL CONSIDERATIONS

This chapter contains an unusual assortment of findings, which do not fit together easily and which certainly do not fit easily into the simple paradigms of classical and instrumental conditioning we have described. In this section we shall try to impose some organization on these diverse facts, relying on two theoretical papers, both of which appeared in the *Psychological Review*. The first, by Martin Seligman, appeared in 1970 and is called, "On the Generality of the Laws of Learning." Seligman argues that laws of learning formulated on the basis of observation of one species in one situation cannot be generalized to other species and other situations without severe modifications. The second article, by John Staddon and Virginia Simmelhag, appeared in 1971 and is called, "The Superstition Experiment: A Reexamination of its Implications for the Principles of Adaptive Behavior." We have already discussed the data that Staddon and Simmelhag collected; but in their paper they also advance a theory that interprets, not only their own data, but also much of the data discussed in this chapter, in terms of broad evolutionary principles.

Preparedness

The evidence of differences in associability has led Seligman to define a dimension he calls *preparedness*. An organism may be prepared, unprepared, or contraprepared to form a given association—preparedness presumably reflecting the survival value of the association for the species as a whole. In this view, Garcia's rats are prepared to associate tastes with sickness but unprepared or even contraprepared to associate tastes with electric shock. Similarly, Konorski's dogs are prepared to associate directional stimuli with directional responses but unprepared or contraprepared to associate directional stimuli with "go–no go" responses. A contraprepared association is one the organism shows extreme resistance to learning. A canary, for instance, might be contraprepared to associate the image of a cat with anything but danger, although even such learning is not impossible. Preparedness does not refer to a hard-and-fast category but to a dimension along which associations may vary.

Preparedness is measured by ease of learning—for instance, number of trials to reach a certain probability of responding—but stands, according to Seligman, for something more than just ease of learning. Seligman speculates that the way in which an organism learns a prepared association differs from the way in which it learns an unprepared association. Some evidence indicates that there may be different rules of learning for prepared and unprepared associations. For instance, prepared associations may be learned with long delays, may extinguish more slowly once learned, may be less subject to interference from other stimuli, may be learned even under anesthesia, and may be learned by humans despite "knowledge" to the contrary (as when people are afraid of heights, snakes, and certain other natural phenomena even while admitting that their fears are irrational).

To be really useful, the concept of preparedness would have to summarize some group of characteristics that prepared associations show and unprepared associations do not. As it stands now, there is little evidence that properties such as long-delay learning are common to all easily learned associations. Until a set of rules is found consistent from one easily learned association to another, or until a common underlying physiological mechanism is found for easily learned associations, the concept of preparedness will be limited in usefulness except as a synonym for ease of learning.

Seligman intends the concept of preparedness to be a stimulant to further research which would formulate laws appropriate to prepared, unprepared, and contraprepared associations and would discover exactly how preparedness limits learning. There is a danger, however, that when an attempt at learning fails, the concept of preparedness will cause the teacher or learner to focus wholly on the organism doing the learning and not at all on its environment. When a child fails to learn the multiplication tables, is it because he was unprepared to learn them or because his teacher was unprepared to teach them to him? Certainly both are responsible. Even with simpler learning situations it is not always clear where the problem lies. To take an example from the beginning of this chapter, it was once thought that pigeons could not learn to escape electric shocks by pecking a key. The association in question is that between key-pecking and shock reduction. Is this association unprepared? One might suspect so, but when electric shock is increased gradually pigeons easily learn to peck to escape and even to avoid shock. (See Figure 7.4, columns 4 and 5). *Now* the pigeon is seen to have been prepared to learn to peck a key to escape shock. What counts, obviously, is the way the stimuli are presented as well as the way the organism is constructed.

Many of the methods we use to teach animals and humans various associations are traditional, the results of historical accident. It is tempting to define preparedness in terms of these traditional techniques, and then when learning does not occur, to blame the failure on the organism rather than the technique. But a new technique, if it works, soon becomes standard and what seemed unusual at first soon becomes simple. A child may seem unprepared to learn a given subject unless unusual methods are used. But once the unusual methods become usual the child is seen to have been prepared all along. The prominent developmental psychologist Jerome Bruner has claimed that no subject is too difficult to be taught at some level to any child, no matter how young. This would seem a more constructive attitude to have, in general, than the attitude that some organisms simply can't be taught certain things. And it is an attitude that, despite the material in this chapter, is not out of line with the facts.

Behavior and Evolution

Staddon and Simmelhag, in their complex experimental and theoretical article, draw an analogy between the processes of evolution and learning. It has been noted many times that reinforcement promotes learning of instrumental responses in much the same way that natural selection promotes the survival of adaptive organisms. (See Figure 5.3.) But Staddon and Simmelhag carry the analogy further. Pointing out that behavior and the mechanisms by which it is modified are part of biological inheritance, they suggest that evolutionary principles may underlie both production and selection of behavior.

Evolution depends on two kinds of principles. First there are the principles of *variation,* such as the laws of genetics, which ensure phenotypic diversity. These principles are responsible for the shapes of the original population distributions in Figures 1.17 and 5.3. Then there are the principles of *selection,* which, operating through the population's interaction with the environment, permit certain members, and not others, to survive. In order to see how Staddon and Simmelhag arrived at their comparison between the evolution of species and the evolution of behavior within the lifetime of a single organism, we must review their experimental findings.

In their experiment, Staddon and Simmelhag presented food to pigeons at fixed 14-second intervals. The food came every 14 seconds regardless of the behavior of the pigeon. This program of periodic free food presentation elicited two sorts of behavior, *interim* and *terminal.* Interim behavior usually consisted of grooming or exploring the cage. Terminal behavior occurred during the period when food was likely to be delivered and usually consisted of pecking. From these observations and those of similar experiments with other organisms, Staddon and Simmelhag classified the sorts of behavior likely to be interim and terminal, and speculated on the function of these two classes of behavior. The sorts of behavior likely to be interim are those which will produce some reinforcement when a principal source of reinforcement is improbable. In the apparatus of this experiment there were few external sources of reinforcement other than the food delivered every 14 seconds. But the pigeons could still groom themselves or hunt along the floor for stray pieces of food. These, in fact, were the interim responses observed. If other opportunities had been available, the pigeons would have exhibited a greater variety of behaviors during this period. Data from studies of *adjunctive* and *aggressive* behavior, in which the subjects—usually pigeons or rats—have been provided opportunities for other interim behaviors, show that during such interim periods acts such as drinking, fighting, and sex increase markedly. In the absence of these opportunities the pigeons would have tried to escape from the situation. When escape is impossible, the pigeons groom or hunt on the floor or in the hopper for stray pieces of food. In other words, interim behavior with respect to one reinforcer (food in this case) consists of the search for other reinforcers during the period when the first reinforcer is improbable. Terminal behavior, on the other hand, consists usually of responses appropriate to the reinforcer. When the reinforcer is food, pigeons peck during the terminal period.

This alternation between interim behavior during periods of low reinforcement probability and terminal behavior during periods of high reinforcement probability, Staddon and Simmelhag claim, corresponds to genetic laws of variation of biological evolution. That is, the natural variation in interim and terminal responding corresponds to the natural variations of genes in the reproduction of species. Almost all of the behavior discussed in this chapter, and the behavior involved in classical conditioning as well, falls into this category. In Figure 7.4, row IV, labeled "behavior elicited," should, according to this theory, be labeled "terminal responses observed." The generation of these responses corresponds to laws of variation and is strongly dependent on the biological makeup of the behaving organism. Classical conditioning would be the occurrence of the terminal response, row IV, given the prior conditions, rows I (organism), II (reinforcement), and III (stimulus conditions). A *prepared* association, in Seligman's terms, would be observed when the conditions of rows I, II, and III make the terminal response, noted in row IV, occur in the presence of the stimulus, row III. (In Garcia's experiment, column 11, this response would be suppression of drinking and the stimulus would be tasty water.) An *unprepared* association would be observed when the conditions of rows I, II, and III do *not* make the terminal response, row IV, occur in the presence of the stimulus, row III. (In Garcia's experiment, column 12, this response would be suppression of drinking and the stimulus would be bright-noisy water). Of course, this explanation does no more than the preparedness explanation to account for easily learned associations. It only relates prepared associations to elicited behavior (interim and terminal responses). Thus, Seligman's notion of preparedness is not contradictory to Staddon and Simmelhag's theory, but rather complementary to it.

To complete our discussion of the principles of variation we need to know how interim and terminal responses varied in the Staddon and Simmelhag experiment. Interim responses were highly variable throughout the several months of experimentation (one 15-minute session each day). Sometimes the pigeons would preen, sometimes they would circle the floor or flap their wings, and so on, during the interim period. Terminal responses were variable at first, the pigeons occasionally putting their heads into the hopper during the terminal period; but as the experiment progressed the terminal responses became more fixed and all the pigeons uniformly settled down to moving along

the front wall, where the food hopper was, and pecking. At the beginning, the
pigeons shifted several responses from the interim to terminal periods and back
again. It was almost as if they were trying out various terminal responses. Once
they selected pecking as a terminal response, however, it remained the most
frequent terminal response for the rest of the experiment, with only occasional
brief shifts to other terminal responses.

Even when reinforcement is contingent on behavior the principles of variation (including instinctive mechanisms such as fixed-action patterns and associative mechanisms such as classical conditioning) govern what interim and
terminal responses will occur. What, then is left for the other evolutionary
principles, analogous to natural selection, which Staddon and Simmelhag call
the *principles of reinforcement?* Very little i. deed. When reinforcement is made
dependent on some particular behavior it can act only to prevent that behavior
from being shifted from a terminal response to an interim response. The reinforcement contingency does not strengthen the response, according to Staddon
and Simmelhag. It simply prevents that response from being shifted into the
interim category (it props up the response), just as natural selection does not
directly strengthen any trait but merely prevents that trait from dying out.
When reinforcement is made dependent on a naturally occurring terminal
response, as when a pigeon's peck is reinforced, training is easy. When reinforcement is made dependent on another response, such as preening, which
would normally occur only during the interim period, training is more difficult.
Following a behavior like preening by food reinforcement makes it ipso facto
a terminal response. On one hand, making food dependent on preening tends to
preserve preening as a terminal response according to the principles of reinforcement. On the other hand, the principles of variation will act to substitute
another more appropriate terminal response such as pecking. This conflict
makes training much more difficult than when food is dependent on pecking in
the first place.* When, as with negative autoshaping, food is dependent on not-
pecking, the conflict is extreme, with pecking and not-pecking alternating as
the principles of variation and reinforcement compete.

Extinction occurs automatically when reinforcement is withdrawn, according to Staddon and Simmelhag, because the prop that was keeping the response
from being shifted out of the terminal category is removed. With reinforcement
dependent on a terminal response, behavior during the terminal period will
vary less widely. Only the reinforced response will be a terminal response.
With reinforcement maintained but the relationship of reinforcement to behavior removed, terminal responding will still occur but will be more variable;
responses other than those previously reinforced will more or less frequently

---

*But not impossible in all cases. If simply making reinforcement dependent on an interim
response (like preening) does succeed in making that former interim response a stable terminal
response, we can expect to observe a new set of interim responses. This may be the way in which
we generate wholly new behavior such as that involved in "insight."

appear during the terminal period. With reinforcement removed entirely, only interim responding will occur and behavior will be still more variable. When we observe previously reinforced responses to decrease during extinction we are observing the increase in variability. Other responses appear as well as the one previously reinforced.

Thus the Staddon and Simmelhag theory ties together the facts of instrumental and classical conditioning with the ethological facts discussed in Chapter 3 and the biological limitations discussed in this chapter. How well does the theory accommodate the facts? Not too badly, but as yet it is mostly speculation. It will be tested as new data come to light that must fit into the theory without straining it. Whether such accommodation will be easily made remains to be seen. Regardless of the success or failure of this particular way of organizing what we know about behavior, some such organization will be necessary to deal with the host of facts emerging from empirical work.

APPLICATIONS IN BEHAVIOR THERAPY

Since this chapter is mostly negative in emphasis, it contains few new techniques that can be applied in behavior therapy. Nevertheless, two topics mentioned in this chapter have received clinical attention.

Preparedness and Phobias

It has been theorized that phobias are acquired through classical conditioning. The object of the phobia (for example, a snake) is the CS. The US is either a primary aversive stimulus or another stimulus that has been associated with a primary aversive stimulus (second-order conditioning). But an objection to the simple classical-conditioning theory is that phobias seem to be much more frequently acquired with certain objects than others. Many people have snake phobias but few have lamb phobias. Since lambs are at least as commonly encountered as snakes, they should have had equal opportunity to be associated with unpleasant US's and therefore equal opportunity to elicit fear on their own. Why don't they? Seligman has speculated that humans might be innately predisposed—that is, prepared—to fear certain types of things. Fear of snakes, heights, and closed spaces, for example, might once have been biologically useful for humans, and natural selection might have operated so that people who easily acquired these fears survived longer than those who did not. Thus we are prepared to fear snakes and unprepared to fear lambs. This is not to say that we are born with a fear of snakes, but rather that we are born with a disposition to acquire such a fear through classical conditioning. Pathological fear of snakes would then be due either to an unusually high preparedness or to an unusually extensive experience of a correlation between snakes and other fear-eliciting stimuli (or of the US, pain, itself).

As yet there is no evidence for or against these speculations about the origin of phobias.

The Aversive Control of Alcoholism

Classical-conditioning procedures have been applied to the treatment of alcoholics, with mixed results. The objective of the treatment has been to pair stimuli linked to drinking alcohol (CS's) with an unpleasant US so that the alcoholic will experience unpleasant CR's while drinking and thus stop drinking. There has been some difference of opinion about what sort of US to use. Occasionally electric shock has been used as the US. Occasionally a drug has been given that causes the subject to become ill and vomit shortly after drinking. Neither method has been entirely satisfactory. Both work well during conditioning, but extinction, in many cases, has been too rapid to allow the alcoholic to become socially rehabilitated before he starts drinking again.

Garcia's experiments suggest that both US's together might work better than either alone. The shock US tends to be associated with visual and auditory stimuli—the sight of the bottle, the sight of the whisky glass, the clinking of the ice, and so on. But a determined alcoholic can well overcome particular sights and sounds and still get a drink into his mouth. Since, as Garcia has shown with rats shock may fail to become associated with taste, the alcoholic can drink without experiencing further unpleasant sensations. The illness-inducing US, on the other hand, does not become associated with sounds and sights, and so with the drug US alone no aversive stimuli are produced until the liquor is actually tasted. By then it may well be too late: it is as easy to swallow the unpleasant-tasting liquid as to spit it out.

But with both shock and the illness-producing drug as combined US's, aversive CS's would come from several sensory modalities and follow along the entire course of drinking. The complex of aversive CS's might act to recondition aversive CR's to any particular element of the complex that extinguished by itself (by means of second-order conditioning), and the complex might thus be much more resistant to extinction than with either shock or illness-producing drug alone. Again, this is purely speculative. Experiments to test these speculations have not yet been done.

BIBLIOGRAPHY

This was an easy chapter to write, mostly because a single book was available that contains much of the material covered. The book, edited by Martin E. P. Seligman and Joanne L. Hager, is *Biological boundaries of learning* (New York: Appleton-Century-Crofts, 1972). Most of the articles listed below are reprinted in Seligman and Hager's book with, in addition, several other articles on the subject. Another book on the same subject has recently been published that contains original articles by workers in this field. Edited by R. A. Hinde and J. Stevenson-Hinde, it is titled *Constraints on learning: Limitations and predispositions* (London: Academic Press, 1973).

Following is a list of the articles referred to in this chaper:

Bolles, R. Species-specific defense reactions and avoidance learning. *Psychological Review*, 1970, *77*, 32–48.

Breland, K. and Breland, M. The misbehavior of organisms. *American Psychologist*, 1961, *16*, 681–684.

Brown, P., and Jenkins, H. Auto-shaping of the pigeon's key peck. *Journal of The Experimental Analysis of Behavior*, 1968, *11*, 1–8.

Dobrezecka, C., Szwejkowska, G., and Konorski, J. Qualitative versus directional cues in two forms of differentiation. *Science*, 1966, *153*, 87–89.

Garcia, J., Ervin, F., and Koelling, R. A. Learning with prolonged delay of reinforcement. *Psychonomic Science*, 1966, *5*, 121–122.

Garcia, J., and Koelling, R. A. Relation of cue to consequence in avoidance learning. *Psychonomic Science*, 1966, *4*, 123–124.

Perin, C. T. A quantitative investigation of the delay-of-reinforcement gradient. *Journal of Experimental Psychology*, 1943, *32*, 37–51.

Reynolds, B. The acquisition of a trace conditioned response as a function of the magnitude of the stimulus trace. *Journal of Experimental Psychology*, 1945, *35*, 15–30.

Rozin, P. Specific aversions as a component of specific hungers. *Journal of Comparative and Physiological Psychology*, 1967, *64*, 237–242.

Seligman, M. E. P. On the generality of the laws of learning. *Psychological Review*, 1970, *77*, 406–418.

Seligman, M. E. P. Phobias and preparedness. *Behavior Therapy*, 1971, *2*, 307–320.

Staddon, J. E. R., and Simmelhag, V. L. The superstition experiment: A reexamination of its implications for the study of adaptive behavior. *Psychological Review*, 1971, *78*, 3–43.

Thorndike, E. L. *Animal intelligence.* New York: Macmillan, 1911.

Williams, D., and Williams, H. Auto-maintenance in the pigeon: Sustained pecking despite contingent non-reinforcement. *Journal of The Experimental Analysis of Behavior*, 1969, *12*, 511–520.

We reprint here the remainder of the Staddon and Simmelhag article (the beginning of the article is at the end of Chapter 3). In this part of the article Staddon and Simmelhag compare learning with evolution. They compare the variation of behavior with variation of species, and they compare reinforcement of behavior with natural selection of species. The *laws of variation* they talk about are laws governing behavior under various conditions of extinction as defined in Chapter 5. The *laws of reinforcement* Staddon and Simmelhag propose are the most controversial part of their theory. According to Staddon and Simmelhag, reinforcement acts not to strengthen behavior but to *preserve* behavior that already exists. This article presents an extended parallel between behavior and evolution. Although the reader may not want to draw this parallel as far as Staddon and Simmelhag do, it is interesting to see how far it *can* be drawn. Previous theorists have noted the similarity between behavior and evolution, but none have explored the implications of such similarity as deeply as have Staddon and Simmelhag.

Supplemental Reading for Chapter 7

THE "SUPERSTITION" EXPERIMENT:
A Reexamination of its Implications for the Principles of Adaptive Behavior
Part II

J. E. R. Staddon
Virginia L. Simmelhag

NATURE OF THE TERMINAL RESPONSE

The data from both FI and VI schedules of food presentation indicate that the probability of the terminal response at different postfood times was a function of the probability of food delivery at those times: the probability of the terminal response increased just in advance of increases in the probability of food delivery, and decreased just after decreases in that probability. Thus, on the FI schedule, the terminal response began at postfood times greater than about 8 seconds, corresponding to a probability of food delivery of zero at times less than 12 seconds, and one thereafter. On the VI schedule, probability of food delivery was zero at postfood times less than 3 seconds (the shortest interfood interval in the VI sequence), and increased thereafter. Correspondingly, the birds began their terminal response after 2 seconds or so of postfood time and continued until food delivery. The data for Birds 29 and 47 on the VI schedule provide additional confirming evidence. Both birds showed a small decline in the probability of the terminal response between Seconds 12 and 17 of postfood time, accompanied by a brief reappearance of an interim activity

NOTE: Part I of this article appeared after Chapter 3.

Reprinted from *Psychological Review*, Vol. 78, No. 1, pp. 16–43. Copyright 1971 by the American Psychological Association. Reprinted by permission.

(between Seconds 13 and 16) in the case of Bird 47. This brief decrease in the terminal response, and accompanying reappearance of an interim activity, corresponds to the zero probability of food in the region of postfood time between 13 and 21 seconds (because the VI sequence used had no interfood interval between 13 and 21 seconds in length—see Method). Catania and Reynolds (1968) showed a similar relationship between rate of key pecking and probability of reinforcement, as a function of postreinforcement time, on a variety of conventional (response-dependent) VI reinforcement schedules. This similarity and the similarities between the response-independent and response-dependent conditions of this experiment emphasize that the terminal response must be regarded as a discriminated operant in Skinner's (1958) sense.

Herrnstein (1966) reported an experiment in which the rate of key pecking on response-independent FI 11 seconds was lower than on response-dependent FI 11. However, in the present experiment, considering just the terminal response of Pecking on magazine wall (R_7), we found no evidence for a difference in either probability or rate of response favoring the response-dependent procedure. Indeed, rate of key pecking (defined as switch operations) under the response-dependent FI was generally lower than the observer-defined rate of pecking under the response-independent FI because many pecks failed to break the switch contact. On the other hand, because the location of pecking was much more variable under the response-independent condition, a comparison between key pecking (in the response-dependent condition) with pecking on a comparable area of the magazine wall (in the response-independent condition) would show more responding under the response-dependent condition. This result raises the possibility that the effect of the response-dependency, in operant conditioning experiments using interval reinforcement schedules, may be largely one of determining (perhaps imperfectly) the *location* of pecking, rather than either its form or its frequency of occurrence.

NATURE OF THE INTERIM ACTIVITIES

Falk (1969, 1970) has coined the term *adjunctive behavior* for a variety of activities that are induced in a number of different animal species (rats, pigeons, monkeys, chimpanzees) by intermittent schedules of reinforcement. These activities generally occur just after reinforcement, when the reinforced (i.e., terminal) response is not occurring. However, the important variable in determining their temporal location seems to be the low probability of further reinforcement in the immediate postreinforcement period (rather than the interruption of eating), since they also occur following brief stimulus presentations on second-order interval schedules (Rosenblith, 1970), following each response on spaced-responding (differential reinforcement of low rates) schedules (Segal & Holloway, 1963), during time-out periods (Wüttke, 1970), only after the last pellet when a number are delivered consecutively at the end of each FI (Keehn, 1970), and later in the interval during long FI schedules (Segal, Oden, & Deadwyler, 1965). They are not elicited (e.g., by frustration) in any obvious sense, since they take some time to develop (Reynierse & Spanier, 1968). They are related to motivational

systems, since a number of activities—for example, polydipsia (excessive drinking), pica (eating nonfood material), wheel running, and schedule-induced aggression—may occur more or less interchangeably depending on the presence of appropriate stimuli; and animals will learn an operant response in order to obtain an opportunity to engage in one of these activities (Falk, 1970).

The interim activities in the present experiment appear to reflect the same causal factors as adjunctive behavior: they occur at times when reinforcement is not available and the terminal response is not occurring; they occur on both response-dependent and response-independent schedules (cf. Azrin, Hutchinson, & Hake, 1966; Burks, 1970; Flory, 1969); and they occur on both FI and VI schedules. Adjunctive behavior requires appropriate stimuli (water for polydipsia, wood shavings for pica, etc.) to which it is directed and by which it can be modified, within limits. This is unlikely to be a crucial difference, however, since appropriate stimuli were not available in the present experiment (had water been available, schedule-induced drinking would almost certainly have been observed in lieu of the interim activities; cf. Shanab & Peterson, 1969), and behavior resembling interim activities has occasionally been reported under conditions when most animals show adjunctive behavior, thus

[this rat] was atypical in that it did not develop polydipsia . . . exhibiting instead a number of stereotyped behaviors, like rearing and running to the corners of the experimental chamber, between reinforcements [Keehn, 1970, pp. 164–167].

We return to a theoretical account of interim and adjunctive behavior in the concluding section.

An analogy can be drawn between the terminal and interim activities here and the classical dichotomy between consummatory and appetitive behavior (Craig, 1918). Thus, pecking, the stable terminal response, is a food-elicited (consummatory) activity in pigeons, and the interim activities were quite variable, as might be expected of appetitive behavior. Moreover, the variability of the sequences (as measured by the number of "forks" in the sequence) was greatest at the beginning of the sequence and decreased toward the end (cf. Figure 2). More or less unlearned sequences terminating in consummatory acts show a similar reduction in variability toward the end of the sequence (e.g., Morris, 1958).

In a similar vein, Falk (1970) has compared adjunctive behavior with displacement activities (Tinbergen, 1952):

In both adjunctive behavior and displacement activity situations, the interruption of a consummatory behavior in an intensely motivated animal induces the occurrence of another behavior immediately following the interruption [p. 305].

At the present stage of knowledge, these comparisons do little more than group together a number of puzzling phenomena that cannot as yet be convincingly explained, either by ethological principles or by the Law of Effect. We can choose either to accept these behaviors as anomalies within our present conceptual system, hoping that further research will show how to reconcile them, or revise the system in a way that will accommodate them more naturally. The first alternative is becoming increasingly hard to maintain, as it becomes clear that these behaviors are of wide occurrence, and as they continue to resist attempts to explain them in conventional terms. Polydipsia is the most widely studied adjunctive behavior, and Falk (1969) summarizes research results as follows:

It is not explicable in terms of any altered state of water balance initiated by the experimental conditions. It cannot be attributed to adventitious reinforcing effects. Since it cannot be related to abnormal water losses, chronic internal stimulation arising from unusual states . . . or from injury to the central nervous system, the overdrinking would be classified clinically as primary or psychogenic polydipsia [p. 587].

A revision of the conceptual foundations of operant behavior, which will deal naturally with these behaviors, as well as guide research into more profitable channels, seems called for.

DEVELOPMENT OF THE TERMINAL RESPONSE

The development of the terminal response provides some clues toward an alternative conception. Changes in the terminal response throughout acquisition rule out an unqualified application of the Law of Effect as a description of the process. For example, three of the four birds made the response Head in magazine at a higher frequency and for a larger fraction of the total time than any other response, for the first few sessions of exposure to the superstition procedure (either FI or VI, depending on the bird). This behavior was also the one most often contiguous with the delivery of food. Yet during later sessions, it dropped out abruptly and was replaced by Pecking. Thus the development of Pecking as terminal response resembles the findings of Williams and Williams and of Breland and Breland, much more than it does the strengthening of an emitted response, in Skinner's terms, by the automatic action of food as a reinforcer. In all these cases, the presentation of food at a predictable time resulted, after training, in the regular occurrence of a food-related behavior in anticipation of food delivery, quite independently of the demand characteristics of the situation (i.e., the reinforcement schedule). Given that food is a stimulus that elicits pecking by pigeons, the appearance of pecking, in anticipation of food, in the present experiment is an instance of the principle of stimulus substitution (Hilgard & Marquis, 1940). The stimulus is, of course, a temporal one (postfood time), and the situation is analogous, therefore, to Pavlovian temporal conditioning (Pavlov, 1927), both operationally and in its conformity to the substitution principle. Therefore, it is tempting to attribute the appearance of pecking to a classical conditioning mechanism, and leave it at that.

A number of considerations suggest that this explanation will not suffice, however: (*a*) The behavior of one bird (29) is a partial exception. He showed a terminal response (Head in magazine) different from Pecking, although this response was metastable (Staddon, 1965), in the sense that it was displaced by Pecking following a schedule shift. In addition, Skinner's results and informal observations in a number of laboratories indicate that the superstition procedure may generate behaviors other than pecking that persist for considerable periods of time. Presumably, many of these behaviors are terminal responses, in our sense, and, metastable or not, they cannot be dismissed in favor of a Pavlovian account of all terminal responses in supersitition situations. (*b*) The results of Rachlin (1969), who was able to obtain spontaneous key pecking by means of the auto-shaping procedure of Brown and Jenkins, but using electric shock-reduction rather than food as the reinforcer, also complicate the picture, since it is not clear that pecking is elicited by shock, as it is by food. The results of Sidman and Fletcher (1968), who were able to auto shape key pushing in rhesus monkeys, are also not readily explicable by stimulus substitution. (*c*) Williams and Williams (1969) note that the directed nature of the key peck in the auto-shaping situation is not readily accommodated within a Pavlovian framework:

the directed quality of the induced pecking does not follow naturally from respondent principles (see also Brown and Jenkins, 1968). It is unclear, for example, why pecking would be directed at the key rather than the feeder, or indeed why it would be directed anywhere at all [p. 519].

A similar objection can be raised here, since the terminal response of pecking was always directed at the magazine wall, although it is important to notice that this objection is more damaging to an interpretation in terms of classical conditioning than one couched simply in terms of stimulus substitution. (*d*) Finally, there is the problem of the skeletal nature of pecking. Ever since Skinner's (1938) original suggestion, it has become increasingly common to restrict the concept of classical conditioning to autonomically mediated responses. Some criticisms of this convention are presented below, and Staddon (1970a) has argued against the operant/respondent and emitted/elicited dichotomies. For the moment, let it be said that the objection to the skeletal nature of the response is only a problem for an interpretation of the development of pecking in terms of classical conditioning, as traditionally conceived. It does not conflict with a stimulus substitution interpretation.

In summary, it is clear that while the principle of stimulus substitution describes the development of the terminal response in a majority of cases, and is more successful than an appeal to Pavlovian principles modeled on the salivation reference experiment, it is not adequate as a universal account. We turn now to the possibility of a general scheme to deal with these anomalous facts.

EVOLUTION AND LEARNING

Objectively considered, the subject matter of the psychology of animal learning—the behavior of animals—is a part of biology. This commonality does not extend to terms and concepts, however. Although the ethologists have investigated unlearned behaviors in a variety of species, learning remains almost exclusively the possession of psychologists. Consequently, the theoretical foundations of the study of learning, such as they are, have evolved almost independently of biology. It is now 15 years since Verplanck (1955) wrote: "the structure of the theory of unlearned behavior and that of learned behavior must prove to be similar if not identical [p. 140]," but little progress toward a unified set of concepts has been made. Yet the facts discussed in the previous section seem to demand an interpretation within the context of adaptive behavior as a whole.

The principles of evolution by natural selection provide a unifying framework for biology. Pfaffman (1970) has recently commented:

I am impressed by the extent to which evolution, the genetic machinery, and biochemistry provide for biologists a common language and unity of theory that overrides the molecular versus organismic debate within biology. In contrast, it is obvious that there is no unified theory of behavior for all students of behavior [p. 438].

These considerations—the commonality of subject matter between biology and animal psychology, the probable common basis of learned and unlearned behavior, the unifying role of evolutionary processes in biology—all suggest the application of evolutionary principles to the psychology of learning in animals. In recent years, several papers have drawn attention to the similarities between evolution and learning (e.g., Breland & Breland, 1966; Broadbent, 1961; Gilbert, 1970; Herrnstein, 1964; Pringle, 1951; Skinner, 1966a, 1966b, 1969), but no version of the evolutionary approach has proved influential as yet. The main reasons for this failure, perhaps, have been the comparative effectiveness of traditional versions of the Law of Effect in dealing with the limited phenomena of laboratory learning experiments and the lack of a substantial body of facts clearly in conflict with accepted theory. To some extent, of course, the second factor reflects the first—although it would be cynical to speculate that the kind of experiments psychologists do are often such as to preclude data that might go beyond current theory. In any event, neither of these reasons now holds true.

The growing number of facts on autoshaping, instinctive drift, adjunctive, and superstitious behaviors are not readily accommodated within traditional views.

In addition, the history of the Law of Effect as a principle of *acquisition* (as opposed to the steady state, i.e., asymptote) has not been a distinguished one. Little remains of the impressive edifice erected by Hull and his followers on this base. We are no longer concerned with the production of learning curves, nor with the measurement of habit strength or reaction potential. Hullian theory has proven effective neither in the elucidation of complex cases nor as an aid to the discovery of new phenomena. Indeed, the opposite has generally been true: new learning phenomena such as schedules of reinforcement, learning, and reversal sets, etc. have typically been the result of unaided curiosity rather than the hypothetico-deductive method, as exemplified by Hull and his students. This represents a failure of Hullian theory rather than a general indictment of the hypothetico-deductive method, which has proven every bit as powerful as Hull believed it to be—when used by others (e.g., Darwin, cf. Ghiselin, 1969). A similar, although less sweeping, verdict must be handed down on stochastic learning theory, which represents perhaps the most direct attempt to translate the Law of Effect into a quantitative principle of acquisition. With the exception of predictions about the steady state, such as Estes' ingenious deduction of probability matching (Estes, 1957), the early promise of this approach as a way of understanding the behavior of individual animals has not been fulfilled. It seems fair to say that the rash of theoretical elaboration that has occupied the years since Thorndike first stated the Law of Effect has told us almost nothing more about the moment-by-moment behavior of a single organism in a learning situation. Although the alternative we will offer may be no better than earlier views, it does accommodate the anomalies we have discussed—and the need for *some* alternative can hardly be questioned.

The close analogy between the Law of Effect and evolution suggests an approach that may be a step toward the general framework which the psychology of learning so obviously lacks. At the present stage of knowledge, this approach is simply an analogy, although a compelling one, and cannot yet be called an evolutionary theory of learning. However, it provides a beginning and may lead to a truly evolutionary account which can securely imbed the study of learning in the broader field of biology.

BEHAVIORAL VARIATION AND REINFORCEMENT

The Law of Effect, suitably modified to take account of advances since Thorndike's original formulation, can be stated so as to emphasize acquisition, or the steady state, and learning (e.g., S–R bonds), or performance. We will take as a point of departure a neutral version of the law that emphasizes performance in the steady state, as follows: "If, in a given situation, a positive correlation be imposed between some aspect of an animal's behavior and the delivery of reinforcement, that behavior will generally come to predominate in that situation." The term "correlation" is intended to include cases of delay of reinforcement and experiments in which the response acts on the rate of reinforcement directly (e.g., Herrnstein & Hineline, 1966; Keehn, 1970). This formulation does not take account of more complex situations where more than one behavior and more than one correlation are involved (i.e., choice situations), as these complications do not affect the present argument. A discussion of three aspects of this law—(*a*) the initial behavior in the situation before reinforcement is introduced, (*b*) the process whereby this behavior is transformed into the dominant reinforced behavior, and (*c*) reinforcement—follows:

(*a*) The behavior in a situation before the occurrence of reinforcement reflects a number of factors, including past experience in similar situations (transfer), motivation, stimulus factors (e.g., novel or sign stimuli), and others. We propose the label "principles of behavioral variation" for all such factors that originate behavior. These principles are analogous to Darwin's laws of variation, corresponding to the modern laws of heredity and ontogeny that provide the phenotypes on which selection (analogous to the principles of reinforcement, see below) can act. Thus, the term "variation" is intended to denote not mere variability, but the organized production of novelty, in the Darwinian sense.

(*b*) Transition from initial behavior to final behavior is the traditional problem of learning theory and, as we have seen, is essentially unsolved at the level of the individual organism. However, it is at this point that the analogy to the mechanism of natural selection becomes most apparent. Broadbent (1961) makes the parallel quite clear:

Since individual animals differ, and those with useful characteristics [with respect to a particular niche] survive and pass them on to their children, we can explain the delicate adjustment of each animal's shape to its surroundings without requiring a conscious purpose on the part of the Polar bear to grow a white coat. Equally each individual animal [under the Law of Effect] tries various actions and those which become more common which are followed by consummatory acts [i.e., reinforcement] [p.56].

Thus, the transition from initial to final behavior can be viewed as the outcome of two processes: a process that generates behavior, and a process that selects (i.e., selectively eliminates) from the behavior so produced. Since there is no reason to suppose that the process which generates behavior following the first and subsequent reinforcements is different in kind from the process that generated the initial behavior (although the *effects* will generally be different, see Extinction, below), we can include both under the head of principles of behavioral variation. We propose the label "principles of reinforcement" for the second, selective process.

(*c*) As we have seen, the Darwinian principle of selection is analogous to the process that transforms initial behavior into final behavior—the "principles of reinforcement." The notion of reinforcement (more exactly, the schedule of reinforcement) itself is in fact analogous to an earlier concept, one that preceded evolution by natural selection and can be derived from it: the Law of Conditions of Existence, that is, the fact that organisms are adapted to a particular niche. This is apparent in the form of the statements: "The Polar bear has a white coat *because* it is adaptive in his environment." "The pigeon pecks the key *because* he is reinforced for doing so." It is important to emphasize this distinction between *reinforcement* and *principles of reinforcement,* and the analogous distinction between adaptation to a niche and the process of selection by which adaptation comes about. In the case of adaptation, the process of selection involves differential reproduction, either through absence of a mate, infertility, or death before reproductive maturity. In the case of reinforcement, the distinction is less obvious, since the principles of reinforcement refer to the *laws by means of which* behaviors that fail to yield reinforcement are eliminated, rather than the simple fact that reinforced behaviors generally predominate at the expense of unreinforced behaviors.

Thus, both evolution and learning can be regarded as the outcome of two independent processes: a process of variation that generates either phenotypes, in the case of evolution, or behavior, in the case of learning; and a process of selection that acts within the limits set by the first process. In both cases, the actual outcome of the total process is related to, but not identical with, the material acted upon: phenotypes reproduce more or less successfully, but a gene pool is the outcome of selection; similarly, behaviors are more or less highly correlated with reinforcement, but learning (i.e., an alteration in memory) results.

The three aspects of this process—variation, selection, and adaptation—have received differing emphases at different times, depending on the prevailing state

of knowledge. Before Darwin, adaptation, in the form of the Law of Conditions of Existence, was emphasized, since the only explanation for it—the design of the Creator—was not scientifically fruitful. Following Darwin, selection, both natural and artificial, received increased attention, in the absence of firm knowledge of the mechanism of variation (i.e., inheritance). With the advent of Mendelian genetics, variation has been most intensively studied (this is one aspect of the "molecular vs. organismic" debate referred to by Pfaffman).

In terms of this development, the study of learning is at a relatively primitive level, since the Law of Effect, although a great advance over the level of understanding which preceded it, simply represents the identification of environmental events—reinforcers—with respect to which behavior is adaptive. Lacking is a clear understanding of both selection (the principles of reinforcement) and variation (the principles of variation).

Space precludes exhaustive elaboration of all the implications of the classificatory scheme we are suggesting. However, in order to provide some context for our account of the facts already discussed, it seems essential to briefly summarize some possible candidates for principles of variation and reinforcement. It should be obvious that current knowledge does not permit the categories used to be either exhaustive or clear-cut.

Principles of behavioral variation.

1. Transfer processes: One of the main sources of behavior in a new situation is obviously past experience in similar situations. Transfer has been most exhaustively studied under the restricted conditions of verbal learning (e.g., Tulving & Madigan, 1970), but the principles of memory thus derived—proactive and retroactive interference, primacy and recency, retrieval factors, etc.—are presumably of general applicability. With few exceptions (e.g., Gonzales, Behrend, & Bitterman, 1967), these principles have been little used to

interpret animal learning experiments. Other principles of transfer are stimulus and response generalization (induction) and what might be called "compositional transfer," in which several past experiences are combined to generate a novel behavior, as in insight learning and other forms of subjective organization of past input.

2. Stimulus substitution: This principle, which is usually identified with Pavlovian conditioning, has already been discussed as a description of the origin of the terminal response of Pecking. It may also describe the origin of the metastable terminal response Head in magazine, since this response is also elicited by food under these conditions, and the animal which showed this response most persistently (Bird 29) had had considerable experimental experience. The difference in the persistence of Head in magazine in the case of this bird, as compared with others, cannot be explained in this way and might reflect a difference in other transfer processes. The final dominance of Pecking, in every case, may reflect a special susceptibility of consummatory responses to the stimulus substitution principle, or the action of other transfer principles in this particular situation in ways that are presently unclear. The indefinite persistence of key pecking following only three peck-contingent reinforcements, found by Neuringer (1970b), tends to support the simpler conclusion, as does the data of Wolin (1968), who reports a similarity between the topography of operant pecking for food or water reinforcers, and the appropriate unconditioned response. We return later to a general discussion of this principle in relation to these data (p. 391).

3. Preparatory responses: This principle is also frequently associated with classical conditioning, and in that sense is related to, and to some extent overlaps with, the stimulus substitution principle. Thus, some conditioned responses, such as salivation, can be equally well described by either principle. Others, also respondents (such as heart rate, which increases following electric shock, but usually decreases in anticipation of it [Zeaman & Smith, 1965]) may be classified as preparatory responses. Skeletal responses observed in classical conditioning situations are often preparatory in nature (see discussion of classical conditioning, below).

4. Syntactic constraints: There are often sequential constraints among behaviors, so that a given behavior is determined by some property of the sequence of preceding behaviors. Examples are spontaneous position alternation observed in rats and other rodents, stimulus alternation observed in monkeys on learning set problems (e.g., Levine, 1965), and sequential dependencies observed in most species which cause responses to occur in runs rather than alternating randomly (e.g., position habits and other perseverative errors). Human language provides the most developed example of syntactic constraints.

5. Orienting responses: This category includes all those transient behaviors, such as exploration, play, curiosity, etc., that expose the organism to new stimuli and provide the possibility of transfer to future situations.

6. Situation-specific and species-typical responses: Certain situations seem to call forth specific responses, which are often typical of the species rather than the individual and do not seem to depend in any obvious way on any of the other principles of variation such as transfer, etc. Examples are the species-specific defense reactions discussed by Bolles (1970), which occur in fear-producing situations, the tendency to peck bright objects shown by many birds (Breland & Breland, 1966), and the digging shown by small rodents (Fantino & Cole, 1968). Other examples are given by Glickman and Sroges (1966).

Principles of reinforcement.

Before the discovery of the mechanism of inheritance, evolution could be explained only in terms of a goal—adaptation—and a means sufficient to reach that goal—variation and selection; the genera-tion-by-generation details of the process were obscure: "Our ignorance of the laws of variation is profound [Darwin, 1951, p. 170]." We are at present equally igno-rant of the mechanisms of behavioral variation. Since learning must usually involve constant interplay between varia-tion and reinforcement, we are not yet in a position to suggest anything specific about the moment-by-moment details of the process, either in its variational or selective aspects. However, just as Darwin was able to say something about selection by pointing out the adaptive role of var-ious structures, so it is possible to learn something about the selective role of reinforcement by looking at steady-state adaptations to fixed conditions of rein-forcement, that is, reinforcement sched-ules. On this basis, we suggest the following tentative generalizations about the effects of reinforcement:

1. Reinforcement acts directly only on the terminal response; activities which occur at other times (interim activities, adjunctive behavior, etc.) must be ac-counted for in other ways, to be discussed later. This assertion is perhaps closer to a definition than an empirical generaliza-tion, since it is equivalent to the assertion that the terminal response may, in gen-eral, be *identified* as the activity occurring in closest proximity to reinforcement in the steady state. Identification is, of course, no problem in conditioning situa-tions that *enforce* a contingency between some property of behavior and the deliv-ery of reinforcement. However, we will show later that there is no empirical or logical basis for separating situations that do impose a contingency between re-sponse and reinforcement from those that do not (see Classical Conditioning, below).

2. Reinforcement acts only to elimi-nate behaviors that are less directly cor-related with reinforcement than others. This generalization, like the first, is also more like a definition, since all that is *observed* (under consistent conditions of reinforcement) is the eventual predomi-nance of one behavior over others—which is consistent with either a suppressive or a strengthening effect. As Skinner (1966a) points out in a summary of the Law of Effect:

Thorndike was closer to the principle of nat-ural selection than the [usual] statement of his law. He did not need to say that a response which had been followed by a certain kind of consequence was more likely to occur again but simply that it was not less likely. It even-tually held the field because responses which failed to have such effects tended, like less favored species, to disappear [p. 13].

Unfortunately, Skinner, and most other behaviorists, elected to follow Thorndike in considering reinforcement to have a positive, strengthening, or "stamping-in" effect. One of the main purposes of the present paper is to suggest that this deci-sion was a mistake and has given rise to a number of problems and controversies that can be avoided if the effects of rein-forcement are considered to be purely selective or suppressive.

There are three kinds of argument which support a purely selective role for reinforcement. The first, and most impor-tant, is that the overall conceptual scheme which results is simpler and more easily related to biological accounts of behavior than the alternative.

The second point is that situations such as extinction and shaping by succes-sive approximations that might seem to require an active role for reinforcement can be interpreted in a way that does not require anything more than a selective effect. This point is discussed later (see Extinction, below).

The third point is that the superstition and related experiments suggest that the response contingency imposed by most reinforcement schedules is not essential for the production of *some* terminal re-sponse, but only for the selection of one response over others, or for directing a response which would probably predom-inate in any case—as in key pecking by pigeons. Our failure to find a consistent difference in rate of observer-defined pecking between the response-dependent and response-independent conditions of the present superstition experiment supports this view, as does a recent finding that the contingency between electric shock and responding is not necessary to the generation of behavior maintained by intermittent shock delivery to squirrel monkeys (Hutchinson, 1970; Stretch, personal communication, 1970).

The usual interpretation of the fact that there is a terminal response in the superstition situation, despite the absence of response-contingency, is the notion of accidental strengthening of a response by contiguity with the delivery of reinforcement. Here we consider the general implications of adventitious reinforcement as an explanation, and its incompatibility with the notion of reinforcement as selection. Other problems related to adventitious reinforcement are discussed later (see Acquisition, Classical Conditioning).

First, adventitious reinforcement implies failure of constancy, in the sense that the animal is presumed to be unable, because of the stamping-in mechanism of reinforcement, to distinguish between real and accidental correlations between his behavior and the occurrence of reinforcement. This is a strong assumption, in view of the adaptive utility of the constancy process and its ubiquity in perceptual and motor mechanisms. In perception, a similar failure to distinguish changes in sensory input that are produced by our own behavior from changes that are independent of behavior might cause us to perceive the world as rotating every time we turn our head. It is of course true that on the basis of one or a few instances the animal may not be in a position to be certain about the reality of a contingent relationship between his behavior and reinforcement—and this kind of sampling limitation might account for a transient superstitious effect. It is less convincing as an account of a long-term effect.

Second, if reinforcement is considered as purely selective, it *cannot* be invoked as an explanation of behavior when *no* imposed contingency exists between reinforcement and behavior (i.e., in the *absence* of selection). To do otherwise would be like taking a population of white mice, breeding them for 20 generations without further selection for color, and then attributing the resulting white population to the results of "accidental selection." In this case, as in the case of response-independent reinforcement, the outcome reflects a characteristic of the initial population (i.e., the mice gene pool, the nature of the organism), and not a nonexistent selection process.

In short, the notion of adventitious reinforcement is not a tenable one. The extent to which reinforcement can be invoked as an explanation for behavior is directly related both to the degree of *imposed contingency* between response and reinforcement and to the opportunities for that contingency to have some selective effect (i.e., the number of contingent reinforcements). If there is no contingency, or if few contingent reinforcements have occurred, the resulting behavior must owe more to principles of variation than to the selective action of reinforcement. On the other hand, if many contingent reinforcements have been delivered during a protracted period of shaping, the final form of behavior is obviously much less dependent on *particular* principles of variation, and the role of reinforcement (selection) may properly be emphasized.

3. There is considerable evidence for the generality of a principle implicating relative rate or proximity of reinforcment as the fundamental independent variable determining the spatial and temporal location of responding in steady-state conditioning situations. Thus, Herrnstein (1970) has recently reviewed a number of operant conditioning experiments involving differential reinforcement of simultaneous (concurrent schedules) and successive (multiple schedules) choices which support the idea of relative reinforcement rate as the independent variable most directly related to the rate of key pecking in pigeons. Shimp (1969) has presented an analysis which is formally

different from Herrnstein's, but which also implicates differences in reinforcement rate as the crucial variable. An extensive series of experiments by Catania and Reynolds (1968) suggests a similar (although less exact) relationship between rate of pecking and relative temporal density of reinforcement on interval reinforcement schedules. Jenkins (1970) summarizes a series of studies with a discrete-trials procedure that led him to suggest relative proximity to reinforcement as an important determiner of the tendency to respond in the presence of a stimulus. Staddon (1970a) has suggested a similar principle to account for positive "goal gradients" that underlie the effects of reinforcement omission on a variety of interval schedules.

4. The concept of reinforcement implies a capacity to be reinforced. The fact that a given stimulus may be reinforcing at one time, but not at another, requires the idea of a *state* corresponding to each class of reinforcers. The independent variable of which the strength of most of these states is a function is deprivation with respect to the appropriate class of reinforcers (food deprivation for the hunger state, water for thirst, etc.). This will not do for most negative reinforcers (e.g., the removal of electric shock), however, since there is no obvious counterpart to deprivation in this case. It is also unlikely that deprivation is the only independent variable sufficient to alter the strength of states associated with positive reinforcement. For example, evidence is discussed later in favor of reciprocal inhibitory interaction between states as a possible factor in polydipsia and other adjunctive behavior. Interactions of this sort may also alter the strength of states for which there is no deprivation requirement, as in audio anaesthesia (Licklider, 1961).

Thus, one may hope for a set of principles of reinforcement that will deal both with the proper classification of states and with the interactions among them.

The theoretical vocabulary of learning is full of terms with an uneasy conceptual status somewhere between explanation, definition, and category label. This terminology, which is not coherent or internally consistent, makes it difficult to approach particular topics with an open mind. It is too easy to dismiss an experimental result as due to adventitious reinforcement or respondent conditioning without, in fact, having any clear understanding of what has been said. Simply defining everything operationally is of little help in this situation, since a set of definitions is not a theory. And a theory, in the sense of a system of concepts that is internally consistent and coherent, is what is required if we are to be sure, in particular cases, whether we really understand a phenomenon—or are merely substituting one mystery for another, with the assistance of an opaque vocabulary.

What we are proposing is too primitive to be called a theory in this sense. However, it does offer a system of classification that makes it difficult to have the illusion of understanding a phenomenon if comprehension is really lacking. In the following section, some implications of this scheme are shown in three major areas: acquisition, extinction, and classical conditioning. This is followed by a brief discussion of possible difficulties of this approach. With the aid of this groundwork, it will then be easier to return to a general account of the superstition and related experiments in the concluding section.

ACQUISITION

The number of trials necessary for learning is one of those perennial problems that seems to defy resolution. Appeal to data is not conclusive because learning curves are sometimes incremental and sometimes steplike. Even in particular cases, theory is not conclusive either, since with sufficient ingenuity, theoretical accounts of both kinds of curve may be constructed on the basis of either one (or a few) trial learning assumptions or incremental assumptions involving thresholds. We turn now to the possibility that the issue is a consequence of the stamping-in view of reinforcement and becomes less urgent once that view is challenged.

A comment by Skinner (1953) on the necessary and sufficient conditions for the development of superstition provides an illustration:

In superstitious operant behavior . . . the process of conditioning has miscarried. Conditioning offers tremendous advantages in equipping the organism with behavior which is effective in a novel environment, but there appears to be no way of preventing the acquisition of non-advantageous behavior through accident. Curiously, this difficulty must have increased as the process of conditioning was accelerated in the course of evolution. If, for example, three reinforcements were always required in order to change the probability of a response, superstitious behavior would be unlikely. It is only because organisms have reached the point at which a single contingency makes a substantial change that they are vulnerable to coincidences [pp. 86–87].

Even within the framework of the stamping-in view, it is clear that the truth of this statement depends on a tacit assumption that responses will not generally occur more than once unless followed by reinforcement. If a given response can be relied on to occur at least 20 times in succession, even without reinforcement, then 3-trial, or even 10-trial learning might well be sufficient to insure its acquisition under the conditions of the superstition experiment. The assumption that responses will occur only once in the absence of reinforcement is a strong assumption about syntactic constraints, in our terminology. Moreover, it is contradicted by the results of the Williams

and Williams study (1969), which show indefinite persistence of pecking in the absence of any contiguous relationship between pecks and reinforcement. There is no reason to suppose that a similar persistence is not characteristic of other behaviors (e.g., position habits), although pecking may be more persistent than most. Thus, the finding of superstitious terminal responses, or of indefinite pecking following just three response-contingent reinforcements (Neuringer, 1970b), need imply nothing about the number of trials necessary for learning.

These considerations suggest, as a minimum, the need to take variation into account in discussions of the "speed of conditioning," since rapid acquisition may either reflect an unpersistent response that is really learned rapidly, or a very persistent one that may be learned quite slowly. No inferences about "speed of conditioning" can be drawn solely on the basis of speed of acquisition without information about the frequency and pattern of a given behavior to be expected in a given situation (which may include predictable delivery of reinforcement) *in the absence of contiguity* between the behavior and reinforcement. In practice, since information of the required sort is rarely, if ever, available, it seems wise to defer the issue of speed of learning until behavioral variation has been much more thoroughly studied.[1]

Thus, the moment-by-moment details concerning the effect of reinforcement remain uncertain until much more is known about variation. In the meantime it seems more parsimonious and less likely to lead to fruitless controversies

---

[1]Problems of this sort are not solved by referring to a hypothetical "operant level" because (*a*) this level is often zero in the absence of a history of reinforcement in the situation; (*b*) it is rarely constant, as the term level implies; and (*c*) the problem of the origin of this level is thereby simply evaded.

about "speed of conditioning," continuity versus noncontinuity, etc. to assume that the appearance of one behavior, rather than another, at a certain time or place, always requires explanation in terms of principles of variation, with only the *disappearance* of behaviors being attributable to the effects of reinforcement.

This general approach is not novel. It resembles both Harlow's (1959) account of learning-set acquisition in terms of the progressive elimination of error factors, and certain versions of stimulus-sampling theory (Neimark & Estes, 1967). In Harlow's terms, as in ours, one-trial acquisition is a phenomenon that depends on the existence of factors that make the correct behavior much more probable (and persistent) than others (i.e., upon principles of variation). In the learning-set case, these factors are embodied in the prior training procedure, which progressively selects for an initially weak behavior (the "win stay, lose shift" strategy) at the expense of the initially much stronger tendencies to approach particular stimuli. A lengthy process may not be essential, however, for principles of variation involving insight ("compositional transfer," see above) may serve the same function, if they are available to the animal. The important point is the shift of emphasis away from the supposed efficacy of some stamping-in mechanism, the action of which must remain obscure in the absence of knowledge about variation, to the principles of variation that determine the strength of behaviors in advance of contiguity with reinforcement.[2]

EXTINCTION

Extinction is often used as a test for

---

[2]Memory has not been separately discussed in this account of acquisition because it is embodied in most of the variational and selective processes we have described. The argument of the present section suggests that a separate account of memory may have to await advances in our knowledge of these processes.

"what is learned" during a training procedure, as in generalization testing (Guttman & Kalish, 1956), and testing for control by temporal factors (Ferster & Skinner, 1957; Staddon, 1970b). Under these conditions, it is assumed that behavior is determined almost entirely by transfer from the base-line condition. Providing the difference between the extinction and training conditions is not too great, either in terms of environmental factors (the stimulus situation is not too different) or temporal factors (the extinction is not prolonged), this assumption can be justified by the reliability and predictability of the behavior usually observed.

When these conditions are not satisfied or when the training preceding extinction has not been protracted, this reliability is not usually found. On the contrary, extinction under these conditions is usually associated with an increase in the variability of behavior (Antonitis, 1951; Millenson & Hurwitz, 1961). This increase in variability is exactly what would be expected if, as we have suggested, reinforcement has a purely selective effect: in these terms, training involves a progressive reduction in variability under the selective action of reinforcement (centripetal selection, see below), so that absence of reinforcement (extinction) represents a relaxation of selection—with an attendant rise in variability. We turn now to a brief account of the effects of changes in the amount and direction of selection in evolution, which may shed some further light on the properties of behavioral extinction.

Darwin (1896) comments on the effect of domestication as follows:

From a remote period to the present day, under climates and circumstances as different as it is possible to conceive, organic beings of all kinds, when domesticated or cultivated, have varied. . . . These facts, and innumerable others which could be added, indicate that a change of almost any kind in the conditions of life suffices to cause variability . . . [Vol. 2, p. 243].

Although Darwin sometimes (erroneously) interpreted this observation as reflecting a direct effect of changed conditions on the reproductive system, it can be interpreted in modern terms as due to a relaxation of selection. This is clear from the concept of *centripetal selection* (Haldane, 1959; Mayr, 1963; Simpson, 1953), which refers to the fact that selection under *un*changing conditions, if long continued, acts to weed out extremes, rather than systematically to shift population characteristics in any particular direction:

When adaptation is keeping up, selection at any one time will be mainly in favor of the existing type. . . . In such cases, the intensity of selection tends to affect not the rate of change but the amount of variation [Simpson, 1953, p. 147].

Thus, a *change* in conditions will generally involve a shift *away* from centripetal selection, with its tendency to reduce variability, and will often lead, therefore, to increased variability. The most obvious example of the effects of relaxation of selection in evolution is degenerating or vestigial structures, that are no longer being selected for:

It is so commonly true that degenerating structures are highly variable that this may be advanced as an empirical evolutionary generalization [Simpson, 1953, p. 75].

We have already noted that the onset of variability in extinction is often delayed. A similar delay in the effect of changed conditions is often apparent in evolution, Darwin (1896) notes:

We have good grounds for believing that the influence of changed conditions accumulates, so that no effect is produced on a species until it has been exposed during several generations to continued cultivation or domestication. Universal experience shows us that when new flowers are first introduced into our gardens they do not vary; but ultimately all, with the rarest exceptions, vary to a greater or less extent [Vol. 2, p. 249].

Similar delays have also been reported in experiments on artificial selection (Mayr,

1963). These delays seem to reflect what has been termed "genetic inertia" or "genetic homeostasis" (Mayr, 1963), that is, the tendency for a gene pool which is the result of a long period of consistent selection to resist changes in the direction of selection. A similar mechanism in behavior might account for the dependence of variability in extinction on the duration of the preceding training period, which was referred to earlier: The amount of variability might be expected to be greater and its onset sooner following a brief training period than after one of longer duration. Genetic homeostasis also seems to be involved in the phenomenon of reversion, to be discussed next.

Not all of the variation which occurs either in behavioral extinction, or following a change in the conditions of life in evolution, is wholly novel. A relatively common effect, for example, is the reappearance of what Darwin terms "ancestral types," that is, phenotypes which predominated earlier in phylogeny but which have been selected against more recently. This is the phenomenon of reversion which, because of his ignorance concerning heredity, Darwin (1896) found among the most mysterious of evolutionary processes:

But on the doctrine of reversion . . . the germ [germ plasm] becomes a far more marvellous object, for, besides the visible changes which it undergoes [i.e., phenotypic expressions], we muct believe that it is crowded with invisible characters, proper to . . . ancestors separated by hundreds or even thousands of generations from the present time: and these characters, like those written on paper with invisible ink, lie ready to be evolved whenever the organisation is disturbed by certain known or unknown conditions [Vol. 2, pp. 35–36],

Thus, one effect of a relaxation of selection is a more or less transient increase in the relative influence of the distant past at the expense of the immediate past. In the behavioral extinction, this should involve the reappearance of old (in the sense of previously extinguished) behavior patterns; that is, transfer from conditions preceding the training condition at the expense of transfer from the training condition.[3] In both cases, evolution and behavior, the effect of the change in conditions may be expected to depend on variables such as the magnitude of the change and the time since the preceding change.

The analogy from Darwin suggests that any considerable change in conditions should increase variability, yet a change in reinforcement schedules that includes an *increase* in reinforcement rate is not usually thought of as producing an increase in variability. This apparent contradiction is resolved by noting that an increase in rate of reinforcement, in addition to changing conditions, also increases the rate of selection (since the analogy assumes reinforcement to have a purely selective effect). Thus, variability may be breifly increased, but since the rapidity of selection is also increased, the net effect may be small. An analogous (but impossible) phenomenon in evolution would be to decrease the time between generations at the same time that conditions are changed. This would speed up the attainment of a new equilibrium and minimize the increase in variability generally associated with changed environment.

The increase in variability due to extinction is most directly put to use in the process of shaping by successive approximations. Frequently, following the first few reinforcements delivered during a "shaping" session, the effect is simply an increase in the range and vigor of behavior. This change can be viewed as being due to the interruption of eating

(cf. Mandler, 1964), however, rather than any direct strengthening effect of reinforcement (which we are questioning in any case). In terms of the foregoing analysis, the conditions following the first reinforcement should be optimal for an increase in variability: the change is large (from continuous eating to absence of food) and the training procedure is of short duration (the 3–4-second eating bout), so that time since the preceding change is also short. As food continues to be delivered intermittently, selection occurs and variability decreases.

We have been suggesting a purely selective (rather than strengthening, stamping-in, or energizing) role for reinforcement. The present discussion suggests that such an essentially passive role is compatible with a number of phenomena—extinction, the activating effects of isolated reinforcements—that may appear to demand a more active role for reinforcement. This compatibility was established by drawing attention to similar phenomena in evolution, where the purely selective effect of the conditions of life (analogous to the schedule of reinforcement) is unquestioned. However, no *necessary* identity between the genetic mechanism, which is responsible for the effect of changed conditions on variability in structure, and whatever process is responsible for analogous effects in behavior, is intended. Any process for the production of variation that incorporates some latent memory of past adaptations is likely to show similar effects.

CLASSICAL CONDITIONING

Our scheme has strong implications for the distinction between classical (Pavlovian, respondent) and instrumental (operant) conditioning, to the extent that the distinction goes beyond procedural differences. Classical conditioning is often thought of as a paradigmatic instance of the primary process of learning: "The [learning] process appears to be based entirely on temporal contiguity and to

---

[3]Other than clinical accounts of regression, we have been able to find only one published report of this effect—in an account describing shaping porpoises to show novel behaviors (Pryor, Haag, & O'Reilly, 1969). However, we have frequently observed it while shaping pigeons: if a pigeon has been trained in the past to perform a variety of responses, the increase in variability during extinction of the most recently reinforced response generally includes the reappearance of earlier responses.

have classical conditioning as its behavioral prototype [Sheffield, 1965, p. 321]." The salivation "reference experiment" can be interpreted as prototypical in at least two ways that are not always kept separate. The first (which has some similarities to our position) is referred to by Sheffield—the notion that learning depends solely on temporal relationships. Guthrie's aphorism that the animal learns what he does" is a related idea. It is not easy to find a definitive account of this position, but it may perhaps be summarized by saying that reinforcement or reward is simply necessary to ensure that some behavior occurs in a conditioning situation. Principles involving temporal relationships (contiguity) then ensure that whatever occurs will transfer from one occasion to the next.

The second way in which classical conditioning is discussed as prototypical is in terms of the rule that relates the conditioned and unconditioned responses. Pavlov (1927) emphasized stimulus substitution as the distinctive property of the situation: the response originally elicited only by the UCS is later made to the CS. Subsequently, two kinds of departure from this rule have been pointed out: (a) Even in the salivation experiment, there are other readily identifiable components of the conditioned response that do not fit the stimulus substitution rule. These preparatory responses (Zener, 1937) are largely, but not exclusively, skeletal (rather than autonomic). (b) Even in the case of salivation and other autonomic responses, the CR is rarely identical to the UCR (i.e., a redintegrative response), so that components of the UCR may be missing from the CR. More serious are differences in direction of change between CR and UCR, which may not even be consistent across individuals, as in heart rate and respiratory conditioning (Martin & Levey, 1969; Upton, 1929; Zeaman & Smith, 1965).

Partly because of problems involving preparatory responses, classical conditioning has increasingly been restricted to autonomically mediated responses. There were two bases for this restriction: the apparent difficulty of conditioning skeletal responses by the operations of classical conditioning and according to the stimulus substitution principle (cf. Skinner, 1938, p. 115), and the supposed impossibility of conditioning autonomic responses via the Law of Effect. This is clear from Kimble's (1961) comment:

Obviously the common expression, "*the* conditioned response," is misleading, and probably in important ways. At the same time it should be recognized that the behavior described by Zener [preparatory responses] was almost certainly instrumentally, rather than classically, conditioned [p. 54].

The force of this argument is lost once the susceptibility of autonomic responses such as salivation to operant conditioning is demonstrated.

The foregoing facts are sufficient to show the error of continuing to regard classical conditioning as a unified process, much less as an explanatory element in accounts of operant conditioning. If classical conditioning is a single process, then it must be describable by principles of operation that apply to every instance. As we have seen, even stimulus substitution, the most general such principle, fails to apply in every case. Many, but not all, the anomalous cases are skeletal responses—which suggested that perhaps the notion of a single process could be preserved by restricting the term to autonomic responses. The only independent basis for this is to segregate skeletal and autonomic responses on the grounds that operant conditioning of autonomic responses is impossible. Since this is now known to be false (Miller, 1969), the only remaining basis for excluding skeletal responses from the class of classically conditionable responses is their failure to conform to the principle of stimulus substitution. But, in addition to being tautologous (classical conditioning simply becomes equivalent to learning via stimulus substitution), this fails because many autonomic responses do not conform to this principle and, based on the work of Brown and Jenkins and of Williams and Williams, at least one skeletal response—pecking in pigeons—does obey it (other possibilities are leg flexion and eyeblink). Thus, the class of classically conditionable responses can be defined neither in terms of the neural mediating system (autonomic vs. skeletal) nor in terms of adherence to a particular principle of learning.

The only remaining feature common to all the situations labeled as classical conditioning is the procedure itself. Research in this area has tended to focus on the properties of the temporal relationship between CS and UCS that are necessary and sufficient for the CS to acquire the power to elicit the conditioned response, and a consensus appears to be emerging that the crucial factor is the extent to which the CS is a predictor of the UCS (Rescorla, 1967). However, the notion of predictiveness does not appear to differ from *relative proximity* (of the CS to the UCS, or of a stimulus to reinforcement) which, as we have seen (Principle of Reinforcement 3, above), is a factor of wide applicability in operant conditioning. Thus, for all practical purposes, classical conditioning may be defined operationally as a class of reinforcement schedules that involve presentation of reinforcement independently of the subject's behavior.

We conclude, therefore, that the division of the field of learning into two classes—classical and instrumental conditioning—each governed by separate sets of principles, has no basis in fact. As an alternative, we suggest an analysis based on the principles of behavioral variation and reinforcement we have already discussed. In terms of this analysis, all adaptive behavior is subsumed under an expanded version of the Law of Effect, and a given situation is to be understood in terms of two factors: (*a*) the reinforcement

schedule, that is, the rule prescribing the delivery of reinforcement, or, more generally, stimuli, in relation to the behavior of the organism, and (*b*) the nature of the response under consideration. In terms of such an analysis, the properties normally considered as distinctive of classical conditioning may, once attention is directed to the question, be seen as due in part to a reinforcement schedule that happens to prescribe no correlation between the delivery of reinforcement and the subject's behavior, and in part to the special properties of responses such as salivation (see Implications 2 and 3, below).

Implications

Several puzzles become clearer once classical and instrumental conditioning are no longer regarded as separate processes:

1. In the earlier discussion of auto-shaped pecking, Williams and Williams noted that "the directed quality of the induced pecking does not follow naturally from respondent principles." Since we question this framework as a general description of anything outside the salivation experiment, its inability to deal with this particular situation poses no problem. The appearance of key pecking in the auto-shaping and superstition situations is, of course, not fully understood. It may reflect a special susceptibility of consummatory responses to the principle of stimulus substitution, as suggested earlier, or the action of transfer principles in ways that reflect something in common among the past histories of most pigeons. Similarly, little can be said about the directedness of pecking until the conditions under which this response is, and is not, directed have been more fully explored; although the results so far (with pigeons and monkeys) suggest that skeletal responses may always be directed. Rather than attempt to explain (or explain away) these characteristics, the best course seems to

be simply to observe and classify these and other behaviors under a variety of response-independent and response-dependent schedules, in the hope that hypotheses can be devised that have more hope of generality than anything that can be inferred from the scanty data presently available. We return to these issues in the concluding section.

2. There is little doubt that most autonomic responses are more easily conditioned by response-independent schedules than by response-dependent ones. However, this need not imply the existence of two different kinds of conditioning. It can as well be interpreted as reflecting the existence of internal controlling factors that are not amenable to the principles of reinforcement. Because of these fixed factors, these responses are not as free to come under the control of external stimulus factors as are skeletal responses that perform no function in the internal economy of the organism. Moreover, this principle can be extended beyond autonomic responses to deal with any response that is strongly connected to any stimulus, internal or external. Thus, in a recent discussion of operant conditioning of drinking, Black (1970) writes:

This discussion suggests that one dimension along which responses might be classified with respect to operant conditioning is the degree to which they are constrained from being changed by operant reinforcement by the properties of the neural subsystems of which they are a part. The regulatory systems can vary from very simple reflexes, such as the knee-jerk, to complex instinctive ones, such as those involved in courtship. The main point is not the complexity of the subsystems but rather the extent to which they limit the conditions under which operant reinforcement will work [p. 267].

Segal (1970) has made a similar suggestion in a thoughtful discussion dealing with a number of the points raised in the present paper.

As an example, the difficulties associated with demonstrating operant conditioning of heart rate can be viewed as analogous to the problem of acquiring control over an operant response that is already under the control of other variables, that is, such schedules are really concurrent rather than simple schedules. The heart rate problem is perhaps analogous to training an animal to alter his rate of bar pressing to receive food, while pressing the same bar is also necessary to obtain another reinforcer (such as oxygen or heat). Even without considering the problem of interactions among drives, one would not be surprised to find rather weak control by the food reinforcer.

3. Williams (1965) recorded salivation in dogs while they were bar pressing for food reinforcement on both fixed-interval and fixed-ratio reinforcement schedules. He found that the onset of salivation within each interreinforcement interval approximately coincided with the onset of bar pressing in the fixed-interval case, but began *later* than bar pressing on fixed-ratio. This interesting result is incompatible with an explanation of the operant response in terms of an underlying classical conditioning process. However, it may be understood in terms of the view we have been proposing by assuming that (*a*) the occurrence of each response (bar pressing or salivation) is separately and independently determined by the conditions of reinforcement peculiar to it, and (*b*) both responses tend to occur at times of greatest relative proximity to reinforcement (Principle of Reinforcement 3) In the fixed-interval case, these two assumptions predict a similar time of occurrence for both behaviors, because time since the beginning of a trial is, for both responses, the best predictor of reinforcement. However, in the fixed-ratio case, it is apparent that no matter what determines the time of onset of bar pressing, once it has stabilized its onset provides a better

predictor of reinforcement than does trial time (since the fixed number of responses making up the fixed ratio take an approximately fixed time). Thus, at asymptote our two assumptions imply that salivation should be reliably delayed with respect to bar pressing on fixed-ratio, but not on fixed-interval, as Williams reports.

However, there is no reason to expect this delay early in training, since the animal is not in a position to learn the cue significance of bar pressing until it has more or less stabilized. This expectation is also confirmed by Williams (1965), who notes that the delayed onset of salivation in the fixed-ratio case "emerged only after repeated exposure to the schedules [pp. 344–345]."

On the basis of a failure to find salivation *preceding* bar pressing on a spaced-responding ("controlled latency") procedure, Williams (1965) concludes that "the hypothesis that the two measures are independent may be rejected [p. 347]," which contradicts Assumption *a*, above. However, since *both* responses are assumed (Assumption *b*) to occur at times of greatest relative proximity to reinforcement, and reinforcement *cannot* occur *before* a bar press if it is always contingent upon bar pressing, there is no reason to expect salivation reliably to precede bar pressing under conditions where the common reinforcement for both responses depends on bar pressing alone. Thus, the apparent asymmetry between salivation and bar pressing observed by Williams may simply reflect an assymmetry between the conditions of reinforcement for each response, and need not imply any fixed internal linkage between them.

4. Recently, considerable attention has been devoted to avoidance of particular foods conditioned by a nauseous experience (induced by insulin or X rays) taking place several hours after ingestion (Garcia, Ervin, & Koelling, 1966; Kalat & Rozin, 1970; Revusky & Bedarf, 1967; Rozin, 1969). Since the CS–UCS interval

in these experiments is considerably longer than is customary in classical conditioning experiments, these data are even less congenial to a Pavlovian analysis than the auto-shaping results. They hint at the existence of a number of unsuspected built-in linkages between response systems and various salient stimuli. Such linkages are not unexpected from a broad evolutionary point of view that sees principles of variation and reinforcement as behavioral characteristics that are separately selected for, and bear as much (or as little) relationship to one another as do morphological characteristics.

DIFFICULTIES OF THE PROPOSED CLASSIFICATION

Science is conservative and, quite correctly, resists most attempts to alter an established theoretical framework. We have already tried to show that the number of anomalies facing current learning theories is sufficient to justify a search for alternatives. Nevertheless, the radical appearance of the scheme we suggest is a substantial obstacle to its consideration. It is important, therefore, to point out that it is little more than an extension and reorganization of familiar concepts, that is, reinforcement, S–R behavior units, learning principles such as transfer, and ethological observations on species-related behaviors. The difference is therefore largely one of emphasis and selection rather than the introduction of wholly novel ideas.

Any discussion of evolution and learning naturally brings to mind the learning-instinct issue. There is no simple parallel between this dichotomy and anything in the scheme we propose. The origin of every behavior is supposed traceable to principles of variation; if, for example, in a particular case a principle of transfer is involved, one might want to say that the behavior is learned. However, the question must then simply be asked again about the previous situation from which transfer has supposedly occurred. In this way, almost any question about the relative roles of heredity and environment will involve unraveling the whole of ontogeny. This conclusion will not be unfamiliar to ethologists (cf. Beach, 1955).

It is also important to emphasize that we have not been directly concerned with the evolution of the capacity to learn; although it may be that increasing knowledge of variation will shed light on this issue.

One objection that may be raised to the proposed scheme is that it is derived from and deals explicitly only with positive reinforcement. However, a recent account of behavior sustained by negative reinforcement (Bolles, 1970) is in perfect agreement with our position. Bolles points out that some activities are much more easily conditioned than others in avoidance situations, and these are the unconditioned activities that normally occur in a variety of potentially dangerous circumstances. These species-specific defense reactions, in Bolles' terminology, occur in advance of reinforcement (i.e., the avoidance of electric shock)—in our terms, they are determined initially by one of the principles of behavioral variation. The lack of arbitrariness of the response is perhaps more obvious in avoidance than in any other situation because of the complexity of the schedules involved: the animal must usually learn something about the pattern of occurrence of an intermittent aversive event, in the absence of responding, before he is in a position to detect alterations in that pattern correlated with his own behavior. Although a similar situation prevails in all reinforcement schedules, the change to be discriminated seems considerably easier both in appetitive conditioning, where the shift is from zero reinforcement in the absence of responding to reinforcement following every response, and in escape, where it is from continuous presence of the aver-

sive stimulus in the absence of responding to complete absence following each response. Bolles suggests other reasons, related to the limited opportunities for avoidance (in the schedule sense) in the wild life of small mammals, and thus the limited opportunities for the capacity to avoid to be selected in phylogeny.

The strongest point in favor of our proposal is its promise of parsimony. Consequently, the most damaging criticism that can be directed against it is the absence of firm specification of the principles of reinforcement and variation. This appears to allow the creation of such principles at will, enabling us to explain everything—and nothing. There are two defenses against this criticism. First, we again emphasize the tentative nature of the principles we have suggested. The overlap among the principles of variation, particularly, suggests that our list is provisional. Second, there is the strong possibility that clear recognition of the distinction between variation and reinforcement may be essential to further advance. In defense of this proposition, we first briefly discuss some examples from synoptic accounts of current learning theory, which show it to incorporate few safeguards against multiple explanations for phenomena. Since our scheme of classification is at least internally consistent and forces one to relate each new principle of variation to others that already exist, it has some advantages in this respect. Second, we discuss the controversy between cognitive and behavioristic theorists regarding the role of structure in behavior, in relation to a similar controversy in the history of evolutionary thought. The persistence of this controversy and its amenability to analysis in terms of variation and reinforcement suggest that our classification may be of some value despite its incompleteness.

1. Hilgard and Marquis (1940) list as principles of reinforcement: stimulus

substitution, expectancy, and the principle (law) of effect. It should be apparent from the earlier arguments that the Law of Effect is the result of the combined effect of both variation and reinforcement, stimulus substitution is a principle of variation, and expectancy refers to a general characteristic which can be imputed to most learning. Consequently this set of terms allows for considerable uncertainty in application to particular situations. For example, our analysis of the Williams and Williams experiment (see p. 391) makes use of both stimulus substitution and a principle of reinforcement analogous to what Hilgard and Marquis mean by the Law of Effect. Yet the same situation could also be analyzed in terms of expectancy; and it appears to be incompatible with the Law of Effect as traditionally understood. Progress since 1940 has not been dramatic, as illustrated by a list of "elementary conditioning processes" inventoried by Jenkins (1970) in connection with his work on cyclic reinforcement schedules: generalization, delay of reinforcement, conditioned reinforcement, unconditioned effects of eating, frustration effects, effects related to "behavioral contrast." Despite the number of these processes and the lack of any obvious relationship among them, Jenkins finds that they are unable to account for some rather simple features of his data, which require a description in terms of the relative proximity of a stimulus or a response to reinforcement as a major determiner (see Principles of Reinforcement, above).

2. There is a history of fruitless controversy between many behaviorists, who place little emphasis on the structural properties of behavior, and students of cognitive processes, who see structure as the most interesting and important behavioral attribute (cf. Staddon, 1967, 1969, for a discussion in relation to operant conditioning). The distinction between variation and reinforcement can shed

some light on this issue, which can be illustrated by briefly considering the contrasting views of Skinner and Chomsky (Chomsky, 1959; MacCorquodale, 1969) on the causation of learned behavior.

Chomsky's major concern is with principles of variation, in our terms, as is clear from his emphasis on the rule-governed nature of language (see Principle of Behavioral Variation 4, above).

Skinner's position is less obvious, but becomes clear from his account of the shaping of behavior (Skinner, 1953); he writes:

Operant conditioning shapes behavior as a sculptor shapes a lump of clay. Although at some point the sculptor seems to have produced an entirely novel object, we can always follow the process back to the original undifferentiated lump, and we can make the successive stages by which we return to this condition as small as we wish. At no point does anything emerge which is very different from what preceded it. The final product seems to have a special unity or integrity of design, but we cannot find a point at which this suddenly appears. In the same sense, an operant is not something which appears full grown in the behavior of the organism. It is the result of a continuous shaping process [p. 91].

For Skinner, apparently, moment-to-moment variation in behavior is small in magnitude, and essentially random (in the sense that it is unrelated to the final goal) in direction. Behavior is the result of the "accumulation . . . of indefinite variations which have proved serviceable" in Darwin's phrase. The similarity to natural selection is further emphasized by Darwin's (1951) account of the evolution of complex structures:

If it could be demonstrated that any complex organ existed, which could not possibly have been formed by numerous, successive, slight modifications, my theory would absolutely break down [p. 191].

In the history of evolution after Darwin, the rediscovery of Mendel's laws led to a retreat from gradualism in favor of a saltationism that traced evolutionary progress (especially evolutionary novelty) to large changes (mutations) of a more purposive sort (cf. Mayr, 1960). This position is closer to the view of Chomsky and other cognitive theorists, who tend to stress the importance of insight and other rules of composition that can produce sudden jumps in behavior.

The history of evolution has not supported the saltationist view. Fisher (1930) showed that large changes are much less likely to be adaptive than small ones, and Haldane and others have shown by a variety of arguments that the time available for evolution by the selection of small variations is more than sufficient to account for the observed differences among taxa: "The saltationism of the early Mendelians has been refuted in all its aspects [Mayr, 1960, p. 350]."

At a superficial level, therefore, these comparisons might appear to favor Skinner's gradualism and emphasis on reinforcement (selection), to the detriment of the cognitive position. This is probably unjustifiable for two main reasons. First, detailed analysis of complex problem solving clearly indicates the insufficiency of random variation as an account of the process (e.g., Neisser, 1967). The heuristics that are employed may, of course, be attributed to past learning based entirely on random variation. However, this suggestion meets with quantitative difficulties when applied to the development of language—the best-studied example of rule-governed behavior. Although calculations in this area are of limited validity in the absence of established principles of variation (analogous to Mendelian genetics), the attempts that have been made seem to indicate that the time available in ontogeny for the development of language is incompatible with any kind of learning by random variation (Chomsky, 1962; McNeill, 1968). This negative result is the opposite of Haldane's affirmative conclusion on the

sufficiency of small mutations as a basis for phylogenetic changes. It suggests that neither the heuristics employed in complex problem solving, nor the rules of syntax, need to be built up entirely de novo during ontogeny.

Second, the relationship between evolution and learning is such as to allow greater flexibility to learning. This is because natural selection can only be a response to small differences in "fitness": the most fit genotype will tend to prevail, although the species as a whole may thereby be led into an evolutionary blind alley. In terms of contemporary accounts of goal-directed mechanisms, natural selection represents a hill-climbing process (Minsky, 1961) and has no provision for prediction. This is clear in a familiar analogy due to Sewall Wright (1931) which shows the relationships among selection, structure, and variation. He pictures the field of possible structural variation as a landscape with hills and valleys. The range of variation present in a population of organisms is represented by a closed area on this landscape. Selection pressure is represented by the gradient (upward slope) of the landscape, so that each *peak* is an adaptive optimum for a given constellation of characters; valleys represent unstable equilibria yielding so-called centrifugal selection. If the area representing a given species includes a single adaptive peak, selection will be centripetal, so that the species will tend to cluster more and more closely around the peak. Thus, small mutations are more likely to lead to improvements in fitness than large ones (with a limiting probability of .5, as Fisher, 1930, has shown), and the consequent predominant role of such small differences in fitness in the evolutionary process becomes obvious.

Learning is not so limited, however, because the principles of variation can be weighted to take account of regularities in the past history of the species (these are

Skinner's, 1966b, "phylogenic contingencies"); that is, behavior need not occur at random in advance of reinforcement, but can reflect a priori probabilities that have been selected for during phylogeny. Other more complex strategies of this sort may also be built up by natural selection, giving learning a predictive capacity largely denied to evolution itself. Thus, although learned behavior reflects differences in reinforcement rate, just as evolution reflects selection on the basis of relative fitness, it need *not* be generally true either that small changes in behavior are more likely to be adaptive than large ones, or that the direction of change is unrelated to the final goal—as Skinner's account implies, and as is usually (although not invariably) the case in evolution. However, since the more elaborate principles of variation must themselves be built up step-by-step by natural selection, it is to be expected that the pattern and range of behavioral variation must bear some relationship to the phylogenetic status of the organism: "higher" organisms, such as man, are likely to have developed more complex principles of variation than "lower" organisms, such as the pigeon.

Thus, the major focus of the argument between Skinner and Chomsky is not on the importance of reinforcement, but about the complexity of the principles of variation that determine the nature of behavior in advance of reinforcement. Since Skinner derives his ideas from work on rats and pigeons, and Chomsky from the study of human language, there are considerable grounds for a disagreement, especially if its basis is not clearly perceived by either party. Clear conceptual separation of variation from reinforcement makes this kind of confusion much less likely.

CONCLUSION

The argument so far has served to draw attention to a number of generaliza-

tions about steady-state conditioning situations:

1. Most such situations involve some times and stimuli associated with relatively high reinforcement probability (e.g., the period at the end of the interval on fixed-interval schedules), and others associated with relatively low reinforcement probability (e.g., the period at the beginning of the interval).

2. The *terminal response* (a discriminated operant in Skinner's terminology) is restricted to periods of relatively high reinforcement probability. This distribution of the terminal response with respect to time and stimuli corresponds to a principle of reinforcement that relates the strength of a response to the relative frequency, density, or proximity of reinforcement associated with that response (Catania & Reynolds, 1968; Herrnstein, 1970; Jenkins, 1970).

3. The type, as opposed to the temporal and stimulus location, of the terminal response in situations involving both response-dependent reinforcement and response-independent reinforcement is determined by the interaction between principles of variation (e.g., transfer, stimulus substitution) that describe the occurrence of the response, in advance of reinforcement, and principles of reinforcement that determine whether it will persist or not (selective function of reinforcement).

4. Periods of low reinforcement probability are generally associated with *interim activities,* resembling appetitive behavior. If appropriate stimuli (goal objects) are provided, stereotyped *adjunctive behavior* (e.g., polydipsia, pica; Falk, 1969) takes the place of the more variable and relatively undirected interim activities.

5. Both terminal response and interim activities are more correctly labeled as predisposing conditions or *states* rather than behaviors, since in the absence of response dependency, the type of activity falling into these categories is not fixed.

Thus, drinking, wheel running, fighting, pecking, and a number of other activities may be either terminal or adjunctive behaviors, depending on historical and stimulus factors (Segal, 1969b; Skinner, 1959; Skinner & Morse, 1958). Directing factors for adjunctive behavior are the availability of appropriate goal objects (see above), and factors related to reinforcement that render some kinds of activity more probable than others: for example, polydipsia appears to partially displace both adjunctive wheel-running (Segal 1969a) and chewing-manipulatory behavior (Freed & Hymowitz, 1969) in rats (in situations with food as terminal reinforcer), even when both supporting stimuli are concurrently available.

The Terminal Response

We have already discussed the probable role of principles of variation such as stimulus substitution in describing the origin of terminal responses such as Pecking and Head in magazine in the superstition situation. Before turning to the more complex matter of the interim activities, a word should be said about the paradoxical results of the Williams and Williams (1969) study, in which they found persistent pecking at a brief stimulus, ending in reinforcement, despite the fact that a key peck terminated the stimulus and thus prevented reinforcement. In terms of our analysis, this situation pits reinforcement and variation against one another; thus, (*a*) the predictable delivery of food at the end of each presentation of a brief key stimulus may be a sufficient condition for the occurrence of key pecking in that stimulus, by the principle of stimulus substitution. But, (*b*) because of the response-contingency, the occurrence of a peck turns off the stimulus, omitting reinforcement on that occasion, and thus reducing the overall reinforcement rate. In turn, this reduction in reinforcement rate will, via Principle of Reinforcement 3, tend to re-

duce the tendency to make any terminal response, including pecking, in that situation. This process will continue until the tendency to peck has been sufficiently reduced to allow the key stimulus to continue unpecked until the delivery of reinforcement, which will again provide the occasion for the operation of the stimulus substitution principle, making pecking likely once again. Thus, an equilibrium will be established at a rate of pecking higher than zero, but less than the rate which would obtain if pecking had no effect on reinforcement rate. Extinction of pecking takes place if key pecking prevents reinforcement, but does not turn off the key stimulus, because the predictability of reinforcement, and thus the necessary condition for the operation of stimulus substitution, is thereby destroyed. Under these conditions, variation and reinforcement combine to weaken the tendency to peck, which therefore declines relatively rapidly.

The data on "instinctive drift" reported by Breland and Breland (1961, 1966) are also compatible with this kind of analysis.[4] However, their results strongly suggest that too much stress should not be laid on the apparent identity we (and others, e.g., Brown & Jenkins, 1968; Williams & Williams, 1969; Wolin, 1968) have found between the topography of the terminal response and the (uncon-

---

[4]The delayed appearance of the food-related behaviors in the Breland and Breland situations (as compared to the relatively rapid emergence of pecking in auto-shaping experiments) reflects the fact that food delivery could not become predictable (the necessary condition for the operation of the stimulus substitution principle) until after the animals had learned to produce it by making the required "arbitrary" response. However, once this initial response was learned (via principles of variation other than stimulus substitution), the stage was set for the operation of stimulus substitution, which could then override the original learning.

ditioned) response made to the terminal reinforcer. As in the case of adjunctive behavior (discussed below) and behavior elicited by general stimulation in reinforcing brain areas (e.g., Glickman & Schiff, 1967; von Holst & von Saint Paul, 1963), the effect of the experimental procedures we have described appears to be the induction of a *state* (in our terminology) or "mood" (von Holst & von Saint Paul) which makes some kinds of activity much more likely than others but preserves some flexibility in the animal's mode of response to the stimulating environment.

For example, Breland and Breland (1961) describe two situations, both showing "instinctive drift" in chickens, but only one of which conforms to the stimulus substitution principle. In the first case, the chicken pecked a ball which he had learned to project (via a remote firing mechanism) at a target—a hit being immediately followed by food. The history of contiguity between the moving ball and reinforcement and the similarity of the responses to both ball and food (i.e., pecking) fit easily into the stimulus substitution paradigm. In the second case, however, the chicken was reinforced for a chain of responses, the last of which involved standing on a platform for 15 seconds. After training, the chicken showed vigorous ground scratching while standing on the platform. This response has no topographic resemblance to pecking food, but is, of course, a universal food-getting behavior in chickens and typically occurs in the vicinity of food.

These examples, and others discussed by Breland and Breland (e.g., raccoons "washing" poker chips, porpoises swallowing manipulanda, pigs "rooting" tokens, etc.), as well as exceptions to stimulus substitution in the auto-shaping literature (e.g., Rachlin, 1969; Sidman & Fletcher, 1968), are compatible with a more general notion, to the effect that the stimulus (temporal or exteroceptive) most predictive of reinforcement comes to control a state or mood (the terminal state) appropriate to that reinforcer. The particular activity which occurs during the terminal period will then depend on principles of variation, which take into account *both* its motivational properties (e.g., food-related activities become more likely if the terminal reinforcer is food), *and* the nature of the stimulating environment; that is, the nature of the terminal state determines what stimuli will be effective in eliciting what behavior. Thus, the Breland and Breland chickens pecked when the stimulus defining the terminal state was appropriate (in some sense) for pecking, but scratched when it was not; pigeons peck the key in auto-shaping experiments, but (based on our results) are slower to peck in the superstition situation—presumably because an appropriate target is not provided. Similarly, Glickman and Schiff (1967) reviewed a large number of studies of behavior induced by direct brain stimulation which suggested that the effect of stimulation at a particular site is to induce a predisposing motivational condition or state which may lead to a variety of behaviors depending on the presence or absence of appropriate supporting stimuli. More recent work (e.g., Valenstein, Cox, & Kakolewski, 1970) further emphasizes the similarity between the terminal state and behavior induced by central stimulation:

Hypothalamic stimulation does not activate only one specific behavior pattern. The stimulation seems to excite the substrate for a group of responses that in a given species are related to a common state [Valenstein et al., 1970, p. 30].

Within this more general framework, stimulus substitution becomes a special case, which simply reflects the fact that the response normally made to the terminal reinforcer often becomes highly probable when the animal is in a terminal state corresponding to that reinforcer, and will occur if minimal environmental support is provided.

INTERIM ACTIVITIES AND ADJUNCTIVE BEHAVIOR

The principles of variation and reinforcement so far discussed refer to the origin and maintenance of the terminal response. The interim activities (including adjunctive behavior) require a separate although complementary account, to which we now turn.

There is as yet no general agreement on the causal factors underlying adjunctive behavior (i.e., behavior occurring during the interim period on a variety of intermittent reinforcement schedules). As we have already noted . . . , data presently available appear to rule out simple physiological interpretations (Falk, 1969), although they do not clearly point to any alternative. Some help is offered by the similarities between adjunctive behavior and displacement activities: the same explanation should be adequate for both. Possibilities are also somewhat restricted by general functional considerations. In the present section, we state a tentative general hypothesis and its empirical basis in what is presently known of adjunctive behavior. The relationship of this hypothesis to accounts of displacement behavior and to general adaptiveness is discussed in the following section.

The hypothesis may be stated in the form of three propositions:

1. The interim and terminal periods correspond to states, in the sense described earlier, defined by (*a*) the class of reinforcer or reinforcers that are effective at that time, and (*b*) the applicability of principles of variation appropriate to that class of reinforcer (e.g., food-related behaviors are likely to occur during the food state, defense reactions during the fear state, etc.).

2. The terminal state corresponds to the terminal reinforcer; the state during the interim period corresponds to *all other reinforcers*, although all need not be equally effective. The linkage between terminal and interim states is assumed to be direct and reciprocal, so that the strength (defined below in terms of *rate*) of activities during the interim period is *directly related* to the strength of the terminal response.

3. The strength of the terminal response is directly related to the "value" of the reinforcement schedule; that is, to relative rate and amount of reinforcement and to motivational factors (e.g., deprivation).

As a consequence of the reciprocal interaction between the terminal and interim states (Proposition 2) and the dependence of the terminal response on the value of the reinforcement schedule (Proposition 3), the strength of behaviors associated with the interim period will be determined both by the value of the terminal reinforcement schedule, as well as by the value of the reinforcers proper to them.

The notion of the interim and terminal periods as states (Proposition 1) has already been discussed. The dependence of the strength of the terminal response on variables related to the value of the reinforcement schedule (Proposition 3) should also encounter no opposition. It remains to show, first, that reinforcers other than the terminal reinforcer are effective during the interim period; second, that a number of different reinforcers may be effective at this time; and third, that the direct relation between the strength of the terminal response and the strength of adjunctive behavior implied by Propositions 2 and 3 has some basis in fact. Evidence for the effectiveness of reinforcers other than the terminal reinforcer, during the interim period, comes largely from studies of polydipsia (excessive drinking), induced by intermittent schedules of food reinforcement, as follows: (*a*) Consummatory behavior (e.g., drinking) occurs in the presence of the appropriate goal object (water) during the interim period on a variety of schedules. (*b*) This goal object can reinforce operant behavior:

If water is not freely available . . . concurrently with a food schedule, but is available in small portions contingent upon the completion of a fixed-ratio schedule, polydipsia is acquired and will sustain large fixed-ratios [Falk, 1970, p. 297].

Azrin (1964, reported in Falk, 1970) has found similar schedule control, in pigeons, by a bird provided as target for schedule-induced aggression. (*c*) Polydipsic drinking can be both increased and decreased by appropriate alteration of the palatability of the liquid available (Falk, 1964, 1966). (*d*) Polydipsia is usually reduced by using liquid terminal reinforcers. In the cases where the liquid used is at least as reinforcing to a hungry rat as dry food pellets (e.g., liquid Metrecal, condensed milk, liquid monkey diet; Falk, 1964, 1966; Hawkins, Everett, Githens, & Schrot, 1970; Stein, 1964), this decrease may be attributed to a direct effect on the thirst system (state), due to the water content, as in water preloading (see below). Wesson oil as terminal reinforcer is also less effective than food pellets in producing polydipsia (Stricker & Adair, 1966), although it contains no water, but is probably also less reinforcing and may reduce polydipsia for this reason (see Propositions 2 and 3). (*e*) Acquisition of polydipsia can be prevented by presession stomach loads of water (Chapman, 1969, reported in Falk, 1970), although established polydipsia is little affected. This kind of effect is also found with food-motivated terminal responses which, once established, will continue to occur at a somewhat reduced rate even in the presence of ad lib food (Neuringer, 1970a).

That more than one reinforcer is effective during the interim period is suggested by the facts that (*a*) the interim activities (which occur in the absence of appropriate goal objects) have no consistent direction and are not obviously related to any particular reinforcer; (*b*) a variety of goal objects—water, wood shavings, another animal—are sufficient to elicit appropriate consummatory reactions (drinking, chewing or eating, aggression); (*c*) physiological data, suggesting short-term reciprocal interactions between hunger and thirst drives which were induced centrally by electrical or chemical stimulation (Grossman, 1962; von Holst & von Saint Paul, 1963), indicate a possible mechanism for the simultaneous effectiveness of reinforcers other than food at nonfood times (interim periods) and food at food times (terminal periods). While it is as well to be cautious in generalizing both across species and from physiology to behavior, these hypothalamic mechanisms are evidently quite similar in birds and in mammals (cf. Åkerman, Anderson, Fabricius, & Svensson, 1960), and recent work supports the similarity between schedule-induced drinking and drinking induced by direct hypothalamic stimulation implied by these comparisons (Burks & Fisher, 1970). This kind of reciprocal interaction suggests that at a time when activity motivated by hunger is suppressed (e.g., during the period of interim activities on a food schedule), activities motivated by thirst might be facilitated.

That the effective reinforcers during the interim period are other than the terminal reinforcer is suggested both by the nonoccurrence of the terminal response at that time and by data reported by Segal (1969b) showing a shift in the status of drinking—from an adjunctive behavior, occurring early in the interval, to a terminal response, occurring largely at the end. The changeover took several experimental sessions, but it suggests that in the steady state, the same activity is unlikely to occur during both terminal and interim periods, as might be expected if these periods are associated with the action of different reinforcers.

Propositions 2 and 3 in combination imply that the strength of adjunctive behaviors, like that of the terminal response, should be directly related to the "value" of the reinforcement schedule, as indexed by motivational and reinforcement variables. The evidence in favor of this deduction is as follows: (*a*) With the interreinforcement interval held constant, the amount of polydipsic drinking in a session of fixed length is inversely related to body weight (Falk, 1969). Similar results have been reported for schedule-induced attack and air licking (Falk, 1970). (*b*) Postpellet pause (until the onset of polydipsic drinking) increases as a function of the interval duration (Segal et al., 1965). (*c*) Rate of licking within a drink bout tends to decrease as a function of interval length (Segal et al., 1965). (*d*) Rate of polydipsic drinking is increased by increasing the size of food reinforcement (Hawkins et al., 1970). Hawkins et al. attribute a contrary result by Falk (1967) to session length differences between the one- and two-pellet conditions of Falk's experiment. (*e*) Polydipsic drinking falls off drastically at fixed-interval values longer than about 3 minutes (Falk, 1966; Segal et al., 1965). Falk (1966) also reports a *direct* relationship between polydipsia (measured as total amount drunk per session) and fixed-interval length over the range 2–180 seconds. However, based on the results of experiments indicating the relative constancy of ingestion rate within a drinking bout in rats (Davis & Keehn, 1959; Schaeffer & Premack, 1961; Stellar & Hill, 1952), and the different times available for polydipsic drinking under different fixed-interval values, Falk's finding of a direct relationship between fixed-interval value and total amount drunk over part of the range, is compat-

ible with an overall *inverse* relationship in terms of *rate* of drinking. This inference is confirmed by recent data reported by Hawkins et al. (1970) which show a monotonically decreasing ingestion rate as a function of fixed-interval length, over the range 1–5 minutes. Given that overall ingestion rate is probably better than total amount drunk as a measure of the tendency to drink, this finding is both consistent with the deduction from Propositions 2 and 3 and more easily reconciled with other measures that indicate an inverse relationship between tendency to drink and frequency of reinforcement. Falk's finding that total amount drunk is maximal at intermediate interval values may reflect, therefore, an optimal balance between two factors: tendency to drink, which decreases as interval value increases, and time available for drinking, which increases with interval value.

The above account, in terms of interaction between motivational systems (states), seems to be the simplest that can presently be given of both adjunctive behavior and displacement activities. Its relationships to these activities, to the ethological interpretation of them, and to general functional considerations are discussed in the next section.

ADJUNCTIVE BEHAVIOR AND DISPLACEMENT ACTIVITIES

Most behavioral and morphological characteristics are adaptive, in the sense that they can be directly related to the reproductive fitness of the organism in its natural environment. Morphological exceptions to this rule are either the result of "correlated variation," in Darwin's phrase, or are vestigial characters, in the process of being lost. In neither case do they show the ubiquity and reliability that distinguish adjunctive and displacement activities. It is very likely, therefore, that these behaviors reflect a function, or functions, of considerable adaptive value to animals in the wild. What might this function be?

Learning theories generally consider the organism to be motivated by one thing at a time, for example, hunger, thirst, exploratory drive, etc. In like spirit, most learning experiments are designed to ensure the predominance of one kind of motivation at the expense of all others. In the wild, however, animals must allocate their time among a variety of activities so as to both satisfy current wants and anticipate future ones. It is reasonable to assume that there has been considerable selection pressure favoring an optimal balance among the various possibilities.

We have already noted the fact, related to stimulus discrimination, that animals tend to make the terminal response only at times when reinforcement is likely. This fact, and the principle of reinforcement based on it, might seem to reflect some kind of Law of Effort, since responding at times or places when reinforcement never occurs is obviously wasteful. However, a considerable weight of evidence suggests that the Law of Effort is not a major psychological principle, since it is easy to devise situations in which animals make many more responses than necessary (cf. Ferster & Skinner, 1957). A Law of Effort principle would also not explain active *avoidance* of situations associated with nonreinforcement.

A more plausible alternative is that these facts are related to animals' need to budget their time effectively. In these terms, a time, or stimulus, reliably associated with the absence of a given reinforcer provides information just as useful as a time perfectly correlated with the delivery of that reinforcer, since it permits the animal to attend to present and future needs other than the one associated with the absent reinforcer. However, other potentialities of the environment cannot usually be sampled as long as the animal remains in the vicinity of the un-

available reinforcer. One might expect, therefore, that natural selection will have fostered the development of a mechanism to ensure that animals avoid places at times when, on the basis of past experience, they have learned that reinforcement is not forthcoming.

Evolution is notoriously opportunistic in the sense that adaptation is achieved by whatever structural or functional means happen to be available. In the present case, we suggest that the means for ensuring that animals will not linger in the vicinity of food (or other reinforcers) at times when it is not available may be provided by the facilitation of drives other than the blocked one (Propositions 2 and 3); that is, that the relative aversiveness of the stimuli in the vicinity of food, during the interim period, may be a *direct effect* of the simultaneous suppression of the food state and facilitation of states associated with other reinforcers. In the wild, such facilitation will usually ensure that the animal leaves the situation to seek other reinforcers. Moreover, once the animal has left the situation, generalization decrement will ensure that the effect of factors acting to facilitate these other drives is reduced, restoring the animal to a state appropriate to his condition of deprivation and allowing him to take advantage of new opportunities to satisfy the previously blocked drive.

In experimental situations showing adjunctive behavior, however, the animal is *kept in the vicinity of the withheld reinforcer,* both by the physical restraint of the enclosure and, perhaps more importantly, by the properties of the reinforcement schedule. Since enclosure size has not been explicitly investigated, one cannot be sure of the relative importance of these two factors. In our laboratory, we have often observed animals on time-based schedules and noticed that pigeons tend to turn away from the key during the no-pecking phase of schedules such as the fixed-interval, which yield a period of no pecking followed by pecking. Figure 1 [page 148], which shows the birds' orientation (R_1) as a function of postfood time, is a quantitative record of this effect. However, the avoidance of the key is much more complete on schedules which require pecking followed by no pecking (temporal go-no go schedules, Staddon, 1970a, 1970b), presumably because the no-pecking period is terminated by an external event (delivery of reinforcement) rather than by the bird returning to the key to peck. These observations provide some evidence both for the tendency of pigeons to avoid the key at times when key pecking is not reinforced and for the restriction placed on this tendency by fixed-interval schedules.

In situations involving external (rather than temporal) stimuli, there is also considerable evidence for the aversive character of stimuli associated with non-reinforcement when they occur in a context associated with reinforcement (e.g., multiple and concurrent reinforcement schedules; cf. Beale & Winton, 1970; Catania, 1969; Terrace, 1966).

Thus, the temporal locus of adjunctive (and interim) behavior coincides with a period when, by other measures, the situation is aversive to the animal so that he will withdraw from it if he can. Studies of schedule-induced escape have shown that animals will learn to make a response during the interim period on fixed-ratio schedules that has the effect of removing them from the situation, even though the frequency of the terminal reinforcement may thereby be reduced (e.g., Azrin, 1961; Thompson, 1964). The present argument suggests that these data may reflect a general property of interim periods, although experimental results with other schedules are presently lacking.

Falk (1969, 1970) has ably summarized the similarities between adjunctive behavior and displacement activities, which include the apparent "irrelevance" of both kinds of activity, their association with situations in which a strong drive is blocked, and their modifiability by available stimuli and conditions of deprivation other than the major drive (cf. Morris,

1954; Rowell, 1961; Sevenster, 1961). A study by McFarland (1965) concerning displacement pecking induced by preventing drinking in thirsty doves further emphasizes the "state" property of displacement behavior:

The evidence for the view that this pecking belongs to the feeding system . . . [is] as follows: 1. Total time spent pecking is increased by the presence of grain. 2. Time spent pecking is partly replaced by time spent at a specific food getting activity, when the birds have previously been trained to obtain food in this way. 3. Food deprivation . . . increases the time spent pecking when grain is present, and this effect is counteracted by [prefeeding] [p. 298].

The interpretation of adjunctive behavior that we have presented is very similar to the disinhibition hypothesis concerning displacement activities first suggested by Andrew (1956). Hinde (1966) summarizes this view as follows:

When mutual incompatibility prevents the appearance of those types of behaviour which would otherwise have the highest priority, patterns which would otherwise have been suppressed are permitted to appear [p. 279].

Displacement behavior is usually exhibited in approach-avoidance conflict situations (e.g., territory defense, birds returning to the nest after an alarm, etc.) when the animal is consequently *prevented from leaving the situation*. We have already seen that during the interim period on intermittent reinforcement schedules, animals are also restrained in the situation both by the enclosure and, probably, by the properties of the schedule. Both situations therefore meet the conditions necessary and sufficient, by our hypothesis, for the *elevation* (rather than merely disinhibition) of motivational states other than the blocked one, leading in the schedule case to adjunctive behavior, and in the approach-avoidance case to displacement, redirection, or vacuum activities—the particular activities being a function of the strength and nature of the blocked response, the proximity to the goal, the stimuli available, the past history of the animal, and the duration of the blocking. This modification causes no difficulty in application to displacement behavior and meets theoretical objections to certain forms of the disinhibition hypothesis raised by McFarland (1966).

Finally, our account of the adaptive significance of adjunctive behavior, as a reflection of the integrative capacities of the organism which enable it to strike an efficient balance among a number of activities, finds a counterpart in McFarland's (1966) account of the significance of displacement behavior:

Thus it is suggested that the functional significance of displacement activities is that they are the by-product of a mechanism which enables animals to break away from a specific course of action, when progress in that course of action comes to a standstill [p. 231].

We conclude, therefore, that interim, adjunctive, and displacement behaviors may be grouped together on the basis of similar functional properties, similar probable causal factors, and similar adaptive role.

In summary, the argument relating to the interim period is as follows: (*a*) Extant data on adjunctive behavior are consistent with a tentative general interpretation in terms of interactions among motivational systems (states). (*b*) On the basis of general adaptive considerations, we have suggested the probable existence of a mechanism which enables animals to budget their time efficiently (e.g., by giving up temporarily ineffective activities). (*c*) McFarland has suggested that displacement and other "irrelevant" activities may reflect the action of such a mechanism. (*d*) Falk has pointed out the extensive similarities between adjunctive and displacement activities. (*e*) McFarland's suggestion may therefore be extended to interim and adjunctive behaviors, both on the basis of their restriction to the aversive interim period. Thus, the general interpretation of adjunctive behavior offered earlier gains additional support from the resemblances between adjunctive and displacement activities, from its similarity to the disinhibition hypothesis for displacement activities, and from its adequacy as a mechanism for enabling the animals to budget their time efficiently.

EPILOGUE

This ends our outline of conditioning. We have dealt with both terminal periods —which, we suggest, reflect a Law of Effect process that can best be understood by analogy with evolution by means of natural selection—and interim periods— which may reflect a mechanism enabling animals to allocate their activities efficiently. Learned behavior, under the relatively simple conditions of reinforcement schedules at least, is viewed as reflecting the sequencing, with respect to time and stimuli, of terminal and interim periods; and the scheme is therefore potentially comprehensive, although necessarily incomplete as to details.

Our proposal is founded on the belief that the most distinctive thing about living creatures is the balance they maintain among a number of tendencies to action, each one adaptive, yet each destructive if pursued to the exclusion of others. This emphasis on the *integration* of behavior has required that the scheme attempt to be comprehensive and that it relate in a natural way to biological and physiological considerations. Such merits as it possesses lie not in formal elegance or precision, but in an ability to organize otherwise unrelated facts and to suggest gaps where others may possibly be found.

REFERENCES

ÅKERMAN, B., ANDERSSON, E., FABRICIUS, E., & SVENSSON, L. Observations on central regulation of body temperature and of food and water intake in the pigeon (*Columba livia*). *Acta Physiologica, Scandinavica,* 1960, **50**, 328–336.

ANDREW, R. J. Some remarks on behaviour in

conflict situations, with special reference to *Emberiza* Spp. *British Journal of Animal Behaviour,* 1956, **4,** 41-45.

ANTONITIS, J. J. Response variability in the white rat during conditioning, extinction, and reconditioning. *Journal of Experimental Psychology,* 1951, **42,** 273-281.

AZRIN, N. H. Time-out from positive reinforcement. *Science,* 1961, **133,** 382-383.

AZRIN, N. H. Aggression. Paper presented at the meeting of the American Psychological Association, Los Angeles, September 1964.

AZRIN, N. H., HUTCHINSON, R. R., & HAKE, D. F. Extinction-induced aggression. *Journal of the Experimental Analysis of Behavior,* 1966, **9,** 191-204.

BEACH, F. A. The descent of instinct. *Psychological Review,* 1955, **62,** 401-410.

BEALE, I. L., & Winton, A. S. W. Inhibitory stimulus control in concurrent schedules. *Journal of the Experimental Analysis of Behavior,* 1970, **14,** 133-137.

BLACK, A. H. Constraints on the operant conditioning of drinking. In, *Schedule-induced and schedule-dependent phenomena.* Vol. 2. Toronto: Addiction Research Foundation, 1970.

BOLLES, R. C. Species-specific defense reactions and avoidance learning. *Psychological Review,* 1970, **77,** 32-48.

BRELAND, K., & BRELAND, M. The misbehavior of organisms. *American Psychologist,* 1961, **16,** 661-664.

BRELAND, K., & BRELAND, M. *Animal behavior,* New York: Macmillan, 1966.

BROADBENT, D. E. *Behaviour.* London: Methuen, 1961.

BROWN, P. L., & JENKINS, H. M. Auto-shaping of the pigeon's key-peck. *Journal of the Experimental Analysis of Behavior,* 1968, **11,** 1-8.

BURKS, C. D. Schedule-induced polydipsia: Are response-dependent schedules a limiting condition? *Journal of the Experimental Analysis of Behavior,* 1970, **13,** 351-358.

BURKS, C. D., & FISHER, A. E. Anticholinergic blockade of schedule-induced polydipsia. *Physiology and Behavior,* 1970, **5,** 635-640.

CANE, V. Some ways of describing behaviour. In W. H. Thorpe & O. L. Zangwill (Eds.), *Current problems in animal behaviour.* London: Cambridge University Press, 1961.

CATANIA, A. C. Concurrent performances: Inhibition of one response by reinforcement of another. *Journal of the Experimental Analysis of Behavior,* 1969, **12,** 731-744.

CATANIA, A. C., & REYNOLDS, G. S. A quantitative analysis of the responding maintained by interval schedules of reinforcement. *Journal of the Experimental Analysis of Behavior,* 1968, 11 (Pt. 2), 327-383.

CHAPMAN, H. W. Oropharyngeal determinants of non-regulatory drinking in the rat. Unpublished doctoral dissertation, University of Pennsylvania, 1969.

CHOMSKY, N. A review of B. F. Skinner's *Verbal behavior. Language,* 1959, **35,** 26-58.

CHOMSKY, N. Explanatory models in linguistics. In E. Nagel, P. Suppes, & A. Tarski (Eds.), *Logic, methodology and philosophy of science: Proceedings of the 1960 International Congress.* Stanford: Stanford University Press, 1962.

CRAIG, W. Appetites and aversions as constituents of instincts. *Biological Bulletin of the Marine Biological Laboratory,* Woods Hole, Mass., 1918, **XXXIV,** 91-107.

DARWIN, C. *The origin of species.* Oxford: The University Press, 1951. (Reprinted from the sixth edition, 1972).

DARWIN, C. *The variation of animals and plants under domestication.* New York: Appleton, 1896. 2 vols.

DAVIS, J. D., & KEEHN, J. D. Magnitude of reinforcement and consummatory behavior. *Science,* 1959, **130,** 269-270.

ESTES, W. K. Of models and men. *American Psychologist,* 1957, **12,** 609-617.

FALK, J. L. Studies on schedule-induced polydipsia. In M. J. Wayner (Ed.), *Thirst: First international symposium on thirst in the regulation of body water.* New York: Pergamon Press, 1964.

FALK, J. L. Schedule-induced polydipsia as a function of fixed interval length. *Journal of the Experimental Analysis of Behavior,* 1966, **9,** 37-39.

FALK, J. L. Control of schedule-induced polydipsia: Type, size, and spacing of meals. *Journal of the Experimental Analysis of Behavior,* 1967, **10,** 199-206.

FALK, J. L. Conditions producing psychogenic polydipsia in animals. *Annals of the New York Academy of Sciences,* 1969, **157,** 569-593.

FALK, J. L. The nature and determinants of adjunctive behavior. In, *Schedule-induced and schedule-dependent phenomena.* Vol. 2. Toronto: Addiction Research Foundation, 1970.

FANTINO, E., & COLE, M. Sand-digging in mice: Functional autonomy? *Psychonomic Science,* 1968, **10,** 29-30.

FERSTER, C. B., & Skinner, B. F. *Schedules of*

reinforcement. New York: Appleton-Century-Crofts, 1957.

FISHER, R. A. *The genetical theory of natural selection.* Oxford: Clarendon Press, 1930.

FLORY, R. Attack behavior as a function of minimum inter-food interval. *Journal of the Experimental Analysis of Behavior,* 1969, **12**, 825–828.

FREED, E. X., & HYMOWITZ, N. A fortuitous observation regarding "psychogenic" polydipsia. *Psychological Reports,* 1969, **24**, 224–226.

GARCIA, J., ERVIN, F. R., & KOELLING, R. Learning with prolonged delay of reinforcement. *Psychonomic Science,* 1966, **5**, 121–122.

GHISELIN, M. T. *The triumph of the Darwinian method.* Berkeley: University of California Press, 1969.

GILBERT, R. M. Psychology and biology. *Canadian Psychologist,* 1970, **11**, 221–238.

GLICKMAN, S. E., & SCHIFF, B. B. A biological theory of reinforcement. *Psychological Review,* 1967, **74**, 81–109.

GLICKMAN, S. E., & SROGES, R. W. Curiosity in zoo animals. *Behaviour,* 1966, **26**, 151–188.

GONZALEZ, R. C., BEHREND, E. R., & BITTERMAN, M. E. Reversal learning and forgetting in bird and fish. *Science,* 1967, **158**, 519–521.

GROSSMAN, S. P. Direct adrenergic and cholinergic stimulation of hypothalamic mechanisms. *American Journal of Physiology,* 1962, **202**, 872–882.

GUTTMAN, N., & KALISH, H. I. Discriminability and stimulus generalization. *Journal of Experimental Psychology,* 1956, **51**, 79–88.

HALDANE, J. B. S. Natural selection. In P. R. Bell (Ed.), *Darwin's biological work.* Cambridge: University Press, 1959.

HARLOW, H. F. Learning set and error factor theory. In S. Koch (Ed.), *Psychology: A study of a science.* Vol. 2 New York: McGraw-Hill, 1959.

HAWKINS, T. D., EVERETT, P. B., GITHENS, S. H., & SCHROT, J. F. Adjunctive drinking: A functional analysis of water and alcohol ingestion. In, *Schedule-induced and schedule-dependent phenomena.* Vol. 1. Toronto: Addiction Research Foundation, 1970.

HERRNSTEIN, R. J. "Will." *Proceedings of the American Philosophical Society,* 1964, **108**, 455–458.

HERRNSTEIN, R. J. Superstition: A corollary of the principles of operant conditioning. In W. K. Honig (Ed.), *Operant behavior: Areas of research and application.* New York:

Appleton-Century-Crofts, 1966.

HERRNSTEIN, R. J. On the law of effect. *Journal of the Experimental Analysis of Behavior,* 1970, **13**, 243–266.

HERRNSTEIN, R. J., & HINELINE, P. N. Negative reinforcement as shock-frequency reduction. *Journal of Experimental Analysis of Behavior,* 1966, **9**, 421–430.

HILGARD, E. R., & MARQUIS, D. G. *Conditioning and learning.* New York: Appleton-Century, 1940.

HINDE, R. A. *Animal behaviour: A synthesis of ethology and comparative psychology.* New York: McGraw-Hill, 1966.

HUTCHINSON, R. The production and maintenance of behavior by shock and shock-associated stimuli. In R. Ulrich (Chm.), The maintenance of responding through the presentation of electric shocks. Symposium presented at the meeting of the American Psychological Association, Miami, September 1970.

JENKINS, H. M. Sequential organization in schedules of reinforcement. In W. N. Schoenfeld & J. Farmer (Eds.), *Theory of reinforcement schedules.* New York: Appleton-Century-Crofts, 1970.

KALAT, J. W., & ROZIN, P. "Salience": A factor which can override temporal contiguity in taste-aversion learning. *Journal of Comparative and Physiological Psychology,* 1970, **71**, 192–197.

KEEHN, J. D. Beyond the law of effect. In, *Schedule-induced and schedule-dependent phenomena.* Vol. 1. Toronto: Addiction Research Foundation, 1970.

KIMBLE, G. A. *Hilgard and Marquis' conditioning and learning.* New York: Appleton-Century-Crofts, 1961.

LEVINE, M. Hypothesis behavior. In A. M. Schrier, H. F. Harlow, & F. Stollnitz (Eds.), *Behavior of nonhuman primates.* Vol. 1. New York: Academic Press, 1965.

LICKLIDER, J. C. R. On psychophysiological models. In W. A. Rosenblith (Ed.), *Sensory communication.* Cambridge: M.I.T. Press, 1961.

MACCORQUODALE, K. B. F. Skinner's *Verbal behavior:* A retrospective appreciation. *Journal of the Experimental Analysis of Behavior,* 1969, **12**, 831–841.

MANDLER, G. The interruption of behavior. *Nebraska Symposium on Motivation,* 1964, **12**, 163–219.

MARTIN, I., & LEVY, A. B. *The genesis of the classical conditioned response.* Oxford: Pergamon Press, 1969.

MAYR, E. The emergence of evolutionary novelties. In S. Tax (Ed.) *The evolution of life.* Vol. 1. Chicago: University Press, 1960.

MAYR, E. *Animal species and evolution.* Cambridge: Harvard University Press, 1963.

McFARLAND, D. J. Hunger, thirst and displacement pecking in the barbary dove. *Animal Behaviour,* 1965, **13,** 293-300.

McFARLAND, D. J. On the causal and functional significance of displacement activities. *Zeitschrift für Tierpsychologie,* 1966, **23,** 217-235.

McNEILL, D. On theories of language acquisition. In T. R. Dixon & D. L. Horton (Eds.), *Verbal behavior and general behavior theory.* Englewood Cliffs, N.J.: Prentice-Hall, 1968.

MILLENSON, J. R., & HURWITZ, H. M. B. Some temporal and sequential properties of behavior during conditioning and extinction. *Journal of the Experimental Analysis of Behavior,* 1961, **4,** 97-106.

MILLER, N. E. Learning of visceral and glandular responses. *Science,* 1969, **163,** 434-445.

MINSKY, M. Steps toward artificial intelligence. *Proceedings of the Institute of Radio Engineers,* 1961, **49,** 10-30.

MORRIS, D. The reproductive behaviour of the Zebra finch (*Poephila guttata*), with special reference to pseudofemale behaviour and displacement activities. *Behaviour,* **6,** 271-322.

MORRIS, D. The reproductive behaviour of the Ten-spined Stickleback (*Pygosteus pungitius* L.). *Behaviour,* 1958, Supplement VI, 1-154.

NEIMARK, E. D., & ESTES, W. K. *Stimulus sampling theory.* San Francisco: Holden-Day, 1967.

NEISSER, U. *Cognitive psychology.* New York: Appleton-Century-Crofts, 1967.

NEURINGER, A. J. Many responses per food reward with free food present. *Science,* 1970, **169,** 503-504. (a)

NEURINGER, A. J. Superstitious key pecking after three peck-produced reinforcements. *Journal of the Experimental Analysis of Behavior,* 1970, **13,** 127-134. (b)

PAVLOV, I. P. *Conditioned reflexes.* (Trans. by G. V. Anrep.) London: Oxford University Press, 1927.

PFAFFMAN, C. The behavioral science model. *American Psychologist,* 1970, **25,** 437-441.

PRINGLE, J. W. S. On the parallel between learning and evolution. *Behaviour,* 1951, **3,** 174-215.

PRYOR, K. W., HAAG, R., & O'REILLY, J. The creative porpoise: Training for novel behavior. *Journal of the Experimental Analysis of Behavior,* 1969, **12,** 653-661.

RACHLIN, H. Autoshaping of key pecking in pigeons with negative reinforcement. *Journal of the Experimental Analysis of Behavior,* 1969, **12,** 521-531.

RESCORLA, R. A. Pavlovian conditioning and its proper control procedures. *Psychological Review,* 1967, **74,** 71-80.

REVUSKY, S. H., & BEDARF, E. W. Association of illness with prior ingestion of novel foods. *Science,* 1967, **155,** 219-220.

REYNIERSE, J. H., & SPANIER, D. Excessive drinking in rats' adaptation to the schedule of feeding. *Psychonomic Science,* 1968, **10,** 95-96.

ROSENBLITH, J. Z. Polydipsia induced in the rat by a second-order schedule. *Journal of the Experimental Analysis of Behavior,* 1970, **14,** 139-144.

ROWELL, C. H. F. Displacement grooming in the Chaffinch. *Animal Behaviour,* 1961, **9,** 38-63.

ROZIN, P. Central or peripheral mediation of learning with long CS-US intervals in the feeding system. *Journal of Comparative and Physiological Psychology,* 1969, **67,** 421-429.

SCHAEFFER, R. W., & PREMACK, D. Licking rates in infant albino rats. *Science,* 1961, **134,** 1980-1981.

SEGAL, E. The interaction of psychogenic polydipsia with wheel running in rats. *Psychonomic Science,* 1969, **14,** 141-144. (a)

SEGAL, E. Transformation of polydipsic drinking into operant drinking. A paradigm? *Psychonomic Science,* 1969, **16,** 133-135. (b)

SEGAL, E. Speculations on the provenance of operants. In, *Schedule-induced and schedule-dependent phenomena.* Vol. 2. Toronto: Addiction Research Foundation, 1970.

SEGAL, E., & HOLLOWAY, S. M. Timing behavior in rats with water drinking as a mediator. *Science,* 1963, **140,** 888-889.

SEGAL, E., ODEN, D. L., & DEADWYLER, S. A. Determinants of polydipsia: IV. Free-reinforcement schedules. *Psychonomic Science,* 1965, **3,** 11-12.

SEVENSTER, P. A causal analysis of a displacement activity (Fanning in *Gasterosteus Aculeatus* L.). *Behaviour,* 1961, Supplement IX, 1-170.

SHANAB, M. E., & PETERSON, J. L. Polydipsia in the pigeon. *Psychonomic Science,* 1969, **15,** 51-52.

SHEFFIELD, F. S. Relation between classical conditioning and instrumental learning. In W. F. Prokasy (Ed.), *Classical conditioning: A symposium.* New York: Appleton-Century-Crofts, 1965.

SHIMP, C. P. Optimal behavior in free-operant experiments. *Psychological Review,* 1969, **76**, 97-112.

SIDMAN, M., & FLETCHER, F. G. A demonstration of auto-shaping with monkeys. *Journal of the Experimental Analysis of Behavior,* 1968, **11**, 307-309.

SIMMELHAG, V. L. The form and distribution of responding in pigeons on response-independent fixed and variable interval schedules of reinforcement. Unpublished master's thesis, University of Toronto, 1968.

SIMPSON, G. G. *The major features of evolution.* New York: Columbia University Press, 1953.

SKINNER, B. F. *The behavior of organisms.* New York: Appleton-Century, 1938.

SKINNER, B. F. "Superstition" in the pigeon. *Journal of Experimental Psychology,* 1948, **38**, 168-172.

SKINNER, B. F. *Science and human behavior.* New York: Macmillan, 1953.

SKINNER, B. F. Reinforcement today. *American Psychologist,* 1958, **13**, 94-99.

SKINNER, B. F. An experimental analysis of certain emotions. *Journal of the experimental Analysis of Behavior,* 1959, **2**, 264.

SKINNER, B. F. *Cumulative record.* New York: Appleton-Century-Crofts, 1961.

SKINNER, B. F. Operant behavior. In W. K. Honig (Ed.), *Operant behavior: Areas of research and application.* New York: Appleton-Century-Crofts, 1966. (a)

SKINNER, B. F. The phylogeny and ontogeny of behavior. *Science,* 1966, **153**, 1205-1213. (b)

SKINNER, B. F. *Contingencies of reinforcement.* New York: Appleton-Century-Crofts, 1969.

SKINNER, B. F. & MORSE, W. H. Fixed-interval reinforcement of running in a wheel. *Journal of the Experimental Analysis of Behavior,* 1958, **1**, 371-379.

STADDON, J. E. R. Some properties of spaced responding in pigeons. *Journal of the Experimental Analysis of Behavior,* 1965, **8**, 19-27.

STADDON, J. E. R. Asymptotic behavior: The concept of the operant. *Psychological Review,* 1967, **74**, 377-391.

STADDON, J. E. R. Inhibition and the operant. A review of G. v. Békésy, *Sensory inhibi-*

tion, and F. Ratliff, *Mach bands: Quantitative studies on neural networks in the retina. Journal of the Experimental Analysis of Behavior,* 1969, **12**, 481-487.

STADDON, J. E. R. Reinforcement after-effects. In, *Schedule-induced and schedule-dependent phenomena.* Vol. 2. Toronto: Addiction Research Foundation, 1970. (a)

STADDON, J. E. R. Temporal effects of reinforcement: A negative "frustration" effect. *Learning and Motivation,* 1970, **1**, 227-247. (b)

STEIN, L. Excessive drinking in the rat: Superstition or thirst? *Journal of Comparative and Physiological Psychology,* 1964, **58**, 237-242.

STELLAR, E., & HILL, J. H. The rat's rate of drinking as a function of water deprivation. *Journal of Comparative and Physiological Psychology,* 1952, **45**, 96-102.

STRICKER, E. M., & ADAIR, E. R. Body fluid balance, taste, and postprandial factors in schedule-induced polydipsia. *Journal of Comparative and Physiological Psychology,* 1966, **62**, 449-454.

TERRACE, H. S. Stimulus control. In W. K. Honig (Ed.), *Operant behavior: Areas of research and application.* New York: Appleton-Century-Crofts, 1966.

THOMPSON, D. M. Escape from S^D associated with fixed-ratio reinforcement. *Journal of the Experimental Analysis of Behavior,* 1964, **7**, 1-8.

TINBERGEN, N. "Derived" activities: Their causation, biological significance, origin, and emancipation during evolution. *Quarterly Review of Biology,* 1952, **27**, 1-32.

TULVING, E., & MADIGAN, S. A. Memory and verbal learning. *Annual Review of Psychology,* 1970, **21**, 437-484.

UPTON, M. The auditory sensitivity of guinea pigs. *American Journal of Psychology,* 1929, **41**, 412-421.

VALENSTEIN, E. S., COX, V. C., & KAKOLEWSKI, J. W. Rexamination of the role of the hypothalamus in motivation. *Psychological Review,* 1970, **77**, 16-31.

VERPLANCK, W. S. Since learned behavior is innate, and vice versa, what now? *Psychological Review,* 1955, **52**, 139-144.

VON HOLST, E., & VON SAINT PAUL, U. On the functional organisation of drives. *Animal Behaviour,* 1963, **11**, 1-20.

WILLIAMS, D. R. Classical conditioning and incentive motivation. In W. F. Prokasy (Ed.), *Classical conditioning: A symposium.*

New York: Appleton-Century-Crofts, 1965.

WILLIAMS, D. R., & WILLIAMS, H. Auto-maintenance in the pigeon: Sustained pecking despite contingent non-reinforcement. *Journal of the Experimental Analysis of Behavior,* 1969, **12,** 511–520.

WOLIN, B. R. Difference in manner of pecking a key between pigeons reinforced with food and with water. In A. C. Catania (Ed.), *Contemporary research in operant behavior.* New York: Scott, Foresman, 1968.

WRIGHT, S. Evolution in Mendelian populations. *Genetics,* 1931, **16,** 97–159.

WÜTTKE, W. The effects of d-amphetamine on schedule-controlled water licking in the squirrel-monkey. *Psychopharmacologia* (Berlin), 1970, **17,** 70–82.

ZEAMAN, D., & SMITH, R. W. Review of some recent findings in human cardiac conditioning. In W. F. Prokasy (Ed.), *Classical conditioning: A symposium.* New York: Appleton-Century-Crofts, 1965.

ZENER, K. The significance of behavior accompanying conditioned salivary secretion for theories of the conditioned response. *American Journal of Psychology,* 1937, **50,** 384–403.

Chapter 8

Secondary Reinforcement and Stimulus Control

Instrumental conditioning depends primarily on the relation between a behavioral event and a significant environmental event, either reward or punishment. But significant environmental events may also act as unconditioned stimuli, becoming associated with other environmental events via classical conditioning. These other events, or conditioned stimuli, may then play a secondary role in instrumental conditioning.

Consider the example of the bakery, in which eating bread is the significant event (reinforcer). The sight and smell of the bread, through prior association with eating bread, have become conditioned stimuli. Paying for the bread has become a learned instrumental response. If paying occurred only in the presence of the sight and smell of the bread, these stimuli would be said to *control* the response. And when these same stimuli—sight and smell—intervene between paying for, and eating, the bread, they are said to act as *secondary reinforcers* of the response. Such interactions between classical conditioning and instrumental conditioning occur frequently, in the laboratory as well as in everyday life.

SECONDARY REINFORCEMENT

Suppose that we can agree—regardless of our position on the question "What is an instrumental reinforcer?"—that a certain event and a certain response can be set in a reinforcement relation to each other. We may attribute the action of the reinforcer to need reduction, tension reduction, or some other cause, or we may simply have found previously that this particular event reinforces this particular behavior in this particular organism. Such an event is then defined as a *primary reinforcer.** It may have occurred to the reader by now that there are few human actions that are directly reinforced by primary reinforcers such as food. Even if we adopt Premack's view that reinforcement consists of a higher-valued event dependent on a lower-valued event, it would be hard to find any higher-valued event following most of our daily activities. We work for such things as food, clothing, and shelter, but these items bear no clear-cut relation to our work. Instead, a series of other stimuli—clocks and calendars, which tell us how long we are working, and counters such as bank statements and check-book balances, which tell us how much food, clothing, and shelter we can buy—intervene between work and what we are working for.

What is the function of these stimuli? Where primary reinforcement or punishment is always directly contiguous with behavior, or where the relation between them is vivid and constant, secondary reinforcers serve no function. But where the relation between responding and reinforcement is tenuous or variable, secondary reinforcers serve a useful function—they increase the salience of the relationship. They can do this in two ways: (1) they can signal that the response has just been made, and (2) they can signal that the reinforcer or punisher is about to occur. We shall consider these two functions of secondary reinforcement in turn.

Secondary Reinforcers as Feedback

When rewards or punishments are dependent on behavior but the behavior is not well defined, secondary reinforcers provide feedback telling the subject that a response (as the experimenter has defined it) has just been completed. In experiments with pigeons, pecks at a key are typically followed by feedback clicks to tell the pigeon that the peck is of sufficient force. Similarly, the light on an elevator button tells the person waiting that his press on the button has effectively called the elevator. Such feedback stimuli are especially important when the response has little feedback of its own. There are many sorts of behavior that provide little or no feedback. We are unaware of our heart rate, the size of the pupils of our eyes, the state of our brain waves, and the state of most of our internal organs (unless something is wrong with them). These responses are subject to instrumental conditioning when they are measured and feedback is provided as to their state. The feedback (a stimulus following responses) provides information about the relation between response and primary reinforcer.

---

*Premack's theory of reinforcement declares that any event may be a primary reinforcer under the proper circumstances. This is consistent with our assumption, in this section, that the given circumstances are such that certain events are primary reinforcers of the responses in question and others, which we shall call neutral stimuli, are not reinforcers (they may be very weak reinforcers or punishers).

Neal Miller and his students at Rockefeller University have instrumentally conditioned autonomic responses in animals. For instance, when an animal's heart rate is measured and the animal is given feedback and reward only when its heart rate varies within a certian range, the heart rate tends to stay within that range more than it does if rewards are delivered randomly. The characteristic of autonomic behavior that normally makes instrumental conditioning difficult may be lack of feedback to the behaving organism.

This area of research holds the promise that people may be able to learn to keep blood pressure, stomach acidity, and other autonomic functions at nonharmful levels provided they receive feedback informing them of the state of these functions. Such feedback could be provided electronically. Indeed, this procedure is already being used in behavior therapy, as we shall see later in this chapter.

Whether the autonomic responses are directly conditioned or whether the conditioning is mediated by some other response (as when an actor gets himself to cry by thinking of the death of a loved one) is not yet clear. It is conceivable, for instance, that the animals trained to control heart rate are actually learning to move their muscles in a certain way and that their heart rate changes only as a result of the muscular movement. However, some experiments have shown that when rats' skeletal muscles were paralyzed by the drug curare, instrumental conditioning of their heart rate was actually better than without curare. Evidently, far from mediating autonomic conditioning, skeletal responses actually hindered conditioning. Nevertheless, central nervous system activity still goes on during curare paralysis and could have mediated conditioning.

Second-order Schedules of Reinforcement

We have indicated previously that a response can be defined in any arbitrary way. The responses studied in the laboratory have mostly been simply manipulandum operations such as pecks at a key by a pigeon or presses of a lever by a rat. But even if we confine ourselves to manipulandum operations for the time being, there is no reason why a response must be a *single* manipulandum operation. For instance, it is possible to define a response as 10 presses of a lever and then to reinforce responses (10 presses each) just as one would reinforce responses defined as single lever-presses.

Such an arrangement is called a second-order schedule of reinforcement. In a second-order schedule there is a component schedule, such as FR-10 or VI-5', that defines the new response unit. Completion of the requirements of the component schedule results, not in primary reinforcement, but in a signal (usually a brief tone or brief light flash) indicating that a component is completed. These components then function as responses themselves within a superordinate schedule that provides primary reinforcement. For instance, the component schedule might be FR-10 for lever-presses of a rat. The superordinate schedule might be FI-3'. In this case, feedback would be provided after every tenth lever-press, and the first unit of 10 lever-presses completed after 3 minutes had elapsed from the time the schedule began would produce primary reinforcement. The entire component is the response, the lever-press is just a fraction of the response. For convenience, subresponses such as lever-presses within second-order schedules will be called *fractional responses.*

Consider two types of fixed-ratio schedules of reinforcement. One is a normal FR-100 schedule, in which 100 responses—say, pecks by a pigeon—are required to obtain food. The other is a second-order schedule that requires 10 pecks, not for food, but for a brief flash of light. After 10 flashes of light, food is given. Both schedules effectively require 100 pecks for food. The only difference between them is that the second-order schedule provides signposts, so to speak, along the way. Such a second-order schedule for a pigeon is like the schedule by which a bubble gum company gives a child a certificate for each 10 wrappers he sends in and then gives him a prize for 10 certificates, as opposed to simply giving a prize for 100 wrappers.

Is there a difference between the two types of schedules? It turns out that there is a tremendous difference. The behavior of the subject, be it pigeon or child, with the second-order schedule is the same as if it consisted of 10 fixed-ratio schedules of primary reinforcement. Figure 8.1 shows (idealized) cumulative records of a pigeon on an FR-100 schedule of food reinforcement and a pigeon on a second-order schedule in which 10 FR-10 components are required. There are two aspects to performance on second-order schedules to

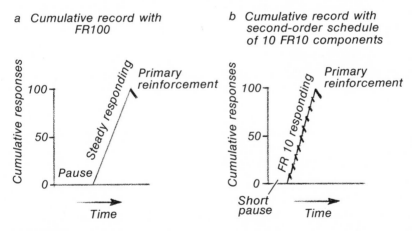

FIGURE 8.1
Hypothetical cumulative records comparing performance with (a) a normal FR-100 schedule of primary reinforcement and (b) a second-order schedule consisting of 10 FR-10 components, each followed by a brief stimulus. The tenth component is followed by primary reinforcement. Note that the pause is shorter with the second-order schedule and that the overall response rate is faster than with one primary reinforcement alone.

note. First, fractional responses in the component conform to the usual pattern of responses on that schedule of primary reinforcement. If the component is an FI schedule, the cumulative record pattern of fractions will be scalloping. Second, considering the entire component as a response, the pattern of responses conforms to the superordinate schedule. Thus, in a second-order fixed-interval schedule of fixed-interval schedules there would be a scalloping between as well as within components.

Second-order schedules sometimes generate very high overall rates of the fractional response. The number of fractional responses with a second-order schedule is usually somewhere between the (lower) amount that would be obtained with the superordinate schedule only (no feedback) and the (higher) amount that would be obtained if each component schedule were reinforced with primary reinforcement. Often these very high rates of fractional responses can be obtained on second-order schedules with very little primary reinforcement. Thus the bubble gum company might get children to buy more bubble gum by instituting a second-order (certificate) program than by just giving prizes for 100 wrappers.

Considering the strong effect the secondary reinforcers (the feedback stimuli) in second-order schedules seem to have on responding, we should first ask whether they acquire this effect by being paired contiguously with primary reinforcement. The question may be answered by comparing behavior under the two types of schedule illustrated in Figure 8.2. Type I pairs the stimulus with primary reinforcement and type II does not. If pairing of the feedback stimulus with primary reinforcement is necessary for feedback to act as secondary reinforcement, then in type II, where pairing is absent, the feedback should not increase responding. The results of experiments using type II second-order schedules, however, have uniformly shown that the effect of the feedback stimulus on both pattern and rate of the fractional response is very similar to the effect of primary reinforcement itself (although the rate is usually somewhat

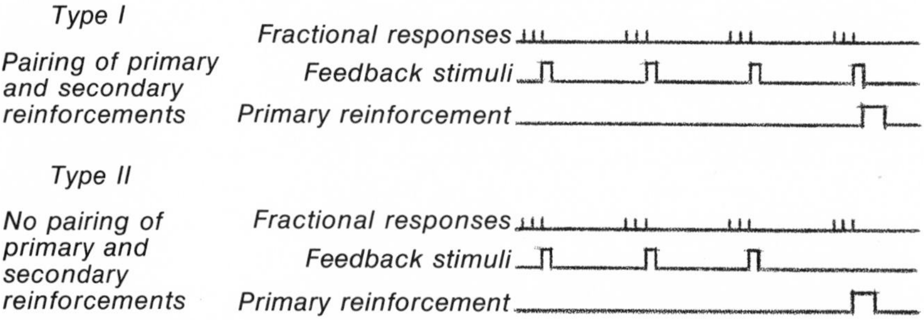

FIGURE 8.2
Two types of second-order schedule. Both types consist of a superordinate schedule of FR-4 and a component schedule of FR-3. In Type I, primary and secondary reinforcement are paired. In Type II, primary and secondary reinforcement are *not* paired.

less than with type I). Contiguous pairing is thus not necessary for secondary reinforcement to affect responding in second-order schedules, although contiguous pairing does increase the fractional response somewhat.

A molar theorist might explain the potency of secondary reinforcers by noting that the pattern of fractional responding appropriate to each component is correlated with primary reinforcement even though primary reinforcement is delayed. A more molecular theorist would look for mediating events between the stimuli and eventual primary reinforcement. Later in this chapter we shall consider what such mediating events might be.

Secondary Reinforcers as
Signals in Reinforcement Delay

Since instrumental conditioning depends on a learned relation between a response and a reinforcing (or punishing) event, anything that makes the relation stronger will aid in learning. We have just discussed one way to strengthen the relation, by providing feedback for the response, that is, a stimulus that invariably follows the response. Another way, which we shall take up now, is by providing a stimulus that invariably precedes the reinforcer. As we noted earlier, when response and reinforcer are already contiguous, secondary reinforcement serves no instrumental function. But when response and reinforcer are not contiguous, as when primary reinforcement is delayed, a secondary reinforcer preceding primary reinforcement speeds up learning considerably. A secondary reinforcer during the delay period can completely cancel out the deleterious effect of delay on learning. For instance, in an early study of delay of reinforcement with rats in a maze, the food reward was buried under sawdust in the goal box. Reward was delayed by the time the rats had to dig through the sawdust to get the food. The rats learned to run through the maze just as fast with the sawdust as without it. The sawdust, which itself was now invariably followed by reward, served as a sort of promissory note for the rat—a signal that food was coming.

An experiment involving chimpanzees working for poker chips, carried out by John B. Wolfe in 1936, illustrates the effect of secondary reinforcement on performance during delay of primary reinforcement. Wolfe trained chimpanzees to press a lever to get a poker chip and then to deposit the chip in a slot to get a grape. The sequence of events is shown in Figure 8.3a. The poker chips in this experiment served as secondary reinforcers—their presence was invariably followed by food. The chimpanzee in this situation is much like the television quiz show winner who is presented with a check instead of prizes: although the check is only a piece of paper, the recipient is as rewarded as the person who receives a refrigerator or television set because he will be able to cash the check and get the prizes in the future. When Wolfe arranged a delay between acquisition of the poker chip and its insertion in the machine (Figure 8.3b), the chimpanzee responded just as fast to get poker chips as when there

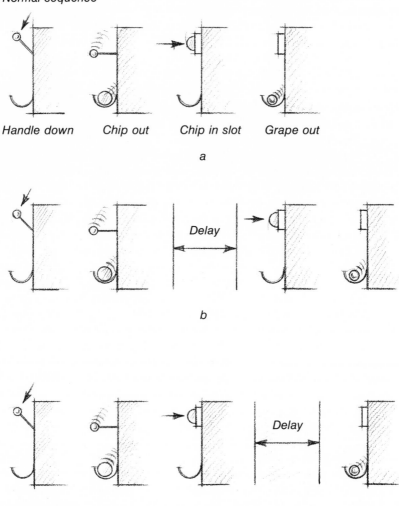

Normal sequence

Handle down   Chip out   Chip in slot   Grape out

a

Delay

b

Delay

c

FIGURE 8.3
How the point of delay affected lever-pressing in Wolfe's experiment. (a) Normal
sequence without a period of delay. (b) Delay between collecting chip and
inserting it in slot. In this sequence, the chimp has the chip during the delay,
and the delay does not slow down the chimp's lever-pressing. (c) Delay between
placing poker chip in slot and collecting grape. In this sequence, the chimp has
no chip during the delay, and the delay does slow down lever-pressing.

was no delay. However, when Wolfe arranged a delay between insertion of the poker chip and delivery of the food (Figure 8.3c), so that the chimpanzee had to wait during the delay period with no poker chip in its hand, responding for poker chips fell off sharply.

Do Secondary Reinforcers Acquire
the Properties of Primary Reinforcers?

We have discussed two ways in which secondary reinforcers may be employed in instrumental conditioning. After some relation between a response and a significant environmental event (primary reinforcer) has been set up, a stimulus may be inserted between the response and the reinforcer, related either to the response, as feedback, or to the reinforcer, as a signal. In both cases the stimulus (the secondary reinforcer or punisher) now enters into a relationship with the significant event—a relationship we have defined as classical conditioning. In other words, in both cases the stimulus becomes a CS. When the CS intervenes between the response and primary reinforcer, does it actually take on the characteristics of the primary reinforcer, becoming reinforcing in itself? For example, in the experiments with rats and chimps discussed above, do sawdust and poker chips become valuable in and of themselves, through their association with primary reinforcement? This possibility has been much discussed and investigated. The evidence indicates, however, that secondary reinforcers do not take on the characteristics of primary reinforcers. That is, they do not change in value themselves because they are associated with an event of higher (or lower) value.

As an illustration, let us suppose that there are two hotels identical in all respects except for one thing. In hotel A each meal is invariably preceded by a dinner bell. In hotel B the same meals are served, each preceded by a dinner bell, but the boy who rings the dinner bell frequently rings the bell between meals as well as before each meal. In both hotels the same meals are served, but in hotel B there are many more dinner bells. Given experience with both hotels which hotel do people prefer? Surely hotel A. Meals are primary reinforcers and since each meal in both hotels is always preceded by a dinner bell, dinner bells must be secondary reinforcers. In hotel A there are fewer of these secondary reinforcers than in hotel B. In hotel B people no doubt spend more time walking toward the dining room, but one might expect people to prefer hotel A where dinner bells reliably precede meals. In other words, one might expect secondary reinforcement (dinner bells) to be valuable in this case only insofar as it is followed by primary reinforcement (meals).

An experiment by Richard Schuster with pigeons parallels the situation of the two hotels.

Schuster allowed his pigeons to choose between a few minutes of exposure to either of the following two conditions:

A. A condition in which pecking a key occasionally (on a variable-interval schedule) produced a blue light and buzzer followed by food (corresponding to hotel A).

B. A condition identical to the first (in which pecking produced the blue light and buzzer followed by food) except that, in addition, pecking sometimes produced extra pairs of blue lights and buzzers that were not followed by food (corresponding to hotel B).

Figure 8.4 illustrates the choice the pigeons were required to make. Suppose, on a given exposure to condition A for 1 minute the pigeon pecked the key 60 times, and 3 of those pecks were followed by a blue light and a buzzer, followed in turn by reinforcement. Thus, there were 3 primary reinforcements each preceded by a secondary reinforcement. Suppose on a given exposure to condition B for 1 minute, the pigeon also pecked the key 60 times. In condition B suppose 15 of the pecks produced a blue light and buzzer, but only on 3 occasions was the signal followed by food. Thus, there were again 3 primary reinforcements, each preceded by a secondary reinforcement, but there were 12 extra secondary reinforcements.

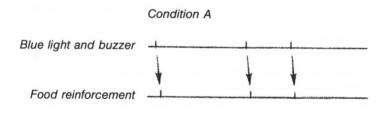

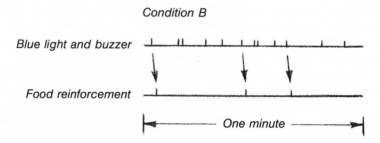

FIGURE 8.4
Examples of the two conditions between which pigeons chose in Schuster's experiment. (All reinforcements are shown by ticks.) Condition A: each reinforcement is preceded by a secondary reinforcement. Condition B: each reinforcement is preceded by a secondary reinforcement plus extra secondary reinforcements.

Schuster reasoned that if the buzzer and blue light had the properties of primary reinforcers, the pigeons should prefer condition B, in which there were more of them, but if they were only reinforcing to the extent that they signalled, or promised, food, the pigeons should be indifferent or actually prefer condition A, in which the promise was more reliably fulfilled—that is, in which the contingency and correlation relationships between the signal and the food were stronger. Schuster found that although the pigeons pecked more during condition B, they chose condition A when given a choice, indicating that the buzzer and light were only reinforcing to the extent that they reliably indicated that food was to come.

The idea that secondary reinforcers take on the properties of primary reinforcers is another version of the idea, discussed in Chapter 4, of stimulus substitution, according to which the CS becomes equivalent to the US. Just as the evidence is against stimulus substitution, the evidence is also against the notion that the secondary reinforcer takes on the value of the primary reinforcer.

Secondary Reinforcement and Information

One useful way to characterize secondary reinforcers is in terms of their power to give the subject information about the coming of a primary reinforcer. We may talk figuratively here about "promissory notes," "cues," and "signals," but there is a more exact way of specifying how much information a certain event in the environment conveys to a subject—that is, in terms of the degree to which that event reduces uncertainty.

One of the first studies to show that a secondary reinforcer only works if it gives information about the primary reinforcer was done by David Egger and Neal Miller. This study was rather negative in character in that it showed that a stimulus that did *not* provide information about the reinforcer was *not* a secondary reinforcer even though it was contiguous with the primary reinforcer (food, in this case). The two experimental conditions are shown in Figure 8.5. With condition A, a stimulus, S_2 (either light or tone), was paired with food for a hungry rat. S_2 lasted for 2 seconds. After S_2 had been on for half of a second, another stimulus, S_1 (a tone if S_2 was a light; a light if S_2 was a tone), was presented along with S_2. In terms of information, S_1 was largely redundant. It provided little more information than S_2 alone (although S_1 did localize the US temporally somewhat better than S_2). After exposure to condition A, the rats were trained to press a bar for food reinforcement, the bar-pressing was then partially extinguished (for 10 minutes) by removing food, and then for half of the rats each bar-press was followed by S_2 and for the other half each bar-press was followed by S_1. Egger and Miller found that S_2, the informative stimulus, showed much greater secondary-reinforcing strength (the rats pressed the bar many more times when S_2 was produced) than S_1, the redundant stimulus.

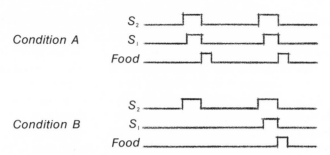

FIGURE 8.5

Diagram of Egger and Miller's experiment on secondary reinforcement and redundancy. In Condition A, S_1 is redundant and proved to have low value as a secondary reinforcer. In Condition B, S_1 is not redundant and proved to have high value as a secondary reinforcer. [From Egger, M. D. and Miller, N. E. Secondary reinforcement in rats as a function of information value and reliability of the stimulus. *J. Exp. Psych,* 1962, *64,* 97–104. Copyright 1962 by the American Psychological Assn.]

An entirely different result was found after condition B of Figure 8.5. In this condition S_1 was sometimes paired with S_2 and sometimes not, but the food was only presented when S_1 was presented. Although S_2 did give some information about food (the rats were never fed in the absence of S_2, but sometimes they were not fed even in its presence) S_1 gave more information (the rats were never fed in the absence of S_1 and always fed in its presence). After condition B, rats pressed more times to get S_1 than to get S_2.

Both Schuster's experiment and Egger and Miller's experiment showed that signals do not become secondary reinforcers unless they are informative. In Schuster's condition B, and in S_2 of Egger and Miller's condition B, the extra signals actually subtracted from the informativeness of the signals that did precede food. In Egger and Miller's procedure A the redundant signals (S_1) provided little information not already provided by S_2.* Now we turn to the

---

*The attentive reader will wonder how the Wagner-Rescorla model might handle the results of these experiments. The degree to which a stimulus becomes a secondary reinforcer should parallel the degree to which it becomes an effective CS in ordinary classical conditioning experiments. Both Schuster's and Egger and Miller's experiments could be interpreted in terms of compound stimuli. In Schuster's experiment the background stimuli of condition A plus the blue light and buzzer form one triple compound stimulus; the background stimuli of condition B plus the blue light and buzzer form another compound. During conditions A and B some subsets of the compound are subject to conditioning and some to extinction. In Egger and Miller's experiment some additional assumptions are necessary about what happens to conditioning *during* a signal when the US is delayed. The working out of these explanations is far beyond the scope of this book. It is fair to say that the Wagner-Rescorla model can handle information-type experiments with some difficulty. This difficulty, so far, makes it more parsimonious to look for other, more molar, explanations for the efficacy of information. One such explanation is described on the following pages.

question (already touched on by Schuster's experiment) of preference for informative versus noninformative situations.

There is some evidence that organisms prefer situations where uncertainty about reinforcement is low to situations where uncertainty is high, even if the two situations involve the same reinforcement. (Schuster's experiment is one example.) A study by Gordon H. Bower, Jim McLean, and Jack Meacham was called "The Value of Knowing When Reinforcement is Due." The experimenters made pigeons choose between two identical reinforcing conditions. Their experiment is illustrated in Figure 8.6. In condition A, reinforcement was delivered on one of two fixed-interval schedules, a fixed-interval 10-second (FI-10″) schedule or a fixed-interval 40-second (FI-40″) schedule. Which of these schedules was in effect was determined randomly. The key was yellow during both schedules, and there was no signal to indicate which of the two FI

Condition A

On half of the exposures to Condition A, the key was: *and reinforcement was delivered on a 40-second fixed-interval schedule.*

|————————————————————|
40″   Food

On the other half of the exposures to Condition A, the key was: *and reinforcement was delivered on a 10-second fixed-interval schedule.*

|—————|
10″ Food

Condition B

On half of the exposures to Condition B, the key was: *and reinforcement was delivered on a 40-second fixed-interval schedule.*

|————————————————————|
40″   Food

On the other half of the exposures to Condition B, the key was: *and reinforcement was delivered on a 10-second fixed-interval schedule.*

|—————|
10″ Food

FIGURE 8.6
Bower, McLean, and Meacham's experiment on the value of knowing when reinforcement is due. Pigeons chose between Conditions A and B.

schedules was in effect. In condition B, reinforcement was also delivered on one of two fixed-interval schedules, and which of these two schedules was in effect was also determined randomly. However, if the pigeons chose condition B, the key turned red when the FI-40″ schedule was in effect and green when the FI-10″ schedule was in effect.* The experimenters argued that the pigeons were choosing between an informative and a noninformative situation. Condition A provides no information about the schedule in effect, whereas condition B provides information. In other respects the two conditions are identical. The pigeons showed a strong preference for condition B, the one with more information about reinforcement.

It is to the extent that secondary reinforcers convey information about reward that they, themselves, can be reinforcing.

Experiments with noxious stimuli have yielded similar results. Given a choice of being shocked without warning or having each shock preceded by a signal, rats choose the signalled shock. Pietro Badia and his students at Bowling Green State University in Ohio have found that the signals are so important that rats choose the signalled shocks even when they are several times as intense, several times as long in duration, or several times as frequent as unsignalled shocks. The rats in Badia's experiments could press a lever to change from an unsignalled to a signalled condition. Each press of the lever gave the rat 3 minutes of exposure to signalled instead of unsignalled shocks. Pressing the lever had no effect on the rate of shocks (just as in Schuster's or in Bower, McLean, and Meacham's experiment, the pigeons could not get more or less food). The response being studied only produced a signal. Such a response is called an *observing response.* Observing responses have been studied in many contexts with both positive reinforcement and punishment. The findings demonstrate conclusively that animals prefer events such as food and shock to be signalled.

Why are signalled events preferred to unsignalled events? In other words, why is information reinforcing? A strict behaviorist might reply that it just is, and then go on to discover how the parameters (relative duration of signal, type of signal, type of event signalled) affect various types of observing responses in various organisms. But we may speculate here a little about why information should reinforce observing responses. One fairly obvious theory is that when an event is signalled it can be prepared for. That is, food may be more valuable if some salivation can take place before the food is ingested. Similarly, responses geared to withstanding shock, such as freezing or adjusting physiological processes, may make the shock less aversive.

At the end of Chapter 3 (Patterns of Behavior) we discussed an experiment by Staddon and Simmelhag that may throw some light on the role of signals

---

*Choice in the Bower, McLean, and Meacham experiment (and in the Schuster experiment) was measured by pecking during still another condition when two responses were available, one leading to condition A and the other to condition B. These are, technically, concurrent chain schedules and will be described in detail in Chapter 10.

preceding significant environmental events. In that experiment food was delivered to hungry pigeons at fixed intervals. Thus, food delivery may have been predictable by internal, temporally correlated stimuli. The pigeon's activity was markedly different just before the food (they made "terminal" responses such as pecking) from their activity when food was unlikely (they made "interim" responses such as preening and scratching). Suppose we assume that the following rank order holds for the values of the three events for a hungry pigeon: (1) food, (2) intrinsic value of interim activities, (3) intrinsic value of terminal activities. We are assuming that terminal activities are valuable only insofar as they add to the value of food, but that if they are not followed by food they are of least value (reflecting our observation that terminal activities do not occur when no food is probable). Interim activities, such as preening and scratching, do have some intrinsic value, since when no food is available the pigeon engages in them rather than doing nothing. A signal preceding food (and, by analogy, shock) thus causes the pigeon to budget its time efficiently, restricting terminal activities to the signal period and leaving the rest of its time for the higher-valued interim activities. When Staddon and Simmelhag did remove the predictability of food (by presenting it at variable intervals) the pigeons spent more time at terminal activities (which was presumably wasted when the food did not come) and less time at interim activities. The same reasoning applies to low-valued events like shocks. If an interval is divided into shock-free (safe) and shock-likely (danger) periods, interim activities can occur freely during safe periods and preparation for shock need only occur when shock is likely. In experiments with signalled food and signalled shock the signal divides the experimental session into two periods, one of higher value and one of lower value. With food the signal delimits the higher-valued period and with shock the signal delimits the lower-valued period. The signal in both cases provides the opportunity for terminal (preparatory) responses. The absence of the signal in both cases provides the opportunity for interim responses.

Efficient budgeting of time governs use of secondary reinforcers in everyday life as well as in the laboratory. People, in general, like to know in advance when the significant events in their lives, whether good or bad, will occur, not only so that they can prepare for them, but also so that they can spend the periods when these events are improbable not anticipating or worrying about them. A good doctor or dentist warns a patient when it's going to hurt, not only so that the patient can prepare for the pain but also so that the patient can relax the rest of the time.

Secondary Reinforcement and
Frequency of Primary Reinforcement

One question of current interest is to what extent the frequency of signalled reward or punishment (food or shock) affects observing responses (responses that produce signals but do not influence frequency of food or shock). A function showing rate of observing responses for food (obtained by Derek Hendry

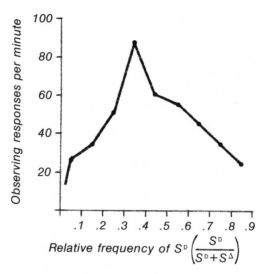

FIGURE 8.7

The rate of observing responses as a function of the probability (relative frequency) that an observing response would produce an S^D (a discriminative stimulus signalling availability of reward) as opposed to an S^Δ (a discriminative stimulus signalling absence of reward). [From Hendry, D. P. Concluding commentary. Hendry, D. P. (Ed.) *Conditioned reinforcement.* Homewood, Ill. The Dorsey Press, 1969.]

with chimpanzees) is shown in Figure 8.7. The low values at the left and right show that signals are useless when the event they are supposed to signal never occurs or always occurs (for example, a weather report would be useless if the weather were always the same, if it were always or never raining). Signals are useful, that is, support observing responses, only when the experimental session is divided into more and less valuable parts.

Note that the maximum of the function of Figure 8.7 is to the left of 0.5 on the abscissa. This means that the chimpanzees found the signal for food most valuable when food was relatively infrequent. That is, when rewards are infrequent information seems to be more valuable than the same amount of information when rewards are frequent (for example, the weather report would be listened to more when there are few sunny days than when they are many sunny days).

STIMULUS CONTROL

Stimulus control is another term for stimulus discrimination. If an organism comes to respond one way in the presence of a stimulus and another way in its absence, then that stimulus is said to "control" the organism's behavior, much as a traffic light controls traffic.

Stimulus Control in Classical Conditioning

We have already discussed stimulus control (discrimination) in classical conditioning. Recall the experiment by Shenger-Krestovnikova in which dogs were taught to respond differentially to circles and ellipses. (Figure 4.10). The circles (CS's) were followed by food powder; the ellipses were not. At first dogs salivated when either circles or ellipses were presented; later they came to salivate only when circles were presented (except when the circles and ellipses were almost identical). From one point of view, the dogs learned to discriminate between the circles and ellipses. From another point of view, the circles gained control of the dogs' salivation.

The most common form of discrimination conditioning consists of alternating two stimuli (like the circles and ellipses), one followed by the US and the other not followed by the US. Because this form of discrimination conditioning is so common, special terms have been coined for the stimuli: the stimulus followed by the US (the circle) is called the CS^+; the stimulus not followed by the US (the ellipse) is called the CS^-.

There are also other ways to establish stimulus control in classical conditioning. For example, instead of circles followed by food (and ellipses followed by no food), Shenger-Krestovnikova's experiment might have had circles followed by more food and ellipses followed by less food. The dogs then might have come to respond during exposure to both circles and ellipses, but to respond more to the circles. Alternatively, Shenger-Krestovnikova might have made the amount of food proportional to the roundness of the ellipse (In Figure 4.10, (b) would be followed by the least food, (c) by more food, (d) by still more food, and (a) by the most food.) The dogs might then have come to salivate in proportion to the roundness of the stimulus. Still another alternative would have been to follow circles by food and ellipses by electric shock to the paw. Then circles might have come to elicit salivation and the ellipses, withdrawal.

Stimulus Control in Instrumental Conditioning

In classical conditioning the CS is itself associated with a significant event (the US). In instrumental conditioning, however, neutral stimuli may be associated, not with an event, but with a relation between two events: between behavior and reinforcement (or punishment). A good example of a stimulus serving such a secondary function in human behavior is an out-of-order sign on a Coke machine. This sign tells us about the *relation* between dimes and Cokes but is not itself necessarily associated with either. Signs that signal a relation between response and reinforcement are called *discriminative stimuli*.

As in classical conditioning, the most common discrimination procedures in instrumental conditioning involve alternate presentation of two stimuli. In the presence of one stimulus, reward is obtained; in the presence of the other, reward is not obtained. Again as in classical conditioning, the stimuli for this special discrimination procedure have special names. A discriminative stimulus that signals a positive correlation between responding and reward is called an S^D ("ess dee"). A discriminative stimulus that signals the absence of reward regardless of responding is called an S$^\Delta$ ("ess delta"). Figure 8.8 shows this common discrimination procedure with the two types of conditioning.

It is important to note that alternation of stimuli signalling reinforcement and no reinforcement (as in Figure 8.8) is only one of many discrimination procedures—only one form of stimulus control. A discriminative stimulus may signal any relation between responding and reinforcement. The color of the sky in the morning, for example, gives an indication of whether a trip to the beach that afternoon will be reinforced by the opportunity to swim. But blue skies in the morning do not guarantee fair weather, nor do grey skies guarantee rain. Blue skies signal one relation between response and reinforcement, grey skies another. Thus, although we may decide not to go to the beach on a grey day,

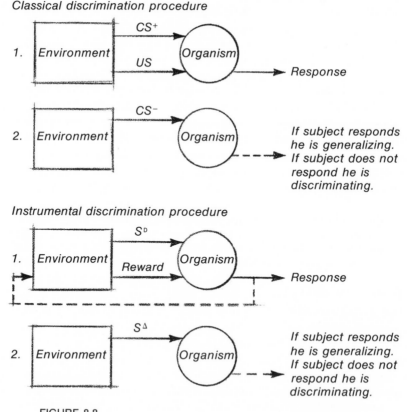

FIGURE 8.8
Discrimination procedures for classical and instrumental conditioning.

such a signal is not, properly, an S^Δ because it is possible that our response (going to the beach) would be reinforced (by nice weather at the beach) even when skies are grey in the morning.

Successive Discrimination and Simultaneous Discrimination

Within the confines of instrumental conditioning, discrimination has been studied in two ways. One way, called *successive discrimination,* consists of alternately presenting two different discriminative stimuli. The other way, called *simultaneous discrimination,* consists of presenting two discriminative stimuli together. The alternating green and red of a traffic light, telling us to go in the presence of the green and stop in the presence of red, is an example of successive discrimination. The adjacent green and red lights marking open and closed toll booths on a highway or bridge are an example of simultaneous discrimination; they tell us not whether to go or stop, but whether to go one way or another. In general, simultaneous-discrimination situations can produce finer distinctions in responses to stimuli than successive-discrimination situations. There are two reasons for this greater sensitivity of simultaneous discrimination. First of all, the stimuli themselves are easier to tell apart when presented simultaneously. It is easier, for instance, to tell a darker from a lighter shade of grey when the two greys are adjacent than when they are seen at different times. Secondly, even when the stimuli are clearly distinguishable, simultaneous procedures tend to create greater differences in performance than successive procedures because in simultaneous procedures a response to one stimulus precludes a response to the other.

It is easy to see how simultaneous discrimination is more sensitive than successive discrimination in everyday life. At home, where dinner is simply put before someone, he often has the choice only of eating it or going hungry. Observing a person's eating habits at home may tell you little about his preferences for food, since many people will eat whatever is put in front of them rather than go hungry. In a restaurant, however, a choice is available, and eating one food often precludes eating another. Here, the same person is likely to be more "discriminating." In the chapter on choice we shall discuss this difference in more detail.

Testing for Control by S^D and S^Δ

Let us return to the procedure illustrated in the lower part of Figure 8.8. Two discriminative stimuli are alternated. One (the S^D) signals a positive correlation between responding and reinforcement. The other (The S^Δ) signals a zero correlation, with no reinforcement programmed, regardless of responding. The behavior usually observed under these conditions is straightforward: responding during the S^D, no responding during the S^Δ.

A particular instance of such discrimination, involving a pigeon and a key, is illustrated at the top of Figure 8.9. The pigeon's pecks are reinforced when

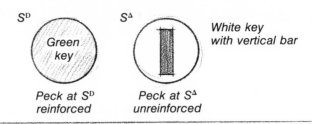

FIGURE 8.9
Procedures for testing control by S^D and S^Δ.

the key is green (S^D) and not reinforced when the key is white with a vertical bar (S^Δ). After alternate exposure to the two discriminative stimuli, the pigeon comes to peck at the key when it is green and not to peck at the key when it is white with a vertical bar.

What has the pigeon learned about the two discriminative stimuli? Consider these three alternatives:

a. The pigeon learns to peck when the key is green (S^D).
b. The pigeon learns not to peck when the key is white with a vertical bar (S^Δ).
c. The pigeon learns to peck when the key is green *and* not to peck when the key is white with a vertical bar.

A parallel set of questions could be raised about virtually any discrimination. A little boy may be rewarded for kissing his mother and not rewarded for kissing his father. Does he learn (1) to kiss his mother, (2) not to kiss his father, or (3) both? Which alternative the boy learns depends on what he ordinarily does. If he ordinarily kisses nobody, he must learn to kiss his mother, but need learn nothing specific about his father. If he ordinarily kisses everybody, he must learn not to kiss his father, but need learn nothing specific about his mother. If he ordinarily kisses some people, he must learn to kiss his mother *and* not to kiss his father.

The same sort of reasoning applies to the pigeon. If it ordinarily does not peck, it must learn to peck the green key. If it ordinarily pecks, it must learn not to peck the white key with the vertical bar. If it sometimes pecks, it must learn both.

Whether alternative (a), (b), or (c) applies in any given case depends on the organism (both its species and its previous experience), the stimuli, the reinforcement, the response, and the relation between the reinforcement and the response. The question that concerns us here is how to test the alternatives.

Alternatives (a) and (b) imply that one of the stimuli has no effect. Alternative (a) implies that the S^Δ has no effect, and alternative (b) implies that the S^D has no effect. One way to test these alternatives is the experiment shown in Figure 8.10.* The rationale for the test follows a somewhat complicated argument. The stimulus that is supposed to have no effect is varied. If it is argued, as it is in alternatives (a) and (b), that one of the stimuli has no effect, then its variation also ought to have no effect. If, on the other hand, varying both stimuli, in successive operations, has the effect of producing variation in behavior, then alternative (c) must be correct.

An important practical point of the tests is that the S^D and S^Δ must be capable of separate variation along different continua. In the illustration in Figure 8.10, the continuum is color for the S^D and angle of the bar for the S^Δ. Suppose otherwise, that the S^D and S^Δ varied along the same continuum—that the S^D was a simple white key and the S^Δ was a grey key, on a continuum of brightness. Then in the test phase, any new stimulus (a new shade of grey) would be a variation of both the S^D and the S^Δ. If the pigeon pecked less during the new stimulus, there would be no way of knowing whether it was because the stimulus was less like the S^D or more like the S^Δ. In the example in Figure 8.10, on the other hand, where the S^D and S^Δ are on two continua, we can be fairly certain that while the red key is not like the S^D, it is no more like the S^Δ than the green key was.

Another practical problem with the procedure in Figure 8.10 is what to do about reinforcement while the test stimuli are presented. For tests of the efficacy of S^D, for instance, the usual solution is to stop reinforcement altogether during the test and alternate the original S^D and a group of test stimuli varying along the same dimension (color, in the case of the example in Figure 8.10). This would be a simple generalization experiment in which responding would be expected to fall off as the stimuli became more different from the original

---

*Although the results shown in Figure 8.10 are hypothetical, similar experiments with similar results have been done by H. M. Jenkins, W. K. Honig, and others.

Training:

$S^D =$ (Green key)

$S^\Delta =$ (White key with vertical bar)

White key with vertical bar

Presence of S^D signals possibility of reinforcement for peck

Presence of S^Δ signals no possibility of reinforcement

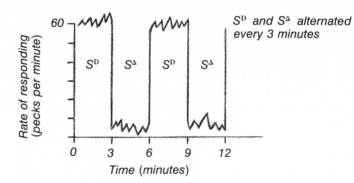

Rate of responding (pecks per minute)

60

S^D S^Δ S^D S^Δ

0   3   6   9   12

Time (*minutes*)

S^D and S^Δ alternated every 3 minutes

Test phase: Reinforcement discontinued. Stimuli alternated. Average rate of responding measured during exposure to each stimulus.

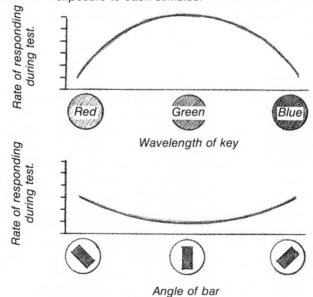

Rate of responding during test.

Red   Green   Blue

Wavelength of key

Rate of responding during test.

Angle of bar

FIGURE 8.10
Hypothetical experiment to test discrimination.

S^D, provided the S^D had an effect, that is, provided either alternative (a) or (c) were true. Otherwise (if alternative (b) were true), responding would not drop off, but would remain at a high value as the color of the stimulus was varied.

For tests of the efficacy of S^Δ, a corresponding procedure is followed. Reinforcements are discontinued, and the original S^Δ is alternated with test stimuli varying along the same dimension (tilt of the bar across the white key in Figure 8.10). This experiment, shown in Figure 8.10 (bottom curve), would test generalization of the S^Δ. Responding would be expected to increase as the stimuli became more different from the original S^Δ provided the S^Δ had an effect (provided either alternative (b) or (c) were true). Otherwise (if alternative (a) were true), responding would not increase but would remain at the same low value as the angle of the bar was changed.

Although the specific experiment of Figure 8.10 has not been performed exactly as described here, enough similar experiments have been performed for us to be certain that in the case described (pigeons pecking a key), alternative (c) is correct. Both S^D and S^Δ gradients have been found. Figure 8.10 shows a hypothetical S^D and an S^Δ test-phase gradient. Usually S^Δ gradients are somewhat shallower than S^D gradients. Some experimenters have speculated that this is because the S^D is the only stimulus signaling reinforcement, whereas the S^Δ shares the property of signalling nonreinforcement with the myriad other stimuli in the pigeon's environment. Since the S^D is unique and the S^Δ somewhat more general, the pigeon is likely to respond in the presence of a new stimulus as if it were another of the general, more common "S^Δ"s. In the generalization test, therefore, the particular S^Δ of training does not produce as much discrimination in responding as the S^D of training.

The gradient in Figure 8.10 obtained from the S^D is called an *excitatory gradient* and the gradient obtained from the S^Δ is called an *inhibitory gradient.**

Generalization Gradients

The degree to which responding is elicited, not just by the discriminative stimulus, but also by other stimuli along the same continuum, is expressed as a *generalization gradient*. Figure 8.11 shows three hypothetical generalization gradients, which could have been obtained with either classical or instrumental procedures. Gradient A, the flat gradient, shows that no stimulus control was attained by the discriminative stimulus over the response measured. Another way to express the effect represented by a flat gradient is to say that the subject paid no attention to the stimulus. Gradient C would indicate that sharp stimulus control was attained and the subject paid close attention to the stimulus. Using the language of "attention", however, to describe generalization gradients is somewhat dangerous. If it is understood that attention refers only to the re-

---

*The notion that inhibition is associated with nonreinforcement comes from Pavlov's conception of extinction as a positive inhibitory process (see Figure 4.8).

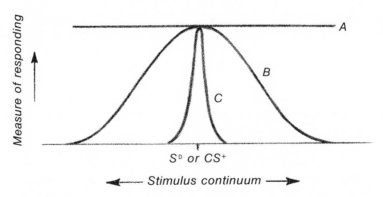

FIGURE 8.11
Three hypothetical stimulus-generalization gradients. Gradient A is flat, showing no stimulus control along the continuum being explored. Gradient B is "typical," and gradient C is very sharp, showing precise stimulus control along the continuum being explored.

sponse being measured, then the word is safe to use. But many people will assume that if a subject is paying no attention to a stimulus, the generalization gradients as measured by all possible responses will be flat. Sometimes generalization gradients are flat for one response but sharper, like gradient B or even C, when other responses are used to measure generalization. For instance, a pigeon that is trained to peck a key in response to a certain frequency of tone (the S^D) may then peck at the same rate with all tones used in a generalization test, producing a flat gradient (like gradient A of Figure 8.11). It is nevertheless possible that other responses, such as the pigeon's brain waves, its pupil dilation, its orientation to the key, and the number of incipient pecks (not actually completed), might still show sharp gradients like B or C around the S^D. It would seem that the pigeon must have been paying some attention to the stimulus if the stimulus could control *some* responses. Saying that a stimulus did or did not control a certain response simply describes the slope of the generalization gradient for that response. Saying that the subject did or did not pay attention to the stimulus is an inference about other gradients for other responses.

It is a truism that the more similar a new situation is to an old one the more likely an organism is to do in the new situation what it did in the old one. If a rat has been trained to run in a red alley with smooth floors it is less likely to run in a green alley with rough floors than in the original alley. This decrease in the probability of a response is called a *generalization decrement*. To say that a generalization decrement has occurred is merely to say that a non-flat gradient has been obtained. Thus, observation of "generalization decrement"

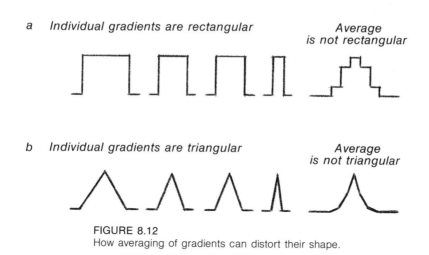

a   *Individual gradients are rectangular*   *Average is not rectangular*

b   *Individual gradients are triangular*   *Average is not triangular*

FIGURE 8.12
How averaging of gradients can distort their shape.

and observation of "stimulus control" mean the same thing—that the generalization gradient is not flat.

Generalization gradients may be obtained with individuals or groups. For example, a group gradient might be obtained in instrumental conditioning by training 100 rats to run down a grey alley for food and then extinguishing the response in 10 groups of 10 rats each in alleys of different brightness. The number of trials required for extinction would be most for the group receiving extinction training in the conditioning alley; fewer trials would be required for groups receiving extinction training in brighter or darker alleys.* The disadvantage of group gradients is that the average of a group of subjects may not reflect the gradient of any single subject. For instance, Figure 8.12 shows that the average of a group of individual rectangular or triangular gradients does not retain the shape of the gradients of which it is composed.

Generalization gradients for individual subjects may be obtained by methods such as those shown in Figure 8.10, in which the S^D is alternated with other stimuli without reinforcement. The problem with individual gradients obtained in this way is that since reinforcement is discontinued during the test the subjects' responding tends to slow down as the test proceeds. Thus there will be more responding during whatever stimulus is presented early in the test and less responding during whatever stimulus is presented later in the test, than there would ordinarily be. Another way to put it is that an extinction curve is superimposed on the generalization gradient. A way of handling this

---

*Probably the rats would run more in brighter alleys than darker alleys equally different (physically) from the alley of training. The tendency to respond more vigorously with more intense stimuli regardless of their similarity to the training stimulus is called "stimulus-intensity dynamism." This action of the stimulus to directly cause responding parallels the direct action of certain reinforcers, which we discussed in Chapter 7.

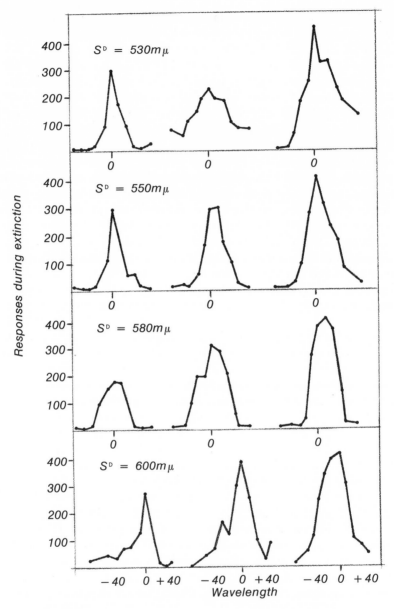

FIGURE 8.13
Individual generalization gradients from 12 of the 24 pigeons used by
Guttman and Kalish. Four different wavelengths (S^D's) illuminated the key.
The abscissa indicates by how many *nm* (mμ) the test stimuli differed
from the S^D. [From Guttman, N. and Kalish, H. Discriminability and stimulus
generalization. *J. Exp. Psych.*, 1956, *51*, 79–88. Copyright 1956 by the
American Psychological Assn.]

problem is to reward the subject during training on a schedule such as a VI-2′ or VI-3′ schedule, which provides reward very infrequently. Because of the tendency for extinction to be very slow after partial reinforcement (remember Humphreys' paradox) all the generalization testing may be done before extinction has progressed too far. If the different stimuli are presented to the subjects in various scrambled orders and the gradients for each subject do not differ on the basis of the order of the stimuli, then we can be fairly certain that the extinction curve had minimal effect on the generalization gradient.

Figure 8.13 shows a series of individual generalization gradients obtained during extinction in an experiment by Norman Guttman and Harry Kalish with pigeons pecking a lighted key. The experimenters obtained their generalization gradients by first rewarding the pigeons on a variable-interval schedule while the S^D was being presented, then removing reward entirely and measuring responses with the former S^D and with all the test stimuli higher and lower in wavelength. Another technique which results in much sharper gradients is to continue to reward the pigeon for pecking the key whenever the S^D is presented but not to reward the pigeon when the other test stimuli are presented. This method was used by Donald Blough to obtain the gradient for a single pigeon shown in Figure 8.14. The average gradient of six pigeons obtained by Guttman

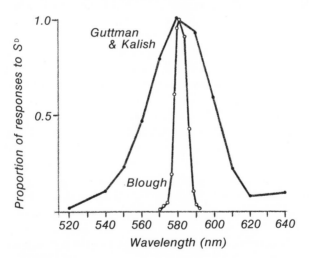

FIGURE 8.14
A comparison of two ways to test for generalization. During testing in the Guttman and Kalish experiment pigeons were not rewarded at all. During testing in the Blough experiment pigeons were rewarded for pecking during the S^D but not during the S^Δ. This resulted in a sharper gradient. For comparison the gradients are normalized about the S^D value. [From Guttman and Kalish. *op. cit.*, and D. S. Blough, Stimulus generalization as signal detection in pigeons. *Science*, 1967, *158*, 940–941.]

and Kalish is shown too in Figure 8.14 for comparison. The S^D used by Guttman and Kalish was 580 *nm* (a yellow light projected onto the translucent response key from behind the key) and that used by Blough was 582 *nm*. Blough's pigeon pecked faster than Guttman and Kalish's, but for the purpose of comparing the slopes, the rate of response to the S^D in each experiment is called 1, and the other points are shown as proportions of that rate. Note how much sharper Blough's gradient is than Guttman and Kalish's. Blough's pigeon was rewarded during the test and Guttman and Kalish's pigeons were not rewarded. Evidently extinction increased the range of variability of behavior. In this case the pigeon was more likely to peck at colors other than the S^D during extinction than during reinforcement, just as in Figure 2.13 we saw that a pigeon was more likely to peck at other places along a strip during extinction than during reinforcement.

The increased variability of behavior during extinction is a very adaptive characteristic of behavior. Recall from Figure 5.10 that variability of behavior is necessary in some cases to discriminate between conditioning and extinction. The rule the pigeons seem to be following is the "win-stay, lose-shift" rule—when things are going well keep doing what you were doing before, but when things are going badly change your behavior. This strategy is a good one for maximizing reward in everyday life situations for most animals. Staddon and Simmelhag point out that a similar pattern is found in evolution. When a species is well adapted to its environment, the variability among members seems to be less than when a species is ill adapted.

The sharpness of the gradient also depends on whether the training involves instrumental or classical conditioning. Consider the following experiment: A pigeon in a Skinner box is trained to peck a red key (S^D) for food on a VI-1' schedule of reinforcement. The red key alternates with a white key (S^Δ) during which pecks are not reinforced. Another pigeon is exposed to the same red-white alternation and receives the same food as the first (he is said to be *yoked* to the first pigeon) but no pecking is required. We know from the autoshaping experiments discussed in Chapter 7 that the second pigeon will peck the key too. For the second pigeon the red key is a CS (a signal associated with food), whereas for the first pigeon the red key is an S^D (a signal associated with the relation of pecking and food). Now a generalization test is done for both pigeons; that is, food is discontinued and the color of the key (still alternated with white) is varied about the original red. Whose generalization gradient will be steeper, the S^D or the CS pigeons?[*] To the author's knowledge this experiment has not been done, but a reasonable guess is that the S^D pigeon's gradient would be sharper. Usually, gradients with instrumental conditioning are sharper than those with classical conditioning, although so many variables affect the sharpness of gradients that it is difficult to be sure.

---

[*]The S^D pigeon will peck at a higher rate but we are assuming that steepness is being compared, with rates normalized as in Figure 8.14.

A similar experiment could be carried out with punishment. Suppose, while responding is maintained by a schedule of positive reinforcement, a 3- or 4-second tone is presented during which responses are punished. It is reasonable to assume that responding will be suppressed during the tone, which is a discriminative stimulus for punishment. The same tone may be used with another subject as a CER stimulus (signalling shock independent of responding) superimposed on the same schedule of positive reinforcement. The tones and shocks could be equalized for the punishment and CER subjects. Then, the frequency of the tone could be varied with shock discontinued. The experiment would essentially be symmetrical to the hypothetical experiment proposed with positive reinforcement. The gradients would be upside down like the lower gradient in Figure 8.10. Although this experiment has not been done exactly as described, several punishment and CER gradients have been obtained separately, and when compared the punishment gradients are usually sharper.

Other factors that may influence the gradient are amount of training, motivation, incentive, and schedule of reinforcement during conditioning. Results of experiments with amount of training, motivation, and incentive as independent variables have been ambiguous, indicating that perhaps non-monotonic relationships are involved. For instance, with very little training, gradients are sometimes fairly sharp, then with more training they become flatter and finally steep again. It is possible that the nonmonotonicity has to do with the interaction of classical and instrumental learning—with alternate learning of the relations of the stimulus and response to the significant event. At first, only the association of the stimulus to the significant event may be learned (classical conditioning). Then the association of the response to the significant event (instrumental conditioning) may interfere with the initial learning, during which time generalization gradients would be flatter. Finally, once the instrumental association is well learned the S^D function of the stimulus as it relates to the association of response and significant event may be learned, causing the gradient to become sharper. To draw a perhaps far-fetched analogy, a child who is read to, first learns the association of books with interesting stories, and may be very particular which book is read to him (sharp gradient). Then when learning to read the child may be completely undiscriminating in his choice of books (flat gradient) and finally may again become quite particular as he learns which authors write good books (S^D's) and which authors write bad books (S^Δ's). This sequence, of course, is pure speculation.

The effect of schedules of reinforcement on the sharpness of generalization gradients is much more clear-cut. The more infrequent the reinforcement, the flatter the gradient. Also, the more the schedule requires discrimination based on internal or temporal events (as with drl schedules, for instance) the flatter the gradient. The reason for the flatness with infrequent reinforcement may be the tendency to vary behavior more widely during extinction. The less frequent the reinforcement, the more the situation resembles extinction, and the flatter the gradient will be.

The explanation for the flat gradients produced by temporal discriminations might be similar to the explanation for the relative flatness of the inhibitory gradient of Figure 8.10 as opposed to the excitatory gradient. During training the temporal stimuli come to share with the S^D the property of signalling reinforcement. During testing, these temporal stimuli are present during both S^D and the other test stimuli. The more the S^D has in common with the other stimuli presented during the generalization test, the more the subjects are likely to respond during the test stimuli. When the S^D uniquely signals reinforcement (when no internal temporal stimuli are effective) it has less in common with the test stimuli and therefore there is less tendency to respond while they are present. Again, this is very speculative. Obviously more experiments are needed in this area.

One of the assumptions of the conflict model we discussed earlier is that punishment gradients are steeper than gradients of positive reinforcement. Despite many attempts it has been impossible so far to compare "pure" punishment gradients with "pure" excitatory gradients and keep everything else (motivation, learning, incentive, the response tested, the stimuli varied) constant. This does not mean that meaningful comparison will never be made, but only that so far as we have not developed the behavioral technology to test this assumption directly.

The Lashley-Wade Hypothesis

When Pavlov originally observed the phenomenon of generalization in classical conditioning, he speculated that similar stimuli terminate near each other in the brain, making it possible for excitatory waves from one stimulus to activate another stimulus nearby. This hypothesis was challenged in 1946 when Karl Lashley and Marjorie Wade published an influential paper claiming that the initial effect of stimuli entering the brain is generalized rather than specific. Their paper was based on decortication experiments with rats, which showed learning losses to be correlated with the amount of cortex removed rather than with the specific parts. Lashley and Wade concluded that associations between stimuli must be produced by experience with the stimuli. For example, red and orange are similar, not because they terminate close together in the brain, but because our experience with them is similar. The sun is sometimes red and sometimes orange, but rarely blue or green. The sea is sometimes blue and sometimes green, but rarely red or orange. Our common experience with the red and orange sun makes red similar to orange and our common experience with the blue and green sea makes blue similar to green.

According to Lashley and Wade, generalization between two stimuli occurs only because our previous experience with those stimuli has not sufficiently differentiated them from each other. An implication of the Lashley-Wade hypothesis is that prior to experience a flat generalization gradient across all stimuli will occur and that prior to differential experience within a dimension flat generalization gradients will occur across that dimension. In other words, Lashley and Wade contended that stimulus control is wholly a product of experience.

This hypothesis has proved difficult to test. The usual procedure has been to try to rear a group of animals from birth without experience on some dimension, usually light (that is, to rear them in the dark), then train them to make a response in the presence of a single stimulus on that dimension (say, yellow light), and afterwards to give them a generalization test and compare the results with a similar generalization test on normally reared animals. But this procedure has produced mixed results. When the two groups show the same generalization gradients, supporters of the Lashley-Wade hypothesis frequently claim that the rearing procedure did not succeed in eliminating all possible experience with a dimension. On the other hand, when the dark-reared group shows flat gradients and the light-reared group sharp gradients, as predicted by the Lashley-Wade hypothesis, opponents frequently claim that deprivation of experience with a dimension of stimuli early in life hinders the normal development of the receptors, either permanently or temporarily damaging them, so that animals reared, for instance, under visual deprivation, are effectively blind during testing. When, after almost thirty years, a hypothesis still cannot be meaningfully tested, it is a sign that the hypothesis itself may be meaningless.

A more meaningful argument advanced by Lashley and Wade is that even later in life, after a dimension has already been experienced, flat generalization gradients will be obtained unless the subject has differential experience with that dimension during training. Lashley and Wade phrased their argument in terms of attention. They claimed that if an animal experiences only one single value of a dimension during training it will pay no attention to that dimension. Then, during testing, any stimulus on that dimension will be equivalent to any other, and flat generalization gradients will result. An experiment designed to test this argument was performed by H. M. Jenkins and R. H. Harrison. The experimenters trained pigeons to peck a key and reinforced pecking on a VI-20″ schedule. For some pigeons a 1000 Hz (cycles per second) tone was present throughout training. For other pigeons the 1000 Hz tone was turned on and off periodically. When the tone was on, pecks were reinforced on the VI-20″ schedule (tone-on was S^D). When the tone was off, pecks were not reinforced (tone-off was an S^Δ). Lashley and Wade would have argued that the first group of pigeons were not forced to pay attention to the tone, since they were rewarded continuously, whereas the second group were forced to pay attention, since reward was when the tone was absent. Therefore, the second group should have sharper gradients when tested on a dimension of the tone. This is exactly what Jenkins and Harrison found. Generalization gradients for their two groups of pigeons are shown in Figure 8.15. In Lashley and Wade's terms,

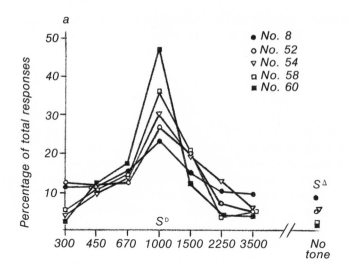

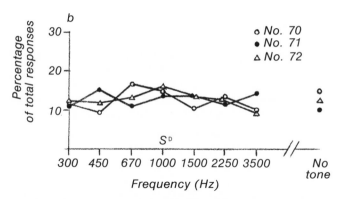

FIGURE 8.15

Comparison of generalization gradients in Jenkins and Harrison's experiment after two types of training. For the pigeons shown in panel a, training consisted of alternation of an S^D (1000 cycle-per-second tone) and an S^Δ (no tone). For the pigeons shown in panel b, training consisted of the S^D alone. Testing was identical for both groups of pigeons (various tones and no-tone during extinction) but the S^D–S^Δ training produced much steeper gradients than the S^D training alone. [From Jenkins, H. M. and Harrison, R. H. Effect of discrimination training on auditory generalization. *J. Exp. Psych.*, 1960, *59*, 246–253. Copyright 1960 by the American Psychological Assn.]

the gradients show that the group with differential training paid more attention to the tone. In more behavioral terms, differential training with the tone sharpened its control of the response.* Note that the differential training was not along the dimension (frequency) of testing, but simply On versus Off. The first question raised by the Lashley-Wade hypothesis—how generalization gradients are shaped in the first place—is still unanswered.

Interaction of Gradients

One of the assumptions of the conflict model discussed in Chapter 6 is that two opposing gradients (spatial or temporal gradients in the case of conflict) subtract to form a resultant gradient. Similar interactions have been investigated with the stimulus-generalization gradients we have just been discussing. Let us first consider the case of two excitatory gradients adding together; then we shall consider the case of an inhibitory gradient subtracting from an excitatory gradient. Figure 8.16 shows, at the left, two hypothetical stimulus-generalization gradients for a pigeon—one that might be obtained with a reddish-orange key as S^D and one that might be obtained with a yellowish-orange key S^D. Suppose reddish-orange and yellowish-orange keys are both S^D's (that is, pecks are reinforced while the key is either color and are unreinforced while the key is dark). We might ask now whether the two gradients actually add or whether they are completely independent. The question becomes interesting when we consider the rate of responding (after training with the two S^D's) during a generalization test when the key is orange. If the gradients add, the rate of response while the key is orange should be equal to the sum of the two gradients (point x in Figure 8.16). This rate would be higher than the rate when the key is either of the two S^D colors in the example shown. If the gradients do not add, the rate of response while the key is orange should be equal to either of the two gradients alone (point y in Figure 8.16).

Tests in which pigeons were trained with two S^D's consisting of colored keys near each other in wavelength have found summation, although complete summation (up to point x) is rare. We should emphasize again here that a higher overall rate of response while the key is a certain color does not necessarily mean a higher tempo of responding. It may reflect higher perseveration (more time spent responding at a constant tempo). Summation of gradients at a stimulus intermediate between two S^D's might reflect some response bursts attrib-

---

*In the Guttman and Kalish experiment the key-color S^D was continuously present during training but nevertheless sharp gradients were obtained. This seems to contradict what Jenkins and Harrison found. The reason for the difference is that the color occupied only the area of the key in the Guttman-Kalish study. Pecks had to be on the key. Thus, the effective S^Δ was the uncolored area around the key. That is, in the Guttman-Kalish experiment, there was *spatial* differential training, so sharp gradients were obtained. For Jenkins and Harrison's pigeons, with the tone continuously on, there was neither spatial nor temporal differential training, so flat gradients were obtained.

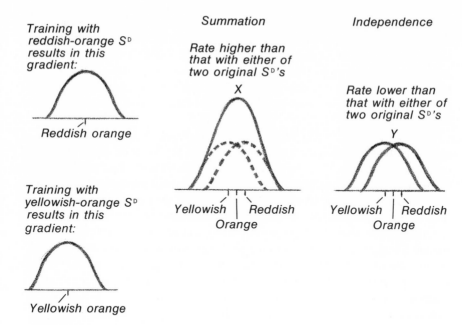

FIGURE 8.16
Training with two different S^D's along the same continuum may result in summation of gradients, in which case intermediate stimuli will generate high rates of responding. Otherwise, if the gradients are independent, intermediate stimuli generate low rates of responding.

utable to one S^D and other response bursts attributable to the other S^D. Some evidence that overall rate of response in generalization tests varies by means of perseveration rather than tempo comes from studies that, during training, present two S^D's with different response requirements. Then, an intermediate stimulus is presented. Will the organism make an intermediate response or will it make some responses of one kind and some responses of the other kind? For instance, a pigeon can be trained to peck at the left part of a strip when the illumination is bright and at the right part of a strip when the illumination is dim. Then, when the illumination is medium will the pigeon peck in the center of the strip or will it peck a little at the right and a little at the left? In several tests with this and analogous procedures pigeons tended to distribute their responses on the right and left only (so much to one S^D and so much to the other) rather than make an intermediate response. One might infer then that the higher rate at point x for an intermediate (orange) stimulus consists of some responses attributable to the reddish S^D and some attributable to the yellowish S^D. It seems that the pigeon pecks at the orange stimulus, not because it is similar to either or both S^D's, but because there is some possibility, however uncertain, that the orange key is *functionally identical* to either the reddish or the yellowish keys. If you were driving through a strange country where the stop signs were red and yellow and you came across an orange sign you would stop, not because the orange sign was similar to a stop sign, but because it might *be* a stop sign. This behavior is consistent with the Lashley-Wade hypothesis according to which generalization gradients are the result of a failure of discrimination training to functionally separate the test stimulus from the S^D of training.

Now let us consider subtraction of gradients. Figure 8.17 shows hypothetical gradients for a pigeon pecking a reddish-orange key as an S^D and a yellowish-orange key as an S^Δ. The S^Δ gradient is drawn flatter and closer to the abscissa than the S^D gradient as in Figure 8.10. The resultant gradient (called a *post-discrimination gradient*) has a peak to the right of the peak of the S^D gradient. This difference in peaks between the S^D gradient alone and the resultant gradient is called a *peak shift*. In a generalization test, after training with the reddish-orange S^D and the yellowish-orange S^Δ a pigeon will peck less at the reddish-orange key than at a red key (the new peak in the gradient).

The peak shift obtained by this method provides a way of describing the phenomenon known as *transposition*. In a transposition experiment the pigeon would be trained, again, with a reddish-orange S^D, and a yellowish-orange S^Δ. Then the pigeon would be given a choice of two keys to peck, the old S^D (reddish orange) and a new, red key. The pigeon would peck the red key more than the reddish-orange key, showing transposition. The Gestalt psychologists claimed that the phenomenon of transposition is an example of "relational learning." The pigeon learns during training, not to peck the reddish-orange

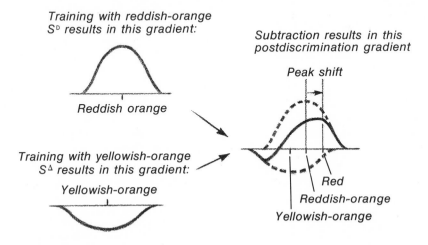

FIGURE 8.17
Training with a reddish-orange S^D and a yellowish-orange S^Δ may result in subtraction of gradients so that the peak of the postdiscrimination gradient is shifted toward red.

key specifically, but to peck the redder of the two keys. Then during testing the pigeon continues to peck the redder key even if it is not the color of the original S^D. The "peak shift," obtained by subtracting gradients, and "relational learning" are two ways of describing the transposition phenomenon. They do not contradict each other since they are at two different levels of analysis, one more molecular (peak shift) and the other more molar (relational learning). It remains to be seen which will ultimately provide the most useful laws and experiments.

Errorless Discrimination

In 1963 H. S. Terrace demonstrated a way of training pigeons to make sharp discriminations without "errors." An error was defined by Terrace as a peck in the presence of S^Δ. Normally, pigeons trained to peck, say, a red key as an S^D will also peck many times at the key if it suddenly turns green. If the green color is an S^Δ, the pigeons will eventually stop pecking the green. The initial pecks at the green are useful in most situations since new stimuli do not always signal extinction. Terrace, by carefully controlling the time and manner of the introduction of S^Δ, found a way to bypass the normally useful tendency of pigeons to peck when the stimulus changes. When the S^Δ was introduced early in training and initially was brief compared with the S^D (5 seconds versus 3 minutes) and much darker than the S^D, pigeons did not peck at the S^Δ stimulus. Then, when the duration and brightness of the S^Δ were progressively increased, pigeons continued to refrain from pecking it even when it finally was just as bright and lasted just as long as the S^D. Thus, the pigeons were finally discriminating between the S^D and S^Δ with hardly any pecks at the S^Δ stimulus. Errorless discrimination has since been obtained with other organisms and other responses by similar techniques. The phenomenon has several interesting consequences. First, pigeons in ordinary discrimination experiments are usually very active during S^Δ when S^Δ is first presented. They strut about the cage excitedly and weave their heads back and forth in front of the key even when not pecking it. Errorless pigeons, however, seem to be quite calm while S^Δ is being presented. Second, postdiscrimination gradients obtained after errorless discrimination do not usually show a peak shift. Of course if S^D and S^Δ are *too* near each other the errorless discrimination procedure will not work. Nevertheless errorless discrimination does work with stimuli (such as reddish versus yellowish orange) that ordinarily yield a peak shift. It is as if the inhibitory gradient did not exist. Turning back to page 434 it seems as if normally trained pigeons learn (c), both to peck during S^D and, by their "errors," not to peck during S^Δ, but that errorless pigeons learn only to peck during S^D and never learn not to peck during S^Δ because the method of training causes them never to peck at S^Δ in the first place. They therefore have no inhibitory gradient and no peak shift is observed.

Compound Discriminative Stimuli (Attention)

We have already discussed, in Chapter 4, a model for the action of compound stimuli in classical conditioning—the Wagner-Rescorla model. The model substitutes a molecular explanation based on individual pairings of CS and US for a molar explanation based on attention to one or another of a pair of cues. The same sort of model could be applied to discriminative stimuli in instrumental conditioning.

When discriminations are established with compound color and shape cues, say red triangle as S^D and green square as S^Δ, subjects may attend to one dimension and ignore the other. For example, George Reynolds trained two pigeons with a white triangle on a red key as S^D and a white circle on a green key as S^Δ. Then the pigeons were tested with four stimuli: white triangle on black key, white circle on black key, uniform red key, and uniform green key. One pigeon pecked only at the white triangle; the other pigeon pecked only at the uniform red key. It is as if one pigeon attended only to shape during training and the other, only to color. It is possible, in Reynolds' experiment, that one of the dimensions was idiosyncratically initially more salient for each pigeon and that a *blocking effect* was at work, with the initially salient dimension blocking the other. It is clear that prior training with a discriminative stimulus on one dimension blocks attention to another dimension added later, just as prior training with one CS blocks attention to another CS added later. Both blocking phenomena may be explainable by the same set of principles, whether "attention" or an extension of the Wagner-Rescorla model to discriminative stimuli.

A perhaps related blocking phenomenon in the area of human attention is known as the *cocktail party effect*. In a crowded room with many conversations going on at once we are able to select one and follow it and ignore (block out) the rest. The ability to follow one conversation imbedded among others depends on many factors, including sex of the speaker, location of the speaker, language, and topic. In general, the more different the voices, the easier it is to follow one of them and the less the rejected voice is perceived (the more it is blocked out). Subjects in "blocking" experiments often cannot identify even the language or the sex of the rejected speaker.

A model for selective attention was proposed in 1957 by Donald Broadbent and has since been modified several times by Broadbent himself and others. In its simplest form the model consists of the Y-shaped tube pictured in Figure 8.18. Stimuli from two sources (two modalities, two dimensions, or two spatial locations) are represented by balls rolling down the branches of the Y and pushing aside the swinging door. (In our terms these dimensions would be embodied in compound CS's or compound discriminative stimuli.) A ball getting through the swinging door and out the bottom elicits a response. (In our terms, getting through to the stem of the Y would be association with a

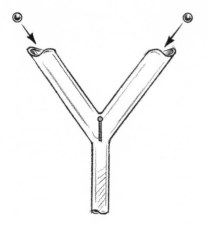

FIGURE 8.18
Broadbent's mechanical model of human attention. Stimulus input into different channels is represented by balls entering branches of a Y-shaped tube. Blocking is represented by the first ball pushing the swinging gate aside, thereby blocking the passage of the second ball. Two balls arriving simultaneously might both be blocked. [From Broadbent, D. E. A mechanical model for human attention and immediate memory. *Psychological Review*, 1957, *64*, 205–215. Copyright 1957 by the American Psychological Assn.]

significant event.) Blocking occurs when one ball pushes the door to one side, closing the stem to the ball in the other branch. A stimulus of high salience or intensity corresponds to a ball that comes faster down the Y and is more likely to block than be blocked. Broadbent's mechanical model is not as precise as the Wagner-Rescorla mathematical model designed to handle analogous facts, but Broadbent's model, crude as it is, does account for many observations in the study of attention. For instance, when two balls reach the door at once they interfere with each other and neither gets through. This corresponds to the confusion that often occurs when two equally strong messages are received at once. Similarly, when a ball is blocked, the blocking is temporary, the door eventually swings back and the ball gets through. This corresponds to the finding that blocked and blocking messages, if they are both short, can both be perceived, the blocking message first and the blocked message later. The Wagner-Rescorla mathematical model would have to be modified to account for such facts. Such reconciliation, now being attempted by psychologists between models for human attention and classical conditioning, is necessary for the progress of psychology as a science.

Stimulus Control in Various Species

If all the species are descended from common ancestors, as evolutionary theory suggests, then it should be possible, under the right conditions, to find resemblances to human behavior in the behavior of other species. Just as the human body has evolved from simpler forms, examples of which abound in the animal kingdom, human behavior must have evolved from simpler forms of behavior, now exhibited by other animals. The study of complex discriminations in animals is thus an attempt to study animal behavior that differs from human behavior, not in its form or quality, but in a few measurable dimensions.

If these dimensions could be discovered we would be able to make more mean-ingful comparisons between the behavior of one species and another.

As we indicated in Chapter 3, there are many obstacles to such a compara-tive psychology. To begin with, how do you equalize responses? A rat can press a lever, but what can a goldfish do that would be equivalent? How do you know that a certain colored light is equally salient, or even visible to ani-mals of two different species? There have been several attempts to get around such problems by designing experimental tasks that require organizing behav-ior in a certain way with respect to the environment rather than making a particular response or discriminating between two particular stimuli. We shall describe here several attempts at devising such tasks. We should indicate in advance, however, that none of them has been completely successful.

Alternation. One of the earliest devices used to study complex behavioral processes in animals was the *temporal maze,* devised by W. S. Hunter. A dia-gram of the maze is shown in Figure 8.19. Starting from point A in the maze, the animal runs to point B and then must turn either right or left. If it turns correctly, it comes around again to point A. If it turns incorrectly, a barrier (indicated by one of the dotted lines) is placed in its way. After a series of turns, alternation (left-right) or double alternation (left-left-right-right) the animal is fed at point A. The more complex the alternation pattern learned, the more intelligent the animal is judged to be. The problem with this procedure is that the particular locomotor response required determines to a great extent how well various animals do at the task. Pigeons do very poorly in the temporal maze shown in Figure 8.19 but very well at double or even triple alternation in key-pecking. For any animal that fails to learn alternation with one response, there may be some other unknown response with which the animal would succeed.

Learning to Learn. If a monkey learns one discrimination problem (say circle-reward versus square-extinction) and is then switched to another prob-

FIGURE 8.19
Floorplan of a temporal maze. The rat starts at A and chooses one or the other branch at B. If the choice is incorrect, a barrier is placed before A and the rat must go back to the choice point. If the choice at B is correct, the rat may run through the maze again. Food reward is given at A for a correct series of choices at B. The series may be alternation (right–left) or double alternation (right–right–left–left).

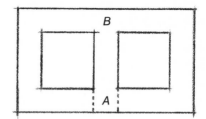

lem (say triangle versus hexagon) it tends to learn the second problem faster and a third problem still faster, until after many problems learning is virtually complete on a single trial. Evidently the monkey has learned something more general than a particular discrimination. It has learned how to solve the sort of problems posed by the experimenter—in other words, it has learned to learn. A monkey and a rat may learn an initial discrimination about equally fast, but the monkey quickly improves with successive discriminations whereas the rat takes almost as much time to learn the thousandth discrimination as it did to learn the first. A graph comparing the percentages of correct responses of various species on the second trial of successive discriminations is shown in Figure 8.20. The learning-to-learn task separates the species nicely, with monkeys doing better than cats and cats doing better than rats. But the tasks were visual discriminations of different sorts. Rats have poor vision. Perhaps they would have done better on auditory or tactual discriminations. Pigeons, which do have excellent visual abilities, do as well or better on visual learning-to-learn tasks as rhesus monkeys. For any animal that learns to learn slowly there may be some unknown stimulus dimension with which it learns to learn faster.

Reversal Shifts. The problem of reversal shifts is related to learning to learn. The animal is first trained with one discrimination (for example, square–reward versus circle–extinction), then the stimuli are switched (square–extinction versus circle–reward), then switched back, and so on. At first, reversals

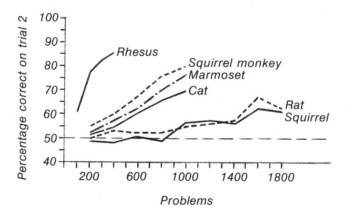

FIGURE 8.20
The learning-to-learn ability of various species. Each subject was given a series of different discrimination problems. The ordinate shows the percentage of correct responses on the second trial of each problem. [From Warren, J. M. Primate learning in comparative perspective. In A. M. Schrier, H. F. Harlow, and F. Stollnitz (Eds.) *Behavior of nonhuman primates, vol. 1.* New York: Academic Press, 1965.]

impair learning of all animals, but with repeated trials, some animals improve to the point that they learn the reversals as fast as they learned the original problems, and sometimes faster. Pigeons, rats, and monkeys all learned to solve reversal problems. After 20 reversals of a simple discrimination they made no more errors than before the first reversal. Fish, however, after 20 reversals did as poorly as they did on the first reversal. It was as if the fish could learn nothing about the molar properties of the reversal itself, but only what they had done on the immediately previous problem. The discrimination task for the fish was to swim up against one of a pair of disks inserted in the water and press the disk with its head. (The discrimination was based on the shape or color of the disk.) The fish was rewarded for a correct response with food dropped into the tank behind it. The problem with this technique was that slight modifications in the experimental procedure brought about significant improvements in performance with successive reversals. One of the modifications consisted of feeding the fish near the disks instead of on the opposite side of the tank. Again, one can never be sure, with a given animal, that all effective training procedures have been exhausted before concluding that the animal can not learn reversal shifts.

It should be noted here than even "simple" discriminations may be analyzed into several subtasks. For instance, the response may be associated with the reinforcer, the S^D may be associated with the reinforcer, other responses and the S^Δ may be associated with extinction, the response and the S^D may be associated with each other, and the other responses may be associated with the S^Δ. On a more molar level, the subject must learn to pay attention to the dimensions along which the S^D and S^Δ vary and to determine how those are correlated with responding and reward as well as how responding and reward are themselves correlated. Thus, even "simple" discrimination tasks are complex, and learning-to-learn and reversal-shift tasks are still more complex.

Many theories have been devised to explain how animals learn discriminations. One theory has it that higher animals learn discriminations in two stages. First they learn which stimulus dimensions are correlated with reinforcement and then, later, they learn the direction of the correlation. The theory implies that we have to learn that the color of traffic lights tells us to stop and go before we learn that red means stop and green means go. Thus, for higher animals learning should not be impaired when reversal shifts (which change the direction of the correlation but not the relevant dimension itself) are done early in training (while, for example, the relation of traffic lights and behavior is being learned but before red–stop and green–go is learned). Lower animals (human children are sometimes included among these) learn nothing about the dimension concerned but only the molecular association of S^D with reward (only red–stop; green–go). Reversal shifts (red–go; green–stop impair the learning of these animals even when they are done early in training.

It should not surprise the reader that such theories have been difficult to test. Results of experiments have been about equally balanced in support and refutation of the theory just described, depending on which of several methods is used to test it. Because of the practical and theoretical importance of discrimination learning, however, and because nearly everyone is convinced that humans differ from other animals such as birds, fish, and insects in their abilities to make complex discriminations, the search for the dimensions of the difference goes on.

Concept Learning. In a sense, all discrimination is concept learning. Even "redness" is a concept because it can be abstracted from other aspects of the environment. So, when a pigeon learns to discriminate red from green it is learning a concept. Alternation, learning-to-learn and reversal shifts all involve more complex sorts of abstractions. We now turn to two experimental paradigms that demonstrate still more complex concept learning in lower animals. Experiments such as these (and others that will be described in the next chapter) make a strictly molecular view of instrumental conditioning difficult to maintain.

The concepts of same and different have been tested with matching-to-sample experiments. First a sample stimulus is presented to the animal, say an "X." Then two comparison stimuli are presented. One is the "X" and the other is an "O." The subject responds by manipulating one of the comparison stimuli. A correct response—a response to the comparison stimulus identical to the sample—is reinforced according to some schedule. An incorrect response is not reinforced and may be punished. Then a new trial starts on which the sample may be an "O." In matching-to-sample problems the subject must learn, to respond not to the X or the O, but to whichever comparison stimulus is the same as the sample. (In a variation of the matching-to-sample experiment the correct response is to the comparison stimulus different from the sample.) Once the matching-to-sample response is established, a delay between the offset of the sample and the onset of the comparison stimuli may be introduced. It is also possible to introduce completely new stimuli to see whether the subject has learned the rule, "Respond to whichever comparison stimulus is the same as the standard." Perhaps surprisingly, pigeons, rats, and monkeys can be as accurate as humans on this sort of task once they learn it. Again, speed of learning and final accuracy depend on the particular stimuli responses and rewards used.

Most experiments in the laboratory use simple discriminative stimuli, such as tones or lights. Yet experiments in concept learning have shown that animals can make much more complex discriminations. Consider the following experiment in which pigeons learned to discriminate between pictures of cars and trucks. Thousands of photographs were taken of vehicles of various kinds. The pictures were then sorted into two groups, those that showed trucks or parts of trucks, and those that showed cars. The pictures were shown in random order to the pigeons, but the same picture was never shown twice to the same pigeon. While the pictures were being shown, the pigeons could peck a key. For some pigeons pecks were reinforced (on a VI schedule) only if the picture represented a truck or part of a truck. For other pigeons, pecks were reinforced only when the picture represented a car or part of a car. In other words, for the first group of pigeons, trucks were S^D's and cars were S^Δ's; for the other group, conditions were reversed. As far as the experimenters could tell, there was no difference between the two groups of photographs other than the car-versus-truck distinction. The two groups of photographs were equally light, equally colorful, and equally complex. Yet, within a few weeks of daily exposure to the photographs, the pigeons came to peck rapidly when they saw a picture of the S^D vehicle, whether truck or car, and slowly or not at all when they saw the S^Δ vehicle. How was this discrimination made? Possibly each pigeon had its own strategy based on some simpler feature of the photographs. Perhaps some counted the axles on the vehicles. Perhaps some recognized the distinctive hoods or fenders of trucks or simply discriminated by means of the vehicles' size. (Since some vehicles were shown close up, however, and some at a distance, a size discrimination would have to be based on the relative size of the vehicle compared to its surroundings.) The complexity of the discrimination can be appreciated when we realize that with all our modern technology, we are now only on the threshold of our ability to build machines to make equivalent discriminations.

Whatever the detailed strategy of the individual pigeons, their molar behavior was consistent (pecking did occur in the presence of the S^D). Furthermore, whatever the strategy of the individual pigeons, their behavior was subject to manipulation in the same way by reinforcing pecks in the presence of the S^D. When differential reinforcement was discontinued, the discrimination deteriorated, and the pigeons responded equally during the two kinds of pictures. For the molarist, this covariance between properties of behavior (responding) and properties of the environment (cars or trucks) is the important part of the experiment.

CHAINS OF BEHAVIOR

A chain of behavior consists of a series of stimuli and responses in which each stimulus serves as a secondary reinforcer for one response and a discriminative stimulus for another response. For instance, the sequence in which a predator hunts for its prey, sees the prey, tracks the prey, kills the prey, and finally eats the prey is a chain as we have defined it. The sight of the prey is both a secondary reinforcer for hunting (it stands between the activity of hunting and the reward of eating) and a discriminative stimulus for tracking (tracking the prey after sighting it leads to reward). Similarly, each stimulus along the route from hunting to eating is a secondary reinforcer with respect to previous responses and a discriminative stimulus with respect to subsequent responses.

Almost no instrumental learning takes place without some chains occurring. For instance, in an alley the sight of the goal box is a secondary reinforcer for running down the alley and a discriminative stimulus for eating food. In a Skinner box, the sound of the food being delivered is a secondary reinforcer for the operant responses in the box and a discriminative stimulus for eating.

In establishing a chain of behavior, the basic rule is to start with the last response, the one that is reinforced with primary reinforcement. If you want to teach a dog to fetch your slippers and drop them in front of you, first put the slippers in his mouth and reward him for dropping them in front of you, then put the slippers in another room and teach him to fetch them. Most complicated animal tricks in circuses are taught this way.

A chain of behavior may be constructed from component schedules of reinforcement. For instance, for a pigeon placed in a Skinner box with a white key, 10 pecks on the white key (FR-10) might produce, not primary reinforcement, but a change in key color to green. Then, pecking on the green key might lead, on a VI-1' schedule, to another change in key color, to red. Finally, a single peck on the red key could produce food.

Chained schedules of reinforcement are similar to the second-order schedules discussed previously, except that with chained schedules the components differ and each is signalled by a different stimulus (white, green, and red key lights in our example), whereas in second-order schedules the components are all the same and signalled, usually, by a brief stimulus change identical from component to component. In chained schedules the superordinate arrangement of components (links) is always fixed, with a certain number and sequence of components composing each chain. In second-order schedules the superordinate arrangement of components may itself be a schedule and therefore may be variable.

The pattern of responding within components of chained schedules, as in second-order schedules, is that usually found when the schedule is programmed alone as a schedule of primary reinforcement. That is, even when an FR schedule is an early or middle component of a chain, animals pause at the beginning and then respond rapidly as with FR schedules of primary reinforcement. The overall rate of responding usually increases from the initial to the terminal links of the chain as primary reinforcement gets closer in time.

In nature there are two kinds of chains. In one, the stimuli signalling the various links are permanently available. For example, consider the stimuli at the various stages of building a chair. If the carpenter stops for lunch after sawing the wood, he does not have to begin again at the beginning when he resumes work. This kind of chain, in which stimuli at each stage remain until the response is completed, is the kind most frequently studied in the laboratory. Another type of chain, less studied but also very common in nature, allows abortion of the response sequence. The example of the predator hunting, seeing, tracking, killing, and eating its prey is one in which appropriate stimuli for each act are available only temporarily. If there is too long a pause at any stage, the chain is aborted without primary reinforcement and must begin again from the beginning.

We have discussed chain schedules at this point in the book for two reasons—because they combine secondary reinforcement and stimulus control, the subjects of this chapter, and because they comprise the theoretical underpinning for the subject of the next chapter, two-factor theory, which attempts to bridge the delays between responding and reinforcement by chains of contiguous events.

APPLICATIONS IN BEHAVIOR THERAPY

Secondary reinforcement and stimulus control have been applied to behavior therapy in several ways. We have already mentioned the use of biofeedback techniques to control physiological functions such as heart rate and brain waves (EEG). Biofeedback has been used in the treatment of various psychosomatic disorders, such as high blood pressure, epilepsy, migraine headache, cardiac arrhythmia, and Raynaud's disease. In migraine headache, feedback of temperature differences between forehead and finger or of small muscle contractions in the forehead seems to help in the alleviation of this condition. In many studies of biofeedback application, however, proper control experiments are needed to ascertain that the biofeedback procedure is not acting as a placebo—that is, that the mere hooking up of the apparatus and presence of a physician is not by itself enough to effect a cure or a partial cure. So far, the promising experimental applications of biofeedback techniques have not been translated into standard clinical practice.

Feedback of various kinds may be useful in behavior therapy. It has been proposed for treatment of sexual dysfuntions in males that a device called a penile plethysmograph, which accurately measures the extent of penile erection, be used to indicate to the therapist and the subject himself the degree of arousal caused by various stimuli (pictures of naked men or women, scenes, stories, and so on). Since the plethysmograph is much more sensitive than physiological feedback, certain sources of arousal, perhaps previously unsuspected, can be identified.

Even in cases where proprioceptive feedback should be adequate, additional feedback by the therapist may be necessary. One school of therapy (that of Carl Rogers) is based largely on verbal feedback by the therapist, who selectively repeats to the patient what the patient has said himself. The therapist repeats those portions of the patient's speech displaying emotional content, on the theory that people are often unaware of their own feelings. Apparently we do not always attend to what we say, even—or especially—when what we say is important to us. Such feedback procedures help bring behavior into a proper relationship with contingencies of reinforcement, which is what behavior therapy is all about.

Behavior therapy has utilized not only secondary reinforcement related to the response side of the response–reinforcer relationship, but also secondary reinforcement related to the reinforcer side. For instance, programs of token reinforcement have been used with success in institutional settings. In these instances a system of exchange is set up whereby certain socially desirable activities such as making one's own bed, doing kitchen chores, or cleaning an area earn tokens for the patients. These tokens are then exchangeable for valued rewards such as extra food or privileges. The point of this treatment is to restore the normal relationship between socially acceptable behavior and rewards, which has been disrupted in some way for the patient. The tokens and even the rewards that the tokens earn, are really secondary reinforcers—stand-ins, so to speak, for real rewards offered by society. It is easy to obtain desired behavior in an institutional setting with the use of tokens. The trick is to phase the tokens out and phase the societal rewards in without disrupting the behavior. This is a trick that behavior therapists are finding difficult to do. Patients often fail to transfer desired behavior from institutional settings to everyday life. Figure 8.21 shows the results of a major program for treatment of alcoholics with aversive techniques (punishment for drinking). The subjects were contacted from 1 to 10 years after treatment. The initial rate of success was very high (88 percent) but of those subjects contacted 10 years after treatment only about 15 percent had remained abstinent. It has long been observed that bad habits come back when the environment in which they were first generated is restored.

The transfer of control from one environment to another comes under the heading of stimulus control. Although serious problems exist in the transfer from one environment to another, some success has been achieved in stimulus control of harmful habits. Careful analysis of the chains of discriminative stimuli and responses in undesirable behavior often suggests ways to get rid of that behavior. Habits such as overeating, cigarette smoking, or alcholism often depend on certain stimuli that have come to control the response. Treatment of such habits is rarely successful unless these controlling stimuli can be identified. For instance, for most people hunger pangs are the signal to start eating and a feeling of fullness, the signal to stop eating. For the overweight, these internal signals are often ignored and an external signal such as seeing pasteries in a bakery window may serve as the signal to start eating and a "clean plate" or an empty refrigerator become the signal to stop (see the description of Schacter's experiments in Chapter 3). For chain smokers, the putting out of one cigarette becomes a discriminative stimulus for the lighting up of another. For alcoholics, environmental events such as certain social settings, watching a sports event on television, or coming home from work may become discrim-

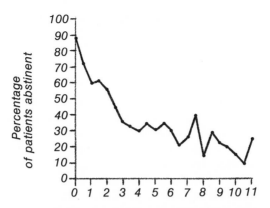

Years since patient received treatment

FIGURE 8.21

The percentage of patients remaining abstinent as a function of the number of years since treatment with various aversive techniques. The points represent *different* groups of patients, who received various treatments at various times. Hence the curve may not represent the probability of any individual remaining abstinent, or the efficacy of any treatment. But it shows that some of the treatments were effective for only one or two years for most of the patients. [From Voegtlin, W. L. and Broz, W. R. The conditioned reflex of chronic alcoholism. *Annals of Internal Medicine,* 1949, *30,* 582.]

inative stimuli for ultimately undesired behavior. The therapist's job here is to identify the stimuli and remove their control over the response, perhaps by extinction, when the reward is easily identifiable, perhaps by punishment of the response, perhaps by rewarding a competing response *in the presence of the controlling stimulus.* Alternatively, when possible, the controlling stimulus could be removed completely.

Sometimes the therapist's job is to sharpen the gradient of stimulus control, retaining the response when it is appropriate but eliminating the response when subtle differences in the stimulus indicate that it is inappropriate. Again, the main problem faced by behavior therapists is transfer from the treatment situation to everyday life.

BIBLIOGRAPHY

There is a vast literature on secondary reinforcement. For a good summary of the issues prior to 1961, see G. A. Kimble's *Hilgard and Marquis' conditioning and learning* (New York: Appleton-Century-Crofts, 1961). For more recent work, see the symposium report edited by D. P. Hendry, called *Conditioned reinforcement* (Homewood,

Ill.: The Dorsey Press, 1969). The article by M. J. Marr, "Second-order schedules," is an excellent review of this topic.

On the topic of stimulus control, another symposium report is available, edited by D. I. Mostofsky. The title is *Stimulus generalization* (Stanford: Stanford University Press, 1965). A more recent symposium, the report of which is edited by R. A. Boakes and M. S. Halliday (see Chapter 6 bibliography), also has material on stimulus control. Other excellent reviews are the chapter on the subject by H. S. Terrace in Honig's, *Operant behavior* (see Chapter 5 bibliography) and the chapters by J. A. Nevin in Nevin and Reynolds' *The study of behavior* (see Chapter 4 bibliography).

The standard texts on behavior therapy (see Chapter 5 bibliography) all have sections on stimulus control.

Following is a list of articles referred to in this chapter:

Badia, P., Culbertson, S., and Harsh, J. Choice of longer or stronger signalled shock over shorter or weaker unsignalled shock. *Journal of The Experimental Analysis of Behavior*, 1973, *19*, 25-32.

Blough, D. S. Stimulus generalization as signal detection in pigeons. *Science*, 1967, *158*, 940-941.

Bower, G., McLean, J., and Meacham, J. Value of knowing when reinforcement is due. *Journal of Comparative and Physiological Psychology*, 1966, *62*, 184-192.

Broadbent, D. E. A mechanical model for human attention and immediate memory. *Psychological Review*, 1957, *64*, 205-215.

Egger, M. D., and Miller, N. E. When is reward reinforcing? An experimental study of the information hypothesis. *Journal of Comparative and Physiological Psychology*, 1963, *56*, 132-137.

Guttman, N., and Kalish, H. I. Discriminability and stimulus generalization. *Journal of Experimental Psychology*, 1956, *51*, 79-88.

Hendry, D. P. Concluding commentary. In *Conditioned reinforcement*, ed. D. P. Hendry. Homewood, Ill.: The Dorsey Press, 1969.

Honig, W. K., Boneau, C. A., Burstein, K. R., and Pennypacker, H. S. Positive and negative generalization gradients obtained after equivalent training conditions. *Journal of Comparative and Physiological Psychology*, 1963, *56*, 111-116.

Hunter, W. S. The temporal maze and kinaesthetic sensory processes in the white rat. *Psychobiology*, 1920, *2*, 1-17.

Jenkins, H. M. Generalization gradients and the concept of inhibition. In *Stimulus generalization*, ed. D. I. Mostofsky. Stanford: Stanford University Press, 1965.

Jenkins, H. M., and Harrison, R. H. Effect of discrimination training on auditory generalization. *Journal of Experimental Psychology*, 1960, *59*, 246-253.

Lashley, K. S., and Wade, M. The Pavlovian theory of generalization. *Psychological Review*, 1946, *53*, 72-87.

Miller, N., and DiCara, L. Instrumental learning of heart rate changes in curarized rats: Shaping and specificity to discriminative stimuli. *Journal of Comparative and Physiological Psychology*, 1967, *63*, 12-19.

Schuster, R. A functional analysis of condition reinforcement. In *Conditioned reinforcement,* ed. D. P. Hendry. Homewood, Ill.: The Dorsey Press, 1969.

Terrace, H. S. Discrimination learning with and without "errors." *Journal of The Experimental Analysis of Behavior,* 1963, *6,* 1–27.

Wolfe, J. B. Effectiveness of token-rewards for chimpanzees. *Comparative Psychology Monographs,* 1936, *12,* No. 60.

Reprinted here is an article by H. S. Terrace, published in the journal *Science,* in which Terrace shows that no inhibitory stimulus control is achieved by the S^Δ of a discrimination between orthogonal (mutually independent) stimuli learned without errors. Some pigeons learned a discrimination with errors and some pigeons learned the same discrimination without errors. All the pigeons show positive stimulus-generalization gradients with no peak shift. (Because S^D and S^Δ are orthogonal, there is no direction of shift of the S^D dimension that would be *away* from the S^Δ.) But only the pigeons that learned the discrimination with errors show a negative gradient as well (as in Figure 8.10, bottom gradient). The pigeons that learned the discrimination without errors show no negative gradient. They never responded during the S^Δ stimulus and they did not respond with other similar stimuli. Terrace argues that the lack of any gradient is evidence for lack of inhibitory control by the S^Δ stimulus. We also reprint a criticism of Terrace's conclusion by J. A. Deutsch and a reply to Deutsch by Terrace.

The issue is, what is the evidence for inhibitory control? Deutsch says that amount of responding is a measure of inhibition. Since the errorless pigeons did not respond to *any* of the stimuli during the inhibitory generalization test, they inhibited responding more than the pigeons that made errors (that did respond during the inhibitory generalization test). Terrace answers that inhibitory control depends on relative, not absolute, responding. We reprint this exchange so that the reader will have a sample of how arguments about scientific issues are conducted. Then, we reprint a small section of an article by J. W. Bernheim, in which Terrace's experiment is criticized on methodological grounds. At this point the reader should be able to understand the issues involved in the arguments well enough to form an opinion. On the basis of his article on conditioned inhibition, reprinted at the end of Chapter 4, what would Rescorla say about the Terrace-Deutsch controversy?

Finally, we reprint an article by John Karpicke and Eliot Hearst that raises another objection to Terrace's experiment, that of a "floor effect." Karpicke and Hearst do find a gradient even with errorless pigeons, showing that errorless discrimination does involve some degree of inhibitory control.

Note that in these articles S^D and S^Δ are referred to, in classical conditioning terms, as S^+ and S^-.

Supplemental Reading for Chapter 8

DISCRIMINATION LEARNING AND INHIBITION
H. S. Terrace

Pigeons learned to discriminate between a white vertical line on a dark background (S+) and a monochromatic circle of light (S−) either with or without responses to S− (errors). Gradients of inhibition, which were centered around S−, and which had greater than zero slopes, were obtained only from those subjects who learned to discriminate with errors. The results indicate that the occurrence of errors is a necessary condition for S− to function as an inhibitory stimulus. This finding is consistent with other performance differences in subjects who have learned to discriminate with and without errors.

During the past decade our knowledge of how a discrimination is acquired has been considerably enhanced by new empirical findings and theoretical analyses. The peak shift and behavioral contrast have both been established as reliable characteristics of discrimination performance. The peak shift, first studied by Hanson (1),* derives its name from the finding that, after subjects are successively trained to discriminate between a stimulus correlated with reinforcement (S+) and a stimulus not correlated with reinforcement (S−), the peak of a generalization gradient does not occur at S+ but is instead shifted away from S−. Behavioral contrast, a phenomenon studied by Reynolds (2), was originally called "induction" by Pavlov (3) and was later referred to as "contrast" by Skinner (4). The term refers to an increase in the strength of the response to S+ that accompanies a decrease in the strength

From *Science*, Vol. 154, pp. 1677–1680, 30 December 1966. Copyright 1966 by the American Association for the Advancement of Science. Reprinted by permission.

*Italic numbers in parentheses refer to numbered references and notes at the end of articles from *Science*.

of the response to S− during discrimination training. Behavioral contrast derives its name from the fact that the rates of responding to S+ and S− diverge. According to classical generalization theory, these rates should converge (5).

Recent experiments on "errorless" discrimination learning suggest a possible relationship between the peak shift and contrast (6). Errorless discrimination learning is achieved by starting discrimination training immediately after the response to S+ has been conditioned with a large S+-S− difference that is progressively reduced to its final smaller value. These experiments show that a subject can be trained to discriminate without the occurrence of responses to S− (errors), and that many characteristics of discrimination performance usually observed after a subject learns to discriminate with errors are absent after that subject learns to discriminate without errors. Neither behavioral contrast nor the peak shift, for example, occur after the subject learns to discriminate without errors (6, 7). Other characteristics of performance that were absent after a subject learns to discriminate without errors are gross emotional responses (8) and the occurrence of errors that are typically observed after the administration of certain tranquilizers (*9*). These differences suggested that S— functions differently after a subject learns to discriminate with and without errors. After a subject has learned to discriminate with errors, S— appears to function as an inhibitory stimulus; after discrimination is learned without errors, S— appears to function as a neutral stimulus.

A theoretical analysis by Jenkins (*10*) of inhibition in discrimination learning suggested a way of directly observing the inhibitory function of S—. Jenkins argued that an inhibitory stimulus can be considered to control the tendency not to respond in a manner analogous to the way that an excitatory stimulus controls responding. The existence of both types of control is determined by varying S+ and S— in a generalization test. Just as the control of excitation is determined by varying S+ and observing to what extent the tendency to respond decreases as the distance between a test stimulus and S+ is increased, the control of inhibition may be determined by varying S— and observing to what extent the tendency not to respond increases as the distance between a test stimulus and S— increases.

In a generalization test in which gradients around both S+ and S— are obtained, Jenkins also points out that S+ and S— should be varied independently of each other so that a change in the distance between a test stimulus and S— does not affect the distance between that test stimulus and S+. This can be done by selecting S+ and S— from different continua. If S+ and S— were from the same continuum, a change in response frequency could be attributed either to a change in the distance between the test stimulus and S+ or to a change in the distance between the test stimulus and S—. Jenkins and Harrison (*11*) and Honig *et al.* (*12*) have obtained empirical gradients of inhibition from individual subjects, after they were trained to distinguish between stimuli from different continua. These gradients serve as an

effective answer to Skinner's position on inhibition, which holds that inhibition is merely another name for a decrement of excitation and that changes in response frequency can be entirely accounted for in terms of different magnitudes of excitation.

The present experiment is an attempt to test the hypothesis that S— does not function as an inhibitory stimulus after a subject has learned to discriminate without errors. Subjects were trained to discriminate, with and without errors, between stimuli from two different continua; the shapes of the gradients centered around S— were then examined. A U-shaped gradient, with a minimum at S—, would indicate that S— was an inhibitory stimulus, while a flat gradient would indicate the absence of any inhibitory function.

The experiment was performed in a standard operant conditioning apparatus (*13*) which contained a single circular key, 2.54 cm in diameter, 10.16 cm above the opening to the food hopper. An optical system, consisting of a high-intensity point source, a collimating lens, and a solenoid-operated dual filter box, could project onto the back of the key any one of 15 uniformly-bright monochromatic stimuli, or a 32-cm white diameter on a black background in any one of nine equally spaced orientations. The half-widths of the monochromatic stimuli were each less than 15 nanometers (nm).

The subjects were eight white Carneaux male pigeons that were maintained at 80 percent of their free-feeding weight throughout the experiment. None had been used in previous experiments.

During the conditioning sessions and the 14 subsequent sessions of nondifferential training, the stimulus on the response key was a white vertical (0°) line on a dark background (S+). At the end of each minute the key was darkened for 2 seconds. These 2-second time-out periods were later used during the discrimination and generalization sessions to change the value of the discriminative stimuli. Responses were never reinforced during the time-out periods. During discrimination training, which began after 14 sessions of nondifferential training, S+ was alternated with S− in a random sequence. For six subjects (birds 131, 138, 140, 141, 142, and 144) the value of S− was 580 nm; for the remaining two subjects (birds 122 and 123) the value of S− was 550 nm. Responses to S+ during both the nondifferential and the differential reinforcement sessions were reinforced on a 1-minute variable-interval schedule, a schedule that reinforced the first response that occurred after an interval whose average value was 1 minute (*13*). Each session was terminated after 25 reinforcements.

During discrimination training each presentation of S+ lasted 1 minute. The duration of S− was also 1 minute, unless the subject responded to S−. Each response to S− delayed the termination of S− for 30 seconds. This procedure insured that responses to S− would not be reinforced by the subsequent appearance of S+.

Since a pilot study indicated that the discrimination between a white vertical line and a circle of monochromatic light can be acquired without errors with no special training, no explicit attempt was made to train the discrimination without errors by progressively reducing the difference between S+ and S−. After the fifth discrimination session, a generalization gradient of wavelength was obtained from each subject. No reinforcements occurred during the generalization test. The stimuli during the wavelength generalization test were 490, 510, 520, 530, 540, 550, 560, 570, 580, 590, 600, 610, 630, 650, and 670 nm. S+ was also presented during the generalization test. The 16 test stimuli were presented in four different random sequences, each time for a duration of 1 minute (*14*). After the first generalization test each subject received four more sessions of discrimination training, after which a generalization gradient of line orientation was obtained.

No reinforcements were given during the generalization test. The test stimuli consisted of lines whose orientations were ±90°, ±67.5°, ±45°, ±22.5°, and 0°. In addition, S− (550 or 580 nm) was also included in the generalization test, which consisted of four random sequences of the test stimuli, each presented for 1 minute. After the second generalization test each subject received three additional sessions of discrimination training. Each subject was then exposed to six sessions of nondifferential training during which only S+ was presented. Each of these procedures was carried out on successive days of experimentation.

Half of the subjects learned the discrimination with few or no errors (birds 123, 138, 140, and 141), while the remaining four subjects (birds 122, 131, 142, and 144) made many responses to S−. The range of the number of responses to S− of the group which was considered to have learned the discrimination without errors was 0 to 19, while the range of errors of the group which was considered to have learned the discrimination with errors was 171 to 1551.

The rate of responding to S+ for all of the subjects who learned the discrimination with errors increased at the start of discrimination training. In three instances (birds 122, 142, and 144) the rate of responding to S+ reached a value that was double the value of the prediscrimination rate of responding to S+. After nondifferential training was resumed, the rate of responding to S+ of each subject decreased and approached the prediscrimination value. The rate of responding to S+ of each of the subjects who learned to discriminate without errors remained unchanged throughout the experiment. The results confirm the findings of earlier experiments (*6*) which showed that contrast develops only when discrimination learning takes place with errors.

The wavelength generalization gradients of each subject who learned to discriminate with errors were U-shaped functions centered around S− (Fig. 1). Each of these gradients was asymmetrical with the longer tail occurring at the short end of the spectrum; the reason for this was not understood. In other respects these gradients confirm the findings of earlier experiments (*11, 12*) which have shown that the tendency not to respond is maximal at S− and decreases as the distance between S− and the test stimulus increases.

The wavelength generalization gradients of the subjects who learned to discriminate without errors (Fig 2) were in each case flat, indicating that for these subjects the value of S− did not affect the tendency to respond.

No systematic differences in the shapes of the gradients of excitation were observed as a function of whether or not the subjects learned to discriminate with or without errors. In most cases the gradients of excitation were peaked around S+. A peak shift would not be expected from the subjects who learned to discriminate with errors, since S− was on a continuum orthogonal to the S+ continuum.

The difference between the shapes of the gradients of inhibition obtained from those subjects who learned to discriminate with and without errors clearly indicates that S− functions differently in each case. After a subject learns to discriminate with errors, S− comes to control the tendency not to respond in a manner that is in most respects analogous but not identical to the control S+ exerts over responding. The flat gradients obtained from the subjects who learned to discriminate without errors indicate that S− did not acquire any differential control over the tendency not to respond. However, responding and other behavior cannot be considered as symmetrical opposites. The generalization gradients shown in Fig. 1 clearly indicate that the number of responses to the wavelength test stimuli was generally much lower than the number of responses that occurred to S+, and that the gradients of inhibition were not

as steep as the gradients of excitation. Jenkins (*10*) has suggested that this asymmetry between responding and other behavior stems from two different ways of classifying other behavior. The first class includes responses antagonistic to key-pecking, for example, turning away from the key or jerking back the head after the onset of S−. The second class of other behavior includes "anything else" or what Skinner would refer to as the absence of excitation, for example, grooming, brooding, or pecking at objects on the floor of the experimental chamber. This second type of nonresponse is controlled by the absence of S+, rather than by a specific value of S−. In testing for the generalization of the tendency not to respond, the experimenter is only able to record when responses occur, but there is no way to determine which type of nonresponse was involved. Only when the responses which define a gradient of inhibition are entirely transferred from the first type of nonresponse (antagonistic) will the gradients of excitation and inhibition be symmetrically opposite. The gradients of inhibition shown in Fig. 1 indicate that this was not the case. These gradients were presumably flattened by the prevalence of the second type of nonresponse.

Although it is not possible to differentiate between the two types of nonresponse, it is nonetheless clear that S− controls the tendency not to respond, that is, it functions as an inhibitory stimulus only after a subject has learned to discriminate with errors. Thus different things are learned after a subject learns to discriminate with and without errors. After learning to discriminate with errors, the subject learns to respond to S+ and not to respond to S−. This finding was demonstrated by gradients of excitation and inhibition, each of which had a slope greater than zero. After learning to discriminate without errors, the subject learns to respond to S+ and not to its absence. S− does not specifically control the tendency not to respond.

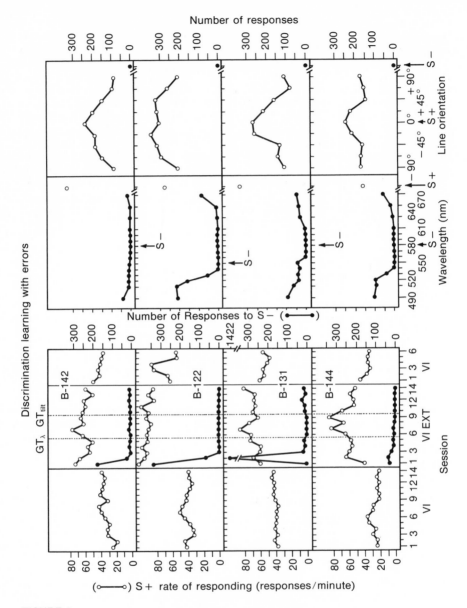

FIGURE 1
(Left) Rate of responding to S+ (open circles) of subjects who learned to discriminate with errors during nondifferential and differential reinforcement sessions, and number of responses to S− (closed circles) during each differential reinforcement session. The vertical lines indicate when discrimination training began and ended and when the wavelength and line-orientation generalization gradients were obtained. GT_λ and GT_{tilt} refer to the wavelength and line orientation generalization tests, respectively. VI and VI EXT refer to the nondifferential and differential reinforcement sessions, respectively. (Right) Wavelength and line-orientation generalization gradients.

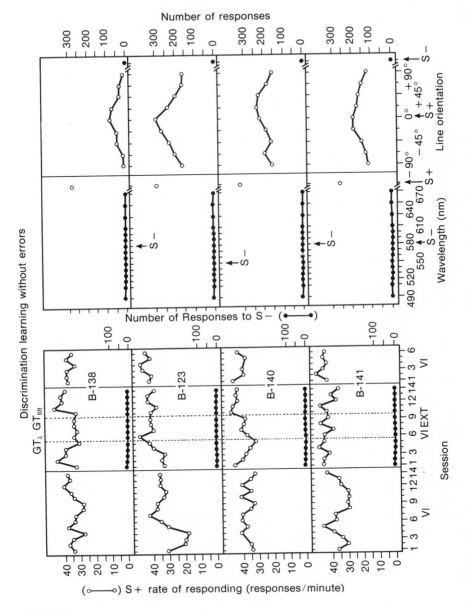

FIGURE 2
(Left) Rate of responding to S+ of subjects who learned to discriminate without errors during nondifferential and differential reinforcement sessions, and number of responses to S− during each differential reinforcement session. Abbreviations are the same as in Fig. 1. (Right) Wavelength and line-orientation generalization gradients.

The differences between the gradients of inhibition of those subjects who learned to discriminate with errors and those who learned to do so without errors are consistent with the finding that a peak shift occurs only after a subject has learned to discriminate with errors. As Spence's model of discrimination learning suggests (5), if an inverted U-shaped gradient of inhibition centered around S— is subtracted from a larger gradient of excitation centered around S+, then the peak of the gradient of excitation will be displaced away from S—. Since discrimination learning without errors results in a flat gradient of inhibition, no peak shift would result when the gradient of inhibition is subtracted from the gradient of excitation.

The occurrence of contrast, however, cannot be accounted for in terms of interacting gradients of excitation and inhibition. An algebraic combination of peaked gradients of excitation and inhibition would result in a divergence rather than a convergence of the rates of response to S+ and S—. The occurrence of contrast after a subject has been trained to discriminate between stimuli from two different continua suggests, however, that responses which are not reinforced may have an effect that is uniformly distributed over all stimuli. According to this view, elaborated by Amsel (15) and Lawson (16), a nonreinforced response to S— results in a general elevation of the gradient of excitation. Subtracting a U-shaped gradient of inhibition from this elevated gradient of excitation would still displace the peak away from S—. This appears to be the simplest way to account for the fact that the peak shift, contrast, and U-shaped gradients of inhibition occur only after a subject has learned to discriminate with errors.

REFERENCES AND NOTES

1. H. M. Hanson, *J. Exp. Psychol.* **58,** 321 (1959).
2. G. S. Reynolds, *J. Exp. Analysis Behav.* **4,** 57 (1961).
3. I. P. Pavlov, *Conditioned Reflexes* (Oxford Univ. Press, London, 1927).
4. B. F. Skinner, *The Behavior of Organisms* (Appleton, New York, 1938).
5. K. W. Spence, *Psychol. Rev.* **44,** 430 (1937; C. L. Hull, *ibid.* **57,** 303 (1950).
6. H. S. Terrace, *J. Exp. Analysis Behav.* **6,** 1 (1963).
7. _____, *Science* **144,** 78 (1964).
8. _____, in *Operant Behavior: Areas of Research and Application,* W. K. Honig, Ed. (Appleton, New York, 1966).
9. _____, *Science* **140,** 318 (1963).
10. H. M. Jenkins, in *Stimulus Generalization,* D. I. Mostofsky, Ed. (Stanford Univ. Press, Stanford, 1965).
11. H. M. Jenkins, *J. Exp. Analysis Behav.* **5,** 435 (1962).
12. W. K. Honig, C. A. Boneau, K. R. Burstein, H. S. Pennypacker, *J. Comp. Physiol. Psychol.* **56,** 111 (1963).
13. C. B. Ferster and B. F. Skinner, *Schedules of Reinforcement* (Appleton, New York, 1957).
14. The correction procedure was not used during the generalization tests.
15. A. Amsel, *Psychol. Rev.* **69,** 306 (1962).
16. R. Lawson, *Frustration: The Development of a Scientific Concept* (Macmillan, New York, 1965).
17. Research supported by NIH grant HD-0930-05 and NSF grant GB-4686.

DISCRIMINATION LEARNING AND INHIBITION

J. A. Deutsch

Terrace's conclusions in his recent report (1) are not supported by the evidence he presents and opposite conclusions seem to follow. He argues that when a subject learns to discriminate between two stimuli (S+ and S−) without errors, the negative stimulus (S−) does not acquire an inhibitory function. He supports this conclusion by showing that there is no generalization gradient around S−, or in other words, that this gradient has zero slope. However, to evaluate this argument we must take into account the absolute values of the points of which the gradient is composed. These are all zero or very close to zero. The animals did not respond in the presence of any stimulus similar to the original S− when they learned without errors. Since they did not respond, and the animal cannot make scores of less than zero, we cannot infer that inhibition around S− is greater than that away from S−. The score at S− cannot be lower than zero when this experimental design is used, and therefore the lack of slope may only reflect this design. We cannot discriminate between an increase or no increase of inhibition at S− with Terrace's data. Can we interpret the zero scores, as Terrace does, as indicating that there is no inhibition when the subject learns to discriminate without

errors? (He states: " . . . it is nonetheless clear that S− controls the tendency not to respond, that is, functions as an inhibitory stimulus, only after a subject has learned to discriminate with errors.") This question can be answered by looking at the scores of the group which learned S− with errors. Their rates of responding are much greater than zero when the stimuli presented moves away from S−. When the subjects learn to discriminate without errors, however, these rates of responding stay at zero or very close to it when the stimuli move away from S−. Therefore, rates of responding to stimuli away from S− are lower when the subjects learn to discriminate without errors than when they learn to discriminate with errors. Since the amount of responding is used as a measure of inhibition, one must infer that there is greater inhibition due to S−, when the subjects learn to discriminate without errors, as the stimulus moves away from S−; but this conclusion is the opposite of that made by Terrace. Far from supporting the evidence that Terrace quotes in favor of the idea that S−, when learned without errors, does not have an inhibitory function, the facts presented in the report cast strong doubt on Terrace's previous interpretations of such data.

REFERENCE

1. H. S. Terrace, *Science* **154,** 1677 (1966).

REPLY TO DEUTSCH

H. S. Terrace

When, given the same set of data, two scientists reach opposite conclusions, it is likely that each used different decision rules. In this case, the data in question are generalization gradients of wavelength that were obtained after a subject was trained to discriminate between a white vertical line on a black background (S+) and a homogeneous circular patch of monochromatic (either 550 or 580 nm) light (S−). The gradients of those subjects who learned the discrimination without errors were flat, with all of the data points having zero or near zero values. The gradients of the subjects who learned the discrimination with errors were U-shaped with minima (of zero or near zero value) located at S−. At issue is the question of how these gradients can be used to measure inhibition. Deutsch (but not this author) states that "the amount of responding is used as a measure of inhibition," and concludes that "there is greater inhibition due to S− when the subjects learn to discriminate without errors," because in the case of errorless learning the "rates of responding stay at zero or very close to it."

The validity of Deutsch's decision rule and conclusions can be questioned on at least two grounds. (i) A low rate of responding can be explained in terms of lack of excitation. Thus, given no additional information, the concept of inhibition is superfluous. (ii) A flat generalization gradient cannot be used as evidence of inhibition for the same reason that it cannot be used as evidence of excitation. The second point follows from the definition of an inhibitory stimulus, first

formulated by Jenkins (1), which states that an inhibitory stimulus is a stimulus which controls the tendency not to respond. To determine whether or not a stimulus controls the tendency not to respond, one varies the stimulus along a stimulus continuum and observes to what extent the tendency not to respond has been affected. Thus, the rationale for determining whether or not a stimulus controls the tendency not to respond (inhibition) is identical to the rationale for determining whether or not a stimulus controls responding (excitation). In both cases one examines the relationship between the frequency of occurrence of a conditioned response and the value of the stimulus. Since, in the present experiment, S+ and S− were selected from different continua, they could be varied independently of one another and it was possible to obtain both excitatory and inhibitory gradients from each subject. A flat generalization gradient that is obtained along the S+ continuum (at either a zero or greater than zero level) usually signifies that there was no stimulus control with respect to the continuum under study. Applying the same logic to a test for generalization along the S− continuum, it seems erroneous to use a flat generalization as evidence of inhibition. I would instead suggest that the flat gradients that were obtained from the errorless group reflect a uniform lack of excitation and that stimuli from the S− continuum should be considered neutral in the sense that they have neither inhibitory nor excitatory properties.

Deutsch also argues that "Since . . . the animal cannot make scores of less than zero, we cannot infer that inhibition around S− is greater than that away from S+." He then concludes: "We cannot discriminate between an increase or no

From *Science*, Vol. 156, pp. 988–989, 19 May 1967. Copyright 1967 by the American Association for the Advancement of Science. Reprinted by permission.

increase of inhibition at S− with Terrace's data." However, Deutsch did in fact conclude that "there is a greater inhibition due to S− when the subjects learn to discriminate without errors as the stimulus moves away from S−." It is nevertheless interesting to explore the significance of the fact that scores of less than zero were not possible. Deutsch's interest in negative scores apparently stems from the Spence-Hull model of discrimination learning which algebraically combines positive quantities of excitation with negative quantities of inhibition at each stimulus value to determine the net strength of the responses. However, in applying this model to experimental data, one must transform the data to produce negative quantities. Responses either occur or do not occur, and the only way one could obtain scores of less than zero would be to subtract an appropriate amount from each response frequency. Gradients of the type obtained in the present experiment would be transformed by assigning zero to the highest value of each gradient and assigning minus signs to all points below the highest point. The amount of inhibition at a given point would be determined by the difference between that point and the highest point. Thus flat gradients would result in zero inhibition and the amount of inhibition represented by gradients of greater than zero slope would be the sum of the differences between the highest point and the remaining points.

What would be gained if one obtained an elevated base line? (By definition, however, this is impossible since once the level of responding along the S− continuum is raised we could no longer have subjects who learned the discrimination without errors.) Suppose that this hypothetical experiment yielded the same type of results as those obtained in the present experiment, that is, flat gradients from those subjects who learned without errors and U-shaped gradients from those subjects who learned the discrimination with errors. If in interpreting these results Deutsch applied the decision rule he used in his letter, he would again have to conclude that there was more inhibition in the case of the errorless group. But whether or not a stimulus has an inhibitory function is determined by whether the tendency not to respond decreases as we move away from S−, and that a flat gradient signifies the absence of inhibitory stimulus control. Thus the design which Deutsch might suggest would result in the same problem of interpretation that arose from his criticism of my conclusion. We are still left with the question of why, given that both groups had an equal opportunity to produce gradients of greater than zero slope, such gradients were obtained only from the group that learned with errors. I have chosen to interpret these findings as indicating that S− functions as an inhibitory stimulus only when a discrimination is learned with errors. This conclusion follows readily from the definition of an inhibitory stimulus as a stimulus which controls the tendency not to respond.

The evidence that Deutsch feels is inconsistent with the data obtained in the present experiment includes the findings that emotional responses in the presence of S− and a peak shift away from S− are only observed after a discrimination is learned with errors. It remains to be demonstrated that these observations are in any way compatible with Deutsch's contention that there is more inhibition associated with S− after a discrimination is learned without errors than after a discrimination is learned with errors.

REFERENCE

1. H. M. Jenkins, in *Stimulus Generalization*, D. I. Mostoisky, Ed. (Stanford Univ. Press, Stanford, 1965).

COMMENT

Joseph W. Bernheim

. . . Terrace's Ss all confronted the same discrimination between a vertical line on a white background (positive stimulus) and a monochromatic nonpatterned stimulus (S−). Some Ss made many errors and some made few errors learning this discrimination; and, . . . an ex post facto assignment to errorless and nonerrorless groups was made. Generalization gradients were then obtained around S− along the wavelength dimension, which was assumed to be orthogonal to the dimension of the discrimination learned. Virtually no responses were made to any of the stimuli in the generalization test for the errorless Ss, while nonerrorless learners showed U-shaped gradients centered on S−. Terrace interpreted the flat zero gradients of errorless Ss to indicate a lack of inhibitory control of S− learned without errors. It is likely, however, that the procedure selected as "errorless" those birds with an initial predisposition not to respond to nonpatterned monochromatic stimuli. In this light the failure to obtain inhibitory gradients from these Ss should be understood simply as the result of a zero baseline.

Deutsch (1967) has taken issue with Terrace's conclusion, and argues that the flat gradients obtained for errorless Ss actually indicate greater inhibitory strength for the errorless S− when compared to the S− learned with errors. This conclusion is likewise unnecessary if one assumes that a different baseline of responding to monochromatic nonpatterned stimuli was the biasing factor in the selection of the two groups.

Terrace's (1966b) data can neither support nor deny the assertion that an errorless S− is not inhibitory, although other evidence put forth by Terrace (1963a, 1963b, 1964, 1966a) argues convincingly to that point. . . .

From *Psychonomic Science*, Vol. 11, p. 327. Copyright 1968 by The Psychonomic Society. Reprinted by permission.

REFERENCES

DEUTSCH, J. A. Discrimination learning and inhibition. *Science*, 1967, **156**, 988.

TERRACE, H. S. Errorless discrimination learning in the pigeon: Effects of chlorpromazine and imipramine. *Science*, 1963b, **140**, 318–319.

TERRACE, H. S. Wavelength generalization after discrimination learning with and without errors. *Science*, 1964, **144**, 78–80.

TERRACE, H. S. Stimulus control. In W. K. Honig (Ed.), *Operant behavior.* New York: Appleton-Century-Crofts, 1966a.

TERRACE, H. S. Discrimination learning and inhibition. *Science*, 1966b, **154**, 1677–1680.

INHIBITORY CONTROL AND ERRORLESS DISCRIMINATION LEARNING

John Karpicke
Eliot Hearst

Pigeons learned to discriminate between a positive stimulus (white key) and a negative stimulus (red or green key, depending on the subject) via Terrace's fading procedure. Generalization tests, conducted with intermittent reinforcement for key pecking at various wavelengths, yielded minima at the value of the negative stimulus in most "errorless" birds. Terrace's contrary finding of flat gradients in errorless subjects probably resulted from a floor-effect (*i.e.*, virtually zero responding) produced by his extinction-test procedure. The present and other findings do not support Terrace's conclusions that the negative stimulus of an errorless discrimination is behaviorally neutral; inhibition apparently develops to the nonreinforced stimulus even during errorless discrimination learning. A negative correlation between stimulus and reinforcer seems the crucial factor in producing an inhibitory stimulus.

Conventional operant discrimination-learning procedures begin with the reinforcement of a response in the presence of one stimulus (S+). After the response is established, another stimulus (S−) is occasionally presented, during which responding is not reinforced. Responses to S− decrease, whereas responses to S+ continue. Terrace (*e.g.*, 1966a, 1972a) labelled S− responses "errors" and attributed certain by-products of discrim-

ination learning (*e.g.*, behavioral contrast, peak shift, "emotional" behavior during S−, and inhibitory stimulus control) to the occurrence of errors. More recently, he traced these byproducts to the "active" inhibition of responding during S− (Terrace 1972b). The role of errors remains important, however, as their reduction or suppression produces active inhibition.

Results of experiments in which pigeons mastered discriminations without making errors have provided the main support for Terrace's position. Procedures for training such errorless discriminations generally involve a gradual increase in the duration and brightness of S−, rather than the sudden introduction of S− at full duration and brightness, as on conventional procedures. This fading technique produces very few errors in some subjects. Terrace reported that when pigeons make fewer than 25 to 40 errors, the byproducts typical of discriminations that are learned with errors fail

This research was supported mainly by National Institute of Mental Health Grant MH 19300. We thank Dexter Gormley for valuable advice. Dr. H. S. Terrace generously supplied unpublished information concerning his prior experiments, which guided our selection of specific procedural details and our criteria for labelling birds "errorless". He also made valuable comments on a draft of the present manuscript. Reprints may be obtained from either author, Department of Psychology, Indiana University, Bloomington, Indiana 47401.

From *Journal of the Experimental Analysis of Behavior*, Vol. 23, No. 2, pp. 159–166. Copyright 1975 by The Society for the Experimental Analysis of Behavior. Reprinted by permission.

to develop. For example, when trained to discriminate between either a white vertical line (Terrace, 1966*b*) or a white homogeneous field (Terrace, 1972*a*) as S+ and some wavelength as S−, and then tested with several wavelength values in extinction, birds that had made errors showed incremental gradients with minima in responding at or near the former S−; errorless birds, on the other hand, produced flat gradients with virtually zero responding. According to some workers (*e.g.,* Jenkins, 1965; Terrace, 1966*b*, 1972*a*), the finding of incremental gradients along an S− dimension orthogonal to dimensions of S+ demonstrates inhibitory control by S−, whereas flat gradients indicate that S− is behaviorally neutral. Therefore, Terrace argued that the flat gradients he obtained after errorless training demonstrate that an "errorless" S− is a neutral stimulus.

Interpretation of Terrace's flat gradients encounters a methodological limitation. Deutsch (1967; see also Hearst, Besley, and Farthing, 1970) pointed out that because Terrace's errorless birds rarely responded to any stimulus value during generalization testing, it was not possible to detect whether reponding was weaker at S− than at other values along the S− dimension. In other words, Terrace (1966*b*, 1972*a*) may have failed to observe incremental gradients around S− in his errorless birds because of a floor-effect produced by the extinction-test procedure.

The present study employed discriminations (a white S+ *versus* S− color) and fading procedures very similar to Terrace's. The major new feature was the use of a *resistance-to-reinforcement* procedure during generalization testing. Hearst *et al.* (1970) suggested that testing with nondifferential reinforcement of responding to all stimulus values may be useful for several reasons, but should be particularly appropriate when extinction procedures produce a floor-effect. Continued reinforcement ought to ensure a relatively high response level along the S− dimension.

METHOD

Subjects

Sixty-one female White Carneaux pigeons were maintained at 75% of their free-feeding weights. Only 31 completed all phases of the experiment. After obtaining an appreciable number (*i.e.,* approximately 20) of subjects that made more than 40 errors ("with-errors" group), we concentrated on filling the "errorless" groups with at least three subjects each, since analysis of errorless learning was the main goal of the present research. Additional birds were dropped from the experiment once they had made approximately 40 errors. A total of nine errorless birds was secured from the original stock of 61 birds. This information is included to indicate the difficulty in obtaining errorless birds, even when we tried to follow Terrace's procedure very closely. Published reports of errorless discrimination learning have rarely, if ever, provided an index of success rates with the procedure.

Apparatus

A Grason-Stadler chamber was modified for pigeons by inserting a black panel 36 cm wide by 32 cm high, with a single response key centered 18 cm from either side wall and 24 cm above the floor. The response key (2.4 cm in diameter) could be transilluminated with either white light or light of 630 (red), 590 (yellow), 555 (green), or 490 nm (blue) by an in-line readout projector (I.E.E. 10-0229, with G.E. 44 lamps). Three-second access to grain was through a hole 6.4-cm square, centered 10 cm below the response key. A force of 15 g (0.15 N) on the key was required to register a response. The floor was constructed of bakelite (23 by 36 cm) and covered by white paper during experimental sessions. Dim general illumination was continuously provided by a G.E. 7.5-W bulb located at the back of the chamber and shielded so that the illuminance on the black panel was approximately 0.05 ft ca (measured by a Photovolt Corp. photometer, Model No. 210). Stimulus intensities were manipulated by variation of resistors in series with the in-line readout projector. The only major apparatus difference compared to Terrace's work was use of the miniprojector, rather than a monochromator, to produce various wavelengths.

Procedure

Training. On Day 1, subjects were trained to eat from the magazine and shaped by the method of successive approximations to peck the white response key. Each of the first 30 responses was reinforced. After conditioning of the key peck, discrimination training began. During 30-sec periods when the key was white, responses were reinforced on a variable-interval (VI) 10-sec schedule; during periods when the key was dark, responses were not reinforced. As detailed in Table 1, the duration of the dark-key presentations was increased from 3 to 30 sec on Day 1.

On Day 2, the duration of each S+ (white key) was increased to 60 sec, and the reinforcement schedule was changed from VI 10-sec to VI 30-sec after the second S+ presentation. Duration of the S− wavelength (red or green, depending on the subject) remained at 3 sec throughout this session, but its intensity was increased in 10 steps from completely dark to an intensity equal to S+. Final equalization of S+ and S− intensities, as well as the determination of approximately equal steps by which the intensity of S− was raised, were based on judgments by independent human observers. The corresponding changes in resistance value are shown in Table 1. For this day and for the rest of the experiment, stimulus presentations were separated by 2.5-sec interstimulus intervals, during which the key was dark.

On Day 3, the S+ component of the schedule was increased to 180 sec and the reinforcement schedule was changed from VI 10-sec to VI 30-sec to VI 60-sec over the first two S+ presentations. Equal intensities of S+ and S− were used and

Table 1 Specific variations in intensity and duration of S− during the three days of fading in S−.

Day	Successive S− Trials	Intensity (ohms)	Duration (sec)
1	1–3	↑	3
	4–7		6
	8–10		10
	11–14	Dark	15
	15–17		20
	18–20		25
	21–30	↓	30
2	1–3	Dark	↑
	4–5	64	
	6–7	47	
	8–9	35	
	10–11	26	3
	12–13	22	
	14–15	16	
	16–17	9	↓
	18–20	5	
	21–30	0 (i.e., brightness equal to that of S+ key)	
3	1–3	↑	3
	3–4		6
	5–6		10
	7–10		15
	11–14	0	20
	15–17		30
	18–20		45
	21–25		60
	26–30	↓	180

the duration of S− was gradually increased from 3 sec to 180 sec, as shown in Table 1. During the first three (fade-in) discrimination training sessions, 30 S+ and 30 S− trials were ordered such that the same stimulus did not appear on more than two consecutive trials.

After Day 3, S+ and S− always remained equal in intensity and duration, and were presented in a quasi-random order, 15 times during each session; no more than three consecutive trials could be of the same stimulus. Throughout training, responses during S− delayed the offset of S− by resetting the S− timer.

All subjects with S− (red) and the first nine subjects with S−(green) experienced the above fading procedure. However, errorless learning proved extremely difficult to obtain with a green S− (26 birds were used without success); there-

fore, the procedure for introducing S−
was modified for the last 10 birds. On
Day 1, S+ was 30 sec, as before, but both
the duration and the intensity of S− were
increased within the session. Over the
first 10 S− trials, duration of the dark
key was increased from 1 to 30 sec; for
the second 10 S− trials, duration was
reduced to 1 sec and intensity was increased over the same 10 steps as for
previous subjects; for the final 10 S−
trials, duration was gradually increased
so that by the end of Day 1, S+ and S−
were the same intensity and duration.
Over the next two days, both stimuli
were gradually increased in duration until
each was 180 sec long.

Testing. Following 14 days of additional
training (15 days for one "with-errors"
bird), with S+ and S− at their full intensity and duration, each subject was
tested for stimulus generalization along
the wavelength dimension. Test values
included 630, 590, 555, and 490 nm. The
S+ was not presented during the test.
Each test was, however, preceded by a
warm-up of four S+ presentations (with
VI 60-sec reinforcement) and four S−
presentations according to the same procedure used in training. Generalization
test stimuli were presented in 12 random-
ized blocks of four stimuli, and each
stimulus presentation was 60 sec in duration. Each bird received one of four
different test-stimulus sequences.

On subsequent days, subjects received
additional generalization tests (with a
variety of different sequences, but otherwise the same procedure). Only the first
test was preceded by a warm-up.

For the first 12 birds (all trained with
a red S−, including errorless Birds 71,
2337, 2643, and 7897 in Figure 3) the test
began with a presentation of S−, which
remained on until the subject responded.
The first two responses were reinforced,
after which this stimulus remained on for
an additional 60 sec while reinforcement
was available on a VI 30-sec schedule.
This schedule remained in force until the

bird had completed one block of four
stimuli in which each reinforcement that
became available during a stimulus presentation was collected during that
presentation. The schedule was then
changed to VI 60-sec for the remaining
stimulus blocks. During generalization
sessions after the first test, reinforcement
was always available on the 60-sec
schedule.

If a subject did not respond to the
first test stimulus (S−) within 2 hr, several free reinforcements were given and
the method of successive approximations
was employed to shape key pecking to the
test stimulus. Thus, these first 12 birds
each obtained at least two response-
contingent grain deliveries at the red S−
before other test stimuli were introduced.
This training at S− was omitted for all
remaining birds, however, because we felt
that it unnecessarily complicated the
experiment.

For the remaining subjects, therefore,
the first test stimulus was not necessarily
the former S−. Reinforcement was
initially available on a VI 30-sec schedule, which was changed to VI 60-sec, as
for previous subjects. All test-stimulus
presentations were 60 sec long, and no
attempt was made to shape responding to
the former S−.

Before testing, each bird was classified as either "with-errors" or "errorless",
according to the general criteria offered
by Terrace (1966a and personal commun-
ications). Only responses to the illuminated S− were considered errors;
responses on the dark key on Day 1 and
interstimulus-interval (ISI) responses
during later sessions were not counted as
errors. In addition, responses during the
first second of S− that followed (very
infrequent) responses during the 2.5-sec
ISI were not counted as errors because
such S− responding appeared to be a
"spillover" from ISI responding. This
additional criterion was suggested by
Terrace (personal communication) and is
analogous to one employed in his early
work to discount S− responses that

appeared to represent a spillover from an immediately preceding S+. A bird was classified as errorless if it made fewer than 35 errors to S−. Generally, once a bird made a burst of responses, or even more than three or four responses during one S−, it continued making errors on subsequent S− presentations and exceeded the 35-error criterion. This limit is also consistent with the general criteria followed by Terrace (personal communication).

There were some procedural differences from Terrace's experiments. In his interdimensional discrimination experiments, Terrace used either 30-sec or 60-sec stimulus durations. However, because we found errorless performance difficult to maintain with 60-sec durations, we used 180-sec stimuli, as in Terrace's earlier experiments (see Terrace, 1966a). Our correction procedure (rarely experienced by errorless birds) also differed somewhat from Terrace's: S-responses reset our S− timer; in Terrace's

experiments, they stopped the timer for 30 to 45 sec.

RESULTS

Of the S− (red) subjects, 13 learned with errors, making between 46 and 1178 errors. Six birds made between one and 22 errors and were considered errorless. Nine S− (green) subjects made between 73 and 528 errors, whereas three made between 30 and 33 errors, meeting our criterion for errorless performance.

Group data for S− (red) subjects during the first day of generalization testing are shown in Figure 1. The two groups displayed very similar relative gradients. The absolute gradients, however, show that with-errors subjects made many more responses during the test than did errorless subjects. This difference in total generalization-test responses was statistically significant ($t = 2.18, df = 17$, $p < 0.05$, two-tailed).

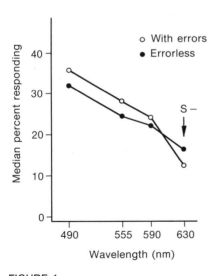
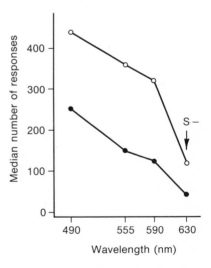

FIGURE 1
Group gradients of relative and absolute wavelength generalization obtained on Day 1 of generalization testing for six errorless and 13 with-errors birds after training with a white S+ and a 630-nm (red) S−.

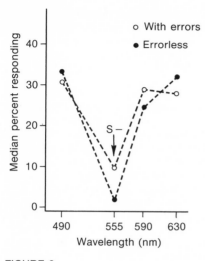 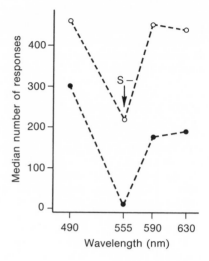

FIGURE 2

Group gradients of relative and absolute wavelength generalization obtained on Day 1 of generalization testing for three errorless and nine with-errors birds after training with a white S+ and a 555-nm (green) S−.

Similar findings are shown in Figure 2 for the S− (green) subjects. As in Figure 1, relative gradients had very similar shapes, and with-errors birds responded more during the tests than did errorless birds. For these subjects, however, this difference in total generalization-test responses was not statistically significant ($t = 1.28$, $df = 10$, $p > 0.20$), perhaps due to the small number of errorless birds.

Gradients for individual errorless subjects are presented in Figure 3. All the S− (red) birds, except 7897, showed maximal responding at the wavelength value (490 nm) farthest from S−, but a clear minimum at S− was present in only three of the six birds. Subject 7897 made eight responses during the first test stimulus (shaping was not necessary) but, even though the first two of these were reinforced, it made only one other response (to 490 nm) during the rest of the test. Figure 4 shows that during further sessions of generalization testing, this bird also exhibited a clear-cut gradient around S−. Gradients for Birds 2337 and 2643 were irregular during further testing and

are not shown; these were two of the three birds whose pecking to the red S− had to be shaped at the start of generalization testing. All three S− (green) birds produced clear incremental gradients around S−. Thus, dimensional control by S− was found for at least seven of the nine errorless birds.

To compare the proportions of with-errors and errorless birds that showed incremental gradients, *i.e.*, a definite minimum at S−, we determined the number of subjects that showed a gradient on one or more of the first four tests. Sixteen of 22 with-errors birds (72.7%) and seven of nine errorless birds (77.8%) showed such gradients. Thus, errorless performance produced incremental gradients at least as often as did with-errors performance.

DISCUSSION

According to the generalization assay for inhibition used by Terrace (1966*b*; 1972*a*), the present finding of incremental gradients around S− suggests that an errorless S− is an inhibitory stimulus. Furthermore, the results of our tests with maintained intermittent reinforcement at all stimulus values imply that the flat gradients Terrace obtained in very similar experiments were due to a floor-effect brought about by his extinction-test procedure. An example of such a floor-effect occurred in the present experiment (Figure 4), in which a bird that made

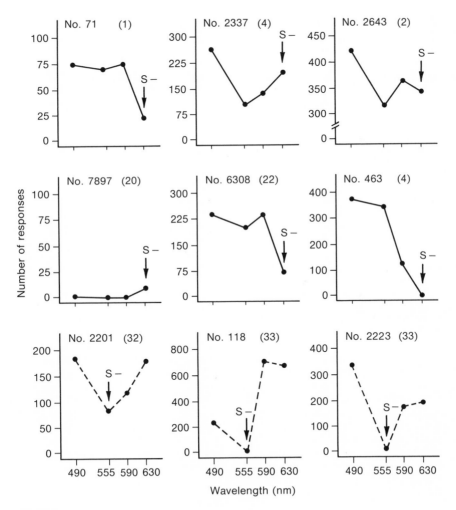

FIGURE 3

Gradients of absolute wavelength generalization obtained on Day 1 of generalization testing for all errorless birds. The upper six graphs are for subjects trained with a 630-nm (red) S−. The lower three graphs are for subjects trained with a 555-nm (green) S−. For each bird, the number of errors is indicated in parentheses.

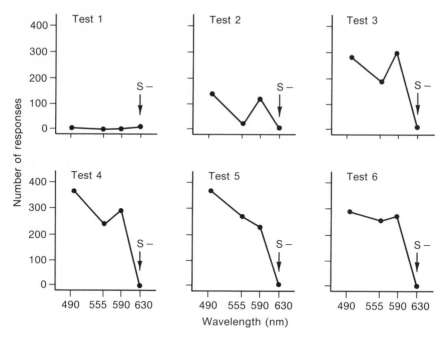

FIGURE 4
Generalization gradients obtained on six successive days after errorless discrimination learning in Bird No. 7897. Control by the S— value (630 nm) was not apparent on the first day, but a clear gradient emerged with continued testing.

only 20 errors during training responded very infrequently during the first session of testing and produced a flat gradient. During further sessions of testing, however, a clear incremental gradient emerged.

Hearst (1972) suggested that incremental gradients may be obtained even when the stimulus producing minimal responding is not inhibitory. For example, a stimulus could merely be less excitatory than the other test stimuli and the obtained gradient would be hard to distinguish from one around an inhibitory stimulus. Hearst proposed that several tests for inhibition, *e.g.*, combined-cue and retardation-of-learning tests (*cf.* Rescorla, 1969), are necessary to determine if a particular training paradigm produces an inhibitory stimulus. Although the present experiment employed

only generalization tests, and was therefore inconclusive according to Hearst's argument, the additional evidence required to establish that an errorless S— exerts inhibitory control comes from other investigators. For example, Lyons (1969) and Johnson (cited by Hearst, 1972) reported that when the S— of an errorless discrimination is superimposed on the S+ from the same discrimination (combined-cue test), large decrements in responding are observed. Although Lyons' procedure for training error-less discriminations (response prevention) differed from Terrace's, Johnson did use Terrace's fading procedure. In experiments involving discriminations established in an autoshaping situation, Wilkie and Ramer (1974) showed that an error-less S— is inhibitory via a retardation-of-learning test; Wessells (1973) found that an errorless S— is inhibitory via both a combined-cue test and a retardation-of-learning test; Rilling (*in press*) obtained incremental gradients around an errorless S—. Thus, there is good evidence, obtained with a variety of assays, to indicate that S— is inhibitory after errorless learning.

Terrace's (1972*a*) argument that reduction or suppression of responding during S— is necessary to establish incremental gradients around S— fails to handle the present results. In fact, one bird (No. 71) made only one error and still showed an incremental gradient. Our generalization gradients obtained from error-less subjects, and the evidence supplied by Lyons, Johnson, Rilling, Wessells, and Wilkie and Ramer indicate that the negative correlation of a stimulus with a reinforcer is crucial in endowing a stimulus with inhibitory properties. Such a negative correlation produces an inhibitory CS— in Pavlovian conditioning (Rescorla, 1969). We suggest that the relationship between a stimulus and a reinforcer is as important in operant conditioning as it is in classical conditioning, and we propose that it is such relationships that mainly produce inhibitory (and excitatory) control, rather than specific-response reduction or suppression (in the inhibitory case) as suggested by Terrace.

In summary, we have argued that Terrace's (1966*b*, 1972*a*) failure to obtain incremental gradients around S— after errorless learning was probably due to a floor-effect, and that findings from our and other experiments indicate that in operant discrimination learning, a stimulus bearing a strong negative correlation with the delivery of reinforcers becomes inhibitory even when discrimination learning occurs with almost no responses to S—.

REFERENCES

Deutsch, J. Discrimination learning and inhibition. *Science,* 1967, **156,** 988.

Hearst, E. Some persistent problems in the analysis of conditioned inhibition. In R. A. Boakes and M. S. Halliday (Eds.), *Inhibition and learning.* London: Academic Press, 1972. Pp. 5–39.

Hearst, E., Besley, S., and Farthing, G. W. Inhibition and the stimulus control of operant behavior. *Journal of the Experimental Analysis of Behavior,* 1970, **14,** 373–409.

Jenkins, H. M. Generalization gradients and the concept of inhibition. In D. I. Mostofsky (Ed.), *Stimulus generalization.* Stanford: Stanford University Press, 1965, Pp. 55–61.

Lyons, J. Stimulus generalization as a function of discrimination learning with and without errors. *Science,* 1969, **163,** 490–491.

Rescorla, R. A. Pavlovian conditioned inhibition. *Psychological Bulletin,* 1969, **72,** 77–94.

Rilling, M. E. Stimulus control and inhibitory processes. In W. K. Honig and J. E. R. Staddon (Eds.), *A handbook of operant conditioning.* Englewood Cliffs, N.J.: Prentice-Hall. (*in press*).

Terrace, H. S. Stimulus control. In W. K. Honig (Ed.), *Operant behavior: areas of research and application.* New York: Appleton-Century-Crofts, 1966. Pp. 271–344. (*a*)

Terrace, H. S. Discrimination learning and inhibition. *Science,* 1966, **154,** 1677–1680. (*b*)

Terrace, H. S. By-products of discrimination learning. In G. Bower and J. Spence (Eds.), *The psychology of learning and motivation,* Vol. 5. New York: Academic Press, 1972. Pp. 195–265. (*a*)

Terrace, H. S. Conditioned inhibition in successive discrimination learning. In R. A. Boakes and M. S. Halliday (Eds.), *Inhibition and learning.* London: Academic Press, 1972. Pp. 99–119. (*b*)

Wessells, M. G. Errorless discrimination, auto-shaping, and conditioned inhibition. *Science,* 1973, **182,** 941–943.

Wilkie, D. M. and Ramer, D. G. Errorless discrimination established by differential autoshaping. *Journal of the Experimental Analysis of Behavior,* 1974, **22,** 333–340.

Chapter 9

Two-Factor Theory

The original models for both classical conditioning and instrumental conditioning depend on contiguity as the mechanism of association. Learning was believed to occur either through contiguity of conditioned stimulus and unconditioned stimulus or through contiguity of response and reinforcer. But contiguity alone does not explain much of complex behavior (Where is the contiguous reward, for instance, for buckling your safety belt in a car?). Even in the laboratory, contiguity does not explain why a rat presses a bar to avoid electric shock, which then does *not* occur, or why a rat takes the first step in an alley when it does not receive a reward until it reaches the goal box.

One way to get around this problem is to abandon the notion that contiguity of any kind is necessary for learning and instead to look for other types of relationships (such as correlation and contingency) to explain learning. This is the tactic of molar-learning theorists, and we have discussed it at several points in this text. But, in adopting a molar theory of behavior, we may lose some of the precision that a molecular theory would provide. Two-factor theory is an attempt to explain learning that does not appear to take place through contiguity in more molecular terms.

Two-factor theory was developed in a systematic way by O. H. Mowrer in the 1950s, but it was based on much prior work of other theorists and researchers. Mowrer retained the notion that contiguity is necessary for learning and, to explain apparent learning without contiguity, postulated chains of contiguous events inside the organism. The two factors of the two-factor theory are, of course, classical and instrumental conditioning. The factors may be overt and easily observable or covert and difficult or impossible to observe. In either case contiguity is assumed to be necessary for both factors. We shall now see how two-factor theory deals with the facts of behavior.

MEDIATING EVENTS

Why does a rat start to run in an alley when the reward does not come until the goal box? Figure 9.1a diagrams the series of stimuli and responses that occur in the alley. Suppose a rat is put into the alley for the first time. It is presumed that through an innate tendency to explore its environment the rat will wander down the alley and make a series of responses (R_1, R_2, R_3, and R_4). For the first few trials the rat moves slowly through the alley and the response sequence need not be anything other than exploration of the alley. Our job is to explain why, with successive trials, the rat will come to run faster and faster. When the rat enters the goal box it sees the food (S_5) and eats it (R_g). Each step toward the goal box is preceded by a certain stimulus and followed by another, so that to get from S_1 to S_2 the rat has to make R_1. Each response (R_1 to R_4) leads to the next stimulus as indicated by the arrows in the diagram. Finally, R_g occurs. The first assumption of two-factor theory is that R_g results in feedback stimuli— notably, the taste of food and the feeling of food in the mouth. It is so likely that such feedback stimuli exist that they are considered as vivid as observable stimuli. (We signify them by a capital letter in Figure 9.1.) The feedback stimuli always accompany eating, and so R_g-S_g always stands for the behavior of eating and its accompanying feedback stimuli. Now R_g-S_g, as a significant event, is both a reward, which can reinforce any response that precedes it, and a US, which becomes associated with any stimulus that precedes it. R_4 is thus reinforced and S_5 (which stands for the stimuli in the goal box) becomes a CS associated with R_g-S_g, which is the US. The conditioned response is r_g-s_g, shown in Figure 9.1b. It is shown in small letters because often it is not observed and may occur wholly within the animal. It may be measurable as salivation or as covert chewing movements made in anticipation of food, but it may also consist merely of unobserved events within the animal's nervous system. In any case, as a response it must be accompanied by its own feedback stimulus of some kind (if the response were salivation, it would produce a feeling of wetness in the mouth). The response is thus always shown with its feedback stimulus as r_g-s_g and never as r_g alone. The r_g-s_g sequence is the building block that two-factor theory uses to connect distant events. It is supposed that r_g-s_g now instrumentally reinforces R_3 and acts as a second-order US for S_4 in the same way that R_g-S_g reinforced R_4 and S_5. Similarly, once r_g-s_g is connected to S_4 it can reinforce R_2 and S_3 and so on back to the beginning of the alley. The final series of connections is shown in Figure 9.1c. As r_g-s_g gets connected successively to more and more distant S's (distant from the goal box) it becomes

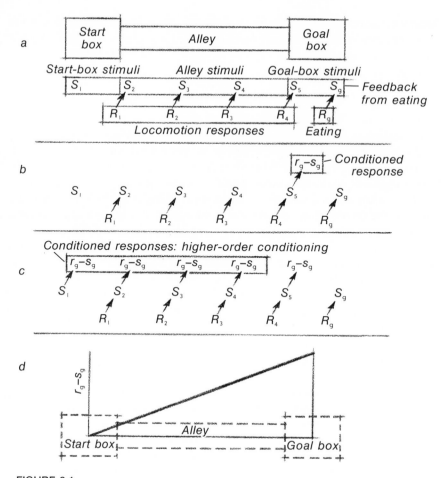

FIGURE 9.1

The two-factor explanation of how a rat comes to run faster and faster down an alley with food reward. Overt responses and feedback stimuli are shown by capital letters. Conditioned responses (r_g's) and their feedback stimuli (s_g's) are shown by lower-case letters. R_g–S_g serves both as an unconditioned stimulus and as a reward. Likewise, each r_g–s_g, established by classical conditioning, rewards the response that precedes it. A gradient of reward is formed, with each step down the alley increasing r_g–s_g.

weaker and weaker. The declining strength of r_g–s_g results in a gradient much like the gradients we discussed in connection with conflict theory. A hypothetical gradient is shown in Figure 9.1d. Here, however, the gradient is not just a convenient way to summarize overt behavior, but represents an actual set of events supposed to take place inside the organism. Just as R_g–S_g is a reward, so is r_g–s_g a reward. A response that changes from a weaker to a stronger r_g–s_g is thereby reinforced. Each response in the sequence of Figure 9.1c is thus reinforced by transition from a weaker to a stronger r_g-s_g. Thus, two-factor theory involves two stages:

1. The acquisition of r_g-s_g by classical conditioning, and
2. the instrumental responses that substitute a stronger for a weaker r_g-s_g.

In the sequences from (a) to (d) in Figure 9.1, the reinforcement for each response develops and the responses begin to occur faster and faster, which is another way of saying that the rat runs faster down the alley. Although we described the rat's movement down the alley as a series of stimuli and responses (often compared to the caroming of billiard balls) the rat's movement actually occurs in a continuous way. No one supposes that the rat makes a response, waits for the feedback stimuli, makes another response, waits for its feedback stimuli, and so on. Rather the process is supposed to occur at such a rapid rate that—just as the still frames of a moving picture blend to produce continuous motion—the individual stimuli and responses blend to produce continuous movement down the alley.

When there is an aversive event (such as electric shock) in the goal box, a symmetrical process occurs. The aversive event serves as an unconditioned stimulus. In the aversive situation, responses that take the rat away from the goal box are reinforced by reduction in aversive stimulation. The first step out of the goal box is reinforced by an actual shock reduction. Further movement away is reinforced by reduction in the strength of r_g-s_g, which is now aversive.

This explanation of positive and negative reinforcement provides a hypothetical mechanism capable of accounting for conflict theory. Where conflict occurs, according to two-factor theory, it does so because of competing response tendencies. Imagine a rat previously both shocked and rewarded by food in the goal box and hovering between R_2 and R_3 in Figure 9.1; the rat would be rewarded for making R_3 by an increase in the r_g-s_g associated with food and rewarded for going back to R_2 by a decrease in the r_g-s_g associated with shock. Because the rat cannot make R_2 and R_3 simultaneously the opposing tendencies conflict.

Two-factor theory relies on the notion that conditioned responses and their feedback stimuli can take on some of the actual positive and negative properties of unconditioned stimuli and responses, so as to reinforce behavior distant from actual reward. We indicated previously that conditioned responses need *not* be identical to unconditioned responses and that secondary reinforcers need not themselves take on reinforcing properties. It is still possible that such conditioned behavior as the r_g-s_g mechanism could facilitate learning in the same way that other secondary reinforcers do, by providing information that a response has just occurred or that a significant event is imminent. But this notion would be a serious breach of the primary purpose of two-factor theory—to explain association wholly in terms of contiguity.* How seriously two-factor theorists take the notion that the stimuli in an alley or maze take on the properties of unconditioned stimuli may be seen by this passage from a lucid exposition of two-factor theory by Frank Logan and Allen Wagner (1965, p. 94):

> Imagine an animal that has been fitted with two devices which it carries and which do not restrict its movement. When activated, one of the devices automatically delivers small amounts of water into the animal's mouth, the other delivers an electric shock to, let us say, the animal's back. We shall suppose that the rate of water delivery and the intensity of shock may be varied over a specified range.
>
> Having attached such devices to a thirsty animal and habituated him to their operations, let us place the animal for the first time in a complex maze. The question is, can we now, by controlling the water delivery and shocking devices, successfully direct the animal over some selected pathway through the maze? Whenever the animal makes a step in the desired direction we would present him with a small amount of water or increase the amount he is receiving. Whenever the animal makes a movement in an undesired direction we would slow down or stop the water flow. The shocking device may be employed in the opposite manner, that is, movements in the desired direction would decrease and ultimately terminate the shock, or undesired activities would initiate or increase the shock.
>
> Although we as experimenters might have a good deal to learn about the most efficient programming of the stimulation, we would not be surprised if an animal could under such conditions be made to go over the desired path on the *first trial* rather quickly and efficiently, as compared with a similarly naive animal who received no shock or water delivery.
>
> Suppose we now change the conditions somewhat. Prior to placing an animal in the maze, let us give it a number of paired presentations of a distinctive light and an electric shock, as well as a number of paired presentations of a tone and water. When we place the animal in the maze for the first time, rather than attempting to direct its behavior by administering shock and water, we will manipulate the occurrence and intensity of the light and tone. The belief that the animal could with suitable control of the light and tone be directed through the maze, just as with water and shock, provides the basis for a number of theories of incentive learning, all of which are of the fractional goal response variety.

At this point let us pause for a few definitions of terms. The r_g-s_g sequence is called the *fractional anticipatory goal response*. When the significant event in the goal box is a reward, the fractional anticipatory goal response is sometimes called *hope* and written r_h-s_h. We shall adopt this convention here from now on. When the significant event in the goal box is aversive, the fractional anticipatory goal response is sometimes called *fear* and written r_f-s_f. We have waited until now to introduce these terms to show that their definition is wholly within

---

*Any evidence showing that secondary reinforcers are useful only as information is thus evidence against this strong form of two-factor theory.

the sphere of classical and instrumental conditioning and need take nothing from the everyday meanings of "hope" and "fear." In fact just the opposite is true. The meaning of a child's fear of the dark may become illuminated when we consider it in the light of knowledge gained in the laboratory. It is sometimes helpful to interpret such an everyday fear as a conditioned response elicited by stimuli that have previously been paired with an aversive event. As we mentioned previously, such an interpretation suggests a cure for the fear by one or another deconditioning procedure.

Two-factor theory relies on a series of events both outside and inside the organism. The initial event, starting outside the organism, is a stimulus, and the terminal event, ending as overt behavior, is a response. Stimuli are said to cause responses, which in turn cause stimuli, which cause further responses, and so on. For this reason, two-factor theory is an S-R theory. But it is important to realize that for a psychologist the terms "stimulus" and "response" are defined only in terms of the organism's interaction with the environment (as indicated in Chapter 2). When events occur wholly within the organism (and when they occur wholly outside the organism) "stimulus" and "response" have no meaning. An event inside the organism such as a neural impulse from one point to another is neither a stimulus nor a response.* It is simply an event. When two-factor theory speaks of stimuli and responses (such as r_g-s_g) wholly inside the organism, these should be taken only as analogies. An r_g-s_g sequence is an event that can be caused by other events and can itself cause other events but cannot be broken up into stimulus and response components. That is, there is no r_g without an s_g and no s_g without an r_g. Since these two symbols *always* go together and cannot even be conceived apart, it must mean that they stand for a single thing.

We now turn to ways in which two-factor theory has been used to explain avoidance and punishment behavior.

TWO-FACTOR THEORY OF AVOIDANCE

Two-factor theory was first developed to account for avoidance behavior. It is difficult to explain by means of contiguity alone why animals maintain avoidance behavior once they have learned it. Consider the typical sequence of discriminated avoidance. First the subject learns to escape from the shock and then to avoid the shock altogether by responding during a warning signal before the shock comes on. At first, when responses only effect escape from shock, it is easy to find a contiguous reinforcer for the response—the reduction of the shock itself. But later, when shock is avoided altogether, what reinforces the

---

*Or it is *both* a stimulus (to the next nerve) and a response (of the previous nerve), which is to say that the distinction is meaningless within the system being studied, the organism.

avoidance response? A molar theorist would reply that avoidance responses
are reinforced by the negative contingency or negative correlation between
responses and shocks. A molecular theorist must look for contiguous reinforcement. He finds it with two-factor theory. In discriminated avoidance (Figure
9.2) the application of two-factor theory is straightforward. The two factors
correspond to the two stages by which avoidance proceeds: (1) escape from
shock, and (2) complete avoidance of shock. The escape phase (stage 1) consists of three events: first the signal comes on, then the shock and signal are
both present together, then the response turns off both the shock and the signal.
The signal thus acts as a CS and the shock as a US. The conditioned response
is fear, the r_f-s_f of two-factor theory. (Sometimes the classically conditioned
response is not called r_f-s_f but "conditioned fear," "anxiety," or simply, "aversiveness.") This is the first factor, classical conditioning of fear. During the
avoidance phase (stage 2) the signal comes on first, the response then turns off
the signal, and there is no shock; responses in this phase are reinforced by reduction of fear, which goes away when the signal (the CS) goes away. The
second factor is thus instrumental conditioning of the response reinforced by
the reduction of fear. As in the alley, responses are first reinforced by reduction
of shock and then by reduction of fear (turning off a stimulus associated with
shock).

Nondiscriminated avoidance works in a similar way. Here, instead of an
external warning signal, the CS consists of internal stimuli. The subject is
assumed to have a sort of internal clock, which can be reset at each response.
Readings on this internal clock take the place of the warning signal of discrimi-

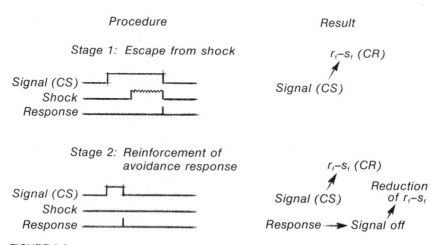

FIGURE 9.2
Two-factor explanation of discriminated avoidance in terms of generation (stage 1) and
reduction (stage 2) of r_f-s_f (fear).

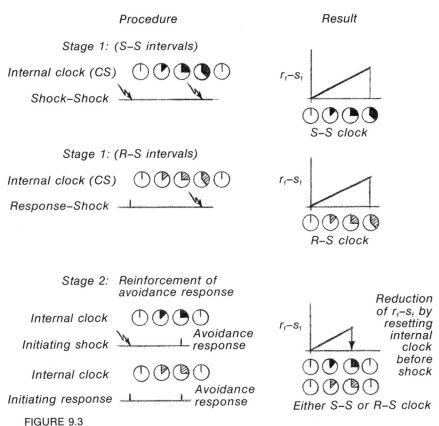

FIGURE 9.3
Two-factor explanation of Sidman avoidance in terms of generation (stage 1) and reduction (stage 2) of r_f-s_f (fear).

nated avoidance.* In the type of nondiscriminated avoidance called Sidman avoidance, before the subject learns to respond, shocks come at regular intervals (the S–S interval). Early readings on the internal clock (given some variability in its movement) will rarely be paired with shocks, but readings at or near the end of the S–S interval will frequently be paired with shocks (Figure 9.3). Thus these readings serve as internal CS's. As the time approaches for a shock, stronger and stronger r_f-s_f's are generated because the readings on the clock have more and more frequently been paired with shock. With the Sidman-avoidance procedure, responses postpone shocks for a given

---

*The reader should not take the notion of an internal clock too literally. It is not like a stop watch with hands that move around in a circle, but rather a sequence of internal events that vary in intensity or quality with time. Such a sequence must exist, otherwise animals would have no sense of time.

period, the R–S (response-shock) interval. Responses will reset the S–S internal clock and start another clock, the R–S internal clock. The production of fear (r_f–s_f) by internal clocks, which start timing from the last shock or the last response, is the first, classical conditioning, factor. This is shown in Figure 9.3 as the first stage. Since low readings are associated with low fear and high readings associated with high fear, a response will be reinforced immediately by reduction of fear (change from a high to a low reading). This is the second, instrumental, factor of two-factor theory as applied to Sidman avoidance. The subject in a Sidman-avoidance experiment is repeatedly building up fear and then having it suddenly reduced, either after being shocked, at first, or after making a response, later on.

Herrnstein-Hineline avoidance, in which responses reduce the frequency of irregularly persented shocks, is subject to explanation by the same two-factor mechanism (Figure 9.4). Again, both responses and shocks reset an internal clock. When shocks reset this clock, its readings are likely to be paired with shock (Figure 5.27, machine A). When responses reset the clock, its readings are less likely to be paired with shock (machine B). Proprioceptive feedback from responses and memory traces of shocks are the internal stimuli that distinguish the response clock from the shock clock. A change from the shock clock to the response clock would be rewarding because it would constitute a change from a more aversive internal stimulus to a less aversive internal stimulus. Thus, the subject will tend to respond after a shock. But in Herrnstein-Hineline avoidance experiments two or more responses are sometimes made in a row without an intervening shock. Why would these occur? As time passes after the last response the memory trace of the proprioceptive feedback fades. In essence, the subject is less certain that a response rather than a shock was the last event. A new response restores the relatively less aversive proprioceptive state, and is thereby reinforced.

The alert reader will have noticed that even two-factor theory does not predict that avoidance behavior will be maintained indefinitely under any of the procedures discussed. Once avoidance responses begin, shocks are no longer presented (except with Herrnstein-Hineline avoidance, which programs shocks at a low frequency regardless of how fast the subject responds), and although responses are still reinforced by reduction of fear, the fear itself is subject to extinction because the CS and US are no longer paired. One would expect, then, that even a well-trained animal would occasionally fail to avoid the shock—and this is exactly what is found. Experiments on avoidance always involve occasional failures to avoid the shock. The two-factor theory would attribute these failures to a weakening of the r_f–s_f response due to presentation of the CS (signal) without the US (shock).

An experiment by Leo Kamin (done in 1957) illustrates the two principal experimental procedures used to test the two-factor theory of avoidance:

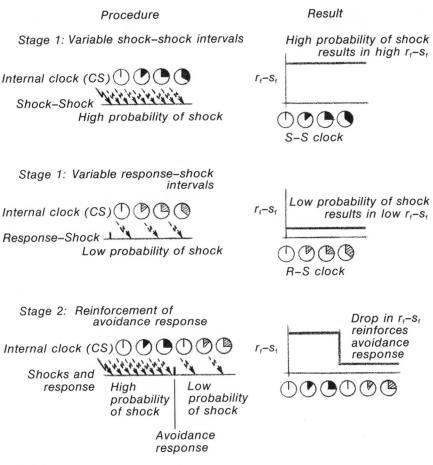

FIGURE 9.4
Two-factor explanation of Herrnstein–Hineline avoidance in terms of generation (Stage 1) and reduction (Stage 2) of r_f–s_f (fear).

1. According to two-factor theory, avoidance responses are reinforced by the termination of a stimulus (the CS) that has been previously paired with shock. Can animals learn a response that *only* terminates the CS but does not actually prevent the shock? Two-factor theory predicts that such learning should be possible.

2. Suppose the response *only* prevents the shock but does not terminate the CS. Two-factor theory predicts that such learning should be impossible.

Kamin's discriminated-avoidance experiment, conducted with four groups of rats, is illustrated in Figure 9.5. The response was running from one side of

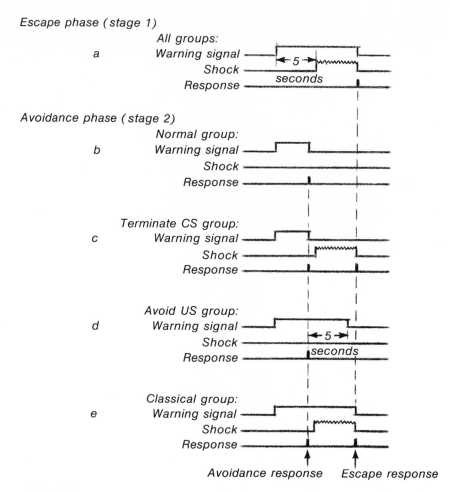

FIGURE 9.5
The procedure of Kamin's experiment to test the two-factor theory of avoidance using four groups of rats.

a shuttle box to the other. The aversive stimulus was shock. The warning signal was a tone. All four groups were subject to shock if they did not respond within 5 seconds of the tone. A response permitted escape from the shock and turned off the tone (Figure 9.5a). The difference between the groups was in what happened if a response occurred during the first 5 seconds of the tone, before the shock came on. For the "normal" group (Figure 9.5b), the avoidance response turned off the warning tone and prevented the shock. For the "terminate CS" group (Figure 9.5c), the avoidance response turned off the warning tone but did not prevent the shock; the shock came on anyway and another response (crossing back into the original compartment) was required to escape it. For the "avoid US" group (Figure 9.5d) the avoidance response prevented the shock but did not turn off the warning tone, which stayed on for 5 seconds and then was turned off. For the "classical" group (Figure 9.5e) the avoidance response had no programmed consequences; the tone stayed on and the shock came on anyway. Another response was required to escape the shock and turn off the tone.

Kamin expected that the normal group would learn the avoidance response and that the classical group would not learn the avoidance response (although they might make a few anticipatory escape responses). The test of two-factor theory would be what happened to the other two groups. Two-factor theory predicts that the "terminate CS" group should learn to respond but that the "avoid US" group should not learn to respond. Figure 9.6 shows the percentage of avoidance responses made by each of the four groups over 100 trials. The results were exactly opposite to those predicted by two-factor theory. The

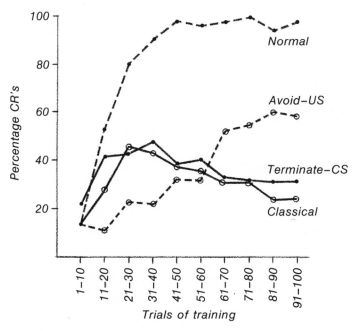

FIGURE 9.6
Percentage of avoidance responses in each of the four groups of Kamin's experiment over 100 trials. [From Kamin, L. J. The effects of termination of the CS and avoidance of the US on avoidance learning: an extension. *Canadian Journal of Psychology*, 1957, *11*, 48–56.]

"avoid US" group performed the avoidance response despite continuation of the overt CS, and the "terminate CS" group responded only slightly (not much more than the "classical" group) despite CS reduction. The experiment indicates that although CS reduction aids in avoidance (the "normal" group avoided more than the "avoid US" group), it is not necessary for avoidance learning as two-factor theory asserts.

It has been pointed out, however, by Kamin among others, that other factors than those overtly programmed may have contributed to the results of Kamin's experiment. Figure 9.5 reveals some extra contingencies in the experiment. The "terminate CS" group could have failed to make many avoidance responses because their avoidance responses were adventitiously punished by the subsequent onset of shock. The "avoid US" group might have avoided, not because the shock was absent, but because the avoidance response was eventually followed by CS termination, albeit delayed by 5 seconds. Nevertheless, the experiment, if it does not conclusively rebut two-factor theory, fails to supply support for it.

It is much more difficult to test the two-factor theory in its application to nondiscriminated avoidance. Here, the hypothesized CS's are internal clocks reset by shocks or by proprioceptive feedback from responses. One attempt to investigate proprioceptive feedback directly was made by E. Taub and A. J. Berman. These researchers trained a monkey in a Sidman-avoidance task and then operated on the monkey's spinal cord, completely severing all proprioceptive connections. Despite the absence of any proprioceptive feedback the monkey, after recovery, maintained avoidance responding. This experiment provides some evidence against the assertion of two-factor theory that proprioceptive feedback is necessary for avoidance responding.

Still further evidence against the two-factor theory of avoidance is the fact that after extended avoidance training almost no signs of fear are observed. Even when signs of fear *are* observed, early in training, they do not come and go with the CS as two-factor theory says they should. Of course, a two-factor theorist might argue that signs of fear are just that—signs. Fear itself might be primarily a central process, which we are now incapable of measuring.

Herrnstein, in a comprehensive review of avoidance called "Method and Theory in the Study of Avoidance," has argued that this vary ability of two-factor theory to explain any conceivable experimental result is a disadvantage of the theory. To be meaningful, a theory should be capable of disproof. With regard to Herrnstein-Hineline avoidance he argues for a molar explanation, saying that two-factor theory is unparsimonious. Instead of attributing avoidance responses to unobserved internal states and then attributing the unobserved internal states to shocks (as in Figure 9.4, derived from Figure 2.19), why not attribute the avoidance responses to the observed relationship (contingency or correlation) between responses and shocks?

TWO-FACTOR THEORY OF PUNISHMENT

When Thorndike's "law of effect" was first published, it had two parts: (1) the positive law of effect stated that connections are strengthened when they are followed by satisfying events, and (2) the negative law of effect stated that connections are weakened when they are followed by annoying events. Later Thorndike revised his theory and, essentially, repealed the negative law of effect. Thorndike had come to believe that punishment simply did not work—that negative consequences did not reduce responding. The advantage of such a belief is that it reduces the four types of instrumental conditioning—positive reinforcement, negative reinforcement, punishment, and omission—to just two: positive and negative reinforcement.* This would indeed be a simpler, and therefore a better, theory provided it could explain behavioral facts as well as the theory that posits both a positive and negative law of effect.

The critical fact that must be explained by anyone who denies the negative law of effect is the apparent efficacy of punishment. The effectiveness of punishment was shown clearly in Figure 5.23. Pigeons that were shocked after pecking a key decreased their responding much more than pigeons that were shocked independently of their pecking, even though the independent shocks were at least three times as frequent (and sometimes more than ten times as frequent) as the peck-dependent shocks. Why is there such a difference between punishment and response-independent shock? It cannot be simply that the shock interferes with pecking because the much more frequent free shocks do not seem to interfere with pecking. A possible answer is provided by the two-factor theory of punishment.

In explaining the two-factor theory of punishment let us stick with the example of a pigeon pecking a key. A peck may be analyzed into a series of subresponses such as lifting head, orienting, rearing back, moving forward, opening beak, and so on, which comprise a chain of behavior such as described earlier in this chapter. The series of subresponses and the events those responses produce are just like those shown in Figure 9.1 except that the gradient established would be avoidance gradient of r_f-s_f. Just as a rat in a conflict situation will run part way down the alley and then stop, the pigeon about to peck a key will begin the sequence of subresponses leading to a peck and then abort the sequence in the middle. Thus, when a pigeon pecks less at a key after pecks are punished, the pigeon is still beginning to peck at the same rate as before—but is aborting some of the pecks before its beak hits the key. Such aborted pecks are not measured by the experimenter, who counts only displacements of the

---

*If one goes further and accepts a relativistic theory of reinforcement, say drive reduction or Premack's theory, then positive reinforcement is the same as negative reinforcement (the reduction of an aversive state) and only a single kind of instrumental mechanism is required. Thorndike himself did not go this far.

key. According to two-factor theory, then, punishment does not decrease the number of responses started—only the number of responses completed.

But why is the sequence of subresponses aborted—if not by punishment of the later subresponses? Two-factor theory provides a ready answer: the response sequence is aborted, not because of punishment, but because of negative reinforcement of another response. Figure 9.7 illustrates the negative-reinforcement process. Figure 9.7a shows how the strength of r_f-s_f increases during a normal response sequence. Figure 9.7b shows what happens if a subresponse late in the sequence is not performed but another response, one not usually followed by an eventual peck on the key, is substituted. This other response (R_0) has feedback stimuli that have never been paired with shock and so are not aversive. The reduction of aversiveness from the feedback stimuli of R_3 to the feedback stimuli of R_0 reinforces R_0. When the pigeon performs R_0 instead of R_4 it is escaping from the aversive feedback stimuli generated by R_3.

To summarize, according to two-factor theory, punishment works not because it reduces the punished response directly, but because it increases some

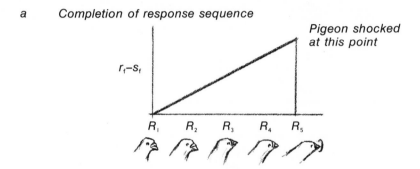

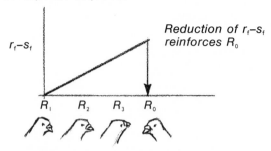

FIGURE 9.7
The two-factor theory of punishment of a pigeon's key-peck. The chain of responses leading to the key-peck generates increasing r_f-s_f. Abortion of the chain is reinforced by reduction in r_f-s_f.

other response, R_0. This other response is reinforced by reduction in aversiveness (r_f-s_f), just as in regular discriminated and nondiscriminated avoidance. As in avoidance experiments, the two factors consist of (1) pairing of a stimulus (a CS) with an aversive US (classical conditioning), and (2) responding that reduces that stimulus (instrumental escape conditioning). With discriminated avoidance the CS is provided by the experimenter. With nondiscriminated avoidance the CS is an internal clock. With punishment the CS is the feedback from the response itself. The CS, in each case, is paired with the aversive stimulus, and the absence of the CS is paired with the absence of the aversive stimulus. (That is, there is a contingency relation between the CS and US.) Punishment differs from avoidance in that with avoidance the avoidance response is actually observed, whereas with punishment the avoidance response (R_0) is inferred from the measured reduction of the punished response. It is conceivable that an R_0 could be observed in punished behavior, but usually none is observed. So strictly speaking, R_0 should be written r_0.

The problems with the two-factor theory of punishment are similar to those of the two-factor theory of avoidance—that events inside the organism are inferred and may be unmeasurable. In the case of punishment, even the avoidance response itself (r_0) is unobserved. The reader must decide for himself whether the parsimony gained by abandoning the negative law of effect is lost when unobserved and potentially unobservable internal states are postulated.

Although it is difficult to test the two-factor theory of punishment directly, an attempt to do so was made by J. W. Mansfield and the author. In a Skinner box fitted with two keys, we trained hungry pigeons to peck first the right key and then the left key to get food. That is, food was given only after right–left sequences and never after right or left key-pecks alone. In this experiment right key-pecks and left key-pecks were subresponses of a right–left sequence, which comprised the complete response. We then punished the pigeons with shock after complete right–left sequences. At the beginning of the experiment the shock was very mild. Then each day the intensity was increased slightly until finally the pigeons stopped pecking the keys. We reasoned that if the two-factor theory were correct, there would be some intensity of shock at which the pigeons would abort the right–left sequence between the right and left peck. At this point the pigeons would peck the right key, stop the response before pecking the left key, and return to pecking the right key again. We expected that as punishment intensity increased, completed responses would decrease as usual but response initiations (pecks on the right key) would not decrease or would decrease very slowly. By analogy, imagine a schoolchild who is punished for getting up out of his seat. As punishment became more severe, the child might actually get up less frequently—but he might *start* to get up just as much, stopping before the teacher noticed him. We found, on the contrary, that as shock intensity increased, the pigeons reduced their pecks on both keys by the same percentage. That is, punishment seemed to reduce initiations as well as completions of the response. It is possible, of course, that at all intensities of shock our pigeons were starting to peck just as frequently but aborting the sequence before even the first peck (on the right key). In such a case, again, we would have to look further and further into the organism to find support for two-factor theory.

FRUSTRATION THEORY

If you look at a rat that has been rewarded in the goal box of an alley and is now undergoing a process of extinction, you will observe that the rat acts agitated, much as the person does who hits and curses the out-of-order Coke machine that has just taken his dime. Such observations, as well as more systematic studies of behavior during extinction, which show that animals will escape from a distinctive alley or chamber in which they have been previously rewarded and in which reward is no longer available, have led psychologists to conclude that instrumental extinction is not just a negative process. Just as, according to Pavlov's theory, extinction of classical conditioning is a positive inhibitory process (see Figure 4.8), extinction of instrumental conditioning also may be a positive inhibitory process.

This inhibitory process has been described in various ways, but the most detailed explanation of its action has been provided by Abram Amsel. According to Amsel, in a situation where reward has been present but is no longer present, an animal emits a response that Amsel calls "frustration." This primary frustration response (symbolized R_F) is said to be elicited by nonreward just as eating is elicited by food and running and jumping are elicited by electric shock.

The critical assumption of frustration theory is that frustration responses are only symptoms, so to speak, of an internal aversive state. Once frustration has occurred, say in the goal box of an alley, it is as if a punishing stimulus such as electric shock were in the goal box of the alley. Like the punishing stimulus, frustration acts as a US, and a series of fractional anticipatory frustration responses are generated in the alley in exactly the same way as fractional anticipatory fear responses would be generated if the rat were shocked in the goal box.

These fractional anticipatory frustration responses conflict with (and subtract from) the fractional anticipatory "hope" responses (previously generated by the reward) and slow down the rat's speed in the alley. Thus, a rat slows down in an alley during extinction, not because the effects of reinforcement have dissipated, but because the effects of reinforcement are opposed by the countereffects of frustration. By extension, any extinction process in any organism generates similar unconditioned and conditioned frustration responses, which oppose and eventually stop the instrumental response.

The contrary effects of primary and conditioned frustration must be distinguished. Primary frustration (R_F) tends to activate the animal. Like electric shock, primary frustration causes increased running and jumping in a rat.

Wherever primary frustration occurs, a rat will tend to run away from that point, with more vigor the closer the rat is to the place of primary frustration. The only difference between primary frustration and mild electric shock in this respect is that electric shock is applied externally and its effects disappear quickly when it is removed, but primary frustration is said to be internal and its effects would dissipate slowly outside of the situation in which it is generated. In fact, primary frustration may persist from one trial to the next so that because of frustration in the goal box on one trial a rat will run faster in the alley on the next trial.

Conditioned frustration, however, like conditioned fear, tends to slow down a rat's running in an alley. This is so because steps toward the goal box increase conditioned frustration (which is aversive), whereas steps away from the goal box decrease conditioned frustration.

Thus, the two factors of frustration theory work in opposite directions for a rat running in an alley. The classical-conditioning factor tends to speed up running because increased activity is the unconditioned response to frustration. The instrumental-conditioning factor tends to slow down running because running toward the goal box increases conditioned frustration and punishes the response. In this respect frustration would be no different from electric shock and other aversive stimuli, which also may have contrary classical and instrumental effects.

Let us now consider what happens, according to frustration theory, when a rat running in an alley is partially rewarded (sometimes not rewarded) in the goal box. We can follow along with our practical example of the Coke machine that only works part of the time. According to Amsel there are four stages:

1. The reinforcement in the goal box generates r_h-s_h in the alley by the mechanism shown in Figure 9.1. In our example, r_h-s_h's are what get us to put a dime into the Coke machine in the first place.
2. In the presence of r_h-s_h the rat is occasionally not rewarded. This generates R_F (frustration) in the goal box. With the Coke machine, depositing the dime does not work and generates frustration.
3. The R_F in the goal box, in turn, generates r_F-s_F* (conditioned frustration) in the alley, again according to the mechanism shown in Figure 9.1. The r_F-s_F acts in opposition to the r_h-s_h and slows the rat down—not enough, however, to prevent the rat from reaching the goal box. A set of hypothetical gradients is shown in Figure 9.8. In the Coke machine example, we now start to feel uneasy even before depositing the dime and hesitate, but being thirsty we deposit the dime anyway.
4. The fourth stage is somewhat more complicated. Because r_F-s_F is not

*Unfortunately, "frustration" and "fear" begin with the same letter. We shall use r_f-s_f for "fear" and r_F-s_F for "frustration."

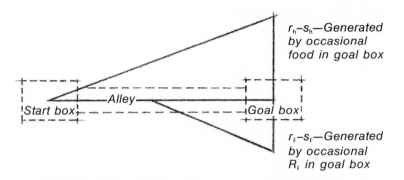

FIGURE 9.8
Hope and frustration gradients with partial reinforcement in the goal box of an alley. First the occasional reinforcement generates r_h–s_h. Then occasional nonreinforcement in the presence of r_h–s_h generates R_F (primary frustration). Then occasional R_F generates r_F–s_F. The gradient above the line (positive) reinforces movement toward the goal box. The gradient below the line (negative) reinforces movement away from the goal box.

strong enough at first to prevent running to the goal box, its occurrence will frequently be followed by food. That is, with partial reinforcement in the goal box, after r_F–s_F is generated, the rat will sometimes run to the goal box in the presence of r_F–s_F and find food in the goal box. Thus, for a rat that receives partial reinforcement r_F–s_F will come to signal food. In the Coke machine example, we will put a dime in the slot even though we feel frustrated, but then the dime will sometimes work and the Coke delivery will reward us. This reward in the presence of conditioned frustration will establish the frustration as an S^D so that in the future the feeling of frustration will come to signal the possibility of reward and actually increase the probability of the response.

The fourth stage, the development of persistence in the presence of frustration, has been used by Amsel to explain Humphreys' paradox in molecular terms. (Humphreys' paradox, introduced in Chapter 5, describes the finding that more responding is made in extinction after partial reinforcement than after continuous reinforcement.) According to Amsel, when a rat in a runway has been fed each time it runs to the goal box, frustration never develops during conditioning. When food suddenly is absent during extinction, primary frustration appears and may actually speed up running in the first few extinction trials, but then conditioned frustration builds up and soon the rat stops running.

With partial reinforcement, however, the fourth step outlined above occurs during conditioning. That is, conditioned frustration was already present before extinction began; the rat has learned to persist in running in the presence of frustration. Eventually this discriminative function of frustration itself extinguishes, but not before many responses have been made during extinction.

To return to the Coke machine example, taken from Chapter 5, the machine in building A, which works all the time, will not generate frustration until it is unplugged. This frustration will succeed quickly in preventing too many dimes from being wasted. The machine in building B, which has been generating frustration all along (by working only occasionally), is also occasionally reinforcing the insertion of dimes in the presence of frustration. After the machine in building B is unplugged, people will continue to experience frustration, and will continue to insert dimes at a high rate—at least for a while.

Frustration theory provides a molecular, two-factor explanation for a phenomenon (Humphreys' Paradox) that was explained in Chapter 5 with one factor—instrumental discrimination between contingencies. The advantage of frustration theory here is that it involves only contiguous relations. The disadvantage is that these relations are said to take place inside the organism where they cannot be observed.

Because frustration theory, like two-factor theory of avoidance and punishment, depends on the existence of several internal events, it is impossible to test directly. Nevertheless, frustration theory does make some predictions about behavior that can be tested, and much research has been done in this area. We can briefly discuss only a small portion of it. First, consider what should happen in the double alley shown in Figure 9.9. The rat runs down the first alley and into the first goal box, then out of the first goal box (through a

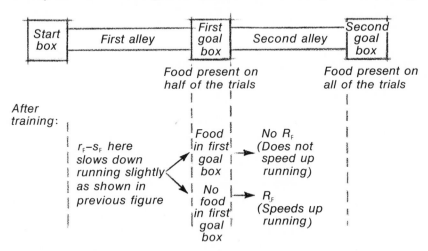

FIGURE 9.9
The double-alley experiment. Partial reinforcement in the first alley slows down running by subtraction of gradients as shown in Figure 8.17. On trials in which no food is present in the first goal box, primary frustration (R_F) speeds up running in the second alley.

back door) into the second alley and then into the second goal box. If food is present on every trial in the second goal box and only on half of the trials in the first goal box, what will the relative running speeds be? Frustration theory predicts that after some training with this apparatus, r_F-s_F should develop in the first alley (with partial reinforcement). In the second alley R_F (primary frustration) will be present for half of the trials (after nonreward in the first goal box) and absent for the other half of the trials (after reward in the first goal box). The rat should slow down in the first alley (because of r_F-s_F) and should speed up in the second alley (because of R_F), compared to another rat that is rewarded on every trial in both goal boxes. Furthermore, the rat that receives partial reinforcement in the first goal box should run faster in the second alley after nonreinforcement in the first goal box (R_F present) than after reinforcement in the first goal box (R_F absent). These predictions have been confirmed when tested.

An experiment by H. M. Adelman and J. L. Maatsch was designed to show that frustration acts like any aversive stimulus in that escape from frustration could reinforce a response. They allowed three groups of rats to jump out of a box and onto a raised platform. The jumping response was reinforced in various ways for the three groups. One group was simply allowed to jump onto the platform; curiosity and escape from the confinement of the box would presumably support responding. A second group was fed on the platform. A third group was rewarded by escape from frustration. This third group was fed in the box (after running down an alley to get to the box), then food was removed from the box. Presumably this group now experienced frustration in the box and would escape. The average latency for the first group of rats (escape from confinement) was 160 seconds; the average latency for the second group of rats (food on the platform) was 20 seconds; and the average latency for the third group (escape from frustration) was 5 seconds. Furthermore, the first group stopped jumping onto the platform almost immediately. The second group, after food was removed, jumped to the platform 60 times and then stopped. But most of the rats in the third group were still jumping onto the platform even after 100 trials. The experimenter's behavior (of putting the rats back into the box) persisted less than the rats' behavior (of jumping out).

Amsel and others have used the frustration mechanism to explain several facts of discrimination learning. Like partial reinforcement, discrimination learning (alternation of S^D and S^Δ) involves occasional reward and nonreward. At first, before S^D and S^Δ are discriminated, they act like the single alley leading to a goal box with partial reward. Both S^D and S^Δ generate r_h-s_h and, in turn, r_F-s_F. As in the straight alley, these two internal events act in conflict. As discrimination training proceeds, however, S^D tends to differentially elicit r_h-s_h, and S^Δ tends to differentially elicit r_F-s_F. These two separate tendencies underlie the two opposing gradients shown in Figure 8.17 and explain the occurrence of the peak shift.

There are two conditions under which the peak shift may not appear. One is extended discrimination training. After many discrimination trials the peak shift is not found. This is consistent with frustration theory. R_F and r_F-s_F would eventually disappear since nonreward is frustrating only in the presence of r_h-s_h. As r_h-s_h comes to be elicited less by S^Δ, so will r_F-s_F. To the extent that hope decreases during S^Δ, frustration must also decrease. Without frustration there will be no inhibitory gradient and, hence, no peak shift. The second condition under which the peak shift may not be found is Terrace's errorless discrimination.* If S^Δ is introduced gradually, no responses are made in its presence; it never generates r_h-s_h; it will never generate r_F-s_F; it will never generate an inhibitory gradient, and no peak shift will occur.

A BRIEF HISTORY OF TWO-FACTOR THEORY

As we pointed out in Chapter 5, both Thorndike and Pavlov in the early twentieth century emphasized the importance of contiguity in learning. In the 1940s at Yale University, Clark Hull, the most influential learning theorist of his time, made learning by temporal contiguity the cornerstone of his system, which attempted to subsume all of learning under a set of geometry-like axioms and postulates. Since two-factor theory provided an explanation of secondary reinforcement, avoidance, punishment, and extinction in terms of temporal contiguity, it assumed a prominent place in learning theory for followers of Thorndike, Pavlov, and Hull. In the United States during the 1940s and 1950s two-factor theory received its fullest exposition and we have summarized some of that exposition above.

The first objections to strict contiguity as an explanatory principle came from Hull's contemporary E. C. Tolman. Tolman argued that relationships more molar than contiguity could be learned, but he retained the requirement that these relationships be mediated by internal events. The mediation Tolman proposed consisted of cognitive events such as "expectancies" and "cognitive maps." During the 1940s there was much argument between "motivational" theorists and "cognitive" theorists about the nature of the mediating events. From the perspective of the present, however, there seems to be little difference between one sort of internal mediator and another.

The first real objection to internal mediation itself as an explanation of learning came in 1950 from B. F. Skinner in a paper called, "Are Theories of Learning Necessary?". In this paper Skinner argued that behavioral observations might be explained best in behavioral terms—without hypothesizing the existence of unobserved events within the organism. Since 1950, the point of view expressed in Chapter 5, that contingencies and correlations could be learned directly, without mediation, has slowly gained acceptance. In the late

---

*Karpicke and Hearst, p. 475, dispute this. To the extent that their evidence is conclusive, it is evidence against Amsel's theory.

1960s two reviews of the avoidance literature appeared that had much to do with the decline of strong two-factor theory and its replacement by the molar view, which explains avoidance, punishment, and extinction in terms of contingencies and correlations. One, by Richard Herrnstein (1969), attacked two-factor theory on the grounds of parsimony, citing especially its awkwardness in explaining Herrnstein-Hineline avoidance. Another, by Robert Rescorla and Richard Solomon (1967), reviewed the direct evidence for mediation in avoidance and concluded that avoidance behavior could occur without any measurable fear and that even when signs of fear were present, the instrumental avoidance response appeared with shorter latency than the fear. How could fear mediate avoidance if fear does not appear until avoidance is already under way? Rescorla and Solomon did argue that although classical conditioning of such internal events as fear, hope, and frustration might not be *necessary* for non-contiguous instrumental conditioning, these internal events do occur and can have strong effects on instrumentally conditioned behavior. This latter view they called "weak" two-factor theory, and we turn to it next.

WEAK TWO-FACTOR THEORY

As it turns out, we have already discussed in some detail two paradigms exemplifying ways that classical and instrumental conditioning may interact. One of these paradigms is CER (conditioned emotional response) and the other is autoshaping. We shall review CER first.

The CER technique and its usual results are shown in Figure 4.3. A tone or a light (or other neutral stimulus) is paired with an aversive stimulus such as electric shock. This CS–US combination is superimposed on a baseline of instrumental conditioning. In most applications of this procedure, the baseline is a variable-interval schedule of food reinforcement, but it may be any instrumental schedule (although different baselines will give different results). The classical conditioning then interferes with the ongoing instrumental response and (usually) suppresses the instrumental response. The degree of suppression is taken as a measure of the classical conditioning.

The autoshaping technique is shown in Figure 7.3b. In that figure a CS (the lit key) is paired with food. In Chapter 7 we explained that this would generate pecking. We should add now that when the autoshaping procedure (CS–food) is superimposed on a variable-interval schedule of food reinforcement, pecking increases during the CS.

Some data from the author's laboratory may illustrate how CER and autoshaping interfere with and facilitate responding on a baseline variable-interval schedule. The procedure is illustrated in Figure 9.10. In this experiment hungry pigeons were trained to peck a key, and key-pecks were reinforced with food on a variable-interval 8-minute schedule. During this baseline-schedule period, the key was lit with a white light. All of the pigeons pecked the white

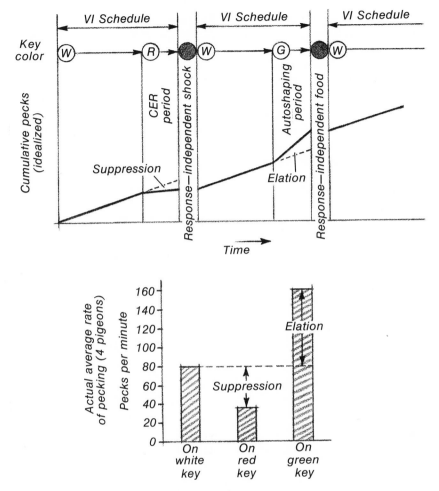

FIGURE 9.10
Procedure and results of an experiment in the author's laboratory showing
suppression of pecking by pigeons during a signal preceding shock (CER) and
"elation of pecking" during a signal preceding free food (autoshaping). The baseline
was a variable-interval 8-minute schedule. Food reinforcements, not shown, were
obtained for pecking during white, red, and green key lights.

key at a slow steady rate and were rewarded occasionally by 3 seconds access to
food. Every once in a while (4 minutes on the average) the key light would
change from white to either red or green for 4 seconds. When the key was red
or green, pecks could still produce food—that is, the variable-interval schedule
was still in effect. At the end of the red key-light signal, however, the pigeons
were shocked for 3 seconds. At the end of the green key-light signal the pigeons received a free food delivery. The red key light, thus, was a CER stim-

ulus, a CS paired with shock, and the green key light was an autoshaping stimulus, a CS paired with food. The CER effect would be a decrease in key-pecking during the red key light. The autoshaping effect would be an increase in key-pecking during the green key light. Figure 9.10 (bottom) shows the average results for the four pigeons. All of the pigeons pecked less during the red light and more during the green light.*

The CER and autoshaping procedures described here are only two of the many procedures used to study the interaction of classical and instrumental conditioning. The following is a list of some of the parameters that have been varied and some of the effects of their variation:

1. *The subject.* CER and autoshaping experiments have been run with rats, pigeons, monkeys, humans, and other animals. Similar procedures some-times have different effects depending on the species of the subject.

2. *The instrumental baseline.* Instrumental baselines have mostly been vari-able-interval schedules with food as a reward. But others such as ratio schedules drl and drh (see Chapter 5), also with food as a reward, have been used. There is also an extensive experimental literature on avoidance and escape schedules with shock. In addition to food and shock reduction, other instrumental reinforcers such as water, tokens, avoidance of black-out (periods of darkness), and avoidance of noise have been used. The schedule and type of reward used will strongly influence what happens when the CS is superimposed. For instance, when the CER procedure is superimposed on a food-reward baseline, the instrumental response is often suppressed during the CS. But when the CER procedure is super-imposed on an avoidance baseline, the instrumental response is often increased during the CS. The rate of positive or negative reinforcement obtained and the rate of response generated by the baseline schedule may also influence the CER or autoshaping effect.

3. *The US.* Just as there have been many instrumental reinforcers used in these experiments, there have been many US's: food, shock, shock reduc-tion, water, and others. One study reported a CER with a caress to the pigeon as the US.

4. *The CS.* Lights and tones have been most popular.

5. *The duration of the CS.* Long CS's tend to have less of an effect (elation or suppression) than short ones, but this is perhaps because the beginning of a long fixed-duration CS serves as a signal for the *absence* of the US and so generates an opposite effect, which cancels out the effect at the end of the CS.

---

*For some of the pigeons red signalled food and green, shock. This was to control for the effects of color on pecking. It was found that color *per se* had little effect. For the sake of simplic-ity of presentation, the data of all pigeons is averaged with the shock signal called red (even if it was green) and the food signal called green (even if it was red).

6. *The time between CS's (the intertrial interval).* In general, the longer the time between CS's, the stronger the effect when the CS is finally presented.

7. *The point at which classical conditioning occurs.* In the procedures we have described, the CS–US pairing has been superimposed on an instrumental baseline. The disadvantage of this procedure is that the US and the instrumental reinforcer both occur in the same situation. Unconditional responses to the US may interfere with instrumental responding over and above any interference by classical conditioning. It is possible, however, to perform the CS–US pairing "off the baseline." With this off-the-baseline procedure, instrumental training is usually given first. Then the CS–US pairing takes place separately without instrumental responding. Then instrumental responding is reinstated and the CS alone is superimposed, without the US. Observations of suppression and elation are taken during the first few CS presentations before extinction (of classical conditioning) has taken effect. The usual finding with the off-the-baseline procedure is that the change in responding is in the same direction (elation or suppression) as with the on-the-baseline procedure, but of less magnitude.*

There has recently been a great deal of theoretical dispute (and consequent research activity) over the basis for the CER and autoshaping interactions. We shall make no attempt to resolve the issues here. New evidence about the nature of these interactions is coming forth steadily now. In a few years, perhaps, enough perspective will be attained to effect a resolution. Meanwhile, all we can do here is try to organize the information as best we can.

Figure 9.11 shows a set of behavioral consequences of the CER–autoshaping experiment with pigeons described in Figure 9.10. The first column shows the contingent relations. The red key light–shock and green key light–food relations represent classical conditioning, and the key peck–food relation represents instrumental conditioning. Internally, however, the classical-conditioning operation may involve instrumental relationships and the instrumental-conditioning operation may involve classical relationships. We have already discussed these hypothetical relationships at various points in this chapter. Let us review them now:

---

*Another procedure that can be followed with off-the-baseline classical conditioning is to pair one CS with the US (this CS is called CS+) and another stimulus with the absence of the US (this CS is called CS−). If the CS+ signals shock (a danger signal) then the CS− would signal signal the absence of shock (a safety signal). The CS− usually acts opposite to the CS+ when it is superimposed on instrumental responding. If the CS+ suppresses responding, the CS− tends to elevate responding. Whether this is because the CS− inhibits the CR normally generated by the CS+ or because the CS− actually generates a new response of its own is a matter of dispute at the present time.

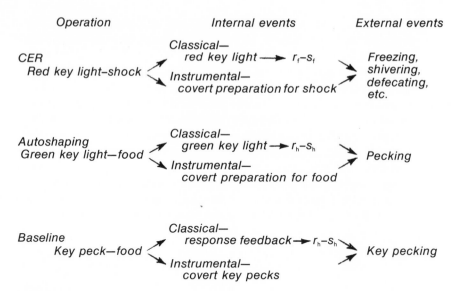

FIGURE 9.11
Hypothetical consequences, internal and external, of the various contingencies in the CER–autoshaping experiment of Figure 9.10. Note that each operation, whether classical or instrumental, may cause *both* classical and instrumental internal events. Interference or facilitation could occur through the interaction of any or all of the internal events with each other or through the interaction of external events with each other.

1. *How the classical-conditioning operation may involve instrumental relationships.* In the section of the previous chapter on secondary reinforcement we discussed why animals should prefer a signalled event to an unsignalled event—that is, why information seems to be valued. One explanation was that the information allows either internal or external preparatory responses to be made so that the value of the signalled event is enhanced. The classical-conditioning operation always involves a signal (the CS) for a significant event (the US). The preparatory responses made during the signal are instrumental responses because they change the value of an environmental event. Some theorists have maintained that *all* classical conditioning can be explained in terms of instrumental preparatory responses. We shall assume here that preparatory responses do occur but that some classically conditioned responses may not be preparatory.

2. *How the instrumental-conditioning operation may involve classical relationships.* In the section of this chapter on strong two-factor theory we discussed what is presumed to happen when an animal performs an instrumental response such as running down an alley, pecking a key, or

pressing a bar. Each response is really a chain of responses producing a series of feedback stimuli. The feedback stimuli from the response are CS's with respect to the instrumental consequences (usually food, in the case of positive reinforcement, and usually shock in the case of punishment) because the response invariably precedes its instrumental consequences. The feedback stimuli generate conditioned responses (r_g-s_g's) of various types (r_h-s_h, r_f-s_f, or r_F-s_F). Some theorists (strong two-factor theorists) have maintained that these conditioned responses (fractional anticipatory goal responses) mediate many instrumental procedures, and some theorists have gone so far as to say that these classically conditioned responses are all there is to instrumental conditioning. We shall assume here that classically conditioned responses do occur in instrumental conditioning but that they need not serve as mediators.

Now, let us consider Figure 9.11 again. The classical-conditioning and instrumental-conditioning operations each may have classical and instrumental consequences inside the organism. Any of the internal events may add to (facilitate) or subtract from (interfere with) any of the other internal events. Any of the external events may add to or subtract from any of the other external events. The possibilities for interaction are numerous, and the theories as to where and how interaction takes place have been just as numerous.

As we said above, we cannot discuss all of the theories of interaction. Instead we shall briefly consider one of the more plausible theories and some of its empirical consequences. This theory was designed to explain the CER procedure only, but it could easily be applied to autoshaping and other interaction procedures. The theory has been recently expounded by J. R. Millenson and P. A. deVilliers. These theorists claim that the interaction between classical and instrumental conditioning takes place, at least in part, at the internal level. They reject the notion that the interaction takes place wholly on the external level because there have been several demonstrations of the same CS–US having opposite effects on the same instrumental response depending on the instrumental procedure that generated the response. For instance, when a light previously paired with shock is presented to a rat pressing a bar on a schedule of positive reinforcement, the bar-pressing is suppressed. But when the same light is presented to a rat pressing a bar on a schedule of negative reinforcement (escape or avoidance) the bar-pressing is often increased. Evidently the responses to the CS (the conditioned responses) do not simply interfere directly with bar-pressing. Interference or facilitation depends on *why* the bar-presses are occurring.*

---

*For this result to be explained in terms of external interactions we would have to assume that bar-presses for food differ in topography from avoidance bar-presses in such a manner that a given CR adds to one kind of bar-press and subtracts from the other. This seems highly unlikely.

According to Millenson and deVilliers, when the CER procedure is used with a positive-reinforcement baseline, the CER procedure generates a negative drive, which subtracts from the positive drive supporting the instrumental conditioning. With a negative reinforcement baseline the CER procedure would add to the negative drive and increase responding. Millenson and deVilliers make no distinction between drive and incentive (see Figure 6.11, which shows how these two concepts may be considered as one) so that with positive reinforcement it is as if the value of the reward were reduced during the period in which the CS is superimposed. Referring again to Figure 9.11, the r_f–s_f (fear) based on the connection between the red key light and shock

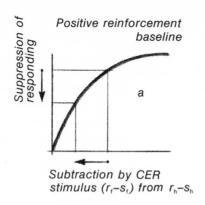
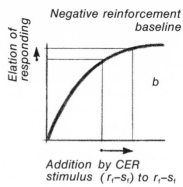

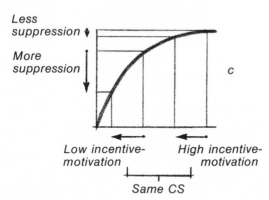

FIGURE 9.12
The effect of superimposing an aversive CS on an instrumental-conditioning baseline (according to the theory of Millenson and deVilliers). Part (a) shows subtraction of r_f–s_f of the CS from r_h–s_h with a positive-reinforcement instrumental baseline. Part (b) shows addition of r_f–s_f of the CS to r_f–s_f with a negative-reinforcement instrumental baseline. Part (c) shows the same CS superimposed on a positive-reinforcement baseline under high and low incentive–motivation. The suppression is greater with low incentive–motivation because of the curvature of the function relating incentive–motivation to instrumental responding.

subtracts from the r_h-s_h (hope) based on the connection between the key-peck and food. Thus when the key light is white the food is valued higher than when the key light is red. The lower value of food during the red key light reduces responding during red as shown in Figure 9.12a. If the pigeon were responding on a schedule of negative reinforcement based on r_f-s_f (fear) motivation, then the addition of a signal previously paired with shock would add to the fear, as in Figure 9.12b, and increase responding. If the function relating incentive-motivation to response rate is curved down (negatively accelerated), as shown in Figure 9.12a, b, and c (for which function there is considerable evidence—see Figures 5.18 and 6.9), then the Millenson-deVilliers theory has certain empirical consequences. These consequences are shown in Figure 9.12c. Millenson and deVilliers predict that with high incentive-motivation conditions a given CS will have less of an effect on responding than with lower incentive-motivation conditions. In a series of experiments with rats pressing a bar for food rewards, this prediction was confirmed. Millenson and deVilliers varied deprivation in one experiment and amount of reward in another experiment. Suppression of food-reinforced responding was greater with the lower motivation or incentive than with the higher motivation or incentive at each of several shock intensities previously paired with the CS.

Whether this finding would also apply to negative incentive-motivation conditions and to the effects of autoshaping and other classical-instrumental conditioning interactions with other organisms remains to be seen. There is no intrinsic reason why interactions cannot occur both internally *and* externally.

BEHAVIORAL CONTRAST

In discussing transient effects of motivation (p. 328) we said that a sudden shift from low to high incentive-motivation conditions often produced a temporarily elevated rate of responding—higher than the rate that would be maintained by the high incentive-motivation alone. Symmetrically, a sudden shift from high to low incentive-motivation conditions causes a temporary drop in responding below what would be maintained by the low incentive-motivation alone. The first of these effects is called *positive contrast*, the second, *negative contrast*. In other words, the response overshoots the level it will ultimately attain and then slowly approaches its final value. The effect is somewhat similar to that of a sudden rise or fall in the price of some popular commodity such as automobiles. When a sharp increase in price is announced there is usually a precipitious drop in sales, but eventually sales climb back up to a level dictated by the law of supply and demand.

Contrast does *not* occur if the change in incentive-motivation conditions is not accompanied by some sort of signal. This is why, perhaps, decreases in price are heavily advertised and increases in price are usually unadvertised. Figure 9.13 shows sudden changes in reinforcement schedules and typical

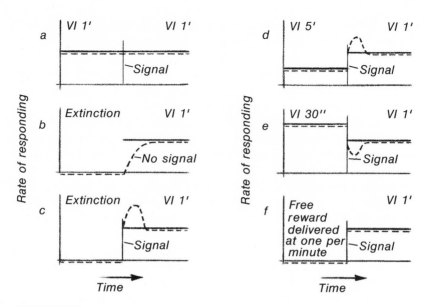

FIGURE 9.13
Response patterns with sudden changes in incentive–motivation conditions. The solid lines represent asymptotic rates of responding and the dotted lines, actual rates of responding. Positive contrast is shown in parts (c) and (d). Negative contrast is shown in part (e). Contrast is found in circumstances where a change in rate of reinforcement is accompanied by a signal. Part (f) shows a free-reward schedule. With this schedule reinforcement is independent of responding. Asymptotic rate of response is zero, but rate of reinforcement may be high. No contrast is found in (f) because rate of reinforcement does not change.

response patterns. In the figure, the asymptotic rate of response is shown by solid lines and the actual rate of response by dotted lines. Transient increases or decreases in responding (above or below asymptote) are shown by deviations of the dotted line from the solid line. Asymptotic responding with the 1-minute variable-interval schedule (VI-1') is shown in part (a). When conditions are changed from extinction to VI-1' with no signal, as in part (b), responding shows no contrast effect. The response rate gradually changes from the old to the new asymptote. When conditions are changed from extinction to VI-1' with a signal, as in part (c), (assuming that the subject has had previous experience with the signal and its associated schedule of reinforcement), the change in responding is much more sudden and a contrast effect is observed.

Why does contrast occur? According to one theory of contrast, the signal plays an important part; this theory sees contrast as an interaction between classical and instrumental conditioning. Suppose a pigeon is pecking a key on a VI-5' schedule of positive reinforcement (as in Figure 9.13d) and a signal (say, a green light) is suddenly presented which indicates a change to a VI-1' schedule of positive reinforcement. The green light has two functions: first, it is an instrumental discriminative stimulus (an S^D) that signals a new relation (a new schedule) between pecking and food; second, it is associated with the increased food like the autoshaping CS we discussed in the last section. Pecking is thus affected by two contingencies—the instrumental contingency between pecking and food and the classical contingency between the green light and food. To return to a previous example, the smell of bread in a bakery is a discriminative stimulus that signals a certain relation between our behavior and eating the bread. But the smell is also related to eating the bread itself. Thus, the smell generates both instrumental responses via instrumental contingencies and conditioned responses via classical contingencies. These two types of responses interact. How they interact depends on which of the alternatives of Figure 9.11 one accepts. Millenson and deVilliers' would say that the incentive–motivation conditions of the two contingencies add to generate the elevated responding, but it may be that the interaction is on a peripheral level, the excitatory effects of the signal increasing the ongoing activity (pecking). In any case, the instrumental effect (without the signal) is slow to appear (as in Figure 9.13b) but long lasting, whereas the classical effect (additional effect due to the signal) is quick to appear but transient.

At this point the reader might ask, Why should the classical-conditioning effect be transient? First of all, the reader should note that there is a difference between "transient" and "transitory." A transient phenomenon is one that occurs at a point of change. If a CS, any CS, is kept on continuously and US's are presented randomly in its presence, it will fail to signal the presence or absence of the US. That is, the contingency between CS and US will disappear. Many experiments have shown that it is the *onset* of the CS that is important in classical conditioning. The continued presence of a CS is largely redundant and thus, as Egger and Miller have shown (p. 425), ineffective.*

But the effect of the CS, although transient, is usually not transitory. To be transitory the conditioned response would have to disappear with continued representations of the CS. Except in cases of rapid habituation, classically conditioned responses are generally not transitory. Thus, our attributing the temporary elevations in rate of response shown in Figure 9.13c and d to classical conditioning (superimposed on an instrumental procedure) is not out of line with the facts of classical conditioning.

Symmetrically, when a signal indicates a sudden lowering of the reinforcement rate, as in Figure 9.13e, the signal acts like a CER signal as well as a

---

*It is true that when the CS is fixed in duration and the interval between CS onset and US is fixed, the conditioned response tends to occur at the end of the interval, but this is because the *real* CS is a combination of the external CS and internal timing stimuli. When the CS is variable in duration, temporal cues do not aid in predicting the US and the conditioned response tends to occur at the beginning of the CS, fading out thereafter. The same is true when the CS is constant in duration and the US occurs randomly within the CS: conditioned responses tend to occur at the onset of the CS.

discriminative stimulus and tends to lower the rate of response.* Like the autoshaping effect, the CER effect is transient, the rate of response eventually rising.

Now, suppose two schedules with their signals, say VI-1' and VI-5', are alternated every few minutes. This alternation procedure is called a multiple schedule and the VI-1' and VI-5' schedules with their signals are the components of the multiple schedule. Figure 9.14a shows how rate of response might vary during each component for long component durations (on the left) and for short component durations (on the right). Figure 9.14b averages responses over each component. Figure 9.14a is hypothetical, but the data of Figure 9.14b come from an actual experiment by C. L. Shimp and K. L. Wheatley. The distance between the average rates of responding increases as the components are made shorter in duration. With very long components the transient rise and fall in rate occupies only a small part of the component and has little influence on rate, but as components become shorter the transient effects occupy a proportionally larger portion of the interval and the difference between the averages widens.†

The theory we have just described views contrast as the result of an interaction between classical and instrumental conditioning; it is only one theory of contrast. Another theory claims that contrast is due, not to the sudden change in reinforcement value, but to the sudden change in response rate. Looking again at Figure 9.13c, it is as if extinction allowed the subject to rest so that the sudden onset of FI-1' released energy stored up during the rest period and resulted in a suddenly elevated rate of responding—like the substitute who comes into a basketball game when everyone else is tired and outruns the opposing team for a while. Whether or not the "rest" theory is taken literally, it is possible that something about the low response rate during extinction (Figure 9.13c) causes the high response rate during the VI-1' schedule. The question boils down to this: Is it the sudden increase in reinforcement rate or the sudden increase in response rate (from extinction to VI-1') that causes contrast? To test this one must separate reinforcement rate from response rate. In Figure 9.13, parts (a) through (e), the two would be expected to vary together. Part (f) shows a way to separate them. Instead of extinction, let the initial condition be a free-reward schedule of reinforcement with food delivered once per minute on the average. This schedule provides the same rate of reward as a VI-1' schedule but with little or no responding. When a signal indicates

---

*We have used the term CER to refer to signals preceding shock, but CER may refer to any signal preceding a low-valued event (including a low rate of reinforcement) in the presence of a higher-valued event.

†With *extremely* short duration components the rates of responding in the two components must equal each other. The signals would alternate faster than responding could adjust. Responses initiated during one signal would carry over into the next signal. Such an interaction is known as *induction*. Induction tends to blur the difference between two temporally adjacent conditions; contrast tends to accentuate the difference.

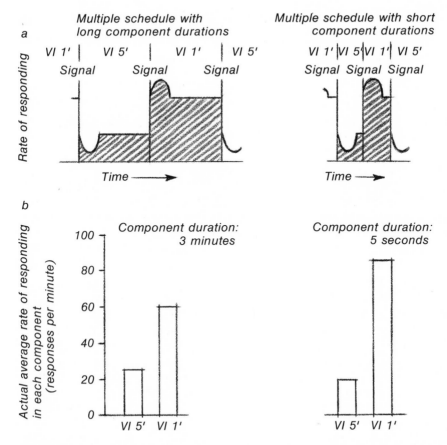

FIGURE 9.14
The difference between rates of response in two components of a multiple schedule is greater when the duration of the components is brief than when the duration of the components is long. Part (a) shows hypothetical responding as the components are changed. The average rate of responding in each component would equal the shaded area divided by the duration of the component. Part (b) shows average rates of response (of three pigeons) with multiple schedules of long and short component durations. Note that the difference in the rates is greater with short component durations. [Data from Shimp, C. P., and Wheatley, K. L. Matching to relative reinforcement frequency in multiple schedules with short component durations. *Journal of the experimental analysis of behavior,* 1971, *15,* 205-209.]

a sudden switch from free-food to VI-1' the asymptotic response rate increases but the rate of food delivery remains the same. The classical–instrumental interaction theory, which sees a change in reward value as the cause of contrast, would predict no contrast in Figure 9.13f, whereas the "rest" theory would predict contrast (a free-food schedule requires as little responding and, hence, as much rest as extinction). When this experiment has been done, contrast is usually *not* found (as diagrammed in Figure 9.13f), confirming the classical–instrumental interaction theory and refuting the "rest" theory.

APPLICATIONS IN BEHAVIOR THERAPY

Two-factor theory was one of the first areas in which learning theory was applied to the treatment of dysfunctional behavior. According to two-factor theory much dysfunctional behavior is avoidance behavior, mediated by fear. The difficulty of reducing avoidance behavior by standard extinction procedures has been cited as the reason for the persistence of many dysfunctional behaviors. To take an extreme example, suppose a boy grows up in a family or in a neighborhood where any assertive action, even speaking out of turn, results in a beating. The boy may learn to keep silent in threatening situations, as an avoidance response. This response may persist into adult life where it is no longer appropriate. A behavior therapist who relied on two-factor theory would view his job as getting rid of the fear underlying the avoidance behavior. His strategy might consist of first severely threatening the patient (a measure designed to elicit more fear than the typical threatening situation the patient confronts in everyday life) but then not following the threat with aversive stimulation (an extinction procedure, which should reduce fear). Once fear was reduced, according to two-factor theory, the avoidance response (keeping silent in the face of threat) should automatically disappear since it would no longer be reinforced. Note that this form of therapy would not be used by a behavior therapist who did not accept two-factor theory. An alternative might be to work directly with the desired behavior (training the patient to speak up in threatening situations). The therapist might rehearse with the patient things to say or do in various situations, giving the patient feedback as to when his behavior was or was not appropriate. Here is a case in which the basis for therapy depends directly on experimental findings. The evidence against strong two-factor theory in general would suggest that a therapy based on fear reduction would be less likely to work than a therapy focused on the avoidance response itself. Whether this prediction is actually borne out in clinical experience is another matter. As yet, no clear-cut clinical evidence has been obtained.

Finally, we should say that two-factor theory is at the heart of the systematic desensitization procedure described in Chapter 4. Elimination of fear by systematic desensitization would then be followed by extinction of all those behaviors previously reinforced by fear reduction.

BIBLIOGRAPHY

Two-factor theory is covered fully in M. R. D'Amato's book *Experimental psychology: Methodology, psychophysics, and learning* (New York: McGraw-Hill, 1970). It also forms the central theoretical core for Logan and Wagner's book *Reward and punishment,* cited below. An article by H. Rachlin, "Contrast and matching" (*Psycho-*

logical Review, 80, 217-234 1973), discusses behavioral contrast and compares this phenomenon to the phenomenon of matching discussed in the next chapter. Applications to behavior therapy can be found in J. Dollard and N. E. Miller's *Personality and psychotherapy* (New York: McGraw-Hill, 1950) and in books by J. Wolpe (see bibliography, Chapter 4).

Following is a list of articles referred to in this chapter:

Adelman, H. M., and Maatsch, J. L. Resistance to extinction as a function of the type of response elicited by frustration. *Journal of Experimental Psychology*, 1955, *50*, 61-65.

Amsel, A. Frustrative nonreward in partial reinforcement and discrimination: Some recent history and theoretical extension. *Psychological Review*, 1962, *69*, 306-328.

Herrnstein, J. R. Method and theory in the study of avoidance. *Psychological Review*, 1969, *76*, 46-69.

Hull, C. L. *A behavior system.* New Haven: Yale University Press, 1952.

Kamin, L. J. The effects of termination of the CS and avoidance of the US on avoidance learning: An extension. *Canadian Journal of Psychology*, 1957, *11*, 48-56.

Logan, F. A., and Wagner, A. R. *Reward and punishment.* Boston: Allyn and Bacon, 1965.

Mansfield, R. J. W., and Rachlin, H. C. The effect of punishment, extinction, and satiation on response chains. *Learning and Motivation*, 1970, *1*, 27-36.

Millenson, J. R., and deVilliers, P. A. Motivational properties of conditioned anxiety. In *Reinforcement: Behavioral analyses*, ed. R. M. Gilbert and J. R. Millenson. New York: Academic Press, 1972.

Mowrer, O. H. *Learning theory and behavior.* New York: John Wiley, 1960.

Rescorla, R. A., and Solomon, R. L. Two-process learning theory: Relationships between Pavlovian conditioning and instrumental learning. *Psychological Review*, 1967, *74*, 151-182.

Shimp, C. P., and Wheatley, K. L. Matching to relative reinforcement frequency in multiple schedules with a short component duration. *Journal of The Experimental Analysis of Behavior*, 1971, *15*, 205-209.

Skinner, B. F. Are theories of learning necessary? *Psychological Review*, 1950, *57*, 193-216.

Taub, E., and Berman, A. J. Avoidance conditioning in the absence of relevant proprioceptive and exteroceptive feedback. *Journal of Comparative and Physiological Psychology*, 1963, *56*, 1012-1016.

Tolman, E. C. Principles of purposive behavior. In *Psychology: A study of a science*, ed. S. Koch. 1959, *2*, 92-152.

We reprint here Herrnstein's article on avoidance. This article contains an excellent history of the study of avoidance and of how two-factor theory came into being. Herrnstein argues that two-factor theory is an unparsimonious explanation of avoidance behavior.

METHOD AND THEORY IN THE STUDY OF AVOIDANCE

R. J. Herrnstein

Two-factor theories of avoidance were conceived to explain responding in avoidance procedures that closely resemble the Pavlovian paradigm in superficial features, although differing in the fundamental contingency of reinforcement. Both typically involve an arbitrary conditioned stimulus and a trial-by-trial sequence of pairings between the conditioned and unconditioned stimuli. According to two-factory theory, the instrumental reinforcement of avoidance is based on the Pavlovian reinforcement of a drive state in the presence of the conditioned stimulus. It has been shown, however, that the presence of the conditioned stimulus is not necessary for the occurrence of avoidance responding. A procedure in which the sole effect of the avoidance response was a reduction in the average frequency of occurrence of an aversive electric shock proved to be fully adequate to maintain lever pressing in rats, thereby suggesting that not all avoidance requires two factors. Further experiments with various new procedures suggested that the conditioned stimulus may function as a discriminative stimulus for the avoidance response, rather than as a stimulus whose removal is inherently reinforcing, as two-factor theory requires.

The conditioned reflex was to I. P. Pavlov (1928, pp. 59–60) the final answer to the problem of biological adaptation.

Preparation of this paper, as well as the conduct of the previously unpublished experiments described herein, was supported by grants from the National Science Foundation to Harvard University. The author wishes to express thanks to P. N. Hineline for his generosity in allowing use of some of his as yet unpublished data and for help in formulating some of the notions here advanced. An early and much reduced version of this paper was presented at the 1966 meeting of the American Association for the Advancement of Science, Washington, D. C., as part of a symposium on Aversive Control. The author owes thanks to J. V. Brady for having organized the symposium and for inviting him to participate in it. To another of the participants, D. Anger, special thanks are owed for his vigorous and insightful criticisms of many of the author's theoretical ideas.

From *Psychological Review*, Vol. 76, No. 1, pp. 49–69. Copyright 1969 by the American Psychological Association. Reprinted by permission.

As a mechanist, Pavlov sought a naturalistic explanation for everything an animal did, which had come to mean an explanation in terms of physical processes that could be isolated by the vivisectionist techniques of nineteenth-century physiology. But the behavior of many animals, for example, the dog, precluded any such simple machinery. Dogs clearly differed in what they did and seemed to know even though they might share virtually identical inheritances. The psyche of the dog was, in other words, a sizable obstacle to the progress of a science of adaptation even in Pavlov's day, two and a half centuries after Descartes had initiated modern reflexology in 1664.

The process of conditioning seemed to explain adaptation and also to retain the scientism of Pavlov's lifelong approach to problems. Acid, for example, was a natural stimulus for salivation in the mouth of a dog. Presumably, the excitation of the sensory surface of the mouth was transmitted through the nervous system to the salivary glands. Aside from the multiplicity of the connections within the nervous system, there needed to be no difference between this system and the classical reflexes of tendons and joints. The adaptiveness of the salivary reflexes was readily squared with the dominant biological theory of the time, for Darwin's theory of natural selection implies that adaptive, inherited reflexes would be favored in the struggle for survival. Pavlov's contribution was to show that the elicitation of a response such as salivation was transferred to arbitrary and initially neutral stimuli by temporal pairing. If a dog repeatedly heard a buzzer before getting a dose of acid in its mouth, it would soon begin salivating at the sound of the buzzer. What had taken nature aeons by its old method of natural selection was here accomplished in minutes by its new method—conditioning. The vast advantages conferred on conditionable organisms was more than enough explanation of how this process itself might have arisen on the phylogenetic scene. A conditionable organism is adapted to a changing environment, reshuffling responses almost momentarily so as to keep abreast of the haphazard changes of its circumstances.

Pavlov's notion of conditioning was reminiscent of the classical doctrine of association. From the time of Aristotle, philosophers had been struck by the psychological power of sheer contiguity. The experiencing together of two ideas seems to forge a bond between them so that subsequently one calls forth the other. Though it was distinctive in important ways, Pavlov's theory of conditioning was but one more in a long list of associationisms, stipulating as it did that the transfer of power from one stimulus to the other was based simply on their approximate simultaneity. Pavlov often made clear that he saw his work as an improvement over classical associationism, primarily because of its thorough objectivity.

Unfortunately for the subsequent development of objective psychology, Pavlov's version of associationism left out more than the superfluous subjectivity, for he never brought his experimental skills to bear on the question of the necessary and sufficient conditions for his discovery. Pavlov showed that the pairing of a neutral stimulus with a natural elicitor of salivation, like acid or dry food, creates a new reflex—the production of salivation by the now no-longer-neutral conditioned stimulus. But he did not question what there was about the pairing that was important. Was it, as he said, that the contiguity itself created new pathways within the cerebral hemispheres because regions of simultaneous excitation inevitably become connected? Or was it, as Zener (1937) said, that contiguity sets the occasion when an anticipatory response would be most effective? Zener was arguing that the conditioned salivary response is not identical with the response naturally elicited by the dry food or the acid. The conditioned response is, rather, a readying of the animal for the arrival of the unconditioned stimulus. In the case of dry food or acid, salivation is appropriate both as preparatory response and as terminal response, but not every response in the situation is thus doubly appropriate. The dog does not, for example, ordinarily start chewing until the food itself is in its mouth, even though by strict Pavlovian principles it might start chewing as soon as it starts salivating.

The problem of the consequences of the conditioned response apparently did not concern Pavlov, perhaps because he was engrossed with a response system whose natural consequences are virtually undetachable from its activation. How effective would Pavlov's procedure be if the salivary response does not moisten the food, dilute the acid, or irrigate the mouth? For the salivary response, the consequences are almost inextricably interwoven into the physical properties of the situation. In contrast, Pavlov's countryman, contemporary, and codiscoverer of a new and objective method for the study of adaptation, V. M. Bekhterev (1913), was using a procedure that did not have this peculiar inflexibility.

At about the same time as Pavlov, Bekhterev had also developed a method for producing adaptive changes in behavior. Bekhterev used what has since been called motor, instead of salivary, conditioning. A dog would be exposed to a sequence consisting of some originally neutral stimulus, followed by a painful electric shock to a forepaw. The reflex response to the shock was leg flexion and the adaptive change was the occurrence of leg flexion as soon as the neutral stimulus was presented. Superficially, the difference between Pavlov's and Bekhterev's discoveries was minor, concerning only the physical response—muscular instead of glandular. The similarity in their findings—the shifting of a response from one stimulus to another—tended to make the two situations look still more similar. Nevertheless, it is impossible to tell whether the two procedures are basically similar or profoundly different until something more is said about Bekhterev's experiment. In particular, was the flexion response an effective escape response, which is to say, did it terminate the shock as soon as it occurred; was it, moreover, an effective avoidance response, which is to say, did it cause the shock to be omitted on any trial in which it occurred before the shock was turned on but after the neutral stimulus was presented? In order for Bekhterev's procedure to be comparable to Pavlov's the flexion response would have to have been an effective escape response, terminating an ongoing shock, but never an effective avoidance response, for in Pavlov's procedure, the dog's behavior in no way controlled what stimuli the experimenter presented.

Judging from the accounts published in English (Razran, 1956), the experiments in Bekhterev's laboratory sometimes used one procedure and sometimes another, largely fortuitously. In many later experiments done in the United States using adaptations of Bekhterev's procedure, (e.g., Hull, 1934), the conditioned response did preclude the electric shock. Because of this feature of the

procedure, the term "avoidance training" (Hilgard & Marquis, 1940, p. 58) came into use, for it is obvious that without this feature, the term would be unsuitable. Although it is obvious, it was nevertheless widely unrecognized. Many of the experiments in which there was a genuine avoidance contingency were discussed in strictly Pavlovian terms, as if the necessary and sufficient part of the procedure was the simple contiguity, or association, of conditioned and unconditioned stimuli. An example is Hull's (1929) treatment of the "conditioned defense reaction" as a type of contiguity conditioning even though his discussion reveals it to be an avoidance response.

THE EMERGENCE OF TWO-FACTOR THEORY

Given this setting, the somewhat strange developments in the field of avoidance conditioning starting in the mid-1930's make a kind of sense. The ambiguity in the basic procedure favored a corresponding fuzziness in the theory of avoidance behavior, with the notion of contiguity crucial, albeit unexplicated. Recognition of the ambiguity gave rise to a series of procedural changes that displaced various elements of Pavlov's method until the simple contiguity theory was no longer applicable. The present paper will recount only a fraction of this interplay between method and theory; there have been several outstanding reviews of the literature recently (Mowrer, 1960; Rescorla & Solomon, 1967; Solomon & Brush, 1956).

One of the first investigators to see the conceptual problem and to do an experiment to clarify (if not solve) it was Schlosberg (1934). He compared two procedures for the motor conditioning of the tail-flick response in rats. In one procedure the response precluded the delivery of the electric shock; in the other, it did not. Schlosberg confessed his surprise when he found that the response was conditioned to about the same extent—which, incidentally, was not very well—with the two procedures. Schlosberg, who was at this time formulating two different paradigms for learning—one based on contiguity and the other based on the consequences of the response—was looking for a difference between the two procedures.

In spite of his inability to find a difference between the two major alternatives for motor conditioning, Schlosberg deserves credit for the conceptual distinction. After Schlosberg's paper, it was only a matter of time before someone succeeded in teasing apart the effects of sheer contiguity from those of letting the response influence the sequence of stimuli. The most often cited experiment along this line seems to be the one by Brogden, Lipman, and Culler (1938). It was not, however, the first one after Schlosberg's to show that an instrumental response is more easily conditioned than a noninstrumental one (e.g., Hunter, 1935).

The apparatus used by Brogden, Lipman, and Culler was a running wheel, the standard device for studies of general activity in the laboratory rat. These investigators, however, used guinea pigs and compared the two procedures for motor conditioning labeled A and B in Figure 1. The guinea pigs were in the wheel and could run at any time. Every once in a while, at intervals not precisely specified in the publication, a tone was turned on for 2 seconds, at the end of which a brief, painful shock of prespecified duration was delivered. Most guinea pigs are goaded into running by such a shock, which is what the "response" in Figure 1 refers to. For the guinea pigs in Group A, a running response great enough to rotate the wheel about 1 inch was an effective avoidance response if it preceded the shock. Once the shock came on, nothing could be done to alter it. A dashed line below the shock line without a curved arrow above it indicates a shock scheduled but not presented. (Throughout these procedural figures, it will be possible to compare the shocks that would have been given if the animal had not made the designated response with the shocks that it failed to avoid.) For Group B, then, the occurrence of the running response had no effect on the presentation of shock. The two groups correspond, in other words, to the two versions of Bekhterev's experiment, or, to put it eponymously, correspond to the Pavlovian paradigm and the Thorndikian.

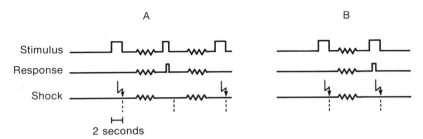

FIGURE 1
Diagrams of the two procedures examined by Brogden, Lipman, and Culler (1938). (A. The instrumental conditioning procedure, in which running in the wheel terminated the conditioned stimulus and avoided the shock. B. The classical conditioning procedure, in which the stimulus and shock were presented on every trial, independent of the response. The shock line shows both the shocks delivered—above the line—and the shocks that would have been delivered but for the occurrence of avoidance responses—below the line.)

The findings were clear-cut. The Thorndikian group, A, learned to respond precurrently and eventually reached virtually 100% performance. The Pavlovian group, on the other hand, while it started out about as well as the Thorndikian, soon fell behind by not improving as rapidly, and later even showed signs of falling back from levels of performance once attained.

The conclusion drawn by Brogden, Lipman, and Culler was that Pavlov's characterization of the conditioning process was wrong because it left out the consequences of the conditioned response, something that was, as noted before, inevitably built into the salivary response, but independently manipulable in the case of motor conditioning. In technical parlance, the experiment was taken as evidence for the law of effect, which was Thorndike's principle, and against the conditioned reflex, which was Pavlov's.

With the publication of this influential paper by Brogden, Lipman, and Culler, the study of avoidance had crystallized as a study in its own right and was no longer merely one of the various conditioned-reflex procedures. From here on, the work of O. H. Mowrer becomes central in the developing theory of avoidance. In a paper published in 1939, when he was at Yale, Mowrer gave a lucid anticipation of the position that he was to defend, in various altered and elaborated versions, until the present. Mowrer presented no new data; he was, rather, putting what was already known about avoidance into a new setting. He spoke about anxiety, rather than avoidance, but he was clearly using the term in a limited sense.

Mowrer's main point in this paper was that Freud, not Pavlov, was right about anxiety. Freud (1936) had concluded that anxiety came from anticipations of danger, and that much of neurosis was concerned with the elimination of anxiety-provoking stimuli. Mowrer saw in Freud a kindred soul, theoretically speaking, for the Yale psychologists around Hull had come to believe that learning in general—hence the learning of a neurosis—could be accounted for by some form of the law of effect. Unlike the Pavlovians, the Hullians would insist that the avoidance response exert some effect, and since in an avoidance procedure the avoidance response is by design not followed by any change in the unconditioned stimulus, the response's effect must be on the animal itself. To quote Mowrer (1939):

> The position here taken is that human beings (and also other living organ[ism]s to varying degrees) can be motivated either by organic pressures (needs) that are currently present and felt *or* by the mere anticipation of such pressures and that those habits tend to be acquired and perpetuated (reinforced) which effect a reduction in *either* of these two types of motivation. This view rests upon and is but an extended application of the well-founded law of effect and involves no assumptions that are not empirically verifiable [p. 561].

The prevailing view in America had reversed itself in the 10 years between Hull's paper and Mowrer's. Hull's original account was strictly Pavlovian, and now his junior colleague was arguing that Pavlov was wrong and that the crucial paradigm was Thorndike's, although he preferred to relate his view to Freud's as regards anxiety. The switch in viewpoint could have been an appropriate reaction to the procedural refinements of the Brogden, Lipman, and Culler experiment or to others like it. It had, indeed, been shown that the strict contiguity required by Pavlov's theory produced less effective motor conditioning than did the instrumental paradigm. The view was, however, to keep changing as further refinements evolved, each carrying the method of avoidance a bit further away from the apparent purity of strict contiguity.

Mowrer himself was one of the leading innovators in this methodological and conceptual evolution. In 1942, he and Lamoreaux (Mowrer & Lamoreaux, 1942) published a monograph on avoidance conditioning. The apparatus was the productive shuttle box, adapted by Mowrer and Miller at Yale specifically for the study of avoidance learning, although it had been used before for just this purpose (Gentry, 1934). The shuttle box is a small rectangular chamber with a metal-grid floor across which electric shock can be presented, a couple of light bulbs or a buzzer, and the means for observing the rat without being observed by it. The Mowrer-Lamoreaux monograph of 1942 examined various temporal configurations in the pairing of the conditioned stimulus with the electric shock. The avoidance response was throughout merely the running of a rat from one side of the chamber to the other. Figure 2 shows as Part A the basic procedure used in this study. Aside from the lack of a precise specification of the duration of the intertrial interval, but which was about 2 minutes on the average, this is now often referred to as "classical" avoidance, showing that too much of our naming of procedures is done without the proper concern for clarity. "Classical" avoidance, then, is not "classical" conditioning—which is just contiguity conditioning—but is the Mowrer procedure of the early 1940s. It is similar to the instrumental condition of the Brogden, Lipman, and Culler study, but adds the extra instrumental feature of an escape

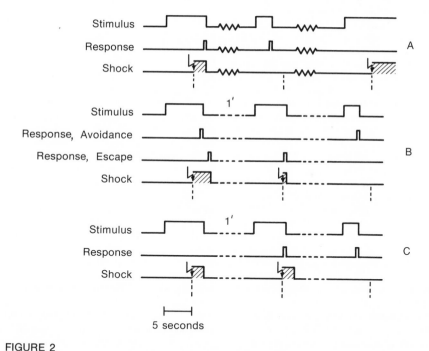

5 seconds

FIGURE 2

Diagrams of three procedures examined by Mowrer and Lamoreaux (1942, 1946). (A. The standard avoidance procedure, in which the response may either terminate the conditioned stimulus and avoid the shock, or, if it occurs after the shock has been turned on, terminate both the stimulus and the shock. B. The shock-avoidance and shock-escape contingencies are divided between two different responses. The avoidance response shuts off the conditioned stimulus and avoids the shock. The escape response shuts off the shock. C. Avoidance with fixed-duration, inescapable shock.)

contingency. Once on, the shock is terminated by the rat's running to the other side. Part A shows an escape response, that is, running with a latency greater than 5 seconds after the onset of the conditioned stimulus; an avoidance response, that is, running with a latency less than 5 seconds and thereby causing the shock of that trial to be omitted, and a trial containing no response, when the shock will stay on presumably until the experimenter is satisfied that nothing useful is going to happen.

The procedural innovation was reflected in Mowrer's (Mowrer & Lamoreaux, 1942) explanation of avoidance, which was now shifting from the monistic position taken in the earlier paper (Mowrer, 1939) towards the dualistic theory long associated with him. He said that the running response is first learned in the situation as a result of the escape contingency in the presence of the shock itself. This learning is of the Thorndikian variety, with the response clearly instrumental in terminating the shock. Next, owing to a presumably Pavlovian mechanism, the response tends to move earlier in time so that it occurs in the presence of the conditioned stimulus, making it an avoidance response. The avoidance response is maintained, said Mowrer, by the escape from the conditioned stimulus itself, which, he further said, becomes anxiety-provoking and is thus reinforcing in its removal. Avoidance conditioning, by this procedure which includes both an escape and an avoidance contingency, is cast in terms of a pair of escape contingencies, one from the shock itself, and the other from the conditioned stimulus, which has become fearsome and therefore motivating. How the stimulus becomes fearsome, Mowrer did not yet try to explain.

The next major procedural change in this development (Mowrer & Lamoreaux, 1946) tested the notion of a pair of escape contingencies. Once again there were three experimental groups, each involving a different arrangement of the avoidance contingency, as shown in Figure 2. Section A is, as already noted, the standard avoidance procedure, consisting of a dual contingency for the running response: At first it is an avoidance response, but after the shock is turned on, it becomes an escape response. Section B is an experimental separation of the two contingencies, which was Mowrer's ingenious method for testing whether there was any necessary connection between the two roles played by the single response in the standard procedure. For 5 seconds before the onset of the shock, running avoids the impending shock and turns off the conditioned stimulus, just as in the standard procedure. Once the shock is on, however, running no longer affects the shock, even though it still turns off the conditioned stimulus. Now, in order to turn off the shock, which would otherwise stay on indefinitely, the rat must jump into the air. The shock-escape response here differs from the shock-avoidance response. In the study, there were, of course, balanced groups to cancel out the factor of response-form per se. Section C is a further demonstration that the shock-escape contingency is not the determiner of the avoidance response. Once on, the shock lasts 2 seconds no matter what the rat does. An avoidance response during the 2 seconds turns off only the conditioned stimulus. This last procedure in effect duplicated that originally used by Brogden, Lipman, and Culler (1938).

The significant finding of the experiment was that having different avoidance and escape responses did not prevent avoidance. Given this, it was no longer possible to argue for any important Pavlovian mechanism involving the response itself; it had been shown that the simple associative process of stimulus substitution, which here would have been nonadaptive, was unable to account for the adaptive performances obtained. While it was true that of the three groups, the anti-Pavlovian one (Group B) learned most slowly and least completely, in the theoretical context of the time, this was far less significant than that the group learned at all.

The suggestion of the experiment was clear: There was some kind of intrinsic reinforcement for the avoidance response in the presence of the conditioned stimulus. A solution was near at hand, but Mowrer was not ready to seize it. He said, as he had in the preceding papers, that the rat was afraid while the conditioned stimulus was on, but he was essentially silent on the sources of the stimulus' power.

Mowrer did not long maintain this uncomfortable theoretical position. In 1947, just 1 year later, he abandoned the single-factor approach and formulated the first two-factor theory explicitly designed to account for avoidance behavior. It was not the first general theory of learning involving two factors, however, as Mowrer carefully pointed out. Schlosberg (1937) had argued, 10 years before, that learning can occur either by Pavlovian conditioning or by the mechanism of the Thorndikian law of effect. And Skinner (1935), with his distinction between operant and respondent conditioning, had also been more than a decade ahead of Mowrer in allowing both Pavlov and Thorndike fractional credit for a theory of learning. The list of anticipators could easily be extended, and perhaps should include Thorndike himself, who had long since (1913) incorporated something like Pavlov's theory into his own under the notion of "associative shifting." But for all of his predecessors, Mowrer was first to describe the union of the two kinds of conditioning discernible in conventional avoidance procedures. He pointed out that the pairing of the conditioned stimulus with the shock is the operational equivalent of Pavlovian conditioning; consequently, if fear is conditionable, it would come to be elicited by the originally neutral stimulus, just as salivation was elicited in Pavlov's experiments. To say that fear is conditionable, which is to say that fear is itself a covert response, seemed to solve the problem of the instrumental avoidance response in all of the procedures examined so far by Mowrer and others. In each procedure, two well-known and presumably well-established paradigms for learning unite to provide the animal with a drive state that is appropriately reduced by the instrumental response. The standard avoidance procedure, with its escape and avoidance components, could now be depicted as a pair of escape contingencies, as, for example, from an electric shock and a loud noise, except that one of the things to be escaped from is a stimulus with only acquired aversiveness.

Mowrer's two-factor theory of avoidance was not accepted without dispute. For some years, theorists debated whether the law of effect explained the conditioning of the fear itself, in addition to the avoidance response, so that only one kind of learning was required. To the majority of psychologists, however, it was just a matter of time and, of course, a matter of research (e.g., Mowrer & L. N. Solomon, 1954) before some version of Mowrer's dualistic account prevailed. Notwithstanding the nuances, it seems fair to group with Mowrer's the theories later espoused by Schoenfeld (1950), Sidman (1953b), Dinsmoor (1954), Solomon and Wynne (1954), and Anger (1963). In all of these theories, an underlying state, said to be produced by Pavlovian conditioning, is altered by the occurrence of the avoidance response, which is thereby instrumentally reinforced. The major difference among them is in the characterization of the underlying state. For Mowrer and R. L. Solomon, "fear" or "anxiety" transfer from the shock to the conditioned stimulus, terms that seemed too laden with excess meaning for Schoenfeld and his former students at Columbia, Dinsmoor and Sidman, as well as for Anger. These more strictly descriptive psychologists preferred to speak of the transferring of "aversion" defined solely by the fact that the removal of the conditioned stimulus appears to maintain the avoidance response.

The evolution away from the Pavlovian paradigm had shown that avoidance is not simply a matter of Pavlovian conditioning as far as the response itself is concerned. Pavlovian conditioning had retreated to that part of the procedure that was still Pavlovian in design—the pairing of "conditioned" and "unconditioned" stimuli—leaving the response to the control of the instrumental contingency. The next evolutionary step, to diminish further these Pavlovian vestiges, was Sidman's novel procedure (1953a), shown schematically in Figure 3. First, it used a continuous session, rather than one broken into trials. Second, it contained no explicit stimulus to signal an impending shock. Instead, the shock was delivered every so often—10 seconds in the diagram—as long as the animal failed to respond. Third, it presented a brief, inescapable shock of fixed duration, instead of a shock that had to be terminated by an escape response. The avoidance response—the depression of a lever—simply postponed the next shock for some further period of time—again 10 seconds in the example shown in the figure. Whenever the animal stopped responding, it would be shocked 10 seconds later and at the appropriate intervals thereafter. The temporal features of the situation were fully specified by two durations: The interval between successive shocks if there were no intervening responses, and the interval between a response and the next shock, again if there were no intervening responses, the "shock-shock interval" and the "response-shock interval," respectively. Sidman found (1953b) that the ease of conditioning and the terminal

rate of responding depend upon the conjunction of values of the two parameters.

In the procedures for which two-factor theory was first developed, conditioned stimuli were unquestionably present, owing to the confounding of instrumental and Pavlovian paradigms, if for no other reason. Sidman's procedure was the first in which the trappings of the Pavlovian method—the trial-by-trial structure marked off by conditioned stimuli—were clearly meant to be absent. But then, in the very first account of his results, Sidman showed how the key Pavlovian ingredients could be located, albeit only by inference since they were not explicitly programmed. He pointed out that anything the rat does, aside from pressing the lever, is paired with the shock. Hence, by Pavlovian conditioning, all of this other, unrecorded behavior will take on the aversive properties of the shock itself. As a result, the Thorndikian paradigm will maintain any activity that terminates or precludes the punished behavior and its associated aversive stimuli. And the only activity that suffices is the avoidance response—lever pressing—itself. Two factors, it would seem, are present here just as they are in Mowrer's procedure. The originally neutral external stimulus of Mowrer's procedure is replaced by the inferred stimuli emanating from non-avoidance behavior. The reinforcement of the instrumental avoidance response is, just as in Mowrer's account, the removal of stimuli that have become aversive through pairings with shock.

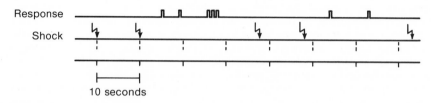

FIGURE 3
Diagram of Sidman's (1953a) avoidance procedure, with shock-shock and response-shock intervals both equal to 10 seconds.

One of the hazards of postulating unprogrammed events is that other theorists may postulate also and do so differently. Anger (1963) has argued that, in addition to the stimuli associated with nonavoidance behavior in Sidman's procedure, the passage of time itself, as measured from the discriminable events in the situation—responses and shocks—generates stimuli. Because of the temporal regularities of Sidman's procedure, Anger further said, these time-stimuli are differentially correlated with shocks and so must differ in their aversiveness. Finally, he said, avoidance responses change the time stimuli to less aversive values and are thereby reinforced in the standard manner for avoidance behavior, which is to say by the removal of conditioned aversive stimuli. Thus, although Sidman and Anger differ in the details of theory, both have relied on two factors, of which one requires the postulation of inferred stimuli.

Virtually all of the modern theories of avoidance involve two factors, one based on the Pavlovian conditioning of a motivational state known by various names (fear, anxiety, conditioned aversion, etc.) and the other based on an instrumental response serving to rid the animal of the motivational state. The current state of knowledge is an advance over what Mowrer encountered towards the end of the 1930s when he first began to express uneasiness with a monolithic Pavlovian framework, as well as over the monolithic instrumental account that he started with. Two-factor theory seems to make good sense out of the original avoidance procedures, with their intermingling of Pavlovian and Thorndikian components. The question now is whether the contemporary extensions of two-factor theory necessitated by new procedures have imperceptibly pushed it over the line into irrefutability. Needless to say, in order to be a useful theory, it must be disprovable. The remainder of this paper presents an argument against two-factor theory on the grounds of its irrefutability and also attempts to formulate an acceptable alternative.

ARE TWO FACTORS NECESSARY?

According to theory, the explicit conditioned stimulus plays a critical role in the maintenance of behavior in avoidance procedures. Mowrer (1960) states the role clearly in a description of a demonstration avoidance experiment:

There is a tendency to say that the subject has learned to *avoid* the shock—hence the term, "avoidance" learning. But this is a rather inexact, abbreviated way of speaking. More precisely, what the rat has learned is (a) to *be afraid* in and of the white compartment and (b) to reduce the fear (and shock, when it is presented) by *running* into the black compartment. Strictly speaking, it is not the *avoidance* of shock that is rewarding to the animal and keeps the running response going. It is rather the fact that the white compartment arouses fear and the running provides a solution to, or *escape from,* this "problem" or drive. The *avoidance* of the shock is a sort of by-product—though, to be sure, a very important one. Action which thus appears to be teleological or "purposeful"—and which, in a sense, indeed is—can in this way be accounted for in a purely causal, or consequential way [p. 30].

Schoenfeld (1950) similarly viewed the conditioned stimulus as crucial:

The avoidance response, by this formulation, is not really avoidance at all, or at least is only incidentally so. Its function is not to avoid, and it is not made "in order to avoid." Rather, it is primarily an escape response, reinforced by the termination of secondary noxious stimuli, including proprioceptive and tactile ones, and possibly also reinforced by the production of proprioceptive secondary positive reinforcers [p. 88].

Figures 1–3 reveal, however, that effective avoidance procedures include a common feature, so obvious as to be taken for granted, but possibly the sole necessary condition for avoidance. In each case, the frequency of shock is reduced by the occurrence of the avoidance response, which is to say, an avoidance response avoids the shock. Truistic as that may seem, it is neither obvious nor trivial whether avoidance would occur when it achieved nothing but shock-frequency reduction. The success of such a procedure would challenge the motivational role of the conditioned stimulus in standard procedures, for having shown that the removal of the conditioned stimulus is not necessary for avoidance, we may wonder if it is sufficient.

In recent years, the standard account has been questioned by a few investigators. Sidman (1962) and Bolles, Stokes, and Younger (1966), for example, have argued that the avoidance of the noxious event is not a mere by-product of the underlying processes, but rather a factor in its own right. Their evidence, however, presents the various opportunities for the postulation of anxiety reduction that earlier extensions of two-factor theory have outlined, either because of the fixed temporal relations (Sidman) or the use of an exteroceptive conditioned stimulus (Bolles et al., 1966). To examine the necessity of two factors, what is needed is the minimum avoidance procedure—one containing no conditioned stimulus, either explicit or plausibly postulated. Either such a procedure is possible or the notion of a conditioned stimulus has retreated out of range of empirical scrutiny. Although conceptually simple, one candidate for such a procedure proves to be unhappily complex in its realization, as shown in Figure 4 (Herrnstein & Hineline, 1966). The heart of the program consisted of a multichannel punched tape that advanced every 2 seconds during the course of an experimental session, irrespective of anything else. At every step of the tape, the apparatus made a decision whether or not to shock the rat, depending on the holes punched into the tape in one or the other of the two operative channels. One channel governed shocks if more recent event was a response; the other channel governed if it was a shock. The postshock channel typically had the higher frequency of holes, which is to say, the higher probability of shock. The rat could shift control from the high-probability channel by depressing the lever. The postresponse channel retained control until the next shock, which could occur at any moment after the response (including, with some frequency, virtually instantaneously) or at any 2-second point thereafter. Responses in the interim had no further effect in forestalling shocks. The parameters of the situation are the two probabilities of shock associated with the two channels and the rate of advance of the tape programmer.

This random-shock procedure is about as far from the Pavlovian procedure as one can get. There is no escape contingency, hence no "unconditioned response" in the usual sense. There are no external stimuli other than the shock itself, hence no explicit conditioned stimuli. There is no fixed temporal relation between responses and shocks; the tape advances independently of the animal's

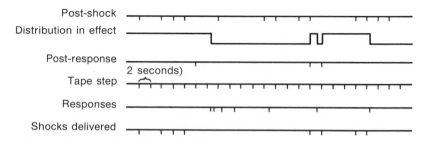

FIGURE 4
Diagram of random-shock procedure (Herrnstein & Hineline, 1966). (See text for explanation.)

response and the distribution of intervals in both channels is drawn from random number tables and changed from time to time to prevent any spurious regularity from developing. If avoidance conditioning required a Pavlovian component, this procedure should be minimal or worse. In contrast, if the reduction of shock frequency is the necessary condition for avoidance behavior, this one comes close to being exactly sufficient, omitting as it does irrelevant stimuli of any sort.

There are various lines of evidence leading to the conclusion that the random-shock procedure is fully effective. All but one of the twenty-odd rats tried with the procedure learned to respond. In contrast, both the Sidman procedure and the standard procedure are plagued by a high incidence of nonavoiders. Black (1963) reports between 10% and 50% failures among rats learning an avoidance response in the standard procedure. In the present author's laboratory, with the same experimental chambers, shock generators, levels of shock intensity, and strain of rats, about 25% nonavoiders are expected with Sidman's procedure. The overall shock rates were comparable to what is typically encountered in experiments using Sidman's technique, which is to say in the range from 3 to 10 shocks per minute. In terms of ease of conditioning, then, the present procedure is clearly not less effective than earlier ones, notwithstanding the absence of a clear conditioned stimulus to mediate the Pavlovian component of two-factor theory.

How else might this procedure be compared in effectiveness with the more familiar ones? The published results with this procedure show that as regards both asymptotic rates of responding and resistance to extinction, the random-shock procedure supports at least as much behavior as earlier procedures, given suitable values of the parameters. Rate of responding has been found to be an increasing function of the amount of shock-frequency reduction whereas resistance to extinction, as measured either by time or

number of responses to extinction, has been found to be an inverse function of the value of this parameter just prior to extinction.[1]

Unlike either the standard procedure or the Sidman procedure, the random-shock procedure precludes a fixed relation between any aspect of the situation, temporal or otherwise, and the occurrence of the shock. There is instead only a statistical correlation between responses and shocks; within a given time period, responses are, on the average, inversely related to shocks. The shock rate is reduced immediately after a response and reverts to the original level at the next shock, which takes place at varying intervals after the response. The procedure could be characterized equally well by changes in the reciprocal of shock rate—shock-free interval. The shock-free interval following a response is, on the

---

[1]Resistance to extinction is therefore inversely related to rate of responding at the start of extinction. It seems that, rather than being measures of response strength, rate of responding and resistance to extinction are here reciprocal measures of the discriminability of the consequences of responding. On the one hand, the smaller the decrement in shock probability caused by a response, the lower the rate of responding, as might reasonably be expected. In the limiting case, with no decrement, the rate of responding goes to zero. On the other hand, a small decrement is likely to make it hard for a rat to detect when the decrement has been shifted to zero, hence the large resistance to extinction.

The persistence of avoidance behavior may generally have more to do with the relative indiscriminability of the shift from training conditions to extinction than with the special processes like "partial irreversibility" (Solomon & Wynne, 1954) that are supposed to characterize aversion. If an animal is avoiding successfully and therefore getting shocked infrequently, the shift to extinction, when the shock is simply withheld, may be expected to make contact with the behavior much more slowly than extinction in the typical paradigm for positive reinforcement. In principle, it should be possible to extinguish avoidance behavior rapidly (as it did under certain conditions here) and positively reinforced behavior slowly by manipulating discriminability.

average, greater than the shock-free interval measured from any other point in time. The average shock-free interval gradually shrinks back to its original value as time since a response increases.

To save itself, two-factor theory must here find, or invent, a stimulus change at the moment of response and, moreover, the change must have the property of fear reduction, aversion reduction, or the like, based on a history of pairing with shock or its absence. There are sufficient opportunities for invention. The animal's response produces an interval of time that is, on the average, relatively free of shocks. Inferred stimuli associated with this period thus replace the more aversive inferred stimuli otherwise present. Another argument might use proprioceptive, rather than temporal, stimuli. Until the rat presses the lever, the nonavoidance behavior is frequently associated with shock. Following the pressing of the lever, the nonavoidance is less frequently associated with shock. Hence, the pressing of the lever again removes an inferred stimulus made relatively aversive by pairings with shock. In either case, two-factor theory seems to be preserved. There are probably other, at least equally acceptable, versions of two-factor theory for the present findings, a clue, perhaps, to the empirical vacancy of an irrefutable theory.

The reason for dwelling on the hypostatizations of two-factor theory is that a pattern emerges. Two-factor theory says, in effect, that an avoidance procedure must contain a potential difference in shock frequencies which is under the control of the animal's behavior and which is signalled by an initially neutral stimulus. In traditional avoidance procedures, the different shock frequencies are indeed sorted out with respect to stimuli, but the random-shock procedure shows that the change in shock frequency is enough by itself to maintain avoidance. The addition of stimuli to parallel the potential difference is, in the light of the random-shock procedure, gratuitous, even though the habit of searching for one may be too ingrained to be immediately abandoned.

With the random-shock procedure, the inferred stimulus is sheer tautology. Observe the argument in terms of conditioned temporal stimuli. The avoidance response, according to theory, must produce a "stimulus" that signals, on the average, an interval of shock-free time greater than the average shock-free interval correlated with the "stimulus" otherwise prevailing. These "stimuli" have no properties other than the very time intervals or shock rates they presumably signal. Unlike the CS of standard avoidance or the temporal regularity of Sidman's procedure, the stimulus for two-factor theory here has but one attribute and that is its statistical relation to shock frequency. To detect these "stimuli," the animal must be reacting to shock frequencies in the first place. Neither the animal, nor our understanding of avoidance, seems to gain by these inferred stimuli. Mowrer (see p. 57) said that the avoidance of noxious stimulation in an avoidance procedure is a byproduct. The real phenomenon, he said, is escape from a fearsome stimulus. The random-shock procedure shows that in at least one instance the avoidance of noxious stimulation is itself effective and need not be mediated by any further stimulation.

The one-factor form of avoidance theory just intimated is but the law of effect itself: A response producing a particular state of affairs is increased in frequency, the state of affairs being here the reduction in shock rate. Mowrer's first (1939) theory of avoidance, it should be remembered, was just such a one-factor theory, as was Miller and Dollard's (1941, p. 50-51). Two-factor theory was an augmentation beyond the law of effect that was supposed to explain how the conditioned stimulus acquired its control over the animal's behavior. Judging from the literature of the period, there was no thought of an avoidance procedure that contained no conditioned stimulus and therefore required no elaboration beyond the law of effect, although the logic of experimentation clearly suggests a try at one. Nor was two-factor theory a notably parsimonious solution, for it substituted unobserved conditioned "emotional" responses—fear, anxiety, and the like—for the problem of the conditioned stimulus.

An experimental alternative to the random-shock procedure is to try to exclude physiologically the postulated "emotional" responses elicited by the conditioned stimulus, as Taub and Berman (1963, in press) have recently done. In one study (1963), they showed that forelimb flexion in monkeys in a trace-conditioning avoidance procedure persisted even after deafferentation of the limb. A trace-conditioning procedure, which eliminated any exteroception at the time of the instrumental avoidance response, made proprioception the crucial dimension of the CS, hence the importance of deafferentation. The monkeys were not permitted to see their forelimb. The fact that the monkeys showed only a temporary disruption as a result of deafferentation was interpreted by Taub and Berman as showing that "stimulus termination theories of avoidance conditioning overemphasize the importance of secondary negative reinforcement [p. 1016]."

The second study cited (Taub & Berman, in press) was a much more extensive assault on two-factor theories. The original finding was reproduced and extended. They showed that monkeys could be taught the avoidance response for the first time after deafferentation. Next, with a group of trained monkeys, Taub and Berman inflicted complete spinal deafferentation, and the avoidance response remained intact. Finally, a single trained monkey, whose deafferentation was subsequently verified histologically, was submitted to further sensory impoverishment. Its cranial parasympathetic system was suppressed with atropine and the vagus nerve was sectioned on one side and blocked with procaine on the other. The monkey had a strong tendency to slip into sleep. However, the experimenters found that when the monkey happened to be awake, or when it was kept awake by

sharp irrelevant stimulation (loud noise, pinching of the face), it executed the avoidance response as before. The authors' own interpretation of the finding is unequivocal:

it will be recognized that under the final conditions avoidance responding proceeded in a situation in which secondary negative reinforcement could not be presented over either proprioceptive, interoceptive [i.e., sympathetic or parasympathetic], or exteroceptive pathways. . . . Proprioception had been, of course, eliminated by total spinal deafferentation, interoception by combined surgical and pharmacological means and relevant exteroception by preventing the animal from viewing its limbs and through the use of a trace conditioning procedure in which the CS could not be response terminated. These results thus call into doubt stimulus termination theories of avoidance conditioning or, alternately, those theories which attribute the acquisition and maintenance of avoidance behavior to the termination of secondary negative stimuli that are, depending on the theory, either proprioceptive (Schoenfeld, 1950), interoceptive (Mowrer, 1947), or exteroceptive in nature [Taub & Berman, in press].

THE CS AS S^D

It has been shown that CS termination is either an unnecessary or an untestable feature of avoidance procedures. Avoidance has been shown where CS termination has been minimized or eliminated as a factor—experimentally (Herrnstein & Hineline, 1966), physiologically (Taub & Berman, in press), and statistically (Bolles, Stokes, & Younger, 1966). However, to show that the Pavlovian component of two-factor theory is not *necessary* is not to prove that it is insignificant in procedures in which a CS is unquestionably present. There still remains, in other words, the question whether the transferring of some unobserved drive state ("aversion" or "anxiety") to the conditioned stimulus is a fact that must be taken into account in procedures that involve such stimuli.

At least a few theorists have expressed dubiety. In Sidman's procedure, for example, the use of a warning signal just before the shock causes the responses to occur during this period rather than at other times. (Sidman & Boren, 1957). As Keehn (1959) has noted, the warning signal should be fearsome, according to two-factor theory, and in Sidman's procedure it can be avoided by a response that occurs prior to its onset. Instead, the rats wait until it is turned on and then terminate it. How, wonders Keehn, can this be if the Pavlovian mechanism is working as it should? Similarly, D'Amato, Fazzaro, and Etkin (1968) present results suggesting that the role of CS termination may be more a matter of feedback for the response than of anxiety reduction. They showed normal acquisition of avoidance for rats whose responses produced a distinctive feedback stimulus instead of CS termination.

Avoidance conditioning as involving stimulus discrimination is not wholly a new idea even among two-factor theorists. Mowrer and Lamoreaux (1951) noted that in the standard avoidance procedure, responding often occurs nonselectively at first, during both CS and the intertrial interval. With additional training, response frequencies during the two periods separate, sometimes approaching the reflexlike elicitation of the CR by the CS and the CS alone. However, they showed that if the CS is only marginally discriminable, animals may never come under the precise control of the CS, resulting in avoidance that tends to occur more or less without regard to the presence of the CS. The authors point out that avoidance usually involves stimulus discrimination, but that the avoidance response may sometimes be in evidence sooner than any sign of stimulus discrimination. At this point, however, the train of discussion gets derailed, with Mowrer (1960, p. 448–449) explaining that the animals must become quickly conditioned to fear the situation as a whole and that the Pavlovian component of two-factor theory is therefore present anyway. Mowrer seems to have overlooked the other requirement of his own two-factor theory, the removal of the CS. If the situation-as-a-whole is func-

tioning as the CS, then how does the avoidance response get reinforced? It seems a logical requirement of the two-factor theory that a stimulus be discriminated out of the complex impinging on the animal, a stimulus whose removal is what reinforces the avoidance response. The nonselectivity of the avoidance behavior in his own study is actually far more damaging to two-factor theory than has apparently been recognized. And conversely, when avoidance responding is selective, the CS is invariably functioning as at least a cue.

What is at question is not whether the CS exerts an effect over responding, for that is indubitable. It is, rather, whether CS termination comprises the reinforcer in the sense meant by two-factor theory, or whether the CS is fundamentally just a discriminative stimulus (S^D), or cue, for reinforced responding, as Keehn (1959) concluded from his consideration of the signaled form of Sidman's procedure. To conclude that the CS is nothing more than an S^D is to conclude that CS termination is insufficient (besides being unnecessary), since an S^D is a stimulus that merely sets the occasion for a reinforcer, which in the case of avoidance is presumably the reduction of the frequency of the aversive event, rather than being itself reinforcing.

Wherever it appears in an avoidance procedure, the CS sets the occasion for the avoidance response. In the presence of the CS, the avoidance response reduces the amount of aversive stimulation; in its absence, the contingency is absent. At least descriptively, the CS in avoidance procedures is functionally similar to the S^D in simple positive reinforcement procedures. In each case, the stimuli divide the experimental session into two interwoven subsessions, defined by different consequences for responding.

The present argument is that even in standard avoidance, in which there is ample occasion for Pavlovian conditioning, the cue function of the stimulus is alone relevant to avoidance. To support this argument it would be necessary to show that whether or not there is a CS, all of the results concerning the avoidance response follow from the instrumental contingencies. This is not to say that there is no Pavlovian conditioning going on during such avoidance experiments, but rather that the classically conditioned responses are not a requirement for the instrumental behavior. We do not attribute the S^D function of a positive discriminative stimulus to Pavlovian conditioning although it is not unlikely that the pairing of an arbitrary stimulus with food may have Pavlovian consequences. For example, the S^D for food-reinforced lever pressing may also cause the rat to salivate, but conceptually the one result is in no way dependent upon the other. And empirically as well, the literature (Rescorla & Solomon, 1967, p. 164–170) does not indicate that Pavlovian conditioning is a prerequisite for instrumental conditioning, nor, for that matter, vice versa.

It is true that most avoidance procedures are not precisely comparable to the usual discriminated operant, for the CS is terminated by the response it controls whereas the S^D usually is not. The difference may, however, be owing to nothing more profound than historical accident and may be of no theoretical significance. Figure 5 shows two avoidance procedures; one is essentially the standard paradigm (A) and the other (B) is a hypothetical arrangement that would mimic a positively reinforced, discriminated operant. Paradigm A comprises signaled avoidance without an escape contingency and may be expected to lead to responding as shown to the right of the break. The avoidance response occurs when the CS is presented and rarely at other times. Paradigm B comprises a train of shocks and the periodic presentation of a stimulus (S^D) in whose presence the response stops the shock for the remainder of its presentation. Paradigm B also has no escape con-

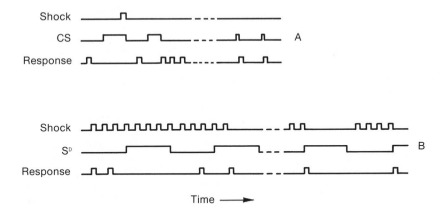

Time ⟶

FIGURE 5

Diagrams of two hypothetical avoidance procedures. (A. Standard avoidance, but with an inescapable, fixed-duration shock. The avoidance response terminates the conditioned stimulus and avoids the shock. The break indicates a period of practice, presumably bringing the performance to its final level. B. An avoidance procedure in which a train of fixed-duration, inescapable shocks may be interrupted by the avoidance response, but only while the stimulus is present. At other times, the shock is unavoidable as well as inescapable. The break again indicates a period of practice, presumably bringing the performance to its final level.)

tingency, which is to say that each shock is of fixed duration. The responding may be expected to be as shown to the right of the break, with a response soon after the onset of S^D and rarely at other times. Since B is just the random-shock procedure under stimulus control and with periodic, instead of random, presentations of shock, it seems a good hunch that responding would be maintained as indicated.

The probable outcome of Paradigm B raises a problem for two-factor theory, although it is obviously in keeping with the idea of the CS as a cue. The S^D is neither terminated by the response, unlike a proper CS, nor for that matter, should it elicit fear any more than its absence does. In fact, once the avoidance response begins to occur, the animal should be, if anything, less afraid in the presence of the S^D than in its absence. However, two-factor theory's problem seems to be, as so often, overcome by a suitable rearrangement of definitions. The CS is, the theory would have to say, not the S^D at all, but a stimulus complex comprising the S^D and the proprioception of not having responded. The occurrence of the avoidance response changes this into another stimulus complex—S^D-plus-the-proprioception-of-having-responded—which constitutes a relatively safe period and thus does not elicit responding. The absence of the S^D also does not elicit responding, but here because responding is ineffective in altering the schedule of shock presentation. As with the random-shock procedure, two-factor theory must again endow stimuli with properties based on shock frequency and then use these properties to explain the animal's sensitivity to shock frequency. In contrast, the idea that the CS is an S^D is readily consistent with the responding in either paradigm.

The presumed outcome of a hypothetical experiment is hardly enough, however, to dislodge a widely held theory. It remains to be shown that in real experiments as well, the CS is not essentially different from an S^D, which is to say that

the contingencies of instrumental reinforcement alone make sense out of the behavior. Would the termination of the CS support avoidance behavior if there were no actual avoidance of the aversive event? In the usual avoidance procedure, the two possible sources of reinforcement are confounded: CS termination and unconditioned stimulus (US) avoidance are in a one-to-one relation. Two-factor theory has said that the latter is a "byproduct" of the former. The present discussion turns this around and asks whether the former has any potency independent of the latter.

Kamin (1956, 1957) obtained responding in the Miller-Mowrer apparatus with rats which *either* terminated the CS without avoiding the US *or* avoided the US without terminating the CS, although neither group was the equal of the rats which did both. It would be a mistake, however, to conclude that CS termination has thereby been shown to be an independent source of response strength. Kamin's experiments used the "standard" avoidance procedure, which means that the rats had to escape from the shock if they failed to avoid it. For the crucial CS-terminating group, there was no shock avoidance, only CS termination, and then, a few seconds later, the shock was presented anyway, and the rats duly escaped. It seems questionable to call this CS-terminating response an "avoidance" response when it could so easily have been a generalized escape response. Moreover, the data indicate a fall-off in the response towards the end of the 100 trials of the study (Kamin, 1957, Figure 1), just as might be expected of a generalized response. The recent study by Bolles, Stokes, and Younger (1966) substantiates this suggestion and also indicates that CS termination has little if any intrinsic reinforcing effect. These investigators showed that the elimination of the shock-escape contingency significantly reduced the number of responses by the CS termination group. In fact, they found no consistent differences between rats that were just terminating the CS without either avoiding or escaping and rats that were neither terminating the CS nor avoiding or escaping. CS termination facilitated responding only for rats that were also avoiding, escaping, or both, a finding that is plausibly considered a response-feedback effect, as Bolles et al. suggest and as D'Amato et al. (1968) have further substantiated with their work.

The lines of defense for two-factor theory had been laid out in Kamin's (1956, 1957) original papers on US avoidance and CS termination and will doubtless be held against the sally from Bolles et al. (1966). The responding apparently due to US termination, said Kamin (and Mowrer, 1960, p. 53), may actually result from the termination of the CS at the end of the CS-US interval and not from the omission of the US at that moment. Moreover, the weakness (or absence) of responding that terminates the CS without avoiding the US, Kamin suggested, is the result of a punishment effect, for the shock is presented on all trials, regardless of the occurrence of a CS-terminating response.

Just as it proved to be peculiarly hard to omit the CS, so it proves to be peculiarly hard to isolate CS termination from the other elements that may affect responding, and for the same reason. Two-factor theorists have allowed themselves to interpret avoidance procedures post hoc, designating as the effective CS whatever would tend to substantiate the theory. If CS termination fails to support responding, it is because a punishment effect has intervened. If responding is supported in the absence of an ostensible contingency for CS termination, it is because the absence is only ostensible—the contingency is said to be there anyway, but delayed.

In this context, two unpublished studies by Hineline are instructive, for they concentrate on the effects of CS termination in a novel way, one that would demand a wholly new reinterpretation for two-factor theory, at any rate. Both procedures used rats in a lever-pressing apparatus in which the lever could be withdrawn and reinserted remotely. In one procedure (see Figure 6), lever pressing had no effect on the overall frequency of shock. An experimental session comprised 300 cycles, each lasting 20 seconds. The rat was shocked 8 seconds after the start of a cycle if no response occurred first. Then, 2 seconds later, the lever was automatically retracted for 10 seconds, concluding the 20-second cycle. (The presence and absence of the lever were correlated with an auditory signal, balanced as to presence and absence across

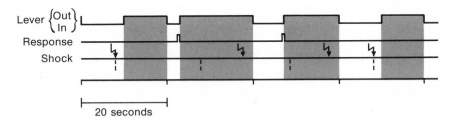

FIGURE 6

A procedure in which the response retracts the lever for the remainder of a fixed 20-second cycle and also postpones, but does not avoid, the shock. (The shock occurs while the lever is absent or present, depending, respectively, upon whether or not a response has occurred in that cycle. There is always one shock in every cycle, and every cycle lasts exactly 20 seconds. The shaded portions show when the lever is withdrawn.

animals.) A depression of the lever during the first 8 seconds retracted the lever immediately, but the shock was not omitted, only postponed. Instead of getting shocked at the usual time, the rat was shocked at the 18th second of a cycle in which it had responded. Once retracted, the lever was never returned until the start of the next cycle. This arrangement kept the cycle fixed at 20 seconds, and the number of shocks per session equal to the number of cycles. Two-factor theory seems to predict that the responding be initially acquired, since it serves to remove stimuli associated with shock. However, once the response is occurring frequently, the shock is being correlated with the absence of the original CS, resulting in drive *induction*, rather than *reduction*, for the response, which might then be expected to diminish in frequency, which, in turn, would restore the conditions for its initial acquisition, and so on. Just how this oscillating state of affairs would finally affect performance is not spelled out by the theory.

In contrast to this complexity, the results of the study were strikingly clear. Every rat tested, including both experimentally naïve and previously trained rats, showed consistent, high levels of responding. In sessions consisting of 300 trials, rats typically responded on more than 260 occasions. The behavior seemed stable and showed no diminution in several months of daily sessions.

The results of the second procedure examined by Hineline (see Figure 7) were in clear contrast. Again, there was a 20-second cycle, with 10 seconds each for the presence and absence of the lever. And as before, a shock was scheduled for the 8th second of a cycle in the absence of responding and for 2 seconds before the end of a cycle if there had been a response. The sole difference was in how long the lever was withdrawn after a response retracted it. In this second procedure, the lever was always absent for exactly 10 seconds, no matter when it was withdrawn. In this way, the occurrence of a response shortened the cycle without eliminating the shock. Unlike the preceding procedure, responses actually *increased* the frequency of shock during a session of given duration, instead of leaving it unchanged. Each response subtracted a period of shock-free time whose duration depended on the locus of response within the cycle—the earlier the response, the greater the increase in shock rate.

Two-factor theory seems to go through about the same steps as before. The response might be acquired because it removes a stimulus associated with shock,

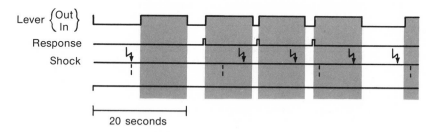

FIGURE 7

A procedure in which the response retracts the lever for 10 seconds. (In the absence of responding, the cycle lasts 20 seconds, but responses shorten the cycle in inverse relation to their latency. The shock occurs while the lever is absent or present, depending, respectively, upon whether or not a response has occurred in that cycle. There is always one shock in every cycle, and cycles last 20 seconds or less. The shaded portions show when the lever is withdrawn.)

but might then diminish in frequency since it precludes the pairing of the CS with the aversive event, which, in turn, restores the original conditions, and so on. In fact, it is hard to find in two-factor theory a precedent for sponsoring any important difference between the two procedures. In both, the nominal CS is terminated by a response. In both, the non-CS gets paired with the shock to the extent that the response occurs. In both, lever-pressing has the maximum delay-of-shock associated with it, compared to any other behavior in the situation.

With the second procedure, however, no rat acquired lever pressing. Rats initially trained to avoid on other procedures, including Hineline's first procedure, soon stopped responding. The difference between the two procedures proved to be crucial—one fully adequate, the other totally inadequate.

For both procedures two-factor theory predicts a fluctuation in responding, since pairings between the shock and *some* stimulus go on no matter what the animal does, but *which* stimulus is paired depends on the animal's behavior. If it responds, the pairings are between the previously safe stimulus and the shock; if it does not respond, the pairings are between the nominal CS and the shock. Hull (1929) noted a similar problem in standard avoidance. If the response is dependent on the shock, then successful avoidance should mean a weakened response, since it prevents the shock's occurring. Later theorists have also wondered how a response can be steadily maintained when its motivating circumstance is removed by its occurrence. The contemporary answers, within the context of two-factor theory, are the notions of "anxiety conservation" and "partial irreversibility" (Solomon & Wynne, 1954). It is worth recalling this answer to see that it is not applicable to the present findings. The problem here is not the preservation of the motivating effects of the CS after the animal's avoidance responding has effectively terminated the pairings that produced the effects in the first place. Rather, it is that the pairings go on unchecked in the present instance, either with the nominal CS or with its absence, depending respectively on the absence of the response or its occurrence. Neither anxiety conservation nor partial irreversibility helps to explain the steady responding here for one procedure and its steady absence for the other, since it is not the *omission* of shock that creates a problem, but its *presence*.

Two-factor theory fails to define the issues here, let alone account for the results. In contrast, the idea of shock-frequency reduction under the control of discriminative stimuli defines the issue exactly and perhaps handles the outcome. Both procedures employ a pair of discriminative stimuli, each correlated with the occurrence of shock according to some routine, much as in a multiple schedule (Ferster & Skinner, 1957). In Hineline's first procedure, the shock is correlated with one discriminative stimulus, (S_1^D) —the nominal CS—such that whenever shock is presented in its presence, the shock rate is necessarily one shock per 10 seconds. (This disregards the rare instances when responses occurred in the 2 seconds following shock and prior to the withdrawal of the lever. Including those instances would only further support the present view.) On the other hand, the shock is correlated with the other discriminative stimulus (S_2^D)—the nominal "safe" stimulus—such that when the shock is given here it is always during some period greater than 10 seconds, since its duration is set at 10 seconds *plus* the remaining duration of the first half of the cycle. To the rat, then, each cycle presents a choice between a pair of stimuli in whose presence the potential shock rates are different. If the rat "calculates" shock rates per stimulus period, rather than for the experimental session as a whole, then the response is reinforced by the reduction in shock rate associated with a response-produced change from S_1^D to S_2^D.

The failure to maintain behavior in Hineline's second study further suggests that the rat is sensitive to shock rates per stimulus condition. Here, it should be recalled, the shock always occurs in a 10-second period, whether in S_1^D or S_2^D. The response, then, produces no change in shock rates when calculated with respect to stimulus periods. Hence, responding here is extinguished or simply not acquired.

The difference between the two procedures may, then, be seen as a difference in the shock rates associated with the two discriminative stimuli in the situation. The response occurs when it is reinforced by a change from a higher to a lower shock rate, as these are correlated with the discriminative stimuli, and not when it causes no such change. For present purposes, however, the main import of Hineline's findings is not to suggest the form of a new theory, but to show that CS termination is by itself *insufficient* to produce avoidance responding.

EMOTION, KNOWLEDGE, AND AVOIDANCE

In fairness to those who have supported two-factor theory, it must be said that more than just the ordinary avoidance results are involved. In particular, various experiments showed that animals learn to terminate a stimulus previously paired with shock, even when the learning does not involve any direct correlation between the response and the shock. For example, May (1948) trained rats to escape from a shock, and then, when no escape was possible, exposed them to pairings of a buzzer and the shock. These rats escaped from the buzzer alone when given the opportunity. Miller (1948) further showed that rats can be taught a new response to escape from the CS. He first had rats escaping from shock in one compartment to another compartment without shock. Next, the rats were taught to turn a wheel or press a par to get out of the compartment without any shock to

goad them. Finally, Brown and Jacobs (1949) showed, perhaps most dramatically, that rats would learn to escape from a CS alone after having experienced only pairings of the stimulus with the shock and no prior escape training.

These findings, and others like them, leave no doubt that it is possible for a stimulus to gain control over a response without having been directly involved in a correlation between the response and a reinforcer, a phenomenon that has been broadly extended recently (Rescorla & Solomon, 1967). And it is not only with negative reinforcers that this possibility has been demonstrated. For example, Estes (1948) and Morse and Skinner (1958) have shown that if animals (rats or pigeons, respectively) first experience pairings of a stimulus with food and then are taught a response to gain food (but not the stimulus), then the stimulus alone will by its mere presence facilitate responding, without regard to food. In a similar vein are the phenomena of sensory preconditioning, in which stimuli also gain control over responses in the absence of a direct contingency between them.

Given a sufficiently broad frame of reference, the problem of the CS in avoidance conditioning merges into the more general problem of what it is that "transgers" or gets "associated" when any stimuli are paired. The classical answer—"ideas"—has long since gone out of fashion and is probably not due for revival, nor is it being advocated here. The Pavlovian answer is that a response transfers. As stated at the beginning of this paper, the observable response was seen by some as the objective handle to the philosophers' associationism. It was in this spirit that Hull originally (1929) wrote about avoidance as a transferring of some response from a noxious stimulus to one anticipating it. The evloution of method and theory has, however, undermined such a simple objectivistic account of avoidance. First the response and then the conditioned stimulus were driven back into the organism, just about where the philosophers had had them in the first place. Is there, at this point any scientific advantage to the Pavlovian vocabulary? It seems no less objective to infer an "expectation" or an "anticipation" as to infer a drive, except for theoretical proclivities toward one sort of concept or the other. Several theorists, in fact, were willing to risk their status among the tough-minded (Hilgard & Marquis, 1940; Osgood, 1950; Ritchie, 1951) and opt for a cognitive approach. However, the data themselves, as Miller (1948) pointed out, do not favor one view over the other:

It seems possible that the potentialities of response-produced stimuli as mediators of secondary generalization and sources of acquirable drive may account for in stimulus-response, law-of-effect terms for the type of behavior which has been described as "expectancy" and considered to be an exception to this type of explanation. If it should turn out that all of the phenomena of expectancy can be explained on the basis of the drive and cue functions of response-produced stimuli, expectancy will of course not vanish; it will be established as a secondary principle derivable from more primary ones [p. 99].

Cognitive theories are, according to Miller, not so much wrong as profligate, at least in comparison to the parsimonious doctrine he was advancing. According to Solomon and Brush (1956) the trouble with cognitive theories is simply that they are not motivational theories:

Anxiety for Tolman is not a drive state but a negative expectation, a knowledge of bad things to come. This type of theory was weak only because it did not have any provision for predicting the development of a specific instrumental avoidance response. Almost any skeletal locomotor response was accepted by Tolman as an index of negative expectations, as S's knowledge of what is to come. To a marked degree, early cognitive theory left the S knowing what was going to happen, but it did not provide him with a mechanism for doing anything useful about it. Nor did it emphasize the motivating properties of emotional conditioning. It was pretty dispassionate; too much so for such a dreadful process as avoidance trainings [pp. 236-237] !

Solomon and Brush were dissatisfied with the CS as a cue because they assumed that cues do not motivate. However, cues in stimulus discrimination procedures routinely produce behavior presumably without possessing drive status, but this is rarely noted in discussions of avoidance.

The argument between the behaviorists and the cognitivists reduces to a choice between imputing emotion or knowledge to the animal at the time of the CS, although the theorists have shied away from such a stark characterization of their dispute. Implicit in the argument has been the idea that the CS is necessary for the occurrence of the response—hence the effects of the CS have been of central concern. However useful the argument has been as a stimulant to experimentation, it probably delayed the discovery that CS termination is neither necessary nor sufficient and that the reduction of aversive stimulation is probably both.

The alternatives—emotion or knowledge—arise in theory, not observation. As far as observation is concerned, the study of avoidance has shown that various configurations of stimuli, responses, and negative reinforcers produce effects that can be summarized in a reasonably small number of paradigmatic findings, which this paper has attempted to survey. In some cases, it may seem reasonable to suppose that the rat is indeed afraid of the CS, but only under the assumption that a rat's or a guinea pig's subjective life is enough like man's to permit a common vocabulary. In other cases, the animal does not seem to be afraid of the CS, as in the signaled version of Sidman's procedure or in Lockard's (1963) demonstration that rats prefer signaled to unsignaled shock. In any event, there is nothing to suggest that the subjective state *explains* the behavior, any more than vice versa. And there is a good deal in psychology's past to discourage such interactionistic speculations.

The theme of the present paper is that the reinforcement for avoidance behavior is a reduction in time of aversive stimulation, the very idea that both Mowrer and Schoenfeld explicitly rejected. At the heart of the argument is the notion that an animal can respond to the rate of occurrence of events in its environment. Fortunately, it is a notion that has support from various sources in the analysis of behavior (Anger, 1956; Herrnstein, 1961, 1964; Reynolds, 1963). The primary complication of this simple picture arises in the effects of cues. Our understanding of cues is far from complete, but it seems better to let the results of further inquiry shape the concept than to preserve a theory that has passed over the line into irrefutable doctrine.

REFERENCES

ANGER, D. The dependence of interresponse times upon the relative reinforcement of different interresponse times. *Journal of Experimental Psychology*, 1956, **52**, 145–161.

ANGER, D. The role of temporal discriminations in the reinforcement of Sidman avoidance behavior. *Journal of the Experimental Analysis of Behavior*, 1963, **6**, 477–506.

BEKHTEREV, V. M. *Objective psychologie.* Leipzig & Berlin: Teubner, 1913.

BLACK, A. H. The effects of CS-US interval on avoidance conditioning in the rat. *Canadian Journal of Psychology*, 1963, **17**, 174–182.

BOLLES, R. C., STOKES, L. W., & YOUNGER, M. S. Does CS termination reinforce avoidance behavior? *Journal of Comparative and Physiological Psychology*, 1966, **62**, 201–207.

BROGDEN, W. J., LIPMAN, E. A., & CULLER, E. The role of incentive in conditioning and extinction. *American Journal of Psychology*, 1938, **51**, 109 117.

BROWN, J. S., & JACOBS, A. The role of fear in the motivation and acquisition of responses. *Journal of Experimental Psychology*, 1949, **39**, 747–759.

D'AMATO, M. R., FAZZARO, J., & ETKIN, M. Anticipatory responding and avoidance discrimination as factors in avoidance conditioning. *Journal of Experimental Psychology*, 1968, **77**, 41–47.

DESCARTES, R. *L'homme.* Paris, 1664.

DINSMOOR, J. A. Punishment: I. The avoidance

hypothesis. *Psychological Review*, 1954, **61**, 34–46.

ESTES, W. K. Discriminative conditioning. II. Effects of a Pavlovian conditioned stimulus upon a subsequently established operant response. *Journal of Experimental Psychology*, 1948, **38**, 173–177.

FERSTER, C. B., & SKINNER, B. F. *Schedules of reinforcement.* New York: Appleton-Century-Crofts, 1957.

FREUD, S. *The problem of anxiety.* New York: Psychoanalytic Quarterly & Norton, 1936.

GENTRY, E. Methods of discrimination training in white rats. *Journal of Comparative Psychology*, 1934, **18**, 227–258.

HERRNSTEIN, R. J. Relative and absolute strength of response as a function of frequency of reinforcement. *Journal of the Experimental Analysis of Behavior*, 1961, **4**, 267–272.

HERRNSTEIN, R. J. Secondary reinforcement and rate of primary reinforcement. *Journal of the Experimental Analysis of Behavior*, 1964, **7**, 27–36.

HERRNSTEIN, R. J., & HINELINE, P. N. Negative reinforcement as shock-frequency reduction. *Journal of the Experimental Analysis of Behavior*, 1966, **9**, 421–430.

HILGARD, E. R., & MARQUIS, D. G. *Conditioning and learning.* New York: Appleton-Century, 1940.

HULL, C. L. A functional interpretation of the conditioned reflex. *Psychological Review*, 1929, **36**, 498–511.

HULL, C. L. Learning: II. The factor of the Conditioned reflex. In C. Murchison (Ed.), *A handbook of general experimental psychology.* Worcester: Clark University Press, 1934.

HUNTER, W. S. Conditioning and extinction in the rat. *British Journal of Psychology*, 1935, **26**, 135–148.

KAMIN, L. J. The effects of termination of the CS and avoidance of the US on avoidance learning. *Journal of Comparative and Physiological Psychology*, 1956, **49**, 420–424.

KAMIN, L. J. The effects of termination of the CS and avoidance of the US on avoidance learning: An extension. *Canadian Journal of Psychology*, 1957, **11**, 48–56.

KEEHN, J. D. The effect of a warning signal on unrestricted avoidance behavior. *British Journal of Psychology*, 1959, **50**, 125–135.

LOCKARD, J. S. Choice of a warning signal or no warning signal in an unavoidable shock situation. *Journal of Comparative and Physiological Psychology,* 1963, **56,** 526–530.

MAY, M. A. Experimentally acquired drives. *Journal of Experimental Psychology,* 1948, **38,** 66–77.

MILLER, N. E. Studies of fear as an acquirable drive: I. Fear as motivation and fear-reduction as reinforcement in the learning of new responses. *Journal of Experimental Psychology,* 1948, **38,** 89–101.

MILLER, N. E., & DOLLARD, J. *Social learning and imitation.* New Haven: Yale, 1941.

MORSE, W. H., & SKINNER, B. F. Some factors involved in the stimulus control of operant behavior. *Journal of the Experimental Analysis of Behavior,* 1958, **1,** 103–107.

MOWRER, O. H. A stimulus-response analysis of anxiety and its role as a reinforcing agent. *Psychological Review,* 1939, **46,** 553–565.

MOWRER, O. H. On the dual nature of learning —A re-interpretation of "conditioning" and "problem-solving." *Harvard Educational Review,* 1947, **17,** 102–148.

MOWRER, O. H. *Learning theory and behavior.* New York: Wiley, 1960.

MOWRER, O. H., & LAMOREAUX, R. R. Avoidance conditioning and signal duration—a study of secondary motivation and reward. *Psychological Monographs,* 1942, **54** (5, Whole No. 247).

MOWRER, O. H., & LAMOREAUX, R. R. Fear as an intervening variable in avoidance conditioning. *Journal of Comparative Psychology,* 1946, **39,** 29–50.

MOWRER, O. H., & LAMOREAUX, R. R. Conditioning and conditionality (discrimination). *Psychological Review,* 1951, **58,** 196–212.

MOWRER, O. H., & SOLOMON, L. N. Contiguity vs. drive-reduction in conditioned fear: The proximity and abruptness of drive-reduction. *American Journal of Psychology,* 1954, **67,** 15–25.

OSGOOD, C. E. Can Tolman's theory of learning handle avoidance training? *Psychological Review,* 1950, **57,** 133–137.

PAVLOV, I. P. *Lectures on conditioned reflexes.* New York: International, 1928.

RAZRAN, G. *Avoidant vs. unavoidant conditioning and partial reinforcement in Russian laboratories. American Journal of Psychology,* 1956, **69,** 127–129.

RESCORLA, R. A., & SOLOMON, R. L. Two-process learning theory: Relationships between Pavlovian conditioning and instrumental learning. *Psychological Review,* 1967, **74,** 151–182.

REYNOLDS, G. S. Some limitations on behavioral contrast and induction during successive discrimination. *Journal of the Experimental Analysis of Behavior,* 1963, **6,** 131–139.

RITCHIE, B. F. Can reinforcement theory account for avoidance? *Psychological Review,* 1951, **58,** 382–386.

SCHLOSBERG, H. Conditioned responses in the white rat. *Journal of Genetic Psychology,* 1934, **45,** 303–335.

SCHLOSBERG, H. The relationship between success and the laws of conditioning. *Psychological Review,* 1937, **44,** 379–394.

SCHOENFELD, W. N. An experimental approach to anxiety, escape and avoidance Behavior. In P. H. Hoch & J. Zubin (Ed.), *Anxiety.* New York: Grune & Stratton, 1950. (Republished: New York, Hafner, 1964.)

SIDMAN, M. Avoidance conditioning with brief shock and no exteroceptive warning signal. *Science,* 1953, **118,** 157–158. (a)

SIDMAN, M. Two temporal parameters of the maintenance of avoidance behavior by the white rat. *Journal of Comparative and Physiological Psychology,* 1953, **46,** 253–261. (b)

SIDMAN, M. Reduction of shock frequency as reinforcement for avoidance behavior. *Journal of the Experimental Analysis of Behavior,* 1962, **5,** 247–257.

SIDMAN, M., & BOREN, J. J. A comparison of two types of warning stimulus in an avoidance situation. *Journal of Comparative and Physiological Psychology,* 1957, **50,** 282–287.

SKINNER, B. F. Two types of conditioned reflex and a pseudo type. *Journal of General Psychology,* 1935, **12,** 66–77.

SOLOMON, R. L., & BRUSH, Experimentally derived conceptions of anxiety and aversion. *Nebraska symposium on motivation,* 1956, **5.** 212–305.

SOLOMON, R. L., & WYNNE, L. C. Traumatic avoidance learning: The principles of anxiety conservation and partial irreversibility. *Psychological Review,* 1954, **61,** 353–385.

TAUB, E., & BERMAN, A. J. Avoidance conditioning in the absence of relevant proprioceptive and exteroceptive feedback. *Journal of Comparative and Physiological Psychology,* 1963, **56,** 1012–1016.

TAUB, E., & BERMAN, A. J. The effect of massive somatic deafferentation on behavior and wakefulness in monkeys. In S. J. Freedman (Ed.), *The neuropsychology of spatially oriented behavior.* Homewood, Ill.: Dorsey Press, in press.

THORNDIKE, E. L. *Educational psychology.* Vol. II. *The psychology of learning.* New York:

Teachers College, Columbia, 1913.

ZENER, K. The significance of behavior accompanying conditioned salivary secretion for theories of the conditioned response. *American Journal of Psychology,* 1937, 384–403.

(Received December 15, 1967)

Chapter 10

Choice

In the psychology laboratory, as well as in everyday life, we need to know how organisms choose between alternatives. In everyday life the need is obvious. A manufacturer has to determine which of several colors or styles of his product consumers prefer. A legislator may wish to determine which of several policies his constituents favor. Researchers in the field of behavior and learning are interested in both (1) how preferences develop, under different schedules of reinforcement, and (2) how existing preferences influence learning. Remember that according to Premack's theory of reinforcement (Chapter 6) a hierarchy of preference, or scale, determines whether one event will reinforce or punish another. This hierarchy must be established by choice experiments.

In this chapter we shall discuss choice between rewards almost exclusively and ignore choice between punishers. There are two reasons for this. First, most of the relevant experiments have used rewards rather than punishers. Second, the results of choice experiments with punishment, like those of punishment experiments discussed in previous chapters, are symmetrical to results obtained in experiments with reward.

MEASURING CHOICE

In the course of treating other topics in this book we have already described, in one way or another, the basic measures of choice. The pupose of this section is to classify the measures of choice and discuss their rationales.

Concurrent Rewards

In discussing Premack's theory in Chapter 6 we used as an illustration the boy whose mother wanted to get him to eat spaghetti by rewarding him with ice cream. To determine which had a higher value for him, spaghetti or ice cream, we suggested the hypothetical experiment of leaving the boy alone in a room with a large bowl of spaghetti and a large bowl of ice cream and measuring how much he ate of each. Such an experiment involves concurrent rewards and is the simplest kind of choice experiment. Another concurrent-rewards procedure was described in Chapter 7 as part of Garcia and Koelling's experiment to determine whether rats preferred tasty water (sweet or salty) or bright-noisy water (licks accompanied by a light and buzz); the rats were tested before and after a classical conditioning experiment. Preference was determined by means of a *two-bottle test;* one bottle contained the tasty water and the other the bright-noisy water. The two bottles were placed in the rat's cage and the rat could drink from either. The bottles were shifted periodically from side to side so that side preferences would cancel out. The amount drunk from each bottle was periodically measured. Figure 7.5 shows that conditioning altered the rat's choice from indifference before the test to a strong aversion to one of the liquids after the test, the particular aversion depending on the conditioning procedure.

Concurrent rewards are commonly used in experiments designed, like Garcia and Koelling's to measure taste preferences. Figure 10.1 shows a typical preference function obtained with a two-bottle test. In this case one bottle contained plain water and the other contained a salt solution. The concentration of the salt solution was varied from day to day. As the concentration was increased from zero the rats began to prefer the salty solution, but eventually the solution became too salty and preference shifted to the plain water. The dependent variable, plotted on the ordinate, is the relative amount of salty water consumed:

$$\frac{\text{Intake salty water (cc)}}{\text{Intake salty water (cc)} + \text{Intake plain water (cc)}}$$

This relative measure, called a *behavior ratio,* is one of the most commonly used choice measures. Complete avoidance of the salt solution would be represented by a behavior ratio of zero, complete preference, by a behavior ratio of 1.0, and indifference, by a behavior ratio of 0.5. The curve shown in Figure 10.1 is fairly typical of taste preferences of various animals, including humans, for various solutions. Sweet solutions, for instance, follow a similar pattern of indifference, followed by preference for the solution, followed by aversion as concentration increases.

Concurrent Instrumental Responses

One problem with the two-bottle test and other tests using concurrent rewards is that it is difficult for the experimenter to control the variables. If the

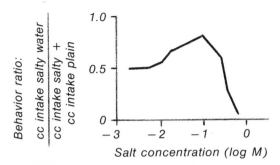

Salt concentration (log M)

FIGURE 10.1
Preference shown by rats for solutions of different
salt concentrations. An ordinate value of 0.5
represents equal consumption of salty and plain
water. Ordinate values above 0.5 indicate more
consumption of salty solutions, and below 0.5, more
consumption of plain water. [From Pfaffman, C., The
pleasures of sensation. *Psych. Review,* 1960, *67,*
253–268. Copyright 1960 by the American
Psychological Assn.]

rewards are available for a long time, the subject might become satiated and
preferences might change. If the rewards are available for a short time, perhaps
not enough responses will occur to provide meaningful data.

An even more critical problem arises when the rewards require different
consummatory responses. Consider, for instance, water and food. A rat licks
at water, but bites at food pellets. Should one measure choice in terms of weight
consumed, volume consumed, number of licks or bites, time spent consuming,
or some other criterion? The concurrent-rewards procedure does not provide
an answer. This problem would have to be faced, also, with the boy eating spaghetti and ice cream. Should our measure of choice be specified in terms of
weight, volume, calories, or bites, or some combination of these parameters?
We can only tell if we can hold one or the other parameter constant while varying the rest. If choice stays constant while that particular parameter (or combination) is constant, we can be fairly certain that we have the right measure.
The concurrent-rewards method does not allow such manipulation of parameters. A method that *does* is the method of concurrent instrumental responses.
To see how this method works, let us consider the T-maze shown at the top
of Figure 10.2.

The T-maze consists of a single central alley down which an animal (usually
a rat) runs until it reaches the cross of the T, where it must choose which of
the two arms to run down next. This point is called the choice point. The two
arms of the T are essentially two separate straight alleys that the rat can choose
between. (Most of the devices that measure choice, are, in fact, combinations of
two or more rate-of-response devices.) At the choice point, the experimenter

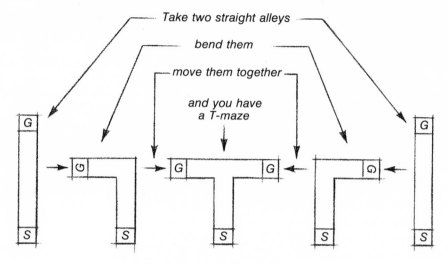

Take two straight alleys

bend them

move them together

and you have
a T-maze

where choice can be measured

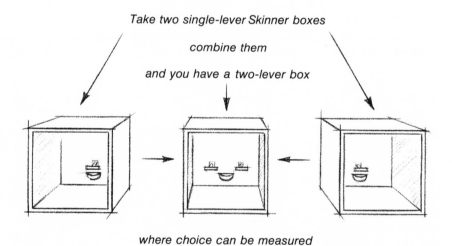

Take two single-lever Skinner boxes

combine them

and you have a two-lever box

where choice can be measured

FIGURE 10.2
In principle, each of these two-choice devices combines two simpler rate-of-response devices.

may provide the rat with a cue—for instance, a card, one side of which is painted red, and the other side green. At the ends of the arms lie two goal boxes, in which the rat may be rewarded or punished. Almost always, the events in the two goal boxes will be different. For instance, when the rat runs down the arm corresponding to the green part of the card it might be rewarded in the goal box with a pellet of food, and when the rat runs down the arm corresponding to the red part of the card, it might be rewarded with 0.1 cc of water. The behavior ratio is simply the fraction of trials on which the rat goes to one side or the other. (For instance, if the left goal box of the T-maze contains food and the right goal box is empty, the animal will learn to choose the left alley on all of the trials. Thus, the behavior ratio is 1.0. If the animal were indifferent between left and right, the behavior ratio would be 0.5; if it always chose the right, the behavior ratio would be 0 with reference to the left goal box).

A fairly obvious example of a combination of two rate-of-response devices into a single device that will measure choice is the Skinner box containing two response levers instead of one (Figure 10.2). Pressing one lever might cause food to be delivered, and pressing the other might cause water to be delivered. The fraction of the total number of presses made on one lever determines the behavior ratio with respect to that lever. As with the T-maze, behavior ratio varies anywhere from 0 to 1.0.

By keeping rewards small and by rewarding the rat according to a schedule of reinforcement that delivers reinforcement infrequently, it is possible to obtain a considerable amount of choice data without satiating the rat.

The feature of the *concurrent instrumental response* procedure that most distinguishes it from *concurrent rewards* is that with concurrent instrumental responses the choice and the consummatory response are separated. Choice responses may be symmetrical while consummatory responses differ. Left versus right or red-side versus green-side or light-side versus dark-side responses (whether turning in a T-maze, pressing levers, or pecking keys) are easier to compare than eating versus drinking. With concurrent instrumental responses it is easier to vary the parameters of the rewards because the experimenter rather than the subject controls these parameters. For instance, instead of giving the boy in our example a big bowl of ice cream and a big bowl of spaghetti, we could give him two levers; pressing one would produce a portion of ice cream, pressing the other, a portion of spaghetti. The various parameters (weight, volume, temperature, calories, and so on) could be controlled for each portion. Choice could be measured by the behavior ratio of lever-presses.

Most of the choice experiments we shall discuss in this chapter involve concurrent instrumental responses, particularly concurrent schedules of reinforcement with rats pressing levers or pigeons pecking keys. Let us consider a specific experiment with pigeons done by A. C. Catania. Catania wanted to study the pigeon's choice between various amounts of food reward. He used a Skinner box fitted with two keys (A and B) and a single hopper. Pecks on each key were reinforced according to a variable-interval 2-minute schedule (VI-2′). Each key had its own schedule of reinforcement and the schedules for the two keys ran concurrently. The pigeon's situation may be compared (with considerable stretching of the facts of nature) to that of a farm girl with two chickens laying eggs at variable intervals of about 2 minutes each. The number of eggs laid would be 30 per hour from each chicken or 60 per hour total. Now, to distort reality a little further, imagine that the girl wants to collect the eggs but cannot tell whether a chicken has laid an egg unless she lifts it up to look. The girl's picking up the two chickens is analogous to the pigeon's pecking the two keys. As long as the parameters of reinforcement (schedule, amount, quality, and so on) are equal, we would expect the pigeons to distribute their pecks equally on the two keys—just as we would expect the girl to pick up each of the two chickens an equal number of times. Catania's pigeons pecked the two keys equally when the amount of reinforcement for pecking each of the two keys was equal (at 4.5 seconds of access to the food hopper). The behavior ratio (pecks on key A divided by pecks on key A plus pecks on key B) was 0.5. Then Catania changed the food reward for pecking key A to 6 seconds and the food reward for pecking key B to 3 seconds. It was as if one chicken were laying eggs twice as large as those of the other chicken. Now the pigeons changed their distribution, pecking twice as much on the key with the larger reward. When Catania reversed the amounts so that pecking key A led to 3-second rewards and pecking key B led to 6-second rewards the pigeons reversed their distribution, now pecking twice as much on key B.

This experiment of Catania's resembles a prior experiment by R. J. Herrnstein. In Herrnstein's experiment, also with pigeons and concurrent variable-interval schedules, the amount of each reinforcement was held constant, but the rate of reinforcement (the value of the variable-interval schedule) was different for each key. (Following along with the farm-girl example, it was as if the eggs were all of equal size but the chickens were laying them at different rates.) Herrnstein kept the total rate of reinforcement constant at 40 per hour but varied the percentage of this total that could be obtained by pecking each key. For instance, when reinforcements for pecking one key were programmed on a variable-interval 6-minute schedule (10 per hour) reinforcements for pecking the other key were programmed on a variable-interval 2-minute schedule (30 per hour). The pigeons could have obtained all 40 reinforcements with almost any behavior ratio of pecks as long as they pecked at each key at least occasionally. But the actual results of this experiment revealed a remarkable uniformity. Figure 10.3 illustrates that the behavior ratio of the pigeons matched the proportion of the 40 reinforcements obtained by pecking each key. Expressed as an equation, within a given session,

$$\frac{\text{Pecks on key A}}{\text{Total pecks (key A + key B)}} = \frac{\text{Reinforcements obtained by pecking key A}}{\text{Total reinforcements (key A + key B)}} \quad (1)$$

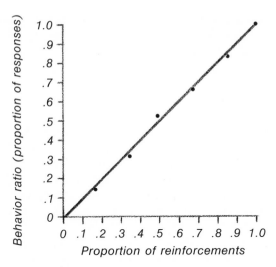

FIGURE 10.3
The relative frequency of responding to one
alternative in a two-choice procedure as a function
of the relative frequency of reinforcement for that
choice. Variable-interval schedules governed
reinforcements for both alternatives. The diagonal
line shows matching between the relative
frequencies. [From Herrnstein, R. J. On the law of
effect. *J. Exp. Anal. Beh.*, 1970, *13*, 243–266.
Copyright 1970 by the Society for the Experimental
Analysis of Behavior, Inc.]

This equation Herrnstein called the *matching law*. It is a pervasive observation in studies of choice and we shall spend most of this chapter discussing it.

Matching of relative responses to relative rate of reinforcement has been shown consistently for pigeons pecking keys, with various schedules of food reinforcement programmed for the pecks. It has also been observed when parameters of reinforcement other than amount (Catania) or rate (Herrnstein) were varied. It has been found when delay of reinforcement was varied, when electric shock punishment suppressed responding, when the pigeons were hungry as in the Catania and Herrnstein experiments, and when they were satiated. It was also observed when pigeons lived in the experimental chamber and obtained all their food by pecking the two keys. It has been observed with rats pressing levers for food reward and for brain-stimulation reward, with monkeys pressing disks for food reward and for morphine injections as reward, and with human eye movements. In the eye-movement experiment done by S. R. Schroeder and J. G. Holland subjects viewed four dials, two on the left and two on the right. Their job was to spot pointer deflections on the dials. They could not see any two dials at once and so had to move their eyes from dial to dial. A response to a dial consisted of an eye movement *to* that dial either from another dial on the same side or from a dial on the opposite side. Schroeder and Holland found that the relative responses to the dials on each side matched the relative rate of pointer deflections on that side.

An experiment by William Baum will illustrate the generality of the matching relationship. Baum was studying behavior of pigeons in the laboratory at Harvard University, but his contact with pigeons was not limited to the laboratory. In his house in Cambridge there was a hole under the eaves and wild pigeons had gotten into a portion of his attic, using it as their loft. Instead of plugging up the hole, Baum decided to take this opportunity to study the pigeons. He brought from his laboratory a panel with two keys and a hopper through which food could be periodically delivered. He installed this panel in his attic in a position above the floor so that the pigeons had access to the front but not the rear of the panel. Just below the front of the panel he attached a bar on which one (and only one) pigeon at a time could perch. The pigeon on the perch could then peck at the keys and eat from the hopper. Behind the panel Baum installed electromechanical programming equipment. At first Baum arranged an autoshaping procedure whereby the wild pigeons would learn to peck a key (see Figure 7.3). Several pigeons learned to peck and eat from the hopper with the shaping procedure running continuously. Then Baum programmed concurrent variable-interval schedules continuously, 24 hours per day. As Herrnstein did in the laboratory, Baum periodically changed the values of the variable-interval schedules so that sometimes one key provided higher rates of food delivery and sometimes both provided equal rates. The schedules ranged from variable-interval 30-second schedules to variable-interval 4-minute schedules. Baum found that between 10 and 20 pigeons took turns pecking the keys, that they pecked mostly during daylight hours, and that the overall rate of pecking was high enough so that only 10 percent of the pecks actually produced food. He also found that the relative rate of pecks (the behavior ratio) matched the relative rate of reinforcements. His results are shown in Figure 10.4. Each pigeon individually could have deviated considerably from matching, but the behavior of the flock as a whole conformed to equation (1).

Are there any situations in which matching is *not* found? Yes there are, and we shall discuss such situations later in the chapter. But first let us consider the implications of matching for measurement of choice. The matching law suggests that concurrent schedules of reinforcement are a good way to measure choice. If we know that twice the rate or amount of a given food results in twice the number of responses on the manipulandum that produces that food, that three times the rate or amount results in three times the number of responses, four times the rate or amount, four times the responsee, and so on, then when we put *different* commodities on the two sides of a concurrent schedule and find that one results in twice the number of responses as the other it is

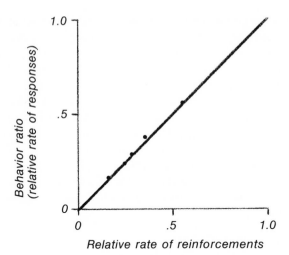

FIGURE 10.4
The relative rate of responding (behavior ratio) to one
alternative in a two-choice procedure as a function of
the relative rate of reinforcement for that choice. In
this case the function is for a group of pigeons living
in William Baum's attic. Variable-interval schedules
governed reinforcement for both alternatives. The
diagonal line shows matching between the relative
rates. [From Baum, W. M. Choice in free ranging wild
pigeons. *Science,* 1974, *185,* 78–79. Copyright 1974
by the American Association for the Advancement
of Science.]

reasonable to assume that the value of the preferred food is twice that of the
other. Concurrent schedules can be used as a sort of scale, then, on which preferences of various kinds can be measured. The balance pans of the scale are
the various rewards contingent on responses on either manipulandum. The
reading of the scale is the relative rate of responding on the two manipulanda.

The Changeover Delay (COD)

Occasionally, with concurrent schedules, subjects do not match relative
responses to relative reinforcement because they develop certain patterns of
switching. For instance, rats, pigeons, and humans tend to switch back and
forth between two alternatives. With several manipulanda arranged in a straight
line, they tend to range back and forth along the line. If, for instance, a pigeon
pecks three keys in the order 1-2-3-2-1-2-3-2-1-2-3 . . . , the middle key
will be pecked twice as frequently as either of the end keys. Patterns such as
these are very common and must be either accounted for in choice experiments
or somehow experimentally controlled. A way to control such patterns is by a
contingency called a changeover delay (COD). The changeover delay arranges

that when the subject switches over from one response to another the reward cannot be obtained for a brief period, usually about two seconds. The first peck at a key after pecking the other key would never be reinforced. Thus, if the pigeon simply alternates or even if the pigeon pecks several times at each key, but switches keys before the COD period ends, pecks would never be reinforced. Once a pigeon starts to peck a key it must keep pecking at that key for at least the COD duration in order to obtain any reward at all.

The COD contingency effectively breaks up patterns of switching and forces the subject to remain with an alternative for at least a little while once it is chosen. Without the COD, patterns such as simple alternation cause relative responding to deviate from relative rate of reinforcement. With a COD of about 2 seconds or more, relative responding usually equals relative rate of reinforcement.*

Concurrent Chains of Responses

Concurrent chains are used to study choice, not between rewards directly, but between various sources of reward. To return to the example of the farm girl and the chickens, we compared concurrent instrumental responses to picking up one or the other chicken to look for eggs. Analogously, a concurrent chain would begin with the girl in the market buying one or another chicken. The initial link of the chain would be her choice at the market. The terminal link would be her behavior, back in the barn, of picking up that *one* chicken she bought and looking for eggs. The critical feature of concurrent chains is that they force subjects to abide by their choices. No longer is the farm girl able to switch blithely from one chicken to another. Whatever chicken she bought, that's the chicken she's stuck with—at least until she goes to the market again. Having a choice between concurrent *chains* rather than concurrent *responses* is like having a choice of hens rather than eggs or having a choice of cooks rather than meals. It might even be compared to choosing a husband or wife rather than spending an evening with a boy or girl. With concurrent chains, choice is for a longer term than with concurrent responses. The considerations that govern the long-term choice may be quite different from those that govern the more immediate choice.

To return to the laboratory, Figure 10.5a shows a T-maze and two alleys. The T-maze alone would be used to study choice between two events in the goal boxes. Each alley alone would be used to study running as a function of events in its goal box. Now suppose we wanted to study choice, not between individual events in the goal boxes of the T-maze, but between the alleys them-

---

*With very large COD values, the COD interferes with the schedule so that reinforcement is considerably less than the nominal rate. For instance, with a VI 1-minute schedule versus a VI 2-minute schedule and a COD of 6 seconds, the actual rates of reinforcement obtained from the two alternatives might be 0.8 per minute versus 1.5 per minute instead of 1 per minute versus 2 per minute. In such cases, the subject matches relative responding to relative rate of reinforcement *actually obtained* rather than to the reinforcement originally programmed.

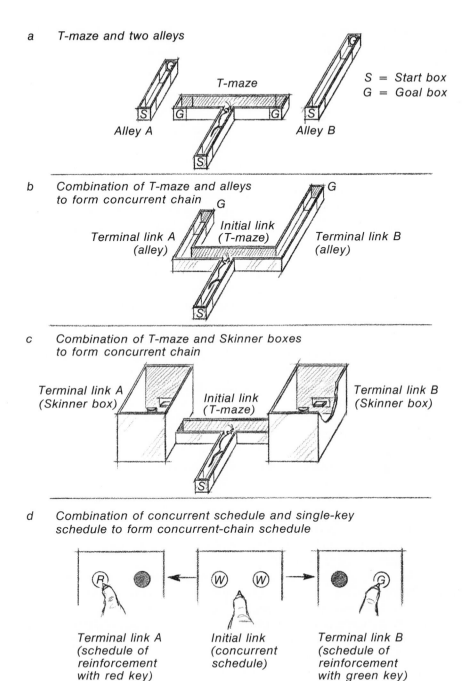

a   T-maze and two alleys

T-maze

S = Start box
G = Goal box

Alley A   Alley B

b   Combination of T-maze and alleys
to form concurrent chain

G

Terminal link A   Initial link   Terminal link B
(alley)   (T-maze)   (alley)

G

c   Combination of T-maze and Skinner boxes
to form concurrent chain

Terminal link A   Initial link   Terminal link B
(Skinner box)   (T-maze)   (Skinner box)

d   Combination of concurrent schedule and single-key
schedule to form concurrent-chain schedule

Terminal link A   Initial link   Terminal link B
(schedule of   (concurrent   (schedule of
reinforcement   schedule)   reinforcement
with red key)   with green key)

FIGURE 10.5
How a choice procedure is combined with two single-response procedures in order to
form a concurrent chain.

selves (with their respective goal boxes). Figure 10.5b shows how the T-maze and the alleys are combined to form a concurrent chain. Now, the rat at the choice point of the T-maze is choosing between the alleys. A chain of responses is required to reach either goal box. First the rat must run to the choice point, then to the alley, then down the alley and into the goal box. The paths to both goal boxes run concurrently until the rat reaches the choice point, and then they separate. This is typical of concurrent-chain responses: only the initial links of the chain are concurrent. At some point a choice is made and the terminal links are experienced separately.

Figure 10.5c shows another type of concurrent chain. Here the rat chooses, not between alleys, but between Skinner boxes. The rat is clearly choosing not only between rewards but between the means by which those rewards are obtained. The difference between the rat in a two-lever box (as in Figure 10.2) and the rat in the concurrent-chain apparatus of Figure 10.5c is very much like the difference between the farm girl in the barn choosing which chicken to pick up to look for eggs and the farm girl in the market choosing which chicken to buy. Once the terminal link of the chain is reached only a single response is available. In the terminal links the experimenter can provide any schedule of reinforcement for lever-pressing. For instance, terminal-link A might consist of a variable-interval schedule, and terminal-link B might consist of a variable-ratio schedule. The rat might be punished for lever-pressing in one terminal link and not in the other. The rat might get free food in one terminal link but have to press the lever for food in the other terminal link. Stimulus conditions might differ in the two terminal links. The concurrent-chain procedure provides great flexibility. With simple concurrent schedules (as in Figure 10.2), conditions of responding are always concurrent. We could not, with simple concurrent responses, tell whether a rat prefers to respond in the presence of a red light or a green light because both lights, concurrently present, would mix and constitute yet a third light, perhaps reddish or greenish. The concurrent-chain procedure, with separate terminal links, allows us to study choice between *any* two conditions without mixing them together.

The apparatus shown in Figure 10.5c, although simple enough conceptually, would be difficult to build, requiring two separate Skinner boxes in two separate locations. Consequently, the apparatus shown in Figure 10.5d is usually used. With this apparatus the events are arranged temporally instead of spatially. The initial link, instead of the choice point in a T-maze, now consists of two concurrent schedules. The subjects tested in this apparatus are usually pigeons. Pecks at either key are not followed by food directly but by entry to one or the other terminal link. Figure 10.6 shows the procedure with pigeons in more detail. During the initial link the pigeon may peck at either of the two keys. Usually both keys are the same color (white, in Figure 10.6). The period of pecking at the two white keys is analogous to the period at the choice point of a T-maze. Not every peck during the initial link will produce a ter-

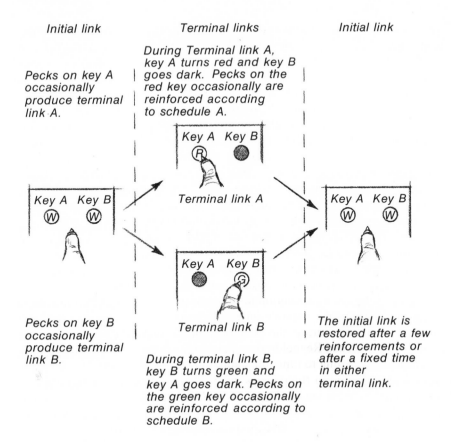

Initial link   Terminal links   Initial link

Pecks on key A occasionally produce terminal link A.

During Terminal link A, key A turns red and key B goes dark. Pecks on the red key occasionally are reinforced according to schedule A.

Key A   Key B

Terminal link A

Key A   Key B

Key A   Key B

Key A   Key B

Pecks on key B occasionally produce terminal link B.

Terminal link B

During terminal link B, key B turns green and key A goes dark. Pecks on the green key occasionally are reinforced according to schedule B.

The initial link is restored after a few reinforcements or after a fixed time in either terminal link.

FIGURE 10.6
Sequence of events in a concurrent-chain schedule of reinforcement.

minal link, but the concurrent schedules during the initial link govern entry into the terminal link. Usually they are variable-interval schedules, and equal for the two keys. When a peck at one of the white initial-link keys produces a terminal link, the pigeon need not move anywhere—the conditions of the terminal link are brought to the pigeon. The terminal link is signalled by the change in color of the key just pecked (to red for the left key or to green for the right key) and by the darkening of the other key. (Pecks on the dark key have no programmed consequences and pigeons rarely peck at them.) After the pigeon has spent the specified period of time pecking the colored key and experiencing the consequences of its choice (the schedule of reinforcement) in the terminal link, the initial link is restored and the pigeon chooses again. Choice is measured by the behavior ratio of pecks on the two keys during the initial link.

To visualize what happens in concurrent-chain schedules, consider an experiment with pigeons by S. M. Autor done in 1960. Autor programmed concurrent variable-interval 1-minute schedules during the initial link. In other words, the pigeons, if they pecked at the two keys during the initial link (when both keys were white), would spend an average of 30 seconds in an initial link before a peck would produce a terminal link. During the terminal link the pigeons obtained food by pecking one key (now either red or green) according to another variable-interval schedule. Autor periodically changed the variable-interval schedule in one or the other of the terminal links. These schedules could vary between variable-interval 3.75-seconds and variable-interval 1-minute schedules, and they could be the same in the two terminal links or different. After spending a period of time in the terminal link (proportional to the average interval between reinforcements in that link) the pigeons were returned to the initial link. Autor measured the rate at which the pigeons pecked the key during the terminal link (when it was red or green) and he measured how they distributed their pecks on the two keys during the initial link (when they were white). The rates of pecking the red and green keys were about what they would have been if the keys were continuously red or green and pecks reinforced according to the particular variable-interval schedule programmed. That is, the pigeons' responding during the terminal links confirmed the experimental findings of Catania and Reynolds varying with rate of reinforcement during the terminal links according to functions similar to those of Figure 5.18. But Autor was mainly interested in the pigeons' choice behavior in the initial link. The pigeons choices are shown in Figure 10.7. Note how similar they are to those obtained by Herrnstein with simple concurrent variable-interval schedules. Again the behavior ratio matches the relative rate of reinforcement. With the simple concurrent schedules used by Herrnstein, choice and reinforcement were intermixed. With the concurrent-chain schedule used by Autor, choice periods (initial link) were separated from reinforcement periods (terminal link). Nevertheless, with both procedures the matching law was confirmed.

We should note here that concurrent-chain schedules were discussed, albeit peripherally, in Chapter 8. Schuster's experiment in which pigeons chose between condition A (blue lights and buzzers preceding all food deliveries) and condition B (extra blue lights and buzzers) illustrated in Figure 8.4, and Bower, McLean, and Meachum's experiment in which pigeons chose between condition A (unsignalled reward intervals) and condition B (signalled reward intervals) illustrated in Figure 8.6, both involved concurrent-chain schedules. In each case condition A and condition B comprised the terminal links; the initial links consisted of two white keys, which when pecked yielded access to one or the other terminal link.

One important characteristic of the concurrent-chain schedule is that it effectively separates the performance within the two schedules from the choice between them, thereby permitting the study of both in the same experiment.

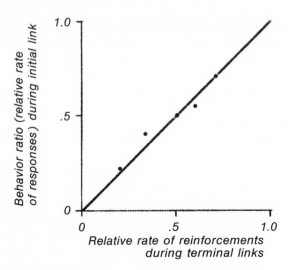

FIGURE 10.7
The relative rate of responding to one alternative during
the initial link of a concurrent-chain schedule as a
function of the relative rate of reinforcement during the
terminal links. [From Hendry, D. P. (Ed.), *Conditioned
Reinforcement,* The Dorsey Press, 1969.]

Performance and choice need not vary together. For instance, suppose terminal-link A contains a drh schedule, in which reinforcements are delivered at one per minute provided a *high* rate of pecking is maintained, and terminal-link B contains a drl schedule, in which reinforcements are delivered at two per minute provided a *low* rate of pecking is maintained (see p. 256 for a description of drl and drh schedules). It is perfectly conceivable that the pigeons would prefer the drl schedule and peck more during the initial link on the key corresponding to the drl than on the key corresponding to the drh, making the behavior ratio during the initial links (the choice) vary inversely with the responding during the terminal links. In fact, one very frequent finding in concurrent-chain experiments has been that choice is independent of the responding performed during the terminal links. Rather, choice is dependent on the reinforcement (or punishment) delivered during the terminal links.

Another important characteristic of the concurrent chain is that even with wide disparities in degree of preference for one terminal link or the other, all terminal links will be entered about equally. This is due to the concurrent variable-interval schedules of the initial link that usually program entrances into the terminal links. With concurrent variable-interval schedules, the more responses on either key, the lower the probability of entering the terminal link corresponding to that key. Thus, if the pigeon pecked on one white key 90 percent of the time, only a few of those pecks would produce the terminal link corresponding to that key, whereas a much higher proportion of the 10 percent of pecks on the other key would produce the terminal link corresponding to it.

Since the only difference between the concurrent chain and an ordinary concurrent schedule is the temporal extent of the terminal links, the concurrent chain becomes more like an ordinary concurrent schedule as the terminal links are reduced in duration. (A corresponding manipulation in Figure 10.5b would be to make the alleys shorter and shorter.) When each terminal link consists of a single reinforcement delivered immediately, the concurrent chain *is* a simple concurrent schedule.

Consider another type of concurrent-chain schedule. Suppose that reinforcement is freely delivered at fixed intervals during each terminal link, with no responses required to produce reinforcement during the terminal links, and that each terminal link ends after a single reinforcement. A corresponding manipulation in Figure 10.5c would be to remove the levers from the Skinner boxes and use the boxes simply as delay chambers, delivering food after a certain time in the chambers. In this case, the concurrent chain is measuring choice between various delays of reinforcement.

By appropriate variation of its parameters, the concurrent chain may be made to mimic the essential features of virtually any study of choice, including those using the T-maze.*

Concurrent-chain schedules may also be used with other responses and other organisms. Consider an experiment done by the author and M. Frankel to study gambling in humans. The subjects, undergraduates at Harvard, were seated in front of a control panel containing five buttons that they could press. These buttons were initially all lit with white light and comprised five choices in the initial link of a concurrent-chain schedule (as opposed to the two choices offered to pigeons and rats in procedures described above). The subjects could press the buttons to obtain any of five separate terminal links. Access to the terminal links was controlled by five separate variable-interval 5-minute schedules. Once a subject entered a terminal link, the button he had just pressed turned red and all the other buttons went dark. In the terminal link the subjects could gamble. Each press of the red button cost the subject a certain number of points, but occasionally presses were followed by a "hit"—the sudden accumulation of a larger number of points (as in a slot machine or roulette game). After a minute in any terminal-link gambling situation the subjects were returned to the initial link. It was as if the subjects could choose between five

---

*The main difference between the T-maze type of concurrent chain shown in Figure 10.5a, b, and c, and the more typical concurrent chain shown in Figure 10.5d is that choice in the former consists of a single response, a left turn or a right turn, whereas choice in the latter consists of repeated responding on the concurrent schedules of the initial link. If the initial-link concurrent schedules were FR1 schedules, in which a single response on either manipulandum produced a terminal link, then the situation of Figure 10.5d would be exactly like that of a T-maze concurrent chain; a peck on the left key would correspond to a left turn and a peck on the right key, to a right turn.

one-armed bandits but once the subjects made their choice, access was barred to the other four machines for one minute. After the experiment, which lasted about a half hour, the subjects could exchange the points for money. Each terminal link consisted of a different gambling situation, varying in probability of a hit and points won per hit. We found that given zero expected value (odds compensated exactly by payoffs), subjects gambled more during the terminal links as probability of a hit increased and that their choice was proportional to the probability of a hit. This means that our subjects gambled more on favorites than long shots and preferred gambling on favorites to long shots even though combination of odds and payoff made the long shots and favorites equally valuable overall. When we varied expected value across the five choices the subjects preferred the higher expected values (average winnings) to the lower. The point of using a concurrent chain in this experiment was that it separated the actual gambling behavior of the subjects from their preference for one gambling situation over another. Once a gambling situation was chosen the subjects had to stick with it for a minute even if they did not gamble.

Two interpretations of choice behavior in concurrent chains have been advanced—one more molar and the other more molecular. The molar interpretation says that choice in the initial links is directly dependent on the parameters of the terminal links, such as rate of reinforcement, amount of reinforcement, and effort expended. This is the interpretation we have implicitly assumed so far. On the other hand, the molecular interpretation says that the parameters of the terminal links give a certain value to the stimuli that signal the terminal link (by classical conditioning) and that responses in the initial link are reinforced or punished by the presentation of these stimuli. For instance, in regard to Figure 10.5c, a molar theorist would say that a rat that turns left at the choice point prefers the *rewards* in terminal-link A to those in terminal-link B, but a *molecular* theorist would say that the rat preferred the *Skinner Box* in terminal-link A to that of terminal-link B, the two Skinner boxes having attained their values by association with the rewards. The advantage of the molecular viewpoint, as noted in the last chapter, is that it preserves association by contiguity. The stimuli that signal the terminal links (the alleys of Figure 10.5a, the Skinner boxes of Figure 10.5b, and the red and green keys of Figure 10.5c) serve as bridges between responses in the initial links and rewards in the terminal links. The molar theorist would argue that such bridges are unnecessary to explain relationships such as the matching of relative rates found by Autor between responding and reward.* The molar theorist would say also that it is up to the molecular theorist to show that the stimuli signalling the terminal links take on

---

*One conceivable advantage of the molecular theory is that it would permit analysis of a complex relation between responding in the initial link and reward in the terminal link into two simpler relations—one between reward and the terminal link stimuli, the other between the terminal link stimuli and responses in the initial link. But since the relation between responding in the initial link and reward in the terminal link is *already* very simple (as Autor found) breaking it into components would provide no real advantage.

some value from the rewards or punishments with which they are associated, and that they serve not only as signals giving information about rewards but as surrogate rewards themselves. We have seen in the previous chapter (when we discussed experiments such as Schuster's, Figure 8.4) that most of the evidence indicates that signals associated with rewards do *not* thereby become rewards themselves.

THE MATCHING LAW

In the choice experiments described so far, a simple relationship has been found between choice behavior and the rewards chosen: *the behavior ratio (the relative rate of responding) equals the relative rate of reinforcement.* This relationship is called the matching law. In this section we shall explore some extensions and limitations of this relationship. In so doing, it is helpful to describe the relationship in terms of simple algebraic equations. Equation (1) says that with two responses, P_A and P_B, and two rewards, Rf_A and Rf_B, the attainment of which depends on the responses, then:

$$\frac{P_A}{P_A + P_B} = \frac{Rf_A}{Rf_A + Rf_B} \tag{1}$$

where P stands for rate of responding and Rf, for rate of reinforcement. It can be shown* that this is equivalent to another expression:

$$\frac{P_A}{P_B} = \frac{Rf_A}{Rf_B} \tag{2}$$

Sometimes it is more convenient to write the matching law in the form of equation (2) than equation (1), especially when more than one parameter of reinforcement is involved. For instance, in certain situations and within certain limits, pigeons and rats are indifferent whether they get large deliveries of food infrequently or small deliveries frequently. That is, the amount of each food delivery and the rate at which deliveries come are interchangeable as long as the overall rate of reinforcement remains constant. The matching law would express this as follows:

$$\frac{P_A}{P_B} = \frac{Rf_A}{Rf_B} \cdot \frac{A_A}{A_B} \tag{3}$$

---

*Simply cross-multiply to get equation (2) from equation (1):

$$P_A (Rf_A + Rf_B) = Rf_A (P_A + P_B)$$
$$P_A Rf_A + P_A Rf_B = Rf_A P_A + Rf_A P_B$$
$$P_A Rf_B = Rf_A P_B$$
$$\frac{P_A}{P_B} = \frac{Rf_A}{Rf_B}$$

where Rf stands for rate of food deliveries and A stands for amount delivered. A reduction of Rf_A could be compensated for by an equivalent increase in A_A so that P_A/P_B would remain the same. Equation (3) was confirmed in an experiment by Allen Neuringer, which measured the rates (P_A and P_B) at which pigeons pecked two keys in the initial link of a concurrent-chain schedule when Rf and A were varied in the terminal links. It is obvious, though, that equation (3) could not be true at extreme values. Some commodities are almost valueless in very small amounts. A single healthy gulp of water is worth more than twice as much dribbling through a clogged-up water fountain. At the other extreme, a little bit of salt on each egg is worth something but large amounts are actually aversive. Obviously, equation (3) has limited applicability.

The form of the matching law in equation (3) is also used in accounting for bias, and we shall turn to this issue next.

Bias

We said before that a choice procedure is like a scale on which two commodities are to be weighed against each other. The behavior ratio is like the reading on the scale: it tells us by how much the value of one commodity exceeds the other for the organism being tested. With a physical scale, imperfections in construction or improper handling can cause the scale to go out of balance. For this reason one has to check a scale for balance before each use. A thorough check would consist of putting equal weights on the two sides, from zero to the maximum the scale will hold, and checking that the pointer reads "no difference" at all values. With concurrent choice procedures imbalances frequently occur. In a maze with equal rewards in both goal boxes, a rat may run to the left more than to the right. In a Skinner box, more responses may be made to one lever than another or more pecks made to one key than another, even though equal reinforcements are programmed on the manipulanda. There could be a number of reasons for such biases: the two alleys or keys may differ in color and the subject may prefer one color; the tension of the springs behind the levers or keys may be slightly different; the rewards themselves may differ slightly if they come from different sources; if rewards come from the same source, the subject may prefer to approach the source from one side rather than the other; the apparatus may be slightly tilted; the prior history of the subject may have differentially rewarded responses to one side; the subject may be built asymmetrically; despite COD procedures, asymmetric patterns of responding may develop; and so on ad infinitum. The experimenter may try to control for some of these imbalances but cannot control for all of them. Sometimes significant biases will creep into an experiment despite the best efforts of the experimenter. Do we have to throw out biased data or is there some way of accounting for bias? William Baum (the man with pigeons in his attic) has devised a way of accounting for bias in choice experiments. In order to understand Baum's technique we must do a little more mathematics. Suppose all those factors for which we have not accounted (color, tilt, spring tension, previous history, and so on) behave in the same way as the factors we do know about; that is, suppose they conform to a version of equation (3) that looks like this:

$$\frac{P_A}{P_B} = \frac{Rf_A}{Rf_B} \cdot \frac{A_A}{A_B} \cdot \frac{\text{Color preference A}}{\text{Color preference B}} \cdot \frac{\text{Tilt A}}{\text{Tilt B}}$$

$$\cdot \frac{\text{Ease of manipulating A}}{\text{Ease of manipulating B}} \cdot \frac{\text{etc. A}}{\text{etc. B}} \tag{4}$$

In other words:

$$\frac{P_A}{P_B} = \frac{\text{Factors accounted for A}}{\text{Factors accounted for B}} \cdot \frac{\text{Bias A}}{\text{Bias B}} \tag{5}$$

where bias is simply another word for "factors unaccounted for." Now if equation (5) is true, we should be able to do the following:

1. Make all the factors we can account for equal to each other for alternatives A and B. Now

$$\frac{\text{Factors accounted for A}}{\text{Factors accounted for B}} = 1.$$

2. Determine P_A/P_B. Now P_A/P_B should equal Bias A/Bias B. Step 2 tells us what the relative bias is, even though we do not know exactly what factors may be causing it.

3. Now vary the factors accounted for. For instance, make Factors accounted for A two times Factors accounted for B. Then, if Baum is correct in his assumptions, P_A/P_B should equal twice the relative bias (henceforth we shall drop the term, "relative"). If Factors accounted for A are made half Factors accounted for B then P_A/P_B should equal half the bias, and so on.

Step 3 is essentially a test of whether the matching law holds for unknown factors as well as for those that have been varied within experiments. Baum has found that many apparent deviations from matching may just be instances of bias. For instance, let us trace the three steps outlines above for a single pigeon that did not seem to match relative rate of response to relative rate of reinforcement with concurrent variable-interval schedules:

1. Set $Rf_A = Rf_B$. In this case the pigeon was exposed to concurrent variable-interval 1-minute schedules of food reinforcement for pecking at two keys.

2. Determine P_A/P_B. With the two schedules providing about equal rates of reinforcement, P_A/P_B equalled 0.65. This would seem to contradict the matching law, which says that P_A/P_B should equal 1.0. But, according to equation (5) bias equalled 0.65.

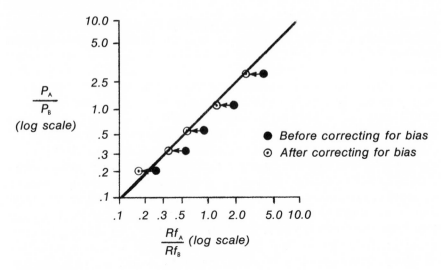

FIGURE 10.8
An example of bias correction in matching. The ratio of responses to one alternative in a two-choice procedure (log scale) is shown as a function of the ratio of reinforcement thereon (log scale). The filled-in circles show the data before correcting for bias. The open circles show what happens when each abscissa value is multiplied by the bias (0.65). The diagonal line shows perfect matching. Ratios and log scales were used in this figure so that the bias correction would move each point the same distance. If the data were plotted as in Figures 10.3 and 10.4 the corrected points (open circles) would still fall on the matching line, but the uncorrected points would form a bow-shaped curve instead of a straight line. [From Baum, W. On two types of deviation from the matching law: bias and undermatching. *J. Exp. Anal. Beh.,* 1974, 22, 231–242. Copyright 1974 by the Society for the Experimental Analysis of Behavior, Inc.]

3. Vary Rf_A and Rf_B. Figure 10.8 shows P_A/P_B, first plotted against Rf_A/Rf_B uncorrected for bias, then after each value of Rf_A/Rf is multiplied by the bias. Notice how much better matching is when bias is taken into account.*

Matching and Maximizing

When choice experiments are made up of concurrent variable-interval schedules, like Herrnstein's (which varied rate of reinforcement) and Catania's (which varied amount of reinforcement), or of concurrent-chain schedules with variable-interval schedules in the initial link, like Autor's, matching is a typical

---

*Baum's method differed slightly from that outlined above. Instead of estimating bias from one point alone (the point where $Rf_A = Rf_B$) Baum estimated the bias from all points. Taking the log of both sides of equation (5), $\log P_A/P_B = \log Rf_A/Rf_B + \log$ Bias A/Bias B. This is a linear relationship between $\log P_A/P_B$ and $\log Rf_A/Rf_B$ with an additive constant equal to the log of the bias. Baum found the best-fitting line when he plotted $\log P_A/P_B$ versus $\log Rf_A/Rf_B$ and estimated the bias as the difference between the best-fitting line and the line of equality between P_A/P_B and Rf_A/Rf_B.

result. When, however, the concurrent schedules are not variable-interval, but variable-ratio, the subjects' behavior is often described as *maximizing* rather than matching. Maximizing is choosing one alternative—the one with the best reward/cost ratio—exclusively. In a T-maze, for instance, which is equivalent to concurrent FR-1 schedules where response A is turn-left and response B is turn-right, rats will learn to choose the side with the bigger reward exclusively. In a Skinner box with two keys, one programmed with an FR-10 schedule and another programmed with an FR-20 schedule, pigeons will peck the first key exclusively. To gain an intuitive grasp of the difference between matching with interval schedules and maximizing with ratio schedules let us return to the farm girl and the chickens. Because chickens lay eggs at variable intervals, the farm girl can do little to speed up or slow down the egg-laying. Even though one chicken might be laying smaller eggs, she might as well collect those eggs too. Thus, she lifts both chickens at least occasionally, not showing exclusive preference for either one. In fact, she will pick up the chickens in proportion to the size of the eggs they lay or in proportion to their rate of laying eggs. This behavior is called *matching*. But egg-laying is a time-dependent process. Let us consider the farm girl at another of her chores, pumping water. Pumping water depends little on time, but a lot on work: the faster you pump, the more water you get. In this sense, pumping water is like a ratio rather than an interval schedule. Now suppose the girl is choosing between two pumps, an efficient one that produces 2 quarts of water for each press of the handle and an inefficient one that produces 1 quart of water for each press. Here the girl would work at the efficient pump exclusively. Why waste effort on the inefficient one? This behavior is called *maximizing*. By devoting herself exclusively to one pump the girl maximizes the return in water for her effort in pumping. Maximizing is typically found with concurrent ratio schedules when the alternatives and rewards are clearly delineated and the subject is exposed for sufficient time to the procedure.*

Does maximizing behavior contradict the matching law? As it turns out, far from contradicting the matching law, maximizing is the only behavior with concurrent ratio schedules that conforms to the matching law. To see how this is so let us return to the girl and the pumps. So far in this book we have avoided talking about organisms *trying* to do anything. What a subject does do in an experiment is much more important than what the experimenter

---

*When we described the experiment by Frankel and the author in which Harvard undergraduates chose between various gambling situations, we indicated that their choice was not exclusive, but distributed across the alternatives. Since gambling situations are equivalent to ratio schedules the reader may wonder why the subjects did not exclusively choose one alternative. The reason is that the choice was presented in a concurrent-chain procedure in which the concurrent initial link schedules were variable-interval schedules. The gambling situations (the ratio schedules) were presented only in the terminal links, which are never concurrent. Had the various gambling alternatives been concurrently available the subjects, with experience, would have chosen one exclusively.

thinks he or she is trying to do. But just for this once let us break our rule. Let us suppose the farm girl has read this book up to this point and, confronted with the two pumps, she is *trying* to obey the matching law. The matching law says that her relative rate of pumping must match the relative rate of water flow. Suppose she tries at first to match by pumping twice as much on the pump that produces 2 quarts per press as on the pump that produces 1 quart per press. Let's say that in a minute she pumps 40 times on the 2-quart pump and 20 times on the 1-quart pump. Her ratio of presses, P_A/P_B, equals 40/20, but her ratio of water from the two pumps, Rf_A/Rf_B, equals $40/20 \times 2/1$, or 80/20. This is clearly not matching. Since in a ratio schedule Rf_A depends on P_A, we can determine what she would have to do to match. For the 2-quart pump Rf_A (in quarts per minute) equals $2 \times P_A$ (in presses per minute). For the 1-quart pump Rf_B equals P_B. So to get matching the girl must find a P_A and P_B so that:

$$\frac{P_A}{P_B} = \frac{Rf_A}{Rf_B} = \frac{2P_A}{P_B}$$

Now, for almost all values of P_A and P_B, it is impossible for P_A/P_B to equal $2P_A/P_B$. The only time this relation holds is when P_A or P_B equals zero—which is to say, when one is chosen exclusively. Thus, in "trying" to conform to the matching law the girl is forced to maximize. Similarly, pigeons, rats, and other animals confronted with concurrent ratio schedules tend to prefer one alternative exclusively. In doing so, their behavior conforms to the matching law; they emit 100 percent of their responses on, and get 100 percent of their rewards from, one alternative. Any other distribution would not be matching. This is not to say, of course, that they are really trying to conform to the matching law, but merely that the matching law is the best way to describe their behavior—even with concurrent ratio schedules.

It is possible that instead of matching relative rate of response to relative rate of reinforcement, organisms could match relative rate of response to some other parameter of reinforcement such as amount of reinforcement per unit of work or to probability of reinforcement. To match probabilities, the farm girl would distribute her presses 2 to 1 on the two pumps. But probability matching is rarely observed.*

---

*In some gambling situations humans are found to match probabilities. These gambling situations usually take the following form: The subject sees two bulbs, one of which will light up when he presses a button. Before he presses he has to guess which one will light. The experimenter varies the relative frequency of one or the other light coming on. Although extensive data has been gathered about this sort of situation, its meaning is not yet clear; however, most of the evidence indicates that subjects who match probabilities (instead of matching rates via exclusive preference) do so because the instructions imply that they must be correct on *every* choice. The only way they can be correct on every choice is to sometimes choose the less probable alternative. In other words, subjects match probabilities only when they are instructed to do so. When subjects are gambling with their own money (rather than hypothetically or for points), they almost always maximize.

To summarize, subjects exposed to concurrent interval schedules tend to distribute their responses across all alternatives, matching the distribution of responses to the distribution of reinforcement over a given time period. Subjects exposed to concurrent ratio schedules tend to emit all of their responses on one alternative. Both sorts of behavior conform to the matching law.

In measuring choice, experimenters usually use concurrent interval schedules because relative rate of response provides a continuous measure of preference. You can find out not only which of two rewards the subject prefers but by how much it is preferred. Concurrent ratio schedules do not provide a continuous measure when choice is between two parameters of a single commodity. Figure 10.9 compares the two measures of choice to two balances, one stable and one unstable. Despite their instability, concurrent ratio schedules are frequently useful in measuring choice. At times we only want to know which of two rewards is preferred, not by how much. When one reward is only slightly preferred, concurrent interval schedules may be too insensitive to measure the slight preference. But concurrent ratio schedules will tend to magnify even the slightest preference. Because concurrent ratio schedules usually result in exclusive preference, care must be taken that when the alternatives are changed, the subject experiences both of the new alternatives. Often this is done by alternating the alternatives separately several times at the beginning of the experimental session before presenting them concurrently.

a   b

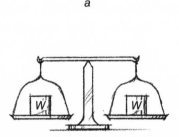   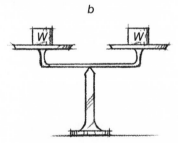

Concurrent interval schedules are like a scale that provides a stable measure of balance where degree of tilt measures degree of imbalance.   *Concurrent ratio schedules are like an unstable measure of balance where the slightest difference in weight causes complete tilt to one side.*

FIGURE 10.9
Concurrent-interval and ratio schedules compared to stable and unstable scales. (a) A concurrent-interval schedule is like a scale that provides a stable balance, where degree of tilt measures degree of imbalance. (b) A concurrent-ration schedule is like a scale that provides an unstable balance, where the slightest difference in weight causes a complete tilt to one side.

The Matching Law as an Assumption

We have seen that matching is a common finding in choice experiments. Now we shall argue that even when matching is not directly observed it may still be convenient to assume that matching underlies all choice. To understand why such an assumption may be convenient, consider again a topic first brought up in Chapter 2—the measurement of responses and stimuli. The matching law says that relative rate of responding equals relative rate of reinforcement—but what responding and what reinforcement?

How do we measure the amount of food reward in an experiment with pigeons? We might program a fixed-interval schedule so that a peck was reinforced every minute, but the pigeon might not peck exactly when the minute was up, so the actual rate of reinforcement would be slightly less than one per minute. Then, the food hopper might be presented for 3 seconds but the pigeon might only eat for 2.5 seconds. Then, of the food the pigeon eats, some of it might not be digested or not tasted. And, of that part digested, what part constitutes reinforcement? The rewards presented by the experimenter can never exactly equal the rewards actually obtained by the subject. On the response side similar problems occur. The pigeon may peck the key but not close the switch; or the pigeon may peck at the key but not hit the key; or the pigeon may start to peck and then be distracted in the middle and not complete the peck. The responses emitted by the subject can never exactly equal the responses measured by the experimenter. Figure 10.10 diagrams the events in the chain from rewards presented by the experimenter to responses measured by the experimenter. When matching is found in an experiment it is, necessarily, between boxes 1 and 4. (We are assuming that the experimenter has taken pains to make box 1 equal to box 2 and box 3 equal to box 4.) But is the matching law intended to apply between boxes 1 and 4 or only between boxes 2 and 3 of Figure 10.10?

As long as matching is found between boxes 1 and 4, as it has been in the experiments we have so far described, the question has no importance. If relative rate of reinforcement, as presented, matches relative rate of responding, as measured, then all the interior relations match as well.* When matching between the exterior boxes, 1 and 4, is *not* obtained, however, we do not know whether the non-matching relation actually found applies between boxes 1 and 2, 2 and 3, 3 and 4, or some combination of these. One strategy is simply to assume that matching applies between boxes 2 and 3 and look for the cause of non-matching between boxes 1 and 2 or 3 and 4. An advantage of this strategy is that it focuses attention on the exterior relations (between boxes 1 and 2

---

*It is possible that they do not match but compensate for each other. For instance, there may be a log relation between boxes 1 and 2 and an antilog relation between boxes 3 and 4. Such a coincidence seems unlikely, but its possibility should be borne in mind.

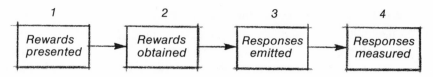

FIGURE 10.10
The chain of events from rewards presented to responses measured.

or boxes 3 and 4), where measurement and control can be modified, rather than on the interior relations (between boxes 2 and 3), where they cannot be measured or controlled.* When this assumption is made, matching becomes a deductive, rather than inductive law—not a principle derived from experimentation, but a premise with which experimental findings can be interpreted. For example, experimenters often find with concurrent interval schedules and pigeon subjects that relative rate of pecking does not quite match relative rate of reinforcement as programmed by the apparatus. However, when the grain deliveries actually received by the subject are used instead of those programmed, matching is more closely approximated. A still closer approximation is obtained when a photocell is placed in the grain hopper to measure the actual time the pigeon spends pecking at the grain. Presumably still closer matching would be obtained if the grains actually eaten were counted. The test of whether matching between boxes 2 and 3 is a good or bad assumption is whether focusing on the relations between boxes 1 and 2, and 3 and 4 yields useful information.

Although many psychologists studying choice do assume, before they begin, that the matching law is true, this assumption is by no means necessary. Another strategy with respect to Figure 10.10 is to assume that our experimental measurement and control are precise enough that the two outer relations (1–2 and 3–4) are either controllable or separately determinable to the extent that they can be accounted for and the quantities in boxes 2 and 3 determined. If we assume, for instance, that the two outer relations are matching relations

---

*A similar problem occurs in psychophysics. The relationship between stimuli presented and subjects' reports of those stimuli may be thought of as composed of a relationship between stimuli presented and stimuli experienced (corresponding to boxes 1 and 2), between stimuli experienced and responses generated (boxes 2 and 3), and between responses generated and reports of those responses (boxes 3 and 4). Relationships between the outer terms are said to be those of outer psychophysics. Relationships between the two inner terms are said to be those of inner psychophysics. The German psychologist G. E. Müller suggested a strategy similar to the one proposed above. He assumed matching between sensations experienced and responses generated (inner psychophysics). He called this isomorphism. It is identical in concept to the isomorphism between the brain and the mind proposed later by the Gestalt psychologists (see Chapter 1). G. E. Müller believed that psychophysics could not progress as a science unless isomorphism was assumed.

(either naturally or through experimental control) then when matching between boxes 1 and 4 is not found it must be because a relationship other than matching applies between boxes 2 and 3. Such other relationships have been proposed from time to time by various investigators. For instance, E. Fantino, one of the most active researchers in choice behavior, suggests that matching (between boxes 2 and 3) only applies in a very limited range of situations, even within the already limited experimental situation of a pigeon pecking keys in a Skinner box. Fantino suggests that the actual relations between boxes 2 and 3 are much more complicated than matching and may vary from one situation to another.

Time Matching

Let us return again to the girl in the barn lifting up the two chickens. Suppose that the chickens are located at two points in the barn, point A and point B. When the girl changes over from lifting chicken A to lifting chicken B she stops lifting chicken A, walks from point A to point B, and starts lifting chicken B. Consider her moving from point A to point B a changeover from A to B and from point B to point A, a changeover from B to A. Let us further suppose that she spends all of her time either at point A or point B or walking between them (which she does rather quickly). Now we can ignore completely her picking up the chickens and just concentrate on how much time she spends at point A and point B. Analogously, with pigeons pecking keys on concurrent variable-interval schedules of reinforcement, we can time how long a pigeon spends at key A and at key B. Figure 10.11a shows hypothetical patterns of pecks on key A, pecks on key B, and reinforcements for pecks on the two keys. The unshaded areas show pecks and reinforcements for key A; the shaded areas show pecks and reinforcements for key B. The moment that a pigeon pecks a key it is considered to be spending time at that key no matter what it actually does, whether it pecks the key fast or slowly or even if it does not peck again. The timer that is recording time spent at key A ignores all pecks on key A that follow other pecks on key A. The timer just keeps running. When the pigeon pecks key B after pecking key A (a changeover) the key A timer stops and the key B timer starts. The pigeon is considered to be spending all of its time either at key A or at key B. The key A timer runs during the unshaded part of Figure 10.11a and its cumulative reading over a session is called T_A. The key B timer runs during the shaded part and its cumulative reading is called T_B. The sum of T_A and T_B is the duration of the experimental session, T_T. When *time* at key A or key B is measured in this way and when pecks are counted as well, the pigeon is usually found to match both relative time and relative number of pecks on the two keys to relative rate of reinforcement. Thus:

$$\frac{T_A}{T_B} = \frac{P_A}{P_B} = \frac{Rf_A}{Rf_B} \tag{6}$$

In this equation T_A and T_B are, respectively, the sum of all the white and grey areas in a session, P_A and P_B are the numbers of pecks at key A and key B, and Rf_A and Rf_B are the numbers of reinforcements obtained by pecking key A and key B. Sometimes P_A, P_B, Rf_A, and Rf_B are considered to be *rates* over the whole session rather than numbers of pecks and reinforcements. In equation (6) it does not matter. To obtain the rate of pecks or reinforcements over the session from number of pecks or reinforcements, simply divide by the time of the session, T_T. Since T_T appears in both the numerator and denominator of equation (6), it cancels out:

$$\frac{\dfrac{P_A}{T_T}}{\dfrac{P_B}{T_T}} = \frac{P_A}{P_B}$$

The finding that time spent responding, as well as number of responses, matches relative rate of reinforcement (equation 6) has several important implications. Before we consider them, however, let us discuss some procedural variations that permit better estimation of times than the one discussed above. One such variation is called a Findley concurrent schedule, after J. D. Findley, who first used it. In Findley's concurrent schedule as used with pigeons, the changeover is accomplished, not by moving from point A to point B, but by making another response altogether, which changes the color of a single key (called the instrumental key) from one corresponding to schedule A to one corresponding to schedule B. With a Findley concurrent schedule, pecking the instrumental key serves as both response A and response B. The schedule in effect is determined by pecking another key, called the changeover key, which serves as a switch, switching from A to B with one peck and back to A with the next. Returning again to the girl and the chickens, we can construct a Findley concurrent schedule for her. Imagine that she got tired of walking from chicken A to chicken B and she devised a sort of lazy Susan with chicken A and chicken B on either side; by turning the lazy Susan she could bring first chicken A and then chicken B within her reach. An observer could (1) count her lifting of the chickens or (2) simply measure the amount of time the lazy Susan is in one position or the other. Changing the position of the lazy Susan corresponds to pecking the changeover key. Lifting chicken A or chicken B corresponds to pecking the instrumental key.

The great advantage of the Findley concurrent schedule over the one diagrammed in Figure 10.11a is that it separates the changeover response from the instrumental response itself. In Figure 10.11a the first response within each shaded or unshaded area serves two functions—it effects the changeover from one key to the other, and it is itself an instrumental response on the new key. With the Findley concurrent schedule, changeover responses are made

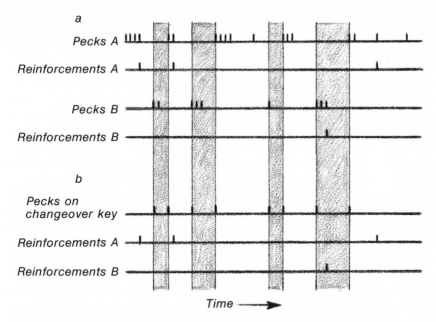

FIGURE 10.11
Part a: Pecks and reinforcements during normal concurrent variable-interval schedules with pigeons. The unshaded areas can be considered time spent pecking at key A, the shaded areas, time spent pecking at key B. Part b: Brownstein and Pliskoff's experiment, using a Findley concurrent schedule with no instrumental response required. The pattern of time spent on key A and key B and the pattern of reinforcements are the same as shown in the normal concurrent schedule above.

only on the changeover key. These responses cannot themselves be reinforced. Instrumental responses are made on the instrumental key when it is red or green, and these responses are reinforced according to schedule A or schedule B. The separation of changeover responses from instrumental responses allows various different instrumental responses to be compared with each other, and even allows instrumental responses to be eliminated. For instance, A. J. Brownstein and S. S. Pliskoff used a Findley concurrent schedule to study preference for various sources of reinforcement without instrumental responding. Pecks on the changeover key in their experiment changed the color of the ambient light but there was no other key to peck. The experiment is illustrated in Figure 10.11b. Reinforcement A and reinforcement B were delivered freely to the pigeon. To get deliveries of reinforcement A, the pigeon had only to peck the changeover key to produce the color of ambient light corresponding to the unshaded area of the figure. Reinforcement B was delivered after another peck on the key. Otherwise, no instrumental response was required. Returning to the farm girl, who is now equipped with a lazy Susan, we find that Brownstein and Pliskoff's procedure would be equivalent to having the eggs themselves on the lazy Susan, without the chickens. Thus, the girl would have to make the changeover response (turning the lazy Susan) to get the eggs, but not the instrumental response (picking up the chickens). In Brownstein and Pliskoff's experiment P_A and P_B were not required, so, of course, they could not be measured; but T_A and T_B could be measured. Matching between T_A/T_B and Rf_A/Rf_B (*time matching*) was found. As with response matching, time matching is a very common finding in choice experiments. It is found with normal concurrent procedures, with Findley concurrent procedures where instrumental responding is required, with Findley concurrent procedures where instrumental responding is not required (Brownstein and Pliskoff), and with Findley concurrent procedures where instrumental responding is required for one schedule and no responding is required for the other. It was found in an experiment by W. Baum and the author in which the pigeon's changeover response consisted, not of pecking at a key, but of crossing from one side of the chamber to another. All a pigeon had to do to get reinforcement A was to be standing on side A. (The report of this study is reprinted at the end of the chapter.)

Time-measuring procedures such as the Findley concurrent schedule are ideal for determining the hierarchies required by Premack's theory of reinforcement. Let's say that we wanted to determine which was more valuable to a rat, running or drinking milk. We could count steps and licks, but since these two responses have different topographies, we cannot say that one step is worth one lick. But if we measure how much *time* the rat spends running and how much *time* it spends drinking milk, the two temporal measures can easily be compared.

Now that we have described time-matching procedures, let us consider some implications of time-matching. In Chapters 2 and 3 we said that much evidence indicates that when responding occurs it tends to occur at a constant rate, or tempo, characteristic of the particular response. Thus, organisms do not respond faster or slower, but mix responding-at-a-constant-speed and not-responding in various proportions, producing a resultant speed that seems to vary. For instance, hungry and satiated rats take different times to run down an alley and hence can be said to have different speeds of running; closer observation reveals that both hungry and satiated rats run at the same speed in the alley *when they run*, but satiated rats stop more frequently in the alley. Equation (6) tends to confirm this observation. Since, according to equation (6):

$$\frac{T_A}{T_B} = \frac{P_A}{P_B}$$

it follows (cross-multiplying and dividing again) that:

$$\frac{P_A}{T_A} = \frac{P_B}{T_B} \tag{7}$$

P_A/T_A is the rate of pecking on key A *when the pigeon is at key A*. P_B/T_B is the rate of pecking on key B *when the pigeon is at key B*. Equation (7) says that when the pigeons are pecking key A, they peck at the same rate as they do when they peck key B. The difference between pecking key A and key B is due entirely to the difference in the time the pigeon spends pecking key A and key B, and not at all to how fast pecking takes place once it has begun. Furthermore, since, according to equation (6):

$$\frac{T_A}{T_B} = \frac{Rf_A}{Rf_B}$$

it follows (cross-multiplying and dividing again) that:

$$\frac{Rf_A}{T_A} = \frac{Rf_B}{T_B} \tag{8}$$

Rf_A/T_A is the rate of reinforcement of pecking on key A *when the pigeon is at key A*. Rf_B/T_B is the rate of reinforcement of pecking on key B *when the pigeon is at key B*. Equation (8) says that the pigeons distribute their time pecking key A and key B so that the rate of reinforcement while they are pecking at each key is the same.

Suppose, for instance, schedule A is a variable-interval 1-minute schedule and schedule B is a variable-interval 2-minute schedule. Given a reasonable rate of responding on each key, $Rf_A = 1$ per minute, $Rf_B = 0.5$ per minute, then $Rf_A/Rf_B = 2$. It appears as if the rate of reinforcement is twice as high for A as for B. But this is true only if:

$$Rf_A = \frac{\text{Number of reinforcements of pecks A}}{\text{Session time } (T_T)}$$

$$Rf_B = \frac{\text{Number of reinforcements of pecks B}}{\text{Session time } (T_T)}$$

That is, it it true if Rf_A and Rf_B are calculated over the entire session. In a 60-minute session, Rf_A would equal 60/60 and Rf_B would equal 30/60. We might calculate Rf_A and Rf_B differently. Let us call the new rates, rf_A and rf_B. These stand for local rates of reinforcement:

$$rf_A = \frac{\text{Number of reinforcements of pecks A}}{\text{Time spent pecking key A } (T_A)}$$

and
$$rf_B = \frac{\text{Number of reinforcements of pecks B}}{\text{Time spent pecking key B } (T_B)}$$

Time spent pecking keys A and B is now under the control of the subject. If the subject's behavior conforms to equation (6), then in a 60-minute session, T_A would equal 40 seconds and T_B would equal 20 seconds. Thus $rf_A = 60/40$

$= 3/2$ and $rf_B = 30/20 = 3/2.$* The exact same reasoning applies to p_A and p_B, local rates of pecking. Just as $rf_A = rf_B$, so $p_A = p_B$.

To summarize what the time-matching results tell us about choice behavior, the organism faced with concurrent variable-interval schedules divides its time in proportion to the overall rates of reinforcement Rf_A and Rf_B, so that $T_A/T_B = Rf_A/Rf_B$. Because time is proportional to reinforcement, local rates of reinforcement (rf_A and rf_B) are equal. Furthermore, the organism responds at a constant rate during T_A and T_B, so local rates of responding (p_A and p_B) are also equal.

This observation gives rise to a somewhat unspecific model, which may nevertheless help the reader to tie together some of the theories in this book. Let us assume that rate of reinforcement, in the absence of other significant variables, determines the value of reinforcement. The local rate of reinforcement rf_A equals the ratio of reinforcements to time spent with reinforcer A. The value of remaining with this reinforcer increases with each reward obtained there and decreases with time. If after a while rf_A falls below any other obtainable local rate, say rf_B, the organism leaves A and goes to B. With concurrent variable-interval schedules, the more time the organism spends at any one response, the lower the value of that response will become with respect to other available responses. The organism is thus seen to be in constant flux, moving from one source of reinforcement to another as the value of that source decreases and the value of other sources increase relatively—much as the lion goes from one waterhole or hunting area to another as their relative values shift.

In choice situations such as those we have been describing in this chapter, switching between alternatives A, B, C, and so on, is free. When constraints are put on behavior, such as a contingency, for example, that "So much time must be spent at A before so much time doing B will be made available," Premack's theory of reinforcement shows how behavior during constraint can be predicted from unconstrained behavior with the same alternatives (see Chapter 6).

Staddon and Simmelhag view behavior with periodic reinforcement as a form of choice, with the animal shifting from interim to terminal responding as the value of the latter increases relative to that of the former. When the pigeons in Staddon and Simmelhag's experiment switched from interim to terminal responding, they were, in essence, doing the same thing as Herrnstein's or Catania's pigeons, which switched from pecking key A to key B—they were switching from a lower-valued activity to a higher-valued activity.

---

*The reader may have forgotten why the pigeon collects all 60 reinforcements from A and all 30 from B even though it spends only part of the session on each key. Remember that concurrent variable-interval schedules run concurrently. Even while the pigeon is pecking key A the timer governing reinforcement B is running. (Similarly, the chicken the farm girl is *not* picking up is still laying eggs—she collects the eggs when she returns to that chicken.)

Secondary reinforcers and discriminative stimuli may be viewed, according to this model, as lines of demarcation dividing situations of different value, enabling the animal to switch from one activity to another at a time and place that maximize overall value of reinforcement.

CHOICE BETWEEN
RESPONDING AND NOT RESPONDING

In a sense, all behavior is choice behavior. We choose between getting up and staying in bed, between going to school and working at a job, between going to the movies and staying home, and so on. Similarly, a rat in an alley can be seen as choosing between running down the alley or staying in the start box, and a pigeon in a Skinner box can be seen as choosing between pecking the key and not pecking it. This much is fairly obvious. The question is whether the behavior of choosing between doing A and not doing A can be analyzed in the same way as the behavior of choosing between alternative A and alternative B.

Let us examine some obvious differences between the two types of choice. First, the choice between A and B may be symmetrical, but the choice between A and not-A is almost never symmetrical. That is, when responses A and B are pecking two keys, or turning down two alleys in a maze, or gambling on one roulette table or another, or buying a green hat or a red hat, the act of choosing A differs from the act of choosing B only in location. But choosing between A and not-A usually involves different acts. A pigeon pecks on key A and key B with nearly the same sort of movement, but a pigeon pecking and not pecking is doing two vastly different things.

A second important difference between choosing between alternative A versus B and between A versus not-A is that the former is rarely exhaustive of all behavior, but the latter always is. The difference is shown in Figure 10.12. When a pigeon is choosing between pecking key A and key B it can also do other things (preening, flapping its wings, and so on) not included in either A or B. But when a pigeon is choosing between pecking a key or not pecking a key it can do nothing else because everything it does other than pecking the key is already included in *not* pecking the key. That is, preening, flapping its wings, and other possible activities are part of the response of not pecking the key once not pecking is defined as a response.*

Given these differences, it would not be surprising if choice between alternatives A and B proved wholly incommensurate with choice between A and

---

*Of course the illustrations given are extremes of a continuum. A and B could be asymetrical choices without being exhaustive. The argument as applied in the following pages to asymmetrical exhaustive choices could also be applied to asymmetrical nonexhaustive choices or symmetrical exhaustive choices. Such applications are fairly straightforward and will not be further pursued.

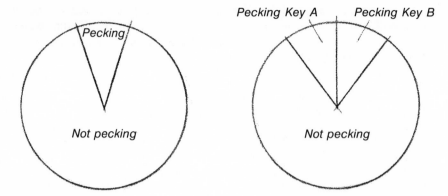

FIGURE 10.12
Division of a pigeon's time into "pecking" and "not pecking" with (left) a single key and (right) two keys.

not-A. Yet, as we shall see, it is possible to view the two types of choice from the same perspective, that of the matching law. Let us start with equation (1) for choice between A and B.

$$\frac{P_A}{P_A + P_B} = \frac{Rf_A}{Rf_A + Rf_B} \tag{1}$$

Now let us substitute not-A for B and see what happens:

$$\frac{P_A}{P_A + P_{not-A}} = \frac{Rf_A}{Rf_A + Rf_{not-A}}$$

Here P_{not-A} stands for all responding other than pecking the key. Note that $P_A + P_{not-A}$ exhausts all the behavior of which the pigeon is capable. That is, the term comprises the complete circle of Figure 10.12. This would hold true regardless of the values on the other side of the equation—so we can substitute for $P_A + P_{not-A}$ the constant k. Now the equation reads:

$$\frac{P_A}{k} = \frac{Rf_A}{Rf_A + Rf_{not-A}}$$

$$P_A = \frac{kRf_A}{Rf_A + Rf_{not-A}}$$

The value Rf_{not-A} stands for all reinforcement other than that obtained from pecking key A. Herrnstein, who first formulated the equation, calls this quantity Rf_0, and we shall henceforth use this symbol. Thus:

$$P_A = \frac{kRf_A}{Rf_A + Rf_0} \tag{9}$$

Equation (9) expresses responding in terms of overall rate of a discrete response (P_A). We can also express responding in terms of the time spent responding (T_A). To convert P_A to T_A, we simply make the constant k equal total session time $(T_T = T_A + T_{not-A})$. Otherwise the equation has the same form as equation (9):

$$T_A = \frac{T_T \cdot Rf_A}{Rf_A + Rf_0}$$

Going back one step,

$$\frac{T_A}{T_T} = \frac{Rf_A}{Rf_A + Rf_0} \tag{10}$$

Equation (10) says that the proportion of the session spent responding equals the proportion of total reinforcements obtained by responding. The quantity T_A/T_T equals *perseveration* of the response. Thus, equation (10) says that perseveration of a response is directly proportional to the rate of reinforcement of that response (Rf_A) and inversely proportional to the total reinforcement in the situation $(Rf_A + Rf_0)$. Similarly, equation (9) predicts that the rate of responding will be directly proportional to the rate of reinforcement of that response (Rf_A) and inversely proportional to the total amount of reinforcement in the situation $(Rf_A + Rf_0)$. According to equations (9) and (10) we should be able to increase responding in two ways:

   a. by increasing Rf_A
   b. by decreasing Rf_0

and we should be able to decrease responding in two ways:

   a. by decreasing Rf_A
   b. by increasing Rf_0

It is easy to vary Rf_A. Figure 5.18 shows how pecking of pigeons increases in rate as Rf_A increases. For each of the pigeons in Figure 5.18 it is possible to establish values of k and Rf_0 so that their rate of pecking (P_A) could be predicted from equation (9), given the rate of reinforcement (Rf_A) provided by the variable-interval schedule.

It is not so easy to vary Rf_0. Ordinarily Rf_0 is the reinforcement for responses other than pecking—for instance, the intrinsic reinforcement of the interim responses of wing-flapping, preening, exploring, and so on. It is difficult to vary these responses directly. However, it is possible that reinforcement for other behavior (Rf_0) would be greater if more other behavior were permitted. For example, more other behavior might be emitted if the Skinner box were bigger. Hence, one way to increase Rf_0 might be to increase the size of the Skinner box. Since according to equations (9) and (10), responding

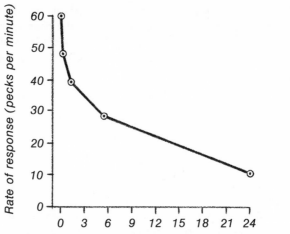

FIGURE 10.13
Rate of pecking a key with a variable-interval 3-minute
schedule (VI-3') of food reinforcement (each reinforcement
consisted of 4 seconds of access to the food hopper) as a
function of the augmentation of R_0 by food provided
independent of pecking the key. Average of eight pigeons.
[From Rachlin, H. C. and Baum, W. M. Effects of alternative
reinforcement: Does the source matter? *J. Exp. Anal. Beh.,*
1972, *18,* 231–241. Copyright 1972 by the Society for the
Experimental Analysis of Behavior, Inc.]

varies inversely with Rf_0, pigeons should peck more slowly with bigger boxes
(and rats should run more slowly in wider alleys). When Skinner boxes have
been made larger, pigeons actually do peck the key more slowly. To the author's knowledge, the experiment with alley size has not been tried.

Another way to vary Rf_0 is simply to augment it by providing free food,
water, or some other commodity. This technique was tried by the author and
William Baum. In addition to the food reinforcements for pecking a key on a
variable-interval schedule, we gave the pigeons extra food deliveries. When we
varied rate of delivery and amount per delivery, we found that the more free
food the pigeons obtained, the more slowly they pecked, as predicted by equations (9) and (10). Figure 10.13 shows the average function relating the amount
by which Rf_0 was augmented and the rate at which the pigeons pecked the
key.* This result makes sense from an economic viewpoint. As an animal gets
more and more food, each additional delivery comes to be worth less (its mar-

---

*When food (free or earned) was made available the response key was darkened (considered
unavailable). When the response key was lit, food was unavailable. Only the time during which
the response key was lit was counted in calculating rate of response.

ginal utility decreases). Thus, to the rich man a $100 gift is less valuable than it is to the poor man. Similarly, to the pigeon already receiving free food, the additional food obtained by pecking the key is worth less than it would be to a pigeon not receiving free food. The more free food, the less a given amount of food "earned" by pecking would be worth and therefore the more slowly the pigeon would peck the key to obtain it.

Thus, responding versus not responding may be considered a choice just like responding A versus responding B. Just as the organism is seen to be switching between A and B as their local values fluctuate, it can be seen to be switching between a state where it is responding and a state where it is not responding as the local values of these two activities fluctuate. Whether it makes sense to view all behavior as choice will depend on how meaningful and consistent the constants of equations (9) and (10) prove to be. If, for a given organism, they vary erratically from one situation to another, then the theory upon which they are based will not be useful. But if they vary consistently with such factors as amount of free reward available, deprivation, difficulty of the response, stimulus properties, other concurrent responses available, and so on, they will provide a useful way to gauge the influence of these variables on behavior.

APPLICATION IN
BEHAVIOR THERAPY: COMMITMENT

One way in which we control our own behavior is by commitment. We sign contracts, join Christmas Clubs, put money in trust funds, and so on. For instance, one way to get yourself to study is to deposit a fairly large sum of money with a friend, asking him to check at random intervals during the evening to see if you are studying, and if he finds you are not, to send the money to a political party with views exactly contrary to yours. This form of self-control involves commitment, a choice whereby one limits choices in the future. The man who signs a contract will have fewer alternatives after he signs it than he did before. Commitment is a choice that guides future behavior and limits future choice.

But why should anyone act in the present to limit his own choice in the future? The answer is that one's values in the present are different from what they will be in the future, and only by agreeing to a commitment can one insure that he will act in accordance with his present values when the future arrives. In the studying example, let's say that the commitment is made the morning before the student intends to study (point A in Figure 10.14). At that time the student rates studying high in his hierarchy of values—certainly higher than going to the movies that night. If you ask the student in the morning, "What do you intend to do tonight, study or go to the movies?" he freely says he will study. But then evening comes. If he has made no commitment (point B in Figure 10.14) going to the movies becomes more and more attractive relative

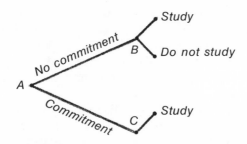

FIGURE 10.14
Sequence of choices involved in commitment
to study.

to studying until finally he goes to the movies instead of studying. The reason for this shift in values is that the reward for studying is delayed, perhaps several weeks, whereas the reward for going to the movies is rapidly approaching. As the delay of the movie reward approaches zero its value grows rapidly and soon exceeds whatever value studying may have. If at point A the student truly values studying higher he will choose to make a commitment since that is the only way (by our hypothesis) he can study (assuming that giving his money to an opposing political party is too aversive to be a feasible alternative to studying).*

Complicated as these shifts in value might seem, they are predicted easily by the matching law. Since the rewards for studying and not studying are difficult to quantify, let us just make them up. Let us suppose, arbitrarily, that the reward for studying is 30 days in the future (the time to the final exam) but that when the reward comes it will be large, perhaps equivalent to one thousand dollars. (This might include part of the cost of an extra year of college plus part of whatever is lost from an extra year of work. It does not, of course, in-

---

*The use of the drug "antabuse" to treat alcoholics may be another example of commitment. We mentioned previously that alcoholics are often given drugs that will make them sick when they drink. These drugs may achieve their effect through classical conditioning—the illness (US) causes the alcohol to taste bad. But antabuse is such a powerful drug and makes the person who drinks alcohol while under its influence so sick that conditioning in the usual sense hardly has a chance to work. If an alcoholic drank more than once or twice while under antabuse a doctor would take him off the drug immediately for fear that his patient would die. The mechanism by which antabuse works is probably more like the commitment strategy of the student than like classical conditioning. The alcoholic takes the drug in the morning when, either because he has a bad hangover or because morning is an unusual time to have a drink, the value of drinking is low relative to the value of alternative rewards. Later that night when drinking increases in value, the antabuse, still in effect, prevents choice and the alcoholic cannot drink. Antabuse illness is thus, like cirrhosis of the liver, a serious aversive consequence of drinking, except that antabuse illness is more clearly defined. For many people cirrhosis of the liver or other aversive consequences are sufficient to prevent excessive drinking. For others, the natural physiological and social aversive consequences are not sufficient. These people become alcoholics. We shall speculate later about how the two kinds of people differ—why some seem to have self-control and others do not.

clude the intrinsic value of studying nor the intrinsic enjoyment of mastering the material.) The movie, say, is worth what it costs, $1.50. The matching law says that the ratio of the value of studying to the value of going to the movies equals the ratio of the rates of reward. Expressing rate of reward in dollars per hour, at point A (12 hours before the movie):

$$\frac{\text{Value of studying}}{\text{Value of movies}} = \frac{\text{Rate of reward for studying}}{\text{Rate of reward for movies}}$$

$$= \frac{\dfrac{\text{Amount of reward for studying}}{\text{Time to reward for studying}}}{\dfrac{\text{Amount of reward for movies}}{\text{Time to reward for movies}}}$$

$$= \frac{\dfrac{\$1,000}{30 \times 24 \text{ (hrs)}}}{\dfrac{\$1.50}{12 \text{ (hrs)}}} = \frac{1.39}{0.125} = 11.11$$

The value of studying is more than eleven times the value of the movies. At point B, $11\frac{1}{2}$ hours later (and $11\frac{1}{2}$ hours closer to each reward),

$$\frac{\text{Value of studying}}{\text{Value of movies}} = \frac{\dfrac{\$1,000}{(30 \times 24 - 11.5) \text{ (hrs)}}}{\dfrac{\$1.50}{(12 - 11.5) \text{ (hrs)}}} = \frac{1.41}{3} = 0.47$$

Now the value of studying is less than half of the value of the movies. Thus, it is not surprising that at point A the student prefers to study, and at point B he prefers to go to the movies. The value of studying remains about the same, 1.40 dollars per hour. But as the movie draws closer, the denominator by which rate of reward (of the movie) is calculated approaches zero and the value of going to the movies grows very, very large. Given this set of values and contingencies, commitment is virtually the only way to guarantee studying.

To show that the choices at A and B do not require ego strength, socialization, or other complex emotional or mental development, Leonard Green and the author designed an experiment with pigeons to duplicate the essential features of the commitment strategy of the student. The procedure is diagrammed in Figure 10.15. At point B, the pigeons were faced with two keys. If they pecked the red key they would receive a small reward immediately (2 seconds of access to the food hopper). If they pecked the green key, they would receive a larger reward (4 seconds of access to the hopper) but delayed by 4 seconds from the peck. At point A the pigeons could make a commitment. Pecking the left key caused a 10-second blackout and then the choice at point B was offered. Pecking the right key also caused a 10-second blackout but then only the larger,

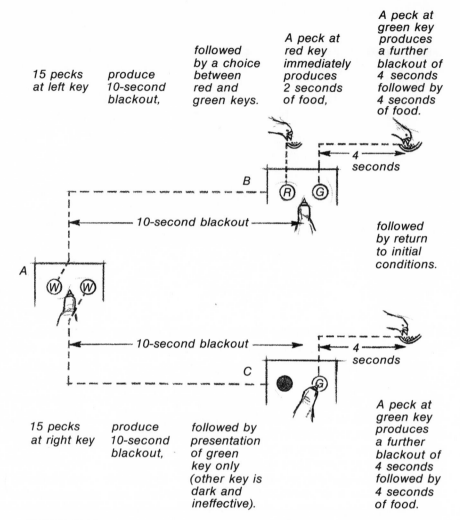

FIGURE 10.15

Experiment of Rachlin and Green, following diagram of previous figure, in which pigeons could choose at (A) between (B) where they could subsequently choose between a small, immediate versus large, delayed reward and (C) where they were committed to the large, delayed reward.

delayed reward was available, at point C. Thus, by pecking the right key the pigeons could commit themselves to obtaining the larger reward.* As with the student studying we can calculate the relative values of the larger and smaller rewards.

---

*Concurrent fixed-ratio schedules were used at A because we wanted the pigeons to exhibit all-or-none behavior typical of such schedules rather than graded choice. We wanted to know which key, left or right, the pigeons preferred rather than by how much. But to insure exposure to both alternatives, several forced trials alternating on the left and right keys preceded the experiment proper. This resulted in less than 100 percent preference for either side at point A during the experiment.

At point A:

$$\frac{\text{Value of larger reward}}{\text{Value of smaller reward}} = \frac{\dfrac{\text{Amount of larger reward}}{\text{Time to larger reward}}}{\dfrac{\text{Amount of smaller reward}}{\text{Time to smaller reward}}}$$

$$= \frac{\dfrac{4}{10 + 4}}{\dfrac{2}{10}} = 1.43$$

The larger reward is worth almost one and a half as much as the smaller. At point B (10 seconds later):

$$\frac{\text{Value of larger reward}}{\text{Value of smaller reward}} = \frac{\dfrac{4}{4}}{\dfrac{2}{0}} = 0$$

The smaller reward is now infinitely preferable to the larger reward.

The behavior of the pigeons in this experiment conformed to the predictions of the equations. At point A the pigeons pecked about 65 percent of the time, on the average, on the key that led to commitment. Thus, most of the time the pigeons ended up at point C and received the larger reward. However, when the pigeons were at point B, they all chose the smaller, more immediate reward 100 percent of the time.

To further test the theory we varied the blackout period between points A and B. The matching equation predicts that as the blackout gets shorter the pigeons at point A should choose the noncommitment side more frequently (the ratio at A becomes more and more like that at B) and eventually receive the smaller reward, and as the blackout gets longer the pigeons should choose the commitment side more frequently and eventually receive the larger reward. Figure 10.16 shows the average function. All of the pigeons tended to choose commitment at point A more frequently as the blackout was increased in duration.

The matching law also predicts what the blackout duration should be when the pigeons are indifferent between commitment and noncommitment. Let us call this duration X, and set the values of the larger and smaller rewards equal:

$$\text{Value of larger reward} = \text{Value of smaller reward}$$

$$\frac{4}{X + 4} = \frac{2}{X}$$

$$X = 4 \text{ seconds}$$

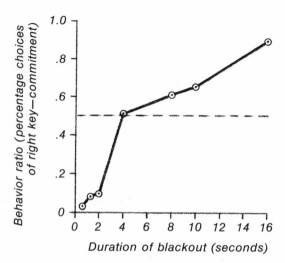

FIGURE 10.16
Behavior ratio of choices of the right key, leading to
commitment, as a function of the duration of the
blackout in Rachlin–Green experiment. The dotted line
at 0.5 on the ordinate represents indifference between
the two white keys. The data shown represent the
median values of five pigeons.

Note that the average curve crosses the line of indifference (behavior ratio
equals 0.5) when the blackout is about 4 seconds. Thus, the pigeons' behavior
conformed to all of the predictions made by the matching law.

What are the essential differences, then, between the behavior of the pigeons
in our experiment and the behavior of the hypothetical student trying to get
himself to study? We can perhaps isolate a few:

1. The time scale. To make sense out of the student's problem we had to
   use a time scale extending over 30 days, whereas with the pigeons even
   the delayed reinforcers occurred within a few seconds of the behavior
   they reinforced. One difference between humans and pigeons, then, may
   be the wider time scale over which events can control human behavior.*
2. The persistence of behavior. For humans a commitment strategy such as
   we have described can serve as a crutch, which is needed only until the
   correlation between behavior and distant rewards has been learned. In
   fact when children were exposed to an experiment similar in structure to
   the one with pigeons just described, the childrens' behavior changed as
   a result of the experiment. At first at point B they chose the immediate

---

*This difference in time scale may also describe the difference between the alcoholic and the
person who controls his drinking.

reward. After experience with the commitment strategy they came to choose the longer, more delayed reward even at point B. In terms of the matching equation, the time denominator over which an appropriate rate of reinforcement is calculated changed for these children from a narrow one, like the pigeon's, encompassing only events within a few seconds of the response, to a wider one that encompassed overall reinforcement over a trial or a session. Another difference between humans and pigeons, then, is the greater plasticity of human behavior. We seem to be somewhat freer of our biological heritage than animals, and more likely to change our patterns of behavior as the environment changes.

3. The nature of the rewards. With humans the primary rewards that control behavior are somewhere in the far past and future. We rely on distant associations between primary rewards and secondary rewards to make effective the secondary rewards we do use. But with pigeons the secondary rewards are almost always associated with primary reward within the experimental situation itself.

4. The complexity of the response. The pigeons in our experiment were exposed to a ready-made commitment strategy. Their responses were simple—peck one key or the other. Humans, on the other hand, often have to invent commitment strategies as well as to use them. The classical example of invention of a commitment strategy is Odysseus' tying himself to the mast of his ship and making his sailors plug their ears with wax so that they might sail past the rocks on which the Sirens lived without being lured by the Sirens' song to sail their ship onto the rocks.

Despite all these differences, there is a similarity of structure between the behavior of the student trying to study and the pigeons in the Skinner box pecking a key for food. They both conform, albeit in different ways, to the diagram of Figure 10.14. In fact, referring back to Figure 1.1, the reader might begin to see that all the behaviors illustrated there are subject to observation, measurement, and control in similar ways. It is such similarities that give purpose to the experimental study of behavior.

BIBLIOGRAPHY

Choice experiments with mazes are described in R. S. Woodworth and H. Schlosberg's book *Experimental psychology* (New York: Holt, Rinehart & Winston, 1954). An early argument that all behavior is essentially choice behavior was made by E. C. Tolman in an article titled "The determiners of behavior at a choice point" [*Psychological Review, 45,* 1–41, 1938].

A review of many studies of concurrent behavior can be found in the chapter by A. C. Catania in Honig's book (see bibliography, Chapter 5).

Fantino's arguments and findings on whether the matching law should be an assumption or a disprovable empirical finding appear in several of his articles in recent issues of the *Journal of The Experimental Analysis of Behavior*. An excellent recent article by D. J. Navarick and E. Fantino (listed below) argues that the assumption behind many choice experiments is that choice is transitive—that is, that if A is preferred to B and B to C then A will be preferred to C. Navarick and Fantino show that in many cases choice is intransitive. They show that intransitivities are more likely when the rewards differ along more than one dimension. This article raises interesting questions with regard to much of the material in this book. If choice between rewards is intransitive in a given case, the rewards concerned cannot be rank-ordered on a scale of value, and the procedures and techniques described here would have to be applied only with great care. There is some question whether they could be applied at all.

Following is a list of articles referred to in this chapter:

Autor, S. M. The strength of conditioned reinforcers as a function of frequency and probability of reinforcement. In *Conditioned reinforcement*, ed. D. P. Hendry. Homewood, Ill.: Dorsey Press, 1969.

Baum, W. M. Choice in free ranging wild pigeons. *Science*, 1974, *185*, 78–79.

Baum, W. M., and Rachlin, H. C. Choice as time allocation. *Journal of The Experimental Analysis of Behavior*, 1969, *12*, 861–874.

Brownstein, A. J., and Pliskoff, S. S. Some effects of relative reinforcement rate and changeover delay in response-independent concurrent schedules of reinforcement. *Journal of The Experimental Analysis of Behavior*, 1968, *11*, 683–688.

Findley, J. D. Preference and switching under concurrent scheduling. *Journal of The Experimental Analysis of Behavior*, 1958, *1*, 123–144.

Herrnstein, R. J. Relative and absolute strength of response as a function of frequency of reinforcement. *Journal of The Experimental Analysis of Behavior*, 1961, *4*, 267–272.

Herrnstein, R. J. On the law of effect. *Journal of The Experimental Analysis of Behavior*, 1970, *13*, 243–266.

Navarick, D. J., and Fantino, E. Stochastic transivity and undimensional behavior theories. *Psychological Review*, 1974, *81*, 426–442.

Neuringer, A. J. Effects of reinforcement magnitude on choice and rate of responding. *Journal of The Experimental Analysis of Behavior*, 1967, *10*, 417–424.

Rachlin, H. C., and Baum, W. Effects of alternative reinforcement: Does the source matter? *Journal of The Experimental Analysis of Behavior*, 1972, *18*, 231–241.

Rachlin, H., and Frankel, M. Choice, rate of response, and rate of gambling. *Journal of Experimental Psychology*, 1969, *80*, 444–449.

Rachlin, H. C., and Green, L. Commitment, choice, and self-control. *Journal of The Experimental Analysis of Behavior*, 1972, *17*, 15–22.

Schroeder, S. R., and Holland, J. G. Reinforcement of eye-movement with concurrent schedules. *Journal of The Experimental Analysis of Behavior*, 1969, *12*, 897–903.

Note that almost all of the cited studies appeared in *The Journal of The Experimental Analysis of Behavior*. The reason for this is that this chapter emphasizes concurrent schedules of reinforcement, an operant procedure, and, *The Journal of The Experimental Analysis of Behavior* is the primary outlet for operant research. But the orientation of the chapter could have been towards maze studies. Although the maze is less flexible than the concurrent-schedule procedure, we have seen that the devices have parallels; so discussions of the two would probably take parallel forms.

We reprint here the article by William Baum and the author, "Choice as time allocation." This article reports an experiment with pigeons in which the reinforced responses were standing on one side or the other of the experimental chamber (symmetrical exhaustive choice). We plotted the pigeons' distribution of time against the distribution of food on the two sides. The point of interest in this experiment is that each pigeon showed some preference for one side or the other (a bias). In accounting for the bias we proposed the general form of matching—of time to reinforcement value—described in the text.

Supplemental Reading for Chapter 10

CHOICE AS TIME ALLOCATION

William M. Baum and Howard C. Rachlin

When pigeons' standing on one or the other side of a chamber was reinforced on two concurrent variable-interval schedules, the ratio of time spent on the left to time spent on the right was directly proportional to the ratio of reinforcements produced by standing on the left to reinforcements produced by standing on the right. The constant of proportionality was less than unity for all pigeons, indicating a bias toward the right side of the chamber. The biased matching relation obtained here is comparable to the matching relation obtained with concurrent reinforcement of key pecks. The present results, together with related research, suggest that the ratio of time spent in two activities equals the ratio of the "values" of the activities. The value of an activity is the product of several parameters, such as rate and amount of reinforcement, contingent on that activity.

Psychology has inherited from reflexology the notion that behavior can be viewed as a mosaic of responses. Skinner (1938) thought of the rat's lever press as a type of reflex. Accordingly, his basic measure of behavior was a count of the number of lever presses made during an experimental session. He computed the frequency of lever presses by dividing the number of presses by the duration of the session. In order to make this computation, he had to treat each lever press as an instantaneous event, as a point in time, having no duration. This assumption implies that two responses could immediately follow one another, with no time intervening. Since each response requires a certain amount of time, however, the minimum interresponse time is greater than zero. When the actual interresponse times approach the minimum interresponse time, the computation of response rate should include a correction for response duration.

Since Skinner's work, experiments on operant behavior have usually treated responses as instantaneous. Indeed, response keys and levers, in conjunction with pulse-formers (that produce short pulses of constant duration) are so commonly used today that available apparatus tends to enforce response counting as the means of measuring behavior.

If we admit that behavior has duration, an alternative scheme of measurement becomes available. Behavior that can be counted can also be timed. Response duration, or time spent responding, can be just as basic a measure of behavior as response frequency.

In some situations the two measures are equivalent. If a pigeon's pecks at a key, for example, were approximately constant in duration, then the key-peck

This research was supported by grants from the National Science Foundation and the National Institutes of Health to Harvard University. We are grateful to Lincoln Laboratory of the Massachusetts Institute of Technology for making available the Lincoln Reckoner, on which most of the data analysis was done. Reprints may be obtained from William M. Baum, Department of Psychology, Harvard University, William James Hall, 33 Kirkland Street, Cambridge, Massachusetts 02138.

From *Journal of the Experimental Analysis of Behavior*, Vol. 12, No. 6, pp. 861–874. Copyright 1969 by the Society for the Experimental Analysis of Behavior. Reprinted by permission.

time would equal that constant duration multiplied by the number of key pecks. If a rat's holding of a lever is reinforced, on the other hand, then lever-holding time might often vary independent of the number of depressions of the lever.

It is usual to select the measure of behavior on the basis of the conditions of reinforcement. If we reinforce at a certain point of time, say, at the moment when the lever has been depressed 5 mm, then it seems natural to count the number of such momentary occurrences as could have produced reinforcement. We might, on the other hand, reinforce while the animal is engaged in some activity, at no particular moment, as when we reinforce being in a certain location and continue reinforcement as long as the animal stays in that location. When such continuous action is reinforced, we tend to use continuous measures of behavior, that is, to measure response time, rather than response number.

Although experimental procedures often carry clear implications for choosing measures of behavior, many experimental situations defy such ready decisions. Bullock (1960), for example, trained pigeons to peck a response key that was not connected to a pulse former, but instead produced reinforcement whenever the key was operated at the same time that reinforcement (on a variable-interval schedule) was due. The pigeons eventually came to hold the key, rather than peck it. Key holding led to a decrease in response rate. Bullock resolved the incompatibility between his measure of behavior and his method of recording behavior by changing his recording, rather than his measure. He found that a pulse former eliminated key holding and restored the response rate to a high level. He might, however, have substituted a timer for his response counter.

Ambiguities of measurement have commonly arisen in the study of responding on fixed-ratio schedule of reinforcement. The assumption that a brief response is instantaneous applies only when the interresponse times are substantially longer in duration than the responses themselves. The "internal coherence" of the bursts of responding typical of performance on fixed-ratio schedules (Mechner, 1958a and b) has led to the suggestion that these bursts themselves be considered as individual units, or "higher-order" operants (Millenson, 1967, pp. 170–172).

A reasonable alternative to this conception of fixed-ratio performance remains to be explored. Fixed-ratio runs are emitted at an almost constant rate (Ferster and Skinner, 1957). The number of responses in a fixed-ratio run determines the duration of the run. As with Bullock's solution to the problem of key holding, an alternative to re-defining the unit of behavior is to change to a different measure of behavior: the time spent responding. When we consider variable-ratio schedules, measuring response time has a decided advantage over counting bursts of responding as units. Performance on variable-ratio schedules includes as high and as constant a response rate as performance on fixed-ratio schedules. The bursts of responding, however, contain a variable number of responses. While it would be difficult to accept response runs of widely different lengths as equivalent units of behavior, it would be easy to think of these variable runs as variable times spent responding.

The notion that a rate of responding defines a continuous activity can be applied to behavior other than performance on ratio schedules: Gilbert (1958) has suggested that local response rate on any type of schedule can be separated from periods of pausing or non-responding. Some experimental evidence supports his contention that long-term response rates are built up from combinations of pauses and periods of responding at a constant rate. Catania (1961) characterized performance on a variable-interval schedule as divided into response "runs" and pauses in responding. He found that time per run, responses per run, and response rate within a run all remained constant in performance on a 3-min VI schedule paired with a variety of other schedules in both multiple and concurrent comparisons. The constancy of the response runs remained even when behavioral contrast resulted in changes in the long-term response rate on the schedule. Catania (1962) found that responding on fixed-interval schedules retains the characteristic pattern of accelerating response rate (the FI "scallop") when paired with a concurrent variable-interval schedule. Since responding on the fixed-interval schedules occurred in bursts, the pattern of acceleration resulted from a gradual decrease in the periods between bursts, rather than a smooth increase in local rate of responding. Such results are not peculiar to concurrent schedules. Blough (1963) showed that in a variety of single-key situations, the majority of interresponse times fall in the range of 0.3 to 0.5 sec. This basic response rate (two to three responses per second) was insensitive to variations in schedule, rate of reinforcement, and extinction. Blough found that variation in long-term response rate, as exhibited in generalization gradients or extinction curves, results from changes in the long interresponse times, that is, the pauses between bursts of responses at the basic rate.

These findings of Catania and Blough suggest that even such brief responses as key pecks tend to group into periods of action that alternate with periods of inaction. They imply that the quantitative relations we have found for numbers of responses can be reasonably reinterpreted in terms of times spent responding.

Herrnstein (1961) found that when a pigeon's pecks on two response keys are reinforced on two variable-interval schedules, the pigeon distributes its pecks between the keys as follows:

$$\frac{NP_1}{NP_1 + NP_2} = \frac{Rf_1}{Rf_1 + Rf_2} \qquad (1)$$

where NP_1 and NP_2 are the numbers of pecks on Key 1 and Key 2 during the course of a session, and Rf_1 and Rf_2 are the rates of reinforcement delivered by Key 1 and Key 2. Equation (1) states that the bird matches the relative number of emissions of a response to the relative rate of reinforcement for the response.

The relative number of pecks in Equation (1) can be rewritten as follows:

$$\frac{NP_1}{NP_1 + NP_2} = \frac{P_1 T_1}{P_1 T_1 + P_2 T_2} \qquad (2)$$

Where P_1 and P_2 are the rates of responding on Key 1 and Key 2, and T_1 and T_2 are the times spent responding on Key 1 and Key 2. Herrnstein (1961) reasoned that since both keys are always simultaneously available in the usual concurrent situation, the time base for calculating the two rates of responding should be the same for the two keys. He assumed, in other words, that in Equation (2) T_1 equals T_2. He therefore expressed the matching law as:

$$\frac{P_1}{P_1 + P_2} = \frac{Rf_1}{Rf_1 + Rf_2} \qquad (3)$$

Equation (3) assumes that the matching law is generated by two simultaneously ongoing response rates. Now, an alternative assumption is to suppose that the pigeon divides its time between the two keys, pecking on one and then the other for a while, but always pecking at the same rate at either key. One may assume, in other words, that in Equation (2) P_1 equals P_2, but T_1 may be different from T_2.

The results of Catania (1961, 1962) and Blough (1963) described above lend support to such an assumption, since they found that the response rate while pigeons are responding is invariant. With a constant response rate, time spent responding determines number of responses.

According to this line of reasoning, the matching law would predict relative time spent pecking at the two keys:

$$\frac{T_1}{T_1 + T_2} = \frac{Rf_1}{Rf_1 + Rf_2} \qquad (4)$$

Although Equations (3) and (4) both predict the observation of Equation (1), they are independent of each other in the sense that either equation may apply in a given situation while the other does not. Distinguishing between the two experimentally is far from simple. In the standard two-key concurrent situation, there is no easy way to measure the time spent pecking at each key. There is no demarcation of time to indicate when the bird is pecking one key, when it is pecking the other, and when it is pecking neither, but engaged in some other activity altogether. One may argue that the time spent pecking a key is just the collective duration of the pecks, but a key peck undoubtedly requires more time than the time during which the bird's beak is actually in contact with the key. The lack of a clear beginning and end to each peck makes its duration difficult to measure. Assuming, however, that the time required for a key peck is approximately constant, as Catania's and Blough's results suggest, then the number of pecks would be an index of the time spent pecking.

A technique used by Findley (1958) allows a more direct approach to measuring the time spent pecking each key in a concurrent schedule. The two choice alternatives are represented by two different colors of a single key. The key color changes when the pigeon pecks a second key, called a changeover key. Instead of changing from one alternative to the other by moving from side to side, as in the standard two-key concurrent situation, the pigeon changes from one alternative to another in Findley's procedure by pecking the changeover key. Findley found that pigeons behaved, with respect to the two key colors, in the same way as they behaved with respect to two separate keys. Catania (1963a) demonstrated that pigeons in a concurrent situation like Findley's match the relative number of pecks on the two keys to the relative rate of reinforcement delivered by the two VI schedules, just as they do in a standard two-key concurrent situation. Equation (1) holds in both situations. Catania (1966) also showed that the pigeons match the relative time spent in the two components to the relative rate of reinforcement. The time spent in a component is not the same as the time spent pecking in the component, but if the pigeons spent the same *proportion* of time responding in both components, then their performance would match relative time to relative rate of reinforcement. Catania's results, therefore, can be expressed either in terms of Equation (3) or in terms of Equation (4).

Brownstein and Pliskoff (1968) showed that in a concurrent situation like Findley's and Catania's, the matching of relative time spent in a component to relative rate of reinforcement occurs in the absence of pecking for reinforcement. In their experiment, the birds' pecks on the changeover key changed the color of a stimulus light, but the reinforcers in each component were delivered independent of the bird's behavior, at the rate determined by the VI schedule. This result presents some difficulty to the interpretation of the matching law as governing relative number of responses. It is difficult to find an appropriate measure of number of responses in Brownstein and Pliskoff's experiment. As noted earlier, it is possible to consider the number of pecks on a key as an index of the time spent pecking the key. In a like manner, it is possible to consider the time spent in a component in Brownstein and Pliskoff's experiment as an index of the number of emissions of some unspecified response. There would be little empirical basis for such an assumption, however.

The experiment described in this paper resembles that of Brownstein and Pliskoff in that it makes use of a non-specific response. It differs from their experiment in the same way that a standard two-key experiment differs from Findley's: the bird changes from one component to another not by pecking a key, but by moving from one position to another. Since the experiment demonstrates the matching relation in terms of time spent in two locations, it supports the interpretation of the matching law as a law of time allocation.

METHOD

Subjects

Six male White Carneaux pigeons were maintained at 80 to 85% of their free-feeding body weights. All had been trained previously with grain reinforcement to peck a key. Four birds, 488, 489, 490, and 496, had a brief period of such training. The other two, 334 and 360, had been exposed to a variety of procedures.

Apparatus

The experimental chamber was 9 in. high, 8.75 in. deep, and 19.75 in. long (229 mm by 222 mm by 502 mm). Each end wall had a 2-in. by 2-in. (51-mm by 51-mm) opening near the floor, behind which a standard solenoid-operated food magazine was mounted. The floor of the chamber consisted of two separate grids, each pivoted on one side and suspended on the other side by a spring. The tension

of each spring was sufficient to operate a microswitch when no weight was on that side. When a bird stood on either side, the floor dropped about 5 mm to release the microswitch on that side: Figure 1 is a diagram of the chamber.

Three lights were mounted above the transparent Plexiglas ceiling of the chamber. A red light was mounted above the left side, a green light above the right side, and a white light above the center.

The chamber was enclosed within a sound-attenuating box and white noise was constantly present. Events in the chamber were controlled and recorded by automatic scheduling equipment in the next room.

Procedure

The birds were placed in the experimental chamber every day for a session that terminated when the sum of the reinforcements delivered by the two magazines equalled 40. A reinforcement on either side lasted 3 sec. During reinforcement, the three lights above the chamber were out; the only light on in the chamber was that illuminating the grain hopper.

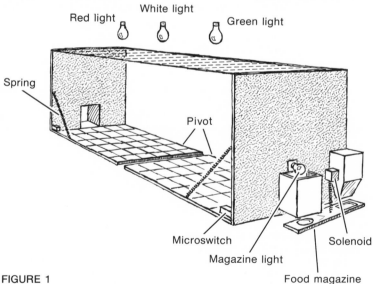

FIGURE 1
The experimental chamber.

At other times one, and only one, of the three lights above the chamber was on.

While a bird stood on the left, the red light alone stayed on. While a bird stood on the right, the green light alone stayed on. If a bird stood in the center, holding both floors down, the white light alone stayed on. No reinforcers were delivered while the white light was on. While the red or green lights were on, reinforcers were delivered only on the side that was lit, at variable intervals, according to the distribution developed by Fleshler and Hoffman (1962). Separate variable-interval timers controlled reinforcements on the two sides. A changeover delay (COD) of 4.25 sec operated whenever a bird changed sides. During the COD, only the white light was on.

These final conditions were gradually approximated over a period of two weeks. At first, the rates of reinforcement on the two sides were about 200 per hour and the COD was absent. The rates of reinforcement were gradually decreased to 30 per hour on each side while the COD was gradually lengthened to 4.25 sec.

The variable-interval timer for each side ran continuously, except from the moment a reinforcement set up for that side to the end of that reinforcement. The timer for one side did not stop during reinforcement on the other side. Reinforcements were scheduled for both magazines no matter where the birds were standing. For a reinforcer to be actually delivered by either of the magazines, however, the bird had to be standing on the side corresponding to that magazine. Thus, in order to produce available reinforcements from both magazines, a bird would have to spend some time standing on each side of the chamber. The two principal data, time on the left and right, were cumulated on two running-time meters. These timers did not run during the COD, during reinforcement, or while the bird held down both floors; that is, they ran only when the red or green light was on.

The variable interval (VI) schedules

studied averaged 8, 4, 2, 1, and 0.5 min. Table 1 shows the situations studied. The first five situations in Table 1 were presented in a repeating cycle, conditions changing every seven days. The relative rate of reinforcement on the left went step by step from one extreme to the other and then back again. Eight weeks were needed to complete a cycle. Three of the birds were always at a position in the cycle opposite to the position of the other three. When one group was at one extreme, the other group was at the other extreme. The birds were on this cycle for nine months. Only the data for the last 13 weeks were analyzed. For half the birds, the last 13 situations occurred in the order: a, b, c, d, e, d, c, b, a, b, c, d, e; for the other birds, the situations occurred in the reverse order.

The last six pairs of schedules in Table 1 were studied after the first five pairs. The birds were exposed to each of these six conditions for two weeks, three birds in the order from f to k (in Table 1), and three in the order: i, j, k, f, g, h. In the transition from the first five conditions to the last six, three birds went from a to i, while the other three went from e to f.

The data were summarized as follows. The times and the number of changeovers were first computed as medians of the last three days of exposure to a set of VI schedules. Since each bird received conditions f through k in Table 1 only once, the three-day medians were the final form

Table 1 Summary of Experimental Conditions

	Schedule on Left (in minutes)	Schedule on Right	Scheduled Relative Rate of Reinforcement on Left
a	VI 8	VI 2	0.20
b	VI 4	VI 2	0.33
c	VI 2	VI 2	0.50
d	VI 1	VI 2	0.67
e	VI 0.5	VI 2	0.80
f	VI 8	VI 0.5	0.06
g	VI 1	VI 8	0.89
h	VI 4	VI 0.5	0.11
i	VI 0.5	VI 8	0.94
j	VI 8	VI 1	0.11
k	VI 0.5	VI 4	0.89

of the data for these conditions for each bird. The first five conditions (a through e in Table 1), however, appeared more than once: a and e were presented twice to each bird, and b, c, and d were presented three times to each bird. The three-day medians for each condition were averaged to produce a single data set for each condition for each bird. To obtain average data, the measures were averaged across birds at this stage in the analysis. All further computations, for the average and the individual birds, were made with the data sets so produced. The independent variables, number of reinforcements received on the left and number received on the right, were computed similarly, except that the original summaries were seven-day averages, instead of three-day medians. It was possible to use seven-day samples because the distribution of reinforcements between the two sides was unaffected by changes in the distribution of time between the two sides. The only interactions occurred during the first few days of the two-week exposures to the last six conditions in Table 1, when the birds were changing from an extreme preference for one side to an extreme preference for the opposite side.

Some symbols appearing commonly in the rest of the paper are defined as follows:

T_1 is time spent on the left side
T_2 is time spent on the right side
T_s is session duration (not including time during which either food magazine was operated)
N_1 is number of reinforcements delivered on the left side during a session
N_2 is number of reinforcements delivered on the right side during a session

RESULTS

Figures 2 and 3 show the principal result of the experiment. For each bird (Fig. 2) and the average (Fig. 3), the logarithm of the ratio of time spent on the left to time spent on the right is plotted against the logarithm of the ratio of the number of reinforcements received on the left to the number of reinforcements received on the right. In such coordinates, direct proportionality between the two ratios will appear as a straight line with a slope of one. If the ratios match, as they would according to the matching law, then the line of slope one would pass through the point (0,0). This line, the locus of perfect matching, appears in each graph in Fig. 2 and 3 as a light line. The heavier lines were fitted to the data points by the method of least squares. The equation of the fitted line is given in each graph.

The slopes of the fitted lines in Fig. 2 vary both above and below one. Their average is 1.00. The slope of the line fitted to the average data (Fig. 3) is close to one. Within the limits of individual variation, therefore, we can conclude that the ratio of times is directly proportional to the ratio of reinforcements.

For all the birds and the average, the line fitted to the data has a negative intercept. Though the line in Fig. 3 may be parallel to the matching line, it falls below it. The negative intercept means that the birds spent relatively less time on the left than the matching law would predict. Since a constant displacement like that in the logarithmic coordinates of Fig. 3 signifies a constant proportion in linear coordinates, the birds showed a constant proportional preference for the right side over the left. The result can be expressed in the following equation:

$$\frac{T_1}{T_2} = k \frac{N_1}{N_2} \qquad (5)$$

where k is a constant less than one. If k were unity, Equation (5) would be identical to the matching law. Since k is not unity, we may say that a biased matching has been found, with the bias expressed by the departure of k from unity. For the average data, k equals 0.60.

Since the birds generally waited for the end of the COD before changing over again, it is reasonable to suppose that the collective time spent during CODs was

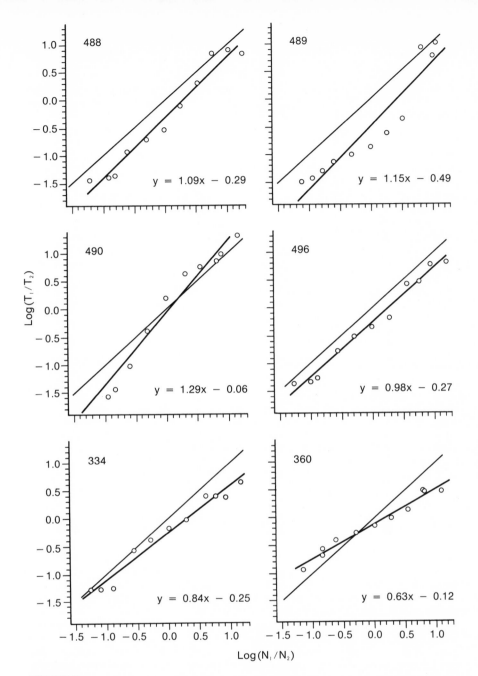

FIGURE 2
Individual data: the logarithm of the ratio of time spent on the left to time spent on the right plotted as a function of the logarithm of the ratio of number of reinforcements received on the left to number of reinforcements received on the right during an experimental session. Each of the six plots shows data for one of the six birds. The heavy lines were fitted to the data points by the method of least squares. The equation of each regression line appears beside it. The light lines have a slope of one and pass through the origin; they represent the performance of perfect matching.

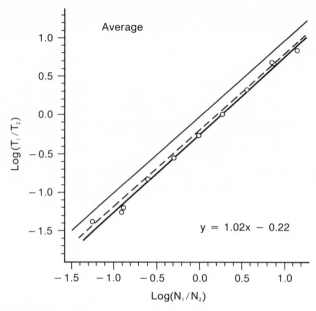

FIGURE 3

Averaged data: the logarithm of the ratio of time spent on the left to time spent on the right plotted as a function of the logarithm of the ratio of number of reinforcements received on the left to number of reinforcements received on the right during an experimental session. The heavy solid line was fitted to the data points by the method of least squares. Its equation appears alongside it. The light solid line has a slope of one and passes through the origin; it represents the performance of perfect matching. The light broken line is the performance predicted on the basis of the data in Fig. 5; a full explanation appears in the text.

equal on the two sides. Adding a constant to two variables will necessarily decrease the variance of their ratio. If the measures T_1 and T_2 in Fig. 2 and 3 had included the collective COD time, the slopes of the lines fitted to the data points would have been less than the slopes of the lines fitted to the data points in Fig. 2 and 3. The slope of the line fitted to the average data with the COD time included was 0.42. Equation (5) applies, therefore, only when the time spent in the COD is excluded from T_1 and T_2.

Catania (1963a) and Rachlin and Baum (1969) demonstrated that in a two-key concurrent situation, the rate of pecking on either key depends only on the relative rate or amount of reinforcement delivered by the key, and is independent of the rate of pecking on the other key. Although Equation (5) specifies the *relative* time spent on either side of our apparatus, it provides no information about the analog to the *absolute* rate of key pecking, the time spent on a side as a proportion of the total session time.

The session time in this experiment is

defined as the sum of the times during which the red, green, or white lights were on, that is, the sum of T_1, T_2, the COD time, and the time spent straddling the two floors. Since the latter was minimal after initial training, the session time closely approximated the sum of T_1, T_2, and the COD time.

Because the COD was fairly long in duration and because the pigeons crossed frequently from one side to the other, the COD time was a significant fraction of the session time (from 16% to 70%, depending on the subject and the conditions of the experiment). It would be possible, then, for the fraction T_1/T_2 to vary as in Fig. 2 and 3, while T_1, for instance, remained constant, all the variation being accounted for by variations in T_2 and the COD time. Despite the relative lawfulness of T_1/T_2 as a function of the reinforcements produced on the two sides of the chamber, there is no *a priori* necessity that T_1 or T_2 individually vary lawfully with reinforcements.

Figures 4 and 5 show plots for individual birds (Fig. 4) and the averaged data (Fig. 5), of the proportion of the total session duration spent on each side as a function of the relative number of reinforcements for that side. The filled circles represent the proportion of time on the left, T_1/T_s, as a function of the relative number of reinforcements on the left, $N_1/(N_1 + N_2)$. The open circles represent the proportion of time on the right, T_2/T_s, as a function of the relative number of reinforcements on the right, $N_2/(N_1 + N_2)$. The two lines in each graph of Fig. 4 and 5, one for time spent on the left (filled circles) and one for time spent on the right (open circles), were fitted by the method of least squares. The equation of each regression line appears alongside its graphical representation.

The relationships depicted in Fig. 4 and 5 appear approximately linear but slightly concave upward. The data from Bird 489, for time spent on the left, constitute an exception to the general rule. The intercepts of the regression lines for

all subjects were small in absolute value. Some were negative, others were positive. The proportion of the session spent on either side appears, therefore, to be approximately proportional to the relative number of reinforcements delivered on that side. The relationships approximated in Fig. 4 and 5 are:

$$\frac{T_1}{T_s} = c_1 \frac{N_1}{N_1 + N_2} \qquad (6)$$

for the left side, and

$$\frac{T_2}{T_s} = c_2 \frac{N_2}{N_1 + N_2} \qquad (7)$$

for the right side, where c_1 and c_2 are constants of proportionality.

For every bird, the data for time spent on the right produced a steeper regression line than the data for the time spent on the left. In terms of Equations (6) and (7), for every bird, c_2 was greater than c_1. This tendency to spend a greater proportion of time on the right than on the left for the same relative rate of reinforcement illustrates again the position preference that appeared in Fig. 2 and 3.

Equations (6) and (7) may be thought of as more basic than Equation (5), since Equation 5 can be derived from Equations (6) and (7). The ratio of Equation (6) to Equation (7) reduces to:

$$\frac{T_1}{T_2} = \frac{c_1}{c_2} \cdot \frac{N_1}{N_2} \qquad (8)$$

Comparison of Equation (8) with Equation (5) indicates that c_1/c_2 should equal k. Because the slopes in Fig. 3 were not all equal to unity, but varied around it, and because of the nonlinearity of some of the individual functions in Fig. 4, only a very rough correspondence exists between the individual constants, k and c_1/c_2. For the average curves, however, where the slope was equal to unity (Fig. 3) the values of k and c_1/c_2 were 0.60 and 0.66. The closeness of these two values is illustrated by the broken line in Fig. 3, which shows the predicted biased matching based on Equation (8) with c_1/c_2 taken from Fig. 5.

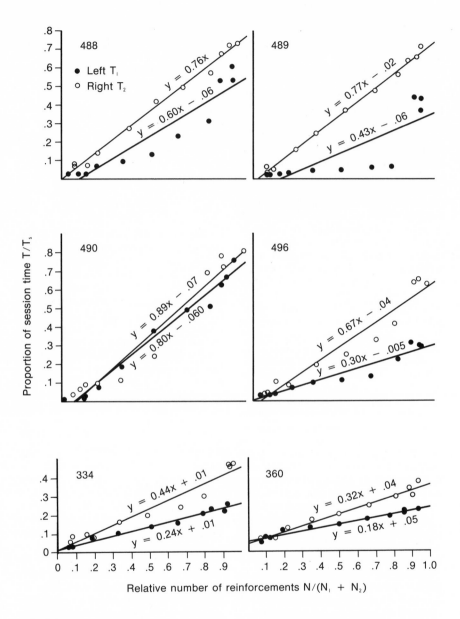

FIGURE 4
Individual data: the proportion of the session time spent on the left (filled circles) and on the right (open circles) plotted as functions of the proportion of reinforcements received on the left (filled circles) and on the right (open circles). The lines were fitted to the data points (open or filled circles separately) by the method of least squares. The equation of each regression line appears alongside it.

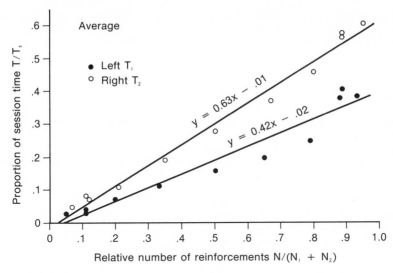

FIGURE 5
Averaged data: the proportion of the session time spent on the left (filled circles) and on the right (open circles) plotted as functions of the proportion of reinforcements received on the left (filled circles) and on the right (open circles). The lines were fitted to the data points (open or filled circles separately) by the method of least squares. The equation of each regression line appears beside it.

Herrnstein (1961) and Brownstein and Pliskoff (1968) found that as the difference in frequency of reinforcement between the two concurrent components increased, the frequency of changeover between components decreased. In the present experiment, four birds, 488, 489, 490, and 496, showed a similar relationship. Bird 334, however, showed no systematic variation in rate of changeover, and Bird 360 changed over most frequently when the rates of reinforcement were most different. All birds showed a tendency to change over more often when they preferred the left side than when they preferred the right side. It may be that the persistent bias toward the right (Fig. 2, 3, 4, and 5), which generally weakened preferences for the left when they occurred, also made these preferences relatively unstable.

DISCUSSION

The present experiment, together with that of Brownstein and Pliskoff (1968), showed that in the absence of reinforcement for any specific response, the same type of law governs the division of an organism's time among the activities in which it engages as governs the distribution of responses among choice alternatives (Herrnstein, 1961; Reynolds, 1963; Catania,-1963a). Catania (1966) found that even when behavior is defined and measured in terms of discrete responses (key pecks), the time allocation matching law still applies. As noted in the introduction, the results of several experiments (Blough, 1963; Catania, 1961, 1962; Mechner, 1958a and b) suggest that series of repetitions of a discrete act (a key peck or a lever press) can be thought of as periods of engaging in a continuous activity (key pecking or lever pressing). Thus, even though behavior in a given situation may be defined and measured as if it consisted of discrete acts, it is still possible to derive continuous measures of behavior in that situation. Laws of time allocation, therefore, are likely to be more widely applicable to behavior than laws of response distribution.

If we accept the idea that the matching law governs time allocation among activities, what can we say about experiments that have demonstrated matching of relative number of pecks to variables other than relative rate of reinforcement? Catania (1963*b*) found that pigeons match relative pecks to relative amount of reinforcement. Chung and Herrnstein (1967) obtained matching of relative pecks to relative immediacy of reinforcement (reciprocal of delay of reinforcement). We can express the three matching laws in terms of time spent pecking at two keys (T_1 and T_2) as follows:

$$\frac{T_1}{T_2} = \frac{Rf_1}{Rf_2}$$

$$\frac{T_1}{T_2} = \frac{A_1}{A_2}$$

$$\frac{T_1}{T_2} = \frac{I_1}{I_2}$$

where Rf_1 and Rf_2 are the rates of reinforcement, A_1 and A_2 are the amounts of reinforcement, and I_1 and I_2 are the immediacies of reinforcement, produced by pecking at Key 1 and Key 2, respectively.

We are now led to ask how these three independent variables might combine to determine choice when they are varied together, instead of one at a time, as Herrnstein, Catania, and Chung and Herrnstein varied them. The simplest possible relation might be multiplication of the ratios of independent variables to produce the ratio of times, as follows:

$$\frac{T_1}{T_2} = \frac{Rf_1 A_1 I_1}{Rf_2 A_2 I_2} \tag{9}$$

The most general form of such a matching law, which would include new variables besides the three already known, would be:

$$\frac{T_1}{T_2} = \prod_{j=1}^{n} \frac{x_{1j}}{x_{2j}} \tag{10}$$

where x_{1j} and x_{2j} are the values of variable x_j associated with Key 1 and Key 2, and there are n such variables, instead of just three, as above. If we define the *value*, V_i, of Activity i as:

$$V_i = \prod_{j=1}^{n} x_{1j}$$

then Equation (10) reduces to:

$$\frac{T_1}{T_2} = \frac{V_1}{V_2} \tag{11}$$

Equation (11) states that pigeons allocate time to any given pair of activities in such a way that the ratio of the times allocated equals the ratio of the values of the activities.

Neuringer (1967) verified Equations (10) and (11) for two variables: amount and rate of reinforcement. He found that pigeons in a two-alternative choice situation matched relative frequency of choice to relative "total access to reinforcement," the product of amount times rate of reinforcement. He found, in other words, Equation (9) with I_1 equal to I_2.

The form of the position preference shown in Fig. 2 lends further support to Equation (10). We do not know what variables determined the preference for the right side over the left. Perhaps the right magazine allowed the birds to eat more during the magazine cycle. Perhaps a greater movement of the left floor when stepped on contributed to the bias. Whatever the determinants, however, the position preference only necessitated multiplying the ratio of the rates of reinforcement by a constant to produce matching. In terms of Equation (10), this constant is either the ratio of two values of a single variable that differed from one side to the other, or, perhaps more likely, the product of several ratios of the values of several variables that differed from one side to the other. The form of the position preference, therefore, suggests that Equation (10) may predict preference with great generality.

We can only hope that other variables that fit into this formulation will be as simple to express as rate, amount, and immediacy of reinforcement. Staddon (1968) suggested that such simplicity may not completely prevail.

REFERENCES

Blough, D. S. Interresponse time as a function of continuous variables: a new method and some data. *Journal of the Experimental Analysis of Behavior*, 1963, **6**, 237-246.

Brownstein, A. J. and Pliskoff, S. S. Some effects of relative reinforcement rate and changeover delay in response-independent concurrent schedules of reinforcement. *Journal of the Experimental Analysis of Behavior*, 1968, **11**, 683-688.

Bullock, D. H. Note on key-holding behavior in the pigeon. *Journal of the Experimental Analysis of Behavior*, 1960, **3**, 274.

Catania, A. C. Behavioral contrasts in a multiple and concurrent schedule of reinforcement. *Journal of the Experimental Analysis of Behavior*, 1961, **4**, 335-342.

Catania, A. C. Independence of concurrent responding maintained by interval schedules of reinforcement. *Journal of the Experimental Analysis of Behavior*, 1962, **5**, 175-184.

Catania, A. C. Concurrent performances: reinforcement interaction and response independence. *Journal of the Experimental Analysis of Behavior*, 1963, **6**, 253-263. (*a*)

Catania, A. C. Concurrent performances: a baseline for the study of reinforcement magnitude. *Journal of the Experimental Analysis of Behavior*, 1963, **6**, 299-300. (*b*)

Catania, A. C. Concurrent operants. In W. K. Honig (Ed.), *Operant behavior: areas of re-search and application.* New York: Appleton-Century-Crofts, 1966. Pp. 213-270.

Chung, S. and Herrnstein, R. J. Choice and delay of reinforcement. *Journal of the Experimental Analysis of Behavior*, 1967, **10**, 67-74.

Ferster, C. B. and Skinner, B. F. *Schedules of reinforcement.* New York: Appleton-Century-Crofts, 1957.

Findley, J. D. Preference and switching under concurrent scheduling. *Journal of the Experimental Analysis of Behavior*, 1958, **1**, 123-144.

Fleshler, M. and Hoffman, H. S. A progression for generating variable-interval schedules. *Journal of the Experimental Analysis of Behavior*, 1962, **5**, 529-530.

Gilbert, T. F. Fundamental dimensional properties of the operant. *Psychological Review*, 1958, **65**, 272-285.

Herrnstein, R. J. Relative and absolute strength of response as a function of frequency of reinforcement. *Journal of the Experimental Analysis of Behavior*, 1961, **4**, 267-272.

Mechner, F. Probability relations within response sequences under ratio reinforcement. *Journal of the Experimental Analysis of Behavior*, 1958, **1**, 109-121. (*a*)

Mechner, F. Sequential dependencies of the lengths of consecutive response runs. *Journal of the Experimental Analysis of Behavior*, 1958, **1**, 229-233. (*b*)

Millenson, J. R. *Principles of behavioral analysis.* New York: Macmillan, 1967.

Neuringer, A. J. Effects of reinforcement magnitude on choice and rate of responding. *Journal of the Experimental Analysis of Behavior*, 1967, **10**, 417-424.

Rachlin, H. and Baum, W. M. Response rate as a function of amount of reinforcement for a signalled concurrent response. *Journal of the Experimental Analysis of Behavior*, 1969, **12**, 11-16.

Reynolds, G. S. On some determinants of choice in pigeons. *Journal of the Experimental Analysis of Behavior*, 1963, **6**, 53-59.

Skinner, B. F. *The behavior of organisms.* New York: Appleton Century, 1938.

Staddon, J. E. R. Spaced responding and choice: a preliminary analysis. *Journal of the Experimental Analysis of Behavior*, 1968, **11**, 669-682.

(Received 24 March 1969)

Index of Names

This is an index of names mentioned in the main text.

Topical Index

This is an index of the topics discussed in the main text. Only the general subjects of the suggested readings are included here.